The Western Dream of Civilization:
The Journey Begins
Volume I

Third Edition

The Western Dream of Civilization:
The Journey Begins
Volume I

THIRD EDITION

Doug Cantrell
David Bowden
Elizabethtown Community and Technical College
Elizabethtown, Kentucky

Mel Weissman
County College of Morris
Randolph, New Jersey

Barbara D. Ripel
Suffolk County Community College
Riverhead, New York

John Moretta
Houston Community College System
Houston, Texas

Donald L. Barlow
Thomas D. Matijasic
Big Sandy Community & Technical College
Prestonsburg, Kentucky

Abigail Press   Wheaton, IL 60187

Design and Production: Abigail Press
Typesetting: Abigail Press
Typeface: AGaramond
Cover Art and Maps: Sam Tolia

The Western Dream of Civilization:
The Journey Begins
Volume I

Third Edition, 2007
Printed in the United States of America
Translation rights reserved by the publisher
10 digit ISBN 1-890919-45-4
13 digit ISBN 978-1-890919-45-0

ABOUT THE AUTHORS

Doug Cantrell is an Associate Professor of History and head of the history program at Elizabethtown Community College in Elizabethtown, Kentucky where he has taught for 15 years. He holds a B.A. from Berea College, an M.A. from the University of Kentucky, and has completed 30 hours toward the Ph.D. He is co-author of *American Dreams & Reality: A Retelling of the American Story* and *Historical Perspectives: A Reader and Study Guide* published by Abigail Press. He also has written numerous journal and encyclopedia articles and contributed book reviews to academic journals. Professor Cantrell also teaches various history courses on the web, and serves as the social science discipline leader for the Kentucky Virtual University, He is listed in *Who's Who in America, Who's Who in the World,* and *Who's Who in the South and Southwest.* In addition, he is former editor of the Kentucky History Journal and past president of the Kentucky Association of Teachers of History.

David Bowden is an Associate Professor of History at Elizabethtown Community College in Kentucky, where he teaches European, United States, and World War II history. He earned a B.B.A. degree in Marketing and an M.A. degree in History from the University of Kentucky. He has taught full-time for Elizabethtown Community College for seven years and previously served as an adjunct faculty member for the University of Louisville and Elizabethtown Community College. David Bowden has published an article on Native American history in the *Chronicles of Oklahoma* and has presented a research paper at the Indiana State University's Conference on Baseball in Literature and Culture. He served as Secretary and then as Community College Representative for the Executive Committee of the Kentucky Association of Teachers of History for six years.

Dr. Mel Weissman is a Professor of History at the County College of Morris, Randolph, New Jersey. Dr. Weissman received his B.A. and M. A. at the University of Illinois, Urbana, Illinois and his Ph.D. in Medieval History from Carnegie-Mellon University, Pittsburgh, Pennsylvania. Dr. Weissman served as visiting professor, teaching a course in Comparative History in the Department of International Relations, St. Petersburg State University, St. Petersburg, Russia, in 1998. Dr. Weissman was awarded a Fulbright Scholarship in 2000 and taught Aspects of a Democratic Society at Mari-State University, Mari-el Republic, Russia. Dr. Weissman has published articles on Carolingian Art, as well as classroom strategies. He is an accomplished violinist, and he and his wife, Peggy, a Director of Public Health Nursing, live in Sparta, New Jersey.

Barbara D. Ripel is Professor of History at Suffolk County Community College, Riverhead, New York. Her B.A. and Ph.D are from SUNY Stony Brook, and her M.A. is from Rutgers University in New Jersey. The *West Georgia Quarterly* published her article on Harbottle Dorr, and *The William and Mary Quarterly* published her research on Early ProSlavery Petitions from the 1780s. Besides her background in American History, Professor Ripel has taught Western Civilization survey courses, Political Science, Anthropology, and Sociology. She recently directed the Honors Program on the Suffolk Campus. In 1998, she received the New York State Chancellor's Award for Excellence in Teaching. In 2002 she received a NEH (National Endowment for the Humanities) Summer Fellowship at Harvard University for an Integrated Study of Eurasia. Dr. Ripel serves as the campus advisor to Phi Theta Kappa, the International Honor Society for Two Year Colleges.

John A. Moretta earned a B.A. in History and Spanish Foreign Language and Literature from Santa Clara University in CA, an M.A. in History from Portland State University in Oregon, and a Ph.D. in History from Rice University in Houston, TX. He is currently Professor of History and Chair of the Social Sciences Dept. of Central College of the Houston Community College System in Houston, Texas. He is also Visiting Professor of History at the University of Houston, Main Campus. He also teaches in the Honors College at UH. Dr. Moretta has published several articles and books during his twenty-two year career in higher education. His biography of Texas lawyer William Pitt Ballinger won the best book award in Texas history (2002) given by the San Antonio Conservation Society and it was runner-up for the best book in Texas history awarded by the Texas State Historical Asso. Dr. Moretta's book did win the best research award given by that same organization for 2001. Dr. Moretta is currently working on a biography of William Penn for Pearson Longman Publishers' Library of American Biography series scheduled for release in spring 2005.

Donald L. Barlow earned a B.S. from Indiana Wesleyan University, and a M.A. and Ph.D in History from Ball State University. He is currently an Associate Professor of History at Prestonsburg Community College in Prestonsburg, Kentucky where he teaches European and American History. Dr. Barlow previously taught at Bartlesville Wesleyan College and Oral Roberts University. He has served on the Board of the Historical Confederation of Kentucky since 1999, and as a District Coordinator of National History Day in two different states since 1985. He was chosen to attend an NEH summer seminar at Yale in 1989, and he participated in a humanities seminar for the University of Kentucky Community College System for the purpose of developing a comprehensive, interdisciplinary approach to the study of history and the humanities for the university and its community college system.

Thomas D. Matijasic earned a B.A. from Youngstown State University, a M.A. from Kent State and a Ph.D. in History from Miami University. He is currently a Professor of History at Big Sandy Community & Technical College in eastern Kentucky. Dr. Matijasic has received three Great Teacher Awards and five NISOD Awards for teaching excellence. He has served as President of the Kentucky Association of Teachers of History and is a member of the Southern Historical Association. In 1994, governor Brereton Jones appointed him to a seat on the Kentucky Heritage Council. He was re-appointed to the Council in 1998 by Governor Paul Patton when his first term expired. Dr. Matijasic has published more than twenty articles and thirty book reviews. He has also contributed entries to the Kentucky Encyclopedia and to reference works published by Salem Press.

PHOTO CREDITS

Special thanks to the following authors for sending their personal photos to be included in this text.

Barbara D. Ripel: 21 (both), 22, 117, 118, 119, 132 (bottom), 133 (both), 134, 184, 188, 189, 280, 293, 353 (bottom).

Tom Matijasic: 258, 261, 264, 265 (both), 266, 267, 268, 270, 271, 277.

Contents in Brief

Contents

CHAPTER TWO
THE GREEKS

CHAPTER THREE
ALEXANDER AND THE HELLENISTIC AGE

CHAPTER FOUR
THE ROMANS

CHAPTER FIVE
THE POST-ROMAN EAST: BYZANTIUM, ISLAM & EASTERN EUROPE

CHAPTER SIX
GERMANIC EUROPE & THE DARK AGE A. D. 378 TO 715

CHAPTER SEVEN
EUROPE UNDER ATTACK: THE EARLY MIDDLE AGES 715-1000

CHAPTER EIGHT
FEUDAL EUROPE, 1000-1215

CHAPTER ELEVEN
FROM FEAR TO HOPE, THE 1300s

CHAPTER TWELVE
THE RENAISSANCE 1350 TO 1650

CHAPTER THIRTEEN
THE REFORMATION

PREFACE

Before we tackle the chronological advance of "Western Civilization," it is important to discuss just what we will be studying. Each word is chosen for specific reasons and the definitions will set the tone, as well as the development of this course.

As we look around the world today in the twenty-first century, the word "western" has acquired many meanings. To some, it is the height of human political, social, and economic progress, and some even add to that the supreme religious interpretation of people's drive to understand their world. The definition certainly represents the settled, urban, materialistic societies of western Europe (possibly minus Spain and Portugal) and the United States. "Western Europe" is in itself a problem to define as the evolution of the nation state has been marked with a sliding group of participants.

Many historians equate western civilization with the rise of the nation state and that political unity certainly directs a definition that can explain participation in the idea of Western Civilization. In the West, nationhood is the product of devotion to a political, economic and social system, such as monarchy or democracy or some combination. It could be described as the "advance" from personal loyalty to institutional loyalty. In "non-Western" formats of society, personal loyalty, loyalty to family, ancestry, and/or tribe are the basis of political organization. This of course breeds a different kind of societal organization, which is on a much smaller and local scale than that of a "nation state." Blood and tradition rule over formal legal systems.

"Civilized" areas kept written records, composed written laws, and produced written histories. They termed their nomadic neighbors "barbarians" (from the Latin term "*barbarus,*" which means strange or foreign) and led future generations to determine those who did not join the ways of the settled populations to be inferior to themselves. The term "civilization" comes from the Latin term "*civitas,*" which means an urban community and also gave us the terms city and citizen. Cities cause the dissolution of family ties and kinship groups because masses of unrelated peoples are gathered together so a different format other than the patriarch or tribal chieftain for their organization is necessary. Individuals in a Western society are not related by blood but by the format of their government, which terms them a "nation," or a "people" rather than a tribe.

We have titled our text as the "Western Dream of Civilization" because the blend of possibilities that form its societies contain many dissident elements in which the notion of "people" and "tribe" create competitions between neighbors, as well as those beyond the borders of Western Civilization. In the United States, we have seen the development of the Civil Rights movements, which include those of African Americans, Amerindians (Native Americans) and other minority groups. In Europe, the struggles between England and France, the Western nations and Central Europe, and the arrival of "barbarians" during various periods, all point to a confrontation between the "civilized peoples" and the nomadic "barbarian tribes."

If, however, we look beyond the political barriers and see the movement of ideas to improve the conditions of humans on earth, we gain a broader picture of the real sense of "civilization." Settled citizen and nomadic trader both contributed to the rise of the Modern World. We see social, economic, and religious trends, which gave and still give meaning to the lives of those touched by both elements. Although this is a text about Western Civilization, the rise of the nation state and the arena in which it still exists and affects our world today, we hope we have presented a balanced picture of the many peoples who have given both meaning and questions to our own place in history. The process of history is really a goal or dream to benefit humanity.

Barbara D. Ripel
Suffolk County Community College
Riverhead, New York

Chapter 1

THE FOUNDATIONS OF WESTERN CIVILIZATION

Early in the written memory of the Mesopotamians and the Hebrews are tales of a Great Flood that nearly destroyed humankind and all the animals. The Hebrews' story of Noah, found in the book of Genesis in the Old Testament of the Bible, is familiar to many people. The Mesopotamian story, however, is less widely known. In the Epic of Gilgamesh, the Mesopotamians tell of Gilgamesh, a ruler of Uruk, who searched for the gods' secret of immortality. In this quest he encountered Utnapishtim, called the Faraway, a formerly mortal man who had been given everlasting life and had gone to live at the place of the sun's transit. Gilgamesh asked Utnapishtim how he had attained immortality, and Utnapishtim recounted the story of the flood. According to Utnapishtim, there was a city on the Euphrates River called Shurrupak that grew old. Meanwhile, the gods too grew old, Anu, Enlil, Ea and the rest. People multiplied, crowding the city and creating a great racket with their noise. Enlil complained to the other gods that the noise made it impossible to sleep and so the gods decided to completely exterminate humankind.

However, Ea warned Utnapishtim of the gods' plan by means of a dream. He told Utnapishtim to give up his home and possessions and to build a boat and thereby save his life. The boat was to have an equal beam and length and a roofed deck. He was also to take into the boat the "seed" of all living creatures. Utnapishtim agreed to build the boat, and he and his household began gathering materials the very next day. On the fifth day of work they laid the keel and ribs and put the planking in place. The boat was square, running 120 cubits on each side, and covered an acre. It had six decks below and a top deck, all divided into nine sections by bulkheads. They gathered up supplies of oil, and, then, caulked and pitched the boat. During construction, Utnapishtim spared no expense in providing feasts, serving plenty of wine and food for the shipbuilders.

Launching the boat proved difficult, but Utnapishtim loaded all his gold, his family and kin, and animals both tame and wild, as well as craftsmen. When the rain came, Utnapishtim boarded and sealed up the hatches. As the gods unleashed the storm, lightning flashed from the torches of the Annunaki, the seven judges of hell. The storm raged the whole day, and even the gods were terrified; the goddess Ishtar bemoaned the decision to destroy humankind. The tempest and flood raged for six days and six nights, but on the seventh day the storm ended, the rain stopped and the sea calmed. Everywhere water covered the land.

The boat grounded on the Mountain of Nisir and remained lodged there for six days. On the seventh day Utnapishtim set loose a dove that found no place to go and returned to the boat. A swallow released did the same. When he released a raven, the waters had receded, and the raven did not return. Utnapishtim opened the hatches, made a sacrifice, and poured out a libation on the mountaintop. The gods gathered overhead. When Enlil became furious that a mortal had escaped the destruction of the flood, Ea castigated Enlil for the carelessness of the flood and, denying that he had anything to do with the man's salvation, said that Utnapishtim had been warned in a dream. Enlil then decided to give Utnapishtim and his wife the gift of immortality.

Chronology
(all dates are approximate and B.C.)

2 million	Beginnings of Paleolithic culture
200,000	*Homo sapiens* appears
by 30,000	Cro Magnon man had emerged
10,000-8000	End of Paleolithic Age
8000-7000	Neolithic Revolution begins Agriculture and pottery developed
4500	Farming villages appear in Holland
3500	Civilization arises in Mesopotamia
3300	The "Ice Man" dies in the Alps
3100	Egypt unified by King Narmer (Menes) Early construction at Stonehenge
2600	The Great Pyramid built at Giza
by 2300s	Indo-European migrations have begun
2371-2316	King Sargon I forms Akkadian Empire
2000-1400	Minoan civilization flourishes
1792-1750	Amorite King Hammurabi rules
1600-1200	Mycenaean civilization flourishes
1490-1468	Hatshepsut rules Egypt
1400-1200	Hittite Empire flourishes
1300-700	Urnfield culture flourishes in Europe
1270	Israelite exodus from Egypt
1200	Invasion of "Sea Peoples" and others Egyptian & Hittite Empires collapse
1000-971	King David rules Israel
814	Phoenicians establish Carthage
700-51	Celtic culture flourishes in Europe
600s	Zoroaster teaches his religion
612	Chaldeans & Medeans crush Assyria
586-538	Babylonian Captivity of the Jews
550	Cyrus the Great begins Persian Empire

Western civilization is the culture, particular worldview, and set of values commonly associated with Europe and the other parts of the world heavily influenced by Europe, such as the United States. Western civilization developed over thousands of years from a wide variety of sources, first emerging as a unique, unified culture in Europe during the region's Middle Ages (the Medieval period), which extended approximately from the fifth through the fourteenth centuries A.D. This textbook examines the history of Western civilization, beginning with its origins in various cultures centered in the Near East, the Mediterranean region, and Europe. The history of Western civilization also includes the ancient Greek and Roman civilizations and continues with the history of Europe from the collapse of the Roman Empire to the present. The story of Utnapishtim and his flood from the Mesopotamian *Epic of Gilgamesh*, as well as the Biblical story of Noah and the Great Flood from the Hebrews, represent great literary and religious traditions that are important contributions of Western civilization to the world. Originating in the ancient world of the Near East, outside the European center of Western civilization, they are good examples of how Western civilization draws on many sources and is the product of cultural interaction, exchange, and inheritance with and from many different civilizations.

The Greek and Roman civilizations, both of which were centered on the continent of Europe, did much to develop early forms of Western civilization. However, the basis of Western civilization extends well beyond the contributions of the Greeks and Romans. Western civilization is built on an extensive foundation of cultural contributions made by various peoples, many of whom lived in places outside of Europe and existed much earlier than the age of Greece and Rome. This chapter examines that cultural foundation upon which Western civilization rests. The ingredients of this extensive foundation derived from five great developments that shaped human culture from the beginnings of human existence up through the days of ancient Greece and Rome: 1) human culture developed over the ages of prehistory, a process in which humans generally advanced in technical skills, artistic creativity, and social, economic, political, and religious complexity and sophistication; 2) civilization arose and developed in Mesopotamia and then spread to, influenced, and interacted with surrounding peoples; 3) around the same time, civilization also arose and developed in the Nile Valley of Egypt and then also spread to, influenced, and interacted with other peoples; 4) people in areas that surrounded the Mesopotamian and Egyptian centers or hearths of civilization, people migrating or infiltrating into these areas, and newly prominent peoples already present in the older areas of civilization made important cultural contributions and assumed an increasingly dominant role in shaping the direction of larger events; and 5) in peripheral areas such as Europe, further removed geographically from the Mesopotamian and Egyptian heartland of civilization, people followed their own pattern of prehistoric development, interacted with the civilized areas, and created a cultural legacy that in important ways helped shape Western civilization.

The rise and contributions of the Greeks and the Romans can be seen as a part of this fifth development, but because of the crucial role they play in Western civilization, they will be treated separately in other chapters. In political forms, economic accomplishments, societal structures, thought patterns, religious systems, and in countless other ways the cultures and societies involved in these five great developments created the basis for later peoples to build upon the creating Western civilization.

PREHISTORY TO THE DAWN OF CIVILIZATION IN THE NEAR EAST

To understand Western civilization, one must begin with the first great development that contributed to it, the achievements of the vast age known simply as prehistory. During this period, humans ever-so-slowly developed, eventually spread throughout the Near East and Europe, as well as other parts of the world, and laid the cultural base for civilization in these areas. Prehistory spans an incredibly long period of time and includes the great majority of human existence, leaving the time since the rise of civilization to represent only a small fraction of the whole. The period begins with the origins of humans and extends to about 3500 B.C. The term "prehistory" is used because this was the era before humans developed writing, therefore, leaving no written records or history. There is no way to know what people thought, felt, and believed about themselves and their world and no way for later generations to effectively discern the interplay of human actions that influenced human events. Traditionally, then, the existence of written records has been viewed as essential to history, and "history" has meant the time written records exist. Prehistory is understood only through analysis of the physical remains of the past, traditionally the material and realm of the archaeologist. In recent years, however, historians have become interdisciplinarians to a much greater degree and have made extensive use of the work and techniques of various social and physical sciences, even for periods for which written records exist. Today, history is defined much more broadly. Through the work and techniques of other disciplines, such as archaeology, anthropology, and sociology, a clearer, more integrated picture of the human past, even in the prehistoric era, is possible.

Early Humans and Prehistoric Achievements

The origin of humans is a concern in examining prehistory since, as noted, the age begins with the origin of humans. While debate and differing interpretations are integral parts of the study of history, the much-debated issue of human origins is not a central topic in the development and history of Western civilization. Modern archaeology and anthropology are engaged in an ongoing effort to trace human origins that has led back millions of years to early hominids. Although scientific disagreement abounds concerning the classification and dating of many remains, the earliest forms of a thinking human or *homo sapiens* apparently appeared between about 500,000 and 200,000 years ago. One major debate concerns Neanderthal people, who lived from perhaps 200,000 years ago to 35,000 years ago. The question whether Neanderthal people were a sub-species of *homo sapiens* that became defunct, remains an integral problem in the evolving *homo sapiens* species, or a separate species altogether. The definite *homo sapiens,* called Cro Magnon, emerged at least 30,000 years ago.

Prehistoric *homo sapiens* eventually developed cultural achievements that laid the foundation for civilization in general and Western civilization in particular. Culture is learned (as opposed to instinctive) behavior that can be passed on to succeeding generations and includes language, clothing styles, religion, forms of government, etc. In the development of human culture, one monumental cultural achievement of early prehistory was the development of tools. The earliest material humans are known to have

used for tools is stone, but this knowledge is based on remains that have both survived over time and been discovered. It is logical that wood, bone, and plant material were used equally as early in human development, but tools made of these organic materials have not survived. Some of the oldest stone tools date back well before the development of *homo sapiens.* Found in the Olduvai Gorge of Tanganyika in Africa, crude, roughly chipped chopper tools have been dated by the potassium-argon method at about 1,750,000 years ago. Stone tools were such a dramatic and important element of much of prehistory's physical remains that archaeologists have named the major prehistoric periods the Old and New Stone Ages, which using terms based on Greek roots are designated Paleolithic and Neolithic periods respectively. Some scholars also include a transitional Middle Stone Age, or Mesolithic period.

Another monumental achievement of prehistory was the development of spoken languages. Being able to speak and thereby express not only emotion but also information allowed humans to more effectively pass on ideas and knowledge from one person to another and from one generation to the next. While it is debatable whether spoken or written language was the more important achievement, certainly spoken language was profoundly important in the advancement of human beings.

The Paleolithic Period

The Paleolithic age lasted from the beginning of human culture, perhaps two to three million years ago, to about 10,000 B.C. In this period, humans depended on hunting and gathering for food, developed increasingly refined tools of stone, wood, bone, antler, natural fibers and other materials, and organized themselves into social units of families and of hunting bands. As early as 500,000 years ago, humans had sought out caves for shelter and had learned to use fire. They eventually began to bury their dead with care and included ornaments and other items in the graves, indicating religious beliefs including perhaps a belief in life after death. In this long period, cultural development and advancement occurred slowly. Many of the most significant advances occurred in the Upper Paleolithic era, from about 35,000-40,000 years ago to the end of the Paleolithic. In this period that coincided with the rise of anatomically modern *homo sapiens* like the Cro Magnon, humans developed many specialized tools, such as tools for making other tools, and began decorating and refining their tools.

The earliest surviving art dates to this period, appearing before 25,000 years ago. Small, stylized carvings of women with exaggerated breasts, hips, and pregnant bellies, such as the so-called *Venus of Willendorf,* have been interpreted as having religious purpose, perhaps in a type of fertility cult, but regardless show a capacity to think conceptually and symbolically since the statues are stylized, not realistic. Cave paintings, such as those at Lascaux in France and Altamira in Spain, realistically portray game animals like mammoths, horses, deer, and bison. These paintings have been interpreted as efforts on the part of Paleolithic people to influence the hunt by magic but may also be an expression of artistic impulse and creativity.

Much of the Paleolithic era was characterized by a similar culture that prevailed over large areas. In the Paleolithic culture, people typically gathered fruits, nut, berries, and other edible plants and hunted large game animals such as bison or now-extinct mammoths that thrived in the plentiful grasslands. One reason for the cultural similarity over large areas was that during

much of the Paleolithic period the Northern Hemisphere experienced the Ice Age, geologically known as the Pleistocene epoch. Between about 1.6 million years ago and 10,000 years ago, continental ice sheets periodically advanced and receded in the form of glaciers. The climate that prevailed in Europe and much of Asia was cooler and wetter than at present, and grassland covered much of the unglaciated areas of the continents. When the last period of glaciation ended, the climate warmed up, ocean levels quickly rose, and many areas that formerly received plenty of rainfall became arid. As a result, climate changes led to diverse environments, and the great grasslands became much less common. Many species of the large game animals that Paleolithic people depended upon became extinct or relatively scarce. The appearance of a variety of different climate zones and environments and the decline in the availability of big game led people to adapt and change their culture in response. To survive, some people altered their way of life in different ways, depending on the new climate and environment they happened to face. Thus, climate differentiation led to cultural differentiation and diversity. Probably one of the responses to changing environments was the development of agriculture, an innovation so important that it is one of the key factors marking the transition from the Paleolithic to the Neolithic period.

The Neolithic Revolution

The cultural changes and achievements of the Neolithic period have been called the *Neolithic revolution* since these achievements occurred in a remarkably short period of time (compared to the pace of change in the Paleolithic period) and fundamentally altered the nature of human life. In many ways these revolutionary Neolithic developments made possible the creation of civilization. The developments of the Neolithic revolution happened at different times in different places and to a differing extent. Some cultural areas classified as Neolithic did not develop all of the achievements of the Neolithic revolution. For the Near East, the Neolithic period began about 8000 B.C. and extended to about 3500 B.C. when the rise of civilization brought bronze tool-making capability.

Although humans achieved various skill refinements and cultural developments in the Neolithic period, a handful stand out as being most important. First is the development of agriculture. Agriculture, the deliberate cultivation of plants, particularly for food, arose in several different places around the world, apparently independently, such as the Indus River Valley in India, Central America, and the Near East. The earliest of these areas to develop agriculture evidently was the Near East, the hearth of agriculture that influenced Western civilization. Around 10,000 B.C., in the Levant (the area along the eastern coast of the Mediterranean Sea in what is today Israel and Syria) and in the hilly region on the western slope of the Zagros Mountains along the modern Iran-Iraq border, hunter-gatherers began to practice what has been called broad-spectrum gathering. In this approach, peoples in these regions took advantage of different naturally occurring plant and animal resources available in the varied ecosystems present in these two areas. Apparently, people stayed in one place and used plants available in one season in one nearby area and then exploited another resource available in a different season in a different nearby area. For example, near the Zagros Mountains, settled communities in the summer used wild goats and sheep from the mountains and in the winter used wild pigs and cattle that roamed the lower elevations, while

also taking advantage of wild wheat and barley that grew in the hill country valleys. Eventually, around 8000-7000 B.C., people were making deliberate efforts to grow certain grains and even to select and plant seeds from the naturally occurring varieties that were most desirable. Agriculture was born.

With agriculture, settled populations could grow larger as a steadier, more reliable, and potentially surplus food supply became the norm. An on-going debate among scholars concerns whether settled life led to agriculture or agriculture led to settled life. As with most such controversies, the answer probably lies in the middle, with a mutually reinforcing, simultaneous development of both agriculture and settled life occurring together, as in the example of the Zagros region. To be sure, in most ecosystems, to practice agriculture in any significant way people had to stay in one place to tend the crops, harvest them, store the surplus, and be able to use the surplus. As agriculture-based settled life emerged, social classes evolved since agriculture allowed the accumulation of wealth. Some people grew wealthier and more powerful than others. It also led to more complex organization and government as larger populations and closer contact generated more disputes that needed resolving and regulating. As competition for resources like land and water increased with the population, the need for greater and more formal defense also evolved.

The emergence of settled life and the rise of villages and towns is another of the monumental Neolithic era developments. With larger populations and the need for remaining in one place that accompanied the adoption of agriculture, Neolithic people began living together in larger, permanent settlements. For example, at Jericho, near the northern end of the Dead Sea, between about 8000-7000 B.C., a sizeable community developed with a population of about 3000 covering an area of about eight acres. There people lived in round houses made of mud brick built on stone foundations. The town was encircled by defensive fortifications consisting of a ditch, impressive stone walls, and towers. Çatal Hüyük, a town in southern Turkey that developed between 6500-5600 B.C., eventually grew to 32 acres in size. There residents grew grain, raised sheep, wove wool into cloth, and mined black obsidian in the nearby mountains. Permanent villages and towns of growing size like Jericho and Çatal Hüyük characterize the evolving culture of the Neolithic period.

Agriculture, with the surplus food supply it created, also freed some members of a community to specialize in and devote more time to non-food-producing tasks like toolmaking. People had more time to think, plan, and experiment. This led to various innovations and advances such as weaving. One of the earliest known woven fabrics was evidently made of hemp and dates to the eighth millennium B.C. The surplus food supplies provided by agriculture and the greater production of goods that specialized labor created also stimulated greater and more complex trade as farming communities bartered their products for other items they lacked. Finally, the fact that agriculture created a portable way of life meant that agricultural peoples could spread into many areas, including areas where hunting and gathering might have been inefficient.

In another key Neolithic development occurring not long after 9000 B.C. at about the same time and in about the same places as the development of agriculture, people began to domesticate animals. The domestication of animals, or animal husbandry, involved taming, keeping, selectively breeding, and managing certain species of animals like sheep, cattle, goats, and pigs, which provided humans with a more consistent and potentially larger supply of meat, skins, bones, and other animal resources such as wool than hunting provided. Domestication also gave access to dairy products that enriched the human diet and provided a source of power for all sorts of tasks like transportation that would remain vital to human society until the widespread availability of the internal combustion engine in the twentieth century A.D. Unlike agriculture, animal husbandry did not require a sedentary lifestyle, and many groups led a nomadic life, herding their animals from place to place.

Another of the significant developments of the Neolithic period was the invention of pottery, apparently invented in the Near East around 7000 B.C. The knowledge and skill of pottery making spread slowly, only becoming generally known and practiced in the sixth millennium B.C. Pottery facilitated the storage and transport of surplus foodstuffs and liquids and became an important item in trade. It also provided an outlet for artistic expression as decoration and elaboration of style developed. For archaeologists and historians, pottery proved to be an invaluable tool for dating sites and tracing ties between communities and cultures since different material composition and styles are tied to certain places and eras. Pottery making was also one of the first uses of the wheel.

By the end of the Neolithic period, people had fully mastered the making of tools of stone, refining these tools, and applying them to new uses. People had also begun to experiment with and use potentially much more useful "rocks," the ores that provided metals like copper and tin. The mastery of stone toolmaking and experiments in rudimentary metallurgy placed humans on the verge of yet even more dramatic technological achievement, the development of alloys like bronze that accompanied the rise of civilization and further revolutionized human life.

Over the course of the Neolithic period, humans demonstrated a remarkable capacity to learn, innovate, and adapt a set of abilities with which they dramatically altered the character of life. Eventually in various places around the globe, some groups of people were able to push developments even further and brought about a level of cultural sophistication called civilization. The earliest peoples known to have created civilization lived in the Near East in the river valleys of Mesopotamia and Egypt. As great as these early civilizations' accomplishments were, however, remember that they were built on the achievements of Neolithic peoples.

Traditionally, historians defined a civilization as an advanced culture demonstrating certain significant capabilities and characteristics. Usually, these prerequisite achievements include the ability to write, advanced metallurgy skills (e.g. the ability to produce and use alloys such as bronze), and the existence of urban life with all the things that go along with it, such as larger, more concentrated populations, sophisticated and complex social structures, governments, economies, and technical abilities. The exercise of defining civilization has often involved much cultural judgement, with implications that if a culture does not have certain things, such as writing, then it is inferior. Today, many scholars would likely agree that a culture might still be called a civilization even if it does not demonstrate some of the key characteristics and so the term civilization may often be used interchangeably with culture. Still, understand that around 3500 B.C. some Near Eastern peoples had begun to develop cultures that in their complexity and level of skills set them apart from their Neolithic ancestors and neighbors. While one could debate whether these cultural achieve-

ments on the whole were beneficial or detrimental, bad or good for humanity, they were the most significant developments of the human story up to that time and continue to impact life today. The rise of civilization in Mesopotamia and its spread and impact on neighboring peoples is the second of the five great developments of the prehistoric and ancient periods this chapter will examine.

THE RISE AND INFLUENCE OF MESOPOTAMIAN CIVILIZATION

The earliest known civilization in the world and one of the key elements of Western culture arose in the harsh environment of Mesopotamia. Mesopotamia, which in Greek means "the land between the rivers," lies between the Tigris and Euphrates Rivers primarily in modern Iraq. Agriculture, one of the precursors of civilization, had been first developed in areas near Mesopotamia, such as the Zagros Mountains and the eastern coast of the Mediterranean. Due to geographic conditions, securing a living by farm-

ing in Mesopotamia was not easy. Some scholars have argued that it was the need to surmount great difficulties in Mesopotamia that provided the stimulus required to forge civilization.

Since geographic conditions played a central role in the rise and especially in the spread of civilization, it is important to preface the history with a geographic overview of the region. The Tigris and Euphrates Rivers arise in the mountainous region between the Black and Caspian Seas and flow roughly southeast to their marshy deltas where they empty into the Persian Gulf. For much of their northernmost courses, these rivers cut through rugged terrain, often forming steep-walled cliffs. But as the rivers flow south, they leave this landscape behind and enter arid plains where rich alluvial soil is deposited. Here the fertile soil meant agriculture was definitely possible with adequate rainfall, but rainfall was generally deficient. The rivers offered a potential solution to agriculture's problems in this dry climate, but harnessing the life-giving waters required much energy and ingenuity. Moreover, the rivers were subject to violent, destructive, and unpredictable floods, making irrigated farming a difficult and uncertain prospect. Adding one more element to the challenge of life in Mesopotamia, the area lies in what is basically a crossroads between three continents and has few natural barriers to movement of peoples, and so inhabitants were often subject to migrations, raiding, and invasion of other peoples.

Sumerian Civilization

Still, here in Sumer, the southern part of Mesopotamia, the people called Sumerians developed the earliest known urban civilization and one that powerfully influenced the Near East for three millennia and made major cultural contri-

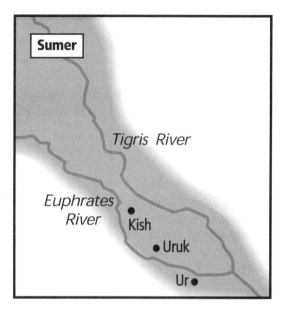

butions to Western civilization. Of uncertain origins and speaking a language related to no other now-known language, the Sumerians seem to have moved into the region sometime in the fifth millennium B.C. and subjugated or overwhelmed the Subarians and other earlier inhabitants. By around 3500 B.C. the Sumerians had begun to make key advances. Devising, developing, and taking advantage of bronze technology, which involved alloying copper together with tin, the Sumerians made superior weapons and tools.

They also developed the monumentally important ability to write. Some evidence indicates that the Sumerians may have derived their writing from the earlier Subarians. Regardless of who originated the early, rudimentary writing, the Sumerians pushed its development forward so that by 3500 B.C. they were using pictograms, simplified drawings that represented a concept, and by 2000 B.C. they had developed a phonetic set of characters. The Sumerian script was used by imprinting a clay tablet with a reed instrument to make wedge-shaped marks. The

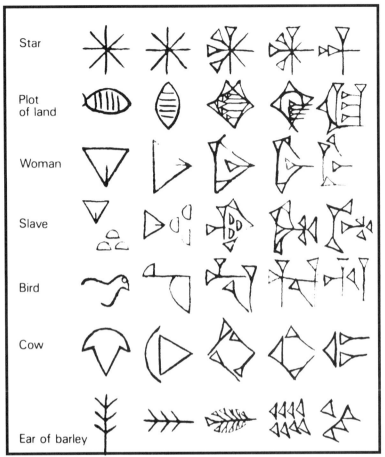

Writing developed from pictogram to cuneiform. Scribes began writing in horizontal lines instead of columns.

characteristic wedge shape inspired the modern term for the script, cuneiform, which is from the Latin word for wedge. With eventually some 350 characters, cuneiform was difficult to learn and master, which meant that only a few in society could devote the effort required to learn and use it. Nevertheless, cuneiform proved so revolutionary and useful for commerce, government, and religion that for thousands of years the script would be adopted and adapted by other Near Eastern peoples for writing their own languages.

As population increased in the region of Sumer and as the demands of wrenching a living from Mesopotamia changed, some Sumerian

villages, particularly those with special religious significance, grew into towns and then into cities. In many areas, as the cities grew, more distant areas of the outlying countryside became unpopulated. One driving force behind the growth of cities was the need to organize and raise significant numbers of people for constructing and maintaining the irrigation and flood control systems that made agriculture possible in the region. The need for protection from nomads and neighboring towns also tended to push people together into concentrated cities. Uruk, for example, rose from an approximate population of 10,000 around 3500 B.C. to about 40,000 by around 3000 B.C. A dozen or so other cities had arisen by 3100 B.C., including Umma, Lagash, and Ur.

In creating these earliest cities, the Sumerians also created complex new patterns of life for dealing with the unique circumstances cities presented. From about 3100 B.C. to 2400 B.C. the basic political unit was the city-state, comprised of the city and the surrounding territory it controlled. Each city-state was independent of the others and, in fact, often warred with the others in competition for territory and the scarce resources of the region. Though early forms of government varied, eventually each city-state was ruled by a king, or *lugal,* in Sumerian, who derived his power from religious authority. Each city was believed to have been founded by a particular god who then protected that city. The lugal was the agent of the city's god, assigned to carry out the will of the patron deity.

Closely connected to the governmental power of the lugal was the temple complex and priesthood of the city, which together exercised great influence over life from organizing irrigation to managing food distribution to commanding vast resources. As evidence of the importance of the religious system in Sumer, by 2000 B.C. most Sumerian cities each sported a prominent example of monumental architecture dedicated to their gods called a ziggurat. A ziggurat was a large mound or tower constructed in tiers, made of mud brick veneered with baked brick, and topped with a temple structure. At Ur, the ziggurat was over 120 feet tall and covered about 2000 square feet at its base.

Sumerian religion in many ways reflected the realities of the harsh conditions and uncertain life the people faced. The Sumerians practiced polytheism, or belief in many deities, that in its basic outlines and in many of its specifics continued to have strong influence in the Near East for 3000 years. The gods and goddesses were associated with certain attributes, cities, forces, activities, and aspects of nature and were arranged in a hierarchical pantheon, with some minor deities having power over things like leatherworking. Other deities had prominent positions and were important to virtually all Sumerians. The original god, An, who beget the other deities, was seen as the sky god and represented authority. Enlil, literally "Lord Air," was the storm god and the god of life. He created the place in which life existed by separating the sky from the earth and represented force. It was Enlil, later known as Marduk, who was responsible for the disastrous floods that threatened Mesopotamians. The earth god was Enki, "Lord Earth," who brought order to life, represented wisdom, and provided the sweet waters that sustained the civilization. One of the most popular goddesses was Inanna, called Ishtar by the Semitic peoples around Sumer, who was the fertility goddess responsible for ensuring the fertility of nature every spring.

The Sumerian deities were anthropomorphic, having the shape of humans, and lived as potentially immortal, super-powerful versions of humans. They had needs, such as food; they experienced emotions, such as anger; and they interacted with one another much as humans did. They were capricious, not being bound by any set of rules or obligations to humans; they could do as they liked. Humans were created to serve the needs of these gods, but even faithful service had no guarantee of reward. Rituals, ceremonies, prayers, hymns, sacrifices, and other activities were performed in an effort to appease the gods and hopefully bring blessings, but the capricious deities might not be satisfied. One of the biggest burdens involved in serving the gods was the support, through labor or sacrificial gift, of the temples and their elaborate priesthoods and numerous attendants and other workers.

Myths, some of which are found in tales like the *Epic of Gilgamesh*, which dates from sometime before 2000 B.C., explained the natural, divine, and human worlds and provided insight as to how humans should conduct themselves or what the important values were. Collections of proverbs and precepts provided advice for living. Incantations helped bring about desirable events, and various methods of divination helped people decide what future course of action to take. A rich literary heritage developed as Sumerians and later Mesopotamians wrestled with questions about the gods and how to please them. However, the Sumerians concluded that regardless of how one had lived, at the end of life no pleasant afterlife awaited, just darkness and a return to clay. Any benefits gained from following the dictates of religion, therefore, had to be enjoyed in this life. As the *Epic of Gilgamesh* pronounces, "only the gods live forever under the sun, as for mankind, numbered are their days, whatever they achieve is but wind." Obviously a strong strain of pessimism flavors the Sumerian and later Mesopotamian religion, just as it likely permeated its adherents' uncertain lives.

The complex social structure of Sumer's cities also reflected the significance of religion. At the top of the hierarchical class system were the rulers, nobles, and priests who controlled much of the city's power and economic resources. Next, with much less wealth than the upper class but with some degree of personal freedom, came the commoners including artisans, merchants, soldiers, and free landowning farmers. At the bottom of this legally recognized structure were the slaves and the large population of dependent rural farmers who labored for others. One persuasive explanation for the development of this social class structure is that the religious and military elites, who were largely responsible for forging the cities, providing the protection the

cities offered, and elaborating the religious justification for the cities' existence, encouraged and, indeed, forced much of the migration into the cities. The powerful position of these elites grew greater as they commanded the labor and production of many of the new city dwellers. Regardless, such social stratification has many parallels in other eras.

Sumerian and later Mesopotamian society also developed stratification along gender lines. Whereas Neolithic culture had seen apparent equality of status and sharing of roles between men and women, urban society saw women hold private authority within the household over children and servants but exercise authority in the world outside the home with less frequency. Certainly women could own property and perform other public roles, but the male-dominated pattern came to prevail.

Akkadians, Amorites, and the Rise of Empire

In creating their urban civilization, the Sumerians established a basic cultural pattern that spread and came to characterize Mesopotamia and much of the Near East as a whole for 3000 years. But peoples other than the Sumerians would be the heirs, refiners, and transmitters of this culture. One of the earliest examples of these cultural heirs were the Akkadians. To the north of Sumer, semi-nomadic Semitic-speaking people from northern Arabia moved into the area around Akkad and followed and adopted the Sumerian model in developing a set of city-states with a similar culture. The Semitic languages included Akkadian, Hebrew, and Canaanite and are related to modern Arabic and Hebrew tongues.

A remarkable figure, Sargon I (c. 2371-2316 B.C.), brought about a successful but temporary end to the prevalence of the city-state in

Mesopotamian political life and introduced the larger, more complex concept of empire. Sargon, whose mother allegedly put him in a reed basket and set him adrift on the Euphrates, served at one time as the cupbearer to the king of Kish. After seizing power in Kish, Sargon conquered the chief Sumerian city-states of Umma, Ur, Lagash, and Uruk. He then pushed on conquering all of Mesopotamia and extending his power into Syria, reaching the Mediterranean Sea. Ruling this large, ethnically and culturally diverse empire from his capital at Akkad, Sargon developed methods for establishing more effective control. He adopted a grander title "King of the Four Regions," and he tolerated existing culture and institutions while replacing ruling elites with his own.

Sargon's descendants maintained political unity of this empire until c. 2200, providing a very important opportunity for the Sumerian civilization to be spread throughout a much larger area than its original hearth. After about 2200 B.C. Mesopotamia saw a brief interlude where city-states reasserted their independence. But before long, the trend toward larger political entities resumed. For a time, the Sumerian city-state of Ur gained control of Sumer. Ur-Nammu, a prominent king of Ur in this period, produced the first comprehensive law code, which set forth crimes and their respective punishments, generally consisting of fines.

Around 1800 B.C. another Semitic people, the Amorites, centered at Babylon, began their rise to dominance. Their greatest king, Hammurabi (c. 1792-1750), put together an empire stretching from the Persian Gulf to the Mediterranean Sea in an arc of territory that included all of Mesopotamia. Of the many contributions of Hammurabi, perhaps one of the most interesting was his written law code. Hammurabi's Code, given by the authority of

no less a god than Marduk, was carved on a great stele and placed in a central, public location. The laws of this code demonstrated the social class differences inherent in the society in that it provided for different punishments for the same crime depending on the class of the victim and of the perpetrator. In contrast to earlier Mesopotamian law, many of the punishments were very harsh and were retributive, seeking to punish the criminal in a way that fit the crime. For example, if a bartender watered down drinks, he was to be watered down: his punishment was to be death by drowning. If a burglar was caught in an all-too-common effort to dig through the mud walls typical of homes, he was to be killed and buried within the wall he had attempted to breach. Nonetheless, Hammurabi's code provided important steps toward a just system in that the same punishment was provided for within a social class. All people belonging to a particular class were to be treated the same. Justice was also served simply by the fact that this code was written down and publicly displayed. Having the laws in writing made it more difficult for a judge to arbitrarily assign punishments.

Mesopotamians from the Sumerians to the Amorites contributed many other accomplishments to human cultural development and to Western civilization. In mathematics, Mesopotamians developed many practical mathematical tools for doing such things as figuring compound interest or calculating the areas of various geometric shapes. Their hexageismal system with its base number of 60 still influences Western life, with the division of days and hours being an excellent example. In architecture, Mesopotamians understood the use of arches, vaults, domes, and columns. Skilled sculptors produced three-dimensional statues, fine carvings in seal-making, and jewelry. Mesopotamians compiled a great deal of knowledge in areas ranging from calendar-keeping and medical knowledge to geography and astronomy.

Like previous empire builders, the Amorites eventually lost their hold on Mesopotamia and Near Eastern power. Neighboring, infiltrating, and culturally descendant or connected peoples came to steer the course of history in many ways. The Hittites, a rising power to the north of Mesopotamia in the region of Asia Minor, finished off the Amorite's Babylonian empire by around 1600 B.C. However, like previous cultural heirs of the early Sumerians, the Hittites and later peoples such as the Kassites, Assyrians, and Chaldeans borrowed and adapted many features of Mesopotamian civilization. This civilization's great vitality and influence persisted in strength up to near the time of Christ. Long before these successors to Mesopotamian civilization made their contribution to Western civilization, however, another great ancient civilization had arisen in another river valley of the Near East and had extended its cultural and political influence outward into the Eastern Mediterranean world, including the Levant and Syria.

THE RISE AND INFLUENCE OF EGYPTIAN CIVILIZATION

While the Sumerians and their successors forged civilization in the crucible of Mesopotamia, to the west in another, more hospitable river valley on the continent of Africa, the Egyptians developed their own civilization. The Nile River, hearth of this civilization, flows about 800 miles from the first cataract to the Mediterranean Sea through desert that stretches eastward to the Red Sea and beyond into the Arabian peninsula and westward into the Sahara. In combination with defensive measures taken by the Egyptians, these deserts and the cataracts to the south and the Mediterranean Sea to the north provided effec-

tive insulation from invasion throughout most of Egypt's ancient past, allowing Egyptian civilization to develop a unity and stability undreamed of in Mesopotamia.

With regular, predictable flooding occurring advantageously between harvests, the Nile moistened and deposited rich silt along its narrow valley and broad delta, making possible a highly productive agriculture. This agriculture still required much organization and hard labor in constructing and maintaining canals and dikes and fighting the advancing desert sands. Also, the Nile could occasionally prove fickle. Nonetheless, Egyptian agriculture was a key foundation of civilization there and centuries later drew envious comments from Greek writers.

Egyptian History and Development

Settled life first arose in Lower Egypt, the wide delta region in northern Egypt where the Nile splits into several branches as it flows north into the Mediterranean. Sometime around 4000 B.C. villages appeared on the western fringe of the delta. Upper Egypt, the narrow southern region of the Nile Valley south of the delta to the cataracts, developed settled life somewhat later but this region would be the first to centralize politically and develop a higher level of culture. Upper Egypt was interacting with Mesopotamia by about 3200 B.C. and had developed a pictographic form of writing.

Over time Lower and Upper Egypt developed into two separate kingdoms. Sometime around 3100 B.C. these two regional kingdoms were unified under a single ruler, later titled *pharaoh*. Traditionally, credit for this unification is given to the semi-mythical king Narmer, also called Menes. Unification ushered in a period of almost three millennia during which the unique Egyptian civilization remained stable and contributed much to the history and culture of the Near East and eventually Western civilization.

Historians traditionally divide Egyptian history into various periods based on thirty-one dynasties of pharaohs. The Predynastic Age ended about 3100 B.C. with Egypt's unification, which began the Archaic period that ran from 3100-2700 B.C. and included the first and second dynasties. The Old Kingdom, incorporating dynasties three through six, lasted from 2700-2200 B.C. and saw the development of the basic patterns of Egyptian civilization, including the divine rule of the pharaoh, the construction of the pyramids, a centralized bureaucracy, and a stratified social structure. Many aspects of Egyptian life cemented during the Old Kingdom persisted to the end of ancient Egyptian sovereignty.

The stability of the Old Kingdom was temporarily interrupted by the rise of political and religious rivals who challenged the pharaohs' authority in the First Intermediate Period that lasted from 2200-2050 B.C. and involved dynasties seven through ten. Stability was restored around 2050 B.C. with the rise of the eleventh dynasty, which initiated the Middle Kingdom. This phase of Egyptian history was marked by land reclamation efforts, defeat of the Nubians who threatened from the south in present-day Sudan, and the extension of Egyptian influence into Palestine and Syria.

Weakened by internal problems, the Middle Kingdom and twelfth dynasty came to an end around 1800 B.C. In this weakened state, a poorly understood group of invaders of mixed Semitic and Asian background, the Hyksos, conquered part of Egypt around 1630 B.C. In the Second Intermediate Period (1800-1570 B.C.), comprising the thirteenth through seventeenth dynasties, the Hyksos influenced Egyptian culture. They ruled as the fifteenth dynasty and introduced the compound bow and horse-drawn war chariot that remained a key part of Egyptian military practice. However, the Hyksos did not seem to interfere much with Egyptian culture beyond politics, and their presence was of limited duration. By about 1570 B.C. Egyptians had driven the Hyksos out of Egypt and the New Kingdom had begun.

The New Kingdom or Empire period of Egyptian history spanned the centuries from about 1570-1085 B.C. and included dynasties eighteen through twenty. The New Kingdom saw the capable rule of the female pharaoh Hatshepsut (1490-1468 B.C.), the sister and wife of Thutmose II. The reign of Amenhotep IV (1364-1347 B.C.), who changed his name to Akhenaten and unsuccessfully attempted to implement a sort of rough monotheism, falls in the New Kingdom as well. Akhenaten was succeeded by the boy pharaoh, Tutankhamen, (whose famous undisturbed tomb captivated the Western world in the twentieth century) under whom Akhenaten's monotheism was abandoned.

In this age Egyptian pharaohs such as Ahmose I (1552-1527 B.C.) extended Egyptian power and influence south into Nubia and north into Syria along the Mediterranean coast as far as the Euphrates River. The northward expansion of power brought Egypt into deeper contact with other Near Eastern peoples and into conflict with the Asia Minor-based empire of the Hittites that had defeated the Amorite's Babylonian Empire. In the end this conflict became a stalemate. The Egyptian pharaoh, Ramses II, and the Hittite king, Hattusilis III, made the world's first known nonaggression treaty in 1284 B.C., which formalized the fact that neither was able to unify the Near East under one power. Ironically, neither power retained its position for long, as around 1200 B.C. waves of infiltrating and invading peoples from the

The Great Sphinx features the head of a man and the body of a lion. The Great Sphinx was built at the same time as the Giza Pyramids. The Sphinx measures 240 feet in length and stands 66 feet tall. At its widest point it measures 13 feet 8 inches.

north shifted the course of history in the civilized world of the Near East and eastern Mediterranean. Egypt went into decline as a political power and entered a Postempire Period (1085-332 B.C., dynasties twenty-one through thirty-one) that saw Egypt's defeat by first Assyria, then Persia in 525 B.C., and then by the Macedonian Alexander the Great in 332 B.C.

Egyptian Civilization

The remarkably stable civilization forged by the Egyptians has many features, only some of which can be surveyed here. In government, the Egyptian pharaoh provides a contrast to the Mesopotamian pattern of kingship. While Mesopotamians viewed their rulers as agents of the gods, Egyptians saw their pharaohs not only as rulers pursuing divine interest but as gods themselves. This concept set the pharaoh up with a good deal of authority. This authority was supplemented with widespread use of bureaucracy, with usually active and interested in-

volvement of the pharaohs themselves, and with art and architecture. The ability to command the construction of the monumental pyramids illustrates the pharaohs' power, and the amazing nature of the pyramids themselves must have reminded Egyptians of the importance of the rulers for whom these structures were built. In art, the pharaoh is inevitably pictured as a giant in contrast to other people.

A chief objective and concern of the pharaoh was to preserve and ensure *ma'at* in Egyptian society, a goal that was highly regarded. *Ma'at* was the principle of right order, justice, and harmony that should prevail in society and the cosmos. This included the proper relationships between people. Pharaoh's orders preserved *ma'at* and, therefore, must be carried out. The stability of the social and political order was bolstered by this principle.

Though they held great power, one limit on pharaohs' power came from the fact that despite being gods, they were also bound by the tenets of the Egyptian religion. This religion developed an elaborate priesthood that could and did conflict with royal designs and had a powerful influence with the mass of Egyptian society. Another limit to the pharaohs' power, as with many other kings in other ages, was the potential rivalry of local or regional nobles.

With his ultimate power, the pharaoh and his royal family capped the Egyptian social structure. Pharaoh ordered and organized life, directing religion, agriculture, construction projects, flood control and irrigation systems, and maintenance of food supplies. To help carry out his rule, the pharaoh had a corps of ministers, priests, and bureaucratic officials. The Egyptian priestly class, as in other Near Eastern societies, was high in the social order and played an important role in the life of the civilization, performing various functions from carrying out the rituals and ceremonies of religion to maintaining the burial places of the pharaohs and managing temple complexes. A royal temple honoring Ramses III built at Medinet Habu employed a residential staff of governors, officials, and scribes who oversaw the temple's manufactories, landholdings, cattle herds, and fleet of ships, as well as fifty-six towns in Egypt and nine cities outside the homeland.

The wealthy nobility also joined priests and royalty at the top of the social structure, followed in the New Kingdom by a class of professional soldiers. For the wealthy, life was pleasant in material terms. Their meals usually included meat, fruit, and wine. The elaborate homes of the wealthy were beautified with surrounding gardens. Also indicative of the lifestyle to which the nobility were accustomed, tombs, dating as far back as the second dynasty, had bathrooms provided for the afterlife of the tomb's occupant.

A significant gap separated the wealthy classes from the rest of society. Among the other classes in Egyptian society were prosperous ru-

Egyptian writing was based on pictograms. Ancient pictographs were colorfully painted using red, yellow and blue.

ral farmers; urban artisans, merchants, and scribes; and the large class of peasants. Slaves also formed a group in Egyptian society, though not exactly a social class. Obviously life for these classes varied, with some living in moderate comfort and others in less enviable circumstances. The poorer Egyptian might live in a small shed constructed of mud bricks with only some rudimentary furniture and a few pottery vessels for furnishings. The basic foods for most Egyptians were bread made from barley or emmer and a barley beer. In fact, the term "barley and beer" often was used in denoting the amount of wages or salary. Vegetables like onions added some variety to meals.

Egyptian society, in contrast to most ancient societies such as the Mesopotamian, Greek, Ro-

Paintings in the Egyptian tombs depicted the lifestyle to which the nobility were accustomed. In this painting servants carry items to fill their pharaoh's tomb.

man, and Hebrew, afforded women greater status and more equality in public matters. For example, Egyptian women could own and bequeath property, testify in court, and instigate legal proceedings. They operated businesses, sometimes served as scribes and treasurers, and even, as Hatshepsut has already illustrated, ruled the country in one exceptional case. Indeed, the lineage of the royal dynasty was traced through both the mother and father. To be sure, women's public role was still limited in Egyptian society. For example, formal education was closed to women, a situation that barred most from entering the professional bureaucracy since literacy was required for these important positions. In another telling example, when Hatshepsut ruled, she had herself represented as a sphinx with a beard and took on other male characteristics. On the whole, however, Egyptian women's status contrasted favorably with many of the other societies of the day, which gave women virtually no public role, some treating women like a form of property.

Hieroglyphics, the name given to Egyptian writing that means "sacred carvings," are another important feature of Egyptian civilization. It is likely that Egypt borrowed the idea of pictographic writing from contact with Mesopotamia. Egyptian scribes, however, created their own pictographs and ultimately evolved a useful script that combined pictographs with phonetic symbols. The Egyptians painted or carved hieroglyphics on walls and in stone in various places, such as in temples, royal tombs, or other places of religious significance, thus leading to "sacred carvings." However, the more common method

The stair-step pyramid of Zoser was so named because of its stairlike appearance. Archaeologists estimate that its construction took at least twenty years.

of using the script was to write it on sheets or rolls called papyri. Papyri were made by laying out crisscrossing layers of the fibers of the reed-like papyrus plant that grew abundantly along the Nile, then soaking, pressing, and drying the material. Though the source material is different, our word paper and its use derive from the Egyptian papyri.

Egyptian hieroglyphics are the center of an intriguing story of historical mystery and discovery. Until the nineteenth century A.D., the history of ancient Egyptian civilization was shrouded in mystery. Although many physical remains, such as the pyramids and thousands of artifacts including many hieroglyphic materials,

survived, use and knowledge of hieroglyphics had long since died out and no one could read the undeciphered script. In 1798 General Napoleon Bonaparte of France invaded Egypt, bringing with him not only his army but also scientists, mathematicians, and engineers to study, chart, and catalog various Egyptian things. In 1799, a group of Napoleon's scientific team discovered at Rachid, known also as Rosetta, a piece of black basalt on which three inscriptions were carved, one in hieroglyphics, one in the common demotic script of ancient Egypt, and one in Greek, which could be read. Along with thousands of other objects, the French transported this "Rosetta Stone" back to France. There, the

Rosetta Stone would provide the young French scholar Jean Francois Champollion with the key to solving the mystery of hieroglyphics. Champollion guessed that the three inscriptions all contained the same text, decided that hieroglyphics operated phonetically, worked from the known Greek inscription, and by 1822 after fourteen years of working on the problem had deciphered hieroglyphics.

Ancient Egyptian civilization also featured great skill and ability in the arts, crafts, and architecture. Egypt, unlike Mesopotamia, had plenty of native stone to use for various purposes—limestone, porphyry, granite, and flint. For example, using flint-tipped drills, craftsmen made paper-thin jars by hollowing out rock crystal. Pottery was commonly available by 2600 B.C., and copper was in use by about the same time. In sculpture, relief carving, and painting Egyptian artists developed unique forms and styles that while changing little over time remained fresh. Architects demonstrated their skill in palace and temple construction. The hypostyle hall temple style made generous use of columns that were modeled to good artistic effect on plants such as the lotus, palm, and papyrus.

The ultimate example of Egyptian skill and technical ability is the pyramid. Most of the pyramids built in Egypt were constructed during the Old Kingdom, and all of the larger ones were built in this period. While being built, they consumed great resources of time, human effort, materials, organization, and skill. The first pyramid was the stair-step pyramid of King Zoser, the founder of the Old Kingdom, constructed at Sakkara. The Great Pyramid of Khufu (or Cheops) at Giza, built around 2600 B.C., is one of the most impressive structures of any age. The four sides of this pyramid were set to be 756 feet long at the base and were constructed to within

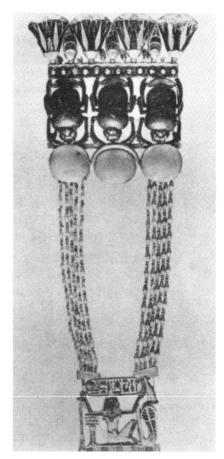

Ornate jewelry was often placed in the pharaoh's tomb. Items placed in the tomb were presumably for use in the after life.

a few inches of square. The sides are also oriented to the four cardinal directions, accurate to within 1/12 of a degree. Covering more than 13 acres, containing some 6 million tons of stone, involving over 2,300,000 blocks of limestone weighing about 2.5 tons each, the Great Pyramid stands 481 feet high, making it the tallest building in the world for nearly 4500 years.

The purpose behind the pyramids was both political and religious. Pyramids served as monuments for the god-king pharaohs and as elaborate tombs for helping preserve and protect their mummified bodies. Venerating past kings on such a scale certainly emphasized the importance of the current king, and the exercise of centralized power needed to successfully build the pyramids enhanced pharaohs' ability to rule. Preserving and attending to the mummified bodies of dead pharaohs held great religious significance because this was important for the immortality of the pharaohs and, therefore, of Egypt itself. The Egyptians believed the *ka,* or spirit of a past pharaoh, could return to his body, and pyramids helped make this possible in grand style.

The pyramids then demonstrate not only the great power of the pharaohs but also the influence and significance of religion in the life of ancient Egypt. Political power, the social structure, and the preservation of social order, as well as literature, philosophy, art, and architecture, all revolved around religion. Originally, Egyptian religion began as a simple polytheism with each city or area having local gods and deities personifying natural forces. With the political unification of Egypt came the evolution and fusion of many deities. Many Egyptian deities that

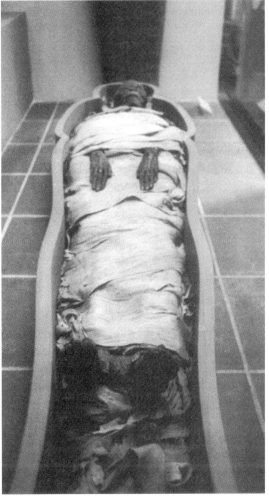

Mummification was an important step in the process of preparing the body for the afterlife. This process was practiced for over three thousand years. This Egyptian mummy and organ jars are displayed in an Egyptian museum in Turin, Italy.

had had animal forms became more or less anthropomorphic, perhaps retaining an animal head or other feature. Many of the guardian deities were merged into the most important god, Re (Ra), the sun god, who was later called Amon or Amon-Re. Another god of great importance, Osiris, resulted from the merger of various fertility deities.

In the Old Kingdom, though the worship of other deities was important, the cults involving Re and Osiris attained great significance. The most important was the cult of Re, the sun god associated with righteousness, justice, truth, and morals. The beliefs and practices associated with Re sought to ensure the immortality of the Egyptian state and the people. The pharaoh was a central figure in this cult since, as a man, god, and ruler, he was the nexus between people, the state, and the gods. Pharaoh was the human form of the falcon god, Horus, son of Osiris. Mummification, elaborate entombment in pyramids or temples or other fitting structures, and attending to the needs of the pharaoh's ka helped guarantee the immortality of the Egyptian state.

The cult of Osiris would eventually, in the Middle Kingdom, provide the means by which ordinary Egyptians could gain access to immortality in a pleasant life after death. Osiris was the fertility god personifying the growth of vegetation and the life-giving powers of the Nile River. According to myth, Osiris had been a kindly ruler who taught people agricultural and other skills. His evil brother, Set, killed him and cut his body into pieces. Isis, the sister and wife of Osiris, collected his scattered components, put them together and brought him back to life. After regaining his kingdom and ruling for a time, Osiris went on to the netherworld where he served as a judge of the dead. Osiris' son, Horus, exacted vengeance for Osiris' murder by killing Set. This legend, with its tale of the death

The pharaoh's coffin was taken by priests into the pyramid and placed inside a sarcophagus. This is an Egyptian sarcophagus.

and resurrection of Osiris, originally explained the life cycle of plants and the seasonal flooding of the Nile, things vital to the agricultural people of the Nile Valley.

Over time, Osiris came to have a more personal meaning for Egyptians as his cult became the means by which they could attain life after death. In the Middle Kingdom Egyptians came to believe that the dead would appear before Osiris and face three stages of judgement based on the life they had lived. During this judgement, they declared their innocence of certain sins, proclaimed their virtues, and had their heart weighed against a feather to determine whether they had told Osiris the truth. Those who passed the test received entrance to the Elysian fields where they would have an easy life of pleasure, while those who failed were consigned to a dark existence of hunger and thirst. This cult not only provided something very personally meaningful to adherents—the possibility of immortality—and placed ethical demands on life in the here and now but also reflected an optimistic outlook that Egyptian stability, order, and cultural longevity certainly fostered.

Later on, an elaborate priesthood developed around the cult of Osiris that catered to Egyptian efforts to attain life after death. Priests sold charms to hide people's true nature from Osiris and prescriptions written on papyri that could be placed in tombs to help the dead enter the Elysian fields. Collectively, the individual inscriptions on these papyrus scrolls are referred to as the Egyptian Book of the Dead and offer an excellent example of the Egyptian religious literary tradition.

Though many other beliefs and practices collectively formed Egyptian religion, one other religious development deserves mention. In the New Kingdom, the pharaoh Amenhotep IV (1364-1347 B.C.) and his wife, Nefertiti, attempted to impose a major religious revolution on Egypt. Giving up the traditional focus on worship of Amon-Re, Amenhotep IV worshipped Aten, the god represented by the disk of the sun, exclusively. This pharaoh changed his name to Akhenaten, meaning roughly "it pleases Aten" and moved his capital from Thebes to the new capital of Akhetaten, meaning "the horizon of Aten." It seems that Akhenaten tried to squash the worship of other deities, and this

has led some to call this religious reform an attempt at monotheism. Akhenaten's religious restructuring was not monotheism, however, since he also still cast himself as a deity whom the people were to worship. The attempt to denigrate previously revered deities and their cults created a backlash, especially in the priesthoods of the various cults affected. After Akhenaten's death, under the reign of Tutankhamen, the religious restructuring was reversed, the capital returned to Thebes, and an attempt made to remove all the vestiges of Akhenaten from Egyptian history by striking his name from monuments and king lists.

Around 1200 B.C. the Egyptian Empire of the New Kingdom went into a long political and imperial decline from which ancient Egyptian civilization never recovered. This decline was aided by the influx of waves of peoples into various parts of the Mediterranean and Near Eastern world. The Egyptians recorded the disruptive impact of what they called "Sea Peoples." This invasion or infiltration was just one part of a larger process of cultural interaction and diffusion that had been in progress for some time as civilization in the Near East matured and other peoples interacted with this civilization. The spread of Near Eastern civilization to neighboring areas and peoples and the contributions made by these peoples as well as by infiltrating and invading groups such as the various Indo-European speaking peoples comprise another of the five great developments of the ancient world.

THE INFLUENCE OF NEIGHBORING, INFILTRATING AND OTHER PEOPLES

Peoples and kingdoms located around the Mesopotamian and Egyptian heartlands of civilization had from the earliest days of civilization actively influenced developments within the heartlands. Semitic nomads in the Levant and Arabia continually contributed to the shifting cultural milieu of the Near East. The Semitic Akkadians, for example, had seized the initiative and united Mesopotamia in the twentieth-fourth century B.C. However, the Akkadians adopted and adapted most aspects of the Sumerian-originated culture, which survived and thrived. And Mesopotamia remained the vital political and cultural center even while its culture was spread outward. Egypt too stood as the other vibrant, primary center of civilization. However, under the influence of the older civilizations of the Near East, by around 2000 B.C. cultures and kingdoms like the Hittites, Minoans, Mycenaeans, Phoenicians, and Medeans had begun and would continue to rise in neighboring areas such as Asia Minor, the Aegean and eastern Mediterranean Seas, the Balkan Peninsula, the Levant, and east of Mesopotamia in Persia. As a part of this development waves of newcomers from the north, most speaking Indo-European languages, migrated into these neighboring areas where they provided the source for several of the rising cultures and kingdoms just mentioned. In later waves these and other newcomers, including the Dorian Greeks and the "Sea Peoples," such as the Philistines, also infiltrated and pressed into the civilized Near East as well as various parts of Europe. In successive periods, these neighboring cultures and infiltrating peoples would increasingly assume leadership of cultural development, driving the events, cultural exchange, and larger political trends in the greater eastern Mediterranean and Near Eastern world. Ranging from empires like that of the Hittites to small kingdoms like that of the Hebrews to city-states like those of the Phoenicians, these groups would make striking and fundamental contributions to Western civilization.

Indo-Europeans

Many of the peoples who established kingdoms in areas neighboring the older heartland of civilization spoke languages that are a part of a large family of related languages called Indo-European that have a common origin. The original speakers of the common proto-Indo-European language are not known definitively since they were not literate. Evidence points to the steppe region north of the Black and Caspian Sea as their original homeland. For example, vocabularies with terminology for horses and their uses but lacking a word for "ocean" certainly point to an inland origin. Many of the Indo-European speakers had warrior elites, used horses in warfare, and had a particular chieftain-oriented political system without hereditary kingship, all of which represent cultural contributions beyond language that these groups made to the areas outside their homeland in which they settled.

Beginning perhaps as early as 5000 B.C., but certainly by the middle of the third millennium B.C., Indo-European speakers began to migrate out of their original homeland and into various parts of Europe, Asia Minor, the Near East, and as far east as India. They took varying dialects of the Indo-European tongue with them. Virtually all of the modern European languages are a part of the Indo-European language family, including the Germanic, Slavic, Celtic, and Romance language groups that include English, French, Russian, and Spanish. Classical Greek, Latin, and Sanskrit are Indo-European as are Persian, Hindi, and Urdu.

Asia Minor and the Aegean World

Before the Indo-European migrations began to have a significant impact on developments in the civilized world of the Near East, areas such as Asia Minor, the Aegean Sea, and Balkan Peninsula that bordered the older centers of civilization felt the cultural impact of contact and exchange with the Near East. Between about 3000 and 2000 B.C. in western Asia Minor, several warlike societies developed, each having a fortified settlement that controlled a particular territory and each having a metalworks for producing the weaponry needed for defense. Some of the earlier phases of settlement at the site of Troy on the Asia Minor coast near the Aegean opening of the Hellespont (Dardanelles) Strait provide an example of these societies. The bronze metal-working capability of these societies illustrate the influence of the civilized Near East on this region. To carry on metal-working in this locale, however, required that the copper and tin needed for producing bronze items be imported since no regional sources existed. The demand of these warlike societies for these metals helped stimulate a vigorous trade in the Aegean Sea and eastern Mediterranean.

This trade network included peoples in various places in Europe to the west and north in Germany and Britain who supplied tin. The involvement of Europe in this trade is an important development in the prehistory of Europe proper. The central web of this trade network involved people on the Greek Peninsula, who traded such items as olive oil and wine, and on the Aegean Islands such as Naxos and Melos in the Cyclades Islands group, which ring the southern end of the Aegean. Developing c. 3000 B.C. and persisting until c. 1550 B.C., Cycladic culture eventually developed great skill in lead- and silver-working, which provided important items to the trading economy and contributed to general cultural development as their metalworking techniques spread north to the Greek mainland and south to the island of Crete in the Mediterranean Sea.

Crete eventually dominated this trade network, and the wealth generated from the trade helped Crete's culture become increasingly sophisticated. By about 2000 B.C. a flourishing civilization developed centered on Crete called Minoan after the legendary King Minos of Crete. The Minoan civilization thrived on the regional trade until about 1400 B.C. By that time another civilization had arisen to the north that challenged Minoan domination of Eastern Mediterranean trade. This civilization, called Mycenaean because its greatest site was found at Mycenae in Greece, originated with Indo-European speakers of a dialect of the Greek language who moved southward down the Balkan Peninsula into Greece around 2000 B.C. The Mycenaean civilization was the first civilization to develop in Europe and was also one of the early examples of the increasingly important role Indo-European speakers played in shaping Western civilization. Eventually, the Greece-based Mycenaean civilization dominated trade in the regional trade network formerly controlled by the Minoan civilization, and it became a forerunner of the classical Greek civilization. The story of the Minoan and Mycenaean civilizations, therefore, is a major part of the history of Greek civilization, treated in Chapter Two. It should also be noted that further west in the Mediterranean, other Indo-European groups, such as the Latins, moved into the Italian Peninsula and played a similarly important role in the history of Roman civilization, treated in Chapter Three.

The Hittites

Among the earliest of the Indo-European speakers to move south into regions surrounding the old Near Eastern centers of civilization and rise to prominence were the Hittites. The Hittites, whose language is the earliest example of a written Indo-European language, moved into and settled in central Asia Minor (Anatolia or modern Turkey) beginning around 2300 B.C. Establishing a capital at Hattusas (modern Boghazkoy), the Hittites first brought nearby areas under their control. Then, around 1600 B.C. King Mursilis I temporarily expanded Hittite power across northern Syria and into Mesopotamia, a move that finished off the Amorites' Babylonian Empire. Hittite control of Babylonia did not outlast the reign of Mursilis. The Kassites, a nomadic people from the mountainous region northeast of Mesopotamia, moved into the region and dominated the area for about 400 years during which time Mesopotamia played little role in the more significant developments in the Near East.

With more lasting success, the Hittites began to forge a larger empire around 1400 B.C., controlling not only their Anatolian base but also northern Syria and parts of the Levant as far south as Palestine by the reign of Suppiluliumas in the mid-fourteenth century B.C. Encroachment into the Levant was in part motivated by resistance to Egyptian moves during the New Kingdom to expand in this area.

The Hittite governmental system involved hereditary monarchy and later exaltation of the king in imitation of the Near Eastern pattern of divinely connected or deified monarchy. The Hittite king served as supreme judge, general, and chief priest. Suppiluliumas, a Hittite king contemporaneous with Akhenaten of Egypt, was influenced by Akhenaten's religious maneuverings and began using the solar disk (which Akhenaten's god Aten represented) as a symbol and insisted that he be called "My Sun." Beginning with Suppiluliumas, Hittite monarchs were deified upon death. Much of the power of Hittite government was exerted in economic controls such as craft production and price regu-

lations. Title to land was held by the king or city governments with grants made in exchange for military service and the obligation of cultivating the land. This practice of using land grants to gain support of warriors for the state set the warriors at the top of society. The Hittite three-tiered social structure consisted of the land-holding warrior aristocracy, artisans, and peasants.

In administering their empire, the Hittite kings typically appointed royal governors to oversee conquered cities. Hittites became the ruling aristocracy and, by and large, left local culture intact. In fact, although the Hittites contributed key elements to the cultural mix of their empire, such as providing women a larger religious and social role than their neighbors and the unique practice of cremating their deceased kings, they adopted many features of Mesopotamian civilization, including cuneiform script, various deities and religious practices, and hereditary kingship. Perhaps of most importance, the Hittites expanded the area under the influence of civilization.

As people like the Hittites moved into the Near Eastern region and began to assume a major role in shaping larger developments, the process of cultural transmission became more significant. It was by no means a given that Near Eastern culture would predominate as neighboring groups infiltrated the region. Part of the dynamics of cultural exchange is that people like the Hittites were willing to adopt and adapt cultural features they found attractive. Another component, however, is that some groups acted as intermediaries between more advanced areas and less advanced peoples like the early Hittites. The Hurrians, who forged the Kingdom of Mittani, are one example of a group that played a valuable intermediary role. Centered in northwest Mesopotamia and flourishing between about 1550 and 1350 B.C., the Mittani kingdom transmitted much of the older Mesopotamian civilization to the Hittites.

One of the most profoundly significant cultural developments associated with the Hittites was a closely guarded state secret that the Hittites for obvious reasons did little to spread. This achievement was the development of iron-working skill and technology. Iron, called the democratic metal because its ore is much more common in the earth's surface than the tin and copper required for bronze making and, therefore, is cheaper and more widely available, eventually revolutionized tools and weaponry and their related activities. The Hittites were producing iron in significant quantities by 1500 B.C., and other powers in the Near East were interested. In the thirteenth century B.C. the Hittite king, Hattusilis, showed his reluctance to share iron technology in an ancient arms deal negotiation. In correspondence with an Assyrian king, he wrote "As for the iron which you wrote to me about, good iron is not available. . . . That it is a bad time for producing iron I have written. They will produce good iron, but as yet they will not have finished. When they have finished, I will send it to you. Today I am dispatching an iron dagger to you." Iron's greater strength and durability, wider availability, and other advantages meant that bronze as the primary metal for tools and weapons was on its way out as soon as knowledge of how to smelt and work the newly discovered metal became more widespread.

This dispersion of iron technology proceeded apace with the collapse of the Hittite Empire around 1200 B.C. At this time a chaotic series of migrations and disturbances lasting for about a half-century and involving new waves of Indo-Europeans, as well as other groups, engulfed the Near East and eastern Mediterranean. While the events of this era are not well understood, the raiding and migration shook up the existing order and helped bring about the collapse of the Hittite and Egyptian empires, as well as the Mycenaean civilization in Greece and the Aegean Sea mentioned earlier. The Hittites continued to survive in small states until being absorbed by neighboring peoples like the Indo-European Lydians to the west and the Semitic Assyrians to the south by the end of the eighth century B.C. A shrunken and declining Egyptian state persisted despite temporary subjugation by the Assyrians until being conquered by Persia (Indo-Europeans) in 525 B.C. In the Aegean region, the folk movements or invasions involved raiding by the mysterious "Sea Peoples" as well as the migration of groups like the Dorian-dialect Greeks into Mycenaean areas, which facilitated the collapse of the Mycenaean civilization and inaugurated the Dark Age of Greek history. There long distance trade declined precipitously while literacy in Greece all but disappeared.

The Age of Small Kingdoms

In the Near East, the nearly four-century-long power vacuum resulting from the Hittite and Egyptian imperial collapse created the opportunity for smaller kingdoms and groups, such as the Phoenicians and Hebrews, to thrive. Eventually, other imperial powers rose to replace the Hittites and Egyptians, but in the meantime these smaller kingdoms and groups made monumental cultural contributions to Western civilization. The folk movements also brought new groups into the Near East, the Aegean Sea, and the eastern Mediterranean world, providing additional cultural ingredients to the forming foundation of Western civilization.

In the Levant and the areas to the east toward Mesopotamia and the Persian Gulf, various nomadic and semi-nomadic peoples, primarily Semitic in language, had for centuries existed on the edges of the civilized Mesopotamian and Egyptian heartlands and had adopted various aspects of those civilizations. Canaanite city-states based on agriculture or trade, such as Jericho and Ugarit, dotted the Levant. The people of Ugarit, a city that flourished c. 1400-1200 B.C., developed a literature in their mixed Semitic and Indo-European language using about thirty characters from the cuneiform script to represent individual consonant sounds. This marked the development of the first true alphabet, an achievement that could change the world if its use spread. Ugarites used their excellent harbor as a base for trade with the Egyptians, Hittites, and Mycenaeans. With the invasions of the Sea Peoples around 1200 B.C., however, Ugarit collapsed as the area suffered severe disruption.

The Indo-European Philistines, one group of the Sea Peoples, posed a disruptive threat. Moving into the Near East, the Philistines first attempted to penetrate into Egypt but were repulsed and settled in the nearby area to the north that today takes its name from them: Palestine. Bearing iron weapons, the Philistines represented a powerful military force in the region and flourished in centers like Gaza until about 1000 B.C. when the Israelites began to dominate the area. The conflict between the Israelites and the Philistines was one of the more prominent episodes in Biblical history: Goliath in the story of David and Goliath was a Philistine warrior.

To the north of the Philistines, between the sea and the mountains of Lebanon, remaining Canaanites developed a thriving city-state civilization that survived independently into the eighth century B.C. The people of this civilization were known as the Phoenicians and provide an excellent example of how smaller states were able to contribute to the larger develop-

ments of the era in ways of prime significance for Western civilization. Much of the Phoenician contribution stemmed from the fact that they were expert merchants and seamen. From cities such as Byblos, Tyre, and Sidon, Phoenician ships plied the Mediterranean Sea exchanging not only their wares but also their Near Eastern culture. For example, the papyrus paper that Phoenicians traded to the Greeks from the port city at Byblos led the Greeks to adopt "byblos" as their word for paper and then "biblion" for book.

More significantly, at about the same time that scribes in Ugarit developed their alphabetic script, the Phoenicians perfected an alphabetic script of their own based on Egyptian hieroglyphics. Written with pen and ink on papyrus, the Phoenician alphabet's twenty-two characters representing consonant sounds could be easily learned and written and opened the potential for literacy to virtually everyone. Significantly, because of the widespread Phoenician trade connections, the Phoenician alphabet spread to other peoples who adapted it for their own languages. Most notably, this Phoenician script was passed to the Greeks, who added characters for vowel sounds. Greek colonists in southern Italy transmitted the script to the Etruscans and Romans, and Roman modifications were passed down to Western Europe and are the basis for the modern Western script used in Western Europe and the Americas today. In Greece, the adaptation of the Phoenician alphabet led to the modern Greek script and related Cyrillic scripts of Eastern Europe.

Another major result of Phoenician trading was their establishment of colonies throughout the Mediterranean. The Phoenicians established Citium on Cyprus, Panormus on Sicily, Ibiza in the western Mediterranean, and even ventured beyond the Straits of Gibraltar into the Atlantic to establish Gadir (Cadiz) on the western coast of Spain. The most famous of the Phoenician colonies, however, was Carthage, founded on the Tunisian Peninsula of North Africa in 814 B.C. The city of Carthage was defended with walls 40 feet high and 30 feet thick. The harbor lay within a sheltered area of the North African coast and was accessed through a narrow 70-feet-wide passage that was protected by large iron chains stretched across the opening in times of danger. A 300-yard long wharf located outside the inner harbor added to the capacity of the port. Carthage survived as a thriving trading center well after the Phoenician city states on the Levant were subsumed by later cultures, and the colony eventually established an empire of its own in the western Mediterranean. Later, the city-state of Rome on the Italian Peninsula rose to rival Carthaginian power and proved to be its nemesis.

Another of the Semitic peoples who flourished in the period after 1200 B.C. were the Arameans, who lived in several smaller kingdoms between the Lebanon Mountains, the Euphrates River, and the Arabian Desert. From cities like Kadesh, Damascus, and Palmyra the Arameans established control of the land-based trade networks connecting various parts of the Near East. The language used by these successful traders, Aramaic, became a universal language that speakers of many different tongues could use to communicate with one another. Aramaic was still in common usage at the time of Christ.

The Hebrews

In terms of their cultural legacy for Western civilization, probably the most significant group of Semitic peoples flourishing in the post-1200 B.C. era were the Hebrews, known after their exodus from Egypt as the Israelites, from whom the Jews of Classical, Medieval, and Modern

times derived. Like many peoples at the time in the area of Palestine, Jordan and Syria, the Hebrews were originally primarily nomadic herders. The Hebrews may indeed be at least one group of the people called Khapiru or Habiru mentioned in various Hittite and Egyptian sources beginning around 1900 B.C. as being wanderers and raiders. The term seems to be a general designation referring to nomadic peoples rather than a particular ethnic group. According to the Hebrews' history, found in the Jewish Torah and the Old Testament of the Christian Bible, they originated with a patriarch named Abraham from "Ur of the Chaldeans" who made a covenant or agreement with his God that promised to make a great nation of Abraham's descendants.

Uniquely, the Hebrews eventually recorded their history in a written, consecutive account tracing back to their origins so as to show what they viewed as the unfolding of God's plan for His chosen people. This historical account of their past is intertwined with material central to their religion and religious identity—including ritual and moral law, proverbs, prophesy, poetry, praise, and their belief in one God to the denial of all others. While like the Homeric epics of Greek civilization, the religious component of the Hebrew tradition must be evaluated by the individual as a matter of faith. While the evidence points to about 850 B.C. as the earliest point at which the Hebrews wrote down elements of their chronicle, much of the broad historical outline of the history recorded in the Hebrew tradition—the major events, developments, and historical figures involved—have substantial corroboration from other sources and evidence.

The Hebrew patriarch, Abraham, may have left the Mesopotamian region around 1800 B.C. and migrated with his troupe and herds into

Canaan. According to Hebrew history, Abraham's grandson, Jacob, who took the name Israel, had 12 sons from whom, according to the Hebrew tradition, were descended the 12 tribes of Israel. Sometime about 1600 B.C., around the same time of the Hyksos invasion of Egypt, some of the Hebrews migrated into Egypt where they lived peacefully for a time. According to Hebrew tradition, their descendants were eventually enslaved but were led out of Egypt in the "exodus" about 1270 B.C. by a man with the Egyptian name of Moses. One line of historical argument is that Moses and his followers were not connected to the Abrahamic Hebrews but rather adopted that heritage as their own after the exodus. Nevertheless, according to Hebrew tradition, while in the wilderness of the Sinai Peninsula under Moses' leadership the Israelites, as the Hebrews were now called, refreshed the Abrahamic covenant. In this revamped covenant, the Israelites promised to follow and obey Abraham's God, whom Mosaic law now designated YHWH (conventionally translated with vowels as Yahweh or Jehovah), while receiving Yahweh's protection and blessing as His chosen people in return. To make clear what obeying Yahweh meant, the Israelites received the law of Moses, which included many ritual requirements such as detailed sacrificial formulas and dietary restrictions, as well as ethical demands like the Ten Commandments, which prohibit such things as idolatry, adultery, murder, and lying.

After Moses, the Israelites moved into Canaan in Palestine where they expended a great deal of effort in fighting first the Canaanites and then the Philistines for possession of the region. During much of this struggle the Israelites were organized into 12 tribes and headed by religious leaders called judges. Around 1025 B.C., the 12 tribes adopted a single king, Saul, who ruled the Israelites under a unified monarchy until his

suicide about 1000 B.C. Saul was succeeded by David, who ruled c.1000-c. 971 B.C. David led the Israelites in a series of victories over the Philistines, driving them into a narrow strip along the coast of the Mediterranean and establishing the Israelite state as a stable kingdom extending from the northern boundary of Egypt in the south along the Jordan River northward into Syria, with Jerusalem serving as its urban capital. In his reign from c. 971-c. 931 B.C., David's son and successor, Solomon, presided over the zenith of Israelite prosperity and political success. Solomon ordered construction of an impressively appointed temple in Jerusalem as the center of worship of Yahweh.

Solomon's construction program, as well as his attempt to live as impressively as other Near Eastern kings, meant heavy taxation and labor demands for the Israelites. Solomon also participated in several diplomatic marriages and allowed his foreign wives to continue in their native religious cults. Upon Solomon's death, the kingdom split with the ten northernmost tribes forming the Kingdom of Israel centered at Shechem. The remaining two tribes continued as the Kingdom of Judah with Jerusalem as their capital. In this era, religious leaders, called prophets, arose decrying the various examples of kings and others who through their immorality strayed from the covenant with Yahweh and called upon the people and leaders to reform themselves. The prophets' tradition not only emphasized an interpretation of Hebrew history that explained success and failure in terms of the Hebrew adherence (or lack thereof) to the covenant but also provided an important legacy of opposition to absolute royal authority, arguing that even a king is not above the law.

Weakened after the split, the two kingdoms eventually fell prey to larger powers that arose in the Near East. The Assyrians conquered the northern Kingdom of Israel in 722 B.C., deporting thousands of the inhabitants to Mesopotamia. This left only Judah, whose people came to be referred to as Jews. Judah survived the Assyrians by submitting to them as a client kingdom but were conquered themselves by the Chaldean or Neo-Babylonian Empire (so-called in contrast to the Old Babylonian empire of the Amorites). The Neo-Babylonian Empire arose in the late seventh century B.C. in southern Mesopotamia and helped destroy the Assyrians in 612 B.C. After Neo-Babylonian King Nebuchadnezzar II (604-562 B.C.) defeated Judah in 586 B.C., the Neo-Babylonians destroyed the temple of Solomon in Jerusalem, burned the city, and hauled off the Jewish elite into exile in Babylon. This Babylonian Captivity, as it was called, came to an end when the Persians, a rising empire to the east, defeated the Neo-Babylonian Empire and permitted the Jews to return to Jerusalem in 538 B.C.

The Babylonian Captivity transformed the Hebrew faith, a process of refinement that produced Judaism as it is called today. During the period of exile, preserving their Jewish identity in a foreign land became a paramount goal for the captive Jews. These Jews used their religious heritage as the rallying point in trying to hold on to their identity, focusing on studying the law and their past. Since it was no longer possible to worship at the temple, intense study of the Hebrew law of Moses, now called the Torah, in houses of study or *synagogues*, became the centerpiece of Jewish religious activity. They analyzed their defeat, determining that it was the people's failure to uphold the covenant that had led to their catastrophe, not any shortcoming on the part of Yahweh. They emerged fully committed to the idea that Yahweh was the one and only God and that adherence to the covenant was crucial.

After the Babylonian captivity, some of the exiled Jews returned to Jerusalem, rebuilt the temple, and pursued a revival of Jewish piety. Leaders of this revival continued to emphasize ethnic purity and the study of and adherence to the Torah as the central features of the Hebrew faith. One group of leaders who strongly adhered to the Torah in the post-exile Jewish religion were the Pharisees. The Pharisees developed the Mishnah, or second law, an oral law for use in interpreting and protecting the Torah. The Talmud of later Jewish faith grew out of this tradition; it consists of the Mishnah and its interpretation, called the Gemara, produced over several centuries. The Pharisees also believed in bodily resurrection, angels, and devils and included several books of Hebrew prophecy in their Torah. Another sect of Jewish leaders, the Sadducees, developed in opposition to the Pharisees. These landowners and aristocratic priests took a conservative view of the Torah, insisting that only the first five books of the Bible—Genesis, Exodus, Leviticus, Numbers, and Deuteronomy—be included. They also disagreed with what they viewed as new ideas in the Pharisees' interpretation of the Torah, including the belief in resurrection. As the Jews continued to live as subjects of foreign states in the centuries after return from exile, a prophecy that God would send a savior, or *messiah* ("anointed one"), to redeem and save His people gained particular attention and importance. Other sects developed partly in anticipation of the messiah. The politically active Zealots opposed foreign rule and eagerly waited for the coming of a political messiah to lead them to military victory and independence. The monastic Essenes withdrew from the world and lived communally in isolated areas such as the cliffs along the northwestern shore of the Dead Sea while they waited for the prophecies to be fulfilled.

The historical significance of the Hebrews and their cultural descendants does not lie in their political achievements but rather in the dominating legacy of their religious, ethical, and literary tradition. The Hebrew faith, as represented by Judaism, which it evolved into, today forms one of the major Western and world religions and gave rise to two other major world religions, Christianity and Islam. Both of these faiths view their one God as being the same God the Hebrews worshipped, and both profoundly influenced Western civilization. Christianity would become the dominant faith of Western civilization, while ironically Islam would serve as a counterpoint to Christianity, being viewed by European Christianity in the Middle Ages as a competing, infidel faith, a view that led Europe into conflict with Islam in the Crusades. The idea of having just one god, a belief called *monotheism*, is one of the most important contributions of the Hebrews to Western culture, a contribution made by this people who lived in a time and place in which polytheism was the rule. Much of the religious struggle of the Hebrews concerned the tension between the monotheistic ideal and the desire of individuals to follow other gods.

Other aspects of the way in which the Hebrews viewed their one God are important to understand. In the Hebrew conception, God was omniscient, omnipotent, and eternal, meaning that the deity was all-knowing, all-powerful, and had existed before anything else and would always be. When, according to Hebrew tradition in Exodus, Chapter 3, Moses asked God who He was, Yahweh replied "I am who I am," a cryptic reply that conveys some sense of the mysterious eternity of God in the Hebrew view. The Hebrews also saw their God as transcending nature; rather than believing Yahweh represented some natural force or was found in some

feature of nature like the sun, they believed that He had created nature and existed above it. Despite the lofty, almighty nature of their God, the Hebrews also believed He was a good and caring God who was concerned about His people, was directly involved in their lives, and moreover followed an ethical code by making promises to act in a certain way. This certainly contrasted with the capriciousness of the Mesopotamian deities who gave no guarantees that human ritual or sacrifice would secure protection.

The notion and importance of the covenant in Hebrew religion also represent a significant contribution to Western civilization. The covenant, combined with the Hebrew view of God as omnipotent, has at times stimulated a powerful sense of confidence among Jews and their theological cousins, Christians and Muslims. Belief in an all-powerful God along with a strong sense of assurance that this God will protect and defend if terms of an agreement with Him are followed creates the feeling that nothing is impossible and has led zealous people to accomplish amazing things.

The covenant was also important in another way. The notion that man was supposed to follow rules set down by a deity was not unique to the Hebrews. However, the particular moral character of the Hebrew's requirements combined with the notion that man had a choice in the matter, that humans could choose to obey or to disobey, have powerfully influenced the Western approach to law and Western views of the causes of immorality as well as various social problems like poverty; one powerful strain in Western thought holds that an individual's condition results from the person's choices. This idea that the individual has *moral autonomy* was refined in the exile and post-exile developments in Jewish religion, when the catastrophe of defeat and exile was blamed on the people breaking the covenant. To be sure, the Hebrew tradition holds that consequences result from the choice made, but it is still seen as an individual's free choice. In the Mesopotamian religion's ideal, people existed to serve the gods and obedience was expected and assumed with no notion of an agreement on the part of humans to do so. The Hebrews believed, for example, that God gave the first man and woman (Adam and Eve in the Hebrew tradition) the power to choose obedience or sin. The difference is subtle but important.

The Hebrew's particular moral, ethical, and legal standards, though certainly having elements in common with other Near Eastern and European peoples, have strongly shaped the worldview and basic moral code of much of the Western world, particularly in areas where Calvinistic Protestant Christianity had strength because Calvinism emphasized adherence to many of the Old Testament moral strictures. The literary tradition of the Old Testament has profoundly shaped Western literature and language since for centuries Biblical stories were the staple of Christian Europe's literary and symbolic diet. In Medieval and Renaissance art, characters and themes from the Hebrew tradition abound. Michaelangelo's *David* is but one example. In sum, the modern Western world derives not only much of its religious heritage from the small ancient nation of the Hebrews but also much of its legal, ethical, literary, and artistic culture.

Other Peoples

In addition to the Phoenicians, Arameans, and Hebrews, many other peoples found a niche in the Near East and neighboring areas in the post-1200 B.C. world and made significant contributions to civilization. Centered in southern Mesopotamia, the Neo-Babylonians who flourished in the seventh and sixth centuries B.C. and conquered the kingdom of Judah, as mentioned earlier, were excellent astronomers. They kept minute records of eclipses, charted the heavens, and mathematically calculated the length of the year, influencing much astronomical work that came after them. Their capital, Babylon, with its massive walls wide enough to accommodate two chariots riding abreast, was a wonder of the ancient world, covering some 500 acres and boasting a population of more than 100,000. There, Nebuchadnezzar II built fabulous temples and a terraced roof garden, the famous Hanging Gardens.

Another group contributing to the continuing development of civilization was the Lydians. Centered on the city of Sardis near the Aegean coast of western Asia Minor, the Lydian Kingdom arose, flourishing in the 600s B.C., and established an empire extending over approximately the western half of Asia Minor. Fabulously wealthy, Lydian kings like Croesus took advantage of rich mineral deposits, such as the gold found in the Pactolus River. An important contribution to civilization attributed to the Lydians is the invention of coinage, which facilitated trade by providing a medium of exchange with an accepted value. The early Lydian coins, called *staters*, a term that meant "standard" and was originally a unit of weight, were made of a natural mixture of gold and silver called *electrum*. The earliest Lydian coins were apparently minted in the 600s B.C. and by the mid-500s B.C. coins were in widespread use by Greeks who adopted the practice from their Lydian neighbors. The Lydians were overcome by the rising Persian empire in 546 B.C.

Lydia's King Croesus was a great admirer of the Greeks, and he faithfully followed many Greek customs.

The Assyrian Empire

While groups like the Neo-Babylonians and Lydians made definitive contributions to civilization, the two most important groups in terms of political power and influence were the Assyrians and Persians, who revived and expanded the concept of empire. After a period of about 400 years after 1200 B.C. in which there was no dominant imperial power in the Near East, a group of Semitic people in a kingdom centered on the city of Assur along the Tigris River in Mesopotamia began to put together a revival of imperial power that outmatched any prior effort of the Ancient World. The Assyrians and their empire not only revived the larger political entity of empire but created the first actual empire, making an effort to integrate disparate peoples and cultures into a new whole rather than simply ruling over conquered city-states.

Originally, the Assyrians were Semitic farmers, traders, and herders who had settled around Assur by the middle of the third millennium B.C. Living as they did in the open northern Mesopotamian region, the Assyrians faced a nearly constant struggle against invaders and raiders, including the Akkadians, Amorites, Kassites, Hittites, Mitanni, Arabian nomads, and mountain raiders from the north and east. In the process of surviving, these people developed into formidable warriors, a characteristic that was enhanced by their adoption of iron weapons and chariot warfare techniques. After the disruptions of c. 1200 B.C., the Assyrians began to use their military prowess to conquer neighboring peoples. Their king, Tiglath-Pileser I (c. 1115-1077 B.C.), pushed Assyrian power west through northern Syria to the Mediterranean coast, northwest into much of the former Hittite domain, and southward into lower Mesopotamia. Providing a hint of the Assyrian tendency to boast, Tiglath-Pileser I then assumed the title of "King of the World, King of Assyria, King of all the four rims of the earth." Although these gains were lost in the rule of his immediate successors, later Assyrian kings such as Tiglath-Pileser III (744-727 B.C.) and Sargon II (721-705 B.C.) regained these territories and more, ruling over an empire that at its height included in a great arc of the ancient Near East Egypt, Palestine, Syria, eastern Asia Minor, Mesopotamia, and territory eastward to Persia.

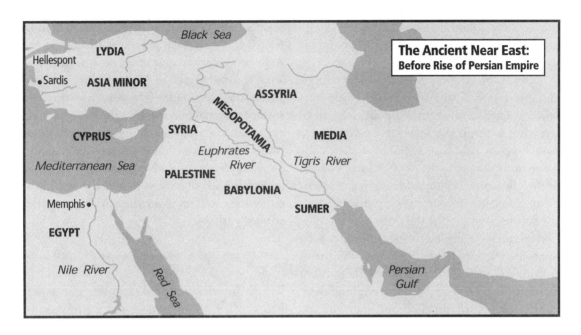

One of the most important accomplishments of the Assyrians was the way they administered their empire. The pattern of Assyrian conquest and administration would serve as an important example for later empire-builders. Assyrian imperial practice had several components. First, the Assyrians used appointed provincial governors and bureaucratic officials to oversee the various parts of their holdings, collect taxes, and enforce written law codes. Communication with and among these officials was enhanced by a postal system and road network linking key centers of the empire.

Second, to conquer territory and maintain control the Assyrians used a professional army combined with a militaristic ideology, which gave them a cohesive and effective force. All able-bodied Assyrian men had to serve in the army, and men from subject peoples were formed into units under Assyrian generals. These soldiers were among the best equipped in the world, for the Assyrians were the first to use iron weap-onry on a large scale. They developed highly effective siege weapons that could batter down the walls of cities that resisted. Cavalry units and chariot forces rounded out the Assyrian military capabilities. Tiglath-Pileser III added an effective religious ingredient to Assyrian militarism. Under this king, the Assyrian god, Ashur, emphasized one command: an order to enlarge the empire. In this way, military duty was also religious duty.

A third component of the Assyrian approach to empire was an effort to break down old regional identities and establish a universal identity tied to the empire. In this vein, the Assyrians removed and resettled many of the peoples they conquered so as to undercut their cultural independence. Israelites were moved to Mesopotamia. Some 18,000 Arameans were marched to Syria while 30,000 Syrians were deported to the Zagros Mountains northeast of the Euphrates River. In a more constructive approach, the Assyrians also adopted Aramaic as a *lingua franca*, a common language that could be used in all parts of the empire regardless of what languages were spoken locally.

Finally, making the Assyrians most famous and greatly hated, they used an extremely brutal, calculated, and advertised policy of official terrorism to instill fear and enforce compliance with Assyrian rule. In accounts of their conquests and campaigns, the Assyrian kings boasted of their brutality. Ashurnasirpal flayed the skins off of the nobles of one resistant city, piled up the corpses, and draped the skins over the pile. Outside another city, he cut off the heads of the opposing warriors and built a tower with them. A third city suffered the loss in battle of 3000 warriors. Captives had it even worse; from these poor souls Ashurnasirpal cut off limbs, hands, noses, and ears. He cut off heads and hung them on trees around the city. In account after account Assyrian kings described such ghastly treatment of foes. The main contribution of Assyrians to the art world, their relief carvings, were most often used to trumpet their military and hunting skill. Palaces at Nimrud and Nineveh were adorned with carved depictions of battle scenes showing the bodies of dead and wounded foes scattered over the ground. The simple message of the Assyrians was submit or face horrific consequences.

For all the effectiveness of Assyrian policy, the terrorism obviously created one major problem: it did not engender much love for Assyrian rule. If the Assyrians faced a serious threat, they were unlikely to receive much aid and comfort from their brutalized subjects who were more liable to join a rebellion or assist an invader. By the late 600s B.C., Assyria had overextended itself by acquiring more territory than it could effectively manage. At this juncture, the Neo-Babylonian Chaldeans and the kingdom of Medes located to the east of Mesopotamia joined

together and crushed the ferocious Assyrians in 612 B.C. Few tears were shed; in fact, the Assyrians received a bit of their own medicine. The Assyrian capital at Nineveh was destroyed and burned to rubble. The Assyrian army and royalty were slaughtered, and the Assyrian state ceased to exist. The capital city of Nineveh slumbered for centuries buried in the desert sands, awaiting discovery and excavation by modern archaeologists who have retrieved a wealth of cuneiform tablets from the royal library destroyed with Assyria.

The Persian Empire

The Medes who helped destroy Assyrian power had unified a kingdom in the region east of Mesopotamia in the middle of the seventh century B.C. The Medes and their neighbors, the Persians, who lived to the south near the gulf that bears their name, were Indo-European speakers. They likely arrived in this area that today is Iran as part of the larger Indo-European migrations. Both the Medes and the Persians were excellent horse breeders and attained notoriety for this and their riding skill. At first, the Median kingdom was more powerful than the Persians and had subjugated their southern neighbors, though the Persians did continue to have their own king. Eventually, in the middle of the sixth century B.C., Cyrus the Great, one of the Persian kings, was able to lead the Persians in conquest of the Medes, making Media the first *satrapy* or province in what ultimately became the largest empire the world had known.

Cyrus came to the Persian throne in 559 B.C., conquered Media in 550 B.C., and pushed westward into Asia Minor, taking control of that region, including the Lydian kingdom that incorporated Greek colonies on the Aegean coast of Asia Minor. After turning his attention to the east and conquering a huge section reaching as far east as the Indus River Valley on the border of India, Cyrus then took Mesopotamia, defeating Babylon in 539 B.C. After Cyrus died in 530 B.C., his son, Cambyses (530-522 B.C.), conquered Egypt with the assistance of ships supplied by the Phoenicians. Under Cambyses' successor, Darius I (522-486 B.C.), who unsuccessfully attempted to subjugate the Greek city-states on the Balkan Peninsula in Europe, the Persians solidified their empire and its administration. The empire lasted until the Greeks under the leadership of the Macedonian king Alexander the Great conquered it in the late fourth century B.C.

Beginning with Cyrus, the Persians developed their own approach to empire administration that had elements in common with the Assyrian imperial method but differed in critical ways. These Persian imperial policies went a long way toward creating an ideal of empire that saw the larger political structure of empire as beneficial and desirable, thus stretching the development of political thought in directions that in later times significantly changed Greek conceptions and set the stage for the success of the Romans in ruling a heterogeneous empire that incorporated the entire Mediterranean world and much of Europe.

In administering their empire, the Persian kings divided the territory into provinces called *satrapies*. Over each of these they appointed a governor called a *satrap*, which means "protector of the kingdom." The satraps were very powerful within the province, having control of the military and civilian government. To keep an eye on the satraps, the Persians sent inspectors, responsible directly to the king, out into all parts of the empire to see that royal policies were being followed. The Persians, like the Assyrians,

depended on efficient communications but developed an even more impressive system. The great Royal Road stretched 1677 miles from Sardis near the Aegean coast in Asia Minor to the chief Persian capital at Susa in Iran. Along the length of this road a series of postal stables were established at frequent intervals so that messages could travel at top speed by fresh horses over the entire distance. Other roads connected the major cities of the empire.

Like the Assyrians, the Persians promoted the notion of the empire as a unified entity. For example, Darius borrowed the Lydians' invention of coins and introduced a standardized coinage throughout the empire, which, in addition to the protection and stability of Persian rule, promoted trade and commerce and presented a concrete benefit of Persian administration. This marks an important contrast to the Assyrian style. While the Persians had a powerful and effective military and used it to quell rebellions, they did not promote or emphasize this approach. In striking contrast to the terrorism of the Assyrians, Cyrus the Great initiated the Persian policy of treating conquered peoples generously to win their support, and other Persian kings promoted the benefits of peace, stability, and security that belonging to the empire could bring.

The Persians made many important cultural contributions beyond the realm of political practices, but one of the more important was the religious legacy that Persia left through the influence of its empire. During his reign, Persian king Darius I was converted to a religion called Zoroastrianism that had not long before developed in Persia. Although Darius did not spread Zoroastrianism by force, he promoted it and helped contribute its legacy to the religious thought of the Near Eastern world in which Christianity soon developed.

Upper-class Persian women led comfortable lives. Women apparently received little or no education, however, and for the most part led secluded lives.

Zoroastrianism takes its name from its founder, a little-known figure called Zoroaster or Zarathustra, who lived around 600 B.C. According to the *Zend-Avesta*, which is the religion's sacred book, Zoroaster was born in Azerbaijan and as a child began to have visions. After spending the early part of his adulthood living in the wilderness, Zoroaster at the age of 30 began preaching a new religion. Zoroaster taught that there was only one true god, who he called Ahura-Mazda. Ahura-Mazda represented good in the world and was locked in a struggle with an evil spirit called Ahriman, or Angra Mainyu. This struggle was played out in the free choices that people made in their lives. A person could choose to be good and follow Ahura-Mazda or to be evil and follow Ahriman. The *Zend-Avesta* spelled out the virtues, such as pure thoughts, good works, and righteous deeds that people should strive for, as well as the evils they should avoid, such as lying. Religious laws in the *Zend-Avesta* also included some excellent hygienic rules. According to Zoroastrianism, Ahura-Mazda would ultimately prevail over the evil Ahriman and then sit in judgement of

people. People who had chosen good over evil in their lives would be rewarded with a life after death in paradise, while those who had followed evil would be punished in an endless night.

Zoroastrianism offers some striking parallels with Christianity, which would arise about 600 years later. The juxtaposition of a righteous god with an evil spirit mirrors the Christian struggle between God and Satan. Like Zoroastrianism, Christianity envisions a final judgement at which the choices people have made will be called to account and the reward of eternal life offered. And like Zoroaster, the central figure of Christianity, Jesus of Nazareth, began his ministry of teaching at the age of 30. While the precise connection between Zoroastrianism and Christian thought is not known, Persian sponsorship of Zoroastrianism made it a part of the general religious milieu of the Near East that affected the development of Christian ideas several centuries later.

The Persians are the last examined of the many peoples neighboring or infiltrating the older zones of civilization who began as early as the third millennium B.C. to make their mark on the larger developments affecting the history of Western civilization. This larger role played by peoples centered or originating outside the original heartlands of civilization became an increasingly powerful development beginning around 1200 B.C. as the then prevailing power structure dominated by the Egyptian and Hittite Empires collapsed, allowing smaller kingdoms to make important contributions and setting the stage for the revival and more complete fulfillment of the notion of empire by the Assyrians and Persians. The Persians, being one of the Indo-European peoples who migrated into the Near East, offer an excellent example of the dynamics that these infiltrating and neighboring peoples added to the development of Western civilization. As the Persians became powerful and influential, uniting the old centers of civilization and much of the neighboring areas in a single political entity, those old centers increasingly faded in their power and influence.

DEVELOPMENT IN PERIPHERAL AREAS: THE PREHISTORY OF EUROPE

Over the great span of time in which Neolithic culture evolved into civilization in the Mesopotamian and Egyptian heartlands, further away, on the periphery of the civilized world in Europe proper, people lived and shaped changing cultures that in their own way contributed a great deal to the development of Western civilization. The development and contributions of these peoples are important because they lived in Europe itself, the place where Western civilization would ultimately take shape. It is also important to precede the history of developments in Europe with a geographical overview.

The Geography of Europe

Europe, with slightly less than four million square miles of land, is the smallest of the bulky landmasses called continents. Its boundaries stretch from the Arctic Ocean in the north, the open Atlantic Ocean in the west, to the Mediterranean and Black Seas in the south. The eastern boundary is not so clear, and disagreement on the subject has led some scholars to question whether Europe should be considered a separate continent at all. However, the generally accepted eastern limits of Europe follow roughly along the crests of the Ural and Caucasus Mountains.

This European landmass is essentially a large peninsula fringed with several smaller peninsulas and nearby islands. The resulting proximity of and access to the sea have shaped much of its history. For example, the Mediterranean Sea has served to connect peoples of Europe, Asia (including the Near East), and Africa, providing a highway for trade, travel, migration, and invasion for millennia. The topography of the land itself varies greatly. In addition to the plains of the Hungarian basin and scattered other areas, a great arc of plains extends across much of France and the nearby island of Great Britain through the Low Countries across northern Germany and into the vast spaces of eastern Russia. Regions of hilly terrain also abound, including the Scottish highlands, Brittany and the Massif Central in France, and much of central and western Germany. Mountain ranges too impose important impacts across the continent from the Kjölen Range of Norway, the Pyrenees bordering the Iberian Peninsula, the Apennines of the Italian Peninsula, the Dinaric ranges of the Balkans, the Carpathians of eastern Europe, and the spectacular Alps of south-central Europe.

Other geographic features deserve mention. Rivers such as the Rhone, the Loire, the Seine, the Rhine, the Elbe, the Oder, the Vistula, and the Danube have provided important avenues of travel, trade, and invasion. The relative openness of eastern Europe made it easy for migrating or invading peoples from further east to move westward into Europe. Finally, while rivers, hills, and mountain ranges divide Europe in different ways, one of the most important divisions is the separation of Mediterranean Europe from northern Europe by the Pyrenees, Alps, and Carpathians.

The mountains forming this division have made travel and trade between the north and the south more difficult (though certainly not impossible, especially since the Rhone Valley provides an important gap in the division). More important is the difference in climate that accompanies the division. In the Mediterranean area, summers are typically dry and hot, while winters are usually wet and moderately cool. North of the mountains the climate is significantly wetter and colder, with rainfall occurring year round. When differences in soil types and resulting vegetation patterns are also considered, the climate differences helped produce important historical differences in culture between the two regions. The north had an abundance of timber in many areas, while the Mediterranean faced shortages. Olive trees thrived in Mediterranean Europe but could not be cultivated north of the mountains. Wheat did not ripen as easily in the north as it did in the Mediterranean region so other grains were often cultivated. While these few examples point out the major cultural difference between the north and the Mediterranean, keep in mind that the two regions were connected by trade and travel. Both would become incorporated into Western civilization.

The Spread and Characteristics of Neolithic Life in Europe

Because most of the peoples in Europe proper—on the periphery of the civilized world—were not literate until Roman influence was felt around the time of Christ, this section is essentially a look at the later prehistory of Europe proper, a prehistory that is nonetheless rich in cultural accomplishments and contributions. When Neolithic innovations such as agriculture first emerged in the Near East beginning around 8000 B.C., Europe was not as culturally advanced. But under the influence of contact with the Near East and through other processes of exchange and cultural evolution, European peoples developed the basic features of Neolithic life. Most of the major advancements, such as farming and metal-working technology, followed a basic pattern of spread from east to west.

Based on archaeological evidence, economies based on producing food, rather than procuring food by hunting and gathering it, first emerged in Europe around 6000 B.C. Farming, including both agriculture and animal domestication, appeared first in Crete, Greece, and Bulgaria, areas in southeastern Europe closest to the Near East, and then spread westward. Settled, village-based life also accompanied the spread of farming economies as people built and rebuilt on the same site over generations. For example, at the Karanovo site in Bulgaria, the tell, or mound of remains from a series of settlements built on the same site, accumulated to a height of over 12 yards, indicating a very long period of settled use. The size of settlements also grew; the earliest site at Knossos on Crete was about an acre in size but by the end of the Neolithic period the site was nine times that large.

The spread of Neolithic villages through Europe followed two primary lines of advance.

One line, characterized by rapid movement, followed the northern Mediterranean coast. By 5600 B.C. settlements were established in Italy and by 4000 B.C. in southern France. The people establishing villages along this line were likely both farmers and sailors/fishermen. The other line along which farming villages spread was the loess soils of the Danube and Rhine River Valleys where the advancing farmers practiced a type of slash and burn agriculture in this heavily forested, temperate region of Europe. By 4500 B.C. farming villages appeared in Holland, and shortly after 4000 B.C. they emerged in western France. In France the two streams of settlement flowed together, and around 3500 B.C. farmers were crossing to Britain and Ireland. By 3000 B.C. farming villages had spread over most of the British Isles.

With the spread of farming villages across Europe came several important cultural developments. First, by about 3000 B.C. a broad cultural unity that had characterized early Neolithic Europe was fragmenting as cultural regions developed. Also defensive works began to appear by this time as people settled in particular territories and saw the need to protect their homes and animals from competitors made more common because of population growth. Another significant cultural development was the rise in Iberia, France, and Britain of complex religious practices. From Spain to Denmark in the period c. 3500-2500 B.C. Neolithic peoples built collective tombs by laying large stone slabs inside mounds of rubble and dirt. The attention paid to the dead in such burials indicates a belief in life after death. These people of the Western part of Europe also created various sacred sites of impressive sophistication. The stone temples at Malta and various stone alignments in Brittany and Britain are good examples, but the more famous examples are the circular henge monuments such as the one at Avebury on the Salisbury Plain in England known as Stonehenge.

Though in ruins today, Stonehenge inspires speculation and awe with its familiar horseshoe of megaliths (huge solid rocks) standing upright inside a larger circle of upright megaliths, both at one time laid with additional megaliths capping and connecting the column-like uprights. While today people often associate Stonehenge with the Celtic religious tradition of druidism, and the site may very well have been used by ancient Celtic peoples for religious purposes, Stonehenge apparently was constructed in three phases well before the rise of Celtic culture in Europe. Archeological investigation has determined that the first construction at the site took place around 3100 B.C. The first construction, which did not involve circular stone settings but rather the construction of a circular ditch and embankment on the interior side of the ditch, was apparently used for about 500 years and then abandoned. About 2100 B.C., in a second phase of construction, the entrance to the circular site was aligned approximately with the summer solstice sunrise and this alignment enhanced by the construction of an avenue leading to the site along the line of the sunrise. Though later dismantled, about 80 bluestone pillars weighing about four tons each were laboriously brought some 240 miles from the Preseli Mountains in Wales and set upright in two concentric semicircles. The third phase of construction occurred in stages with the first stage beginning about 2000 B.C. and the last stage falling about 1550 B.C. While various other features were constructed in the third phase, at its beginning, around 2000 B.C., the megalithic horseshoe and circle of uprights capped by lintel stones were imported and erected. These sarsen stones, approximately 75 in number, weighing as much as 50 tons, and extending up to 30 feet in length,

Stonehenge is a favorite spot for tourists. However, people are no longer allowed to touch and climb on the stones.

came from the Marlborough Downs 20 miles to the north and were carefully shaped to fit together with mortis and tenon joints. This was a remarkable achievement of transportation, engineering, and craftsmanship.

The purpose of Stonehenge and other such monuments is exceedingly unclear and various theories have been advanced. One theory regarding a circular henge monument in France argued that that site was originally a cattle pen. A popular theory that Stonehenge was an elaborate calculator of eclipses and the calendar has been roundly criticized by scholars. The ruined state of the monument makes it impossible to determine what astronomical alignments may have been incorporated in the construction. It is safe to assume that Stonehenge had some important religious purpose for those who built and used

it. Regardless, its construction indicates the sophistication and great skill of Neolithic Europeans.

Another cultural development in Neolithic Europe was the spread of metalworking skills, such as the mining of ores and extraction of metal from the ores where these deposits existed. Copper was used for ornaments and weapons. As with farming and settled life, the earliest metalworking activity in Europe appeared in the Balkans, closest to the Near Eastern centers of civilization, as early as 3000 B.C. Metalworking activity spread to the eastern Alpine region and Thuringia, and by 2400 B.C. Neolithic Iberians were extracting, alloying, and casting copper at Almeria, Algarve, and Alemtejo. In one of the most intriguing recent archaeological finds, the excellently preserved body of a

Neolithic man was found in 1991 in the Alps on the Austrian-Italian border after a collapse of part of the edge of a glacier. Known as the "Iceman," this individual died, perhaps of an arrow wound, as he traveled through the mountains. About 25-35 years old at his death, the Iceman's body was frozen about 5300 years ago (c. 3300 B.C.) in an avalanche. In addition to flint-pointed, feather-tipped arrows and a flint dagger, the Iceman was carrying a copper axe blade, making him a good example of the blending of stone-age technology with emerging metal usage at an early point.

Despite the advancement of culture in various parts of Europe, the level of civilization developed first in the area of Europe closest to the Near East: the eastern Mediterranean Sea and the Greek area of the Balkan Peninsula where the Minoan civilization centered on Crete and the Mycenaean civilization in Greece arose. Both of these civilizations were economically based on the elaborate trade that closely networked the Aegean and eastern Mediterranean world. For the rest of Europe this trade was very important for it stimulated a great deal of economic activity throughout Europe because of the demand it created for European resources. Northern Germany, Amorica, and Britain supplied valuable tin needed for smelting bronze. Ireland and Spain produced gold, while the Baltic Sea region in the north supplied amber. An elaborate system of production and exchange developed within Europe and this economic vitality allowed flourishing cultures to develop in Amorica, Wessex, Germany, northern Italy, and Denmark.

The Urnfield Culture

Around 1200 B.C. the trade and economic demand of the Aegean world collapsed as the Sea Peoples and other groups disrupted the eastern Mediterranean and Near East. Central and western Europe were significantly impacted by the collapse of the trade network. People in Europe had to find other activities or markets and likely forged much closer economic and cultural ties with each other. In part as a result of the collapse of the Mycenaean market and in part due to the influx of Indo-Europeans into Europe in the second millennium B.C., a new culture called the Urnfield culture developed in Hungary in the thirteenth century B.C. and eventually spread to parts of Poland, Germany, the Alps, and Italy, so that by about 1000 B.C. all these areas had a similar culture that was influencing neighboring areas like France, the Low Countries, Spain, and Britain.

The Urnfield culture, flourishing from about 1300-700 B.C., dominated this whole region and was characterized by several important features. The term "Urnfield" comes from the burial practices of this culture. The dead were cremated and their remains placed in urns that were then buried in cemeteries along with various grave goods. These burials indicate that the Urnfield peoples had little disparity in wealth, as the various burials all received about the same amount of attention and contained a similar amount of grave goods. Another important characteristic of the Urnfield culture is that the people spoke dialects of the Celtic branch of the Indo-European language family. This culture then is the immediate source culture of the Celtic culture.

In the 700s B.C. changes began that transformed the Urnfield culture and created the Celtic culture in the process. For one thing, greater disparity in wealth became evident. In this period some urns were buried with much more attention and wealth in the form of grave goods than others. The evidence for the use of horses increases dramatically as such items as bridle fittings turn up with increasing frequency. The exact causes of these changes are uncertain, but the movement of peoples from further east, where horse use was well established, into central and western Europe as part of the larger Indo-European migrations likely explains much of the transformation.

The Celts

Regardless of why the changes happened, they resulted in the formation of the Celtic culture. The Celtic culture emerged between the 700s B.C. and about 450 B.C. in what archaeologists label the Halstatt Phase (from the location of an early excavation site). This cultural period marks the first European culture to be a part of the Iron Age. Celtic culture continued to develop in the LaTène phase from 450 B.C. until the rising Roman civilization swamped native culture, a process that happened at different times in various areas of Celtic Europe.

The history of Celtic Europe, about which a substantial amount is known primarily through a rich archaeological record, historical accounts written by Greek and Roman observers, and the ancient Irish sagas set down in writing in the eighth century A.D. by Irish monks, can be divided into three main periods. The first period from about 700-400 B.C. was characterized by a wealthy aristocracy that controlled and profited from the production and trade networks that had by this time once again connected Europe to the civilized Mediterranean world. Originally, aristocratic power was centered in Bohemia and the upper Danube Valley. Then the center shifted first to a zone between Stuttgart and Zurich in the sixth century B.C. and finally to the middle Rhine and Marne Rivers region in the middle of the fifth century B.C. These shifts are probably tied to the establishment of the Greek colony, Massilia, at the mouth of the Rhone River, and the flourishing development of the Etruscan civilization, one of the source cultures of Roman civilization, in northern Italy.

The aristocratic elite centered themselves on fortified earthworks called hillforts, such as one located at Heuneburg, to help protect their wealth and defend their position. The tremendous wealth of this aristocracy is evidenced by their burials. Typically, wealthy individuals were buried on a finely made funerary cart set along with various possessions of great value in a timbered chamber that was topped with a barrow of dirt. At Vix in France, one such burial included a huge five-feet-tall bronze krater used for holding wine that had been imported from the Mediterranean. Interestingly, this Celtic practice developed near the time that some Indian cultures in North America began burying their dead along with grave goods in earthen burial mounds.

Over the course of the 400s B.C. the power of the aristocrats began to break down as the archaeological record shows big disparities in burials decrease, old fortified centers go out of use, and evidence of movement and disruption increase. The second phase of Celtic history is a period in which large, often wholesale migrations occur. From about 400-180 B.C. many Celtic tribes collectively moved to new areas. Perhaps the fact that under the aristocrats much wealth was being buried in graves rather than redistributed in the economy forced groups to seek better economic opportunities elsewhere. Growing population or over-exploitation of the environment could have led to similar pressures. Many movements took place in this era, but two examples will illustrate. One group of Celts crossed the Alps into northern and then central Italy where they sacked the city of Rome around 390 B.C. They stayed in the region until the

Romans defeated them in the Battle of Bologna in 191 B.C. Another group moved east and south across the Danube into the Balkan Peninsula and to the Black Sea. One element of about 20,000 of these Celts crossed over into Asia Minor, raided for a while, and then settled in the region that eventually took its name from them: Galatia.

These major migrations were significant in two fundamental ways. First, the movement of Celts into previously settled regions caused no end of disruption, fear, and reaction. For example, after the 390 B.C. sack of Rome, the Romans built the huge 10 kilometer-long Servian Wall to defend against future Celtic attacks. Second, the migrations stimulated a tremendous amount of cultural interaction that helped shape the culture of both the Celtic peoples and the areas they moved into. For example, as a result of contact with the Celts, Mediterranean states often employed Celts as mercenaries, having been impressed by the Celts' fighting skills. On the other hand, having been exposed to the urban life of the Mediterranean world, Celts, in the third stage of their history, settled down and formed larger towns and small cities, a settlement practice that the Celts had not previously followed.

The third stage of Celtic history began around 180 B.C. and extended, if political measures are used and the continent of Europe is the focus, until 51 B.C. when the last of the independent Gallic tribes (the Roman name for the Celts was Gauls) under the leadership of Vercingetorix were defeated by the Romans at Alesia as Rome extended its power north of the Alps. If on the other hand, cultural vitality and sense of identity are the criteria used to determine the end of the last period of Celtic history, then an argument could be made that the last period continues today since strong elements of Celtic culture survive in certain parts of Europe, such as in Ireland. Certainly by the end of the first century after Christ, the Celtic culture had in most areas of Europe so blended with the Roman or other cultures that it does not make sense to give it a separate identity. In this last period, the Celtic migrations ended and Celtic groups settled down, came into closer and more on-going contact with the civilizations of the Mediterranean world and merged into a blending cultural mix that along with Roman and Germanic elements would form the direct basis of the early Western civilization of Medieval Europe. In addition to the increased cultural blending, this period saw more settled life among the Celts that resulted in growing towns and small cities called oppida.

The Celts, whom the Greeks called Keltoi, certainly captivated classical observers. Their long hair especially drew comment. The official Roman name for the province of Gaul was Gallia Comata, meaning literally "shaggy-headed Gaul." The Celts impressed classical observers in various other ways as well. Celts were admired or feared for their noisy, ferocious fighting style and their innovations such as the trimarcisia, a three-man cavalry unit. Julius Caesar admired what he called the *murus gallicus*, a type of defense works that fortified Celtic oppida and hillforts.

The Celts were not an empire nor in any sense a unified people. They were composed of a number of different tribes such as the Boii, Helvetii, Aeudi, Arverni, and Scordisci, each having its own government, customs, and other cultural features but all sharing some broad cultural similarities. One of the more obvious cultural features the Celts shared was their languages, which were different dialects of a common Celtic language. It is difficult to generalize about features of Celtic society. Celts did typically have a class structure with wealthy warriors occupying the top position. Celtic tribes seem to have originally been governed under a form of hereditary monarchy, but eventually leaders were apparently selected out of the warrior elite, who formed a sort of oligarchy that built on networks of dependency relationships formed by wealthy and powerful Celts with folks of lesser means. Druids, who were learned intellectuals and priests, formed a class in some Celtic societies.

The Celtic economy was quite diversified. Celts were generally quite rural and made their living farming such crops as wheat, barley, and oats, raising animals like cattle, swine, and chickens, and hunting to supplement the diet. The Celts bred hunting dogs that assisted in the hunt and provided an object of trade as well. Trade was an important component of Celtic economic life. The Celts traded salt, various iron products, tin, gold, silver, bronze, amber, furs, grain, slaves, and hunting dogs in a well-developed system of commerce with the Mediterranean world in exchange for various manufactured goods like bronze vessels, pottery, glass, coral, and the popular wine, which the Celts drank undiluted, contrary to Mediterranean custom.

Celtic culture developed its own style and character that made a valuable contribution to many aspects of life, not the least of which is the interpretive, lively, and sinuous art expressed in carvings, statuary, jewelry, and metal objects. Many features of Celtic culture deeply influenced Western civilization, though these are often difficult to discern because of the fact that Roman civilization blended with the Celtic before the emergence of Western civilization. Geography

and religion provide two good examples. A modern map of Europe shows many large cities such as London, Budapest, Paris. Though other examples could be listed, each of these cities rest on sites that were originally Celtic oppida. One of the modern religious traditions associated with Catholic Christianity of Medieval Europe is Halloween (All Hallow's Evening) and All Saint's Day celebrated at October 31/November 1. Many of the practices associated with this date on the Christian calendar are derived from Celtic practices associated with the same date. The Celtic seasonal ceremonies of Samhain (November 1) marked the end of the old year and beginning of the new, a limbo period of chaos when the spiritual and physical worlds intermingled and the normal order of life was out of balance. The belief that ghosts and goblins stalk the earth on Halloween playing tricks on folks provides just one example of a direct cultural link with the rich Celtic heritage that is part of the extensive foundation of Western civilization.

This chapter has examined five great developments: the prehistoric development of humans that set the stage for civilization, the rise and influence of Mesopotamian civilization, the rise and influence of Egyptian civilization, the development and contribution of various peoples neighboring or moving into the older centers of civilization, and finally the developments in Europe itself that preceded the Greeks and Romans. In these five great developments, then, the building blocks of Western civilization were laid. The development of Western civilization, carried forward by the Greeks, Romans, and later Europeans rests on the foundation thus established.

Suggestions for Further Reading

Mary Boyce, *Zoroastrians: Their Religious Beliefs and Practices* (1984).

John Bright, *A History of Israel* (1972).

A. Rosalie David, *The Ancient Egyptians: Religious Beliefs and Practices* (1982).

Margaret Ehrenberg, *Women in Prehistory* (1989).

Richard N. Frye, *The History of Ancient Iran* (1983).

Thorkild Jacobsen, *The Treasures of Darkness: A History of Mesopotamian Religion* (1976).

T.G.H. James, *An Introduction to Ancient Egypt* (1990).

Arthur Bernard Knapp, *The History and Culture of Ancient Western Asia and Egypt* (1988).

Samuel N. Kramer, *History Begins at Sumer* (1981).

Richard E. Leakey, *The Making of Mankind* (1981).

J.P. Mallory, *In Search of the IndoEuropeans: Language, Archaeology and Myth* (1989).

J. Maxwell Miller and John H. Hayes, *A History of Ancient Israel and Judah* (1986).

Sabatino Moscati, *The Face of the Ancient Orient* (1962).

Leonard R. Palmer, *Mycenaeans and Minoans* (1980).

Georges Roux, *Ancient Iraq* (1980).

W.W. Hallo and W.K. Simpson, *The Ancient Near East* (1971).

Barbara Watterson, *Women in Ancient Egypt* (1991).

Raymond Weill, *Phoencia and Western Asia to the Macedonian Conquest* (1980).

Robert J. Wenke, *Patterns in Prehistory: Humankind's First Three Million Years* (1990).

Chapter
2

THE GREEKS

It was the year of the great invasion, 480 B.C. The greatest power in the world, Persia, was sending an army of at least 150,000 men plus a huge navy of over 100 ships to take revenge on the Athenians because they had humiliated the Persian army ten years earlier at Marathon. Many of the Greeks decided to give in and try to get the best deal possible from the great emperor, Xerxes. Who could blame them for wanting to save their own lives, or perhaps avoid slavery in a distant land, which was worse than death for these free people?

Only thirty-one out of hundreds of Greek city-states (poleis) joined in an alliance to stop this seemingly unstoppable force. Many must have called them fools and argued that they would bring the wrath of the great king down on all as a punishment for their vain opposition. Sparta, which had the most formidable army in all Greece, was chosen to lead this alliance, known as the Greek Alliance. As the Persian army crossed the Hellespont (Turkish Straits) and marched around the northwest end of the Aegean Sea, every city-state in its path surrendered without a fight. But when they turned south along the coast, they came to a narrow pass about 50 feet wide, Thermopylae. This was the place that the Greeks had been chosen to halt the Persian invasion. King Leonidas, one of two kings in Sparta, was the chosen leader of the Greek armed forces. He had 300 Spartan soldiers with him but a total of about 9,000 men to hold the pass. Since the Greek soldiers were equal to the Persian troops man to man in courage and skill, the larger Persian army could gain no advantage from their greater number. According to Herodotus, the "Father of History," who wrote the **History of the Greek and Persian War** *and is our main source for this event, Xerxes waited for four days, as he expected them to capitulate. When they didn't, the attack began and went on for two days, The Persian army could not break through despite sending in the king's special bodyguard called the "Immortals" by Xerxes.*

Then a Greek from a polis that was not allied against Persia offered to show the Persians a mountain path that would bring the Persian troops out on the far side of the pass and dislodge the Greeks from their defensible position. This was done during the second night. By morning of the third day, it was clear that the Greeks must abandon their position or die. Leonidas commanded most of the allies to retreat but he determined that he and his 300 men, along with 400 Thebans which he forced to stay as hostages (to insure that their polis did not go over to the Persians), would stay and fight to the death. Another 700 Thespians, who would not abandon him, also remained by his side. Strange as this action might seem to modern civilians, Leonidas refused to retreat to gain glory for Sparta and because Spartans were never supposed to retreat. His polis had sent him to defend that place, and he would not break that command. Furthermore, he had a religious reason in that the oracle (source of divine revelation to the Greeks) at Delphi had foretold "that either Sparta must be overthrown by the barbarians or one of her kings must perish." He and his men fought to the death that morning, and Herodotus tells us that they fought with such fury that the enemy "fell in heaps." At last Leonidas fell in the battle. There was a great struggle for his body, which was won by the Greeks after four counterattacks were made to drive the Persians back so they could carry his body back with them. The remaining Greeks retreated to a small hill in the narrowest part of the pass. They formed a circle to protect their backs and fought to the last man, except for the Thebans who surrendered after Leonidas' death. Herodotus described it thus: "Here they defended themselves to the last, such as still had swords using them, and the others resisting with their hands and teeth; till the barbarians . . . overwhelmed and buried the remnant which was left beneath showers of missile weapons."

The defiant courage of these men was perhaps best expressed by a Spartan named Dieneces who heard a fellow Greek from Trachinia complain before the battle began that the monstrous army they faced would produce so many arrows that they would darken the sun. Dieneces answered "Our Trachinian friend brings us excellent tidings. If the Medes darken the sun, we shall have our fight in the shade." Their heroic stand won not only the admiration of all Greeks at that time, but it has echoed down the centuries to inspire and touch human beings even today.

Chronology
(all dates B.C.)

2,900	Minoan Period
2,000	First Palace at Knossos
1,900	First appearance of Greek-speaking people on the mainland
1600-1150	Mycenaean Period
1,400	Linear B tablets first appear on Crete
1,200-1,150	Mycenaean palace culture is destroyed
1,150 -750	The Greek Dark Age
776	First Olympic Games are held
750	Homer writes *Iliad* and *Odyssey*
750-500	The Archaic/Lyric: Poleis develop and expand through colonization
725-710	First Messenian War
657	Cypselus takes over Corinth as Tyrant
650	Second Messenian War followed by Lycurgan Reforms
621	Draco publishes first law code in Athens
594	Solon reforms the law code of Athens
546-527	Pisistratus is Tyrant of Athens
510	Hippias, son of Pisistratus, is deposed and Athens is free of tyranny
508-501	Cleisthenes brings democratic changes to Athenian constitution & politics
500-323	Classical Age
499	Ionian poleis revolt against Persian rule and Athens sends military assistance
490	Persian War begins; Athenians defeat Persians at Marathon

480	Second Persian invasion of Greece:
479	Battles of Plataea and Mycale
478	Delian League formed
474-462	Cimon is the leader of Athens
467	Cimon defeats Persians at the Battle of the Eurymedon River
465-463	The revolt of Thasos
462	Pericles becomes the leader of Athens
460-445	First Peloponnesian War
449	Persian War ends
431-404	Second Peloponnesian War
405	Spartans destroy Athenian fleet at Aegospotami
404	Second Peloponnesian War ends Thirty Tyrants rule Athens under Sparta
403	Democracy restored in Athens – Tyrants driven out
399	Socrates' trial and execution
400-387	Spartan war against Persia
395-387	Corinthian War
387	Plato founds the Academy
378	Second Athenian Confederation formed
371	Thebes defeats Sparta at Leuctra – end of Sparta's hegemony of Greece
362	Battle of Mantinea – death of Epaminondas and of Theban hegemony of Greece
350	Appearance of Corinthian columns in architecture

HELLENIC CULTURE AND CIVILIZATION

Greece is a land of mountains with little arable soil that can be used for farming. These mountains were barriers to political unity, causing communities to form that were unique and fiercely independent. While the communities of the interior region of this rugged extension of the Balkan Peninsula were isolated by geography, a brief look at a map of Greece will immediately impress the observer with the fact that it is surrounded by water.

Jutting out into the Mediterranean Sea, this peninsula is cut off from Anatolia (modern Turkey) by the Aegean Sea to the east, from Italy by the Ionian Sea to the west, and from Africa and the Middle East by the Mediterranean Sea itself. Because of this extensive coastline, many Greeks were seafaring people, particularly those who had direct access to the sea. Eventually the Greeks expanded north into the Black Sea and around the Anatolian coast of the Aegean to the east, over the Ionian Sea west to southern Italy, and on across the Mediterranean to North Africa and what is today southern France and Spain. These people naturally turned to the sea for their livelihood, developing skills in fishing, boat building, seamanship, and trade.

Their position astride a peninsula, which forms a spearhead into the heart of the sea, led the Greeks quite naturally to share not only the economic goods of the region through trade but also cultural and religious developments as well. Greek sailors and merchants frequently traveled to Egypt and the ports of the Near East where they learned new ideas about religion, technology, and other aspects of culture. Some historians of ancient Greece stress this process of transferal of knowledge from other parts of the world when they describe the cultural development of the Greeks. Others emphasize the self-develop-

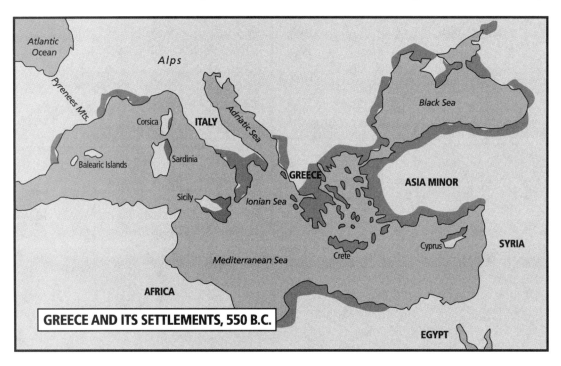

GREECE AND ITS SETTLEMENTS, 550 B.C.

ment of these people instead of seeing them as being dependent on outside influences. We cannot say with certainty, which of these was predominant, but most historians would agree that there was a mixture of the two, which produced Hellenic (Greek) culture and civilization.

The Minoans (1900-1150 B.C.)

Whether the development of Hellenic civilization is interpreted as spontaneous self-development, the spreading of civilization from Mesopotamia, the Near East and Egypt, or a blending of the two, it is on the island of Crete that we find the first advanced civilization in this region. Sir Arthur Evans, an early archeologist who discovered the site of a palace at Knossos, named the Minoans after the legendary ruler of Crete, King Minos. The Minoans developed Bronze Age technology shortly after 3000 B.C. These people traded with the Egyptians, Hittites, and other peoples of the Mediterranean Sea. The Minoans extended their influence into the Aegean Sea islands by establishing colonies and thus trade. Much about Minoan society and culture is unknown today. However, continual archaeological work provides new information, which slowly fills in missing pieces of the puzzle of what they believed and practiced religiously, and how they lived in society and with their neighbors of that time and place. The evidence is clear that the Minoans loved creature comforts, as we do today, and that they were able to build complex buildings up to five stories tall with many rooms, running water, and beautiful fresco paintings on the walls. The palace at Knossos is known as a labyrinth, or maze, because it had so many rooms in it that strangers could easily get lost. This was reinforced by a Greek myth, which claimed that King Minos exacted a tribute of Athens each year, seven young

men and seven maidens, who disappeared in the maze to be eaten by the Minotaur who was part man and part bull. The bull was very important in the Minoan religious belief and ritual system. Rodney Castleden, author of *Minoans: Life in Bronze Age Crete,* describes the bull-leaping rituals of the Minoans as a rite of passage for males and females that symbolized human struggle with, and obedience to, their deity.

The first palace at Knossos was built around 2000 B.C. Castleden argues that the palaces were actually temples and that these temples were the center of religious, social, and economic activity, led by the priests and priestesses, much as the Mesopotamians did at that same time. About 1700 B.C., an earthquake destroyed the building. It was rebuilt on an even grander scale and survived until a catastrophe occurred in 1470 B.C. with the eruption of a volcano on the island of Thera, 50 miles to the north. The resulting earthquake, tidal wave, or a combination of the two caused major destruction on Crete and damaged the temple/palace at Knossos extensively, as well as many other buildings on the island. Within 100 years, the Knossos building was abandoned. This period marks the end of a dominant Minoan culture, which was then replaced by the mainland center of Mycenae.

Before moving on to the Mycenaens, let us note several other significant Minoan developments. First, they developed or adopted several forms of writing, which are preserved on tablets today. So far, the written records that are readable only reveal business transactions of the palace/temples. No literature revealing the way they lived and thought has been discovered, but there is hope something will be unearthed in future excavations that will unlock the mysteries of these important people. The Minoans used hieroglyphics apparently adopted from the Egyptians and a non-Greek language, which has not been deciphered, called Linear A. Around 1400 B.C. another written language named Linear B appeared, which Briton Michael Ventris deciphered in 1952. This language was Greek and as far as we know now was used for record keeping. The appearance of this language indicates the increasing importance of the Greek Mycenaens to the Minoans. In fact, most historians believe that the Mycenaens took over Crete, either peacefully or by force, around 1400 B.C.

The Minoans have been interpreted by many scholars, beginning with Evans, as a peace-loving people due to the lack of walled cities. An alternative view is that, like England, the Minoan walls of defense consisted of her ships. Seemingly there was no need to defend themselves against each other, so as in any stable, strong country, forts and walled cities were not necessary. Again, Castledon takes a contrarian view of the peace-loving inhabitants of Crete. He finds that recent archaeological evidence shows a darker side to Minoan society. Castledon cites new frescoes that reveal naval battles, armor in graves, and evidence of the sacrifice of teenage boys. He theorizes that Minoans produced art that portrayed themselves and nature idealistically, not as they really were, just as Victorian Britons preferred flowers and bric-a-brac while conquering and exploiting other people in their empire.

Perhaps the last word on the Minoans should be about women in their society. Women are noticeable in Minoan culture as goddesses and priestesses. The Great Mother Goddess, a bare-breasted fertility symbol, was accepted as the chief deity. It is not known whether this female dominance in the religious world transferred to the secular world, but it is reasonable to conclude that women in Minoan society held a higher status and were closer to equality with men there than anywhere else in ancient society. This widely-held view is supported by the existence of a chief god that is female and by the prominent portrayal of women in art who are shown as engaging in a wide range of activities.

The Mycenaeans (1600-1200 B.C.)

The Minoans had a great impact on mainland Greece through trade and cultural exchange. The mainland people spoke a language that was Indo-European in origin, an early Greek form of language, which corresponds to the Linear B tablets. Once again, there is no written history or literature of these people. They appear to have invaded Greece shortly after the beginning of the second millennium B.C. While the name of Mycenae is used to represent the mainland Bronze Age civilization, these early Greeks spread across the Peloponnesus and the Attic Plain, establishing the cities of Pylos, Thebes, Athens, and Tiryns. Mycenae was known as the home of King Agamemnon in Homer's *Iliad*. Thus, it was the first mainland site to be identified and excavated by Heinrich Schliemann, the German businessman/archeologist who set out to prove that Homer's tale was not just a myth.

Mycenaean civilization was centered in the city, and political control was in the hands of powerful kings. Even at this early stage of Greek development, there was no political unification. Individual city-states, which included the surrounding territory, were the norm then as well as later during the classical period. Existing art and artifacts make it very clear that this was a warrior society. Shaft graves, which were used for burial from about 1600 to 1500 B.C., contained hundreds of bronze swords, daggers, arrowheads, shields, and other weapons of war. These graves also contained beautiful jewelry and items made of gold and silver. In fact, the

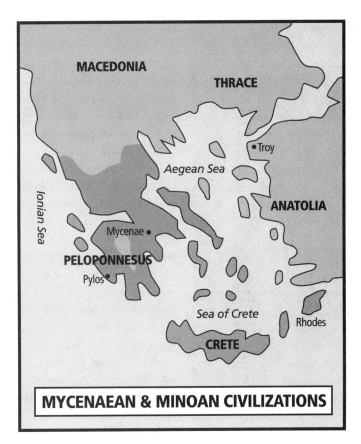

MYCENAEAN & MINOAN CIVILIZATIONS

Mycenaean kings lived in fine palaces and developed a high standard of living with complex methods of economic production and trade.

A new type of grave marks the second general period of Mycenaean development around 1500 B.C., known as the beehive, or Tholos tombs. These tombs were built with large blocks of stone, which were cut to fit perfectly. One of the large lintel stones is estimated to weigh over one hundred tons. The best known of the tombs is the Treasury of Atreus. The vault of this tomb is over 40 feet high and was only surpassed in size by the building of the Pantheon in Rome 1500 years later. This vault, which has stood for over 3,000 years, attests to the wealth and power of the kings of that era and to the architectural skill of this civilization.

The Mycenaeans flourished from about 1600 B.C. to 1200 B.C. As we have already noted, they came to dominate the Minoans by 1400 B.C., perhaps as a result of the volcanic devastation to Crete from the explosion of Thera. Egyptian records show that the Mycenaeans sometimes raided their shores and at other times traded with them. In fact, the people of mainland Greece replaced the Minoans as traders who ranged across the Mediterranean Sea. Homer's *Iliad* tells the story of their siege and eventual ransacking of the city of Troy. This event is estimated to have taken place at around 1250 B.C., if, indeed, the Greeks are the cause of the destruction of Troy at that time.

Then Mycenaean civilization fell apart and disappeared into a Dark Age where writing and

The epic poems, the *Iliad* and the *Odyssey*, attributed to Homer, were important examples of European literature. According to Homer, the kidnapping of Sparta's Queen Helen by a Trojan prince supposedly provoked the war. Whether this part of the legend is factual remains unknown.

higher forms of political organization and cultural achievement ceased to exist. The cause of the fall of the Mycenaeans is uncertain. The Greeks themselves told of an invasion by the Dorians, a less civilized people from the north that spoke a different dialect of the Greek language. These Dorians, according to the legend, teamed up with the Heraclidae and eventually overran the Peloponnesus, except for Athens and the Attic Plain. Greeks from the west and south fled to the east through Athens to the islands of the Aegean Sea and to the coast of Asia Minor, now known as Turkey. There they were known as Ionian Greeks, and the west coast of Asia Minor became Ionia.

Some scholars theorize that the Mycenaeans fell apart from within. They believe that bands of Mycenaean marauders began to attack the Greek kingdoms, perhaps as part of a rebellion against the over-centralized system of economic and political control exercised by the kings. It is important to note that this came at a time when groups known as the "sea peoples" overran the Hittite kingdom to the east in Asia Minor about 1200 B.C. and attacked Egypt and the coastal cities of the Mediterranean. Thomas Martin, author of *Ancient Greece* and an important American scholar of this period today, argues that the internal conflict explanation is the most plausible. He finds that there is evidence that the "sea peoples" were composed of different groups, which could very well have included Greeks from the mainland, as well as from the islands. All historians agree that, whatever the cause, the period after 1200 B.C. witnessed the destruction of Mycenaean palaces and the widespread movement of people.

The Dark Age (1150-750 B.C.)

For the next 200 years, there was chaos and economic insecurity as the centralized systems of the kings in their palaces were destroyed, and the population of Greece shrank. The only record of this period is archaeological evidence, since the Greeks lost their knowledge of writing. According to that record, this was a period where less land came under cultivation, and people re-

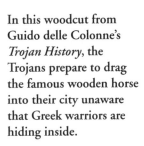

In this woodcut from Guido delle Colonne's *Trojan History*, the Trojans prepare to drag the famous wooden horse into their city unaware that Greek warriors are hiding inside.

lied more on the herding of animals to make a living. This naturally led to constant movement by small bands of people with their animals as they searched for new pastures. They lived in small huts that were built for temporary use. The days of great architecture and cultural advancements in the arts were over.

By 1000-900 B.C. the chaos and destruction had ended, and life for the Greeks became more stable. The increase of wealth is apparent from the valuable objects uncovered in burial sites. Iron weapons and tools began to replace those made of bronze. The first Geometric style art appeared by 850 B.C., so-called because of the use of geometric forms, such as circles and rectangles, used to form parallel bands around the vase or other decorated objects. Agricultural production began to increase as did the population, and Greece began to emerge into a new age.

The Archaic Age (750-500 B.C.)

The Greeks adapted the Phoenician alphabet to the sounds of their language by the end of the Dark Age, and the resulting literature informs us about Greek life and culture. Homer is considered the father of Greek literature. His epic poems, the *Iliad* and the *Odyssey*, were gathered from tales of heroes passed down orally for generations. The subject of the *Iliad* is the Trojan War, which was set in the Mycenaean period about 1250 B.C. Homer, whether he was one person as the Greeks believed or several people, wrote these stories about 400 years after the events took place. We can tell that some of his facts about the Mycenaeans are correct, but the lifestyle and values portrayed in these tales are taken from the Dark Age Period. It is believed that Homer lived at the end of that period in about 800-750 B.C., and that he and the poets who passed these tales on to him placed Mycenaean events and people within the context of their own time.

The *Iliad* and the *Odyssey* describe a tribal, rural society led by chieftains who governed them with the assent of their warriors. The Greeks had assemblies, and certain constitutional limits of power were applied to their governments

Winners at the Panathenaic games received awards and honor. This nineteenth-century reconstruction of the north section of the Parthenon's Ionic frieze inaccurately depicts a judge crowning a chariot driver. More recent scholarship suggests that the man is a marshal in the Panathenaic Procession who is signaling for the driver to stop so as to avoid running into the marchers ahead.

in many cases, although this was never a uniform development since each group evolved their own local laws and customs as a result of their political independence. Their society was organized along class lines and was dominated by the nobles. Below the nobility were the freemen who owned small farms. The lowest class consisted of slaves. The noble code of values placed excellence (arete) at the top of the list of virtues. One was to excel in courage and the physical attributes, whether in battle, sports contests, or public speaking. This code of excellence emphasized the individual warrior but also bound him to the honor of his fathers and his family.

The Olympic Games

This code of excellence led to competition not only in battle but also in sports. The Olympic games began in 776 B.C. and lasted for over a 1000 years. They were held at Olympia to honor Zeus, father of the gods, so there was a strong religious connection to the games. Held every four years, the games provided a common cultural heritage for all Greeks, as did the gods and their religious observances. Although in the beginning competitors were individuals who sought excellence for themselves in the panhellenic games that were open to all Greeks, over time this changed and became an effort to gain honor for the community.

The Polis

During the next 250 years, the Greeks developed their characteristic political organization called the polis. The polis was a community usually considered to be a group of people who were descendants of a common ancestor. Although translated as the word city-state, many of these poleis (plural form of the word) were actually just small towns of less than 2,000 people, but they included the surrounding countryside and perhaps several villages. The original center of a polis was an elevated citadel where the people of the area could gather to defend themselves. In Athens, this area was called the Acropolis. Later, the Athenians built their temples on this hill. Eventually some of these villages grew to become cities of some size. Athens was the largest city in Greece, and it grew to about 155,000 people by the fourth century B.C., while Sparta only had a population of 40,000.

Overtime a marketplace developed, the agora, where the members of the polis traded goods and discussed politics. Each male citizen was expected to participate in these discussions and the decision-making process of the polis. Women were members of the polis socially, legally, and religiously, but they were excluded from direct participation in politics. In fact, the modern word "politics" derives from the word polis, as do other words we use today, such as metropolis and police.

Each polis was independent from the others and developed its own particular laws and policies in war and peace. This independence was preserved by fierce loyalty to the polis, preventing the development of a unified Greece and leading to eventual subjugation by more powerful forces. While they worshipped all the gods, each Greek polis had one that presided over and protected it. The members of the polis, in return for that protection, were obligated to honor the god in special religious observances. The uniqueness of each polis provided its citizens with an identity, which they seldom willingly gave up. In fact, exile was one of the worst punishments possible for a member of a polis. Socrates, the famous philosopher, chose death when he could have slipped away from prison and fled from Athens because he thought exile from his beloved polis was worse than death.

The Hoplite Phalanx

The polis included the ideal of equality before the law for all of its members, whether they were rich or poor. Through this ideal of equality, which was unusual in the ancient world, the political inclusion of all male members of society must have been effected. However, citizenship and equal rights did not exist for slaves and metics, which were foreigners who had been granted limited rights to live and work in the polis. Many historians believe that the emergence of a citizen-army toward the end of the eighth century played a critical role in this political development. This new style army was composed of common citizens who were wealthy

Zeus, leader of the Greek gods, is depicted in this bronze statue dated to c. 450 B. C. His right hand once held a thunderbolt, one of his chief symbols.

enough to buy their own weapons and armor. These heavily armed soldiers were called hoplites. They stood shoulder to shoulder and used their shields to form a rectangular wall called a phalanx, which was usually eight ranks in depth. The hoplite's main weapon was the spear, but each man also carried a sword for hand-to-hand combat. As long as the men of the phalanx maintained discipline, they were almost unbeatable except by a stronger hoplite phalanx. This method of battle gave the Greeks a military superiority that they would not surrender until the Romans improved it centuries later.

The hoplites became necessary to the defense of the polis, replacing the older style aristocrats who fought as "heroic" individuals with great skill. This development gave them an importance that could not be denied by the nobility. This evolution in military tactics and the type of people who performed them may not have been the only cause of political rights being extended to all male citizens because the poor could not afford to buy armor, yet, they were included in many of the poleis, and it must have been one of the major causes.

Most of the poleis of Greece, and it is estimated that there were 1,500 of them, followed a similar pattern of development during the archaic age from 750 to 500 B.C. In the beginning, most poleis were under the control of the nobles. Some had kings who might be elected or were hereditary, but they were part of the aristocratic system of government. From 700 B.C. until 500 B.C. most of the poleis were taken over by tyrants. These tyrants were often members of a leading noble family who aspired to gain power for personal reasons, such as revenge against their enemies. They were assisted by economic and social changes, which destabilized society and caused a crisis that these men used to gain control in an unconstitutional manner.

A rising population, the growth of wealth from new sources such as trade, the flow of new ideas and knowledge from the outside world, and the development of hoplite warfare combined to pave the way for tyranny.

Greek tyrants often played a positive role in the development of democracy and in providing a higher standard of living for the people of their poleis. Since they had to appeal to a broad political base to gain and keep control, the tyrants often extended economic development and trade. They built temples and other public buildings in their cities to provide jobs and income for the poor while undoubtedly lining their own pockets and those of their friends. Most important of all was the role they played in the destruction of aristocratic power. When the aristocrats were driven out, as they were all over Greece by 500 B.C., democracy replaced them. Not all poleis turned to democracy, as we shall see, for there were those who followed the Spartans in an oligarchical form of government. Before turning to the divergence between Athens and Sparta in their form of government, an element of this period needs to be considered that was very important to the spread of Greek culture: the colonization movement that began around 750 B.C. and continued for about 200 years. Due in some cases to population pressure and in others to the revival of trade, Greeks aggressively colonized around the shores of the Mediterranean Sea along the coast of North Africa, Spain, southern France, and the Black Sea. Before establishing a colony, the leaders of a polis always consulted their gods. Those who went to the colony were expected to retain ties to their mother polis (metropolis) even though they were to become an independent polis. The colony was never supposed to join in a war against the mother polis. Instead, they were to trade with them and honor the same religious festivals.

The tyrants played an active role in the colonization process, providing new opportunities to members of their poleis while relieving growing pressures at home. Colonization provided several long-term benefits. It increased trade, stimulated the production of new goods, reduced the population pressures in the Greek homeland, and helped to avoid civil wars while providing new opportunities for people who otherwise would have been trapped in the old socio-economic system. Even more important to the development of Western civilization was the spreading of Greek culture around the Mediterranean world.

Sparta

Sparta was one of the leading poleis of Greece. Its development was different from Athens, a rival to Sparta in many ways. Sparta was similar to most of the other poleis in the beginning. Their government was aristocratic and as descendants of the Dorian invaders, they held the original inhabitants as slaves. In 725 B.C. during the first Messenian War they turned to conquer neighboring Messenia, which was located in the southwestern corner of the Peloponnesus. They took the land of Messenia and reduced the people to slavery. These slaves, called Helots, were owned by the state. They were bound to the land where they lived, and their role in life was to till the soil and produce goods for the Spartans. The total number of slaves was far greater than that of the Spartans by a ratio of about 10 to 1.

The great change in Spartan development came in 650 B.C. when the Helots rose in rebellion and almost destroyed Sparta with the help of some neighboring poleis, such as Argos in the Second Messenian War. Once this threat was defeated, the Spartans realized that they were going to have to give up Messenia or completely change their social structure to maintain control. They chose the latter, and the result was a disciplined, militaristic society. In that new society, all adult males constantly trained for war from the age of seven, when they were taken from their mothers, until they reached the age of sixty. As a result, the Spartan army was a professional force, which was ready to march at a moment's notice to put down rebellion or destroy an invading army. The internal threat of a Helot rebellion forced them to be very conservative in their foreign policy because the army had to remain close to home.

The Spartans became very conservative in politics and social development in some ways, while in others they were liberal for the times. For example, while the Spartans never accepted democracy nor the cultural advancements in philosophy, literature, and the arts, they allowed women a certain amount of freedom to learn, compete in sports, or oversee property that was forbidden to other Greek women. The conservative form of government they produced was unique. The Spartans had a "mixed constitution" that included three forms of government. The first part was a monarchy with two equal kings that were hereditary in that they came from two royal families but were elected by the assembly. The second part of the government operated on the principle of an oligarchy (rule of the few), and representative government existed in an assembly composed of all male warriors who were over 30 years of age. This strange combination was guided by a council of 28 elders who were over the age of 60 plus the two kings. It was this body that seemed to lead the government of Sparta based on oligarchical principles. This council, known as the gerousia, presented all proposals to the assembly, which could then vote for or against them. The assembly probably accepted the proposals of the gerousia most of the time, but on occasion it voted against these proposals. It now is considered to have been more powerful than earlier historians concluded. If the gerousia saw that a proposal was generating opposition in the assembly, they could withdraw it. The assembly also had limited power to amend these proposals.

In addition to the legislative powers of the assembly, it also annually elected five overseers (ephors). These men were chosen from the members of the assembly and were originally supposed to provide a balance to the power of the kings and council. They could bring charges against the kings, and they convened and presided over meetings of the assembly and the gerousia. The ephors were given the responsibility of seeing that the law was followed in all things, which was a very important emphasis of the Spartans. Eventually the ephors were given control of foreign policy, oversight of the kings in war, and the prevention of uprisings by the Helots. This system of government was very stable. The Spartans attributed their form of government and the changes in their society to a man named Lycurgus, the lawgiver. There is doubt today that this was the work of one man. Instead, it appears to have developed over time as a reaction to the Second Messenian War.

Despite the control of the state over the individual, which forced conformity to the ideals of the polis, many Greeks admired the Spartan constitution and way of life. The Athenians, who seemed the opposite of the Spartans in so many ways, admired them too. The philosopher, Plato, used Sparta as the model for his ideal polis in the *Republic*.

The Spartans continued to expand their control of the Peloponnesus by defeating their neighbors in war. In these cases they required an alliance with the defeated polis, which made the polis promise to follow Sparta's foreign policy

Plato joined Socrates' circle and saw his mentor condemned to death. From then on Plato sought to vindicate Socrates by constructing a philosophical system based on Socratic precepts.

and provide a given number of warriors in case of war. This Peloponnesian League, as it is known by historians today, included all of the poleis of the Peloponnesus except Argos. Through this league Sparta gained protection from invasion while it became the most powerful polis in all Hellas.

Athens

Athens is the other polis that we use as a model for the Greeks. In fact, Athens is synonymous with Greece for most people because Western civilization inherited the political ideal of democracy that the Athenians developed. Athens went through these stages of political development in the Archaic Age. The monarchy was replaced by aristocratic rule early in the seventh century. The people of the Attic Plain (Attica) slowly combined into one polis with four tribes and several clans and brotherhoods called phratries. The nobility owned most of the land and ran the government through a council known as the Areopagus and elected magistrates (archons).

Late in the seventh century the Athenians began to experience internal dissension due to a growing crisis in agriculture. Evidently the soil became depleted, resulting in small farmers going into debt due to lower yields of crops such as wheat and barley. As they failed to make payments to the aristocrats, they lost their land and their freedom, since many became slaves to pay for their debt. In 632 B.C. an attempt was made to overthrow this government and establish a tyrant. The attempt failed, but the basic cause of unrest continued until in 621 B.C. the legendary lawgiver, Draco, established harsh laws, which were written and made public for the first time. Draco's laws were so harsh that it is said they were written in blood. Even today we use the term "draconian" to signify harsh treatment.

Still the pressures of poor agricultural production, a growing population, and enslavement of their own people led to the development of a society ripe for revolution. In 594 B.C. Solon was elected as the sole archon for one year and given special powers to deal effectively with the growing crisis. He reformed the constitution to restrain the excessive power of the aristocrats. He canceled debts of the poor and stopped the practice of using people as collateral for loans, which had resulted in growing numbers of Athenians becoming slaves. Solon encouraged trade abroad and industry at home, in part, by offering citizenship to foreign craftsmen. He altered the constitution, dividing Athens into four groups based on wealth. While archons could only be elected from the two wealthiest groups,

the third class of hoplites could sit on a new council of 400, made up of 100 men from each tribe. This council was supposed to represent the people and limit the power of the aristocratic Areopagus. The Thetes were the poorest class. They could vote in assembly for the archons and members of the Areopagus, as well as all matters brought to the assembly. They could also sit on a new court of appeals. Solon retired voluntarily from what was practically a dictatorship, warning the nobility to voluntarily restrain their abuses of the common people. Then, he left to live abroad to escape the stress of appeals that were made to him for help. Solon's name, today, is a synonym for wisdom or a wise man.

The basic problems persisted, however, until Pisistratus became tyrant in 560 B.C., and again in 556 B.C., then permanently in 546 B.C. until he died in 527 B.C. Pisistratus fit the norm for tyrants in Greece. He won control and kept it by force, but he also had to improve the economy and social conditions to avoid rebellion. Therefore, he used public works to keep people employed, built temples to the gods to gain religious support, and supported the arts and artists. Pisistratus strengthened his government at the expense of the power of the aristocrats, thus opening the way for truly democratic rule later. His son succeeded him but became harsh as a ruler, and in 510 B.C. the Spartans intervened and deposed him.

In the power struggle that followed, Cleisthenes emerged the winner. Cleisthenes was a noble by birth but a democrat at heart. He was the founder of democracy in Athens, an ironic outcome of the Spartan intervention and a development of which they disapproved. In 508 B.C. Cleisthenes reorganized the basis of representation by making the deme the basic unit of government. He increased the number of tribes to 10 and increased loyalty to the polis while

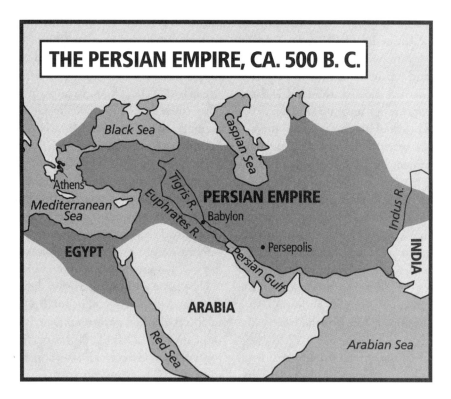

THE PERSIAN EMPIRE, CA. 500 B. C.

reducing old regional and aristocratic rivalries. A new council of 500 replaced the old council of 400 with each tribe electing 50 members. This council proposed legislation to the assembly and supervised public finances and foreign policy. The assembly was composed of all free males, and it had final authority in all things. Democracy had arrived in Athens and would spread to other poleis throughout Greece.

The Persian War

The Greeks were blessed with relative isolation and thus were free to develop their way of life in each independent polis until the fifth century B.C. As noted earlier, the Greeks had expanded across the Aegean Sea to the coast of Asia Minor (Turkey) during the early Dark Age as people fled the chaos and invasions. During the sixth century, the Greek poleis of Ionia were over-run by an expanding Persian Empire. By 540. B.C., all of Ionia had been added to that empire. In 499 B.C. the Ionians rebelled with the support of ships and warriors from Athens and Eretria. The Persians had the rebellion under control by 495 B.C., but Darius, the Persian Emperor, decided to punish the mainland Greeks who had interfered in what he considered to be an internal affair.

The first Persian War began in Ionia, but in 490 B.C. the Persian navy transported an army to strike directly at Athens and Eretria. The Athenians met and defeated the Persian forces on the plains of Marathon under the brilliant generalship of Miltiades. The defeat of the Persian army gave the Athenians self-confidence for they had beaten the forces of the most powerful empire in the world, and they had done it without the Spartans! (Eretria did not fare so well; it was defeated, and its people were sent far away to Persia, probably as slaves.) This confidence directly contributed to the achievements of Athens in the "Golden Age" of the Classical period.

The Persians waited ten years before they made a second attempt to invade Greece and take revenge on Athens. By that time their goal was revenge and control of the whole Greek peninsula. Sensing this, some of the Greeks banded together in a rare display of unity to fight the invader. Darius was dead by that time, and his successor, Xerxes, gathered a mighty army of perhaps 150,000 or more men, and a navy of 600 ships. Ironically, much of this navy consisted of ships and men from the Greek Ionian poleis, since they were part of the Persian Empire. In 480 B.C. the invasion began. One of the leaders of Athens, Themistocles, had foreseen this danger and built additional ships, so that the Athenian navy had 200 ships. Yet with its allies included, there was only a total of about 333 Greek ships to face that massive armada. Xerxes' strategy was to march his army from Asia Minor across the Hellespont and along the coast until it reached Athens. The navy would be used to supply the army and destroy the Greek navy.

The Greek League, consisting of only 31 out of about 1,500 total poleis , chose Sparta as their leader in this war. As the Persian army approached the narrow pass of Thermopylae to the north of Athens, a legendary battle took place between the Greek warriors that included 300 Spartans led by their king, Leonidas, and the Persian army. Unable to defeat the Spartans and their allies at the pass where numbers were no advantage, the Persians found a Greek to guide them along a mountain path, which brought them out on the far side of the pass. Believing that the gods had decreed that a Spartan king must die to preserve their freedom, Leonidas sent the allies back to Athens while he and his men fought to the death. When the Persians reached Athens, the city had already been evacuated. The Persian army burned it as an act of revenge and probably to crush Greek opposition. However, they did not understand the spirit of the people they were attempting to conquer. The Greek navy met the larger navy of the Persians nearby at Salamis and defeated it decisively. Then, in 479 B.C. the Greek army led by Pausanius, the Spartan general who had replaced Leonidas, met the Persian army at Platea. General Mardonius, son-in-law of Xerxes and his best general, was killed, and the Persian army was routed despite their overwhelming numbers. In 478 B.C. the Ionians convinced the Spartan king, Leotychidas, who was in command of the Greek forces, to cross the Aegean and attack the Persians in Ionia. In 478 B. C., the Greek navy won the battle of Mycale, which finished the destruction of the Persian navy. The Persians abandoned Ionia, and Greece seemed to be safe once more. The Persian Wars and the retreat of the great empire of Asia were momentous events not only in the history of Greece but of Western civilization. The defeat of the greatest power in their world gave the Greeks unprecedented self-confidence and led them to achievements in politics and the arts that still influence Western culture today.

THE CLASSICAL AGE (500-323 BC)

Women, Children and Slaves

Women were dominated by men in the Greek world. That was the norm in most societies then and for most centuries since. The woman was considered to be "loaned" by her family to that of her husband for the purpose of bearing male heirs. Unwanted children were exposed to the harsh natural elements and allowed to die. The majority of these were females for they were considered less desirable than sons, and some were imperfect male babies.

The military society of the Spartans especially demanded that males be perfectly healthy and strong, and any babies found to be defective were left to die. Infanticide, along with their unusual style of marriage where men did not live at home but in the barracks and actually had to sneak out at night to visit their wives to enjoy physical intimacy without being caught, led to a declining population in Sparta. As was mentioned earlier, Spartan women lived a life of relative freedom, both from the drudgery of menial housework and the rearing of children, which was done by the Helot slave women, and allowed to participate in sports and run the business affairs of the family. (Boys went to military camp at age seven to stay.) The Athenians were shocked at what they claimed were the loose morals of Spartan women, who were not sheltered by their absent husbands and thus could more easily indulge in sexual affairs Some husbands would lend their wives to another man from their military unit for procreation if that man's wife could not bear children. Spartan girls kept in good physical condition like their male counterparts and were supposed to be among the most beautiful women in Greece. Condemned by Greeks from other areas for their loose morals, nude sports and loose clothes that revealed far more of the body than other Greek women were allowed to show, the Spartan women were noted for winning at sports and running the economy while their husbands spent their entire lives in the army until they were 60 years old.

Most Greek women were expected to live very differently. They were to stay quietly in their homes supervising slaves if they had any, bearing and raising their children, and caring for their husbands. In his *Funeral Oration*, Pericles described the best woman as the type that was "least talked about by men, whether for good or bad." Women could not vote or participate in public political debates or sit on juries, even at the height of Athenian democracy. If they were not prostitutes (these were usually slave women) or courtesans, who were considered high class female "companions," then the Greek woman's chastity was prized and protected by the males of her family.

This was the accepted view in that society, although the poor working class woman enjoyed greater freedom because she had no slaves to do her house work, go to the market and raise the children for her. As a result, women of that class had to have more social contact just to live. But the traditional view set forth in their laws, customs and literature has come to be challenged by women historians as a result of the women's revolution today. While one radical view of young Athenian wives probably went too far when a historian claimed in 1971 that they were undisciplined nymphs, there is the growing recognition that women from Athens were less secluded and had a wider range of social contacts and experiences than has been considered the norm. Certain religious festivals that women took part in, like the *Haloa* festival, featured ribald jokes and replicas of private male parts. Still, most Greek women followed the mores of their polis, but perhaps not as completely as was once thought to be the case.

Children in Sparta have been mentioned above. The military training of the boys was harsh (A young man had to catch and kill a helot before he was accepted as a full soldier in the Spartan army.) and included the idea that mothers expected their sons to come home with their shields (which means they had not thrown them away to run and escape) or on them as a corpse. The rigors of their training and the general lack of any type of luxury in the lives of all people there, not just soldier boys, provides the basis for the term "Spartan" to this day. However the younger boys from 7 until they reached the age of 17, experienced the lighter duty of learning to dance and sing, and of course do gymnastics and compete in sports.

All children were a part of their polis and took part in the religious festivals, learning the proper way to behave and how to fulfill the roles expected of them. Boys began to train for military duty early in life, for each polis had to defend itself against its neighbors as well as enemies from further away. Naturally boys helped their fathers and girls helped their mothers and learned skills from them that were necessary for them to live. All children in working families before the present time, had to help with household chores or work at something to help the family survive. While the children of the rich and famous aristocrats would be expected to avoid menial labor and gain an education along with learning the martial arts, working class children had to work hard from early in their lives, and they could not expect to receive a formal education nor would poor boys be able to learn military skills or become citizens in some of the poleis if their family was too poor to afford the cost of the helmet, sword and shield necessary to join the hoplite army, for usually each man had to provide his own equipment. Slave children would have worked their entire lives unless they could earn their freedom. Slave boys and girls would have experienced what we would consider to be abuse as they became sex objects to their masters.

Slaves were a major component of the Greek economy and indeed of their entire society. The Spartans held an entire group of their neighbors as state slaves. These people basically lived without protection and could be killed at the whim of a Spartan citizen, who of course was male. Undoubtedly the Spartan women were tough on these people too, for toughness was a trait of the Spartans. The helots rose in rebellion several times, partly with the assistance of the Athenians in those times that they were at war with Sparta. Those rebellions were the worst nightmare of the Spartans and the reason that their men were members of a professional army most of their adult lives.

Female slaves have already been mentioned in relation to prostitution, housework, and child rearing. The male slaves worked in the fields as did female slaves, and they also worked in the mines, did heavy construction, ran shops, were rowers on the triremes (the basic naval vessel during the classical age, that had three levels of seating for the rowers who were the main means of propulsion during battle) and in general were indispensable to the Greek economy and cultural achievement. Slaves made up a large portion of the population even in Athens. In fact without them to do the dirty work of their society, the Greeks would not have had the leisure time to make their great contributions in literature, philosophy, politics, or art and architecture to Western Civilization! People who fell into debt at times were sold as slaves to pay for that debt, but normally they came from foreign countries as a result of purchase due to the age-old practice of selling the people of conquered countries as slaves. Slaves were quite often teachers and other educated people, or skilled workers who plied their trade for their master, sometimes making enough on the side to earn their freedom. Zeno, the originator of the Stoic philosophy, was a slave who earned his freedom.

The Delian League

With the defeat of the Persians, the Greeks of Ionia and the Aegean Sea islands formed a defensive alliance with Athens known as the Delian League, knowing that the Persian threat was not over. The league was named after the sacred island of Delos, where they met in 478 B.C. Athens was chosen as the leader of the Delian League because the Spartans refused to accept a commitment that would place their armies far from the Helots at home and because Athens was the largest polis and the greatest naval power among the allies. By 467 B.C., the remaining Greek cities under Persian control were liberated by the league, and Persian forces were driven back into the interior of Asia Minor.

Over time the Delian League became the Athenian Empire. The smaller city-states in the league increasingly converted their obligation to provide men and ships for the common defense into cash payments. The Athenians provided not only their own contribution of ships and men for the league's naval forces, but they also used the cash payments to supply substitute ships with trained crews. Athens had the largest population of any member of the Delian League with a large pool of laborers who sought work as rowers, and she had the skilled shipbuilders who were capable of building the necessary warships in large numbers. More and more, the men of Athens came to rely on the military activities of the Delian League as a source of income. Since they dominated the Athenian assembly, which in turn dominated the Delian League assembly, the league and its activities reflected the Athenians' desire for an active policy. Furthermore, no polis was allowed to withdraw from the league since contributions provided an income for Athens and the original oath bound them to remain members of the league forever. The Athenians

A bust of Pericles

had the means and motive to compel rebellious members to remain in the league.

In 465 B.C. the polis of an island in the Aegean Sea, Thasos, decided to withdraw from the Delian League. Cimon, the son of Miltiades, victor at Marathon, was the leading Athenian statesman and general of the day. He laid siege to Thasos for two years before the "revolt" was put down. Thasos was forced to remain in the league and pay a huge tribute and fines while losing her own navy. Cities had already begun to level the charge against the Athenians that they desired to take over all of Greece. Athenian actions seemed to confirm that suspicion to a growing number of Greeks. This suspicion, coupled with Spartan distrust of Athens' democratic form of government and jealousy on both sides, led to a series of wars among the Greeks that would eventually destroy the Greek way of life.

The Peloponnesian War

Under the leadership of Cimon, the Athenians sought to maintain good relations with Sparta and her Peloponnesian League. The Spartans, however, did not like the democratic tendencies of the Athenians, whose constitution continued to change whereas the Spartans remained stable and unchanging. Democracy, of course, could undermine their control of the Helots, which threatened the entire Spartan way of life. In 462 B.C., following a gigantic earthquake two years earlier that killed many Spartans and allowed the Helots to rebel, Sparta called on the Athenians for help to end the siege of Mt. Ithome where the Helots were holding out. Cimon won the reluctant permission of the Athenian Assembly to take an army of hoplites to assist the Spartan army. The Spartans sent them home soon after they arrived, according to Thucydides, the great chronicler of the wars, in his *Peloponnesian Wars,* because they feared the "revolutionary spirit" of the Athenian soldiers might only make matters worse with their slaves. The Athenian assembly was enraged at this affront.

While Cimon was in the field for the Spartan campaign, his political adversary, Ephialtes, stripped the Areopagus of much of its political power, leaving it to function only as a court with limited jurisdiction over certain crimes. A whole new system of courts using juries consisting of the male citizens of Athens was put in place by the Ephialtic reforms. Ephialtes was assassinated by reactionaries, and the following year, 461 B.C., Cimon was ostracized due to the disfavor he had gained over the insult Sparta had given

to the Athenians. With his pro-Spartan influence removed, the Athenian-Spartan relationship deteriorated further. Athens formed an alliance with Argos, the enemy of Sparta, and then accepted Megara as an ally. Megara had been a member of the Peloponnesian League but due to a boundary dispute with Corinth, another member of that league, the Megarians left to become an ally of Athens with the hope that they might win the territorial dispute.

With Cimon gone, the anti-Spartan, democratic party was clearly in power. Its leader was the young Pericles, a descendant of Cleisthenes, founder of Athenian democracy. Pericles was an aristocrat who wanted to broaden the democratic base of the Athenian constitution. Under his leadership the assembly passed legislation that allowed the hoplites to become archons, the highest office in the polis. They began the practice of paying jurors so poor men could afford public service. The assembly of Athens made the final decision for all things, including war or peace. Public officials were openly criticized and could be removed from office as Pericles was when people lost faith in him.

While pursuing democracy at home, Pericles and his supporters were unwilling to back down when the Spartans demanded that they end their alliance with Megara. This led to the First Peloponnesian War (460-445 B.C.) when the Athenians seemed to gain the upper hand. They took advantage of their alliance with Megara to fortify the northern end of the isthmus that connects the Peloponnesus to the Attic Plain, occupied an island in the Saronic Gulf, and gained control of the area known as Boeotia. Then, as the Athenians seemed to have the upper hand in the war, they over-reached themselves by joining with the Egyptians who rebelled against Persia in 460 B.C. Victorious at first, they were defeated in 455 B.C. and lost an entire fleet of ships and men. As a result of this defeat, some of Athens' allies in the Delian League took advantage of this moment of weakness to rebel. Athens moved the treasury from Delos to Athens for safety, but they also began to keep one-sixtieth of the annual contributions for the building or repair of temples that had been destroyed in the fighting. This money was used to help pay for the building on the Acropolis, such as the Parthenon. Cimon was recalled from exile, and a 5-year truce was agreed on with Sparta. This gave the Athenians time to rebuild their fleet, and in 450 B.C. Cimon led a 200-ship fleet to attack the Persians in Cyprus. He defeated the Persians but died the following year. In 449 B.C. the Persians and the Delian League ended the war. Persia accepted the Greek states as independent of their control except for Cyprus.

The five-year truce with Sparta did not hold. Argos in 451 B.C. revoked her treaty with Athens and made a 30-year treaty with Sparta. The Boeotia and Megara rebelled, Sparta invaded, and Pericles accepted a 30-year peace. For about 15 years, the peace lasted while Pericles (elected Archon a total of 30 times) reorganized what was now the Athenian Empire. This was the Golden Age of Athens. Democracy reached its fullest development, though it excluded women, slaves, and metics, or foreigners. The Acropolis reached the form that we see the remains of today, with buildings and sculptures that still inspire us with its beauty and technical perfection.

War broke out again in 431 B.C. after a series of conflicts between the two alliances, which resulted in an invasion by Sparta and her allies. The Athenian strategy under Pericles' leadership was to attack with her navy along the coast of the Peloponnesus against the Spartan forces. Athens relied on her empire for food and income through trade while defending herself with walls that held off the Spartans. The Spartans

invaded each year, burned, and destroyed the crops, then went home when the Athenians refused to battle. From 431 to 404 B.C., with intermittent periods of truce, war continued until Athens was forced to surrender.

Pericles planned the defensive strategy and expected that Sparta would be forced to ask for peace in one to three years, due to the empire's attacks on Sparta's allies. This might have worked, but a great plague struck Athens in 429 B.C., and one-third of Athens' population died, including Pericles. The Athenian generals followed Pericles' plan and placed strategic bases to surround, blockade, and attack such poleis as Megara, Pylos, and Messenia. At Pylos in 425 B.C., the Athenians won a major victory and trapped a group of over 400 of Sparta's warriors on an island. Sparta was facing yet another Helot revolt, and those men were a significant part of their forces, so they sued for peace. Two Athenian political parties had emerged by that time. Nicias favored continuing Pericles' more conservative policy while Cleon and his followers wanted a more aggressive approach. Cleon won, and Athens refused the Spartan peace offer, opting instead for total victory since the peace plan offered no real guarantee of security for Athens. Some historians conclude that this policy resulted from Athenian pride and aggressiveness, causing them to over-reach the limits of their power and resources. The Greeks, of course, would have appreciated that interpretation and called it hubris, which offends the gods and leads to defeat.

Whatever the cause, the more aggressive policy of Cleon failed as Athens attempted to invade and conquer neighboring Megara and Boeotia. A truce was agreed upon in 432 B.C. Then, a Spartan general, Brasidias, attacked in the areas of Thrace and Macedonia on the northern coast of the Aegean. He took the important ally and colony of Athens, Amphipolis. General Thucydides commanded the naval forces of the area, so he was blamed for the defeat and sent into exile as punishment by the assembly. Thucydides wrote the *Peloponnesian Wars* in exile, which provide us with the most important source of information about this epic war. Thucydides, unlike the earlier historian, Herodotus, does not explain the war in terms of the gods and religious forces; rather, he gathered evidence in a scientific manner and attempted to explain causality in terms of human behavior.

The Athenians tried to retake Amphipolis in 422 B.C. Both generals, Cleon of Athens and Brasidias of Sparta, were killed in the failed attempt. Nicias now asked for peace, and the Spartans agreed in 421 B.C., but some of their allies, such as Megara, refused and so remained at war with Athens. The peace terms demanded that both sides give up captured territory. Brasidias had followed a policy of urging rebellious members of the Athenian empire to revolt. Now some of those poleis did not want to return to the empire, and the Spartans would not force those poleis to rejoin. Thus, the terms of the peace were not fully carried out by both sides.

This war was fought in terms of ideology, meaning a fight between those who wanted democracy and those who wished to return to oligarchy, as well as for power. At Corcyra, the civil war continued after the Peace of Nicias and brought a bloody massacre to the inhabitants of that island. Both sides continued to lure the allies of their opponent to join them, and the young Alcibiades, who was related to Pericles, involved Athens in several ventures during this period of tense peace.

In 415 B.C. Alcibiades persuaded the Athenian Assembly to begin the war again by attacking and conquering Sicily. The expeditionary force at Syracuse was totally lost by 413 B.C., including about 200 ships and 50,000 men. This time Persia joined the war, as well as Sparta, which was an ally of Syracuse. Alcibiades, who had been recalled to answer charges that he had acted in an irreligious manner, escaped to Sparta, advising them as to ways to defeat Athens. He then moved on to advise the Persians, who were providing money to the Spartans. Under Lysander, the victorious general of Sparta, the Peloponnesian League began to build a navy and cut off Athenian trade and their supply of grain from colonies in the Black Sea coastal area. The Spartan fleet destroyed the Athenian fleet at Aegospotami in 405 B.C. Athens surrendered unconditionally in 404 B.C. An oligarchy was put in power whose members came to be known as the Thirty Tyrants, and the walls of Athens were torn down. Her fleet was gone, as well as her empire.

Spartan and Theban Hegemony

Following the end of the Peloponnesian War, the struggle for power among the Greek city-states continued. At first, Sparta was dominant, but other city-states, such as Corinth, Thebes, and Athens, resented her insolent treatment and banded together to end Spartan rule. This resulted in the Corinthian War of 395-387 B.C. Athens took advantage of these events to rebuild her walls and fleet. Spartan hegemony was destroyed by the Thebans defeat at the Battle of Leuctra in 371 B.C. The Peloponnesian League was broken up, and the Helots freed, as Thebes replaced Sparta as the dominant power.

Meanwhile, Athens had put together the Second Athenian Confederation. This confederation, and what remained of the Peloponnesian League, met Thebes at the Battle of Mantinea in 362 B.C. The Thebans won the battle but lost their great commander, Epaminondas. Without him they returned to their former po-

The remains of the Dionysus Theatre are frequently remodeled and expanded. By the mid-fourth century B.C., the facility held an estimated 14,000 spectators.

sition. Athens briefly regained power but without a threat from Sparta or Thebes, the other city-states began to secede from Athens's second empire. The Greek poleis continued arguing and fighting, while to the north a new power began to emerge, which eventually united them by force. The Macedonians changed the Greek world forever.

CLASSICAL CULTURE

Despite the wars and instability of the Classical Age, which has been defined as 500 B.C. to 323 B.C., it was the Athenians greatest period of cultural creativity. With the defeat of the Persian army on the plains of Marathon, the greatest power of their world, the Athenians gained confidence in themselves, believing they could do anything. "Man is the measure of all things," said the Sophist Protagoras, and the Athenians believed it. As a result, along with the wealth extracted by the state slaves from the silver mines at Laurium and from their "allies" in the Delian League, the Athenians achieved new heights of perfection in the arts, literature, and philosophy.

Literature

The epic poems of Homer and the mythological stories of the gods are the basis of Greek literature. Concern about ethical values and the forming of good citizens to build the good community underlay much of the Greek effort in the arts. That was especially true of poetry, which then became drama acted out on the outdoor theater, which was synonymous with Greek culture. Many of the Greek city-states promoted competition in drama, with the winner's play enacted in the public theater, usually as a part of the yearly religious festivals. The tragedy, the oldest form of drama, was probably first developed at Athens. This poetic drama dealt with serious issues in the context of religious mythology. At Athens these plays were performed as a part of the yearly festival honoring the god Dionysius. They included interaction between human beings and the gods often resulting in violence and irreconcilable conflicts. The audience was forced to consider their own flaws as humans and the possibility of self-destruction through hubris, or pride and overconfidence. Especially talented dramatists were Aeschylus (525-456 B.C.), Sophocles (496-406 B.C.), and Euripides (485-406-B.C.). With Euripides, the tragedy began to evolve toward the concerns of the person and his/her own psychological make up.

Comedy was introduced at the festival of Dionysius in the early fifth century. The best known to us, because we have some of his complete plays, is Aristophanes, who lived from 450 to 385 B.C. Known as Old Comedy, Aristophanes and his contemporaries wrote plays of political satire aimed at well-known leaders like Pericles. Comedy developed similar to tragedy and eventually turned to the personal love story in the Hellenistic Age.

History is the earliest form of prose literature. Herodotus is known as the "Father of History" and he was discussed earlier in relation to the Persian War. His account of that epic struggle is the first written history. Thucydides, too, has been discussed earlier as we considered the Peloponnesian War. His method of objective analysis and critical use of sources set the standard for writing history from that day until now.

Philosophy

The word "philosophy" means the pursuit of wisdom, not simply knowledge, and the philosopher is one who seeks or pursues wisdom. The Greeks were not the first people to produce wisdom literature, and surely they were not the first people to pursue the truth, but they were the originators of philosophy as a rational, systematic field of study. Beginning in the sixth century B.C., and sometimes referred to as Pre-Socratic philosophy, Greek philosophy before the Classical Age dealt with the origins and physical nature of the universe. Thales of Miletus is the earliest known philosopher. He undoubtedly encountered several ideas in Egypt, which he brought back and taught in Greece, such as astronomy, geometry, and that water was the basic substance of the universe. Empedocles of Acragas in the fifth century B.C. believed that there were four basic elements in the universe: air, water, fire, and earth. Another theory put forward by Leucippus of Miletus and his pupil, Democritus, was that all things are composed of tiny building blocks called atoms. Anaximander developed the idea of evolution and thought that the universe was a limitless, constantly expanding system. Hippocrates, the father of medicine, began using the empirical method in science, basing conclusions on rational evidence after careful experimentation and observation. Finally, Pythagoras believed that the basis of the universe was mathematical. He also believed that the earth orbited the sun.

During the fifth century, Sophists traveled and taught certain skills, such as rhetoric, for pay. Their use of rational analysis of human be-

Socrates not only pursued knowledge and the meaning of life but also shared both with his fellow citizens, spending hours asking and answering questions.

havior and beliefs was disturbing to many people. They questioned everything and some went so far as to question the basis of law and religion. These were fundamental values of the polis, and this school of philosophy with its questioning of all things helped to undercut the basis of the polis and bring on the crisis of that institution, which was central to the Greek way of life. The Sophists argued that truth was relative, not absolute, and that the end justified the means. The Sophists, who gave us the term "sophistry" (subtly deceptive reasoning or argumentation), also gave us the term that has been used to symbolize the achievements of both the Classical Age and the Renaissance. Protagoras, the leader and probably the originator of the Sophists, placed human beings at the center of the cosmos, sug-

gesting that they determined their own truth and could do anything they chose to do.

A number of Greeks agreed with this new emphasis on man rather than on the universe but were troubled by the Sophists' rejection of eternal or absolute truth. That was akin to a rejection of the gods, and while the Greeks of the fifth century had become more cynical of the religious myths, the worship of the gods was still a deeply ingrained value of the citizens of the polis. Charges of impiety could be used to bring down an opponent, resulting in punishments ranging from public dishonor to exile or death.

Socrates, an Athenian who lived from 470-399 B.C., is considered to be the father of philosophy. He was a humanist, for he centered his philosophy in the quest for truth to improve the soul and lead a just life in the polis. He believed that knowledge led to a life of virtue because the person who knows what is right will choose to do the right or virtuous thing. Socrates held no view similar to the later Christian doctrine of the sinful nature, but he did believe that ignorance was evil and caused people to lead unjust lives.

Socrates conducted his search for truth by questioning the citizens of Athens and causing them to examine their own assumptions, beliefs, and actions. If he found contradictions among these beliefs and actions, he was quick to point it out, but he did it in such a way that the person being questioned realized their own ignorance of the truth. This method of teaching by asking questions is called the Socratic method. Socrates' reliance on reason to discover the virtuous life did not preclude his belief in absolute truth, which he was searching for, but it did cause him to question the Greek understanding of the gods who acted in unethical, immoral ways according to religious mythology. Socrates rejected that kind of religion but affirmed a higher deity that was just and ethical.

His questioning of people and the gods, along with his rejection of democracy at the very time that Sparta forced oligarchy on Athens with the rule of the Thirty Tyrants at the end of the Peloponnesian War, led to trouble for Socrates. Since the traitor, Alcibiades, had been one of his students, as well as two of the thirty tyrants, his opponents claimed that he had corrupted the youth of the city and introduced strange gods. Socrates was convicted by a jury of 501 men and condemned to die. Socrates refused to leave the polis where he had lived for 70 years. He argued that he had taught obedience to the law all of his life, and he would not throw away the work of a lifetime just to exist as a foreigner in an-

other country for a few more years. One of the most poignant scenes of classical age literature is that of Socrates drinking the poison hemlock while he speaks with some of his disciples about truth and the virtuous life to the very end.

Plato, who lived from about 428 to 347 B.C., was a devoted student of Socrates. He recorded Socrates' death scene in the *Crito*. It is largely through the writings of Plato that we learn the philosophy of Socrates. Plato accepted the political philosophy of Socrates that rejected democracy and called for a system in his *Republic* that was led by a few wise men or women, the guardians. His ideal estate granted equality to men and women and was based on ability and achievement of knowledge through systematic education. Plato abandoned the practice of politics after the death of his teacher, convinced that the mobocracy of Athens would do the same thing to any honorable man.

Plato's basic philosophical position on truth is that it is absolute. He is known as a philosophical idealist because he believed that the things we see in material form are only imperfect reflections of the ideal or perfect form, which exists beyond this world. Later, Christianity would equate that place of perfection with Heaven and the Power who established the ideal forms with God. In 386 B.C. Plato began his academy where he taught philosophy, mathematics, and astronomy. Considered the first college in the history of Western civilization, the academy lasted for 900 years and laid the foundation for education.

Aristotle, who lived from 384 to 322 B.C., was a student of Plato and studied with him at the academy. Later he opened his own school in Athens, the Lyceum. Aristotle was born in Macedonia where his father was a doctor to the king. Eventually, Aristotle became a tutor to the son of the king of Macedonia. That young son

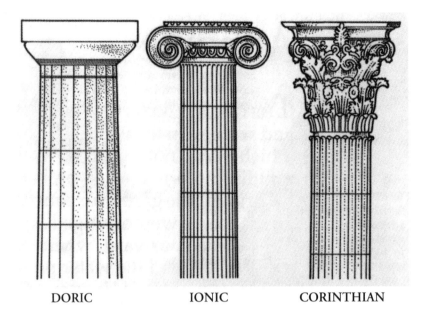

DORIC   IONIC   CORINTHIAN

The Doric style is sturdy, and its top (the capital) is plain. This style was used in mainland Greece and the colonies in southern Italy and Sicily. The Ionic style is thinner and more elegant. Its capital is decorated with a scroll-like design. This style was used in eastern Greece and the islands. The Corinthian style was seldom used in the Greek world, but often appeared in Roman temples. Its capital is elaborate and decorated with acanthus leaves.

was Alexander, known down through history as "The Great."

Aristotle is important for his scientific approach to gathering knowledge about the natural world and placing it in a systematic form for study and practical use. He and his students applied this in many fields of knowledge, such as politics, where they gathered 158 copies of constitutions. Today, only one out of the original 158 remains in existence, which is the Athenian constitution. This brilliant yet practical scientist-philosopher believed the goal of life was to find happiness. Finding balance between extremes in life, or the golden mean, is the way to achieve that happiness. Aristotle was more comfortable with democracy and tended to see men as good and capable of self-government in the polis. His written works that still exist include the *Politics* and *Metaphysics*.

One other branch of philosophy that deserves mentioning is that of the Cynics. This school of philosophy taught that one should reject wealth and physical comfort and live the simple life close to Nature to find the good life and wisdom for the individual. Diogenes (400-325 B.C.) is the best known of the Cynics, and he was famous for his rudeness and filthy, unkempt personal attire. He wore rags, lived in a barrel, and rejected formal study for the simple lifestyle.

Classical Art

In the field of aesthetics, the Greek artists established the highest standard of excellence. While

The Parthenon ruins as they appear today.

they produced beautiful things for everyday use, such as jewelry, the greatest art was produced in architecture and sculpture. Painting was also important for their public buildings and sculptures, however, the paint has been completely erased by time, and we cannot determine its quality.

Architecture

Greek achievement in architecture in the Classical Age affects us still. The symmetry, balance, and order that are characteristics of the religious temples built on the Acropolis of Athens, cause one to gaze in awe at the beauty created by those architects of long ago. The basic construction of a temple like the Parthenon was post-and-lintel with many columns in front and along the sides to hold up the roof. These temples were decorated with carvings of their patron god or goddess, as well as scenes from mythology about the gods and heroes. The Parthenon had seventeen columns along each side and eight on each end. It was different from many of the other temples because the Athenians, full of confidence after defeating the Persians, decorated this temple to Athena with freestanding sculptures of recognizable, contemporary Athenians. Three styles, or orders, of columns developed over time. The oldest, the Doric column, was used in building the Parthenon. This was the largest of the columns and stood directly on the stone floor. Larger at the bottom than at the top, the gradually tapered shape made the columns appear to be straight. The Doric column was simple in style with no intricate carving. The Ionic column came next in development and was a thinner, more graceful column with a scrolled capital. The Corinthian column was basically the Ionic column with a capital that had intricately carved leaves on the capital. Both the Ionic and Corinthian columns were set on a base that in turn sat on the stone floor. The Greeks put their best work into the public temples instead of fine homes and palaces.

Sculpture

Beginning with the more formal, one might even say bland and impersonal, sculpture of the Archaic Age, the Greeks began to experiment with little, individual changes, like a smile or changing the stance of the legs. By the Classical period, this innovativeness brought a new freedom to Greek sculpture. The search for ideal beauty brought them to portray the nude human body, male and female, in lifelike detail where muscles rippled across the chest, legs and arms of the ideal athlete. Myron's *Discobolus* in 450 B.C. portrays a discus thrower in motion, represented by two intersecting arcs that give the impression of a bow that is drawn the moment before the arrow is released. Phidias, the famous fifth-century artist who decorated the Parthenon, and Praxiteles of the fourth century achieved perfection in rendering the human form both real and sensually idealistic at the same time. Not until the Renaissance were great artists again able to approach their skill and vision in portraying the human form.

CONCLUSION

This chapter covers a long period of history, beginning with 3,000 B.C. and ending in 30 B.C. Bronze Age technology had begun to develop on the island of Crete at the beginning of this period. It was not until 2,000 B.C., however, that the history of the Minoans emerged. This period has no known written record, and the interpretation of their history is based completely on archeological evidence. The Minoans were influenced by the contemporary Mesopotamian and Egyptian civilizations and, in turn, spread their culture to the Greek mainland where it blended with the native culture to produce what is known today as Mycenaean culture. This an-

cient Aegean civilization reached a high level of development including writing, urban centers, centralized government, advanced engineering skills demonstrated by the building of extensive palace-temples, international trade, and the appreciation of aesthetics as seen in the beautiful frescoes on palace walls.

A Dark Age followed the fall of that civilization where knowledge of earlier accomplishments faded, and the culture sank to a more primitive level of existence. Legends of that great period lived on, however, and by 750 B.C. Homer had written the great literary epics of the *Iliad* and the *Odyssey*. These epics provided a unified set of religious beliefs about the gods and basic values such as arete, or excellence, that were basic for Hellenic culture.

Believing they must strive to excel in all things led the Greeks to great heights of human accomplishment. One of the greatest of those accomplishments, which certainly affects our world today, was the development of majority rule or democracy. Within their independent poleis the Greeks realized a new concept of citizens, not as subjects but as responsible partners in the defense and governance of their social order. Despite the successful evolution of that concept, it also had a dark side. There was continual warfare and independence among the poleis, which prevented Hellenic unity and led to the demise of the polis and democracy.

The Greeks achieved great things in the arts, literature and drama, philosophy, and science, particularly at Athens, during the Golden Age of the fifth century. Perhaps their greatest achievement was in the emphasis they placed on human beings and their ability to inquire after the truth and find it. This philosophy, known as humanism, placed humankind at the center of all things, believing that human beings could discover truth through rational inquiry.

Suggestions for Further Reading

John Boardman, *Greek Art* (1985)

J. Boardman, J. Griffin & O. Murray eds., *Greece and the Hellenistic World* (1986)

W. Burkert, *Greek Religion* (1977)

A.R. Burn, *The Lyric Age of Greece* (1960)

Paul Cartledge, *Agesilaus and the Crisis of Sparta* (1987); *The Spartans* (2002); (ed) *The Cambridge Illustrated History of Ancient Greece* (1998)

Rodney Castleden, *Minoans: Life in Bronze Age Crete* (1990); *Mycenaeans* (2005)

John Chadwick, *The Mycenaean World* (1976)

James Davidson, *Courtesans and Fishcakes* (1997)

M.I. Finley, *The Ancient Economy*, 2nd Ed. (1985); *Ancient Slavery and Modern Ideology* (1980); *Politics in the Ancient World* (1983)

Y. Garlan, *Slavery in Ancient Greece* (1988)

Michael Grant, *The Classical Greeks* (1989)

P. Green, *The Greco-Persian Wars* (1998)

Victor Hansen, *The Western Way of War* (1989); *A War Like No Other* (2005)

Herodotus, *The Histories*

B. Hughes, *Helen of Troy* (2005)

Donald Kagan, *The Outbreak of The Peloponnesian War* (1969); *Pericles of Athens and the Birth of Democracy* (1991)

G.B. Kerferd, *The Sophistic Movement* (1981)

Thomas R. Martin, *Ancient Greece: From Prehistoric to Hellenistic Times* (1996)

J.D. Mikalson, *Athenian Popular Religion* (1983)

D. Brendan Nagle, *The Ancient World: A Social and Cultural History* (1979)

S. Pomeroy, *Goddesses, Whores, Wives, and Slaves* (1975)

Barry Strauss, *The Battle of Salamis* (2004); *The Trojan War* (2006)

Thucydides, *History Of The Peloponnesian War*

Chapter
3

ALEXANDER AND THE HELLENISTIC AGE

Alexander the Great

Archimedes (287-212 B.C.) is one of the major scientist/mathematicians of the Hellenistic Age, which is also the Golden Age of science in the ancient world. He was born in Syracuse, a Greek colony in Sicily. His father was an astronomer and he sent his son to study in Alexandria, Egypt, the center of scientific study in the world at that time, due to the great library and museum built there by Ptolemy I. Everyone has heard the story of his discovery of the 1st law of hydrostatics, which deals with the idea that a solid displaces an equal amount of liquid, which can be used to determine the weight of the solid item. He realized this as he climbed into a bath and saw the water rise. Ecstatic that he had solved the problem he had been wrestling with, Archimedes is supposed to have run naked through the streets of the city shouting "Eureka," which means "I have found it" in Greek. This man evidently possessed the power of concentration to such a degree that he didn't even realize he had forgotten to put on his clothes!

That same power of concentration when applied to solving scientific problems and allied with his genius produced so many things that we still use today. He calculated the value of pi, the approximate area of circles without calculus, and according to a webpage dedicated to him:

He found the area and tangents to the curve traced by a point moving with uniform speed along a straight line which is revolving with uniform angular speed about a fixed point. This curve, described by r = aq in polar coordinates, is now called the "spiral of Archimedes." With calculus it is an easy problem; without calculus it is very difficult.

Archimedes applied his knowledge to machines, such as the screw of Archimedes, which could be used to raise water as a modern pump does from mines, wells, or the hold of a ship. He built compound pulleys and catapults, as well as other weapons of war. Polybius, a Greek historian who wrote about the rise of Rome, described the use of his catapults to bombard their ships during the Second Punic War with lead weights and rocks, and another machine that picked up the Roman warships with grappling hooks and using the compound pulley, dumped the contents of the ships including the sailors and soldiers on board into the sea when they attempted to bridge the walls of the city from their ships. This broke up the Roman attack from the sea on his city, and when his catapults of varying sizes were used against troops attacking by land, the Romans had to give up the attack. Eventually the Romans took Syracuse by a surprise attack and according to Plutarch:

Archimedes, who was then, as fate would have it, intent upon working out some problem by a diagram, and having fixed his mind alike and his eyes upon the subject of his speculation, he never noticed the incursion of the Romans, nor that the city was taken. In this transport of study and contemplation, a soldier, unexpectedly coming upon him, commanded him to follow to Marcellus, which he declined to do before he had worked out his problem to a demonstration; the soldier, enraged, drew his sword and ran him through.

In this case, his powers of concentration led to his death!

Chronology
(all dates B.C.)

359-336	Philip II of Macedon's reign as king
338	Battle of Chaeronea, Philip II gains hegemony of Greece
336	Philip II assassinated and his son, Alexander III (the Great), becomes king; Aristotle establishes the Lyceum
334-326	Alexander the Great invades Persia, Battle of the Granicus River
333	Alexander and his army of Greeks win the Battle of Issus
331	Alexander wins the Battle of Gaugamela-final defeat of the Persian Emperor
326	Alexander's forces reach the Indus River but mutiny and refuse to go on
323	Death of Alexander the Great
322	Death of Aristotle
320-301	Establishment of the Antigonid kingdom
310	Alexander's son murdered, Zeno founds school of Stoicism at Athens
307	Epicurus founds his school of philosophy at Athens
306-304	Seleucid and Ptolemaic kingdoms established
342-290	Menander lives and writes New Comedy style drama
310-230	Aristarchus of Samos – astronomer who develops helio-centric theory
300	Euclid's *Elements of Geometry*, Museum of Alexandria with great library
287-212	Archimedes of Syracuse develops the basis of physics
276-194	Eratosthenes, founder of mathematical Geography
272	Library of Alexandria destroyed by fire
238-227	Attalus I, king of Antigonid kingdom of Pergamum defeats the Gauls
225	*Dying Gaul* sculpted for the monument of Attalus, example of Hellenistic emotion and portrayal of the individual in art
214-205	King Philip V of Macedonia fights first war with the Romans
200-118	Polybius, Greek historian who writes a history of Rome during the Punic and Greek wars
190	*Winged Victory of Samothrace*
168	Rome conquers the Antigonid dynasty to rule Macedon
150	*Venus de Milo*
146	Roman conquest of Corinth
133	Attalid kingdom of Pergamum bequeathed to Rome on the death of the last king
100	*Laocoon and His Sons* by Polydoros, Hagesandros, and Athenodoros of Rhodes
64	Rome conquers remains of the Seleucid kingdom
30	Death of Cleopatra VII; Rome adds Egypt to its empire; End of the Ptolemaic line of monarchs and the Hellenistic Age

THE HELLENISTIC WORLD
AND CIVILIZATION

The Hellenic period was a time of intense development of Greek culture and a period of conflict between the poleis. The world of the individualized polis as the basic political unit of Greece gave way in the fourth century to the period of the cosmopolitan world empire of the Macedonian, Alexander the Great. The term Hellenistic refers to the three century period from the death of Alexander in 323 B.C. to the death of Cleopatra, the last Macedonian ruler of Egypt in 30 B.C. During this period, Greek culture was diffused throughout the eastern Mediterranean region, including Egypt and the Near East, in the wake of Alexander's army as he invaded and conquered the Persian Empire. Earlier historians dating from the 19th century interpreted this to mean a fusion of the local cultures in the East took place with the Greek culture, forming a new synthesis dominated by the superior culture of the Hellenes. It has long been noted that this blending was not perfect and often seemed to be superficial at best, with the Greeks forming a separate ruling class.

Others have recently come to question this view and instead see the Hellenic conquerors as acting like normal imperial conquerors who imposed their culture on their subjects, but the spreading of their *superior* culture took place incidentally rather than deliberately, and it was only accepted by those who hoped to gain personally from their compliance. Peter Green, a well-known Greek historian, is among those who have adopted this view. He found that almost no Greek literature was translated into the Persian, Egyptian, or other eastern languages and the same was true in the other arts and to a lesser degree in the sciences, and thus little integration of ideas took place. The one great excep-

tion was the Romans who came from the West and conquered the Hellenistic kingdoms, but in turn were conquered by the Hellenes intellectually. The Romans admired and accepted Hellenic culture despite some resistance to it by the older Romans, who saw it as being degenerate due to the nudity and debauchery of the Greeks at that time.

During this period, Sparta, which had retained a certain amount of autonomy, slowly decreased in power as her pool of available warriors dropped to 700 or less, and she had to look for allies and at times hired mercenaries to defend the Peloponnesus. The city states she had dominated broke free of Spartan control, and 1st the Macedonian kingdom and then the Romans defeated and gained control of Sparta as well as the rest of Greece. This was the period of Roman expansion in Italy culminating in the wars with Carthage and the great struggle with Hannibal during the 2nd Punic War. Some Greek kings allied with Carthage while others such as Sparta allied with the Romans. Regardless, all would become part of the Roman Empire by the end of the Hellenistic Age, and democracy was nowhere to be found in Greece.

Philip II of Macedonia and
Alexander the Great

In northeastern Greece, there arose a king with the skill, knowledge, political ambition, and boldness necessary to build his kingdom into a powerful force. Philip II (359-336 B.C.) of Macedonia overthrew his infant nephew to become king. Philip had lived in Thebes during his youth when that polis was at the height of its power under Epiminondas. He learned not only Greek culture (the nobility of Macedonia considered themselves to be Greek, and the royal family claimed to be descendants of Heracles) but also the military skills of the Greeks. The Macedonians spoke a dialect of the Greek language and admired Greek culture. With Philip's ambition and military-organizational skill, he began to build a superb fighting force. Unlike the citizen-soldier of the polis, the Macedonian army was a professional army because Philip, as king, was able to fund it with money from the gold mines of Macedonia and Thrace. Philip employed the phalanx of the Greeks in his army, but he used a more open formation with longer pikes. He relied on the cavalry, who was placed on the flanks of the phalanx, to protect them and to over-run the flanks of the opposing army. This proved to be a superior form of organization of the army and lead to victory after victory. The cavalry were Macedonian nobility, called *Companions,* who fought on horseback. They lived with the king and fought beside him, developing an extreme loyalty to him.

Philip began to involve Macedonia in the internal politics and wars of the poleis when he convinced the leaders of Thessaly in the 350s B.C. to elect him as the leader of their confederacy. This was a cunning move, giving him legitimacy as a Greek leader. In the 340s B.C., he led the armies of the Thessalonian confederacy in battle against the Phocians, who had a long-running dispute with Thessaly, called the Holy War over the oracle of Apollo at Delphi. Defeating the Phocians, Philip then took over not only Phocis but Thessaly as well. He gained control of Thrace along the northern coast of the Aegean Sea adjacent to the Hellespont. By the late 340s B.C., Philip had bribed, cajoled, or forced the northern and central poleis of Greece to submit to his leadership. Philip began to call for a united Greek and Macedonian army to invade the Persian Empire as revenge for the Persian War over a century before. His main detractor was Demosthenes, the great orator of Athens. Ath-

ens was no longer the powerful polis she had been a century earlier, for her empire was gone and her population was declining. Philip needed the resources of southern Greece, in addition to those he already controlled, to carry out his plan of building a great empire. Demosthenes rallied Athenian opinion with his warning that Greece would lose her freedom to this "barbarian" king, and he won Thebes over to this point of view. However, in 338 B.C., Philip's coalition defeated the Athenian alliance at the battle of Chaeronea, ending the independence of the poleis of Greece. Chaeronea was an important turning point in Greek history. Philip granted generous terms to the city-states, giving them autonomy over local affairs but requiring them to follow his foreign policy and join a league that was formed in 338 B.C. The following year, the Greek representatives met at Corinth and declared war on Persia. Before he could carry out his plan, Philip was assassinated and replaced by his oldest son, Alexander.

Alexander, King Philip's son, was present at the Battle of Chaeronea in 338 B.C. and led the cavalry charge that broke the Athenian-Theban line. With the death of his father, Alexander took the Macedonian crown and quickly put down revolts in Greece. He destroyed the city of Thebes in 335 B.C. to intimidate other city-states and establish his control. Although he was only 20 years old, Alexander gathered his forces, which included men from all of Greece as well as Macedonia, and in 334 B.C. he crossed the Hellespont into Asia Minor. He had been advised to wait until he was married to insure the continuance of the royal line, but he was determined to strike immediately.

Alexander inherited many of the exceptional qualities of his father. As a student of Aristotle in Athens, he had demonstrated his intelligence. Like his father, he was ambitious and bold. He

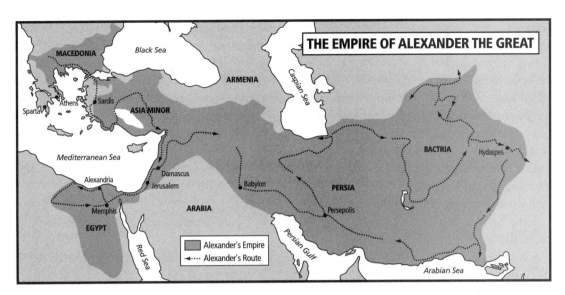

was a masterful general who led his men into battle rather than sending them from behind the lines. He ate and slept with his soldiers and won their loyalty. Alexander had an iron will and the discipline and courage to back it up. Enthusiastically accepting Hellenic ideals, Alexander slept with a copy of the *Iliad* under his head, along with a dagger for protection. He saw himself as the hero, Achilles, and believed that he was chosen for greatness. Upon crossing the Hellespont, Alexander drove his spear into the earth, claiming it like a Homeric hero as "won by the spear."

Leading an army of 30,000 foot soldiers and a cavalry of about 5,000, Alexander invaded an empire far greater in size than all of Greece to fight an army that was several times the size of the combined Greek and Macedonian army. The first serious battle was fought at the Granicus River in 334 B.C. Alexander hazarded his life by leading the cavalry charge across the river and straight into the Persian army line, causing it to break and giving him the victory. In doing so, he almost lost his life, but by such courage he led his men to victory. After defeating and scattering the Persians, young Alexander led his army south along the coast, liberating the Greek city-states and depriving the Persian navy of ports.

In 333 B.C., King Darius met Alexander in battle at Issus with an army three times the size. With good luck, a superior strategy, and courageous leadership, Alexander's smaller army destroyed the army of the great king. In this battle Alexander again led a cavalry charge. The morale and discipline of the Persian army disintegrated, and Darius fled for his life back into the heart of his kingdom, leaving his wife and daughter behind. Alexander treated them with courtesy and won them over, along with many people of the empire.

Alexander's next strategy was to move south along the coast of the Mediterranean Sea, taking Egypt rather than immediately pursuing King Darius. He captured Egypt with relative ease and was deified as the son of Ammon (their equivalent of Zeus) after laying siege to the ancient city of Tyre and destroying its walls, a feat that no one else had been able to do in 700 years. Darius put another army together and met Alexander's forces at Gaugemela in 331 near the site of what had been Ninevah in northern

Mesopotamia. Once again, Alexander's army smashed the Persian army, and the great king fled. That was the last flight of Darius. One of his officers, hoping to gain favor with Alexander, killed him. When the man brought the king's head to Alexander for reward, Alexander had him put to death because of his disloyalty. Alexander found all of the wealth needed to fund his empire at Persepolis, the Persian capital. After confiscating the gold, jewels, and other rich goods, he burned the royal city to symbolize the revenge of Greece and to destroy the loyalties to the center of the old empire.

Alexander pushed on across the Persian Empire into the northeast where in Bactria (now a part of Afghanistan and Uzbekistan) he married the princess Roxane to confirm an alliance with the Bactrians. He also established one of the many cities bearing his name, as he usually did, but this one was named Alexandria Eschate, which means "farthest Alexandria." He tried to conquer the area of modern India, crossing the Indus River and in 327 B.C. led his army through the Khyber Pass. They had now been gone from home for about eight years, and his troops refused to go any further. Although Alexander evidently had heard of China from Aristotle, and must have planned to go all the way to the sea, he listened to his mutinous troops and turned back. As he traveled down the Indus River, Alexander was injured. He had thrown himself into the front of a battle and to motivate his troops, climbed over the wall of the city being attacked and fought alone when his troops would not act with the aggressiveness that he demanded. His warriors were forced to come to his rescue or let him die due to their dishonorable cowardice. They rescued Alexander but not before he received a spear wound that must have punctured his lung during the fight. As a result, Alexander lay near death for several

days. Eventually he was able to travel, and they moved south to where the Indus River flows into the sea. He sent part of his party around the coast while the remainder crossed the desert to return to the center of Persia. Once back in Persia, Alexander the Great began to make his plans to consolidate and expand his empire, but the following year in 323 B.C. he died at the early age of 33 years. His son was born a few months after his death.

Hellenistic Cities and Kingdoms

With the death of Alexander, his generals began a struggle for power that ended in the formation of three major kingdoms. All of the royal family were murdered or executed, including Roxane and her son. One of Alexander's generals, Ptolemy, took control of Egypt and established the 31st dynasty of pharaohs. There the great city of Alexandria, first established by Alexander, became a center of cosmopolitan living and education with one of the great libraries and academic centers of the ancient world. Ptolemy's last and best known descendant in modern times was Cleopatra.

The second general, Antigonus, ruled Macedonia and some of the Greek city-states of northern Greece. He established the Antigonid dynasty. The remainder of Greece was divided between two leagues of city-states that survived until the Romans conquered them in the second century B.C.

The third kingdom was the heartland of the old Persian Empire that stretched from Asia Minor on the Aegean/Mediterranean Sea through Mesopotamia to India. Seleucus founded the Seleucid Dynasty that lasted until the Romans conquered it, though it had lost considerable territory in the east by that time. This kingdom experienced an influx of thousands upon thousands of Greek immigrants who brought their culture with them.

Alexander was the first to induce people to leave their homes in Greece and resettle in his new empire as a part of the governing class necessary to run it reliably and harmoniously. He also seemed to see this as an opportunity to Hellenize that part of the world, since he believed in those values so strongly, at least in the beginning. Realizing the importance of establishing a permanent basis for his empire, Alexander decreed that all were to be citizens of the empire and equal members of the state. This gave rise to the belief in the "Brotherhood of all mankind" and some have interpreted Alexander as a visionary who wanted to establish a world where all men were brothers, under his rule, of course. He urged his soldiers to follow his example and take wives of the region they were in, evidently hoping to blend not only culture but races, despite the fact that some of them had wives back in Greece. After his death, this movement of people from Greece and Macedonia continued, blending the Greek and Eastern culture to form the culture we know as Hellenistic. The Greek language was used among the educated ruling class, but Eastern ways of living and religion were established in most other ways. A truly urban society developed due to emphasis being placed on the cities and the events held there, despite the fact that most people lived in rural areas. This was a cosmopolitan world where people and goods moved about with considerable ease. Their loyalty was no longer to the polis or local region but to the person of the king and the kingdom in which they lived.

The economy tended to thrive at first. The Greeks implemented crop rotation and irrigation, leading to more efficient and productive use of the land. But the main advances came in industry and trade, as goods were made in one place and shipped over wide areas with fewer obstacles to the flow of trade. For example, many thousands of shipping pots (amphoras) made in Rhodes have been found in Egypt. The island of Delos handled the transshipment of many goods, including ten thousand slaves per day. As time passed, there was a tendency to rely more and more on slaves, making it difficult for the poor to compete and make a living. Gradually poverty increased and the separation between the upper class and the lower classes widened.

Religion and Philosophy

Politically, the Greeks accepted the new reality of monarchy with powerful, even absolute, kings, who took on aspects of being gods in the East. The Greeks turned away from the polis to individual pursuits of pleasure and personal escapism. Emphasis increasingly was placed on the inner-self and personal gratification. Outwardly, people became more fatalistic but inwardly they turned to the mystery religions, which gave them the hope of a better life after death, included elaborate rituals involving their emotions and providing catharsis (emotional release), and provided an ethical guide for their actions. Greek religious practice was based on the gods of the polis and as a result, was essentially meaningless to other people. In the East, Greek religious practices never took root among the common people and soon died out. Even in Greece, people were looking for inner fulfillment in their lives. They often found it in one of three major mystery cults: Isis, the goddess of the Nile who renewed life, Mithra, the god of life-eternal, and Serapis.

Still, the religion changed very slowly, for the Greeks held to the ways of their fathers instinctively. One scholar who has studied the religious practices of Athens during the Hellenistic period, Jon Mikalson, found that following their defeat at Chaeronea, the Athenians actually experienced a revival of the old religious faith in their gods, and that for the next couple of hundred years they maintained much of the essence of the classical era religion. Thus, he and others who challenge the idea that Greek religion declined or changed in ways that prepared them for the coming of Christianity, find considerable continuity in Greek religion in some of the poleis they have studied carefully. Yet Mikalson admits that eventually the foreign cults did become popular, but they were accepted within, or adapted to, the framework of religion that already existed.

Philosophy followed a similar pattern of appealing to the individual's need for fulfillment and happiness during the Hellenistic Age. Of course, philosophy was largely the domain of the educated upper class. Epicurus lived in Athens (342-271 B.C.) and taught that pleasure was the goal of life. Pleasure, however, was the absence of pain, not uncontrolled indulgence of the appetites, for that often leads to pain. The Epicureans believed that one should ideally escape the busy life and avoid things like politics. Epicurus taught that there is no life after death, for the soul, as well as the body, is made up of atoms, which disintegrate back into the universe upon death. This philosophy of avoidance fit the age. Politics as the purpose of life was gone, as was the city-state. The earlier polis had become simply a local unit of an empire.

Stoicism is the other major philosophy that came out of the Hellenistic Age. A freed slave, Zeno (333-262 B.C.), taught the brotherhood of all men and the existence of reason and universal law because there is a divine providence that rules over all and determines the destiny of each person. The duty of each person is to live the virtuous life, bear your fate without flinching and take action to make the world around

you a better place. The Stoics believed that God is in Nature and in each person, and the result was to treat human beings with greater respect. Through self-control, one could find happiness, or at least tranquility. This philosophy was the opposite of Epicureanism except for the finding of tranquility for the inner soul. It was accepted by the ruling classes and fit in with the idea of the cosmopolitan kingdom or empire, whose subjects were to serve the state for the good of all.

Two other philosophies, the Cynics and Diogenes, opposed conformity and pleasure of any kind. Instead, they taught that the simple life was best. Whatever came naturally should be followed, whether it was defecating or fornicating in public. Crudeness was completely acceptable for the Cynics. Skepticism claimed that one couldn't know the truth for certain, so one should not worry. Acceptance of things as they were was the result.

Science

The Hellenistic Age was certainly a productive age for science. Why did it occur? First, it was based on the rational inquiry of the Greek philosophers, particularly Aristotle. Second, it received the support of Alexander the Great who brought a number of scientists along on his triumphal invasion of Persia to collect flora and fauna, among other kinds of scientific data, and later the support of the Ptolemies in Egypt. Finally, the cross-fertilization of knowledge from the East with that of the Greeks led to the sharing of knowledge and greater development. Alexandria in Egypt became the most advanced center for the study of science. The greatest library in the ancient world developed with over 500,000 volumes before it was destroyed in 272 A.D. Scientists found employment, a scholarly atmosphere, and resources for research at the first Museum (which means "place of the Muses") there.

In astronomy, Aristarchus (310-230 B.C.) set forth the theory that the earth revolves around the sun, although later the competing theory by Hipparchus won out and the geocentric model was believed to be correct, until Copernicus disproved it 1,700 years later. In geography Eratosthenes (276-194 B.C.) estimated the circumference of the earth close to the actual distance, which meant that he anticipated the earth being a globe, rather than flat.

In mathematics, Euclid (383-325 B.C.) compiled a textbook on geometry, *Elements of Geometry,* one of the most important texts on math ever produced. Archimedes (287-212 B.C.) was an important researcher who calculated the value of pi. He also worked on catapults and developed the screw of Archimedes in physics. He also wrote *On Plane Equilibriums*, a description of levers and their principles and discovered the displacement of a liquid by a solid could be used to determine the weight of the solid. Scientists and mathematicians produced a clocklike mechanism referred to as the Antikythera, named for the island where a shipwreck produced this analog device. X-rays have revealed that the device had metal gears and pointers, which could predict the motion of the planets and probably served as an aid to navigation. In a sense, it was a forerunner of the computer.

In medicine and anatomy, Herophilus learned the functions of arteries and veins and described various organs like the cerebrum, cerebellum, optic nerve, uterus, ovaries, and the prostate. Erasistratus, the founder of physiology, explained how the valves of the heart function and described the difference between the sensory and motor nerves.

Literature and Art

The library at Alexandria became the center of literary effort during the Hellenistic Age. Much of the work was dry, scholarly writing, and over 1,100 writers have been identified. The development of cataloguing and the use of literary criticism were necessary for intellectual development, academic pursuits similar to those that are so important today in colleges and universities throughout the world. Apollonius in the third century B.C., wrote *Argonautica,* which tells the story of Jason and the Golden Fleece. Theocritus (310-250 B.C.), a Greek poet like Apollonius, wrote thirty-two poems and developed the idyll, a poetic form that pictures rural life. This was the age of the New Comedy. Menander (342-290 B.C.) wrote one hundred comedies that dealt with love intrigues and sentimental themes, using a witty, polished style. Finally, Polybius (203-120 B.C.) wrote a forty volume *Universal History* of Rome, covering the period 221-146 B.C. Only five volumes remain today. Polybius is considered to be very accurate. He wrote a great deal about the two Punic Wars in that series. Eratosthenes wrote a chronology of important events from the Trojan War to the second century B.C.

Architecture was affected by the development of the Hellenistic monarchies, for they had plenty of money. The simple Greek temple of the Classical Age was replaced by public structures built on a magnificent scale. Size and lots of ornamentation were characteristics of the period. The Temple of Zeus, which was built at Athens, was 363 feet long and 182 feet wide and was considered by many to be a wonder of the ancient world. The giant-sized lighthouse, or Pharos, at Alexandria, and the massive library are examples of buildings built on a grand scale not only to perform an important service but

This large black-figured amphora, jar, made in Attica during the Classic Age, shows artisans working in a bootmaker's shop.

also to project the power and glory of the king who built it. Of the *Seven Wonders of the World,* two were built during the Hellenistic Age. The first was the Pharos and the second was the Colossus of Rhodes, the huge bronze sculpture that stood astride the entrance to the harbor.

Sculpture became increasingly emotional and dramatic, such as the *Dying Gaul.* In *Laocoon and His Sons,* the realism of the priest and his sons being strangled by the serpents is interwoven with the emotional impact of the death struggle that the artist displayed by exaggerating the muscles and portraying agony on the faces of the victims. Particularly good examples of realism are the *Boxer, Drunken Old Woman,* and *Old Market Woman.* The latter is a bent and

bowed older woman with a mole on her face. Praxiteles in the Classical Age would never have portrayed such a person. This realism would point the way to the art of the Roman world.

CONCLUSION

The Hellenistic period saw a major change take place in the dominant political concept of the times. With the conquest of Greece by the Macedonian kings, Philip and Alexander the Great, the independent poleis were incorporated into an empire and the ideal of democracy was replaced by that of individuals as subjects of a vast empire, or kingdoms that were cut out of the cloth of Alexander's empire. This led quite naturally into the later "world" empire of Rome. The loss of the polis caused people to turn inward for individual satisfaction in religion, philosophy and the arts.

The Hellenistic Age provided a higher standard of living for many in the beginning, but it also saw a growing disparity between the rich and the poor. This period saw an even greater development and application of scientific knowledge. The emphasis on individual fulfillment was demonstrated in the growth of the mystery cults, the individuality, realism and emotion in the arts, and the philosophies of Epicurus and Zeno. Beyond the achievements in the arts and sciences of that age, probably the greatest is the dissemination and preservation of Hellenic culture for the Roman Age and beyond that time to all of later Western civilization.

Suggestions for Further Reading

John Boardman, *Greek Art* (1985)

J. Boardman, J. Griffin & O. Murray eds., *Greece and the Hellenistic World* (1986)

Paul Cartledge, *Alexander the Great: The Hunt for a New Past* (2004); *Ancient Greece* (1998)

M.I. Finley, *The Ancient Economy*, 2nd Ed. (1985)

Robin Lane Fox, *The Classical World* (2006)

Peter Green, *Alexander the Great* (1972); *From Alexander to Actium* (1990)

Peter Green ed., *Hellenistic History and Culture* (1993)

A.A. Long, *Hellenistic Philosophy: Stoics, Epicureans, Skeptics* (1974)

Thomas R. Martin, *Ancient Greece : From Prehistoric to Hellenistic Times* (1996)

J.D. Mikalson, *Athenian Popular Religion* (1983); *Religion in Hellenistic Athens* (1998)

D. Brendan Nagle, *The Ancient World: A Social and Cultural History* (1979)

J. Onians, *Art and Thought in the Hellenistic Age* (1979)

F.W. Wallbank, *The Hellenistic World* (1981)

Chapter 4

THE ROMANS

Gaius Caligula (12 A.D. - 41 A.D.) or "little boots" came to the throne in 37 A.D. He was given the nickname Caligula "Bootikins" or "little boots" because of the little soldier's boots he wore as a child. While the name is innocent, his brief four years as Emperor were marked by psychosis, unbridled promiscuity, incest, cruelty, as well as delusional visions of his own divinity.

He was described as being very unattractive, tall and pale, with a very thin neck and spindly legs. His hair was thin, and he was bald on the top. His face was ugly, and he seemed to have made his appearance even worse by practicing all manner of horrible expressions in front of a mirror. Thus, the emperor was neither healthy in body nor mind. As all emperors, he was a megalomaniac and expected unlimited flattery from his associates.

Caligula had a most "unusual" sexual appetite, even for a Roman emperor. He was known to have homosexual relations, as well as having an incestuous relationship with his sisters. His poor sisters were also prostituted to some of the emperor's favorites. By the time he was thirty (the last year of his life) Caligula had been married four times. The last of his marriages was to Caesonia, a mother of three children. Poor Caesonia was paraded in the nude before his friends. He threatened to have her tortured to find out why he cared for her so devotedly. Caligula was a sadist!

Caligula considered himself quite a warrior, as well as entertainer. "He often danced at night, and once, at the close of the second watch, summoned three senators of consular rank to the palace. Arriving half dead with fear, they were conducted to a stage upon which amid a tremendous racket of flutes and heel-taps, Caligula suddenly burst in, dressed in cloak and ankle-length tunic, performed a song and dance and disappeared as suddenly as he had entered."

One of his favorite actors, Apelles of Ascalon, lost the favor of Caligula, and the emperor had him beaten, finding it amusing to compliment him on the melodious tone of his screams. By 39 A.D. Caligula's behavior had caused discontent throughout Rome. The cost of maintaining the royal lifestyle led to new taxes on food, as well as the income of prostitutes and pimps.

Finally, it was too much for anyone to stand. The senior praetorian officer, the military tribune, Cassius Chaerea, a man who had been deeply insulted by the jokes at his expense, joined a plot to assassinate Caligula. The emperor had joked of the officer's sexual conservatism. In addition, whenever the emperor offered his hand for Chaerea to kiss, it amused Caligula to move his fingers in obscene ways. On 24 January 41 A.D. in a passage beneath the palace, Chaerea and two other officers assassinated Caligula. Sadly, this was followed by the murder of the emperor's wife, Caesonia, and their baby daughter.

Caligula had made a terrible mistake by underestimating the growing power of the Praetorian Guard, alienating them and the Senate. Caligula's murder would, unfortunately, establish the precedent of violence associated with the making or removing of emperors. In January 41 A.D. Gaius Caligula's uncle, Tiberius Claudius Nero Germanicus, became emperor.

Chronology

c. 507   Tarquin expelled the beginning of the Republic.

c. 494   First Secession of Plebeians. Establishment of tribunes.

471   Tribal Assembly established

451-450   The Twelve Tables

264-241   First Punic War

218-201   Second Punic War – Hannibal

149-146   Third Punic War

146   Destruction of Carthage

73-71   Revolt of Spartacus

60   First Triumvirate – Pompey, Crassus, Caesar

59   Full Consulship of Caesar

49-45   Civil War

44   Dictatorship and assassination of Caesar

43   Second Triumvirate: Octavian, Antony, Lepidus

36   Octavian is victorious over Lepidus

31   Defeat of Antony and Cleopatra by Octavius at Actium. Egypt annexed.

27 BC-14 AD   Octavian Augustus

6 BC – 4 BC   Birth of Jesus

66-70   First Jewish revolt

79-81   Titus

115-118   Jewish revolts

132-135   Second Jewish Revolt

161-180   Marcus Aurelius

249-251   Persecution of Christians

257   Renewed persecution of Christians

303-311   Great persecution of Christians

312   Constantine I the Great defeats Maxentius at the Milvian Bridge

312-337   Constantine I the Great and Licenius (d. 324)

313   Toleration to Christianity – Edicts of Milan

324-330   Eastern Capitol at Constantinople

325   Council of Nicaea – Establish Nicene Creed

363-364   Julian the Apostate – Restoration of Paganism
Jews told they could rebuild Temple of Solomon

373-397   Ambrose, bishop of Milan

395-430   Augustine bishop of Hippo in North Africa writes *Confessions*, *City of God*, hundreds of letters

404   Ravenna on Adriatic becomes new capitol of Western Empire

Extending from north to south, the Apennine Mountains are a spiny ridge dividing the Italian Peninsula into fertile plains on its western slopes to more arid climate on the eastern slopes. It was in this peninsula that Rome would be established, develop, and emerge as a great empire. Rome's development, as is true of other civilizations, was significantly affected by geography and climate. The Italian peninsula is comprised of a number of unique geographical features. Basically, Italy is divided into two distinct areas: the northern continental and southern peninsular. Continental Italy measures approximately 350 miles east to west and no more than 70 miles from the Alps in the north to the Po River to the south. The Alps have a series of passes and, therefore, did not afford a serious barrier to migrations from the north. The Po River rises in the Alps and empties into the Adriatic Sea 350 miles to the east. The alluvial plain created by the river and its many tributaries had great agricultural potential once the inhabitants acquired the technology to drain and clear the land for cultivation.

Peninsular Italy is 650 miles in length but no more than 125 miles in breadth. Because of the Apennines, this part of Italy is crisscrossed with hills and valleys. Eventually the Apennines swing to the west forming the toe of Italy at Calabria and to the north and east forming the heel in Apulia.

At no point do the Apennines reach above the snow line. These mountains, however, are not benign as they are the scene of volcanic activity: Stromboli, Etna in Sicily, and Vesuvius near the Bay of Naples have been active for millennia. These volcanoes can wreak havoc as in the case of Pompeii, but they are also beneficial as volcanic ash increases soil fertility.

By the third millennium B.C., having adopted eastern Mediterranean agricultural methods, Italy and its people began to advance. This early development, however, floundered when at the end of the second millennium B.C., Italy, Greece, as well as Asia Minor, experienced barbarian incursions. These barbarian attacks isolated Italy from contacts with the East. These peoples from the north were hunter gatherers, fisherman, and farmers. They had knowledge of copper and eventually learned to smelt bronze. They may also have been the first to introduce an Indo-European dialect into Italy.

The geography of Italy, its long coastline and the passes through the Alps, subjected it to all manner of influences. Migrations from the north and colonial movement from the east met here on the Italian peninsula. That Rome imposed its will over this diverse landscape is remarkable.

The Etruscans

Much of the native traditions and cultural diversity that existed in the Italian Peninsula have disappeared. Among the various peoples there appears to have been great differences in social organization, religion, language, culture, and ethnicity. Greeks in the South, Bruttians in the toe of Italy, Samnites to the north, and a hodgepodge of small tribes, Latins, Umbrians, and Sabines, in the interior, all played a part in Rome's development. The most significant and crucial for Rome, however, was Etruria. From the eighth to the end of the sixth century B.C. northern and central Italy was dominated by the people of Etruria, the Etruscans. Archaeological evidence provides us with a picture of a sophisticated urban civilization

The center of Etruscan life was located between the Arno River on the north, the Tiber River in the south and east, and the Mediterranean to the West. These people dominated much of the northern and central Italian Peninsula from the mid-eighth to the end of the sixth century B.C. As seafarers, they traveled the coast of the Italian Peninsula and beyond. Their pottery, called buchero ware, has been unearthed in many archaeological sites in Southern Italy and Sicily. The Etruscans would make a significant impact upon the early development of Rome, especially in areas of engineering and religion.

What remains a mystery about the Etruscans is their place of origin. Some scholars suggest that the Etruscans were part of an earlier Villanovan culture whose center was in the area of Bologna. The Greek historian, Herodotus, around 450 B.C. provides us the earliest accounts of the Etruscans. It is Herodotus' opinion that their place of origin was Lydia in Western Asia Minor (present day Turkey). According to Herodotus, the Etruscans, "after voyaging past many peoples they came to the land of the Ombrici where they built cities…." Whether Herodotus is to be considered accurate remains a matter of debate. Others historians, like the first century B.C. Greek historian Diogenes of Hallicarnasus (31 B.C.), argued that they were native to the Italian Peninsula. Wherever their place of origin, they continue to be a fascinating and mysterious people. Unfortunately there are just too many pieces of the puzzle missing to do any more than guess. From the artifacts and paintings found in their tombs a picture emerges of a fun loving, sophisticated, and sensual people.

The Etruscans practiced religion similar to their contemporaries. The world, nature, was alive (animate) where the will of the gods could be determined through the practice of divination (reading of signs found in the livers of sacrificial animals.) Archaeology has discovered wall paintings that show the Etruscans at play, dancing, eating, and participating in athletic competition. The sarcophagi (burial containers) often depict husband and wife in a leisurely pose and suggest that women played an active role in society.

A major difficulty in attempting to gain a clearer picture of the Etruscans is the mystery associated with their language. Because they used the Greek alphabet Etruscan funerary inscriptions can be read. Apart from that, the language is an untranslatable maze of hisses and clicks. Even with approximately 10,000 scraps of Etruscan inscriptions, the language remains a mystery. These people stare at us through their vibrant art that presents a visual bright and colorful image of luxury, dancing, music, dining, playing, and women in beautiful jewelry. These same wall paintings also show women enjoying a high status in the community. Etruscans were unique in affording women an open role in society.

Early Rome learned much from the Etruscans and by the end of the sixth century B.C. was ready to throw off their control. By that time the villages on the Tiber had become a town. The traditional date of 509 B. C. marks when Rome freed itself from their Etruscan overlords and their last king, Tarquin the Proud, and established the Republic. In the future, the Etruscans would eventually be absorbed into Roman society. They left behind artifacts that displayed that decline—surreal art, sculpted huddled figures clinging to one another—all indicating their defeat. The future belonged to Rome, pupils who far surpassed their Etruscan leaders.

Rome's Location

Western civilization is indebted to our Roman ancestors. Rome, tutored by Etruscans and nurtured by the Greeks, surpassed them both in the areas of law, engineering, and organization.

In the mid-seventh century B.C. the area that became Rome was controlled by the Etruscans. Their influence is seen in the introduction of agricultural techniques, commerce, and production of trade items. It was sometime in the seventh or sixth century B.C. that the scattered villages on the banks of the Tiber River combined to form a city.

Rome's geographical location provided the fledgling city many natural advantages. The land of the nearby Latin plain was extremely fertile and able to support a growing population. Located on a series of hills above the flooding of the Tiber added security for the city. As the Tiber opens to the sea, it became a commercial avenue for Roman trade. This advantageous location gave Rome a key position to monitor all travel along the western side of the peninsula. In Italy's center, Rome would become the heart of the Peninsula.

THE PERIOD OF THE REPUBLIC 509 B.C. TO 27 B.C.

Two Legends that Trace the Foundation of Rome

The creation of Rome is rooted in the legend of the twins Romulus and Remus. The story relates that the two brothers were illegitimate and that their mother set them adrift on the Tiber River. Taken under the protection of their patron deity, Mars, these legendary figures overcame all obstacles and performed all manner of heroic deeds. Saved by the intervention of Providence, they were suckled by a she wolf and raised by the shepherd Faustulus. Upon reaching manhood, Romulus established a village on the Palatine hill. Remus, his twin, was not idle as he attempted to establish a settlement on an adjoining hill. Then, in order to acquire wives,

the new settlers attacked the neighboring Sabines and carried off their women.

By the beginning of the third century B.C. the legend of the two brothers had become an accepted tradition, explaining Rome's foundation. In the Forum a bronze statue was erected of a she wolf suckling the twins.

The other legend that explained Rome's foundation has a Greek origin. The Greeks, or Hellenes, had become aware of Rome by the fifth century B.C. Greek mythology offered any number of foundation stories concerning Rome. In one account the sons of the Greek hero Odysseus, as a result of his encounter with the enchantress Circe, were the founders of Rome.

The one that had great popularity described how Aeneas, a survivor of the Trojan War, settled the hills above the Tiber. By the end of the fourth century B.C. the Aeneas legend had become another accepted part of Roman tradition.

Information regarding the earlier period of Roman history is derived from archaeology, the study of linguistics, and religion. In order to note continuity such evidence is then applied to written sources when they appear in the third century B.C. The earliest period, during Etruscan control, is lacking in written sources. With the appearance of the Republic c.509 B.C. and the succeeding two centuries some written materials have survived. Here are some examples:

1. The Code of the Twelve Tables: The traditional dating for this code of laws is 450 B.C. Roman jurists cite the Code as furnishing legal precedents into the last century before the birth of Christ. Tracing references in Roman sources to the Code is an important element in developing a picture of the early Republic.

2. Executive Records: This refers to business transactions, procedural rules of Roman magistrates and priests, and especially census records.

3.   Resolutions of the Senate: The Roman historian Livy reports that from the mid-fifth century B.C. Senate resolutions were recorded and deposited in the temple of Saturn.

4. Individual Statues: Unfortunately such evidence is scanty. Some copies of treaties have survived but are insufficient in numbers.

The Early Republic: Expansion of Rome and Its Control of the Italian Peninsula

During this period of expansion in Italy, Rome underwent internal organizational changes. The government of the Republic had to adjust to an ever-increasing population and satisfy the *plebeians* (the <u>many</u>) who struggled against the patrician monopoly of authority.   Two consuls replaced the Etruscan king. The consuls had supreme authority (*imperium*), but each had the power to *veto* (I forbid) the acts of the other. During crises a dictator would be chosen to deal with the threat but could serve no more than six months; the power would then be returned to the Senate.

The Senate was comprised of three hundred members representing the Patrician class and appointed by the Consuls. Their duty was to be advisory to the Consuls and their appointment was for life. No legislation could become law unless approved by the Senate. Made up of patricians interested in maintaining their authority, the Senate was extremely conservative.

The Assembly

In its earliest form citizenship referred to freemen who resided in Rome. Eventually the privileges of citizenship extended to all inhabitants of Italy and finally, during the reign of the Emperor Carracula in the third century A.D., to all peoples of the Empire. Citizens were those who enjoyed all the "Latin rights" and privileges of Rome. They also served in the army and paid taxes.

Besides the Senate there were two tribal assemblies, the *comitia curiata* and *comitia centuriata*. Citizenship was the qualification for selection for one of these assemblies. Those who sat in the *comitia curiata* were selected from tribes while the *comitia centuriata* represented the military. The Assembly elected the two consuls and had the power to veto over their decisions. They did not have the authority to initiate legislation, as they were limited to voting on measures that were presented to them. Dominated by the Patrician, the Assembly followed the lead of their conservative patrons.

Early Roman government attempted to curtail any single group from taking control. The Assembly elected the consuls but did not have the authority to initiate legislation. Their role was limited to accepting or rejecting proposals from the consuls.   Members of the Assembly were quite likely clients of upper-class patricians. The *patricians*, who occupied the Senate, were a powerful military class and, because of that role, they dominated the Early Republic. The Senate, with its lifetime membership, was politically conservative and was interested in keeping its privileges.

During the Early Republic, class distinctions became more pronounced. In addition to the patricians were craftsmen, merchants, peasants, laborers and wealthy non-patricians. These groups became known as the *Plebeians* (the many).

As a result of this imbalance of authority, tensions arose between the patricians and plebeians. Economic, military, political, and social exploitation led the plebeians to threaten to secede from Rome and establish an autonomous state. With no other recourse, the Patricians agreed to Plebeian demands for more representation and protection.

THE TRIBUNE AND
TWELVE TABLES

As a result of the Plebeian revolt, new officers called *Tribunes* became spokesmen for Plebeian interests.

Plebeian assemblies were organized for the annual election of ten officials from their class. These assemblies could also initiate legislation that was in the interest of the Plebeians.

The tribunes were obviously men of considerable standing in Rome. They could intervene on behalf of any plebe that was being unjustly treated by a patrician or high official. They had the right of veto to actions considered unjust. The role of the tribunes was so important that any person who disregarded their veto or harmed them was executed.

Following the example of the Greek city-states two centuries earlier, Rome codified its laws and published them in the Twelve Tables. Around the year 450 B.C. a commission of ten magistrates (decemvirs) was established to codify the laws. Though only fragments of the Twelve Tables have survived, we can re-create something of their content and purpose.

The Twelve Tables: The laws extent of the laws inscribed in this document dealt with matters of public and private life. The laws regulated the obligations and rights of family and property. It also addressed and described offenses against the community.

It is interesting that the Tables contain some harsh and primitive regulations, for example, where money compensation was not agreed upon after an offense the grieving party was free to assault the offender. Witchcraft was punished, especially when crops were blighted. Creditors had the right to "carve up the body" of a debtor who failed in fulfilling his obligation.

There were also laws of a moderate nature. The conservative Roman was very concerned about public order and its maintenance. This, however, did not indicate that Rome, at this time, was a police state, as individual rights were likewise protected. Wives and children, under special circumstances, could be emancipated from the control of the male head of the family. The unsanitary practices of burying or burning the dead within city precincts were forbidden. Most significantly, blood feuds were forbidden, and capital punishment became a matter for the courts. The Popular Assembly became the court of final appeal, especially in cases involving capital punishment.

For the most part the laws of the Twelve Tables attempted to secure an orderly community. They were never repealed and were considered the safeguards for the Plebian against arbitrary judicial proceedings of the Patricians. Here are two examples of change:

1. Magistrates could not execute a prisoner before the convicted exercised the right of appeal.

2. High officers in the priesthood, exclusive for Patricians, became open to Plebeians.

THE MIDDLE REPUBLIC 264-133 B.C.

It is during the Middle Republic that Rome emerged as a major force in the power alignments of the Mediterranean. Rome had expanded during the Early Republic and achieved domination of the Italian Peninsula. Rome's superior military organization, tactics, and discipline were the most important factors in its success. Rome had convinced itself that expansion was to ensure defensible borders rather than planned aggression. By the third century B.C., therefore,

Rome had succeeded in subjugating its closest Latin neighbors, as well as those to the north up to the Po River Valley. Rome was now in a position where, if challenged, it would prove a relentless adversary.

The Punic Wars represent one of the high water marks of Roman history. By the middle of the third century B.C. Rome had successfully extended its control over a major portion of the Italian Peninsula. In the extreme south, just off the toe of Italy and across the Straits of Messina is the island of Sicily. As events unfolded, two powers attempted to gain control of the island, Rome and Carthage, the great commercial sea power of the Western Mediterranean. Beginning in 264 B.C. and ending over 110 years later, Rome and Carthage were involved in three major vicious wars.

Located on the coast of North Africa Carthage is only 130 miles from Sicily. By the fourth century B.C. Carthage had established a commercial monopoly in the Western Mediterranean. With the outbreak of hostilities in 264 B.C. no one could have foretold the momentous ramifications of these conflicts.

Over the following two decades Rome and Carthage fought vicious sea battles. The Romans, unaccustomed to naval warfare, learned seamanship the hard way, as these engagements led to horrible losses in men and ships. On both sides fleets were built, destroyed in engagements or storms, and then rebuilt. The dogged resilience of Rome, however, eventually forced Cartage to sue for peace in 241 B.C.

In Polybius' history of Rome, he described this war as the most vicious ever fought. Roman leadership was inadequate as the Consuls lacked knowledge of naval warfare. While Rome was learning from experience, the fate of defeated Carthaginian generals was execution by crucifixion. Compromising the effectiveness of Carthaginian commanders who did achieve any success was suspicion of a political agenda. As a result, the Carthaginian government failed to send reinforcements. Thus, military success did not lead to victory and the war dragged on.

Rome, exhausted by the war, finally achieved victory and annexed Sicily. With that Rome took a fateful step that carried the Republic into an unforeseen future. The first Punic War made Rome a naval power with commercial and political interests in the Western Mediterranean. The first Punic War had opened the way for Rome to become an imperial power.

The Second Punic War

Of the three Punic Wars it is the second one that has captured the imagination and piqued the curiosity of students, military analysts, scholars, as well as the general public. Hannibal, the son of Hamilcar Barca, crossed the Alps in the winter of 218 B.C. and attacked Rome. There, in Italy, for the next 15 years the armies of Hannibal defeated every Roman army sent against him. From the extreme north to the southern heel Hannibal's troops crossed and recrossed Italy. Victory in battle, however, did not mean victory in war and in 201 B.C. Hannibal and Carthage had been defeated.

Following the first Punic War Carthage had developed the commercial and military resources of Spain where rich silver mines were discovered and exploited. In addition to the mineral resources Spain's population of mixed Celtic and Iberian stock was known for its hardiness and fighting ability. These would be the men that provided the core of Hannibal's army that he threw against Rome, the hated enemy.

Unlike many conflicts where the victors offer terms to the defeated, the Punic Wars aroused such a passionate hatred between the adversaries that victory for one meant annihilation for the other. With revenge in his mind Hannibal left his base of operations in Spain in 218 B.C., crossed the Rhone River above Marsiglia (Marseilles), slipped by the Roman legions that were sent to stop him, and in the winter of 218-217 B.C. made his famous crossing of the Alps. His army, numbering forty thousand, was led by Carthaginian officers and included Numidian cavalry with thirty-seven elephants from North Africa, Iberian infantry, and Gauls. As a result of Hannibal's brilliant leadership, this multi-national army became a formidable adversary.

Rome never thought the Alps could be crossed, especially in winter conditions. To their surprise, in the spring of 217 B.C. Hannibal's army, now reduced to 27,000 because of losses during the treacherous crossing, descended into the valleys of northern Italy. Two months later all of northern Italy had been over-run. The Romans had suffered a defeat at the battle of the Trebia River and the revived Carthaginian army had grown to 50,000. Later in the same year Rome suffered another defeat at Lake Trasimene where two legions were lost along with their commander Flaminius.

The most famous battle and bloodiest encounter in all of Roman history occurred in 216 B.C. On a flat plain near a place known as Cannae, 60,000 Roman legionnaires were confronted by Hannibal's army of 40,000. With a hot wind blowing in their faces the Roman army was lured into a deadly trap. Hannibal had deployed his troops in a convex formation presenting a crescent formation to the attacking Roman legions. What the legions were unaware of was Hannibal's reinforcing of the flanks of his army. He stationed himself in the middle of the line where he also kept the one surviving elephant. Hannibal had discovered that the smell of elephant unnerved the Roman horse thus being a factor in upsetting the effectiveness of the Roman cavalry. As the legions moved forward to attack, Hannibal slowly withdrew drawing the Romans deeper into the center of the line that was slowly taking on a concave shape. When the Roman legions were in the trap Hannibal moved his flanks catching the Romans in a pincer movement. Despite fierce resistance, Rome lost 50,000 men and one Consul in the bloodiest defeat in its history.

In spite of this tragic defeat Rome was able to continue the war and within a short period fielded a new army. After Cannae Rome adopted delaying tactics and refused to be drawn into a major battle. Thus, no battle was conclusive, and the war dragged on for another decade. Rome counterattacked by sending an army to Spain where it cut off the logistics that were so vital to Hannibal.

A serious blow to Hannibal came in 209 B.C. when a relief army was intercepted in northern Italy. Leading the army was Hannibal's brother Hasdrubal, who died with most of his men. Hannibal was informed of the loss when his brother's head was catapulted into his camp.

In 204 B.C. the Roman commander Scipio landed in North Africa to bring the war directly to Carthage. In the following year Hannibal returned to Carthage and in 202 B.C., at the battle of Zama, deserted by the Numidian king, Masinissa, the Carthaginian army was defeated. Hannibal escaped and was pursued by Rome to the East where he eventually committed suicide rather than become a Roman trophy. As Michael Grant so eloquently observed: "He is one of the world's most noble failures, an altogether exceptional man who took on, in deadly warfare, a nation empowered with rocklike resolution—and that nation proved too much for him."

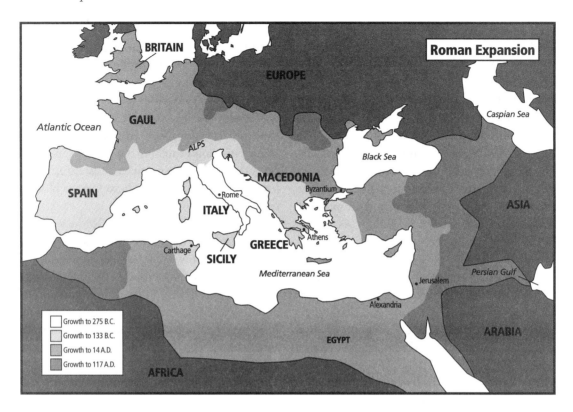

The Third Punic War

Rome was not finished with Carthage and when circumstances allowed, a final chapter to a century of warfare took place. The specter of Hannibal still haunted Rome. Goaded on by the veteran of the second Punic War, M. Cato, who concluded his speeches in the Senate with a call for the destruction of Carthage, Rome moved against Carthage in 149 B.C. This war ended after four years of vicious campaigning. Under the generalship of P. Cornelius Scipio Aemilianus, grandson of Scipio Africanus, who had defeated Hannibal at the Battle of Zama, Carthage was forced to surrender. Its few remaining inhabitants (50,000) were sold into slavery, and the city was razed to the ground. Upon its site salt was sown in plowed furrows, and a

Roman Pontifex Maximus (high priest) cursed the land. It was with this act that the ghost of Hannibal was finally exorcised.

THE LATER REPUBLIC: 133 B.C. to 27 B.C.

The last century before the birth of Christ, however, was not harmonious but an era of violence, murder, and civil war. The small Republic located on seven hills overlooking the Tiber River had become a mighty state, republic in name only, for Rome now governed an Empire. A burgeoning world state required great skill in governing, and Rome was challenged to figure out how that was to be accomplished.

The traditional date—133 B.C.—marks both the opening of the Late Republic as well as a century of violence for Rome. The violence resulted from unresolved social and economic conditions. Political compromise proved useless, only illuminating the weakness of the bickering Senatorial oligarchy. The answer would be to replace the Republic with monarchy, and that is precisely what happened. The period of change was punctuated in bloody factional quarrels. Attempts had been made to address the economic problems that caused such hardship for the peasants. Two brothers, Tiberius Sempronius Gracchus and Gaius Gracchus had attempted to address the economic and social ills that were evident throughout Roman society. The failure to address these economic and social problems would be a key factor in the eventual collapse of the Roman Republic. The careers of these two men were full of tragedy. Their attempts to improve the living conditions of the dispossessed underclass had tragic results. The wealthy landowners considered the political and economic policies as a direct challenge to their traditional authority. The end for both men and the core of their supporters was assassination and summary execution.

Soon after Tiberius Gracchus became Tribune in 133 B.C. he initiated a program of land reform by proposing a limitation on acreage to be held by the wealthy. Going further he sought to parcel and distribute to the poor the remaining public lands. Tiberius was deeply worried about the growing problems faced by the landless. He believed that a revived hardy peasantry, returned to the land, would become the recruiting ground for the army. Unfortunately Tiberius' heavy handed methods of pushing through his legislation alienated the Senate and a violent confrontation took place. An ex-consul led a group of Senators and their clients into the Assembly where Tiberius and 300 of his supporters were clubbed to death. This was the first time in many centuries that civil unrest had led to this kind of blood shed. The violence of Tiberius's death was an ominous sign for the future. The Roman oligarchic system had been challenged, and though it had survived, it had been seriously shaken.

THE END OF THE REPUBLIC

In the last century before the birth of Christ, the problems for Rome were multiplied as Germanic tribes, attracted to the temperate climate of the Mediterranean, moved into southern Gaul. The resulting wars had a significance beyond the military campaigns and strategies of battle. The stress of war exposed the weakness of senatorial government while offering any opportunist military commander an avenue to political control. The resulting challenge to the traditional political structure indicated the dramatic changes that were taking place. Unfortunately for Rome its entire political history would be marred by violence. This will become abundantly clear when the Republic becomes an empire and when aspiring emperors rose and fell as they used or became victims of the assassin.

It was at the end of the second century B.C. curing the Consulships of C. Marius that the army of Rome was transformed from volunteers to a professional military juggernaut. Under Marius' reforms the legions were changed in organization, tactics, and weaponry. Marius opened the army to general enlistment of the lower class proletarian who saw military service as a means of escape from economic hardship. A peasant conscript enlisted for six years and might return to a ruined farm. Why return? Thus, it became imperative for commanders to furnish their legions opportunities for enrichment through booty and gifts (donativa). Each legion of 6000 was divided into cohorts and within each cohort the centurions. As a result, the legions became filled with conscripts rather than volunteers. These new legionaries expected their generals to provide for them, both during and after their term of service had expired.

Throughout the centuries of Rome's dominance the legions proved, time and again, to be the model of discipline, versatility, and efficiency. In other words it was a real killing machine.

The leading military commanders during these final decades were Sulla, Pompey, and Caesar. The problems they faced were extremely sensitive as Rome's arrogance had ignited client resentment into open hostility—the Republic had governed to serve its own self-interests and had used their client states to enrich Rome. What had been suitable for Rome, the city-state on the hills, was not feasible for an Empire. Control of the Mediterranean had not taught Rome to adjust and establish a more inclusive ruling policy. The most glaring error was Rome's refusal to extend citizenship to clients and allies; civil war resulted from that oversight.

Shocked out of complacency, Rome met the challenge by first granting citizenship to loyal allies and then to the pacified rebels. With insurrection over, at least for the time being, Italy, now a part of Rome, developed a culture based on citizenship, the Latin language, and Roman law.

A united Italy, however, did not mean a well-governed Italy. The Senate, inept in leadership, conservative in outlook, and interested in keeping their perquisites, had lost the initiative and had become moribund. The Senatorial oligarchy was split among various factions. The mob was their weapon, and each faction used these clients to intimidate the opposition. The mobs used by the Senate would be used against them by Crassus, Pompey, and Caesar. Faced by crises of their own making, the Senate failed to govern. As a result, the political structure of the Republic collapsed, civil wars resulted, and the Principate was created.

Julius Caesar

Of all the figures that took the stage in this last century before the birth of Christ, none was more formidable than Julius Caesar. In 59 B.C., he became Consul and was a member of the First Triumverate in partnership with Sulla and Pompey. Between 59 B.C. and his assassination in 44 B.C., Caesar led campaigns in Gaul, Britain, Egypt, Thessally, Asia Minor, and North Africa. Possessed with a canny sense of the battlefield, he led his legions to one success after another. His legions, as a result, were absolutely devoted to him.

An impotent government coupled with diminished grain supplies led to rioting; this situation called for a strong leader, and Julius Caesar would answer that call. On 28 July 46 B.C. he was granted dictatorial powers.

Few men in history can rank with Julius Caesar. Brilliant in war as well as politics, he put an end to the Republic. Caesar met the cri-

Julius Caesar's head is graced by a laurel wreath, an ancient symbol of victory, honor, and glory.

teria of the Great Man, someone who, because of his acts, changed history as he molded events.

For all of his brilliance, Caesar was not universally liked. The Senate realized that he had no intention of returning his dictatorial powers. To strengthen his position, Caesar had expanded membership in the Senate from 300 to 700. This increase diluted its prestige and outraged the established families. Believing that their traditional authority was undermined, they murdered Caesar on the Ides of March in 44 B.C. If these disillusioned men thought their act would restore the Republic, they were sadly mistaken. Caesar had responded to a situation, a tension in Rome, created by a moribund government. Rome was a Republic only in name, and the murder of Caesar only served to spark a bloody civil war.

Brilliant as he was, he could not foresee that his ambition and lust for power would place him in mortal danger. His successor would be his grand-nephew Octavian, a man who understood how to wield power and avoid his uncle's fate.

OCTAVIAN 63 B.C. – 14 A.D.

Octavian was only 18 years of age, hardly, one might assume, of sufficient experience and maturity to replace his great-uncle and adoptive father. Slight of build and sickly, Octavian possessed a keen intellect and a will to action. It was the combination of these two qualities that underlied his success. He was a man who coolly and rationally evaluated a situation, considered the variables, plotted a course, and acted. Marc Antony, a close associate of Caesar, was more likely to fill the vacuum of power left by Caesar. Octavian, after a bit of diplomacy, was reconciled with both Antony and Lepidus, another of Caesar's close associates. Their uneasy relationship is known as the Second Triumverate.

Octavia, Antony's wife and Octavian's sister, failed to persuade her husband to abandon Cleopatra and return to Rome.

Octavian, Lepidus, and Antony met in 43 B.C. where the reconciliation took place between Octavian and Antony. The three joined their legions to defeat Cassius and Brutus, creating the Trimverate for a term of five years. (*triumviri reipublicae constituendae*) On November 27, 43 B.C. the Triumverate became official as a tribunician law was passed (*lex Titia*) formalizing their agreement. The Republic continued in name but the real power rested in the Triumverate.

Each of the Triumverate intrigued to become first. In that "game," Octavian proved to be the most adept player. Lepidus quit the field when he left office and retired. Lepidus had intrigued against Octavian but was unsuccessful, and his legions deserted him in favor of Octavian. Pleading for mercy, he was forced to retirement and stripped of authority but allowed to keep the title and office of chief priest (pontifex maximus). He died in 12 B.C. Shortly after 40 B.C. the uneasy relationship between Octavian and Antony unraveled. The catalyst that led to the breach was the Egyptian Queen Cleopatra VII. Antony, married to Octavian's sister, Octavia, had openly abandoned her for Cleopatra. After 37 B.C. hostility between the two intensified leading to a final break in 33 B.C. when Antony ended his marriage to Octavia, the sister of

Antony and Cleopatra are depicted during the Battle of Actium. Actually they commanded separate ships and did not rejoin each other until well after fleeing the conflict.

Octavius. There was no longer any pretense to keep the peace. In 31 B.C. a war began that resulted in the defeat of Antony and Cleopatra at the Battle of Actium. Antony committed suicide and, in 30 B.C., was followed by Cleopatra. Octavian's victory made it clear that the center of power would be in Rome rather than the Hellenized East.

Octavian imposed order, stability, and peace. To be sure, his powers became increasingly dictatorial. But Octavian was too clever to openly establish a dictatorship. He used republicanism and conservatism as important elements in the newly invigorated State. With Italy bound to him by an oath of allegiance, Octavian established a new and basic principal of loyalty to the person rather than to the concept of a State. All of Italy swore the oath to him thus indicating that the person and the State had become one. His success can, in part, be attributed to his society's hunger for peace. If security, peace, and stability were acquired at the price of old freedoms, it was cheaply bought. Old Republican ideals had their moment but had created in the end lawlessness and civil war. The people hungered for peace, and Octavian restored peace. His ability to focus on specific objectives in the face of threats of assassination, corruption in his bureaucracy, and an impossibly large territory to govern is admirable. The difficulty of governing was exacerbated by the great distances and difficult means of communication, as dispatches were sent by boat, by couriers on horseback, or by foot.

Over an empire that extended from Parthia in the east to the Atlantic Ocean in the west, Octavian was a master. The linchpin of his control was his relationship with the army and rule based upon the law. He well understood that his power rested upon the loyalty of the legions, a loyalty that was fickle at best, as the future would attest. For the time being, however, Octavian courted his legions and bound them to him by an oath of loyalty. This practice of requiring the army to swear loyalty to the person of the emperor rather than the office of emperor suited Octavian. Emperors that failed to control the military would never be secure.

By 27 B.C., Octavian's name was supplemented by the titles Augustus and Caesar. These

This fanciful rendering of Cleopatra shows her pressing a poisonous asp to her breast. After her death, Octavian fulfilled her request to be buried with Antony.

titles along with those of chief priest (*pontifex maximus*), first citizen (*princeps civium*), and father of the country (*pater potestas*) made it abundantly clear that the lad of eighteen was now, at the age of thirty-five, the father of his nation, exerting tremendous power. Through it all, Octavian was able to keep his perspective and balance as he never allowed his office to consume him as it would so many of his successors.

Augustus, as the first in a line of Emperors, established standards that would be used to judge his successors. There is much to support the conclusion that Augustus was Rome's first as well as greatest Emperor.

Emperors attempted various practices to ensure a stable procedure of succession. In that they failed, and as a result, there was constant intrigue and manipulation. The unruliness of the army, coupled with the lack of constitutional machinery for transferring power, led to violence and murder, as different aspirants competed for the throne. In effect, Rome failed to establish a method of succession. Roman emperors would have to pay court to the army, particularly the Praetorian Guard, who served as the elite bodyguard of the emperor. Interestingly, it was Octavian who established the Praetorians, and it would be that very same guard that, in the future, would make or remove emperors.

Augustus' military settlement not only secured relative peace within the empire but provided for security in relation to its hostile neighbors. It was during Augustus' reign that the parameters of the Roman Empire were reached. Even though legions pushed beyond the Rhine to the Elbe River, this territory was not pacified and Rome withdrew to the Rhine and Danube where they remained until the western half of the empire collapsed in the fifth century.

Augustus' army of professional soldiers numbered between 250,000+ to 300,000. The le-

This famous statue of Augustus Caesar shows him wearing a general's breastplate with embossed decorations. This statue is found at Prima Porta, near Rome.

gionnaire served for twenty years and then received a pension. During this period of Rome's expansion, sufficient revenue was acquired to defray the expenses of the army. The expense of the army, however, became greater and with no revenues from expansion, the state was forced to make up the difference; the resulting drain upon the economy would eventually become intolerable. Additionally, if pay was late there was the real danger of mutiny and the specter of renewed civil war.

The years following Augustus' death witnessed a succession of men some of whom were capable while others proved unbalanced mentally or psychotic. Irrespective of their mental state, however, all of them were weighed down by the tremendous responsibility of governing. Too much unregulated power just magnified their human weaknesses.

This absence of constitutional means of succession made the position of emperor a prize to be fought over by various claimants. As an example, Nero's death in 68 B.C. was followed by turmoil that is known as the Year of the Four Emperors.

In the following century, the problems of successions became acute, to say the least. Military revolts in favor of one commander over another led to a disastrous half century (235-284). Dozens of men grasped at the imperial throne for a fleeting moment. Those who sought office through assassination were often themselves the victims of assassination. In the face of such violence the Roman Empire continued even as its foundations were being undermined. Controlling the grumbling, tension, and unrest became a major concern of the government. A special police force was responsible for investigating crimes and arresting criminals. The line between tension and mob violence was too easily crossed. Strikes of workers occurred with uncomfortable frequency in such provinces as Asia Minor and Judea, areas where the tensions were especially charged.

Another of the chronic weaknesses experienced by Rome was the financial corruption that gnawed at the State. During the late Republic and continuing into the Empire, Roman provincial officials were known for their greed.

Roman Law

One of the singular and great contributions of Rome was in the field of law. The Empire developed and implemented a system that emphasized the universality of law and mankind. It was a system that bound and protected all citizens of the Empire under the same body of law. It was to be a system that made no distinction of place or residence, whether you lived in Palestine, Egypt, or Britain. The same laws applied. It would be the great compilation of Roman law under the direction of the Emperor Justinian (527-565) that would be revived in medieval universities of the thirteenth century and would become the basis of the French legal system. Roman law was founded upon principles of reason and common sense. Known for its directness and clarity, it was a form of law whose legal precedents were used in the future.

Roman Society

Caesars expressed little sympathy for the underclass. Over the centuries, Roman society became increasingly rigid and top heavy. The state relied on slave labor with the result that the status of freeman was eroded as more and more fell into slavery.

The vast majority that made up the Empire were slaves, peasants, and the urban poor. The huge slave population was the natural result of the territorial expansion during the Republic and the continuing requirements for slaves during the Empire. Slaves, the booty of war, became the cornerstone of Rome's economy and work force.

Slavery was an accepted condition of life in ancient society. The Romans relied upon slave labor almost exclusively. The Punic Wars, campaigns in Asia Minor, and Caesar's wars throughout the Mediterranean brought hundreds of thousands of slaves into Rome. The slave markets of Marsiglio (Marseilles), Greece, and Italy were always busy centers for that trade. In addition to the booty of war, slavery came to those convicted of crimes, debt, or being sold by one's parent.

Slaves performed a number of services for Rome. There were slaves who worked in the home as domestics, some were teachers, professionals, and philosophers—and then there were the gladiators. An educated guess numbers the slaves in Italy during the height of Rome as two million or more; when applied to the overall population of Italy, that number represented one fourth to one third.

During the Republic the brutality and inhuman treatment of slaves by their Roman masters were common. That the average life expectancy of a slave was the early twenties indicates the callous treatment they received. Such a short life expectancy indicates that Roman masters literally worked their slaves to death. In the world of the slave, chains were common and considered an acceptable means of control.

If a slave wanted to be sexually active, permission would first have to be granted, and then the slave was made to pay a tax. With such degrading and appalling conditions, is it any wonder that slaves would run away or rise in rebellion?

Rebellions were suppressed with horrific loss of life. The most famous of the uprisings was that of Spartacus and the gladiators. This rebellion (73-71 B.C.) brought horror to all of Italy. Spartacus was the single greatest threat to Rome since Hannibal and the battles of the Second Punic War. With the crushing of the revolt by the Roman general Crassus, an example was made of the defeated. The Apian Way was lined with six thousand crucified men. This served as a grim reminder of what awaited those who opposed the State.

Eventually the Romans, even with their appetite for cruelty, came to see that slaves were not animals but human beings. Better treatment was encouraged by Stoic ideas that stressed a common humanity and their belief in the existence of a soul. During the reign of Octavian, legislation was passed that protected slaves and required that they be treated more humanely. As an example, slaves could no longer be thrown out to die when they became ill. Octavian's legislation was significant in that slaves were now given a legal status. These changes and those of future emperors attempted to humanize an institution that affected the economy and society of the entire Empire. Law, however, did not make slaves anything other than slaves; they remained property, and as property, they were under the absolute control of their owners.

Roman Religious Beliefs

Official Roman belief was based as much on pragmatism as it was on the adopted Greek family of deities. Jupiter, Minerva, and their supporting cast served as the principle gods of Rome and its emperors. Official religion, however, was proving to be increasingly sterile, unable to satisfy the emotional and/or intellectual wants of the population. The nagging questions refused to go away: Did man have any control over destiny and fate? Was all predetermined and outside human choice and action?

Shortly before the appearance of Christianity, a shift occurred in Roman religion. Roman belief in *Fortune* or chance, with its unpredictability, created tremendous anxiety among many Romans. Many could not bear the thought that life was out of control and beyond understanding. If, however, the god of Fortune were joined with that of *Fate*, then events in one's life might be understood. Many Romans believed that this duality of Fortune and Fate was the common thread that made up each person's life. The unpredictable joined with Fate offered some explanation for success or failure. The Roman could better cope with life when the unexplainable and perplexing could be fathomed.

This pseudo religious system posited a belief in a supreme deity whose essence was everywhere in the Universe. Those who accepted the direction of Fate and Fortune hoped that this divine presence was no longer capricious but purposeful. For the most part, however, this belief system resulted in feelings of lost direction, that life was an aimless wandering.

Astrology

For the vast majority of the Empire, life had to be more than directed by fate, fortune, and the chance happening. For Roman society one such area that would explain and offer direction was astrology. From the best educated to the lowest slave, there was a belief that the sun and planets directed events. The forces of planets and stars directed good or bad luck, sickness or health, and success or failure. Ancient society had rejected the idea of a heliocentric in favor of geocentric. Man, therefore, was in the center of the target. It was a natural extension of that belief to assume that humanity was an important and integral participant in the energy of the universe. The problem was in devising a system that allowed one to understand that place and to discover the laws that directed the heavenly forces.

Decisions to be made and events that occurred, both natural and manmade, were believed to be connected by divine cosmic forces. In a world dominated by unseen forces, it would be astrology, instead of rational science, that be-

came all important. Consider the monumental impact of such a belief system on the emperor's decisions. The significant hold of astrology within the Empire resulted in the distortion of reason.

As the cosmos has always fascinated us, it was no different with the Romans. They were drawn by the mystery presented by the movement of planets and stars, coming to believe that the components of the universe were linked by a universal power. Thus, cosmic "laws" must be directly linked to human behavior.

Rome's most intelligent emperors believed in astrology. Coins proudly displayed the signs of the Zodiac, and astrologers became the intimate advisors of emperors. Dedications of temples, policies of state, and legal decisions might all be determined by first consulting a favorite astrologer. Fate, Chance, Fortune, and Astrology had one thing shared in common, a belief system that was totally mechanistic.

Of equal significance to Astrology was Magic. While not controlling the planets, it was thought to have some effect over lesser invisible forces. Of course, there were skeptics, but the evidence reveals an ongoing belief in any and all systems that promised to control the unseen forces that toyed with life.

Octavian and his successors developed policies that officially sponsored revived state religions. The cults announcing the divinity of the Caesars or the official worship of the sky god Jupiter and his family were to channel Roman patriotic sentiments in support of the State.

Pagan mystery religion was inclusive and religiously tolerant, and one could be a member of as many cults as desired. Some appealed more to women (Isis being the most attractive) and others to men (Myrtha being the most popular among the army).

Christianity

The passion cults originating in Asia Minor and Egypt had a wide appeal throughout the Empire. The most significant and the one that had the possibility of becoming a universal faith was that of Isis, a Savior cult originating in Egypt. By the birth of Christ the Egyptian nature cult to the goddess Isis had evolved into a sophisticated system of belief. Isis was a benevolent deity who, with her male consort Sarapis, promised their devotees rewards in this and the next world. The cult had a priesthood who oversaw and participated in her ceremonials. By the reign of Augustus the cult had come to Rome. Her consort, Osiris, was the god of the underworld, whose rebirth represented the coming of spring. The ceremonies associated with Isis were joyous events, full of drama and spectacle. There were no distinctions of class or sex in this cult, appealing both to men and women.

The religion that defeated Isis and eventually all the others originated in Palestine and is rooted in Judaism. This new faith, Christianity,—as Judaism—was strictly monotheistic. Christianity, a belief system established within the boundaries of the Empire, used the Empire's magnificent roads as avenues for its disciples to preach the gospels and claim the protection of Roman law. Judaism, long before the last century B.C., had fully evolved as a faith. Moses had received the Laws (Torah) from God on Mt. Sinai. By accepting the Laws, the Jews became a covenanting people; they had become God's chosen people to serve as an example through history of what God expected from his believers.

Joshua ben Joseph or Jesus was probably born between 6 and 3 B.C. and was a contemporary of Octavian Augustus Caesar. Our knowledge of his life comes solely from the four Gospels of Mark, Mathew, Luke, and John. The first Gospel was compiled a generation after the crucifixion and the last at the beginning of the second century. Interestingly, none of the Gospel writers had personally known Jesus, but their accounts have a remarkable consistency. The main purpose of the Gospels is to deify and prove Jesus' divinity. The Gospels, therefore, are unlike the Torah that traces God's actions over time.

In 6 A.D., Palestine was annexed by Rome as the province of Judaea. Around 28 or 29 A.D., a man named John the Baptist made his appearance. John preached, as did the Hebrew prophets of old, that the Kingdom of God was at hand. Repentance, a cleansing of the heart, must precede the anticipated Kingdom. At the river Jordan, he performed ritual baptisms that were more than symbolic but represented a permanent and spiritual change in the recipients.

Jesus was one of those who were baptized by John. It would be after his baptism that Jesus began his mission. There was, however, in Jesus' mission a fundamental difference from that of John and the other prophets of Judaism. Where the Biblical prophets anticipated the coming of God's kingdom, Jesus proclaimed that it was already underway. It would be through his ministry, directed by God, that the Kingdom would unfold. This was the core of Jesus' entire ministry, and it is there in all his parables and ethical teachings.

Jesus acknowledged that God's Kingdom on earth was still in the process of occurring but, as other Jewish thinkers, he believed that it was imminent.

Jesus' teaching brought him into conflict with the Pharisees. This group was especially opposed to Jesus' claim that he could forgive sins and that his relationship with God was unique. His followers applauded him as the "anointed one" (*Christos* in Greek). This person, it was

A fanciful depiction of Nero persecuting the early Christians for supposedly starting the great fire of A. D. 64.

believed, would come to the rescue of Israel and would be aided by a heavenly power. For Judaism, this "anointed one," this Messiah, would not be a divine being as that would compromise the absolute monotheism of the Jewish faith. Thus, if Jesus and his followers claimed that he was divine that would be considered idolatry.

In 30 or 33 A.D., Jesus proceeded to Jerusalem, the heart of Judaism, the place of Solomon's Temple. Upon his arrival, he challenged the Sadducees, the most powerful group within the Temple. He claimed that he fulfilled the predictions of the Torah. Jesus, like the prophet Isiah, would be the Suffering Servant.

As a consequence of these actions, he was arrested and accused of claiming to be the Messiah and a threat to the Temple. He was handed over to the Roman governor, Pontius Pilate, who, after some hesitancy, convicted Jesus of sedition and claims of being the king of the Jews. Pilate gave the order for Jesus' execution. Thus began one of history's greatest and most enduring revolutions. What Jesus had failed to accomplish during his life was achieved in his death, as his followers believed that he was resurrected.

The Jewish Revolt (66-73 A.D.) had a tremendous affect upon Judaism and Christianity. The gentile Christians were able to separate themselves from the Jews and the Jewish Christians. The revolt had some initial success because of Rome's preoccupation with civil war following the death of Nero. Once that war ended, along with a peace treaty with Parthia, the Jewish insurgents had no chance. In 70 A.D. Rome turned its full attention and fury upon the rebels and Titus destroyed Jerusalem and Solomon's Temple. This marks the beginning of the Diaspora for the Jewish people, who would have to wait almost two thousand years before their State was again established.

Christians and the Empire

Christians, though small in number and preaching a simple doctrine of love and forgiveness, were not very popular. Initially the Empire viewed the Christians as just another sect. The inclusiveness of paganism would accommodate another sect. The Christians, however, with their roots in Judaism, were strictly monotheistic. In denying the existence of the pagan gods, Christians would be accused of atheism. In refusing to sacrifice to Caesar, they were viewed as treasonous; and, in taking their sacrament of the body and blood, they were considered guilty of cannibalism. From a pagan standpoint, these accusations were appropriate. The Christians preached withdrawal from the world and the imminent return of Christ. Their beliefs were, in so far as pagan Rome was concerned, subversive.

Before the end of the first century, by the reign of Nero the unpopularity of the Christians

resulted in their becoming scapegoats, blamed for the great fire in Rome. Later, the emperor Trajan wanted proof of Christian sedition. Executions were ordered for Christians discovered practicing their faith. Dislike of Christians led to sporadic persecution, particularly in the reigns of Marcus Aurelius, Septimus Severus, and Diocletian.

The zealousness of Christians was not hampered by Roman persecution. The martyrdom of so many acted as a stimulus to attract others to the faith. In the second century, Christian apologists were producing literature aimed at their pagan detractors. Some of this literature supported the State because its strength postponed the end of earthly life. Arguments were made pointing out how many Christians were soldiers and in government bureaucracy. The purpose of this Christian literature was to make the faith intellectually respectable. Greek philosophy, especially Plato, that questioned man's role in the world served as models in the development of Christian theology. Thus, Christianity, its rituals and theology, could appeal to the well-educated pagan as well as the simple peasant.

Constantine the Great

In the fourth century, the emperors Licinius and Constantine issued the *Edicts of Milan*. These edicts granted the Christians religious toleration and return of Church property. It did not make Christianity the sole religion of the Empire. That would occur at the end of the fourth century during the reign of Theodosius the Great. Theodosius received the title "Great" as a result of his making Christianity the official religion of the Roman Empire.

When Diocletian abdicated in 305, he left a political situation that led to yet another civil war. Eventually the contest would focus on Constantine and his ally, Licinius, against Maxentius. At the Battle of Milvian Bridge in 313 on the Tiber River, Maxentius was drowned and his army routed. According to the accounts of Constantine's biographer, Eusebius, Constantine saw in the sky the letters *chi* and *rho*, the first two letters in Greek of Christos. Another account relates that the Emperor saw written by God's hand in the sky the words *in hoc signo_vicenes* (in this sign conquer). These letters, *chi rho* were then emblazoned on the shields of his legionnaires. Constantine attributed his victory to the intervention of the Christian God. The Christian God had answered his request for help with victory.

When Constantine met with his co-emperor,, Licinius and jointly issued the Edicts of Milan probably no more than one-sixth of the Empire was Christian. That number—one-sixth—is attributed to the eastern half of the Empire. Christianity originated in an urban setting and was popular among the urban lower classes. In the west, Christians numbered much fewer because of its rural nature. There were too few large urban centers in the West, and those in existence were distant from one another.

Imperial coinage, until 324, displayed the monogram of Sol Invictus (the Invincible Sun). Constantine, as emperor, also had the title of Pontifex Maximus. As such, he was head of the state's pagan cults. While granting toleration to Christians, he did not make the faith Rome's official religion.

Whether Constantine was a Christian or not has been a topic of considerable debate. This Christian God was a God of power and that was something the Emperor could appreciate. Christians were also well organized and had a successful system of communicating; all that would be of benefit to the Empire.

Without Constantine or some other emperor to champion the cause of this religion, it is doubtful that it would become a powerful force. Constantine, an extremely capable ruler, appears to have been convinced that Christianity would be the faith that could unify the Empire into a single "Catholic" (universal) entity. The Christianization of the Empire was bold, pragmatic, and sincerely religious. Constantine was both a pragmatist who saw in Christianity a potential source for unity. Constantine was also a sincerely religious man who was attracted to Jesus as a personal savior, something not found in paganism.

COUNCIL OF NICAEA 325 A.D.

The matter of correct or orthodox belief and practice was a serious challenge to Christianity. After the death of Jesus, his disciples and followers anticipated his return at any moment. As a result there was no need to develop a formal theology. As the centuries passed and the "second coming" did not take place, it became necessary for the Church to develop a theology (*theos*: God, *Logia*: Knowledge). The issues became even more pressing when differences of opinion on fundamental beliefs created dissension and potential schism within the church. After the Edicts of Milan, the church was able to practice openly, and it was at that time that a great controversy erupted in the church. This conflict was centered on the nature of the Trinity. The faction led by the priest Arius believed that Christ was "created" by God the Father at a specific time. As a result, Christ was not equal to God the Father and thus more human than divine. This doctrine compromises Christ's divinity, calling into question the validity of the crucifixion and salvation. Alexander, and later Athanasius, bishop of Alexandria, opposed Arius.

In response to the inflammatory situation, Constantine called the first ecumenical council that met at Nicaea in Asia Minor in 325. The Emperor presided over the meetings, adding his voice to the proceedings. This council rejected the views of Arius (his belief was called Arianism) and proposed the Nicene Creed, the statement of faith of all Christians to this day.

Christianity, favored by the State, patronized by the Emperor, grew in prestige. Imperial sanctions led to increased conversions among the upper classes, and Christianity was on its way to becoming the dominant faith of Western Europe. The Roman Empire and Christianity were "born" at the same moment. Over the centuries, where one went, so did the other. Eventually Christianity's partner, the Empire in the West, would pass from the scene. The Church remained and by default filled the vacuum once filled by the Empire.

There were believers in various cults into the fourth and fifth centuries that all succumbed to Christianity. Here was a universal faith based on love and, of absolute critical importance, claimed an historic living man as its founder. Christianity's promise is not unlike paganism, with both ceremonies of baptism and communion. The promise of universal salvation irrespective of place or birth was irresistible. Jesus had walked among people, had died, and conquered death. Now his believers awaited his second coming. Christianity, based on Judaism, unlike paganism, was strictly monotheistic. Like Judaism, it had a strict moral code and argued that in Jesus there was the fulfillment of the Hebrew Bible, the Torah, with its promise of a messiah. Christianity was a faith that appealed to both intellect and emotion. Its great church fathers, especially Augustine, did much to incorporate it into a developing theology, the philosophy of Plato. Augustine's *City of God* is a brilliant and critical application of Plato's ideas of the real existing in the idea, existing on an invisible plane. To Christianity this became the Heavenly City.

As emotionally charged as paganism was, there yet existed a separation between religion and reason. With Christianity that separation was replaced with reason in support of faith, reason applied to theology and Biblical *exegesis* (explanation). As a result, brilliant men devoted themselves almost exclusively to working out the difficult issues of theology. Intellectual methods emphasized deductive reasoning. (Beginning with a statement of accepted truth, such as God exists, then all investigation of evidence supports that initial truth. Or, the earth is the center of the Universe! All observed evidence must support that statement of truth. Consider Galileo's imprisonment for arguing that the sun, not the earth, was the center of our solar system. Inductive reasoning does not begin with a statement but with a question: Is the earth the center of the universe?) Western Civilization would have to wait until the Renaissance to witness the eclipsing of deductive in favor of inductive reasoning (the scientific method).

Philosophy

Philosophy, unlike its contemporary mystery cults, offered none of the ultimate rewards of a blissful afterlife. Instead, it was a discipline whose objective was to make the most of life. Philosophic schools, especially Stoicism—a system founded by the Greek Zeno (c. 333-262B.C.) of Citium—furnished rules for living well. These rules were universal, not relative to a particular moment or place. This system was readily adapted to the Roman Empire, a world state tied by universal laws. To the Romans, the Stoics taught the value of moral standards and self-control, as well as the commitment and dis-

Etruscan Aqueduct

cipline to live by those standards. To the adherents of stoicism, man assumes the responsibility to make proper decisions. The gods, therefore, play no role for the stoics as only man possesses that special quality that serves to join all men in a universal brotherhood.

Architecture and Engineering

The average Roman lived in an apartment building or tenement. On the street floor of the tenement or apartment building would be small businesses, such as a bakery, a wine shop, and a religious store. At night the sound of cart traffic made rest difficult, and during the day the crush of people was oppressive. Rents, then as now, depended on location as well as supply and demand. The streets were not safe after dark, and the wealthy only traveled at night with a bodyguard.

These apartment buildings were multi-storied, possible five or six stories high. This followed the formula of one story per ten feet. From the reign of Octavian Augustus, no tenement was built higher than sixty feet. Above the arcades of small shops, a balcony would look out onto the street. To reach the upper floors, there was an external staircase. The Rome of two thousand years ago, with its multi-storied apartments, lacked those conveniences that we take for granted. There were no bathrooms so basic sanitation and bathing were available only at communal centers. These centers were colossal, for an example the basilica of Trajan was almost 300 feet long and 100 feet wide. The great Colosseum, built in the first century A.D., was 620 feet by 500 feet and the arena approximately 300 feet by 200 feet. The arena could accommodate fifty thousand spectators and had a retractable dome.

The baths built by the Romans were large communal centers.

The most common building feature that is identified with Rome is the use of the arch. What magnificent structures, from amphitheaters to aqueducts, drainage tunnels to bridges, bear the unmistakable stamp of the arch. An indispensable part of the construction was Rome's unique and remarkable mortar that had tremendous strength, durability, and uniformity. The mortar was a mixture of a unique volcanic earth called *pozzolana* and waste stone. These elements combined to create a wonderful concrete. Arched bridges were also aqueducts that carried hundreds of thousands of gallons of water through all manner of terrain to urban centers. An aqueduct is an inclined plane that utilizes gravity and a series of conduits to regulate the flow of water.

Latin

Latin was a unique vehicle for communication because it is a language that can express sophisticated ideas as well as the most basic passions and emotions.

Romans expressed themselves in the most personal and intimate of ways. Their literature usually described the actions of individuals and small groups. Latin expressed lofty sentiments of Cicero and Marcus Aurelius, as well as the curses and graffiti on latrine walls.

The educational system of the Republic and empire encouraged and stimulated this personal quality in Roman literature. Education placed special emphasis on rhetoric and the art of public speaking and debate. This type of education stimulated both the art of oratory and writing. Because higher education was confined to the upper classes, the literature produced reflects the interests of that class. The result is that on the one hand, we become familiar with the activities, interests, and philosophy of the upper classes while on the other hand, we are limited in our knowledge of the rest of society.

The greatest contributor to Latin prose was the humanist, lawyer, and follower of Stoicism, Cicero. One of histories most brilliant orators, he used Latin to express subtlety or directness, as the situation demanded.

Virgil continued Cicero's brilliant literary tradition. His themes were broader in scope, asking questions about human suffering and the challenges of life. Of his works the *Aenead* is best known. It is the story of the founding of Rome by Aeneas, a survivor of the Trojan Wars. As Odysseus in Homer's tale, Aeneas wanders the seas after escaping Troy. His adventures take him to the shores of North Africa where, at Carthage, he meets Queen Dido. The queen falls in love with the hero, pleading with him to stay with her. Though Aeneas cares for Dido, he is bound to a higher calling and purpose and must continue his journey. And yet, Aeneas is not a super-human demi-god. He feels sorrow at loss, recognizing that his destiny must bring pain to others. The ultimate message of the Aenead is that irrespective of the obstacles, whether civil war or the duties of office, the great-

The underground chambers of the Colosseum, once covered by the arena floor, are visible in this photo. Slaves and animals were led through underground tunnels and out onto the main area.

est achievement is self-knowledge, sensitivity to the complexity of being, and the will to overcome.

The Last Twenty-one Years

The fifth century A.D. witnessed the final convulsions of the Western portion of the Roman Empire. From the 450's through the 470's Rome was ruled by nine emperors, six of whom where assassinated. The capital was now located at Ravenna on the coast of the Adriatic Sea. The military high command was directed by the German Ricimer. Important as he was, he did not attempt to become emperor. Ricimer, as the power behind the throne, made and unmade emperors over the next fifteen years. These actions led to further political instability. After Ricimer's death (c.472) the German Odoacer became the prominent figure. Odoacer commanded an army of German mercenaries who represented various tribes. This army, originally stationed on the Danubian frontier, had followed their commander to Italy. When they were frustrated in their demands to be recognized as Feodorati (federated troops), they mutinied and, in 476 A.D. proclaimed Odoacer as their king. The emperor Romulus Augustulus was deposed and sent into retirement and the Imperial insignia was sent to Zeno (471-491) the eastern Roman emperor at Constantinople. Odoacer settled his army in Italy, and the Western Empire was now in the hands of barbarians.

Does 476 deserve special acknowledgment as a landmark moment in history or is it just another point on a continuum? Historians are divided on this issue. There is no denying, however, that the last emperor in the West abdicated and the territory controlled by Ravenna, a territory that included Rome, was now just another Germanic kingdom. As Michael Grant states:

"The Western Roman Empire had fallen; or it had become something else. At any rate it was no more."

No new emperor was proclaimed, and Julius Nepos, the remaining claimant to the West, died in Dalmatia in 480.

CONCLUSION

Rome neither appeared in a day nor did it collapse in a day. The process of decay occurred over many centuries. Similar to the death of a great dinosaur, time passed before the diseased body finally succumbed and collapsed.

The Roman poet Rutilius Namatianius c.420 wrote:

No man will ever be safe if he forgets you;
May I praise you still when the sun is dark.
To count up the glories of Rome is like counting
The stars in the sky.

The legacy of Rome did not smolder and decay but remained a living force to affect the future. The heritage of Rome, the majesty that it represented, was to play an integral role in the future of Western civilization. What Rome symbolized was adopted, considered, and modified by the future to meet the exigencies of time and place. Rome is all around us as we study law, view majestic structures, and consider individual choices. Rome is a reminder of the dulling effects of cruelty, as well as striving to achieve the highest goals. When we investigate the following historic period, the Medieval Era, we will be able to note the ongoing presence of Rome—*caput mundi* (Capital of the World).

Suggestions for Further Reading

A.E.R.Boak, *History of Rome to 565 A.D.* (1969)

John Boardman, Jaspar Griffin, and Oswyn Murray, *The Oxford History of The Roman World* (1991)

Julius Caesar, *The Gallic Wars*, (1951)

J.Ferguson, *The Religions of the Roman Empire* (1970)

Robin Lane Fox, *Pagans and Christians* (1987)

W.H.C.Friend, *The Rise of Christianity* (1984)

Edward Gibbon, *The Decline and Fall of the Roman Empire* (1909-1914)

Michael Grant, *The World of Rome*, (1987)

R.M.Grant, *Historical Introduction to the New Testament* (1972)

M.I.Rostovtzeff, *Social and Economic History of the Roman Empire* (1957)

C. Suetonius Tranquillus, *Lives of the Twelve Caesars* (1957)

Chapter 5

THE POST-ROMAN EAST: BYZANTIUM, ISLAM & EASTERN EUROPE

CONSTANTINOPLE

In this chapter we will investigate two remarkable historic developments. First will be an examination of the Eastern Roman Empire, some of its more remarkable emperors and the challenges they faced, their contributions, and the magnificent capital of Constantinople. The second section of the chapter examines the role of the dynamic faith of Islam in the history of medieval Europe, from its beginnings in the desert cities of Arabia to its becoming a major power.

THE SECOND ROME: CONSTANTINOPLE

The Emperor Constantine the Great founded the city named after him in the early fourth century. Constantinople was, of course, more than a city. It became the center, the capital, of the eastern half of the Roman Empire. Located on the shores of the Bosphorus, and at the entrance to the Straits of the Dardanelles, Constantinople became one of the most famous cities in Western history. The moving of the capital indicates that the emperor recognized that the economic and intellectual center of the empire was in the East and not in the West. The wealth of the Orient came to its bazaars and churches. Constantinople was a hub of commerce, as products from the East, India, China, and Persia arrived at its wharfs and commerce houses. The languages of the East and West could be heard on its streets. Its wealth and prestige was a magnet to all who hoped to profit, the conqueror as well as the entrepreneur. Until its capture by

Constantinople's access to the Black Sea and the Mediterranean Sea made it the heart of trade in both Europe and Asia. Merchant ships conducted business and the vibrant economy supported the empire's great expenses.

the Ottoman Turks in 1453, it was a great center of commerce, religion, and learning. It was a city whose history is filled with brilliance, splendor, as well as violence and tragedy.

Fulk of Chartres, a visitor to Constantinople in the eleventh century, wrote his impressions of the City on the Bosphorus, extending between the Golden Horn and the Sea of Marmora:

> O what a splendid city, how stately, how fair, how many monasteries therein, how many palaces raised by sheer labor in the broadways and streets, how many works of art, marvelous to behold; it would be wearisome to tell of the abundance of all good things; of gold and of silver, garments of manifold fashion, and such sacred relics. Ships are at all times putting in at this port, so that there is nothing that men want that is not brought hither.

The *Russian Primary Chronicle* records Russia's conversion to Christianity:

> And Vladimir said to them: 'Go first to the Bulgars and learn about their faith.' They went and arriving among the Bulgars, they saw how evilly things were done there and how they worshipped in the morgue, and they returned to their own land. And Vladimir said: 'Go now to the Germans and see how it is with them also. And from there go to the Greeks.' They went to the Germans and looked at their church service, and then they went to Constantinople and went to the emperor. The emperor asked them why they had come, and they told him all that had happened. When the emperor heard this, he was glad, and sent word to the Patriarch, saying: 'The Russians have come in order to learn about our faith. Prepare the

church and the clergy, and you yourself put on your priestly robes, so that they may see the glory of our God.'

Between the foundation of Constantinople in 330 and the First Crusade in 1095, the history of Byzantium can be divided into four periods. The first begins in 330 and ends in 717 with the accession of Leo III. This initial period witnessed many challenges. The first was the invasions of Germanic tribes, followed by the ongoing struggle with the Persians, the exhausting religious controversies between the Orthodox Church and the heretical sects of Arians and Monophysites, and ultimately the coming of the Muslims and their Islamic faith.

The second extends from 717 to 867 and was a time when the emperors were preoccupied with the threat of Islam. The empire lost its Eastern provinces of Egypt and Palestine to the Muslims but was able to repulse their attacks at the walls of Constantinople. During this period the Bulgars converted to Eastern Christianity, and the empire was torn by the Iconoclastic controversy.

From 867 to 1025 the Byzantine Empire achieved its greatest power. Going on the offensive, it recovered many of its lost eastern territories from the Muslims. Economically Constantinople was the heart of trade between East and West. The Byzantine gold coin, the *nomisma* or *bezant,* served as the standard coin throughout the trading world.

From 1025 to 1095 a series of critical events took place that were too much for the empire to handle, thus marking a turning point in the history of the Byzantine Empire. There were arguments with the papacy that led in 1054 to the great schism of the West from the East. The pope in Rome and the patriarch in Constantinople excommunicated one another, and it remained "on the books" until the 1960s.

Constantinople was strongly walled and surrounded by water, which turned back many invaders.

The Greek areas of Sicily and southern Italy were taken over by Normans who looked greedily at further conquests of eastern territory. A further crisis arose with the invasion of the Turkic Pechenegs and the appearance of newly converted Muslims, the zealous Seljuk Turks. The Seljuks defeated a Byzantine army at the battle of Manzikert in 1071, thus opening all of Asia Minor to their advance.

The second half of the eleventh century witnessed the near collapse of the Eastern Roman Empire. A major strength of the empire had been its centralization of authority and power. During this period, that system began to unravel. As with the Western Empire centuries earlier, great landowners exerted increasing authority over their territories, resulting in a weakening of ties to the center. This greater autonomy, gained by local magnates at the cost of weakening central authority, was a problem that was never overcome.

By the fifth century the situation in the West had become chaotic. As the Germanic confederations were busy quarreling and fighting to gain control of territory, the city on the Bosphorus, Constantinople, flourished with economic, religious, and cultural vitality. When schools had disappeared in the West, Constantinople boasted a university. Where the Church of Rome, with its bishop, came to be the center of Western Christianity, to the East, the emperor considered himself to be head of State and Church, a concept known as *Caesaropapism.*

Constantinople's strategic location acted as a first line of defense against the many waves of

Asiatic hordes. The road to reach the West passed through Constantine's city. From its founding in 330 to its capture by the Sultan Mehmet II in 1453, it had resisted all conquerors. There was only one notable exception and that was the sack of the City by Latin crusaders of the Fourth Crusade in 1204. Between 1204 and 1261 Westerners and the Latin Church ruled Constantinople. But in 1261 the Paleologi dynasty was established and ruled until 1453 when the Ottoman Turks conquered the city.

Constantinople was the seat of one of the five patriarchies of Christianity. (Rome, Alexandria, Jerusalem, and Antioch were the other four.) Christianity is an evangelical (spreader of "good tidings") faith. Missionaries set out from the capital and spread the faith into the Slavic lands. The Russians would be converted in the tenth century to the Eastern form of Christianity. As Rome sent its missionaries into Germany, England, and Gaul, Constantinople sent theirs into Slavic lands. The division that took place between the Latin Church and that of Constantinople by the eleventh century was not confined to the Mediterranean but spread northward dividing West from East as far as the Baltic Sea. What evolved was a split between Western Europe, religiously committed to Rome, and Eastern Europe, religiously committed to Constantinople. The entire history of future strained relations between Western Europe and the Russians is in no small part rooted in this earlier (religious and political) controversy.

Justinian

In more than five hundred years from the reign of Justinian (527-565) until the First Crusade in 1095, the two halves of the Western world traveled different paths. Justinian was the apogee (the high point) of early Byzantine history and in many ways characteristic of the history of the Roman Empire in the East. Justinian's reign was crucial in transforming the Eastern Roman Empire into the Byzantine Empire. Born in 482, he became emperor in 527. The achievements of Justinian and Byzantium had a tremendous impact upon the West. Contributions included art, architecture, law, statecraft, theology, refinements in lifestyle, and the preservation of Greek thought that would be reintroduced to the West in the fifteenth century where it contributed to the Renaissance. One of Justinian's greatest contributions was the reform of the confused legal system.

Justinian was not an aristocrat. He was born to peasant parents near Sardica, deep in the Balkan Peninsula, several hundred miles northwest of Constantinople.

Prior to his elevation he was the power and brains behind the throne of his uncle, the Emperor Justin. Both men, Macedonian peasants by birth, were able to use their positions in the army to rise to the ultimate position of Emperor. Justinian's career was multifaceted as he was the last emperor to campaign against the Germans in an attempt to reconquer the West. Justinian also rebuilt much of Constantinople after the great fire and riots that threatened to dethrone him.

Augusta Theodora

Justinian was a capable, well-educated ruler, but he would have been less of an historic figure if not for his amazing wife, the Empress Augusta Theodora.

The empress was one of those remarkable women in history. A statesperson, she could be manipulative and generous, caring as well as greedy and callous. What we know of Theodora is found in one of history's most venomous personal attacks. Procopius, the secretary of the Justinian's chief military commander, Belisaurius, (instrumental in the reconquest of the West), described Theodora in his *Secret History* or *Anekdota*. Procopius leaves nothing to the reader's imagination in his pornographic accounts of Theodora's sexual behavior. If ever there was a case for defamation of character, the gossip mongering found in this book offers a perfect example. As outraged as he was, Procopius had to admit that Theodora was physically attractive: "Theodora was of handsome countenance and in all other ways attractive, but short, and while of not altogether pale complexion, at least somewhat sallow, and her glance was always keen and sharp."

Theodora's life has already been told in the introduction to the chapter. There was nothing frivolous about her and upon her rise to empress she devoted herself to matters of importance. Though Justinian did not share some of her ideas, especially in her support of the heretical Monophysites (*mono*: one, *thelma*; nature—Christ had a single divine nature, not both human and divine). Her influence resulted in a degree of religious moderation, not persecution.

Justinian, however, never doubted and never wavered from his love and respect for Theodora. A man of vision and grand plans, Justinian could also vacillate and lose confidence. Theodora had the strength and will power to keep Justinian focused on major objectives. Though their faults may have been many, they were a unique Emperor and Empress.

Constantinople's politics in the sixth century, as throughout Byzantine history, was a scene of intrigue, unscrupulousness, double-dealing, and conspiracy. Procopius was accused of profiteering and judicial murder to gain the wealth of the "criminal." The author of the Secret History found little to admire in the emperor, who is described as venal and unscrupulous.

JUSTINIAN AND THE RECONQUEST OF THE WEST

The emperors in the East had never accepted the fact that the West had fallen to Germanic confederations. Viewing themselves as God's vice-regents, they considered the empire to be a gift from God. It was their responsibility to maintain its unity and integrity. By the sixth century, the Eastern Roman Empire became stronger, and Justinian chose to use that strength in a bid to re-conquer the West.

Justinian wanted political and religious unity in the empire. He viewed his military actions as a crusade against Germans who were either pagans or Arian Christian heretics. (Arianism denied the Trinity and considered Jesus to be more human than divine.)

Religious "Orthodoxy" proved a constant source of disharmony throughout the history of Byzantium. In the West, the papacy became sole arbiter of religious correctness. But in the East, the emperor played an important part because his authority was both political and semi-priestly. The emperor could perform religious services that in the West could only be done by priests. He could take the pulpit in church and preach a sermon. Dictating theology and dogma, however, could only be done at an ecumenical council. The emperor's authority was, therefore, not quite total.

Since Justinian and his successors viewed themselves as God's vice-regents, as well as the embodiment of Roman law, the autocratic emperor was above any constitutional restrictions that questioned his policies. As autocrat, the emperor initiated policy and directed his vast and complex bureaucracy. He appointed and dismissed government officials; he was the last court of appeals. This did not place the emperor above the law. His actions were limited by tradition and the coronation oath. If he was found guilty of a heinous sin, the patriarch of Constantinople had the authority to excommunicate him.

Turning his attention to the West, Justinian in a lengthy series of campaigns attempted to reunify the Roman Empire. He was assisted in this monumental undertaking by two generals, Belisaurius and Narses. Their campaigns were successful in defeating the Vandals in North Africa, the Visigoths in Southern Spain, and, after two decades of bloody warfare, the Ostrogoths in Italy.

Justinian has been harshly criticized for turning his attention westward at the expense of the more immediate threats in the East. A Turkic people, the Avars, were raiding across the Danube, and a revived Persian Empire posed a grave danger to the Byzantine provinces in Syria, Egypt, and Asia Minor. This rivalry had gone on for centuries and was both political as well as economic. The Persian Empire was strategically located astride the major trade routes from the East to Byzantium. The wealth in silk from China, and precious stones and spices from the East were all severely diminished because of the

Belisarius brings a captured Vandal to Emperor Justinian. The defeat of the Vandals brought North Africa, which had been overrun by the German Vandals a century before, once more under Byzantine rule.

rivalry between these two powers. In 540, Persia captured and sacked Antioch in Asia Minor, one of the Byzantine Empire's greatest cities. Asia Minor was of immeasurable importance to the Empire as the major trade routes coming from the East crossed that territory.

Law: Corpus Juris Civilis

By the reign of Justinian the legal system had become a confused and murky swamp. The emperor recognized that the laws had to be re-organized and contradictions corrected. To achieve this end, he appointed the legist Trebonian to establish a commission to codify the many laws and codes of the empire. Unfortunately by the sixth century, the law had become chaotic, a jungle of contradictions of interpretation and application. Justinian decided to address the problem. The commission produced the *Corpus Juris Civilis* (Body of Civil Law) that remains a significant legacy of Rome to Western civilization.

Since the re-conquest of the West proved unsuccessful, it cannot be used as a mark of Justinian's greatness. Although military adventurism failed, the codification of law was the singular achievement that affected the future of Western civilization. From its inception the Roman Empire had always been a selective borrower, and the formulation of Roman law was markedly influenced by Greek philosophy and culture.

By the sixth century the emperor and his office were considered the source of law. The *Corpus* was comprised of four separate books. The *Codex* was a collection of all imperial edicts from the reign of Hadrian, including those of Justinian to that point.

The *Edicts* were reconciled, and contradictory ones were eliminated. The *Digest* was a collection of opinions of famous jurists, establishing legal precedents. The *Institutes* was a synopsis of the laws that served as a handbook for law students. The *Novels* (Novellae) included the edicts of Justinian issued since the publication of the *Codex*. Interestingly the *Novels* were written in Greek, rather than Latin, and mark an acknowledgment that there was a new focus and center for the empire—the East and Byzantium.

These books were very important for the development of later Byzantine codes. Following the conversion of the Slavs in the tenth century, their law was directly influenced by Justinian's codes. For the rest of Western Europe from the eleventh century on, Justinian's Code was of great importance as the foundation of their legal codes. (outside of Britain, whose legal system was more directly influenced by Germanic customary law).

Byzantine Religion

Christianity affected all aspects of Byzantine life. Byzantine Christianity was significantly more mystical than Western Christianity. Faith was the bonding agent for all of Byzantine society, and its influence is visible throughout the empire. Architecture, music, art, mosaics, law, and the emperor all display the influence of religion.

As an example, during the reign of Justinian, a raging conflict arose over Monophysitism. The Monophysites favored the belief that Christ had one divine nature. The dual nature of Christ (that he was equally human and divine) had been established in 451 at the Council of Chalcedon. The council's decision established the official position of Christianity into the present day. The Monophysites obviously disagreed and became a serious threat to imperial authority in Palestine, Egypt, and Syria. The Empress Theodora, sensitive to the political implications of alienating this group, as well as possibly favoring them,

This is a modern view of the Santa Sophia. It stands today having survived fifteen hundred years of earthquakes, wars, riots, and fires.

counseled moderation and compromise. Unfortunately, in matters of core religious belief there is often room only for a single truth. Monophysites, as all heresies, would be violently suppressed and persecuted. When Theodora died in 548, Justinian, no longer influenced by his wife, turned to persecution. Thus, in the following century, when the Muslims attacked the empire, the persecuted Christian "heresies" located on the borders of the empire offered little or no resistance to the invaders. Islam promised religious toleration to Jews, Zoroastrians, and Christians, drawing no distinctions between "orthodox" and "heretic."

Justinian's throne in Ravenna, Italy.

The Golden Mosaic of Justinian (top) in Ravenna, Italy and the Saintly Disciples (right).

Art and Architecture

Justinian's career embodies so many facets of the Eastern Empire that it is not surprising that art would be one of his concerns. His reign ushered in the First Golden Age of Byzantine art and architecture. The grandest example of artistic creativity was the construction of one of the world's greatest cathedrals. Hagia Sophia (Holy Wisdom or Christ) was designed and executed under the direction of Anthemius of Tralles, an engineer, mathematician, and architect, with another mathematician, Isidore of Miletus. Built in the basilica Romanesque style, it is modeled after the Greek cross, each arm being the same length and is one of the largest churches in the world.

Mosaic of Justinian and Theodora in Ravenna, Italy.

The interior of Hagia Sophia is ablaze with mosaics, pictures comprised of small pieces of stone or glass set into wet plaster at various angles. The light reflected from their surfaces creates an otherworldly glow to the surroundings. Byzantine churches were Romanesque in design. That style of architecture was represented in structures whose walls were massive to support the vault, thus the windows were small, allowing for a minimum of outside light entering the church.

Hagia Sophia is also a marvel as a successful example of the solutions to a very challenging problem of fitting a dome over a square base. The dome symbolizes the Dome of Heaven and is 180 feet above the floor. Windows, creating the illusion that the dome floats in the air, pierce the circumference of the dome. Procopius reported that when Justinian entered the church, he exclaimed, "Solomon, I have surpassed thee!"

This magnificent basilica, along with the *Corpus Juris Civilis* marks Justinian as one of history's great rulers.

The church of St. Vitale in Ravenna, Italy, is representative of this style affecting European building. St. Vitale has some of the most brilliant mosaics that have ever been created. The mosaics picture the Emperor Justinian and the Empress Theodora in brilliant scintillating golden colors. They stand as if from another dimension, looking out at you, tall, and elegant, surrounded by their court of attendants.

Justinian's Successors

With the death of the emperor in 565 the entire system of government that he had labored so tirelessly to construct disintegrated. Between 565 and 610 the empire was beset with problems of anarchy and plague. It became so difficult that

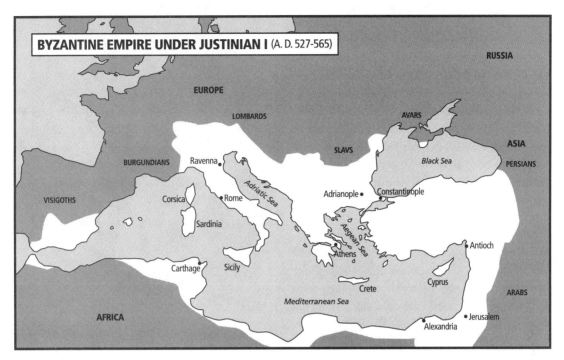

contemporaries thought that they were witnessing the end of the world. Justinian was succeeded by Justin II the Younger (565-578), Tiberius II (578-582), Maurice (582-602), and Phocas (602-610). Internal problems were intensified by the ongoing wars between the empire and the Avars, Slavs in the Balkans, the Lombards in Italy, and the Persians in Asia Minor.

Heraclius (610 – 641)

Heraclius, an Armenian by descent, proved to be a gifted and resourceful leader who came to the throne at a very critical moment in the history of the Eastern Roman Empire. He successfully responded to the military crises that threatened the empire and, at the same time, dealt with chaotic internal affairs inherited from the previous reign.

In 610, Emperor Heraclius came to the throne. Due to Justinian's military campaigns in the West, Heraclius inherited an empire on the verge of bankruptcy. His people were demoralized and the loyalty of the army questionable. The Persians, under their King Khusru II, decided to take full advantage of the Byzantine weakness and attack the empire. During the following ten years, the battles raged between the Persians and the Byzantines. The devastation was tremendous, as the wealthiest cities of the Byzantine Empire were pillaged and famous relics stolen.

Enjoying their victories, the Persians rejected any peace offerings of the emperor. To make matters worse for Heraclius, the Avars and Slavs took this opportunity to invade the Balkans and Greece. It would take a super-human effort if Constantinople were to survive.

The emperor exhibited great leadership and ability during this crisis. He mobilized a fresh army and launched a vicious counteroffensive against the Persians. The threat to Constantinople was extraordinary, as Heraclius fought the Persian navy on the Asiatic side while, at the same time, he defeated a combined army of Slavs and Avars on the European shore. Challenged by these enemies, the empire averted disaster and was able to counterattack.

Heraclius was able to awaken the spirit of his subjects, to turn them from despair to a new commitment to fight their enemies. The battle against the Persians became a holy crusade against the infidel and despoiler of Christian shrine.

In 626, the fighting was renewed when the Persians, allied with the Avars, launched a combined attack against Constantinople. Once again, Heraclius proved capable of dealing with the crisis. He so utterly defeated the Avars that their own empire began to disintegrate, and the subject Slavs rose in rebellion. As a result, the Avar presence south of the Danube was ended.

The defeat of the combined Avar-Persian attack was the turning point of the war. With Constantinople secure, Heraclius turned against Persia. In December 627, he won a great victory over the Persians. As a result, the Persian King Khusru was murdered by his own troops early in the next year. His successor had no taste for war and sued for peace. By the terms of the peace Heraclius reclaimed all the lost provinces, as well as the relic of the True Cross.

The year 629 was a joyful year for the emperor. The Persians had been so totally defeated and shattered that the four hundred year struggle between Byzantium and the Sassanids was finally over. The Persians no longer had the resources or will for aggression. Heraclius had re-established the boundaries of the empire of his predecessor, Justinian.

The emperor now turned his attention to rebuilding the provinces that had been devas-

Heraclius

tated by war. He realized that if the empire was to survive and flourish, Asia Minor must be made secure. To achieve this, he ordered that an interconnected defensive system made up of a line of forts be built in Asia Minor to be garrisoned by local militias and mercenaries.

In his reorganization of the empire it is evident that Heraclius recognized its growing Eastern character. With the decline in Latin and the increasing use of Greek, Byzantium was becoming increasingly Hellenized. Even with these changes, however, the Eastern Roman Empire remained multi-national, whose citizens considered themselves "Romanos" (Romans).

Leo III and Iconoclasm

Less than a century later, the internal stability of the empire was shocked by the decree of Emperor Leo III; in 726 he issued an order to destroy all holy images (icons) of the Virgin, the saints, and Christ. His son, Constantine V, carried his father's policy even further. The issue surrounding the venerations of icons almost tore the empire apart. The Judaic influence present in early Christianity considered any pictures of statues that represented the deity as idolatry (the Second Commandment). In Judaism, the unique oneness of God cannot be physically represented. This theological position had a significant influence on early Christian beliefs and practices. By the fifth century, however, images (icons) of Christ, the Virgin Mary, and the saints were of growing significance in Christian worship. The Christian belief that, in Jesus, the word had become flesh, justified the artistic rendering of images. In fact, the veneration of icons became so much a part of the fabric of Christian practice as to appear idolatrous. From a theological position, the concern was that the veneration of icons compromised worship that was due to God. This argument had been made in a council held in the seventh century. At that same council, it was conceded that the "correct" use of icons was acceptable.

In 726 Byzantine Emperor Leo III, the Isaurian, instituted a policy calling for the removal and destruction of icons from churches (iconoclasm). Leo's motivations may have been religious, as well as political, arguing that his position was in full compliance with Christian tradition. For a half century the storm raged within the empire. The Western provinces and the papacy favored the icons (iconodules) while the East wanted to continue the policy of iconoclasm. Each faction was zealous for its cause, leading to riots and persecution.

A half century later, in 788, the Empress Irene became regent. Irene was from a Western province and, therefore, favored icons. In 787 she convened the Seventh Ecumenical Council that restored the place of icons within Eastern Christianity. The council agreed that

Leo III (left) forbade the worship and display of icons. This imperial act enraged the monasteries, whose monks were fiemly attached to the practice of venerating icons.

icons served as a channel of grace to God and thus deserved their importance for the believer.

Unfortunately, the council's decision did not put the matter to rest. Emperor Leo V in 813 once again instituted a policy of iconoclasm. The passion displayed in the previous century, however, was not rekindled. The iconodules were better organized and with support of the empress, the patriarch formally proclaimed the restoration, once and for all, of the icon. Thus ended iconoclasm, considered by the Eastern Church as its last great heresy

Results of the Conflict

All parties to the iconoclastic struggle were left deeply scarred, angry, and resentful. The papacy never forgave Leo III, who removed Sicily, Southern Italy, and Illyricum from their jurisdiction and placed them under the authority of the patriarch of Constantinople. This was one reason that led the popes to look for a new protector, finding them across the Alps in Gaul (France), the Caroligians.

THE LAND OF THE RUS: KIEV

The appeal of Eastern Orthodoxy, with its pomp and mystery, can be seen in events that led to the conversion of the Slavs of Russia. In the tenth century, the Slavs of Russia accepted and were converted to Christianity. The Byzantine monks, Sts. Cyril and Methodius, were instrumental in achieving this objective. Cyril invented an alphabet for the Slavs that became the major instrument of Slavic culture. In 957, the Grand Princess Olga received baptism in Constantinople. Initial reaction among the Kievan nobility was hostile and fearful of an increase of Byzantine influence and Greek Christianity. It would not be until the tenth century that the Russian people were converted.

The *Primary Chronicle* records the story of Vladimir's embassy to the Muslims, Jewish Khazars, and Greeks of Constantinople. The prince was not sure of the faith he should embrace. His representatives reported to Vladimir:

> When we journeyed among the Muslims, we beheld how they worshipped in their temple, called a Mosque. . . . There is not happiness among them. . . . Their religion is not good. Then we went among the Germans, and saw. . . many ceremonies. . . but we beheld no glory there. Then we went to Greece. {Constantinople}. . . where they worship. . . and we knew not whether we were in heaven or on earth. For on earth there is no such splendor or such beauty.

Prince Vladimir of Kiev converted, along with his people, to Christianity. This conversion was also the result of an already established economic connection between the Russians and Constantinople. The impact for the future would be critically significant as Russia was drawn into the world of Byzantine-oriental culture, economy, and Christianity. Kiev's strategic location on the Dnieper River gave it importance as a trade depot between the Black Sea and the northern trade routes that extended to the Baltic Sea and, thus, to Western Europe.

Kievan Church

Almost from its inception, the Kievan Church was fairly autonomous and not under direct control of Constantinople. While the Metropolitan or Bishop (always Greek) was appointed from Constantinople, the clergy were Slavs. The fact that the Metropolitan was always Greek further strengthened Byzantium's influence in Russia's Christianization.

As a direct result of conversion, Kievan society experienced significant changes, especially in the spheres of law, family, and morals. The still primitive Russians viewed punishment for a crime to be a personal family matter. It was novel to them that punishment for a crime became a state concern.

The destruction of pagan shrines and idols was another obvious result of conversion. They were replaced by Christian symbols. The new class of priests soon exerted great influence throughout the community. The church naturally assumed responsibility for correct behavior, marriage, and proper worship.

Through the church, Byzantine art and architecture came to Kiev. Kiev and later Novgorod to the north became home to brilliant iconographers. Inspired by Byzantium, the artists of these cities produced some of the most spiritual icons of Eastern Christianity.

The Cyrillic alphabet was integrated into all forms of literary expression and education. Translations of religious materials, especially saint's lives and Church liturgies, came from Kievan Russia. Unfortunately for Russia's future history, the contributions of the Golden Age of Greek history were not translated. Russia was ignorant of Socrates, Plato, Sophocles, Aeschylus, and so many others. School children did not know of the adventures of Odysseus or wonder at the medical tracts of Hippocrates, the astronomy of Thales, or the histories of Herodotus and Thucydides. Relying on Cyrillic, very few Russians learned Greek and, as a result, they were ignorant of the inspiring original contributions of classical civilization.

In succeeding centuries, Kiev's fortune was both brilliant and ultimately disastrous. In the eleventh century under the tutelage of Grand Prince Jaroslavl the Wise, Kiev reached its apogee of power. After Jaroslavl died in 1054, the decline began. First the Grand Prince left Kiev and settled near Muscovy at Vladimir. This undermined central government, encouraged nomadic tribes to attack the area, and broke the economic ties of Kiev with Constantinople. The final tragic event for Kiev and Russia was the Mongol invasion. In 1240 Jenghiz Khan entered Russia and sacked the first city of Russia. Thus began centuries of Mongol control.

Each of these events wrote an indelible chapter in the history of Russia and the nature of its people. Because of the contacts with the Eastern Roman Empire, conversion to Christianity, and the conquest by the Mongols, Russia's national character was formed.

Kiev, and eventually all of Russia, would embrace its Byzantine heritage in an intricate network of culture, religion, and economics. Rus-

sia was orphaned when, in 1453, Constantinople fell to the Ottoman Turks. In the following centuries, Russia became increasingly alienated from the West. Culturally, Russia belonged neither to the Orient nor Western Europe but was caught in an in between world. This resulted in a future history where East and West were suspicious and ignorant of one another.

ISLAM

Disaster for the Exhausted Roman and Persian Empires

A new and irresistible force threatened the very existence of the Eastern Roman Empire. Islam exploded out of the Arabian Peninsula, sweeping aside its older and established neighbors. Persia, Palestine, Egypt, Northern Africa, and Spain fell to the new hordes of religiously zealous Muslims, the followers of Allah (God) and his prophet, Muhammad (570-632/3). Within a few years all the eastern provinces, including Crete, Cyprus, North Africa, and Rhodes, were lost to Islam. The followers of Allah went as far West as Tours (near Paris) where they were defeated in 732 by Charles Martel, the grandfather of Charlemagne. Earlier in 717, Emperor Leo III, using a new weapon known as Greek fire (a substance that is combustible when it comes in contact with water) repulsed the Muslim navy beneath the walls of Constantinople. In the following years the Byzantine emperors returned to the offensive and began to reclaim some of their lost territories.

Muhammad

The Muslims were a dynamic new force in the world led by their prophet, Muhammad. Born in 570 in the city of Mecca located in the south-

Muhammad was the prophet of Islam.

ern Arabian Peninsula near the Red Sea. Muhammad was orphaned at the age of 6 and raised by his uncle. Mecca, the city of his birth, was an important religious center, drawing pilgrims to the pagan totems housed in a central shrine, the Ka'bah. The city was also important as a trade center and caravansary (place that organized caravans). Thus, Mecca was the depot for rich goods that were brought from India across the Arabian Sea and from their caravans took the goods north to the borders of the Byzantine and Persian Empires.

The young Muhammad worked in these caravans, traveling the 600 to 700 miles from Mecca to the north and returning. During his travels, he met and was impressed by the beliefs of Jews and Christians. Monotheism (belief in one God) was not something novel to Muhammad and many of his contemporaries, as there was a religious group in Mecca called Hanifs, who believed in a single deity. Judaism appealed to Muhammad because of its emphasis on the oneness of God, a God of Justice, mercy, and love. Christianity also had its appeal in the person of Jesus, who was a loving God who redeemed the world by his sacrifice.

In his twenties, Muhammad accepted the marriage proposal of Khadijah, fifteen years his senior, and a wealthy entrepreneur of Mecca. In his new life, Muhammad continued to work as a merchant for the next twenty years. When he was forty, he began to spend his leisure time enjoying the solitude of the hills that surrounded Mecca where he often walked. Responding to an inner urge, Muhammad would spend time alone, contemplating in a cave on Mt. Hira. It was in that cave that Muhammad experienced his religious epiphany. He believed that God sent the angel Gabriel, who demanded that he recite the divine passages in the name of Allah (God). After some hesitancy Muhammad did as he was told. According to this version, Muhammad was illiterate and repeated Gabriel's instructions to a scribe. Over the succeeding years, the angel continued to dictate God's word to Muhammad. He then shared them with his companions who recorded and collected them in a single book, the Qur'an (or "recitation"). The result is the *Qur'an*, a 114 *sura* (chapter) scripture that has guided the Muslims and a faith called Islam (to submit). The *Qur'an*, to the Muslims, is a direct copy of the same book that exists with Allah (God) in heaven. Allah is said to have dictated that book to Muhammad through the angel Gabriel.

The *Qur'an*, the holy scripture of Islam, is not the book as first revealed by Muhammad. Muhammad related only short and cryptic statements that were full of parables, fables, and visions. It was later, during the Caliphate of Uthman (644-656), that Muhammad's revelations were organized into the 144 *suras* that comprise the *Qur'an*. It is likely that all the legalities and political articles in the *Qur'an* were included after his death. The major concern of the prophet was to emphasize morality and piety.

The elders of Mecca did not respond in a kindly manner to Muhammad's urging that the faithful should face Jerusalem and not the cult shrine of the Ka'bah. Jerusalem was the sacred home of the Jews, and Muhammad initially thought that the Jews would accept him as their long awaited Messiah. When that did not occur, Muhammad was furious and turned his attention—at Gabriel's direction—back to Mecca.

Muhammad did not consider himself divine. He was the Seal of the Prophets in the tradition of Abraham, Moses, and Jesus. But Muhammad did believe that he was the last.

In 622 A.D. Muhammad and a small group of his converts (about forty individuals) fled from Mecca to a town 250 miles to the north, Yathrib, to be renamed Medina (the City of the Prophet). This event is called the Hejira (emigration) and is the first year of the Muslim calendar. During the next ten years until his death in 632 or 633 A.D., Muhammad consolidated his control over Medina, wrote a constitution for Medina, redirected his followers to face Mecca, and carried

out a series of raids against Meccan caravans that led to a brief war between the two cities. His victory led him to reenter Mecca in triumph where he cleansed the Ka'bah of pagan gods, making it the center of Muslim worship. He died shortly after his return to Mecca, leaving a religious heritage that his successors would harness and direct against their Greek and Persian neighbors.

Muhammad had taken a society comprised of warring Bedouin pagan tribes and, with the *Qur'an*, elevated them in a single generation to the level of the other great scripturists of Western civilization: the Jews, Christians, and the Persian Zoroastrians. The Muslims considered that the followers of these faiths were fellow scripturists and extended a promise of religious toleration. Because they made no distinction between the Orthodox and Christian heretic, the persecuted Christian heresies situated on the borders of the empire offered slight, if any, resistance when Islam burst out of the Arabian Peninsula.

Beliefs of Islam

One reason for the popularity of Islam was that its core beliefs could easily be understood and adapted. The Muslim believes that the prophet Abraham is the common father of their faith, as well as Judaism.

Muslim worship is based on the five Pillars of faith, these are:

1. *SHAHADA*: The Muslim, like the Jew and Christian, has a statement of faith that proclaims the oneness of God and that Muhammad is his prophet. This profession of faith is called *SHAHADA*.

2. *SALAT*: The Muslim is directed to turn towards Mecca and pray five times a day. Prayer ceremonies are an expression of worship, devo-

tion, and obedience to the will of Allah. *SALAT* is "the tying of man to God."

3. *ZAKAT*: Like the Jews and Christians, the Muslim is encouraged to give charity to the less fortunate. Zakat is alms given for the love of Allah and is mandatory.

4. *RAMADAN*: This is a month of fasting and prayer during which Muslims are commanded to abstain from food, drink, and sexual activities from dawn to dusk.

5. *HAJJ*: The three Western faiths abound in holy places that attract pilgrims. The Muslim should, at least once in his life, make a pilgrimage to the Ka'bah in Mecca. *HAJJ* is pilgrimage.

Conflict Within Islam

Muhammad died without a male heir; his only survivor, a daughter, Fatima, was married to his cousin, Ali. Thus, Muhammad's son-in-law was his closest male heir.

A tribal council that met to decide who would succeed the prophet passed over Ali in favor of others on four occasions between 632 and 656. Finally, Ali became Caliph in 656, only to be martyred in 661. With Ali's death, power came into the hands of the Syrian Umayyad family. With their capital in Damascus, the Ummayads enjoyed a hundred-year rule that witnessed Islams' greatest military successes and expansion. As a result of the exclusive Arab orientation of the Ummayads, they failed to integrate the more sophisticated Hellenized East and Persian Empire into their bureaucratic system. The Muslims, only a generation earlier, had been nomadic, feuding Bedouin tribes, worshipping their totems and believing that all forces of nature were animate. Now they were conquerors that failed to appreciate the great traditions of their newly conquered and converted subjects. To the Ummayads, these people were MAWALI (sub-

jects), whose only requirement was to pay a tax (JIZYA). Otherwise, they were excluded from any positions of authority, either civilian or military. If they converted, however, they were exempt from these taxes (an obvious incentive).

In 750 the house of Abbas overthrew the Umayyad dynasty. This was a revolution of subject people, especially those Persian and Greek converts to Islam. The new capital was relocated in Baghdad on the west bank of the Tigris River. The Arab garrison armies, the hallmark of the Umayyads, were sent back to Arabia. The cultured and sophisticated Abbasids now directed the future of Islam.

Shi'ites vs. Sun'nites

The problems facing Islam from its inception to the present day are deep and abiding. When Ali was passed over as successor to Muhammad, a split occurred within Islam. Those who followed Ali and supported his candidacy and his offspring became known as Alids or Shi'ites (followers of Ali). The Shi'ites were in the minority and frustrated at their exclusion resorted to violence and assassination. The Shi'ites evolved into mystical sects whose propensity for violence has resulted in explosive insurrections in the Islamic world.

The other group became known as the Sun'nites, a term derived from Sunna (tradition). The Sun'nites accepted the political changes within the Islamic world and offered no objections to the rule of the Caliphs, the Umayyads, or the Abbasids.

The birthplace of Christianity, the urban areas of the East, thus became centers of conversion to Islam. Converts brought with them a wealth of classical knowledge. The treasure of the Golden Age of Greece, the age of Socrates, Plato, Hippocrates, Euclid, and many others were now fused to Islam. As a result, Islam experienced its own Golden Age. Under the leadership of the Abbasid Caliphs, with their magnificent capital on the Euphrates River, Baghdad, the Islamic world, from the ninth thru the eleventh centuries, experienced and produced a brilliant culture. Nothing anywhere in the West was comparable to what occurred in the world of Islam.

ONE EMPIRE, ONE RELIGION, ONE LANGUAGE

The centuries prior to the coming of Islam had witnessed the division of the Mediterranean world and the East into various religions, languages, and variations of monarchy. With the coming of Islam, these political, religious, and linguistic barriers were gone. Now from the gates of India to the Atlantic Ocean, from the sands of North Africa to the Pyrenees Mountains between the Iberian Peninsula and Gaul (France) there was one dominating religion and one language—Arabic. Previous enemies in the Hellenized and Persian East were now drawn together in the same empire. Islam requires that all Muslims be able to read the Qu'ran in Arabic. Thus, Arabic, a magnificent tool of nuance of expression, rich in vocabulary, a language of poetry, literature, philosophy, and science, dominated communication throughout the Islamic world.

Baghdad

One of the great centers of Islamic culture was the city of Baghdad, located on the west bank of the Tigris River. It became the jewel in the crown of the Abbasid dynasty. Located on a fertile plain, where the two rivers, Tigris and Euphrates, are only 20 miles apart, commerce was its lifeblood. The city dominated the major trade routes between the East and the Mediterranean Sea.

The city was established by the Caliph Mansur in 762, and 100,000 craftsmen, assembled from every corner of the empire, worked in its building. Within the city there was a magnificent palace that was entered through a golden gate. A green dome surmounted its main audience hall, 120 feet high. All this elaborate architecture was obviously meant to impress both resident and visitor with the power and wealth of the Caliph.

The Abbasid Caliphs surrounded themselves with an army of bureaucrats and exotic ceremony. While the Umayyad Caliphs had been more accessible to their Arab co-religionists, the Abbasid Caliphs became increasingly isolated, withdrawing into the pleasures of the harem and the intrigues of court life.

The Abbasids were responsible for bringing about the Islamic Golden Age. Baghdad was the destination for the caravans from the Far East and the starting point on to the West. Baghdad was a city filled with all manner of craftsmen who duplicated the luxury items from the Far East, making the city one of great wealth and beauty. Silks, porcelain, and spices arrived from China, precious stones from India, perfumes from Arabia, and grain and linen from Egypt, as well as other valuable items from Persia, Syria, and Africa.

The House of Wisdom

Baghdad attracted more than commerce; Greek and Persian scholars and converts were drawn by the opportunity it offered to study the Greek classics. These converts brought their classical training, translating Plato and Aristotle into Arabic. Letters and envoys were sent to the Byzantine emperor requesting books and manuscripts. A chronicler records that "They sent to the land of Greece people who would procure scientific works…and so brought to light the marvels of wisdom…" The worlds of Hippocrates on medicine, Thales on astronomy, Euclid's geometry, and geography were all translated from Greek into Arabic. This great interest in Greek thought encouraged Muslims to study and advance in many of these areas. A magnificent library of hundreds of thousands of books assisted their inquiry. When this number is compared to the average Western monastic library of dozens, we can appreciate the great difference in the cultural level of the two societies—East and West. The West owes a great debt of gratitude to these Muslim scholars for preserving so much of classical writings.

Decline of the Abbasids

In the ninth century, Seljuk Turks from Central Asia entered the service of the Caliphs. Soon these Turkish guards, much like the Roman Praetorian Guard, were making and removing Caliphs. This resulted in the Caliph's loss of direct political authority. Great Caliphs were followed by men of lesser ability, and soon these men fell prey to palace intrigue and their Turkish guards.

These Seljuk Turks were exceptional horsemen who, on their small horses, employed fleetness and an accurate use of the bow to great affect. The riches and stability of the Byzantine Empire were centered in Asia Minor. The Seljuk's turned their covetous attention to Asia Minor and in 1071, the same year that the Byzantines were defeated by the Normans in southern Italy, they attacked in Asia Minor. The Seljuks, led by Sultan Alp Arslan, defeated a Byzantine army at Manzikert, thus opening Asia Minor to Turkish invasion. The defeat at Manzikert proved deadly for the empire.

Umayyad Spain

In 750 the Abbasids, who were joined by Shi'ites, overthrew the Umayyads and Persian and Greek converts to Islam in the revolution. One Umayyad, Abu-al-Raman I, had the good fortune to escape the massacre of his relatives. Fleeing to Spain, he and his successors reigned there until the fifteenth century.

Umayyad Spain had its capital at Cordova. From there the Caliphs patronized the multiculturalism and diverse religions of their kingdom. Muslim, Christian, and Jew enjoyed the patronage and encouragement of the Umayyads. Spain became the center of a brilliant cultural development. Muslim rulers presided over a flourishing of the arts, architecture, literature, and philosophy. Spain became the cultural transmitter of Aristotle into Europe. The Jews of Spain translated Aristotle from Arabic into Latin and, in that form, it was first re-introduced into Europe. The great Jewish philosopher, Moses Maimonides, wrote *The Guide For the Perplexed*, where he utilized Aristotelian logic into speculation about God. Averroes (Ibn Rishd) wrote commentaries on Aristotle. His work had a direct influence on the brilliant Christian theologian St. Thomas Aquinas, who wrote the *Summa Contra Gentiles* and *Summa Theologica*, using Aristotelian logic to prove the existence of God.

Thus, Islam, wherever it took root, contributed and stimulated culture. There was a cultural exchange, a give and take between Islam and its Byzantine and Western European neighbors. Baghdad acquired texts from Constantinople; Europe re-acquired the Greek philosophers from Spain. Each society, whether reluctant to admit it or not, benefited from the interaction. The backward and truncated Western Europe may have received the most.

CONCLUSION

These were dynamic centuries for the Eastern world. Byzantium experienced its greatest successes and witnessed its tragic decline. Eastern Orthodoxy would attract and then convert the Slavs of Russia, thus creating a future split between Western and Eastern Europe. There was also the appearance and successful expansion of a new and dynamic religion, Islam. From a humble origin in the Arabian Desert this new zealous faith in Allah spread to incorporate major portions of the ancient world, as well as parts of Europe.

Suggestions for Further Reading

Peter Arnott, *The Byzantines and Their World* (1973).

J. W. Barker, *Justinian and the Later Roman Empire* (1966).

Carl Brockelmann, *History of the Islamic Peoples* (1949).

Robert Browning, *Justinian and Theodora* (1971).

Charles Diehl, *Byzantine Portraits* (1925).

S. Franklin and J. Shepard, *The Emergence of Rus 750-1200* (1996).

Francesco Gabrieli, *Muhammad and the Conquests of Islam* (1968).

Hammilton A. R. Gibb, *Islamic Society and the West* (1949, 2nd ed. 1953).

Gustave von Grunebaum, *Medieval Islam: A Study in Cultural Orientation* (1961).

J. M. Hussey, *Church and Learning in the Byzantine Empire 867-1185* (1937).

Romily Jenkins, *Byzantium, The Imperial Centuries A.D. 610-1071.* (1969).

D. A. Miller, *Imperial Constantinople* (1969).

Gregor Ostrogorsky, *History of the Byzantine State* (1957).

Procopius, *The Secret History* (1966); *Qur'an, The* (1949).

N. V. Riasonovsky, *A History of Russia* (1963).

A. A. Vasiliev, *History of the Byzantine Empire* (1952).

G. Vernadsky, *A History of Russia* (2000).

Montgomery Walt, *A History of Islamic Spain* (1965).

Chapter 6

GERMANIC EUROPE & THE DARK AGE A. D. 378 TO 715

ALARIC THE VISIGOTH

In 486, at the age of 20, Clovis summoned his men together on the fields of March in Gaul to decide what to do and who to victimize in the upcoming season for war. (Clovis became king in 481 at the age of 15.) The "fields of March" indicated the month when warfare began as there now was grass for the horses to feed. The men decided to attack a neighboring king, Syagrius. This successful aggression claimed victims of the opposing army, as well the pillaging of churches. "Many churches were despoiled by Clovis's army, since he was, as yet, involved in heathen error." Among the spoils was a beautiful baptismal vase that the bishop requested Clovis to return to the church. To that request Clovis told the messenger that he should follow him to the town of Soissons and there when the booty was allotted to the men, he would ask for the vase and return it to the church. Upon arriving at Soissons, Clovis did as he said he would. In response to his request the men with sense responded that "Glorious king, all that we see is yours, and we ourselves subject to your rule. Now do what seems well-pleasing to you; for no one is able to resist your power." "It would seem, therefore, that the church would have the vase returned when an excitable member of Clovis's army spoke up and said that "You shall get nothing here except what the lot fairly bestows on you." With this the man lifted his battle axe and struck the vase. You can imagine the tension that must have been felt at that moment, as all waited to see what the king would do. Clovis did nothing in response, as he picked up the bent vase and handed it to the representative of the church. The king knew when to act and when to wait.

At the end of the fighting season Clovis called his men together, once again on the field of March, to examine their equipment before sending them back to their estates. As he walked among them and was reviewing their weapons and other equipment he came to the man who had struck the vase earlier in the year. Taking the man's axe, he threw it on the ground, saying that: "No one has brought armour so carelessly kept as you; for neither your spear nor sword nor axe is in serviceable condition." When the man bent over to pick up his weapons, Clovis raised his own axe and drove it into the man's head saying "This is what you did at Soissons to the vase." The men then departed filled with fear and awe of their king.

It was in this way that Clovis made his way in a violent world. It was a time of violence, and he was successful because he was more adept at the game of power than his contemporaries. He exerted himself, as did his contemporaries, to gain power, office, and prestige. Clovis recognized, with the urging of his wife and the bishop Remi of Reims, that through conversion to Christianity he could extend his authority into neighboring territories. When he converted, he was the first to do so and thus was looked upon with favor by both church and community as a rightful sovereign. People living in adjoining territories, under the rule of pagan kings, considered Clovis as the correct alternative to their ruler. Thus, when Clovis attacked those kings, the subjects did nothing to resist but welcomed the Christian king as liberator and protector of faith.

Chronology

306-337	Constantine I
311	Beginning of toleration of Christians in the Roman Empire
354-430	St. Augustine
392	Christianity made Roman religion
410	Visigoths sack Rome
476	Deposition of last Western Roman emperor
c. 480-524	Boethius
c. 481-515	Clovis
498-526	Theodoric the Ostrogoth King of Italy
c. 500-700	Decline of towns and trade in the West
c. 520	Benedictine monastic rule
527-565	Reign of Justinian
532-537	Byzantine church of Santa Sophia
c. 550	*Corpus* of Roman law
610-641	Byzantine emperor Heraclius
630	Muhammad enters Mecca in triumph
715-754	Missionary work of St. Boniface in Germany
726-843	Iconoclasm in Byzantine Empire

The traditional historian's view of the Middle Ages is that following the collapse of the Western half of the Roman Empire in the fifth century, Europe immediately fell into the Dark Ages. The Germans actually did their best to maintain and continue portions of the Roman bureaucratic structure. Germanic chieftains competed with one another in bloody schemes to eliminate their rivals as they sought official recognition from the Emperor in Constantinople. The Mediterranean still carried merchant ships from ports like *Marseglio* (Marseilles) at the mouth of the Rhone River. Of course, there is no denying that a decline in learning and literacy occurred. The Germanic chieftains of the sixth century wanted their new Gallo-Roman subjects to accept them.

The real unravelling of Europe and the great adventure of its survival came in the ninth and tenth centuries after the collapse of the Carolignian Empire and the attacks of the Vikings. That would truly be a time that deserves to be known as an age of rust and iron, a Dark Age.

The event that precipitated the Western Empire towards its final death throes, and one from which they were unable to respond, was the Germanic invasions.

GERMANIC EUROPE

By the fifth century the Rome of the West had gone, to be replaced by various Germanic tribes and their confederations: Ostrogoths, Visigoths, Franks, Bur-gundians, Lombards, and Vandals. In this new world of competition for status and power, the rule was that there was no rule—anything goes. If a plan was successful, that war chieftain or king exerted authority over his own people, as well as the indigenous Gallo-Romans. If the plan failed, the loser was usually killed.

That was the "game," and there were many willing players crowding the European stage.

The Germanic tribes began their migration southward to the temperate Mediterranean around 1000 BC. Migration was probably stimulated by land hunger, as well as the more hospitable climate to the south. Their place of origin was Scandinavia, making them the ancestors of the later Vikings. The period of their great wandering was called the *"Volkerwanderungen."* It ended when they raided the empire in the third century, ultimately causing the Roman Empire to collapse in the fifth century. A series of factors underscore the causes of Germanic movement into the empire: political unrest in Scandinavia, lack of food, and the attraction of the Mediterranean impelled them toward its northern shores. In addition, there were acute problems that arose in the second half of the fourth century, including pressure from tribes further to the north, crude agriculture that depleted the soil, the attraction of the temperate climate of the south and, of greatest importance, the desire to share in the wealth of the empire. The Germans may have despised the legionnaires of Rome's army, but they did not want to destroy Rome's wealth. The lure of rich lands to the south proved irresistible, drawing uprooted and often desperate Germans. Earlier, their migration had been halted by the military campaigns of Julius Caesar in the last century before the birth of Christ.

As the empire weakened in the fourth and fifth centuries, the porous border of the Rhine and Danube no longer presented any problems to the various tribes that looked hungrily at the wealth of Rome. Over the centuries, many Germanic tribes were allowed to settle within the empire as *feodorati* (federated troops). They made up a significant percentage of the Roman army and many of their generals, such as Odoacer and Stilicho, rose to prominence. By the fifth century the empire had Romanized many Germanic tribes and, in turn, been influenced and Germanized by those same tribes.

Centuries earlier the Roman statesman and historian, Tacitus (d.117), had been alarmed by the threat presented by the Germans. In his *Germania*, he wrote that: "Destiny is driving us upon our appointed path. Long I hope that our enemies, if they do not love us, hate one another more." Tacitus' observations were made when the empire was at the height of its power, and his commentaries made no impression.

Europe from the fifth through the eighth centuries was the scene of a long series of invasions. In addition to the various Germanic tribes must be added the Muslims and the Huns, who either threatened or directly invaded Western Europe. The Germans came to stay while the Huns and others were contained near the borders or returned to eastern Asia, as in the case of the Huns.

One of the Teutonic tribes was called *Germani*, another the *Allemanni*. These names are the root of the term German. These *barbarians* (outsiders) called themselves *Theut* (Theoddeutsch) meaning "people" or "the folk." They occupied an area east of the Rhine beyond the Danube and Vistula Rivers.

It is a mistake to consider that all Germans were crude barbarians who desired only to pillage and destroy the Roman Empire. As a matter of fact, those Germanic tribes living closest to the Rhine and the Danube Rivers had adopted much of the culture of the Roman frontier. From hunter-gatherer they had become farmers, merchants, and traders. Rather than attack the empire, they were anxious to be accepted as *federates* (mercenaries) and to be allowed to settle within its borders and enjoy its benefits.

Germanic tribes more distant from the border, unaffected by Roman culture, were vicious and illiterate, barbarians as we have come to define the term. In general, Germans living closest to the empire adopted much of the culture of Roman peasants. Their German cousins, however, were still primitive.

Germanic Invasions

By the late fourth century the empire in the West could no longer resist Germanic pressures. The Rhine and Danube borders that had always been open to trade and controlled migration from Germanic tribes became unstable and eventually indefensible. The invasion of the empire was triggered by events in the great plateau of Central Asia. Huns, a pastoral tribal society related to the Mongols, turned their attention westward. Attila, a warlord, mobilized the Huns, a pastoral tribal society related to the Mongols. The Hunnic chieftain in 370 turned his attention westward and swiftly moved against the Germanic Ostrogoths. The panic and uprooting caused by the Huns created a domino effect, as tribe moved against tribe until a great mass of Germans, the Visigoths, appeared at the Danube River requesting asylum in the empire.

The Goth Jordanes, the historian of the Goths, in his *Gothic History*, describes the horrifying impression made by the Huns: "With small, foul, shaggy faces, seamed with scars, with their clothes rolling on them, wearing helmets on their heads of the skins of wild rats, they ate their food raw, warming the meat by carrying it between their thighs and the backs of their horses."

As a result of the Hunnic attack, the Ostrogothic confederation that had occupied Southern Russia collapsed. The Ostrogoths fled before the Huns and were soon pressuring the Visigoths. Envoys were sent to plead with the Emperor Valens for permission to cross into the empire. At first, Valens hesitated because of their large numbers, possibly numbering 30,000 to 35,000. He eventually gave permission to the Visigoths to enter so long as they sent hostages and surrendered their weapons.

Having crossed the Danube, the Visigoths were subjected to cruel and insulting treatment by the Roman army. Food was rancid, and the prices horribly inflated. Robbery was common, and the final insult was the rape and abuse of Germanic women. Outraged by this treatment, the Visigoths revolted. In 378 a historic and decisive battle occurred at *Adrianople*. German cavalry routed and destroyed the ill-disciplined Roman infantry commanded by the Emperor Valens; underestimating his enemy cost him his life.

After the Visigoths had pillaged the Balkans, they were eventually pacified and settled as *feodorati* (federated troops) within the empire.

Religion

The Germans entered the empire either as pagans, believing in sky gods and simple animism, or Christian Arian heretics. Earlier in the fourth century at the Council of Nicaea, the priest, Arius, and his belief that Christ was more human than divine, was condemned as heresy. The followers of Arius, however, refused to acknowledge their condemnation. Motivated by the evangelical spirit, Arian missionaries went north, crossed the Danube and preached the "Word" to the Germans. One missionary named Ulfilas created an alphabet for them to translate the Gospels into German. These were the ancestors of the Germans who entered the Roman Empire in the fifth century.

Germanic Concept of the State

The *comitatus* (loyal warriors indebted to their leader and protector of his person and treasure) was the basic unit of political association during these formative centuries. The relationship was extremely personal and replaced the Roman model, where fidelity was to the idea of the State and the person of the emperor. It was the sharing of spoils of a military campaign that brought and held these men together. By the fifth century, it was the lure of riches, the pressure caused by the Huns to their rear, and the temperate Mediterranean that led to the serious breaches of the Roman border.

Of the many invaders, the Franks ("proud people"), the last tribe into the empire, were the most successful. By the sixth century their territory extended from the Pyrenees to the eastern shore of the Rhine River. Thus, they occupied Gallo-Roman, as well as Germanic territory. Since they were divided into many tribes, each led by a war chieftain and comitatus, there was little unity among them.

In the fifth century there was a war chieftain named Merovech. Though his origins are shrouded in mystery, historians have concluded that he was an actual historic person. He is reported to have assisted Aetius in 451 at the Battle of the Catalunian Fields against Attila. Merovech founded the Merovingian dynasty, one whose future kings ruled Frankia (Roman Gaul).

The sixth century witnessed the height of Merovingian power. Clovis succeeded his father, Childeric, and became king of the Franks at the age of fifteen. The contemporary and recorder of the history of this period was Gregorovius, Bishop of Tours. In his History of the Franks, he describes the pathologic viciousness of Clovis (or Louis) as he murdered, punished, and assassinated his way to power. Gregorovius, an or-thodox Christian excused Clovis' excesses, de-scribing him as doing "what was pleasing in His eyes…." To Gregorovius, Clovis was heroic be-cause he had converted from paganism to ortho-dox Christianity, as well as acting with political sense and restraint toward his Gallo-Roman sub-jects. While Clovis was bloodthirsty, he was also a man of keen political acumen who was aware of the gain associated with conversion. The first of his Frankish contemporaries to become or-thodox (the Christianity of Rome), he immedi-ately gained the support of the indigenous Chris-tian population. With conversion he could an-ticipate a warm reception in neighboring terri-tories when he campaigned against the pagan neighbors or Visigoth Arian heretics in the south. When Bishop Remi of Reims baptized Clovis, he pronounced: "bow thy head proud Sicamber, burn what thou has worshipped, worship what thou has burned." The new Catholic Christian required no further encouragement and acted

In 409, the war chieftain Alaric led his bands to a final conquest of Rome.

with energy as he extended his control over all of western Gaul. In 511, Clovis was crowned king at Tours and received the coveted rank of Roman Consul or Augustus from the Eastern Roman Emperor Anastasias. This moment has great historic significance as it marked the beginning of the history of Frankland, and the final chapter in the history of Roman Gaul.

As time passed, however, their power was eroded because of the practice of granting land for service. This was in addition to an inheritance practice of dividing the realm among all the king's legitimate. As a result there was chronic civil war. Thus, by the eighth century, the Merovingians were kings in name only with the actual power in the hands of their chief officials, the *maior domus* (mayors of the palace). These officials ruled over the two main divisions of the Merovingian kingdom, Neustria in the West and Austrasia to the East. At the Battle of Tetry (687) the territories were then combined and ruled by Pepin II of Heristal. Pepin's son was the famous Charles Martel (the Hammer), a warrior who defeated an Islamic raiding party at the Battle of Tours in c.732/733.

Unfortunately what Clovis and his immediate successors achieved in unifying much of Germany and Gaul did not survive. The Germanic inheritance practice of dividing the kingdom among the legitimate sons led to its fragmentation into a myriad of smaller Merovingian kingdoms. Thus, by the mid-eighth century, the Merovingian hold on power had become seriously compromised and the kings mere figureheads.

Other Invaders of Gaul

The Merovingians were not the only invader of Gaul. The Arian heretic Visigoths, who had entered the empire because of pressure from the Huns and their defeated the Emperor Valens, were once again on the move. Led by their king, Alaric the Bold, they moved into Italy hoping to pressure the emperor to allocate better land to their tribe. In 410 he entered Rome where he stayed for several days. Again on the move, he planned to march to southern Italy and there cross over to the rich provinces of North Africa. He died before that plan was set in motion, and the Visigoths returned to northern Italy and then to Gaul where they were granted land and settled as *feodorati*. The Visigoths wanted to share in the riches of the empire, not to destroy what they admired. Their migration, however, had another serious consequence as it opened the frontier for other more barbaric tribes to follow.

Eventually the Visigoths left Gaul and settled in Spain where, because of their Arian beliefs, they had little impact upon the Catholics. By the eighth century the Visigoths collapsed when the Muslims invaded Spain in 711. For the next four hundred years, in northern Spain and the fastness of the Pyrenees, there were only small territories ruled by Christian princes.

The Vandals

In the fifth century, two other tribes crossed the Rhine frontier; they were the Burgundians and Vandals. Of the two, the Vandals were primitive, even by the standards of the fifth century. The Burgundians were more peaceful, quietly settling in the Rhone Valley.

Under their king, Gaiseric the Lame, they crossed the Rhine in 406-407 and moved through Gaul, across the Pyrenees into Spain, continuing into North Africa in 429. The great Church Father St. Augustine died in 430 in Hippo during the Vandal siege. (Carthage fell to them in 439 and remained their capital until the Byzantine re-conquest (533-548) during

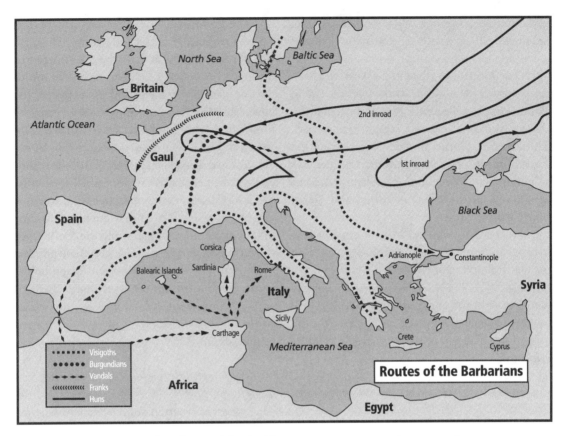

Routes of the Barbarians

Justinian's reign.) From their base in North Africa the Vandals took to the sea. They proved excellent mariners as they pirated in the western Mediterranean. Then in 455, they sailed to Italy and sacked and torched Rome. The extent of their destruction has made their name synonymous with vandalism.

The Vandals were not only vicious, they were also Arian heretics. Their religious beliefs made them antagonistic to Catholics, resulting in massacres of Catholics in North Africa. As a consequence of their actions, the population of North Africa remained antagonistic and when Justinian's armies appeared in the 530s, they met no resistance from the Catholic population. Justinian's General, Belisarius, would eventually crush the Vandals power.

The Ostrogoths

In 500, under the ruthless and capable leadership of their king, Theodoric, the Ostrogoths established their rule over northern Italy. Theodoric admired Roman culture and saw himself as its restorer.

The capital of Theodoric's kingdom was in Ravenna, and from there, he and his people governed Italy as *federates* of the Eastern Roman emperor. The Italians accepted this, as they had become used to Italy being ruled by Germanic representatives of the Emperor.

By the beginning of the sixth century, Theodoric had carefully weaned himself away from his earlier alliance with Constantinople. His aim was to make the Ostrogothic kingdom a Mediterranean power. With that as his goal, he entered alliances with the Franks in Gaul and the Visigoths in Spain.

Theodoric is described in the work of a contemporary Jordanes, *The History of the Goths*. The history is self-serving propaganda that describes Theodoric and the Ostrogoths as descendants of earlier Goths. Jordanes pointed out that Theodoric was a preserver of Roman culture, not a "barbarian." The scholar Boethius, the last intellectual in the West to understand Greek (until the Renaissance), was Theodoric's advisor. His famous work, *The Consolation of Philosophy*, is a summary of theories of ethics from the classical period of Golden Age Greece (fifth century B.C.). He also translated the complete works of Aristotle and Plato into Latin. Until the Renaissance, Boethius' translations were the only source of classical writers available in Western Europe.

Lombards

One of the last tribes to enter and settle in the West, the Lombards were as ferocious as the Vandals. At the end of the sixth century, Pope Gregory the Great (590-604) called the Lombards, as his predecessors had called Attila, the "scourge of God." Paul the Deacon recorded the major source that describes Lombard culture and history. His account is that the Lombards had left Scandinavia to go to Pannonia (Hungary) and then into Italy. Their customary law emphasized *compurgation* (trial by combat) to settle questions of guilt or innocence. These Germanic barbarians were converted to the Arian heretical form of Christianity around the beginning of the sixth century. The Lombards had a deserved reputation for viciousness. The Lombard king, Alboin, made a drinking cup of the skull of the Gepid king.

The Lombards, like others, saw the opportunity for plunder and a food supply in Italy's rich, fertile lands. Once they became masters of northern Italy, they kept apart from the rest of the population. By the end of the sixth century, however, because of the unrelenting efforts of the Church, the Lombards slowly turned from Arianism and began to assimilate. This, however, occurred at a snail's pace. Until the eighth century the Lombards were described as enemies of Catholicism. It was not until the reign of Charlemagne (768-814) that the Lombard rule in Italy came to an end. During the centuries of their rule of northern Italy, they had pillaged more than any of those who had come before them. One historian observes that: "Perhaps no Germanic people had so little to offer to European civilization as did the backward Lombards."

The Anglo-Saxons

There are two written sources that offer some insight into the invasion of England by the Anglo-Saxons, a Germanic tribe from the coast of the North Sea and Frisia: St. Bede's, *The Ecclesiastical History of the English Nation* and *The Anglo-Saxon Chronicle*. A few saint's lives, as well as the letters of Pope Gregory the Great to his missionaries to England, and a few law codes provide the rest of the written sources.

The Anglo-Saxon invasion of England resulted in the virtual destruction of the Celts and their culture. Where other Germanic tribes had eventually assimilated (even the Lombards), the Anglo-Saxons chose to destroy their victims. Whether through conquest, or as some historians suggest colonization, few remnants of Roman culture or civilization survived in Britain. Coming from the area washed by the North Sea, they had little, if any, contact with Rome.

The Angles invaded the English coast, forcing the Celts into remote parts of England. The Angles, along with the Saxons, created their own kingdom.

With the conquest of Britain, the Anglo-Saxons established a number of small, petty kingdoms where feud and warfare became common events. By the ninth century, Britain had not established a unified kingship as had Frankland under the Carolingians. Though the Anglo-Saxons had all but destroyed Romano-British culture, they were affected by the underlying Celtic society and a few remnants of that earlier society.

The Saxons' initial appearance in the British Isles was as hired mercenaries. In his *Conquest of Britain*, Gildas (c.548) described the Saxon entry into Britain. Two leaders, Hengist and Horsa, arrived in 449 in three ships, followed, thereafter, in increasing numbers. Their role as mercenaries did not last, as they turned to savagery, plunder, and conquest. In the *Alfredian Chronicle* (a text that records the En-

glish account of the invasions) the following account is given: in "477 Pelle landed in Britain and his three sons, Cymer, Wlencing, and Cissa, with three ships at the place that is called Cymenes ora; there they slew many of the Welsh and some in flight they drove into the wood that is called Andredesleage." Thus began the subjugation of Britain that lasted for two centuries.

Because there was no racial or cultural synthesis, the British Isles lost its Christianity and returned to paganism. In this culture, the role of war chieftain evolved into a hereditary kingship. Rooted in the ancient *comitatus* relationship, the king was required to call his *thegns* (thanes, kings companions) to meet at a Council of the Wise (*Witan*) where their decisions guided the king. Law was based on gradations of *Wergeld*, depending on the severity of the crime. These early legal developments would have a marked impact on the future development of English common law. Parties bringing a case to be judged had to do so in a public forum. The presentation of evidence had to follow a set procedure where a court made up of ones' peers heard and decided based on the evidence only. The courts, and not the king, therefore, determined law. This is much different from the royal absolutism that appeared in France where Justinian's code was the basis of law.

DEVELOPMENT OF THE CHURCH

Christianity and the Roman Empire were established at approximately the same time in history. Jesus Christ and the first Roman Emperor Octavian (27 B.C. – 14 A.D.) were contemporaries. Advocates of the Christian faith accompanied the developing empire, were protected by its laws, experienced sporadic persecutions, and traveled along its thousands of miles of cobbled highways. When the Western half of the Roman Empire collapsed, the Church, by default, filled the vacuum. Within the hierarchy of the Church were men of intelligence who created a new vision where a universality of faith transcended boundaries. Church leadership would be felt throughout the structure of medieval society.

The Five Patriarchates of the Church

Bishops were assigned to each province throughout the empire. A patriarch, or metropolitan, was above the bishop. The patriarchs directed the entire hierarchy. At first, there were three patriarchs sitting in Antioch, Alexandria, and Rome. When Constantine the Great founded Constantinople in 331 A.D., a fourth patriarch was added, and, finally in 451, Jerusalem became the seat of the fifth patriarch. The early church was ruled by a pentarchy (five heads). All were equal, though it was acknowledged that the patriarch in Rome was first in prestige, not first in authority. Long before Islam surgically removed three of the five, a bitter rivalry among them was obvious. Jealous of one another's prestige, the five patriarchs spent a good deal of time quarreling with one another.

While the patriarch in Constantinople was closely observed by the emperor, the patriarch in Rome had much greater autonomy and, in the eighth century, found a new protector in the new king of the Franks Pepin III, or the Short, the father of Charlemagne (Charles the Great).

In these early centuries of Christianity, the patriarch in Rome did not have jurisdictional power over the territories of the other patriarchs. He could not, for example, appoint or remove bishops. He could not unilaterally decide issues of correct belief.

When the onslaught of Islam removed three of the patriarchs in the seventh century, the field of combat was left to Rome in the West versus Constantinople in the East. In response to the weakening of the Roman Empire, the Church assumed an increasing role until the patriarch of Rome claimed to be supreme head of all Christendom, adopting the Roman-inspired title, Pontifex Maximus: "pope" simply means "little father" coming from the Greek *papas*.

As the fourth century drew to a close, men of exceptional piety, wisdom, and intellect received the title "Father of the Church." Both the Eastern Orthodox and Western Church had remarkable individuals whose lives established a religious standard that inspired their contemporaries, as well as those who later followed.

In the East, the most famous Church Father was St. John Chrysostom ("Golden mouthed") who in 398 became patriarch of

Jerome translated the Bible from the original Hebrew into Latin.

Constantinople. From the pulpit he delivered sermons that both praised and condemned. No one escaped his judgment, whether fellow ecclesiastics, Jews tardy in accepting Jesus, or even the emperor. Particularly in his attacks upon the Jews, Chrysostom argued that a great, not a small difference, separated Christians from Jews. His accusation of *deicide* (killers of God) was a sad link in the chain of a developing Christian anti-Semitism.

St. Jerome (347-420) was a man of learning who is best known for his translation of the Bible into Latin, the *Vulgate* (vulgar-common tongue). His translation became the accepted version throughout the medieval era. A master of the classics of antiquity, he applied their culture to a Christian purpose. Jerome was also a man of great passion who rejected the world as evil because he believed it to be the devil's creation.

In 375 Jerome traveled to the East hoping to experience the rewards of an ascetic life. Unfortunately, in addition to his own asceticism, his rejection of the physical went to an extreme. To Jerome, all sexual intimacy was evil. This neurotic behavior is rooted in an earlier pre-Christian dualism. The Good is associated with light and spirit, while Christianity is associated with soul and heaven. The Bad is, therefore, the opposite focusing upon material selves—the body! Fortunately, for the Christian faith Jerome's rejection of physical intimacy became an undercurrent rather than a dominant practice.

St. Ambrose (339-397), even though he was not baptized, was chosen by the people of Milan as their bishop by popular acclamation, and he was consecrated Bishop of Milan in 374. He served as Milan's bishop for the next twenty-four years. Ambrose was extremely knowledgeable in the classics and did not suffer the guilt of Jerome. Because of his education and skill in rhetoric, Ambrose brilliantly defended orthodox Christianity against the heresy of Arianism, convincing many to return to the Church. His intimate knowledge of pagan writers, especially Plato, made Ambrose a major figure in theology. Even the Emperor Theodosius could not escape the censorship of Ambrose and was forced to do penance on two occasions. When the Emperor Theodosius demanded that rioters who had destroyed a synagogue be punished, Ambrose intervened and argued forcefully and passionately against such action. The emperor relented but a few years later another tragic event occurred that further strained the relations between the two. Rioting had led to the murder of General Butheric, one of Theodosius' officers. The riot had occurred because the general had refused to release from prison one of the mob's favorite charioteers. Theodosius was out-

Ambrose of Milan was among the most brilliant and talented, as well as militant and uncompromising.

raged, and he decided to seek vengeance. The citizens were invited to the amphitheater ostensibly to be entertained. After they were all in place, legionnaires came into the amphitheater and massacred seven thousand men, women, and children. Ambrose once again reprimanded the emperor. Unless Theodosius did penance, Ambrose had no recourse other than excommunication. Theodosius could not justify his action with the argument that he acted to preserve order. His crime resulted in a wanton massacre of innocent men, women, and children.

These incidents transcend the moment, no matter how cruel. The burning of synagogues and the massacre of thousands led to a test of authority and strength. Whose position and argument created precedent, the Church or the

emperor's? The Church in the West lined up its weapons of penance, Christian principles, interdict (suspension of sacraments to the community), and finally excommunication to bring the wayward ruler back in line. Church authority to correct abuses was compromised because the center of imperial authority was also in the East.

The Church of Fathers: Origin, Jerome, Ambrose, and Augustine

Origen of Alexandria (185-253) was a great theologian who influenced the direction of Eastern Orthodox Christianity. Origen was a writer and scholar, as well as an outspoken advocate of his faith.

Unfortunately the zealousness in Origen, as in Ambrose and the others, is characterized by intolerance and fanaticism. Their polimics were specifically directed at the Jews.

Before his conversion to Christianity in 388, Augustine happily indulged in the physical, intellectual, and sensual world of Rome and Milan where he kept a mistress and a child. His study of Hebrew gave him some knowledge of the Pentateuch (first Five Books of the Bible) so that he could debate with Jewish scholars and hopefully illustrate their errors and convert the Jews to Christianity.

Origen believed that every word in the Bible was divinely inspired; otherwise, it would not be there. Where contradictions appeared in the Scriptures, he rationalized the discrepancies by establishing "levels of interpretation." He labored to create a synthesis between pagan rationalism and Judaeo-Christian revelation. The result of this effort was theological philosophy, a pattern of thought that reached its brilliance in St. Augustine.

St. Augustine (354-d.430)

It would take reams of paper and rivers of ink to adequately describe St. Augustine. He was a man of such breadth of intellect that this is but a brief synopsis, a select review of a career that had profound influence on future thinkers.

Augustine was born at Thagaste in Northern Numidia, Africa, into a family where his father was pagan and his mother was a Christian. His mother was the most powerful formative influence in Augustine's life. His father encouraged his education in the classics, but his mother influenced Augustine's moral fiber.

Perhaps because of his mother, Augustine referred to the Church as a "strong woman." This man is justifiably recognized as the most important and creative mind in the development of Christian theology. Next to the Bible, Augustine's *City of God* was the most authoritative work on Christian belief until those of St. Thomas Aquinas eight hundred years later. Augustine was a more attractive personality than his contemporary theologians. Before his conversion to Christianity in 388, Augustine enjoyed and indulged in the physical, intellectual, and sensual world offered by Rome and Milan. Augustine's *Confessions* (written in 397) furnishes an intimate look at his personal odyssey from paganism to Christianity, from infancy to a contemplation of heaven. The *Confessions* must be viewed and read as more than an autobiography for it is a grand statement of Augustine's love of God and God's love for humanity.

Augustine was a teacher of rhetoric with a passionate thirst to discover "truth." His quest followed an interesting path that led from Manichaeanism (belief in a dual force of good/light vs. evil/darkness), to Neoplatonism, and then, influenced by the preaching of Ambrose, to Christianity.

In the 387 he received baptism. In 391, he was ordained a priest, and in 395 he became Bishop of the North African city of Hippo. As bishop, he was unceasing in his efforts to serve his fellow Christians. As an orator and writer, Augustine surpassed most of his contemporaries. He often called a number of secretaries to his office as he simultaneously dictated letters and text to them. He is credited with 113 books, 500 or more sermons, and some 218 letters. His background in Platonism and his conversion to Christianity were immeasurably significant for Christian theology. Augustine achieved a synthesis between the Platonic view that what is *real only exists in the idea* of that thing. For Augustine this perfect and invisible place of Platonic reality became Heaven. Throughout the medieval era *The City of God* was the second most important text to the Bible. This brilliant work of theology was written to counter the accusations of pagans that the tragic sack of Rome by the Visigoths in 410 was due to Christianity weakening the empire. The pagans argued that the Roman gods had abandoned the state. Now defenseless, the eternal city was open to the depredations of the savage Germans. Augustine's response was that there were two cities, the City of God for all those who were saved and the Earthly City, a place of sin, the physical, and the damned. Rome, he argued, did not fall because of Christianity but rather because of the decadence of paganism.

It is uncertain whether Augustine was influenced by the Jewish belief that God's hand is evident throughout history. It is Augustine, however, who believed that from the moment of creation to the final moment, God was at work. Because God was in all things, He created time. If time was good, that indicated that humanity's struggle had purpose and meaning. That this influenced the future of Western civilization is clear in our continual desire to reform society and its institutions. The historian Jeffrey Burton Russell stated: "Augustine's greatness lies in his universality; the immensity, diversity, and complexity of his thought have made him intelligible to men of diverse ages. . . . He completed the intellectual synthesis from which the thought of the Middle Ages proceeded."

Because St. Augustine synthesized his pagan education in Plato, with its emphasis on the invisible universals, with Christianity and its emphasis on heaven, his faith appealed both to the intellectual and the emotional requirements of the faithful. A Christian could be fully committed to his faith and fully engaged in worldly affairs. But what was there for those who desired to abjure the matters of the world and devote themselves to a life of contemplation? For many Christians the contemplative, the ascetic, was more attractive. As an example, in the fourth and fifth centuries in Syria, St. Daniel and his predecessor Simeon Stylites spent decades atop 60 ft. pillars where they gained reputations for holiness and wisdom. Emperors seeking advice, and the humble hoping for miracles, visited the pillar saints. Some of them, like St. Simeon, became celebrities known for their wisdom and miracle working.

Monasticism, however, was more than the escape into the ascetic and contemplative life. A portion of those who found solace in celibacy, prayer, fasting, and withdrawal from the material world gave expression to their own feelings of despair with the economic and social conditions of their world.

Monasticism in the West

It was not until St. Benedict, who established what became a famous monastery at Monte Ca-

sino in 520, that Western Europe had its first remarkable organizer of monastic life. St. Benedict of Nursia (480-543) was born into an affluent Roman family. He abandoned all his worldly possessions for the life of a hermit. His sanctity drew others to him, resulting in his setting down a *regula* (rule) to guide his order. Egyptian St. Pachormius, recognizing that the asceticism of the reclusive hermit monk was too extreme, established communities where monks could live together in a more controlled environment that prescribed hours of prayer as well as manual labor.

Zealous asceticism was more common in the East. Some of these ascetics were extremists. It is as if they were competing with one another to see who could out-mortify the other. These solitary hermit monks were known as *anchorites* ("to go away"). Monk is derived from the Greek *monachos* – "alone." Leaving their homes, families, and material necessities, they lived in extreme conditions with little to compromise their new life of self denial, punishing the flesh, fasting, and prayer, all in hope of recognition by God.

Cenobites – A form of Monasticism

The third and fourth century witnessed a further and more reasonable avenue for the self-denying ascetic. The Benedictine rule emphasized that a monk must live according to the principles of poverty, chastity, and obedience. Benedict rejected the extremism of Eastern monasticism, replacing the extremes of self-mortification and fasting with a brilliant and logical system. Benedict's rule organized a cenobitic style of monasticism where each day was divided into prayer, meals, sleep, and work. Overseeing the common home (*cenobite*) was an abbot (Aramaic *abbas*: father) who had unquestioned au-

Benedict helped to lay the foundations of medieval monasticism.

thority over his community. It was anticipated that the abbot would always rule wisely and justly. Even if that was not the case, the monks were still expected to obey. The monk was expected to be humble in all things and own no worldly possessions. "Let no one in the monastery follow his own inclinations, and let no one…dispute with the abbot…."

Monks lived a hard life. Their clothes were rough homespun, their food simple, and they slept in dormitories. Even their simple sleeping pallets were to be scrutinized by the abbot or seniors in the community to ensure that the monk had no personal items.

Benedict wanted to achieve an environment where moderate observation of religious duties became a pathway to God. Poverty, chastity, and obedience were not meant as punishment but as a lifestyle to free the spirit.

Benedict's rule would be the favored system adopted by all monastic houses of the future. His emphasis on prayer (every three hours) and manual labor (six hours a day) made Benedict's rule the most successful example of the monastic ideal.

The Monastic Role in Culture

Benedict had set aside a portion of each day to study. In an age of seriously declining literacy, it was the monastery that kept learning alive. The monk, toiling in his library, copied and preserved many documents of the classic period that would otherwise have been lost. In the eighth and ninth centuries, under the patronage of Charlemagne and his successor, Louis I, the Pious, monasteries became centers of learning. The Carolingian *scriptorium* (copy center) and the development of a form of writing called *Caroline Minuscule* became the standard of writing and block printing for all succeeding generations. In 817 at the Diet of Aachen, Louis I, the Pious, made the Benedictine form of monasticism official for the entire Carolingian empire. Having achieved such an illustrative position, the Benedictines became among the most powerful forces of religion and culture during the medieval era.

The Papacy

In the case of any developing organization, a hierarchy of authority appears over time, so too with the Church of Rome and the papacy. The claim of the patriarch of Rome to be first in prestige and authority occurred over centuries of acrimonious quarrelling. The other four patri-

Gregory I, pictured in this woodcut, was the most influential of the early popes.

archs (Alexandria, Jerusalem, Antioch, and Constantinople) acknowledged that Rome was first in prestige. According to the "Petrine texts," Christ had said to Peter: "Thou art Peter and upon this rock I will build my church." Peter, martyred in Rome, is, therefore, considered by the Roman Church to be the first Bishop of Rome, the first Pope. Between the first century and the Council of Chalcedon in 451, authority of the papacy had subtly increased. At the Council of Chalcedon, Pope Leo I exerted his authority in settling doctrinal issues. A century later, Pope Hormisdas (514-523) made statements that suggested a future claim of infallibility; ultimately the Church would claim that there was no salvation outside its precincts. The Church believed that it was the sole pathway to heaven.

The chance for the papacy to assert its independence from the control of the Eastern Roman emperor came in the eighth century when the Lombards invaded Italy and took the Byzantine administrative center of Ravenna. That city controlled all of central Italy from the Adriatic to Rome on the Tyrennean Sea. The Pope was, therefore, under the control of the Byzantine governor stationed at Ravenna. With that city lost, the papacy looked for a new protector and found him in Pepin III, the Short, father of Charlemagne, and Mayor of the Palace to the Merovingian monarchy in Gaul (France).

From these early centuries of struggle, the papacy achieved, by the thirteenth century, unimaginable power and authority. Kings and emperors would bow and plead for mercy before the threats of ecclesiastical thunderbolts. The story of this transformation is fascinating.

Pope Gregory the Great (590-604) was the first monk to be acclaimed Pope. His 800 (existing) letters describe his concern for a full spectrum of issues, particularly ecclesiastical matters. Gregory used Church wealth for social welfare—feeding, clothing, administering to the poor, and sending missionaries to distant places.

Gregory's career reflects the growing ignorance of and rejection of the Greek language and the classics, as well as a decline in Latin. He was neither interested in learning Greek, nor concerned with his own ungrammatical Latin. Gregory's theology emphasized the total authority of the Church, rejecting any thought of questioning Rome. Faith and acceptance must come before all else. Thus, miracles of all manners are accepted without question because they reinforce faith. As indicated earlier, the Roman Empire declined in the West. The Church, by default, filled the vacuum. The Church now replaced the bureaucratic structure established by the Romans. As a result, the papacy furnished a model for Christian unity, aided by the zealous commitment of a small army of missionaries and monasticism.

Between the sixth and ninth century the papacy made significant progress in controlling its ecclesiastical hierarchy. Men who led by example, men of intellect, morality, and courage, who would defy, if necessary, emperor and king, were responsible for this progress. As a result, the papacy grew in prestige as it defended orthodoxy against various heresies, established a uniform liturgy, and made every effort to guide the Church through political and religious storms.

CONCLUSION

The invasions of the fifth through the seventh centuries were a period of transition rather than collapse. Rome was transformed. Germanic kingdoms, their laws and customs, took its place. Many of their legal systems combined with those of Rome. Of course, there was decline, but there was also the energy and creativity that accompanied a new cultural amalgam. The future of modern Europe was established during these early centuries of medieval society.

With the triumph of the Latin language and the Roman Catholic faith, continuity was assured. Barbarian incursions and occupation had destroyed Latin education. Roman-Latin culture was replaced by a Christian-Roman culture evident in the literature and philosophy of the medieval era. The philosopher Boethius, with his allegorical description of philosophy and knowledge of Plato and Aristotle, was a precursor of the medieval scholastic. St. Augustine's *City of God* was, aside from the Bible, acknowledged as the most influential theological treatise of the medieval era. St. Benedict of Nursia's (d.543) *Rule* became the most reasonable and successful monastic system serving as the paradigm for the future of all western European monasticism. Cassiodorius (d.583) wrote extensively on the value of higher education, particularly among the clergy, and the *History of the Goths* survives in summary by Jordanes. Gregory the Great (d.604) the last of the great Christian Latin fathers wrote his *Pastoral Care*, instructing bishops on the correct way to govern their dioceses.

These are some of the most significant figures that lived in a world that was gradually being transformed. Incessant and petty wars accelerated decline. These men brought some light to a weakened society. As one historian states: "In a brutal and poverty-stricken society these struggling scholars kept learning alive...."

Suggestions for Further Reading

Frederick B. Artz, *The Mind of the Middle Ages* (1965).

Augustine, *City of God*

T. Baker, *The Normans* (1966).

Boethius, *Consolation of Philosophy*

Norman Cantor, *The Civilization of the Middle Ages* (1993).

W. H. C. Frend, *The Rise of Christianity* (1984).

R. L. Fox, *Pagans and Christians* (1987).

Gregory of Tours, *History of the Franks*

Pope Gregory the Great, *Pastoral Care*

E. James, *The Franks* (1988).

Jordannes, *History of the Goths*

Rosamund McKitterick, *The Early Middle Ages* (2001).

F. Stenton, *Anglo-Saxon England* (1947).

EUROPE UNDER ATTACK: The Early Middle Ages 715-1000

Charlemagne, King and Emperor

Ancient writings have fascinated our modern world. Great effort was put into deciphering Egyptian hieroglyphics and Mesopotamian cuneiform, etc. Another form of writing that has recently captivated Westerners is the "runes" of the Norse invaders who came to the continent in the late eighth century.

The word "rune" seems to mean "a secret whispering." Depending on how the characters are arranged, believers in the system say they can tell the future. These strange marks have been found in stones and monuments among Teutonic peoples. The Norse believed they were given to humans by their gods. In their mythology, the golden age of the gods was destroyed and finally a goddess, Saga, was discovered to help them. (The word "sage" can be derived from her name.) She told them that she was pleased that they sought intelligence and that she had placed the wisdom and eternal truth of the gods on writings across the lands. She instructed men to try to gather them. These runic pictographs were copied and spread by men in the hopes of pleasing the gods and understanding their fate.

Tales of the Norse gods actually have their origin in the legends of the Aryan people, in India. As these peoples moved north and into the Scandinavian peninsula, their lives became even more harsh and so did the tales about their gods. In the most ancient times, two creatures arose: Ymir, the first of the ice giants and the father of all evil, and the cow, Audumla, the mother of goodness. Audumla, licking the ice to survive, discovered Buri, a divine creature, who had been frozen in the ice. By using magic, Buri produced a son, Borr, and these "forces of good" fought against the powers of evil. This war raged for many years with no victor. Finally, Buri met Bestla; they married and had a son, Odin, who, with his brothers, defeated the evil ones. Odin killed Ymir and threw his body into a deep gorge from which he created the universe. From Ymir's flesh Odin created Midgard, a place for humans to live. Ymir's blood was the sea around Midgard, and his eyebrows became a fence around the land. Bones and teeth made the mountains, and his skull was the sky above. Because the world was dark, Odin took sparks and threw them into the sky, making the stars. He placed two larger sparks in chariots to make the sun and the moon; he made a beautiful young woman to ride in the sun chariot and made a handsome young man to guard the moon. The remaining evil gods sent wolves to chase the chariots and that was why they continually roamed the skies.

*As Odin looked upon his creation, he saw that Ymir's body was filled with maggots, both black and white. He turned the white maggots into elves to live on the earth and the black maggots into elves that toiled under the earth to bring out the fruits of the mines. (These are connected to the ideas of J.R. Tolkien in his descriptions of "Middle Earth" in both **The Hobbit** and **The Lord of the Rings.**)*

Odin and Freya had a son, Balder, who was loved by everyone except the evil Loki who seems to have taken on the characteristics of the Christian Lucifer, a fallen, greedy soul who caused trouble. Balder dreamt that he would be killed so his mother made all the world swear to protect him; all but the innocent mistletoe swore to protect Balder, and he became immortal. Loki, however, found that Balder had one weak place (like Achilles) and tricked a blind man to throw mistletoe at Balder. It hit his heart, and he died. Balder descended to the underworld, ruled by Hel (a female god) who said that if Balder were so loved, everyone on earth would be weeping at his death. Hel demanded proof that all were in mourning for Balder's death, but one woman, Thokk (who was Loki in disguise), refused to weep so Balder could not escape Hel's wrath.

Three terrible winters followed; the wolves, chasing the sun and the moon, caught and ate them. Now humans had little hope of surviving; men set off on the journey to find clues to the future so that they might change their fate. It was here that they found Saga, and she revealed that only through their diligence and intelligence would there be any chance of continued existence.

The Runes are considered messages from the gods, written down in a language that is still debated by historians. Some feel it was derived from the Greek traders, as they traveled the ancient world; others see connections with the Etruscan language. Whatever the source, there are many connections to their message to the Western traditions.

One of the more famous runic poems, "The Speech of the High One," shows the broad concepts, which join many cultures.

> *I hung from a windswept tree.*
> *I hung there for nine days and nights,*
> *Gashed with a spear,*
> *An offering for Odin,*
> *A sacrifice for myself,*
> *Bonded to the tree which no man knows,*
> *Or whither its roots may run.*
>
> *No one gave me bread,*
> *No one gave me drink.*
> *I peered down into the depths and*
> *Snatched up the runes,*
> *And with a fearful scream*
> *Fell into a swoon.*
>
> *After I began to thrive,*
> *My wisdom thrived too.*
> *I was joyful and I prospered.*
> *One word led me to another,*
> *One deed led me to another.*

Similarities to Christ on the Cross are obvious, but there are other connections. For instance, this is the event described on the Tarot Card called "The Hangman." Tales across almost every culture talk about suffering as a means to self discovery and "resurrection."

In Nordic tradition, the runes are made into individual characters and arranged and re-arranged hoping to discover information about the future. Today, you can go to the mall and in many card stores, books and packets with rune stones are sold to customers hoping for the same insights the ancient Norsemen sought.

Chronology

550-600	Anglo Saxon conquest of England completed
590	Gregory the Great creates the Latin Church and builds a bigger wall between the East and West
597	Augustine of Canterbury begins mission to England
650	Arabs conquer most Byzantine empire and begin assaults on Constantinople
663	Whitby Council decides Roman Church will supercede the Celtic Church in England
700-900	Northumbrian Renaissance in England
711	Islamic Moors cross Gibralter and conquer Spain from the Goths
714-740	Charles Martel rules as Mayor of the Palace of the Frank Kingdom
732	Battle of Tours; Martel & Franks battle the Moors and they leave France
735	Venerable Bede writes *The History of the English People and Church*
740	Iconoclastic movement begun by the Byzantine Emperor
750	*Beowulf* and *The Book of Kells* are produced
751	Pepin III was crowned the first Carolingian King of the Franks
768-814	Charlemagne's reign as King of the Franks
793	Vikings sack Lindesfarne in England
800	Carolingian Renaissance begins in France; Charlemagne crowned by the Pope
843	Treaty of Verdun splits the kingdom of the Franks between Charlemagne's grandsons
854	Vikings attack Paris but are bought off by tribute
865	Viking Danelaw, the conquest of northern England, begins
870-899	Alfred the Great reigns in England
936	Otto I becomes the Duke of Saxony and King of Germany
954	Danelaw ends in England
955	Battle of Lechfield stops Hungarian expansion
962	Otto crowned Holy Roman Emperor by Pope John XII

When the Germanic nomadic tribes settled into Western Europe and embedded themselves into Roman customs and organization, the "resettlement" of Europe did not stop. In fact it increased, and on every border and coast new influences, in the form of attacks and invasions, brought different people, ideas, and customs into the foundations of Western Civilization. Even from within the old Roman areas, the Germanic tribal groups changed their allegiances and alliances to form new institutions.

THE FRANKS ARE TRANSFORMED INTO THE CAROLINGIAN EMPIRE

Succession is always a problem, and the passing of power from one generation to the next remains a complicated task. All rulers hope to be succeeded by efficient and effective successors, but the system to find such an heir has been difficult in all cultures. In the land of the Franks,

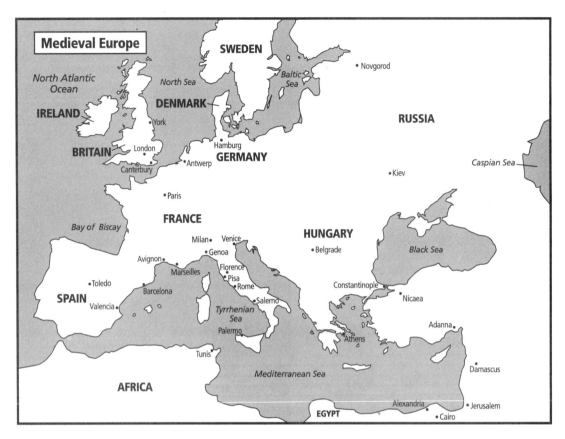

the Merovingian King, Clovis, died in 511. When the last ruler of a generation died, nomadic tradition divided kingdoms among the "brothers" and the sons of Clovis split the kingdom into three parts: Neustria in the north, Burgundy in the south, and Austrasia lying between them. The brothers worked hard at limiting each other's powers and land. The morality and the ability of the Merovingian rulers rapidly declined. The monk historian, Gregory of Tours, described the scene: "The court of the Merovingians was like a brothel; drunkenness was the natural condition of all, wives got their lovers to murder their husbands, and everyone could be purchased for gold." While the royal family fell into debauchery and paid little attention to the task of ruling, the so-called Mayors

of the Palace began to consolidate power. The Pepin family came to dominate the Mayoral position and eventually took power from the Merovingians and formed the Carolingian dynasty.

PEPIN'S DYNASTY

Pepin of Landan was the first of his family to hold the office of Mayor of the Palace of Austrasia. When he died in 639, the title passed to his son, Pepin II. Upon this Pepin's death there was no legitimate heir, and his successor became Charles Martel, his illegitimate son (hence the change from the name Pepin). By now the Pepin family had gained wealth, power, and fame in the kingdom. They continued to consolidate control through their military skills and victories.

Charles Martel (which means "the Hammer") knew how to rule. He organized a standing army loyal to him and ready to fight whenever they were called upon. These soldiers, called *thanes*, were Charles' men and were rewarded with land (*fiefs*) and prestige by their leader. This strengthened Charles' hand in dealing with dissident competitors.

South of the land of the Franks, in 711, invading Islamic troops conquered the Germanic Visigoths in Spain and began building a stronghold on the European continent. As the Islamic forces expanded through Spain, they began raids into France. The Muslims attacked monasteries and churches, which had enough treasure to make it worth their efforts. The rest of the countryside was poor and littered with shacks, hovels, and impoverished peasants and serfs. By 732, however, these raids came as far north as Poitiers, and Charles decided to stop these raids by the "infidels."

History is often the story of the winner, and to some degree there was no winner when the Franks and the Muslims met at Poitiers (often referred to as the Battle of Tours). The Frank strategy was to stop the horsemen of the Muslims by driving sharpened stakes (called Roman stingers) into the ground, which would break a cavalry attack. The battle raged all day with both sides withdrawing to recoup for the next day's attack. According to European records, the next morning the Franks found that the Muslims had disappeared, obviously frustrated by Charles' strategy. Western historians credited Charles with saving all of Western Europe from the clutches of this heathen enemy. Muslim accounts, however, describe their officers making the decision that the poor land of the Franks was not worth fighting for and so they returned to concentrate

on Spanish cities, such as Cordoba and Grenada. The Muslim expansion turned eastward, toward Asia, where converts and riches lay; here they built their empire into rich and powerful states.

Charles' heroism, however, became a legend in France and Western Europe. His descendents would cash in on his supposed success. When the Muslims left the French territory, France took a more aggressive stance against the Islamic invaders. Increasingly Frankish leaders led raids into Spain and contact with the advances and knowledge held by the Muslim world crept slowly into French ways. These raids produced no permanent European hold on Spain until the *Reconquista* (or re-conquest) of Spain was finally achieved in 1492.

The permanent effect of Charles' action was a new form of warfare. He had acknowledged the Muslim advantage of fighting on horseback and the weakness of his own troops who rode horses to the battle but then fought on foot. The Muslims could maneuver their horses because of a device they had learned from the Chinese, the stirrup (a French term meaning "to step up"). Martel adapted this to his soldiers' equipment, and warfare in Europe became dominated by the horseman and cavalry. Soon the heavy weapons of the foot soldiers, such as the battle-ax and javelin, were exchanged for lighter weapons, such as the long sword and the lance. It was a slow process, not completed until the generation of Martel's grandson, Charles, but the character and process of war in Europe changed. Land grants (fiefs), loyalty (fealty) and the military organization became the framework of French society.

The Roman Church was the other ingredient in this mix. Since the fall of the Roman Empire, the Roman Church had supervised the spiritual as well as the political structure of Western Europe. The Church was the major landowner and was in the possession of thousands of

in France and traveled with Charles to the Germanic tribes. He converted thousands of Hessians, Friesians, Saxons, and other tribal groups to Christianity. These pagans had believed primarily in nature gods, but Boniface showed the power of the Christian God by chopping down the Oak of Thor, a huge oak tree worshipped by the Germanic tribesmen. Boniface worked to change long time tribal traditions that allowed for divorce, incest, and polygamy and to get the tribesmen to accept what he considered Christian standards. Charles' support and friendship led Boniface to be an early Church supporter of deposing the Merovingians as the Kings of France.

PEPIN III

By the time he died in 740, Charles Martel was the virtual ruler of all three kingdoms of the Franks. His son Pepin III (also called "the Short") came to the position of Mayor of the Palace with all the powers of a king but not the title. With the backing of Boniface, in 752, Pepin sent a delegation to Pope Zacharias, asking for the title of King of the Franks. The Pope agreed. Pepin called a council of supporting nobles and declared himself King. Legend says that Boniface anointed Pepin, giving him the blessing of the Church, but this might be a latter addition to the historical facts. One problem was that there was still a Merovingian king— Childeric. Pepin captured him (he did not have much support or protection in the face of Pepin's military power and Church support), shaved his head—long hair and beards were Merovingian signs of power (like Sampson)—and locked him up in a monastery until he died. Pepin had now consolidated all the power in France. Again the connection between church and secular leaders was bonded: Pepin's brother, Carloman, who in

horses that Charles needed. The supply of horses gave Charles the mobile army to expand into areas where the people could be converted to Christianity, if not by the Spirit then by force. Churches and monasteries were established in these new areas, and the many new converts built a partnership between the secular and religious leaders, sometimes referred to by historians as the "Cross and Sword" alliance.

Charles Martel's cooperation with the Church was illustrated by his relationship to an English monk, Boniface. The holy man arrived

Frankish tradition should have ruled with him, left for Rome where he became a monk. He eventually moved to the famous Benedictine monastery at Mounte Cassino.

In 754, Pope Stephen traveled to Paris and crowned Pepin III "King of the Franks by the Grace of God and Protector of the Church." He brought Holy Oil to anoint Pepin and his sons so that they were now the legitimate dynasty of the Frankish nation. Although on the surface this simply gave the House of Pepin the throne of France, Stephen had a second reason for blessing the family with his grace: he had political problems with the East where the Byzantine Empire claimed control of central Italy. Through his alliance with Pepin, he now had a powerful army to conquer and control this valuable territory. Pepin soon moved against the Lombards who had threatened the Papacy and with his victory he gave the Church control over most of the northern Italian peninsula. This "gift" was called the **Donation of Pepin** and solidified the relationship between the Franks and the Roman Church, although it added to the strain between the East and West. Besides the military victory, there suddenly appeared a document, the **Donation of Constantine**, stating that Emperor Constantine specified that the Roman Church had secular control over Rome and Central Italy. Both the Pope and Pepin stood behind this document, but it was later (during the Renaissance) proven to be a forgery.

Meanwhile the efforts of Boniface to convert the Germanic tribesmen and bring them under the control of the Frankish King continued. In 754, however, some Friesians murdered the monk as he walked through the forest. The legend was told that he tried to protect himself with his Bible, but the warriors sliced it in two and then killed the defenseless priest. The Christians immediately made him a saint and in his name, St Boniface of Crediton, murdered many Friesians in revenge. The Cross and the Sword were tied together through military might.

CHARLES THE GREAT, KAROLUS MAGNUS, KARL DE GROSSE

The great symbol of the unity of the traditions of the Church, the Germanic Franks, and the traditions of Rome was the person of Pepin's oldest son, who became Charles I in the Carolingian line of French Kings. It is worth studying his life to see the changes which occurred in Western European history. During his lifetime, he preferred the Germanic name Karl and was first called Karl de Grosse (in English, Charles the Great) long after his death his legends transformed him into the Latin, Karolus Magnus, or Charlemagne.

Charles grew to have such importance that he had a contemporary biographer, Einhard, who has left us a glimpse of the great leader. "He was large and strong [6'3 as determined when historians opened his tomb in 1861] and of lofty stature, though not disproportionately tall (his height was well known to have been seven times the size of his foot); the upper part of his head was round, his [bright blue] eyes very large and animated, nose a little long, hair fair, and face laughing and merry. Thus his appearance was always stately and dignified, whether he was standing or sitting." Later comments mark that he wore the native dress of leather with a linen undershirt and a blue cape or robe; he liked foreigners although he would never dress like one (only occasionally would he wear Roman shoes instead of Frankish boots) and he was interested in almost everything. The latter might well be the result of Charles' relationship with his mother. Bertrada, who was perhaps responsible not only for her son's height and large feet (she was sometimes called Bertrada of the Big Foot), was very interested in stories and education. Some historians have linked her to the famous Mother Goose stories, as Bertrada was also called Queen Goosefoot. Charles was always good to his mother and kept her in his household until she died in 783. He was a good father, having most of his 15 (or so) children eat and travel with him.

When Pepin died in 768, he gave the kingdom to his two sons, Charles and Carloman. Einhard states that Charles was always kind to his younger brother but that Carloman was unhappy with the arrangements. Two years later, Carloman died, and Charles was declared King of all the Franks. Meanwhile, Gisela, Charles' sister joined the Church as a nun.

Charles the Soldier

Following the traditions of his father and grandfather, Charles was a strong and effective warrior and enjoyed combat. In a long series of battles and wars, Charles came to rule almost all of the Christian lands (many of which he made Christian) of Western Europe. The exceptions were the British Isles, Spain, southern Italy, and Sicily. He held the titles of King of the Franks and the Lombards, and finally Roman Emperor. His military might included acts of terror to spread the word that Charles meant to rule or to destroy his enemies. In one famous, probably legendary story, Charles found that his son, Pepin the Hunchback, was plotting against him. He dragged the disloyal boy off to the poorest monastery he could find. Later, when others were caught plotting against Charles, he would ask his son for advice; Pepin would reply that he spent all his time weeding out the bad plants so good plants could grow. Charles interpreted this to his own needs and went about killing all the opponents he could find across his domains. With modest forces, he re-conquered the Lombards (his first wife was the daughter of the Lombard King, but he didn't like her and sent her off to a monastery); he totally eradicated the Avars who moved from the East into his territories; battled the Muslims in the Pyrennes, eventually limiting them to Spain; seized Venetia from the Byzantines; annexed the Bavarians; and waged a 30-year war with the Saxons. This last war exemplified the brutal side of Charles. When the war was finally over, he had about 4000 Saxons in his "custody" slaughtered in one day simply to make the point that he had won.

In 778 Charlemagne suffered his only defeat, and it too became part of his legend. While returning from a raid against the Muslims in northern Spain, his troops were ambushed and the rear guard annihilated. This group was commanded by Count Roland and the Franks memorialized the massacre in a ballad, which was finally written down around 1100 into an epic poem, "Le Chanson de Roland" (The Song of Roland). Like most interpretations of tragic events, much of the poem is inaccurate but it did help build the legend of Charlemagne's sacred kingship and shaped ideas of feudal chivalry and courage. In the tale, all the Franks are mercilessly killed although they had fought bravely. Only one faint hearted soul escaped to tell the tale and after he revealed the horrors his comrades met, he was challenged to a duel and killed. The poem continues: "Better dead than a coward be called."

One group that feared Charlemagne and never battled against him was the Vikings. These fierce warriors heard that Charles was too organized and too strong to be defeated and did not land on the French coast during Charles' lifetime. This spared the Franks along the sea coast the horrors that the English and some of the

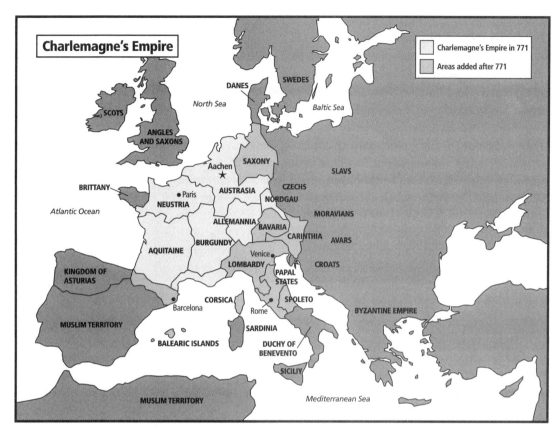

other coastal peoples had to suffer. After Charles died, the Vikings were quick to change this situation. (See below)

Charles as Ruler

Charles knew that keeping control of this huge territory would require organization. Perhaps he had learned some lessons from the traditions of the past Roman system but he had to deal with many new peoples in areas beyond those conquered and controlled by the Romans. On the frontiers of the empire he established military buffers called marks (or marches or margraves). The Ost Mark defended the east; the Nord and Dane Marks defended the North; and the Spanish Mark stood along the Spanish border. The local counts enjoyed powers over their marks, depending on need and their relationship to the King. They had serious responsibilities to maintain peace and order, and, especially, loyalty to Charles.

Across Charles' empire there were a great variety of peoples with different customs and a variety of laws. If this were not challenging enough, there were many long time tribal rivalries that set groups into almost continual skirmishes if not out and out warfare. Keeping stability required a great deal of time, effort and talent from the King. The Merovingians had set up a system where certain local nobles, called *counts*, were empowered to collect taxes, administer justice, and keep order. Charles continued this system, but he sent men loyal to him, *missi domini* (agents of the lord), to supervise these local power holders. As the King aged, he spent less and less time touring his lands and battling opponents and increasingly relied on his emissaries to make sure his rules were observed and loyalty was kept.

Charles also kept the old Germanic court system where each side swore oaths of accusations and denials. When doubt remained, the parties could resort to trial by pain, ordeal, or even combat. Guilty parties often made restitution by paying *wergeld* (literally "man money") to the victims of their crimes. The amount paid depended on the severity of the wounds: death required the highest amount, while putting an eye out of an opponent required a lesser amount as did cutting off a leg, hand or other physical wounds. Wergeld was also adjusted to the age, gender, and social class of the injured party.

For revenue, Charles relied on taxing his many vast and prosperous estates. Local counts collected from their areas and sent a percentage to the royal court. To encourage trade, Charles had a pound of silver divided into twenty parts and minted into coins, known as shillings, thus circulating the first coins in Western Europe since the fall of Rome. This currency was later copied by the Anglo Saxon King (Offa of Mercia) and the unit of currency in Britain today (as well as many parts of the Commonwealth) is still called the pound, which was the weight of twenty shilling coins.

Charles and the Church

The political framework Charles inherited and developed was tightly linked to the powers of the Roman Church. From the time of Clovis, the Frankish rulers had used the Church to secure legitimate rule. Charles' ancestors had done the same and built on the connection. Charles

himself was a devoted Christian and used his military might to convert many across the territories he conquered. His favorite books, read to him at bedtime, were the Bible and St Augustine's *City of God*. As the Frankish government developed so did its ties to the Church. Since literacy was almost equivalent to being a member of the clergy (it has been said that Charlemagne could read but could not write), the Church provided clerks and advisors to the crown. Hence Charles's first decree as king was "A General Warning" to churchmen to end their corrupt and immoral habits of vice, dueling, drinking, gambling, and womanizing. He, however, did not always abide by these laws himself!

Continuing the efforts of Boniface to eradicate pagan practices of divorce, incest, and concubinage (again, he did not have to submit to these rules), he promoted the Church view that sex was to be within marriage. This of course was practical because children would have an identifiable father and mother to take care of them. Monasteries were to follow the rules of St. Benedict (after all, Charles' uncle had given up the throne to become a Benedictine monk). Church courts were to observe canon law, and a common service book was implemented so that reverence to God and the king could be observed throughout the kingdom. Christianity was the major unifier of the Frank kingdom and across its regions, churches and the parish system were imposed upon conquered lands.

In 800, Charles visited Rome and spent Christmas Mass at St. Peter's Basilica (only a wooden structure in those days). During the Mass, Leo III asked the King to kneel and then placed a crown on his head, proclaiming him "Charles Augustus, Emperor of the Romans, Crowned by God." Einhard claimed Charles did not know Leo's intentions and would have stayed away if he had known of the crowning.

The incident still is the subject of great debate, but the fact stands that "Charlemagne" was now lord, by the grace of Leo anyway, over the dominions of Western Europe. There were a number of precedents that should have given Charles a clue that this ceremony might happen. Pope Stephen, who also anointed Charles and his brother Carloman, had crowned Pepin III, his father.

The Pope had political reasons for his act and Charles must have been aware of these, too. The Byzantine Empire, based in Constantinople, still claimed control over central Italy even though the Donation of Constantine claimed that such rule belonged to Rome. The two divisions of the Christian Church were also embroiled in the Iconoclast crisis, the controversy concerning the acceptance of icons and holy images (the second commandment forbid "graven images" of God and the Byzantines were supporters of the idea that no pictures of God were permissible). The Roman Church accepted icons and relics as valid and holy objects to be venerated. By crowning Charlemagne, the Pope enhanced his own authority with inference that whoever put the crown on the king could also remove it.

In Charles' reign, a strong king and a strong church went hand in hand. A few years after the ceremony in Rome, Charles would place the crown on his head and advise his son to follow that tradition. Later, when secular rulers were weak, the Church moved toward supremacy; then stronger kings challenged the Church. This struggle would go on beyond the Reformation.

Charles and the Carolingian Renaissance

Perhaps from the influence of his mother, Charles was interested in education, a topic in which his forefathers had little interest. As his family grew and he aged, he tended to spend more time in the place of his birth, Aachen (also called Aix-la-Chapelle). Earlier, Charles had visited Ravenna, which had been beautified by Emperor Justinian. In Aachen he began to build a city worthy of his own success and position. Charles called artists, musicians, and scholars to his seat of power, and they provided a new cultural impetus to European history. There was the newly built palace, chapel, school and library. These new structures were deliberately copied from the styles of ancient Rome and contemporary Constantinople. A revival of learning and culture flourished at Aachen and began to spread around the empire. Historians call this revival the **Carolingian Renaissance**.

Among the scholars at Aachen was an English monk, Alcuin of York, who directed the palace school. In England, Alcuin had been a student of the "Venerable" Bede and was probably the greatest scholar of the era. He supervised the copying of innumerable manuscripts (there were no printing presses and all written information had to be copied by hand, thus the name "manu-scripts"). He taught scores of students who were sent around the empire to continue the spread of knowledge. Clerics mastered the arts of copying and illuminating (making designs and drawings to explain the texts). These were all done in Latin, in magnificent letters later called the Carolingian script. Alcuin's scholars devised a new, lower case alphabet called "miniscule," which made copying and reading the texts much easier. About eight thousand manuscripts, representing roughly 90 percent of surviving ancient texts, were recorded during the Carolingian Renaissance.

Young nobles came to Aachen and were taught about governing. This not only provided a better trained ruling class but also fostered loyalty to Charles's laws and ideas.

The success of the Aachen school brought Charles to command each monastery and parish church to establish a school and teach the basic elements of reading and computations. Literacy increased dramatically for the first time in many years as schools and libraries appeared throughout the Frank kingdom. By 1050 almost every cathedral in Europe had a school, the later basis of the future universities that would rule the intellectual life of Western Europe through the Renaissance and into the Scientific Revolution and the Enlightenment. This new self-confidence began to change the face of Western Europe and set the stage for a culture that was different from the old Roman and the Byzantine cultures.

Charlemagne's Legacy

After many years of isolation, the European continent began to function as a unit once again. Charles possessed impressive skills of determination and, especially, organization. He was the first ruler to hold an imperial title and as such, he conducted diplomacy with rulers from England to Baghdad. The Abbasid Caliph of Islam, Harun al-Rashid, sent him gifts of a royal robe and an elephant (some historians say the Abbasid sent cast off items to "lesser" rulers, while others claim this was definitely a sign of great respect). His military might and his organizational skills bound numerous Germanic tribes into a cohesive, if fragile, whole. He promoted the Church and spread Christianity, as well as encouraging art, learning and literacy. With just cause, Alcuin called him "the father of Europe."

Charlemagne's weakest asset, however, was his succession. Like the Merovingians before them, the Carolingians, even Charles, birthed inferior and squabbling siblings. Hoping to avoid problems, Charles crowned his only surviving son, Louis the Pious, as his co-emperor before his own death. But even then, the Franks were beginning to churn under the unity imposed upon them, and the more Charles stayed in Aachen, the more they seized local power. Louis, as his nickname implies, was not a warrior who could follow his father's military route to power; he spent his time building monasteries and abbeys. When Charles died in 814, Louis was unprepared to lead the whole empire. In 817, he made his oldest son, Lothair, co-ruler and co-heir of the imperial title but he also gave his two other sons, Louis the German and Charles the Bald, "sub-kingdoms" within the empire. The long nomadic tradition of brothers sharing the inheritance came back with a vengeance, and the three sons plotted against each other and their father. Louis died in 840 and the sons battled until 843. The Treaty of Verdun carved up the Kingdom of the Franks into three parts. Lothair got the imperial title and the Middle Kingdom, including northern Italy; Louis the German took the eastern section (most of present day Germany); and the youngest, Charles the Bald, received the western third (most of present day France). This treaty sym-

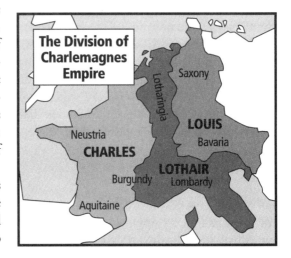

bolized changes in Europe since the old Roman days: it was written in Latin, French, and German, signaling the national and linguistic divisions of the Frank Kingdom as it split into the emerging areas of France and Germany. Lothair died in 855, and the treaty agreement fell apart. His middle kingdom (Lotharingia) was cut up by his less than grieving brothers. The area, partly the modern piece called Alsace Lorrainne, was fought over between France and Germany into the twentieth century.

The Carolingian dynasty ruled Germany until 911 and France until 987, but never again would it produce a great leader like Charlemagne. Names sometimes tell the story of a family, and it certainly does with the Carolingians: later French rulers were called Charles the Fat and Charles the Simple, while their German cousins had names like Louis the Child and Louis the Sluggard. Neither house was capable of controlling the local nobles no less the increasing invasions from other lands. As the Kingdom of the Franks fragmented from within, three outside groups hammered Western Europe from the North, the South and the East, again changing its face and format.

FROM THE NORTH, THE VIKINGS

As the Franks were building an empire that would soon fall apart, the people who had settled in the northern areas, which are now Norway, Sweden and Denmark, were beginning to expand from their frozen bases. Historians have called the three hundred years from 780 to 1070 the Viking Age or the Age of Viking Movement, as these peoples spread their ideas, culture, and terror onto the European mind. The Europeans saw little in the culture of these invaders, and for many years historians perceived them simply as barbaric terrorists who damaged the flow of European culture. Christian chroniclers saw them as priest-murderers and robbers and left no complimentary terms; the Vikings themselves left little written records of their culture and so they stand in history among the fiercest invaders who visited (and stayed) in Europe.

Who were the Vikings? They were the peoples (with emphasis on the "s") of Scandinavia who suffered through frozen winters, short summers (growing seasons), harsh land, and a minimum of sunlight. They had to be tough to survive the corner of the earth into which they had wandered (or were driven). Tribal kings became more general rulers, the King of the Swedes, the King of the Danes, the King of the Norsemen or Norwegians. Although they had embryonic ties that would some day become nation states, such as religion and language, these tribal groups were independent and roamed between the different peoples with little broader loyalties. The pressures of geography and climate made them eke out existences that made physical strength and aggressiveness the only key to survival. If they were farmers, they needed more land to get enough product to survive and trade; if they were traders, they needed to control the routes (land and sea) so that they could get the best bargains; if they were fishermen, they needed bravery and luck to survive the seas; if they were leaders, they needed to be the strongest, boldest, and probably the most bloodthirsty to stay in charge. Yet from early times there were art forms, literature, and "a softer side" that may not have balanced their personalities but certainly gave them a more human form.

As the land refused to support the growing population, the Vikings spread to the sea, building sleek, flat bottomed craft that toured them through the North Sea. They fished and brought their catch back to the shore. As they sought their prey, they encountered lands less formidable

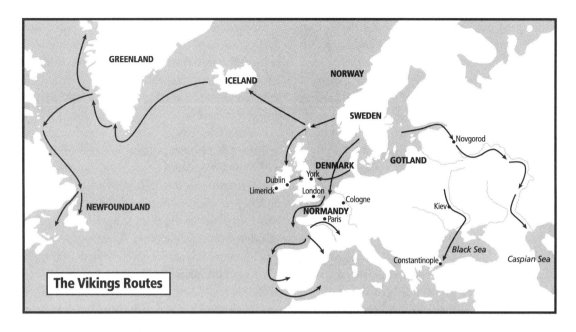

The Vikings Routes

than their own, and they began to raid these areas. The first contact with the Romans was in 5 A.D,, which resulted in some trade, beneficial to both sides. The Viking Runic alphabet has some similarity to the Latin and Greek alphabets. Some art historians see an influence of Roman styles on Scandinavian art. It is clear, however, that most of the attributes of the two cultures were very different from each other and that the nomadic styles of tribal life stayed longer in Scandinavia than on the continent. Thus the raid or trade motif continued among the Vikings after the Germanic barbarians had settled Western Europe.

Historians divide the time of Viking Raids into three periods. The first major attacks were definitely raids to gain wealth and prestige among other Vikings. Although there may have been some previous attacks, the earliest documented Viking raid was in 793 on the monastery at Lindisfarne, England. Here the monks were slaughtered by a small group of bandits who left nothing but the stones of the buildings and the

dead bodies of all the residents. This raiding terror lasted until about 840; it struck terror in all the coastal locations that heard of the horrible treatment of anyone who came in contact with the Vikings. Soon the British Isles and Ireland lived in fear of any Viking ship on the skyline. Charlemagne allegedly stood on the shores of his empire and wept as he saw Viking ships head for the English coast, aware of the impeding death and pillage that awaited the coastal towns and monasteries across the Channel. After Charlemagne's death, the Viking attacks spread to the coast of France. Frisia and Aquitane were targets by 839, and the island monastery of Noirmountier was a favorite spot for the invaders.

The second phase of Viking movement began in Ireland in the 840s when the raiders began to set up permanent bases. There is no evidence of settlement at the spot where Dublin stands, and so it appears the Vikings founded the great Irish city. In 843, some Vikings wintered in Aquitaine and set up a "base." In 844, a

The Vikings were raiders and explorers. Often in settling down, their culture disappeared into that of the surrounding society.

fleet of Viking ships attacked Nantes, Toulouse, Gijon, Lisbon, and Seville. Finally defeated, it returned to Aquitaine, but another fleet was launched and raided North Africa and Mediterranean coasts. Soon some raiders ventured inland, fighting on foot and on horses stolen from the locals. In 854, the Vikings burned the city of Hamburg, far inland.

Settlement and strongholds made the Vikings a different kind of threat. The brothers Olaf and Ivar built towns across Ireland in 853. Danish Vikings broadened their hold on the area into Britain where they dominated the peoples for two hundred years. This era became one of the most unsettled in British history with almost constant struggles for control between the various peoples who had come to settle there.

The Vikings' Early "Victims": the British Isles

The word "England" comes from the slurring of the Roman reference of the land where the Angles lived. The Romans abandoned their control of the island in 410. Twenty years later, groups of Germanic invaders swallowed up the land; the largest of the groups were the Angles and the Saxons. Jutes and many other groups also grabbed up lands once belonging to the Celtic Christian people. The Germanic tribes were pagans and were infamous for their barbarity and fierceness. The Roman reports are a bit ironic since they had hired Angles and Saxons to help them keep order on the frontiers with the Picts and Scots who lived to the north. Between 430 and 600, the Britons fought against the Angle and Saxon mercenaries now turned invaders.

From 430 to 500, the Britons were forced further and further inland by the continual assaults from the Germanic tribes. Around the year 500, the Britons won a now famous battle at Mount Baden, which temporarily halted their retreat. Their heroic leader, "Arthur of the Britons," also called "General Ambrosius

Aurelianus," has been enshrined in Western History as the Arthur of Camelot, the mythical perfect kingdom that goes astray over romance and misplaced love and falls to lesser men.

By 550, the Angles and Saxons resumed their conquests and by 600 the island was theirs. Thousands of native Britons were exterminated, while a few managed to flee to the "Celtic Fringe" areas of Wales, Cornwall, Ireland and Scotland. So complete was this eradication that only 14 Celtic words have survived in English (a few being: the, here, there, is, you, drink, work, dog, and laugh).

Warfare raged almost constantly among the newfound kingdoms. The larger ones swallowed up the weaker ones and borders shifted with almost every battle. By the end of the seventh century, seven kingdoms, known as the "Heptarchy," vied for dominance. The three Angle kingdoms were Northumbria and Mercia in the north and East Anglia (land of the Eastern Angles) along the mid-eastern coast. There were also three Saxon kingdoms: Wessex (land of the West Saxons), Essex (land of the East Saxons) and Sussex (land of the South Saxons). Kent was a kingdom set up by the Jutes along the Southeast coast.

The kingdoms were built on the pagan rituals of their Germanic forefathers. The legal system was based on oaths and trials by ordeal. Feasts were celebrated in timbered mead halls and hailed war victories, as well as hunting successes. Beer brewing and drinking were typical displays of manliness. Poetic tales praised heroes and the pagan gods, as well as encouraging bravery and adventure and loyalties to old traditions and leaders.

There were distinctions between the early Anglo-Saxon kingdoms in England and contemporary ones on the mainland. One difference was the distribution of lands. In Anglo-Saxon England, kingdoms were organized into *hundreds*, blocks of land of 50 to 100 square miles, and subdivided into *hides* of several acres. The hide usually consisted of a farm and the land needed to support a freeman and his family. (In England, a free farmer was called a "yeoman" while in France, he was a "peasant.")

Anglo-Saxon kings periodically held councils of noblemen, which were called the *Witan*. This body advised the king and usually chose or at least approved the successor when the king died. In the seventh and eighth centuries, the most powerful monarchs vied to be the *Bretwalda,* or over-king, of all the Anglo-Saxons. As this tradition emerged, Northumbria and Mercia frequently clashed to establish their monarch as the Bretwalda, but other kingdoms sometimes gained the title. In 1939, archeologists uncovered, at Sutton Hoo, a burial ship of the East Anglia King Raedwald, who died in the 620s. Raedwald was the fourth Bretwalda of Anglo-Saxon England, and the treasures of this burial ship revealed immense wealth and power. The items included an array of weapons, gold coins, and silver and bejeweled vessels from as far away as Constantinople. These discoveries increasingly prove that the early medieval world was more connected than previously thought.

The Anglo-Saxons and Christianity

The Britons had been converted to Christianity before the arrival of the Germanic tribes, but few were left to continue the traditions. Two missionary movements competed for the souls of the Anglo-Saxons, one from Ireland and one from Rome. During the fourth century, St. Patrick had established the Celtic Church in Ireland and from there it spread to the islands off the coast of Scotland. In 563, Saint Columba ("the Apostle of Scotland") founded a Celtic monastery on the island of Iona in the Inner Hebrides. Legend says that Columba settled there because it was the first piece of land from which he could not see Ireland; he had been banished during a trivial religious dispute.

Here he and his followers lived difficult lives but would brave the sea to preach to the Picts on the shoreline across from their retreat. Legend says that when they could not cross to the mainland because of bad weather, they stood on the shores and preached to the seals. One of his followers, St. Aiden, later established the monastery at Lindesfarne where the Vikings would find them in 793.

Celtic Christianity was not the "orthodox" line of the Roman Church so in 597 Pope Gregory the Great dispatched a band of about 40 Benedictine monks to Kent, England (land of the Jutes). Gregory supposedly organized the missionary effort after seeing some blond headed slaves in Rome; when he asked who these beautiful youths might be, he was told they were "Angles," but he declared that they must be "Angels" (*"non Angli, sed angeli"*) and was determined to Christianize their tribes.

The missionaries traveled north through France and heard horror tales about the English pagans—that their favorite meal was Christians! When they arrived in Kent, however, they were greeted by King Ethelbert whose wife was a Christian Frank. The monks were permitted to build a monastery at Canterbury ("fortress of the Kent men") and Ethelbert was baptized along with his nephew, the King of Essex. Once the kings converted, their thanes followed. Conversion to the Church brought immediate, tangible results to both sides. The Church provided kings with literate clerks, schools for the nobility, and connection to the Christianized lands and culture of the continent. The first written law codes (*dooms*) of Anglo-Saxon England, the

Dooms of Ethelbert, appeared after his conversion to Christianity. The first law, not surprisingly, protected the property of the Church. Augustine had led the monks to England, and the Pope rewarded him for this success by making him the first archbishop of England with his Holy See at Canterbury. After he died, he was canonized as St. Augustine of Canterbury and the cathedral that was eventually built around his tomb is still the center of the Church of England (although it is no longer part of the Roman Church).

The conversion of the southern part of the English island by the Roman Catholics slowly but inevitably came into contact with the efforts of the Celtic Church whose missionary work was growing in the north. Although technically a part of the Church of Rome, the Celtic Church operated with a great deal of autonomy and independence. The Celtic Church began and spread to areas outside the old Roman Empire and therefore was not under the Roman system of bishoprics, parishes and dioceses, nor was the bishopric its primary unit of administration. The Celtic Church was centered on monasteries, whose abbots held a higher position than their Catholic counterparts. The Celtic cross and tonsure (haircut of the monks) also differed. The arms of the Roman cross were of uniform width whereas the arms of the Celtic cross widened outward at the ends. Benedictine monks shaved a circle in the top of their heads to imitate Christ's crown of thorns, whereas the Celtic monk shaved bare the front half of the head. Of more serious consequence were their divergent calendars, which meant that the two churches celebrated Christmas, Easter and the Feast Days at different times. Although many doctrinal issues were agreed upon, these different practices were fiercely defended. Of great concern to the Church of Rome, Celtic missionaries were also preaching in northwestern Europe, and the potential existed for the rise of two rival branches of Christianity.

Fortunately for the Church of Rome, a climax and resolution occurred at the Whitby Council of 663, called by King Oswy of Northumbria. Complaining that his Roman Catholic wife observed the Lenten fast while he feasted and celebrated the Celtic Easter, Oswy summoned the spokesmen of each side to Whitby to debate which church should prevail. Celtic monk Coleman urged loyalty to the ways of St. Patrick and St. Columba, whereas Roman Catholic Wilfred countered that the Church of Rome was the true follower of St. Peter, whom Jesus had appointed to hold the keys to the kingdom (the gate to Heaven). With the fear of damnation standing before them, Oswy convinced the nobles to accept the arguments of Wilfred, and the Church of Rome won a crucial victory. As the parish system spread across the seven kingdoms, all Christians claimed to recognize the oneness of the Church, and the Archbishop of Canterbury became the leader of the English Church.

The Northumbrian Renaissance

Following the Whitby Council, Benedictine monks built dozens of monasteries and abbeys in northern England, especially in Northumbria. In the eighth and ninth centuries these new communities became vital and active centers of learning and culture, creating the so-called "Northumbrian Renaissance." Northumbrian monasteries and schools attracted the brightest and best scholars of the day, sent and received monks from throughout Europe, and produced magnificent art, architecture, literature, and illuminated manuscripts. Alcuin of York, the director of Charlemagne's school at Aachen, was

one notable scholar of this era, as well as his English predecessor in France, Boniface of Crediton.

The greatest scholar, teacher and author of the period was a humble monk with the revered name, the "Venerable" Bede (c.673-735). At Jarrow Abbey, in about 731, Bede completed the *Ecclesiastical History of the English Church and Peoples* (one Church, many peoples). This invaluable source of English history argued that the Church was a great civilizing force and stressed the theme of English unity. Bede also popularized the B.C./A.D. dating method that the Roman Church set up in the reign of Gregory the Great.

Another famous literary work was the famous *Beowulf*. Although the oldest manuscript is a tenth century Wessex copy, evidence connects the epic poem to the Northumbrian Renaissance. This 3,000 line poem recorded an old, oral story set in the marshes of Denmark. Combining elements of early Germanic pagan with later Christian ideas, the poem vividly told how the monster Grendel preyed upon drunken revelers in the Mead Hall of the king until it was slain by a valiant hero, Beowulf. The poem's themes of the transience of life, the importance of courage and loyalty, and the dignity in defeat are universal themes that continue through literature even today.

The Danish Vikings in England: The Danelaw, 865-954

By the middle of the ninth century, inroads and settlements of the Vikings began to have an effect on the Anglo-Saxon population. *Beowulf*, like many of the original Angels and Saxons, came to England from the continent, more particularly, Denmark. At the end of the eighth century, a new group of Danes appeared off the coasts of England, the Danish Vikings. In 789, the *Anglo-Saxon Chronicles* tells that three long ships landed on the coast of Wessex. The local "reeve" rode out to see what business these supposed traders wanted and was immediately killed. The nearby town was pillaged. Next the slaughter of Lindesfarne made it clear to all the residents that there was no safe place along the coast. The monasteries of Jarrow and Iona were next. The cry went out "Lord, save us from the fury of the Norsemen!"

In 865, a "Great Army" of Vikings, led by Halfdan and Ivar the Boneless, landed in East Anglia and these invaders came to stay. They easily took East Anglia and marched on to Northumbria, captured York and then went back to East Anglia to ritually murder the king (Edward the Martyr). By 870, the northern Anglo

England, c. 885

Saxon kingdoms simply ceased to exist and the land and people came under Viking control. Instead of the traditional government that the Anglo-Saxons had set up, the area now was subjected to *Danelaw* or literally Danish Law. The defeated English had to pay tribute, *Danegelt,* to their conquerors. Only Wessex in the south precariously preserved its independence and possessed the leadership and spirit to fight back. It was during this period that the only English king to earn the title "the Great" proved his leadership abilities.

ALFRED THE GREAT AND THE CREATION OF ENGLAND

In the turmoil of invasions, succession struggles and competing institutions, the rise of a strong leader is essential to the solution of constant crisis. Heroes like Charlemagne and his English counterpart, Alfred the Great, are part of the Western Tradition.

Alfred was born around 849, second son to King Ethelwulf. When the Danish army first invaded the kingdom of Wessex in 871, his brother, King Ethelred, struggled to hold the Viking force from taking over his kingdom. Alfred was only 23 years old when Ethelred died, and the Witan called him to assume the leadership of his people. He had been Ethelred's chief military leader, second in command of the Wessex *fryd* or army. At first he was successful in defeating the Vikings, but a second encounter was not so lucky for young Alfred. As King, he bought a fragile peace with the Danes, but in 878 the fears of renewed Danish attacks were realized.

After Alfred had paid the Vikings to leave Wessex alone, the Danes split their armies into two groups. Halfdan took his group north and divided up Northumbria among his band. They called for their families in Denmark who came, settled down to farming and collected their Danegeld shares. Later church chroniclers condemned the pagans and said that God punished Halfdan with insanity and an odor unendurable to his men. No other records tell this story.

In the south, closer to Alfred's territory, the other half of the Great Dane army was determined to capture Wessex and finish off the Anglo-Saxons. Led by King Guthrum (Ivan the Boneless's successor), the Vikings launched a swift and merciless attack in January 878. This winter attack completely surprised Alfred, and his army was totally unprepared. The Vikings roamed the area at will, raping, pillaging and burning whatever got in their way. The remnants of Alfred's army scattered and Alfred ran, hiding in the marshes of Somerset. It is here that the famous legend is told about Alfred.

Supposedly the beaten and depressed Alfred showed up at a cottage in the marsh. Here the humble woman of the house welcomed him although she did not recognize the king. One day she had to leave the house to tell her husband some news. Alfred sat on the hearth, lamenting his miserable fate. When the woman returned, she screamed at him: Ca'sn thee mind the ka-aks, man, an' doosen zee 'em burn? I'm boun thee's eat 'em vast enough, az zoon as 'tis the turn. Alfred realized that this was the bottom of the pit he had put himself in: he could not even help an illiterate, impoverished woman. The legend says that after this, Alfred awoke from his cowardly slumber and went back to calling his men to defeat the invaders.

By the Easter season, Alfred's men had built a small fort on the Isle of Athelney and began raiding Viking camps. Another legend about Alfred has him disguised as a minstrel in a Viking village where he gathered vital information about their strength and plans. The *Anglo-Saxon Chronicles* report that seven weeks after Easter,

Alfred the Great
Winchester, England

Alfred's army was organized enough to attack the Viking army at Edington. Alfred's contemporary biography, Asser of St. David, writes that both sides formed tight shield walls. After several clashes, the Viking ranks broke amidst great slaughter, and Alfred's thanes pursued the fleeing Danes to their stronghold. Alfred's victory at Edington in 878 was so complete that King Guthrum agreed to submit to any terms and to hand over for execution as many men as Alfred demanded. Alfred, realizing the victory was complete, exercised kindness to his enemies. He invited Guthrum and his top thirty chieftains to his camp for twelve days of hospitality and amid the gifts and feasting, Alfred persuaded Guthrum to be baptized as his godson. The Treaty of Wedmore of 878 once again temporarily ended the hostilities. Guthrum's conversion from paganism represented the first important Viking king to become a Christian, along with many of his followers.

Alfred, however, was not to be fooled again by the Viking show of compliance. He began building forts all across the area and stocked them with thanes loyal to him. He built a fleet of ships to protect the coasts. These were modeled after the Viking long boats but held twice as many men as the Scandinavian boats. He made a decision to send half the army home while the other half would remain near him and under his command. He established a system wherein every six months, the active members of the army would return home and the other "half" would leave their farms and join the defense of Alfred's domains. He also used the army to build *burgs*, wood and earth barricades, which became forts; these were so common that they were never more than 20 miles from each other (many English towns got their name from being in the place where a "burg" was built).

Alfred's predictions were right. Viking raids continued until 886 when Alfred's men took London and forced Guthrum to accept a new boundary for the Danelaw. Alfred and Guthrum agreed to cut England in two, from the English Channel to the Irish Sea. The new border reduced the Danelaw to territory north of London and liberated a large part of old Mercia from the Vikings. From this point onward, the Danelaw steadily shrank in size and power. Alfred married one of his daughters to a Viking lord from East Anglia; he himself married a

woman from Mercia; and he married other daughters to make alliances around the English island.

To build further unity but maintain control, Alfred divided his nobles into three equal groups and, copying the practice of the Old Testament's King Solomon, required each to reside at court for a month, on a rotating basis. He encouraged the nobles to keep a fighting force ready for deployment at almost a moment's notice, and a group of "professional" soldiers slowly evolved. With these measures bringing more unity to England, some historians have called Alfred the "Charlemagne" of England. He is credited with being the father of the English army, navy, monarchy, and even of England itself. He is, however, mostly remembered for stopping the Viking conquest and setting the stage for a unified England under its own laws, rejecting the Danelaw of the conquerors.

Alfred's legacy was more than military victory over the Vikings. The invaders had left a land weakened by attacks and fearful of the future. Little effort was made to preserve traditions and the history of the peoples of England. Alfred rebuilt the monasteries and abbeys that the Vikings had destroyed. Here, like Charlemagne, he added schools and recruited renowned scholars. Unlike Charlemagne, he himself was a learned contributor to this revival of knowledge; he wrote books and composed works in history, theology, and geography. His biographer, Asser of St. David, said that Alfred was fluent in Latin and English. Alfred, in an effort to make his nobility more literate, had many works translated from Latin to English, including Bede's *Church History of the English Peoples* and Pope Gregory's *Pastoral Care*. This emphasis on learning and literature certainly contributed to the compilation of the *Anglo-Saxon Chronicles*. The *Chronicle* was an historical almanac that started with the year 1 A.D. and originally ended in 892 A.D. Copies were sent to several monasteries and schools where yearly entries were continued until 1154. It continues to be an essential source of information about Anglo-Saxon England.

Alfred set the stage for the formative period of national kingship. He was the first king known to use the term *Angelcynn*, meaning "land of the English folk." He also began coinage that included an impression of him with the title "King of England." Finally the royal family of Wessex became the first dynasty of England, making Alfred the father of the English monarchy. His grandson, Athelstan (reigned 895-939), was the king of a united English kingdom. Every English monarch since Alfred has claimed, many with very weak evidence, to be descendents of Alfred.

Alfred again symbolizes the bond between Church and State. He was a devoted ruler and a dedicated Christian. To keep a balance in his duties to his people and to his God, he had a system in which he would set up special candles. When one candle burned down, he switched from worldly affairs to spiritual devotions. When the next candle burned down, he switched again.

Whereas Charlemagne's rule disintegrated with his death, Alfred's success in bringing unity to the peoples of England has endured. Slowly the Anglo-Saxon and Viking traditions blended into the English nation. The Danelaw decreased significantly under the efforts of Alfred's son, King Edward (reigned 871-924). Edward's son, Athelstan (reigned 895-954), captured York and within 15 years, the Danelaw ceased to exist in England.

Although there was a long trail of terror and destruction, there were benefits from the Vikings' time in England. They stimulated shipbuilding, trade, and town life. Thousands of Viking families, full of energy and resourcefulness, settled down to farming, craft making, and intermarriage among the English. There are over 900 Viking words in the English language—not only the "sk" words like "ski, sky, skill, skin, skirt, etc." but we use the Viking vocabulary today when we say "die, ill, law, egg, bread, want, wrong," and scores of other everyday words.

THE VIKINGS AND THE REST OF EUROPE

The Vikings made their mark on the continent of Europe, as well as England. Significant attacks began around 834, while Charlemagne's weak descendants sat on the French throne. Here, Vikings under the leadership of Ragnan took Paris and retreated only after demanding and receiving 7000 pounds sterling from Charles the Bald. Soon, Viking settlements spotted the French countryside. By 885 and into 886, the Vikings tried to take Paris again, but the French were stubborn. The attacks increased and finally, in 886, Charles the Fat paid the raiders another ransom to stop attacking and leave Paris alone. By 892, the French were organized enough to counterattack the Viking raids. Charles the Simple, king of the West Franks, ended the Viking raids in 911 by giving Normandy to the Vikings. In return, the Viking leader, Rollo, pledged his allegiance to the French crown. He was baptized and defended these lands against other Viking raiders. About 150 years later, descendents of the Normans crossed the sound and took over England when William the Conqueror became King of England.

In Muslim Spain, the Vikings began attacking in 814. They were quickly sent back to sea. There was no putting them off, however, and they soon returned to attack areas along the Iberian Coast and the Mediterranean Sea. The

Muslims were better equipped to defeat these incursions but that did not stop the Vikings from trying to pillage and steal the wealth of the Muslim state.

Viking adventures into Central Europe were more trade related. Here Swedish Vikings established trade routes along the Great Russian rivers, such as the Volga and Dnieper. In some of the major Russian cities, they met the Slavic peoples living there. Historical sources are confusing, but many historians believe that a tribal people called the Rus who had Scandinavian origins founded the territory that became "Russia." The story goes that three Rus brothers were invited (it is not clear by whom) to settle in Central Europe: Rurik settled in Novgorod; and the other two, Sineus and Truvor, settled in Beloozero and Izvborsk. The beginnings of Russian history are in the Kievan area, and it is clear that the first ruling group were of Viking origins. Later Slavic rulers of the area gained legitimacy by marrying Viking mates.

THE SPANISH BORDER WITH THE MUSLIMS

In the fifth century A.D. the Visigoths took the area now called Spain out of the control of the Roman Empire. They settled into farming communities and were not really disturbed until 711 when the Muslim forces crossed onto the European continent by way of the Straits of Gibraltar. The invaders took the area, called Andalusia, and built some of the most beautiful cities that Europe had seen. It was through the Muslim devotion to study, science, and technology that this became a golden age. Cordoba, closest to the Franks, became a central area of learning and architecture. The Great Mosque of Cordoba was begun under Abd-ar-Rahmann in 787. Its long columns of rounded arches built a huge build-

ing, more glorious than any seen in the lands of the Franks. The Alhambra in Granada was built as a citadel and royal palace. These two structures still amaze tourists and city dwellers even today. Muslim Spanish cities, centers of trade, learning and culture, made Paris and London look like outposts on a frontier.

Charlemagne and his descendants made forays into Spain but never could control or drive out the Muslims. It was not until the thirteenth century that the Kings of Castile finally drove the Muslims back toward Northern Africa and not until 1492 that the alliance of Ferdinand and Isabella succeeded in taking Granada for their new kingdom of Spain.

The Muslim forces in Spain, however, moved East and periodically attacked the Mediterranean areas. The Southern coast of France was an easy target, and they invaded Sicily in 827. The island became a springboard to Italy. They forced the evacuation of the Benedictine monastery at Monte Casino. In 846, the Muslims arrived at the mouth of the Tiber River and crushed any resistance in Ostia and Portus. Then they headed for Rome. The only thing that saved central Rome was the old wall and the fact that the Muslims pillaged St. Peters' and St. Paul's from which they carried away some 3 tons of gold and silver. They sacked the outskirts of Rome with such ferocity that the Pope had to take refuge in a fortress converted from Hadrian's tomb. Finally Duke Sergius of Naples defeated the Muslims at sea. The Romans were still afraid, and from 847 to 848, they build the Leonine Wall to protect themselves from future raids.

THE HOLY ROMAN EMPIRE

In Central Europe, where the Germanic tribes originated, the tribal way of life struggled to maintain its traditions but slowly influences from

Small, Roman Post, Sorrento, Italy

the West and the need to centralize power came to the region. Otto I became Duke of Saxony in 936 and began to build his power base. Like the Western kings, most of his success was centered in military victories. He was opposed by his half-brother, his younger brother, and even some of his sons who demanded a share of the power in the nomadic tradition, but Otto prevailed by defeating them in a series of wars called the Ducal Rebellions. By 941 he had replaced the rebels with loyal relatives and supporters. He set up a Church-State alliance, granting large amounts of land to church officials. Otto also boosted his own image across Europe by marrying Edith, daughter of Athelstan, King of England.

The Church in Central Europe became increasingly dependent on Otto's good will and support; Otto appointed many of its officials to direct the Church. In 962, Pope John XII crowned him Roman Emperor, but soon the Pope realized that Otto had too much power over the Church. In the conflict that followed, Otto deposed the Pope and appointed his own "man" to the Holy See, Leo VIII. He then issued the *Privilegium Ottonianum,* which stated that no Pope could be elected without the emperor's approval. This began a period in which the Papacy was controlled by the German states.

Otto used the model Charlemagne had imposed on the area, with representatives of the crown keeping check on the local areas but making sure they were loyal to him. The struggle against his enemies was a sort of cultural clash; he represented the move toward the monarchic principle while they held tightly to the old ideas of tribal rule. Otto won and was later called Otto the Great, first Holy Roman Emperor.

The biggest challenge to Otto's control after he defeated the dukes was the arrival of the last of the plains nomads, the Magyars. This group was a mixture of many tribes from the central Asian plains. Although they are related to the Finno-Ugric language groups, they also had connections to Turkic influences. After roaming the plains for generations, they had blended these influences into a unique culture, which they fiercely defended.

The Magyars followed the path of other nomadic raiders from the Central Asian plains such as the Huns (who are mistakenly called their ancestors, thus the name Hungary), the Ostrogoths (more Germanic than the Magyars), and the Avars, the tribal group that plundered South Russia and the Balkans in the late sixth century. They arrived in the Carpathian Basin about 895 led by Arpad who had been elected chief by the seven tribes. Even today, this historic movement is celebrated in Budapest with a huge statue of the seven tribal leaders led by Arpad into this new and fertile land.

Setting up their base, the Magyars began raids into the old Roman areas of Pannonia and Dacia. Pushing on these borders aroused fear among the peoples of central Europe and the cry went up "From the arrows of the Hungarians, save us, Lord." These land warriors were as fierce and bloodthirsty as the sea people, the Vikings. In 954, they entered the lands of Otto the Great. Only a year later, however, Otto brought his warriors to a battleground near present day Augsburg, Germany. The collision was called the "Battle of Lechfeld" and was so bloody that the banks of the river Lech were called the "Field of Corpses." The defeated Magyars began to cooperate with the powers surrounding them, Otto to the north and west, the Byzantine Empire to the south.

The handwriting on the wall, the Magyars also began to consolidate their political structure. Duke Geza was the first ruler to take firm

St. Stephen, Budapest, Hungary

control of the seven tribes, and when he died in 997, his son Vajk became the King of the Hungarians. He married Gisella, a niece of Otto the Great, and converted to Christianity in 1000 A.D. (changing his name to Stephen after the first Christian martyr). A year later, the Pope recognized Hungary as a Christian kingdom. The Magyars settled down to farming and a period of stability followed.

WOMEN AND FAMILY IN THE EARLY MIDDLE AGES

Medieval Europe was a culture dominated by men. Men were the rulers, the soldiers, and the religious leaders and had the law behind them to rule over every level of women in society. Here and there a few women managed to burst the strict framework of their traditional roles, but on the whole, women were lesser citizens who had to obey, not lead. Men ruled, fought, and determined all the important decisions of the family, tribe, village, or kingdom. There were, however, areas in which women played important roles even if they were under-appreciated.

The cultural systems confirmed the superiority of men. Early medieval society was family oriented, and marriage was the keystone that held it together. There was no sense of romantic love in the choice for mates. To some degree, neither sex had much choice because marriages were alliances and economic unions. Even in the lower classes, men and women married for materialistic reasons: power, land, money, etc. Women had probably less choice then men. Older men in the family, fathers, uncles, older brothers and even nobles with no blood relation, picked out a partner and arranged the marriage. Prospective husbands paid a dowry or bride-price to the bride's family, symbolizing ownership of the woman had passed from one family to another. There were some differences in customs: Roman husbands tended to be older by ten or more years while Germanic couples tended to be closer in age. Of course, the primary emphasis was fertility, but there was also the expectation that the bride would be a virgin. Many children were necessary as infant mortality was high; many women died in childbirth. Unmarried men could join the church or become soldiers, but a single woman was a threat to the social order. Every attempt to marry daughters and widows had to be made.

Marriage was confirmed when it was consummated. In this tradition, the couple were often placed in a bed during the marriage ceremony and made to achieve a physical union.

Fidelity of the bride was essential as only way the parents of a child could be certified. Children needed a father to support and provide for them and illegitimate children, although not rare, were a problem for society. The integrity of the family lineage was important, especially when it came to family inheritance of property and titles. Adultery by the wife was one of the greatest sins, and she could be punished by death, often times in a painful manner. Men, however, were not so punished, and high-ranking Frank men sometimes had several wives, as well as concubines. Charlemagne himself had four wives and six concubines so the rules did not apply to all. If a man were unhappy with his bride for any reason, he could return her, with her dowry, to her family, which was a great disgrace to the woman's future hopes of marriage. Women did not have the same kind of choice and even when she asked for a divorce because of brutal treatment, she was often ignored.

Women were expected to have as many children as possible, even at the risk of their own health and lives. Some women had more than 15 pregnancies, which included stillbirths and miscarriages. Charlemagne's second wife, Hildegaard, bore him nine children in twelve years of marriage, and he wed twice after her death, producing even more children. The importance of motherhood and of women of childbearing age was made clear by the high wergeld they commanded. Wergeld, the compensation owed for unlawful death or injury, was much higher for a woman of childbearing age than for a man of the same age or social group. In all other age groups, the wergeld was much higher for a man than a woman. Invaders to Western groups knew that men prized their child bearing women, and so Vikings and Magyars sought them as war captives. These poor women were not only subjected to the whims and lusts of their captors but they were often sold as slaves to others for more abuse.

Women were expected to be the primary care givers to children (as well as to their husbands). All but the highest of the noble class were expected to contribute to the survival of the family. They helped farm and tend flocks, spun thread, and made clothes. Noblewomen often managed accounts, supervised servants, and ran the households, especially when guests were present. Anglo-Saxon noblewomen gained some legal status and property rights but were still subordinate to their husbands as long as he was alive. While husbands were away on business or at battles, women ran the household and were "masters" of the house; but as soon as the husband returned, she had to return the power to him. If he died, society made certain that she remarried as soon as possible and her new husband took over. As a rule, women worked harder, suffered more, and died younger then the men of society.

Although some Roman women had become prominent, Salic (Germanic) Law did not allow women to be political or military leaders. This old Germanic law was so pervasive that for centuries very few women in Western Europe rose to positions of leadership and authority. (There was no bona fide Queen of the Germanic peoples on the continent until Maria Theresa in 1740—1000 years after the period we are discussing—and she had to fight the War of Austrian Succession to become recognized as a legitimate monarch. England's first ruling Queen, Mary I, ascended the throne in 1553, but her father had been so unsure that Tudor rule would survive with no son, that he broke with the Roman Church to wed another woman (who in turn only produced a princess) and then four other wives to sire an heir.) As late as 1431, the old edicts remained, and Joan of Arc was burned at the stake for leading French men into battle; the charge was not treason or being captured by the enemy, it was heresy.

There were, however, a few women who did slip through the boundaries of sexual roles. Ethelflaed, the daughter of King Alfred the Great, rose above the prevailing circumstances to become a respected leader. She married, through her father's arrangement, Ethelred, the Lord of Mercia, to secure an ally against the Danes. As the Lady of Mercia, she co-ruled with her husband until his death in 911. She governed in her own right for the rest of her life. With her brother, Edward King of Wessex, she participated as an equal partner in battles against the Vikings, personally leading military expeditions. She also helped supervise the construction of burgs. When she died in 918, Mercia united under Wessex, helping to create the emerging English state.

Even in Viking society, a few very exceptional women came to the forefront. Political connections and personality probably played a major role in these exceptions. For instance, Freydis, the daughter of Eric the Red, accompanied her brother, Leif Ericson, on his expeditions to Newfoundland and Labrador in the early eleventh century. When their father died in about 1000 A.D., Leif Ericson had to return to Greenland to rule the Viking colony there. Freydis, in partnership with her other brother, Thorvald, led the Vikings in the New World until they departed in 1024.

Women and the Church

For women, Christianity was a double-edged sword. There is Mary, the mother of Jesus, the kindly sainted woman who submits to the will of God to be honored forever. But there is also Eve, the woman who caused the first sin and because of whom all humankind is damned. The Church "Fathers" made it clear that women tended to be more like Eve than Mary. In the second century, Tertullian wrote to women saying: "YOU are the Devil's gateway. YOU are the first deserter of the divine Law...YOU destroyed so easily God's image, man. On account of YOUR desert, that is death, even the Son of God had to die." St. Augustine said that Eve's sin had created the sexual desire and caste God's original creation into chaos.

A woman had to submit and surrender to be a good, humble Christian servant; little could be said of any assertive woman and any who dared usually became the subject of suspicion long before the famous period of witchcraft trials. It has already been noted that women suspected of adultery were subjected to more punishment than a man was, and that single women were not acceptable members of society. For women who did not wish to marry or were widowed, difficult choices lay ahead.

The clergy had long been an acceptable role for men who did not wish the traditional life of family and was particularly attractive to sons who had little to inherit for the pathway to power could be through the Church. A comparable role for women was not available. On the continent, women did find a place at monasteries because the monks enjoyed having meals made, laundry done, and other "household" chores performed; this service fell to women. Unique to England were the "double monasteries," which housed communities of monks and "nuns" side by side, with the women under the authority of another woman, an abbess (comparable to the male role of abbot). St Hilda (614-680) was a Northumbrian princess who founded Whitby Abbey, England's most famous double abbey. St. Hilda's reputation for wisdom and piety attracted scores of pilgrims and scholars, and Whitby be-

came the center of education for many English bishops. The famous Whitby Council of 663, which settled differences between the Celtic and Roman Churches was held here, probably with St. Hilda's impressive intervention. The abbey also recorded many land donations from women who had been left inheritances from fathers and husbands and showed their devotion to the Church by gifting the abbey with land.

One could make the case that the Church also influenced the lives of women by opposing many of the old pagan practices such as divorce, incest, polygamy, concubinage and maiden burial sacrifice. The image of Eve, however, was never wiped away and was used to make sure that women knew their place in society. Women were feared as seducers of men and had to be kept safe from their own evil personalities. There were severe controls on the notions of sexual conduct. Monogamy was important to the Church and society so that children had a support (meaning financial, not mental) system. Women were often seen as the means to make contracts between men; marriage was never considered a romantic arrangement and if the two parties liked each other, that was simply a bonus.

Since women were seen as child bearers, they were to be virgins and sex was for procreation, not pleasure. The Church denounced any means of birth control, even if the woman's life were in danger. Women had some knowledge of methods to control pregnancy (warm baths, herbal concoctions, and physical exertion after intercourse) but all of these were considered sinful. The Church also claimed that the only acceptable method of conception was the "missionary position," which was so-called because missionaries among the heathen had claimed this was the "blameless path" because animals could not practice it. The Church also denounced as sinful any other methods of contact, as well as foreplay, contact in the daytime, seeing your mate unclothed on Sundays, holidays or during a woman's menstrual days or pregnancy. These restrictions lasted much longer than the Middle Ages.

CONCLUSIONS

The Early Middle Ages was a period of great turmoil, transition, and the triumph of a new blend of influences that brought about great changes in the Western mind and format of society. In every area of Europe invasions as well as internal competitions began the development of national identities, the basis of the later nation states.

Perhaps one of the most important hallmarks of this period was the rise of secular kingship as exemplified by Charlemagne, Alfred, and Otto. Military might was certainly the key to political success, and the period saw the beginnings of feudalism as the military and political organization of Western Europe. Attacks from beyond Europe's borders from the Vikings, the Muslims, and the Magyars left the peoples of Europe dependent on military leaders who could protect them. Secular leadership was military success.

In the middle of the tenth century, a Persian Poet, Abu Mansur Daqiqi, wrote about the requirements for kingship:

There are two things with which men gain a kingdom,
One steel blue and one of saffron color.
One is gold, stamped with the king's name,
The other iron, tempered in the Yemen.
Whoever aspires to kingship
Must have the urge of Heaven,
An eloquent tongue, a liberal hand,
A heart both vengeful and loving.
For kingship is a quarry that cannot be caught
By a soaring eagle or raging lion.
Only two things can make it captive—
A well-forged blade, and mined and minted gold.
Seize it with the sword,
Chain it, if you can, with gold coins.
Whoever has sword, money and luck
Needs neither lofty stature nor royal pedigree,
But only wisdom, munificence and courage
For Heaven to grant him the gift of sovereignty.

In France, the Merovingians degenerated into a weak and useless dynasty while the successors of Charles Martel and Pepin III built on their military success and union with the Roman Church to form a new and dynamic reign under Charlemagne. Charles became great by continuing the tradition of his grandfather and father, storming across Europe with iron and steel. In one description of a siege, Charles' enemy, the King of the Lombards, said that his people had no hope as their city was surround by a wall of iron, with Charlemagne holding the largest iron sword and lance, and all his soldiers dressed in iron to protect them. He claimed that the city fell into terror for the sun set the plains ablaze with the brilliance of the iron weapons. But Charlemagne was more than a warrior. He set up schools and gave away books. He had ancient texts translated, and he converted his captives (although many not willingly) to Christianity. He coined money with his image on it. Although the Carolingians did not succeed in keeping the empire together, they provided monarchs for France and Germany far into the tenth century.

In England, religious settlement (between Celtic and Roman Churches) and the Viking menace propelled Alfred the Great to unifying the Anglo-Saxons into a single kingdom, a task finalized by his heirs in the tenth century. Alfred, too, was a great warrior who had to summon his own courage from the depths of his defeats and depression. He built his success on military strategy. When he defeated the Vikings, he set up a defense system that would keep his victories safe from new attacks. Alfred was also a scholar who sought to develop the English culture and intellectual life. The ingredients of the English traditions came from many sources: Germanic tribes, Vikings, and even some remnants of the original Celtic peoples.

In central Europe, Otto the Great transformed the tribal units into a monarchical system that even held sway over the powerful church in Rome. Finally, Otto I became Holy Roman Emperor through his military victories but he showed benevolence to his victims and, although he did not trust them, led them to settle down and lose some of their barbaric ways. Otto's son followed him, and the line lasted into the next century. The grandiose scheme fell into smaller pieces when the personality and military might of future emperors could not control the local forces, and later wars would continue to boil the mixtures of peoples in central Europe.

Kingship in the early Middle Ages took on a holy aura and began to bring together the areas of Europe into blocks of power. The King was the apex of secular society as the Pope had become the keystone of the spiritual part of Western civilization. The unity of the two became the trademark of Western society. The masses saw that safety in this world depended on a strong military figure who could fight off invaders, enemies, and even bandits. On the other hand, the most important theme for the short lived, poverty stricken peoples, was the Church who held the keys to the Kingdom.

With life short and unpredictable, the Roman Church's message was that this world was a preparation for the next. Suffering on earth would make for a more glorious life in heaven. Not many of the inhabitants of Medieval Europe would trade a moment of earthly glory for an eternity of damnation so the Church tended to dominate. From local priest to Pope, respect and power was commanded from serf to king, and was most often given. Clergy were among the few literate members of society and advised kings, kept the records, preserved the art (and decided its subjects and style), and encouraged the learning that would justify their lofty positions. It was the unifying bond of society and in order to join "Western civilization," one had to be a Roman Catholic.

Charlemagne, Alfred, and Otto were well aware of this loyalty and used it to build their own sources of power. The alliance between Cross and Sword was not always balanced, but it would survive through the period of the Crusades, into the thirteenth century and be finally split with the voices of the Reformation. Meanwhile, the system called feudalism called upon both secular and religious leaders to work together to make Europe a bit more united than the period of "Europe under Attack."

Suggestions for Further Reading

Peter H. Blair, *Roman Britain and Early England, 55 BC-AD 871* (1963).

Peter Brown, *The World of Late Antiquity AD 150-750* (1971).

Rosamond McKitterick, *The Early Middle Ages: Europe 400-1000* (2001).

Glyn Burgess, translator, Song *of Roland,* (1990).

Thomas Cahill, *How the Irish Saved Civilization* (1955).

Einhard (Samuel Turner, translator), *Life or Charlemagne* (1960).

Pierre Riche, (Jo Ann McNamara, translator), *Daily Life in the World of Charlemagne* (1988).

Lewis Thorpe, *Two Lives of Charlemagne* (1969).

Gwyn Jones, *A History of the Vikings* (1984).

Horik Svensson, *The Runes* (1995).

Marshall Poe, *The Russian Moment in World History* (2003).

Simon Keynes and Michael Lapidge, translators, *Alfred the Great: Asser's Life of Alfred the Great and other Contemporary Sources* (1983).

Robert McCrum, William Cran, and Robert MacNeil, *The Story of the English* (1987).

Joel Thomas Rosenthal, *Angles, Angels and Conquerors, 400-1154* (1973).

Michael Swanton, translator and editor, *The Anglo Saxon Chronicle* (1996).

Eileen Power, *Medieval Women* (1997)

Pauline Stafford, *Queens, Concubines and Dowages: The King's Wife in the Early Middle Ages* (1983).

Ernst Kantorowicz, *The King's Two Bodies: A Study in Medieval Political Theology* (William Chester Jordan, editor; reprint, 1997).

Chapter 8

FEUDAL EUROPE, 1000-1215

Norman mounted knights charge Harold's troops in the Battle of Hastings.

Pierre Clergue, The Priest of Montaillou

Records abound of the activities of popes, cardinals, and bishops during the Middle Ages, but there is a dearth of information about the most important cleric of the period: the local parish priest. Occasionally, documentation emerges about such individuals. Such is the case for Pierre Clergue, parish priest of the remote mountainside village of Montaillou in southern France, not far from the Spanish border. In the early fourteenth century, Montaillou had a population of about 200-250 souls, ministered by a single priest. It was not a typical village nor was Pierre a typical priest. Montaillou was poor, backward, and a hotbed of support for the Albigensians. Indeed, it was one of the last bastions in France to cling to the ascribed heresy—not because its inhabitants were zealous followers of the movement but because their community was so isolated and unimportant that it was easily ignored.

Not until the early fourteenth century did Montaillou get the Inquisition's attention. Between 1318 and 1325 Jacques Fournier, bishop of Pamiers, (later the Avignonese pope Benedict XII), conducted a thorough and meticulously recorded inquest to identify and punish Albigensians in his diocese, and his documentation included many detailed interviews with the peasant inhabitants of Montaillou. From these interviews, the modern French historian, Emmanuel Le Roy Ladurie created a pioneering work of social history, **Montaillou: The Promised Land of Error,** *which has been widely praised and widely criticized—the appropriate makings of an interesting book. Ladurie provides, among other things, a vivid portrait of the priest Pierre Clergue.*

Father Pierre was of peasant heritage, but his family was the most powerful and prosperous household in Montaillou. His brother, Bernarrd, was the bayle, or the village's chief secular official. Pierre was literate, articulate, assertive, and, above all, most charming and persuasive. He seems to have performed his priestly duties most conscientiously, saying Mass on Sundays and holy days, hearing confessions regularly, attending diocesan meetings, and collecting tithes. Like the majority of his flock, Clergue was neither a rabid Albigensian nor a fanatical Catholic—he like his parishioners was somewhere in the middle. He was rather fluid in his religious convictions, moving without much strain of conscience between orthodoxy and heresy. Sometimes, he would behave as an Albigensian missionary, reading heretical doctrines to his people. On other occasions he would intimidate his enemies by threatening to accuse them of heresy before the Inquisition. Clergue's most passionate interest, however, was not religious doctrine or any real abiding concern for the physical or spiritual well-being of his charges; it was sex. Fournier's records provide the names of no less than a dozen mistresses, and the list is clearly incomplete. "He scattered his desires among his flock," Ladurie writes, "as impartially as he gave his benediction." And his flock was astonishingly tolerant of his behavior. At least one woman, however, disapproved of Clergue's fornicating habits and told him "You are committing an enormous sin by sleeping with a married woman."

"Not at all," he replied. "One woman is just like another. The sin is the same, whether she is married or not. Which is as much to say that there is no sin about it at all."

One of those who was interviewed by Fournier had this to say about Clergue's activities: "One summer about seven years ago," testified a young woman, named Grazide, "the priest Pierre Clergue came to my mother's house while she was out harvesting, and he was very persistent, 'allow me to have sex with you,' and I said 'all right.' I was very young at the time and a virgin. I think I was about fourteen or fifteen years old. After that, in January, the priest gave me in marriage to my late husband, Pierre Lizier, and after he had given me to this man, the priest continued to have sex with me, frequently during the remaining four years of my husband's life."

Grazide loved Clergue dearly and defended her own innocence with an argument straight out of the southern French troubadours: "A lady who sleeps with a true lover is purified of all sins." And she added, "With Pierre Clergue, I liked it. And so it could not displease God. It was not sinful."

Father Clergue, in turn, declared, "I love you more than any woman in the world"—not only to Grazide but to his other sexual partners as well. Clergue's most serious love affair was with a widow of the lesser nobility named Beatrice de Planisoles. When Beatrice went to the parish church to confess her sins to Clergue, he cut her off with the words, "I prefer you to any other woman in the world" and embraced her passionately. Beatrice managed to elude his blatant sexual harassment and slip away but after a courtship of several months, she finally succumbed. Their relationship lasted some two years, and Beatrice, in her Inquisition transcript, tells of tender moments with Pierre. Sitting beside him by the fire, or sometimes in bed, she would carefully remove all the lice from his body, a ritual known as "delousing" that was both hygienic and an expression of deep affection. She also reported that they committed the deliberate sacrilege of having intercourse in the parish church. In time, however, Beatrice remarried and moved from Montaillou.

Clergue's amorous behavior is a reflection not of medieval society as a whole but of life in an isolated, impoverished mountain village in which the church's dictums on monogamy and celibacy were irrelevant to the inhabitant's daily lives, regardless of occupation or status. "At an altitude of 1,300 meters," Ladurie wryly comments, "rules of priestly celibacy ceased to apply." Nor did religion speak with one voice in Montaillou. Albigensians had an even stricter sexual code than Catholics, but the Aligensian teaching that all sex was wicked deprived many of its followers of a set of sexual standards to which they could realistically aspire.

Father Pierre served for some time as the official representative of the Inquisition in Montaillou. In this capacity he prosecuted some Albigensians but protected others. Eventually, he himself was convicted by the Inquisition—not for licentiousness but for Albigensian leanings. Despite his family's efforts to obtain his release with lavish bribes, Clergue died in prison.

Chronology

955	Otto I defeats Hungarians at Lechfield, securing Europe's eastern border.
1066	Normans win the Battle of Hastings and assume English rule.
1152	Frederick I Barbarossa becomes first Hohenstaufen emperor; reestablishes imperial authority.
1154	Henry II assumes English throne.
1164	Henry II forces the Constitutions of Clarendon on the English clergy.
1170	Thomas a Becket is assassinated.
1176	Papal and other Italian armies defeat Frederick I at Legnano.
1194	Birth of future Hohenstaufen ruler Frederick II, who becomes a ward of the Pope.
1198	Welf interregnum in the empire begins under Otto IV.
1212	Frederick II crowned emperor in Mainz with papal, French and German support.
1214	French armies under Philip II Augustus defeat combined English and German forces at Bouvines in the first major European battle.
1215	English barons revolt against King John and force the king's recognition of Magna Carta.
1227	Frederick II excommunicated for the first of four times by the Pope; conflict between Hohenstaufen dynasty and papacy begins.
1250	Frederick II dies, having been defeated by the German princes with papal support.
1257	German princes establish their own electoral system to elect future emperors.
1270	French King Louis IX, having unified and reformed France, dies a Crusader in the Holy Land.

By the late eighth century, the contours of a new European civilization were beginning to emerge in Western Europe. Increasingly, Europe would become the focus and center of Western civilization. Such dynamism was built upon a fusion of Germanic, Christian, and classical elements. The first, visible beginning of medieval Europe emerged in Charlemagne's Carolingian empire. The agrarian foundations of the eighth and ninth centuries, however, were inadequate for sustaining a monarchial political system. Consequently, a new political and military system based on the decentralization of political power evolved to become an integral part of the political world of the Middle Ages. This new order was called feudalism, and its concomitant social and economic counterpart was called manorialism.

The new European civilization that emerged in the ninth and tenth centuries began to come into its own in the eleventh and twelfth centuries, as Europeans established new economic, social, and political institutions that provided better security and stability for increasing numbers of individuals. The High Middle Ages (1000-1300) was a period of recovery and growth for Western civilization. Both the Catholic Church and the feudal states recovered from the invasions and internal dissension of the Early Middle Ages. New agricultural practices that increased the food supply helped give rise to a commercial and urban revival that, accompanied by a rising population, created new dynamic elements in a formerly static society.

By the fifth century A.D., the town and cities that had been such an essential part of the Roman world declined, and the world of the Early Middle Ages continued to be predominantly agricultural. The late tenth and early eleventh centuries, however, witnessed a renewal of commercialism, leading to the revival of cities. Old Roman sites came back to life while new towns arose at major trading crossroads. Some of these new commercial entrepots were inland cities while others gained preeminence as natural harbors or ports. By the twelfth and thirteenth centuries, both the urban centers and their populations were experiencing a dramatic expansion. Although European society in the Middle Ages remained overwhelmingly agricultural, the growth of trade and cities along with the development of a money economy and new commercial practices and institutions constituted a veritable commercial revolution that affected most of Europe, including many country's political systems. Commerce, cities, and a money economy helped to undermine feudal institutions while strengthening monarchial authority as some medieval kings exerted centralizing authority and inaugurated the process of developing new kinds of monarchial states. By the thirteenth century, European monarchs were consolidating their governmental institutions in pursuit of greater power.

ORIGINS OF FEUDAL EUROPE

The Middle Ages were characterized by a chronic absence of effective central government and the constant threat of famine, disease, and foreign invasions. In this state of affairs the weaker sought the protection of the stronger, and the true rulers became those who could provide immediate protection from rapine and starvation. The term *feudal society* refers to the social, political, and economic system that emerged from these conditions. Feudal society of the Middle Ages was dominated by war lords. What people needed most was the assurance that others could be depended upon in time of dire need. Lesser men pledged themselves to powerful individuals—war lords or princes—recognizing them as superiors and promising them *fealty,* faithful service when called upon. Large warrior groups of *vassals* emerged and developed into a professional military class with its own code of knightly conduct. The result was a network of complex relationships based on mutual loyalty that allowed warlords to acquire armies and to rule over territory whether they owned land or had a legitimate royal title. The emergence of these military organizations, warlords and their retinue of professional military vassals or knights was a necessary adaptation to the absence of strong central government and the predominance of a noncommercial, rural, and agrarian economy.

Vassalage

Feudalism contained two important components: a personal element called *vassalage* and a property element called the *benefice*. These two essential features combined both Germanic and Roman practices. Vassalage originated from Germanic society and was based upon a lord gathering followers to himself on certain conditions, primarily military. In Germanic custom, this relationship between chief and followers was a perfectly honorable one, a relationship between social equals.

Feudalism also contained a property element that was ultimately fused with the personal element of vassalage. In the late Roman Empire, it became customary for great landowners to hire retainers. To provide for the latter's maintenance, the lord gave land known as a benefice, or fief. This granting of land emerged out of a king's or lord's need for fighting men, especially in the newly developing cavalry. Vassals were expected to live on these fiefs, or benefices, and maintain horses and other accouterments of war in good order. Originally, vassals were little more than gangs-in-waiting.

Since vassalage involved the swearing of "fealty," or allegiances, to the lord, a vassal promised to refrain from any action that might threaten his lord's welfare. Most important among the services required of a vassal was military duty as a mounted knight. The Frankish armies of Charlemagne originally consisted of foot soldiers dressed in coats of mail and armed with swords. By the eleventh century a military change had occurred when larger horses were introduced. Earlier, horsemen had been mobile archers and throwers of spears. Eventually, they were armored in coats of mail and wielded long lances that enabled them to act as battering rams. For almost five hundred years, heavily armored cavalry or knights would dominate European warfare. These particular warriors came to have the greatest social prestige and form the essence of Europe's aristocracy.

A knight's service involved a variety of activities: a short or long military expedition, escort duty, standing castle guard, or the placement of one's own castle or fortress at the lord's disposal, if the vassal was of such stature to have one. Frequently bargaining and bickering occurred between lord and vassal over the terms of service. As the relationship between lords and vassals became more formal, limitations were placed on the number of days a lord could require of his vassal's services. By the eleventh century in France about forty days of service a year were considered sufficient. It was also possible for vassals to buy their way out of military obligations by a monetary payment, known as scutage. The lord, in turn, applied this payment to the hiring of mercenaries, who often proved more efficient than contract-conscious vassals.

Beyond his military duty, a vassal was also expected to give his lord advice when requested and to sit as a member of the lord's court when it was in session. Many vassals were also obliged to provide hospitality for their lord when he stayed at a vassal's estate or castle. This obligation was especially important to medieval kings since they tended to be highly itinerant. In addition, a vassal could be called upon for financial assistance when his lord was in obvious need or distress. For example, such would be the case when a lord had been captured by his enemies and needed to be ransomed or when he was outfitting himself for a crusade or a military campaign. Gifts of money might also be expected when the lord's daughters married and his sons became knights.

The lord's obligations to his vassals were also very specific. Foremost was his obligation to protect the vassal from physical harm and to stand as his advocate in public court. After fealty was sworn and homage paid, the lord provided for the vassal's physical maintenance by the granting of the benefice or fief. The fief was simply the material wherewithal to meet the vassal's military and other obligations. It could take the form of liquid wealth, as well as the more common grant of real property. There were also money fiefs, which empowered a vassal to receive regular payments from the lord's treasury. Such fiefs, however, created potential conflicts because they made it possible for a nobleman in one land to acquire vassals among the nobility in another. More often than not, the fief was a landed estate of anywhere from a few to several thousand acres. It could also take the form of a castle, which also varied in size and construction from a simple, crude stone or even wooden tower to an elaborate edifice of the finest stone masonry.

As this system of mutual obligations between lord and vassal evolved, certain practices became common. If a lord acted improperly toward his vassal, the bond between them could be dissolved. Likewise, if a vassal failed to fulfill the requirements of his fealty, he was subject to forfeiture of his fief. Upon a vassal's death, his fief theoretically reverted back to the lord since it had been granted to him to use, not to own as a possession. In practice, however, by the eleventh century fiefs tended to become hereditary. Following the principle of primogeniture, the eldest son inherited the father's fief. If a man died without heirs, the lord could once again reclaim the fief.

By the eleventh century the fief acquired a new dimension involving the exercise of political power. While the fief remained, in essence, a landed estate held from the lord by a vassal in return for military service, increasingly, vassals came to have complete political and legal authority within their fiefdoms. Fief-holding also became increasingly complicated as subinfeudation occurred. The vassals of a king, who were themselves great lords, might also have vassals who owed them military service in return for a grant of land from their estates. Those vassals, in turn, might have their own vassals, who at such a level would be simple knights with barely enough land to provide their own equipment. The lord-vassal relationship bound together both greater and lesser landowners. Historians used to present feudalism as a hierarchy with the king at the top, greater lords on the next level, lesser lords on the next, and simple knights at the bottom, followed by the rest of medieval society, i.e., peasants and serfs. This was only, however, a model and rarely reflected reality. Such a hierarchy implied a powerful king at the top, exercising a substantial degree of authority and control over his kingdom. The reality of eleventh century France, for example, negates this image. The "kings" of France actually controlled no more land than the Ile-de-France, the region around

Paris. By contrast, their supposed "vassals," the dukes of Normandy and Burgundy, controlled far more extensive territory and exercised greater political power and authority than did the kings. Indeed, as will be seen later in the chapter, it will be William, Duke of Normandy, who will conquer England in 1066.

As the centuries passed, personal loyalty and service became secondary to the acquisition of property, especially among the various levels of vassals. In developments that signaled the waning of feudal society beginning in the eleventh century, the fief came to overshadow fealty; the benefice became more important than vassalage, and freemen proved themselves prepared to swear allegiance to the highest bidder. Feudalism, nonetheless, provided stability throughout the Early Middle Ages and aided the difficult process of political centralization during the High Middle Ages. The advantage of feudal government lay in its adaptability. Agreements of different kinds could be made with almost anyone, as circumstances required. The process embraced a broad spectrum of people, from the king to the lowliest vassal in the remotest part of the kingdom. The foundations of the modern nation-state would emerge in France and England from the fine tuning of essentially feudal arrangements, as kings sought to adapt their goal of centralized government and authority to the reality of local power and control. In many countries, it took several centuries for monarchs to consolidate their power and centralize authority in their personage. Constantly obstructing this process were the forces of an entrenched nobility, who believed that the king was usurping power and legitimate authority because he was violating feudal arrangements between himself and his vassals that extended back to the Middle Ages.

THE MANORIAL SYSTEM

Peasants and Serfs

Feudalism rested upon an economic system known as manorialism. The agrarian economy of the Middle Ages was organized and controlled through village farms known as manors. Frequently, a manor and village were synonymous; one agricultural village constituted the lord's estate. Or, a manor might consist of two or more villages. There was no single formula. Manorialism grew out of earlier practices and was especially encouraged by the unsettled conditions of the Early Middle Ages when many peasants gave up their freedom in return for protection.

On manors, peasants labored as tenants for a lord, who allotted them land and tenements in exchange for their services and a portion of their crops. The part of the estate worked for the lord was called the demesne, on average about one-quarter to one-third of the cultivated lands scattered throughout the manor. All crops grown on the demesne were harvested for the lord. The manor also included common meadows for grazing animals and forests reserved exclusively for the lord to hunt in.

Peasants were treated according to their personal status and the size of their tenements. A freeman, a peasant possessing his own land, or hereditary property (property free from claims of an overlord), became a serf by surrendering his property to a greater landowner—a lord—in exchange for protection and assistance. Although the land was no longer his property, he had full possession and use of it, and the number of services and amount of goods he was to supply to the lord were carefully spelled out.

Peasants who entered a lord's service with little real property (perhaps only a few farm implements and animals) ended up as unfree serfs. Such individuals were more vulnerable to the lord's demands for their labor and service, often spending up to three days a week working the lord's fields. Truly impoverished peasants, those who had nothing to offer a lord except their hands, had the lowest status on the manor and were the least protected from exploitation.

The supervision of manors varied considerably. If the lord of a manor was a simple knight, he probably lived on the estate and supervised it personally. Great lords possessed many manors and relied on a steward or bailiff to run each estate. Lords controlled the lives of their serfs in a number of ways. Serfs were not only required to cultivate the lord's lands but also build barns, dig ditches, drain swamps, clear forests, and any other type of work deemed necessary by the lord for his manor's general sustenance and maintenance. Serfs of all classes were subject to various dues, including a share of every product raised by the serfs. Serfs, moreover, paid the lord for the use of the manor's common pasturelands, streams, ponds, and surrounding woodlands. For example, if a tenant fished in the manor's pond or stream, he turned over part of the catch to his lord. If his cow grazed in the common pasture, he paid a rent in cheese produced from the cow's milk. Serfs were also obliged to pay a tithe (one-tenth of their produce) to their local village church. Thus, the lord, who furnished shacks and small plots of land from his vast domain, had at his disposal an army of servants of varying status who provided him with everything from eggs to boots.

Legal Rights

In addition to complete control of their labor, lords also possessed legal rights over their serfs as a result of their unfree status. Serfs were legally bound to the lord's land; they could not leave without his permission. Although free to marry, serfs could not marry anyone outside their manor without the lord's approval. Due to the decentralization of public power that was part of feudalism, lords sometimes exercised public rights or political authority on their lands. This gave the lord the right to try serfs in his own court, although only for lesser crimes (called "low justice"). In fact, the lord's manorial court provided the only law most serfs knew. Finally, the lord's political authority allowed him to establish monopolies on certain services that provided additional income. Serfs could be required to bring their grain to the lord's mill and pay a fee to have it ground into flour. Thus, the rights a lord possessed on his manor gave him virtual control over both the lives and property of his serfs. Weak serfs often fled to monasteries rather than continue to be exploited in such a fashion. That many serfs were discontented is reflected in the high number of recorded escapes. Escaped serfs wandered the land as beggars and vagabonds until they found, if ever, new and more benevolent masters.

AGRICULTURAL REFORMS AND INNOVATIONS IN THE MIDDLE AGES

Medieval Europe was an overwhelmingly agrarian society and remained so for several more centuries, even though by the beginning of the thirteenth century commerce and a revival of town and city life had occurred. The revitalization of trade and urban life was, in large part, the result of important agricultural and technological changes that took place in the eleventh and twelfth centuries that dramatically increased the food supply that preceded and accompanied population explosion. Although some historians have questioned whether the medieval develop-

ments deserve the appellation "revolution," significant changes did take place in the way Europeans farmed.

Although the improvement in climate played an important role in producing longer and better growing seasons, another important factor in increasing food production was the expansion in the amount of land cultivated. This was accomplished primarily by intense clearing of forests. Millions of acres of trees were felled and the land cleared for farming. Cleared forests not only provided more arable land for agriculture but also timber for fuel, houses, mills, bridges, fortresses, ships, and charcoal for the nascent iron industry. Eager for land, peasants cut down trees and drained swamps. In the area of the Netherlands, peasants began to reclaim the land from the sea. Religious orders, such as the Cistercian monks, (a new religious order founded in 1098), proved particularly ambitious in clearing forests, draining marshes, and plowing fields. By the beginning of the thirteenth century, Europeans had available a total acreage for farming greater than any used before or since.

Technological Advancements

Technological advancements also furthered agricultural development. The Middle Ages witnessed an explosion of labor-saving devices, many of which depended upon the use of iron, which was mined in various areas of Europe and traded to places where it was not found. Iron was in demand to make swords and armor, as well as scythes, axeheads, and new types of farming tools, such as hoes, saws, hammers, and nails for building purposes. It was crucial to the development of the heavy-wheeled plow, the *carruca*, which was a great boon to farmers north of the Alps, who unlike their counterparts to the south (Mediterranean and Near Eastern farmers) could not use the *aratum*, a light, nonwheeled wooden scratch plow suitable only for the light soils of those regions. Interestingly, the aratum helped to preserve the family farm as the basic social unit rather than the village in the Mediterranean world. Farmers could afford to have one since it could be pulled by a donkey or a single animal.

Farming north of the Alps, however, required the "carruca" with its iron ploughshare to till the heavy clay soils of northern Europe. The carruca could turn over heavy soils and allow for their drainage. Because of its weight, several oxen were required to pull it. Oxen were slow, however, and two new inventions for the horse made greater productivity possible. A new horse collar appeared in the tenth century. Although horses were faster than oxen, the amount they could pull with the traditional harness was limited because it tended to choke the horse if it pulled too much weight. The new collar distributed the weight around the horse's shoulders and chest rather than the throat and could be used to hitch up a series of horses, allowing them to pull the new heavy plow faster and cultivate more land. The use of the horseshoe, an iron shoe nailed to the horse's hooves, spread in the eleventh and twelfth centuries and allowed for greater traction and better protection for the animal against the rocky and heavy clay soils of northern Europe.

Besides using horsepower, the Middle Ages saw the harnessing of water and wind power to do jobs previously done by human or animal power. The watermill, although invented as early as the second century B.C., was not used much in the Roman Empire, since it was considered disruptive to slave labor and free wage earners. Not until the Middle Ages, with the spread of metallurgical technology, making it easier to build, did its use become widespread. In 1086,

the survey of English land, known as the Domesday Book, listed 6,000 of them in England. Located along streams, they were used to grind grains for flour. Even dams were constructed to increase waterpower. The development of the dam enabled millwrights to mechanize entire industries; waterpower was used in certain phases of cloth production and to power triphammers for the working of metals.

Where rivers were unavailable or not easily dammed, Europeans developed windmills to harness wind power. Historian are unsure if windmills were imported into Europe or designed independently by Europeans. (They were invented in Persia.) In either case, by the end of the twelfth century, windmills dotted the northern European landscape. The windmill and watermill were the most important devices for the utilization of natural power before the invention of the steam engine in the eighteenth century. Their use had a profound impact on the ability of Europeans to produce more food.

Finally, the transition from a two-field to three-field system contributed to the increase in agricultural production. In the early Middle Ages, it was common to plant one field, allowing another of equal size to lie fallow to regain its fertility. Now estates were divided into three parts: one field was planted in the fall with winter grains, such as rye and wheat, while spring grains, such as oats, barley, and vegetables, were planted in the second field. The third remained fallow. By rotating their use, only one-third rather than one-half of the land lay fallow at any time. Crop rotation also prevented soil exhaustion. Grain yields increased to levels that would not be surpassed until the next agricultural revolution that occurred in the eighteenth century. The three-field system was not adopted everywhere. It was not used in the Mediterranean lands, and even in some parts of northern Eu-

Woodcut image of Venice, a leading city in the revival of trade.

rope, the two-field and three-field systems existed side by side for centuries.

Medieval Europe was an overwhelmingly rural society with most people living in small villages. In the eleventh and twelfth centuries, however, new dynamics were introduced that began to transform Europe's economic foundation: a revival of trade, expansion in the circulation of money, the emergence of a new class of craftsmen and artisans, and the concomitant growth of towns. Helping to stimulate these changes were the new agricultural practices and new uses of energy, which freed part of the European population from the need to produce their own food and allowed diversification in economic functions. Merchants and craftsmen could now buy their necessities.

THE REVIVAL OF TRADE

The revival of commercial activity was a gradual process. Although trade had never completely died out in Western Europe, the political chaos and related economic decline of the Early Middle Ages caused large-scale trade to all but disappear. The only amount of substantial trade taking place during those centuries was between Italy and the Byzantine Empire and the Jewish traders who moved back and forth between the Muslim and Christian worlds. By the end of the tenth century, however, individuals were appearing in Europe with both the skills and products essential for a revitalization of trade. Although most villages produced what they needed locally, other items were made that were unique to the region and could be sold elsewhere. These included a variety of goods, such as flax and wool for clothes, wine for drinking and for use in Catholic mass, salt for preserving food, furs for clothing, hemp for rope, and metals for weapons or tools. Some regions and countries became particularly well known for their specialized products: England for raw wool, Scandinavia and Germany for iron, and Germany for silver.

Cities in Italy, most notably Venice in the eighth century, assumed a leading role in the revival of trade. By that time Venice had assumed strong and profitable commercial connections with Byzantium. The city developed a merchant fleet and by the end of the tenth century had become Europe's main entrepot for Byzantine and Islamic commerce. Venetians traded grain, wine, and timber to Constantinople in exchange for silk cloth, which was then sold or traded to other northern Italian communities, which turned the silk into clothing. The Italians furthered their trading enterprises with the advent of the Crusades at the end of the eleventh century. (See Chapter 8) Italian merchants were able to establish new mercantile settlements in eastern ports, obtaining silks, sugar, and spices that they carried back to Italy and the west. Although these items were not entirely new to Western Europe, they were now traded in increasingly large quantities.

While northern Italian cities were enlarging the scope of Mediterranean trade, the towns of Flanders, the area along the coast of present day Belgium and northern France, became the centers for the production of woolen cloth. Flanders' location made it a logical entrepot for northern European traders. Merchants from England, Scandinavia, France, and Germany congregated there to trade their wares for the much desired woolen cloth; England, in particular, became the chief supplier of raw wool for the Flemish woolen industry. Flanders became one of the most prosperous regions in all of Western Europe by the end of the twelfth century, and its towns, particularly Bruges and Ghent, became centers for the trade and manufacture of woolen cloth.

By the twelfth century, both Italy and Flanders had become the leading centers of the trade revival, and it only seemed natural that these two areas witnessed a regular exchange of goods. The dangers and difficulties of sea travel around Western Europe, however, and the expense of overland journeys made such a connection unlikely. Powerful feudal lords and princes, moreover, charged tolls to merchants going through their lands and did not hesitate to plunder caravans carrying goods when they needed money or supplies.

As trade contacts increased, even lords began to see the advantage of promoting trade. The best example of such a change in attitude comes from the counts of the Champagne region in northern France. Beginning in the twelfth century, the feudal counts instituted an annual event of six fairs held in the chief towns of their territory. The counts guaranteed the safety of visiting merchants, supervised the trading activities, and, for their services, collected a sales tax on all goods sold or exchanged at the fairs. The Champagne fairs became the largest commercial marketplace in Western Europe for the exchange of goods between northern and southern Europe and the Byzantine and Muslim East. At the fairs, northern merchants brought furs, woolen cloth, tin, hemp, and honey of northern Europe and exchanged them for the cloth and swords of northern Italy and the silks, sugar, and spices of the East.

Money and Banking

As trade increased throughout Europe in the twelfth century, the demand for coins or the use of money instead of barter increased as well. Without gold mines of its own, Western Europe had few gold coins in circulation before the thirteenth century. Silver and copper coins were most frequently used as money. For several decades Germany had a monopoly on the production of silver coins because it had the richest silver deposit in Western Europe in the Harz

Mountains of central Germany. England also produced coins, the silver penny, called sterling for its stability, and so did France, the pennies of Paris, Tours, and Anjou, together with the English penny became the most widely circulated coins in France and England in the twelfth century.

As trade expanded throughout Europe and competition increased, as more Western European regions emerged as manufacturing/trade centers, the Italian merchants discovered that their trade (if they hoped to maintain their preeminence) required new ways of raising capital and new commercial practices. They created partnerships to raise capital for ships and goods in overseas journeys. The *commenda* was the most common form of partnership, a temporary association amongst a group of related enterprises where one partner contributed money while the other(s) supplied labor and time. If the venture was successful, the partners simple shared in the profits. The Italians also developed insurance to protect their investments, although rates were exorbitant. New methods of credit, such as bills of exchange or notes on credit, were established to circumvent the problem of insufficient reserves of money or the inconvenience of exchanging coins for larger transactions. By the beginning of the thirteenth century the Italians, because of their trade connections with the East, began minting gold coins that became standard in Western Europe over the next few decades. The gold florin of Florence was first struck in 1252 and the Venetian gold ducat in 1284.

Financial matters were complicated by the practice of usury. The Church regarded economic activity as an ethical affair and disapproved of usury, defined as pure interest on a loan. The Church condemned usury in 1139 and damned usurers, as malevolent and unworthy of Christian burial. The Church's attitude was troublesome because the lending of money for

A moneylender works with clients in the center of a medieval fair. Such men were the earliest bankers, issuing loans and credit.

productive purposes was essential to the further expansion and development of trade, manufacturing, and banking. Consequently, Church officials discovered rationalizations and merchants found ways to circumvent the Church's ban. Most economic historians question whether the usury laws actually handicapped Europe's economic growth, although the laws undoubtedly caused many merchants grief and financial hardships.

It should also be noted that banking grew out of mercantile necessity. The existence of many different coinages required professional moneychangers who knew coins' respective values and could exchange them. Soon moneychangers became involved in lending money as well. As merchants accumulated wealth, they were able to hold large deposits of money and function as bankers. Because of their dominance of trade, the richest and most prominent early banking houses were Italian. Italians took the lead in developing the institutions and methods of the new capitalist system. Northern Europeans looked to the Italians as their role models.

In Spain and Portugal, Muslims and Jews dominated banking and financing. Together they dominated the mercantile and banking enterprises of both countries. Since they were non-Christian, the Church could only frown on their activities and not completely shut down their money-lending operations. Muslims and Jews, moreover, had coexisted harmoniously and profitably in both countries for centuries and had become invaluable fixtures in medieval Iberian society. They remained so until the Reconquista finally unified all of Spain under the Catholic rulers Ferdinand and Isabella at the end of the fifteenth century. When that was accomplished, the monarchy along with the Church unwisely decided to drive all non-Christians out of Spain if they did not convert. Most Muslims and Jews refused to convert and were driven out of both countries. Going with them was incredible financial acumen, something Spain and Portugal would sorely need in the centuries to come.

RISE OF MEDIEVAL CITIES

Without question, the most important dynamic resulting from the revitalization of trade in medieval Europe was the emergence of cities and urban life and society. Merchants could not function in a world that emphasized the exaction of labor services and attachment to the land. They needed places where they could build warehouses to store their goods for shipment elsewhere and personal residences that could serve as permanent bases. In short, their livelihood demanded a complete reorientation of their physical environment and existence. Cities did not develop just anywhere. To meet merchants' needs, they were located near sources of protection and alongside rivers or major arteries that provided favorable transportation routes.

Towns in the economic sense, as centers of population where merchants and artisans gathered and exchanged goods, services, and ideas and purchased their food from surrounding areas, had greatly declined in the Early Middle Ages, especially in Europe north of the Alps. Old Roman cities continued to exist but declined dramatically relative to size and population. Many were transformed into administrative centers for dukes and counts or sees or seats for bishops and archbishops. With the revival of trade, merchants began to gather in these old cities, followed by craftsmen or artisans, skilled individuals who saw in these places the opportunity to further develop their trade and produce objects that could be sold by the merchants. In the course of the eleventh and twelfth centuries, old Roman cities came alive with new populations and growth. By 1100 the old areas of these cities had been repopulated; after 1100, the population outgrew the old walls, requiring the construction of new city walls outside the old.

In the Mediterranean world, cities had survived the Western empire's decline and remained viable entities of habitation and commercial centers. After the Moors conquest of southern Spain in the eighth century, Islamic cities had a flourishing urban life, centered in such locales as Grenada and Seville. Urban life in southern Italy also thrived in such places as Bari, Salerno, Naples, and Amalfi. Although greatly reduced in size, Rome, the old capital of the Roman world, had survived as the center of papal administration. In northern Italy, Venice already had emerged by the end of the eighth century as a town because of its commercial connections with Byzantium.

Beginning in the late tenth century, many new towns and cities were established, particularly in northern Europe. The usual pattern for development would be a group of merchants establishing a settlement near some fortified stronghold, such as a castle or monastery. Castles were especially favored since they were usually located along major transportation routes or at the intersection of two such trade routes; castle lords also offered protection (for a fee, of course). If the settlement prospered and expanded, new walls were built to protect it. Most of these new towns were closely tied to their immediate surroundings since they were dependent on the countryside for their sustenance. In addition, they were often part of the territory belonging to a lord and were subject to his jurisdiction. Although lords wanted to treat towns and its folk as they would their vassals and serfs, cities had totally different needs and a different perspective toward life than their rural counterparts.

Townspeople and Self-government

The new class of townspeople did not fit into the structure and pattern of rural life in the Middle Ages. Since they were not lords, they were not subject to the customs that applied to lords. They were not serfs or peasants either and were reluctant to subject themselves to manorial services and mandates, even though many originally came from such ranks. Merchants and artisans needed mobility to trade. Consequently, townspeople were a sort of "revolutionary" group who needed their own identity and laws to meet the different requirements of their lives. Since

townspeople were profiting from the growth of trade and the sale of their products, they were willing to pay to make their own laws and govern themselves. In many instances, lords and kings (especially the latter as they tried to weaken their feudal ties with powerful lords because of their desire to consolidate and centralize power in their own hands) saw the potential for vast new sources of revenues and were willing to grant (more accurately sell) the liberties townspeople were demanding. By 1100 town folk were obtaining charters of liberties from their territorial lords, either lay or ecclesiastical, that granted them the privileges they wanted. In most cases they obtained their goal simply by an outright purchase (one lump sum money payment) or by regular revenues. The rights obtained usually consisted of four basic liberties in their charters: a testamentary right, the right to bequeath goods and sell property; freedom from military obligation to the lord; written urban law that guaranteed the freedom of townspeople; and the right to become a free person after residing a year and a day in the town. The last provision made it possible for a runaway serf, who could avoid capture, to become a free person in a city. While lords and kings granted such basic liberties, they were very hesitant to allow cities the right of self-government. In most cases, the king or lord continued to actually govern the town through an appointed official called a provost, who collected taxes owed and administered the king's or lord's justice and other laws. Some city charters, however, did grant the right of self government. For example, the city of London received such a privilege from King Henry I in 1130. In their charter, Londoners had the right to choose their own officials to govern them. They also had the right to administer their own courts of law. While taxes were still paid to the king, they were collected by the city's appointees, not the king's.

Frequently, urban communities found that their lords were unwilling to grant them all the liberties they wanted, especially self-government. Bishops in cathedral cities were particularly obstinate in retaining their privileges. In these cities, merchants and serfs lived in the same community; to grant freedom meant the loss of the services of the serfs who tilled the fields outside the city. For a bishop to grant self-government to local officials within his city meant the end of his own authority. Where town folk experienced such tenacity, they often took matters into their own hands by forming an association called a commune and, if necessary, were willing to use force to extract from their lay or ecclesiastical lords their rights. Communes were especially effective in northern Italy, in the regions of Tuscany and Lombardy, where townspeople had the support of local nobles, who were just as keen on wresting power from the clergy as were urbanites. With such support, Italian town residents, in cities such as Pisa, Milan, Arezzo, and Genoa, were successful in the eleventh and twelfth centuries of destroying clerical power and establishing complete self-government, which saw the creation of new municipal offices such as consuls and town councils that governed the city in the name and welfare of its citizens.

Although communes were established in northern Europe, especially in France and Flanders, town folk there did not have the support of rural nobles. Revolts against lay lords were usually brutally suppressed; those against bishops, as in Laon in the twelfth century, were more frequently successful. When they succeeded, communes received the right to chose their own officials, hold their own courts, and administer their own cities. Unlike their Italian counterparts, however, which eventually became completely autonomous, self-governing republican city-states, the towns of northern European did evolve

to such status. Instead, in England and France, for example, they remained ultimately subject to royal authority. Medieval cities, then, possessed varying degrees of self-government depending on the amount of control retained over them by the lord or king in whose territory they were located. Nevertheless, all towns, regardless of the degree of outside control, evolved institutions of government for running the community's affairs.

Medieval cities defined citizenship narrowly and granted it only to males who had been born in the city or had lived there for some time. In many cities, citizens elected members of a city council that were responsible for running the city on a daily basis. City councillors not only enacted legislation but also served as judges and city magistrates. Election of councillors was by no means democratic. The electoral process was tightly controlled by the city's mercantile elite— an oligarchy composed of its wealthiest and most powerful families, who came to be called patricians. Councillors were elected from this small cadre of patricians, who kept the reins of government in their hands despite periodic protests from lesser merchants and artisans. In the twelfth and thirteenth centuries, some cities added an executive to the body of councillors, in whose hands was placed the daily governing of the city. Although it varied from town to town, the title of mayor was used to refer to this executive officer. These individuals were either appointed by the king, or lord, or elected from among their ranks by city councillors. In some Italian city-states, the executive known as the podesta, literally a person with power, was brought in from the outside because the city's patricians often feuded bitterly among themselves to decide which of them would assume such control. The podesta was only to rule for one year but occasionally, if he was particularly effective and adept at maneuvering among the city's elite, he was granted a longer tenure, or, if he became especially powerful over the year, he simply established himself permanently by usurping power or taking it by force from the council.

City governments kept close watch over citizens' activities; some historians have used the term "municipal socialism" to describe such scrutiny. To care for the community's welfare and safety, a city government might regulate air and water pollution; provide water barrels and delegate responsibility to people in every section of town to fight fires, which were an ever-present danger; construct warehouses to stockpile grain in the event of food shortages caused by war or bad harvests; and establish and supervise the standards of weights and measures used in the various local goods and industries. Although violence was a way of life in the Middle Ages, urban crime was not a major problem. The community's relatively small size made it difficult for criminals to operate openly. Nevertheless, medieval urban governments did organize town guards to patrol the streets by night and the city walls by day. People caught committing criminal acts were quickly tried for their offenses. Serious infractions, such as murder, were punished by execution, usually by hanging. Lesser crimes were punished by fines, flogging, or branding.

Whatever their condition or degree of independence, medieval cities remained relatively small in comparison to either ancient or modern cities. By the end of the thirteenth century, London was the largest city in England with almost 40,000 people. Otherwise, north of the Alps, only Bruges and Ghent in Flanders had populations close to that figure. Italian cities tended to be larger with Venice, Florence, Genoa, Milan, and Naples numbering almost 100,000. Even the largest European city seemed insignifi-

The shrine of Edward the Confessor in Westminster Abbey.

cant alongside Constantinople or the Arab cities of Damascus, Baghdad, and Cairo. For centuries to come, Europe remained predominantly rural. In the long run, the rise of towns and the development of commerce laid the foundations for the eventual transformation of Europe from a rural and agricultural society to an urban and industrial one.

ENGLAND IN THE MIDDLE AGES

In 1066 the death of the childless Anglo-Saxon ruler, Edward the Confessor (so-named because of his reputation for piety), precipitated one of the most important changes in English political history. Edward's mother was a Norman, giving the duke of Normandy a hereditary claim to the

The most famous account of the Norman Conquest is not a written record but a pictorial one. The Bayeux Tapestry tells the story of Harold of Sessex and William of Normandy through the Battle of Hastings. In the scene at the top, Harold is crowned king of England in Westminster Abbey. In the scene at the right, men cut down trees along the Norman coast to build ships in preparation for the Norman invasion. At the bottom the Normans sack England.

William the Conqueror rides atop his horse during the Battle of Hastings. This was an age when kings were expected not only to lead their armies into battle but also to be mighty warriors, performing extraordinary feats. William of Normandy was certainly such a leader.

English throne. Before his death, Edward, who was a rather weak monarch, acknowledged the Duke's claim and ordered that William's (the Duke of Normandy) ascension to the throne be accepted. In fact, Edward had actually promised William the crown fifteen years earlier. But the Anglo-Saxon assembly, which customarily bestowed the royal power, had in mind a different agenda and vetoed Edward's request. They chose instead, Harold Godwinsson, an Anglo-Dane. Harold claimed that on his deathbed Edward had passed the crown to him when he asked Harold to "look after the kingdom." Based on Edward's rather enigmatic request, Harold as-sumed he was the rightful heir. The Anglo-Saxon lords of England simply did not want to be ruled by a "foreigner." This defiance angered William, who raised an army, crossed the channel and defeated an Anglo-Saxon army, led by Harold, at the decisive Battle of Hastings in 1066. Within weeks of his victory, William was crowned king of England in Westminster Abbey, both by right of heredity and by right of conquest. No sooner was he crowned, than he spent the next twenty years conquering and subjugating the rest of his new country. By the time of his death in 1087, he had made all England his domain.

Alfred the Great instituted the practice of parleying.

As a result of his conquests, every landholder, whether large or small, was now his vassal, holding land legally as a fief from the king. William organized his new English nation shrewdly. He established a strong, centralized monarchy whose power was not fragmented by independent territorial princes. He kept in tact the Anglo-Saxon tax system and the practice of court writs (legal warnings) as a flexible form of central control over localities. He was careful not to destroy the Anglo-Saxon quasi democratic tradition of frequent "parleying"—the holding of conferences between the king and the great lords who had a vested interest in royal decisions.

The practice of parleying was initially instituted by Alfred the Great (r. 871-899). A strong and willful king who forcibly unified England, Alfred relied heavily on his councilors' advice in making laws. His example was respected and continued under the reign of Canute (r. 1016-1035), the Dane who restored order and brought unity to England after prolonged civil war engulfed the island during the reign of the incompetent Ethlered II (r. 978-106). William, although he thoroughly subjugated the Anglo-Saxon nobility to the crown, nonetheless, maintained the parleying tradition by consulting regularly with them about state affairs. The result was the unique blending of the one and the many, a balance between monarchial and parliamentary interests that has ever since been a feature of English government. Although the English Parliament, as we know it today, did not formally develop as an institution until the late thirteenth century, its tradition began with the reign of William the Conqueror.

For administration and taxation purposes William commissioned a county-by-county survey of his new realm, a detailed accounting known as the *Domesday Book* (1080-1086). The title of the book may reflect the thoroughness and finality of the survey. As none would escape the doomsday judgment of God, so none was overlooked by William's assessors.

The Norman conquest of England brought a dramatic change. In Anglo-Saxon England, the king had held limited lands while great aristocratic families controlled vast estates and acted rather independently of the king. By contrast, the Normans established an aristocratic hierarchy where, depending on their status, the amount of land they held was as a fief from the king. William the Conqueror manipulated the feudal system to create a strong, centralized monarchy. Gradually, a process of fusion between the Normans and Anglo-Saxons created a new England. While the Norman ruling class spoke French, the intermarriage of the Norman-French with the Anglo-Saxon nobility gradually merged Anglo-Saxon and French into a new English language. Political amalgamation also occurred as

the Normans adapted existing Anglo-Saxon institutions. The Norman conquest of England had
repercussions in France as well. Since the new
English king was still the Duke of Normandy,
he was both a king (of England) and simultaneously a vassal of the king of France but a vassal who was now far more powerful than his lord.
This "French connection" kept England heavily
involved in French and continental affairs for
several more centuries.

In the twelfth century the power of the
English monarchy was significantly expanded by
Henry II, the first of the Plantagenet dynasty
who reestablished monarchial power after a period of civil war following the death of Henry I,
William the Conqueror's son. Henry II was not
just the king of England. He also became lord of
Ireland, receiving the homage of several Irish
princes after permitting some of his leading
noblemen to occupy parts of that island. Perhaps more important at that moment than the
beginning of English occupation of Ireland was
Henry's acquisitions and footholds in France. He
was count of Anjou, duke of Normandy, and
through marriage to Eleanor of Aquitaine, duke
of Aquitaine as well. Henry's union with Eleanor
created the Angevin, or English-French empire.
Eleanor married Henry while he was still the
Count of Anjou and not yet king of England.
The marriage occurred only eight weeks after
Eleanor's annulment of her fifteen-year marriage
to the ascetic French King Louis VII in March
1152. Although the annulment was granted by
the Pope on grounds of consanguinity (blood
relationship), the true reason for the dissolution
was Louis's suspicion of infidelity—Eleanor, it
was rumored, had been intimate with a cousin.
The annulment cost Louis dearly, who lost
Aquitaine and his wife. Eleanor and Henry had
eight children, five of them sons, two of whom
became the future kings of England, Richard the

HENRY II

Lion-Hearted and John. Yet, Henry, despite his
vast holdings, was still, by feudal arrangement,
a vassal of the king of France! His Angevin empire, as his territory in France was called, made
Henry much more powerful than his lord, the
king of France. Beginning with Louis VII, French
kings saw a serious threat to their own hegemony
in France in this English expansion. Consequently, for the next three centuries, the French
monarchy pursued a determined policy of con-
tainment and expulsion of the English from their
nation. Such an effort was not finally successful
until the mid-fifteenth century, when English
power on the continent collapsed after the Hundred Years' War.

Henry's reign was one of the most important in the early development of the English monarchy. Following his father's death and as a result of the ensuing civil war, royal income declined significantly, and the great nobles, many of whom had resented centralization and the consolidation of monarchial power, used the political chaos to regain their feudal autonomy. Henry, like his grandfather, was not afraid to use brutal force to reassert royal authority. He crushed recalcitrant nobles with ferocity, and once his political hegemony was restored, he successfully implemented administrative reforms and established legal institutions that further strengthened royal government.

First, Henry continued the development of the exchequer or permanent royal treasury that had begun during his father's reign. Royal officials, known as "barons of the exchequer," received taxes collected by the sheriff while seated around a table covered by a checkered cloth (hence, exchequer table), which served as a counting device. The barons gave receipts to the sheriff, while clerks recorded the accounts on parchment that were then rolled up.

Perhaps even more significant than Henry's financial reforms were his efforts to strengthen royal courts and his contributions to the development of English common law. Prior to Henry's legal reformation, justice had been very localized—in primarily county courts and in the courts of the various lords. The king's court had confined itself to affairs relative to the king's rights as a feudal lord. Since William the Conqueror, however, established the king as overlord of the entire kingdom, his successors expanded this jurisdiction to include cases and other legal matters previously handled by the local courts. This expansion or institutionalization of royal legal authority was formalized in 1166 in Henry II's promulgation of the Assizes of Clarendon. The Assizes expanded the number and types of cases to be tried in the king's court. Increased types of criminal acts, as well as property issues, now found their way to the king's court to be heard and tried. Henry's purpose was clear: expanding the jurisdiction of the royal courts extended the king's power and, of course, brought revenues into his coffers. Also, since royal justices were administering law throughout England, a body of common law (laws that prevailed throughout all of England) began to develop to replace the customary law used in county and feudal courts, which often varied from place to place. Henry's systematic approach to legal matters played an important role in developing royal institutions uniform throughout the entire kingdom.

Like his continental counterparts in the twelfth century, Henry became embroiled in the increasing tensions between church and state. Indeed, the most famous (or infamous, depending on which side of the imbroglio one found one's self) church-state controversy in medieval England arose between Henry and Thomas Beckett, Archbishop of Canterbury, the most exalted of all English prelates. The conflict between these two strong-willed individuals centered on two key issues: one, whether the king had the right to punish clerics in royal courts and two, whether legal disputes arising in English courts could be appealed to the papal court for ultimate resolution without royal permission. Since Henry was determined to expand royal power, he viewed such Church prerogatives as an obstacle to his consolidation efforts. Becket, equally determined to sustain Church autonomy by preventing monarchial usurpation of established (and accepted until Henry's reign) Church immunities, asserted that trying clergy for crimes (criminal) in royal courts violated the long-standing right of the Church to try clerics in Church

INNOCENT III

courts. Compounding this church-state power struggle was the fact that Henry and Thomas had been close, personal friends. Becket, prior to becoming archbishop, was one of Henry's closest advisers, and, as such, enjoyed the many "worldly" benefits his position provided. When Henry appointed Becket to be the Archbishop of Canterbury, he expected that Becket, out of loyalty to his friend and king, would do Henry's bidding in all matters. No sooner had Becket put on his archbishop's robes, however, than he underwent a profound spiritual transformation in which he repented for the "sins" he committed while serving as Henry's councilor. To further atone for his past worldliness, Becket decided that he was now religiously obligated to protect the Church's rights. Compromises were attempted between Henry and Beckett, but neither were willing to abandon their respective causes. After Becket excommunicated some bishops who had supported Henry's position, the king, in exasperation, publicly expressed a desire to be "rid" of Becket. Four zealous knights, anxious to please their king, took Henry's utterance literally and on December 29, 1170, assassinated the archbishop at the altar of the cathedral in Canterbury. Becket was martyred by the Church, and three years later canonized as a saint. Henry did public penance for the act and compromised with the Church by allowing the right of appeal from English courts to the papal court. Despite the compromise, Henry had succeeded in strengthening the English monarchy.

Toward the end of his reign, Henry experienced increasing conflict with his nobles over his centralizing policies. Although Henry ultimately crushed the rebels, aristocratic discontent continued into the next century, reaching a climax during the reign of Henry's son, John (1199-1216). Prior to John's ascension to the throne, his brother, Richard the Lion Hearted, ruled England for ten years, most of which time Richard spent in the Holy Land on crusade. Actual power resided with Prince John because of Richard's prolonged absence. Though popular history has vilified John, Richard was just as culpable for policies that aroused aristocratic ire. Burdensome taxation in support of unnecessary foreign crusades and a failing war with France, both of which Richard initiated, turned resistance into outright rebellion during John's regency. Richard had to be ransomed at a high price from the Holy Roman Emperor Henry VI, who had taken him prisoner during his return from the ill-fated Third Crusade. In 1209 Pope Innocent III, in a dispute with King John over the Pope's choice for Archbishop of Canterbury, excommunicated the king and placed England under interdict. To extricate himself and keep his throne, John had to make humiliating concessions, even declaring his country the Pope's fief. The last straw for the English nobility, however, was the defeat of the king's forces by the French at Bouvines in 1214 when John attempted to regain Normandy, which he had lost ten years earlier. With the full support of the clergy and townspeople, English barons revolted against John, forcing him to grudgingly seal the Magna Carta (the Great Charter) of feudal liberties in 1215.

The document limited the monarchial, autocratic power that had been increasing since the Norman conquest, reaching a crescendo with John. It also secured the rights of the many, at least the privileged many, against the monarchy. In the Magna Carta, the privileged preserved their right to be represented at the highest levels of government in important matters like taxation. In short, the Magna Carta was the quintessential feudal document. Feudal custom had always recognized that the relationship between king and vassals was based on mutual rights and obligations. The Magna Carta gave written acknowledgment to that fact and was used in subsequent years to reaffirm the concept that monarchial power should be limited rather than absolute.

THE FRENCH MONARCHY IN THE MIDDLE AGES

The Capetian dynasty of the French monarchy emerged at the end of the tenth century, when in 987, the most powerful noblemen chose one of their own, Hugh Capet, to succeed the last Carolingian ruler of the West Frankish Kingdom (most of present-day France) created in 870 by the Treaty of Mersen. Although they held the title of kings, it was doubtful the Capetians would ever establish their hegemony over all of France. The Capetians controlled as the royal domain only the lands around Paris known as the Ile-de-France. Even that was not entirely under their control; in the eleventh century the

Capetians even failed to curtail aristocratic power in their own immediate region. As kings of France, the Capetians were, by feudal arrangement, to be recognized as the overlords of the great lords of France, such as the dukes of Normandy, Brittany, Burgundy, and Aqutaine and the counts of Flanders, Maine, Anjou, Blois, and Toulouse. As has been seen by the exploits of William the Conqueror, Duke of Normandy, the Capetians supposed "vassals" were considerably more powerful than they were. Thus, much of French political history during the Middle Ages is focused on the conflict that often arose between the Capetians and these powerful lords, as the former attempted to expand their power and authority beyond the Ill-de-France.

In their struggle with their vassals, the Capetians possessed some advantages. As kings anointed by God in a sacred ceremony, they had the enduring support of the Catholic Church. The Capetians also benefited from luck. Their royal domain was so small and insignificant that most of the great lords were not very interested in acquiring it by force, especially since it was ruled by the divinely anointed king of France. The Capetians also proved to be a very "prolific" dynasty. Although the Capetian monarchy did not become officially hereditary until 1223, for generations Capetian kings succeeded in producing sons who shared in ruling and then elected kings before their fathers died.

In the twelfth century, Louis VI "the Fat" (1108-1137) and then his son, Louis VII, were successful in solidifying their control over the Ile-de-France. They further strengthened and added prestige to the crown by allying with the papacy and gaining Church support. Their efforts to expand beyond the Ile-de-France, however, were thwarted, and so by the end of the century, the Capetians' territory was still confined to Paris and its immediate environs. But the Louis's kept the monarchial principle alive, and in the thirteenth century, the Capetian dynasty began to realize the fruits of their labors.

It was during the reign of King Philip II Augustus (1180-1223), Louis VII's son, that the power of the French monarch was extended. Philip realized that the key to Capetian expansion and consolidation of power was to drive the English Plantagenets out of France and then annex their territories to the royal domain. Thus in a series of wars against England, culminating in the decisive defeat of King John at the Battle of Bouvines in Flanders in 1214, Philip was successful in wresting from England, Normandy, Maine, Anjou, and Touraine. By the time of his victory at Bouvines, Philip was not only fighting English but their allies as well, the Flemish and Germans under the leadership of the Holy Roman Emperor, Otto IV.   As a result of these conquests, Philip not only asserted Capetian hegemony over much of northern and central France but in the process quadrupled, royal income. In short, Philip's victory unified France politically around the monarchy and laid the foundation for French ascendancy in the later Middle Ages.

Like his Plantangenet English counterparts, Philip realized how essential it was to centralize institutions of government to rule his new lands. Philip divided his new territories into bailiwicks, each of which was presided over by a bailiff or seneschal. Bailiffs were appointed to provinces close to the original royal domain, the Ile-de-France region, and seneschals to the more remote provinces. Both of these royal appointees administered justice in the king's name, collected revenues, and served the king's interests in a variety of other matters, ranging from the raising of royal troops to providing escorts for dignitar-

FREDERICK II

ies and important clerics. Although most bailiffs came from the middle class, seneschals were barons or knights with military experience capable of commanding royal troops when necessary. Bailiffs, seneschals, and their assistants formed the foundation of the French royal bureaucracy in the thirteenth century.

Philip's successors continued the acquisition of territory but, unlike Philip, did not always use force. Through purchase and marriage the same objectives was achieved: the expansion and centralization of Capetian dominion. Much of the thirteenth century was dominated by the man whom many consider to be the greatest of France's medieval monarchs, Louis IX (1226-1270). A deeply spiritual man, he was later canonized as a saint by the Church, an unusual act by the Church regardless of the century. Although possessing a moral character that far exceeded that of his royal and papal contemporaries, Louis was also at times prey to naivete. Not beset by the problems of sheer survival and a reformer at heart, Louis found himself free to concentrate on what medieval people believed to be the business of civilization.

Although Louis occasionally chastised popes for their crude political ambitions, he remained neutral during the long struggle between the German Hohenstaufen Emperor Frederick II and the papacy (discussed later in the chapter); and his neutrality proved beneficial to the Pope. Louis also remained neutral when his brother, Charles of Anjou, intervened in Italy and Sicily against the Hohenstaufens, again to the Pope's advantage. Urged on by the Pope and his noble supporters, Charles was crowned king of Sicily in Rome and his subsequent defeat of Frederick II's son and grandson ended the Hohenstaufen dynasty. For such service to the Church, both by action and inaction, thirteenth century Capetian kings became the recipients of many papal favors.

Although Louis ruled through the centralized system set up by Philip, he believed it was his duty to God and to his people to personally guarantee their justice and rights. He sent out royal agents to make sure that his bailiffs and seneschals were not abusing their power at the people's expense. Louis also was responsible for establishing a permanent royal court of justice in Paris, the Parlement of Paris, whose work was carried on by a regular staff of professional jurists. Louis made it increasingly difficult for nobles to wage private wars with each other and eventually outlawed the practice, as well as serfdom within his royal domain, the Ile-de-France. He also gave his subjects the judicial right of appeal from local to higher courts and made the tax system, by medieval standards, more equitable. Louis' countrymen came to associate their king with justice; consequently, national feeling, the glue of nationhood, grew very strong during his reign.

Respected by other European monarchs and possessing far greater moral authority than the Pope, Louis became an arbiter among the European powers. During his reign French society and culture became exemplary, a pattern that would continue into the modern period. Northern France became the showcase of monastic reform, chivalry, and Gothic art and architecture. Louis' reign also coincided with the golden age of Scholasticism, which witnessed the convergence of Europe's greatest minds on Paris, among them Saint Thomas Aquinas and Saint Bonaventure.

Sharing in the religious zeal of his age, he played a major role in two of the later Crusades. (see Chapter 8) Both were failures, and he met his death during an invasion of North Africa. It was especially for his selfless but also useless service on behalf of the Church that Louis later received the rare honor of sainthood. Interestingly, the Church bestowed this honor when it was under pressure from a more powerful and less than "most Christian" French king, the ruthless Philip IV, "the Fair."

In the course of the thirteenth century, the Capetian kings acquired new lands to add to the French royal domain, whether by conquest, purchase, marriage, or inheritance. Although the Capetian monarchs imposed their authority on these accretions, they allowed their new subjects to keep their own laws and institutions. Not until the French Revolution of the eighteenth century would the French move toward a common pattern for all of France. Despite the lack of institutional uniformity, by the end of the thirteenth century, France was the largest, wealthiest, and best-governed monarchial state in Europe.

GERMANY AND THE REVIVAL OF THE HOLY ROMAN EMPIRE

In 918 the Saxon Henry I, the strongest of the German dukes of the defunct Carolingian empire, became the first non-Frankish king of Germany. Over the course of his eighteen-year rule, Henry rebuilt royal power with the use of force and conquest. By the time of his death in 936, Henry had combined Swabia, Bavaria, Saxony, Franconia, and Lotharingia into a consolidated political entity. He secured the borders of his new kingdom by stopping Hungarian and Danish invasions. Although much smaller than Charlemagne's empire, the German kingdom Henry created placed his son and successor Otto I (r. 936-973) in a strong territorial position. Otto was just as adept and clever at statecraft as his father. He maneuvered his own king into positions of power in Bavaria, Swabia, and Franconia. He refused to recognize each duchy as an independent hereditary entity, as the nobility increasingly expected, dealing with each instead as a subordinate member of a unified kingdom. In a truly imperial gesture in 951, he invaded Italy and proclaimed himself its king. In 955 he won his grandest victory when he defeated the Hungarians at Lechfeld. This victory secured German borders against new barbarian attacks, further unified the German duchies, and earned Otto the title, "the Great." In defining Western European boundaries, Otto's victories and conquests were comparable with Charles Martel's earlier triumph over the Saracens at Poitiers in 732.

An integral part of Otto's imperial design was to enlist the support of the Church. Bishops and abbots—individuals possessing a sense of universality and because they could not marry, they could not establish competitive dynasties— were the recipients of much royal largesse. They became the king's royal princes and agents. Because these clergy, as royal bureaucrats, received vast estates and immunity from the mandates of local dukes and counts, they found such vassalage to the king appealing. The medieval Church did not become a great territorial power reluctantly. It appreciated such "gifts" while teaching the blessedness of giving.

In 961 Otto, who coveted the imperial crown, put himself in a position to receive it by responding to a plea from Pope John XII (955-964), who was being bullied by an Italian enemy of the German king, Berengar of Friuli. Pope John thanked Otto for his help by crowning him emperor on February 2, 962. Otto, in return for the Pope's "blessing" and recognition, agreed to accept the existence of the Papal States and proclaimed himself their special protector. The Church was now, more than ever before, under secular control. Its bishops and abbots were Otto's appointees and "placemen," and the Pope reigned only in Rome by the power of the emperor's sword. It did not take John long, however, to realize the royal web of entanglement in which he had placed himself and the Holy See. He joined with Italian opposition to Otto, but the emperor retaliated quickly and decisively to John's "betrayal." An ecclesiastical synod over which Otto presided deposed John and proclaimed that, henceforth, no Pope could take office without first swearing an oath of allegiance to the emperor. Under Otto, popes ruled at the emperor's pleasure or whim.

As reflected in these events, Otto shifted the royal focus from Germany to Italy. His successors, Otto II (r. 973-983) and Otto III (r.983-1002), became so immersed in Italian affairs that their German support base ultimately disintegrated, the result of overly ambitious imperial dreams. Otto the Great's heirs should have looked west for lessons from their Capetian con-

A likeness of Frederick I from about 1165.
Frederick Barbarossa called his realm the Holy
Roman Empire, implying a close relationship with
the church.

governments. In England the Magna Carta balanced the rights of nobility against monarchial authority, and in France the reign of Philip II Augustus secured the king's authority over the competitive claims of the nobility. During the reign of Louis IX, France gained international acclaim as the bastion of enlightened, righteous politics and as the center of medieval culture. The history of the Holy Roman Empire, which encompassed northern Italy, Germany, and Burgundy by the mid-thirteenth century, was quite different. Primarily because of the efforts of Hohenstaufens to extend imperial power into southern Italy, disunity and blood feuding became the order of the day for two centuries. It left Germany fragmented until modern times.

FREDERICK I BARBAROSSA

The investiture controversy had earlier weakened imperial authority. After the Concordat of Worms, the German princes held the dominant lay influence over episcopal appointments and within the rich ecclesiastical territories. Imperial power revived, however, with the accession to the throne of Frederick I Barbarossa (r.1152-1190) (Redbeard to the Italians) of the new Hohenstaufen dynasty, the most powerful line of emperors to succeed the Ottonians. The Hohenstaufens not only reasserted imperial authority but initiated a new phase in the contest between popes and emperors that proved even deadlier than the investiture struggle had been. Never had kings and popes despised and persecuted one another more than during the Hohenstaufen dynasty.

Frederick was originally a powerful lord from the Swabian house of Hohenstaufen when he was chosen king. In need of adequate resources to reestablish his control over the German princes, Frederick decided that the best way to

temporaries, the successor dynasty to the French Carolingians. The Ottonians, by contrast, overextended themselves when they tried to subdue Italy. As the briefly revived empire began to crumble in the first quarter of the eleventh century, the Church, long unhappy with Carolingian and Ottonian domination, prepared to declare its independence and exact its own vengeance.

THE HOHENSTAUFEN EMPIRE
(1152-1272)

During the twelfth and thirteenth centuries, England and France developed centralized, stable

generate such income was to pursue an aggressive Italian policy, which he believed would reward him with the needed income to subdue his German rivals. Frederick's plan was to create a new kind of empire. Previous German kings had focused on building a strong German kingdom, to which Italy might be added as an appendage. To Frederick, Germany was simply a feudal monarchy; his chief revenues would come from the much richer Italian states, which would become the center of a "holy empire," as he called it (hence the term Holy Roman Empire). Consequently, Frederick permitted his cousin, Henry the Lion of Saxony and Bavaria, to rule as "surrogate" emperor in Germany but knowing that Henry held the duchies as fiefs of the king, and that the other German princes recognized Frederick as their overlord. Such an arrangement allowed Frederick to concentrate on Italy. He marched an army into northern Italy where he was immediately victorious. His victory, however, proved short-lived. The papacy naturally was opposed to imperial expansion, for it rightfully feared that the emperor intended to include Rome and the Papal States as part of his empire. Luckily for the papacy, Frederick's threat to papal autonomy was resisted by Pope Alexander III, one of the Vatican's most competent and determined twelfth-century popes. While a cardinal (Roland), Alexander had negotiated an alliance between the papacy and the Norman kingdom of Sicily in a clever effort to strengthen the papacy against imperial influence. Perceiving Cardinal Roland to be a very shrewd foe, Frederick had opposed his election as Pope and even backed a schismatic Pope against him in a futile effort to undo Alexander's election. Frederick now found himself at war with the papacy, Milan, and Sicily. In 1167 these allies drove him back into Germany. The final blow to Frederick's imperial ambitions in Italy came a

The Normans had a huge impact on English architecture, such as the Durham Cathedral.

decade later, in 1176, when an alliance of northern Italian cities, known as the Lombard League, soundly defeated the emperor's forces at the Battle of Legnano. In the final Peace of Constance in 1183, Frederick had little choice but to grant the Lombard cities of northern Italy the full rights of self-rule.

Frederick now turned his attention back to Germany where he spent time breaking the power of his cousin Henry the Lion, who violated the emperor's trust by usurping Frederick's authority. Frederick's reign ended with a stalemate in Germany and defeat in Italy. At his death in 1190 he was not, as a ruler, equal in stature to the kings of England and France. After the Peace of Constance in 1183, he seemed himself to have conceded as much, accepting the reality of the empire's indefinite division among the feudal princes of Germany. In the last years of his reign, however, he had an opportunity both to solve his problem with Sicily, still a papal ally, and to form a new territorial base of power for future emperors. The Norman ruler of the kingdom of Sicily, William II (r. 166-1189), sought an alliance with Frederick that would free him to pursue a scheme to conquer Constantinople. In 1186 a most fateful marriage between Frederick's son, the future Henry VI (r. 1190-97), and Constance, heiress to the kingdom of Sicily, sealed the alliance. The alliance proved, however, to be only another well-laid plan that went astray. The Sicilian connection became a fatal attraction for future Hohenstaufen kings. It led them in the end to sacrifice their traditional territorial base in northern Europe to the temptations of imperialism. Equally ominous this union left Rome encircled, thus ensuring papal hostility for decades to come. The marriage alliance with Sicily proved to be the first step in what escalated into a fight to the death between Pope and emperor, resulting ultimately in the complete demise of the Hohenstaufen dynasty.

The period from 1000 to 1300 was a very dynamic one in European history. It witnessed economic, social, and political changes that some historians believe set European civilization on a path that lasted until the eighteenth century when the Industrial Revolution created a new pattern. The revival of trade, the expansion of towns and cities, and the development of a money economy did not mean the end of a predominantly rural European society, but such changes did lay the foundation to new ways to make a living and new opportunities for people to expand and enrich their lives. Eventually they created the basis for the development of a predominantly urban industrial society.

The nobles, whose warlike attitudes were rationalized by labeling them the defenders of Christian society, continued to dominate the medieval world politically, economically, and

socially. But quietly within this world of castles and private power, kings gradually began to extend their powers publicly. Although popes sometimes treated lay rulers as if they were their servants, by the thirteenth century, monarchs were developing the machinery of secular government that would enable them to challenge these exalted claims of papal power and become the centers of European political authority. Although they could not know it then, the actions of these medieval monarchs laid the foundation for the European kingdoms that in one form or another have dominated the European political scene ever since.

Suggestions for Further Reading

Marc Bloch, *Feudal Society*, 2 vols. (1961).

Jean Chapelot and Robert Fossier, *The Village and the House in the Middle Ages* (1985).

Karl Leyser, *Rule and Conflict in an Early Medieval Society: Ottonian Saxony* (1979).

H.R. Loyn, *TheGovernance of Anglo-Saxon England* (1984)

J.P. Poly and Bournazel, *The Feudal Transformation, 900-1200* (1991).

Susan Reynolds, *Fiefs and Vassals: The Medieval Evidence Reinterpreted* (1994).

Alfred P. Smyth, *Alfred the Great* (1995).

Chris Wickham, *Early Medieval Italy: Central Power and Local Society, 400-1000* (1981).

David Abulafia, *Frerderick II: a Medieval Emperor* (1988).

Benjamin Arnold, *Princes and Territories in Medieval Germany* (1991).

John Baldwin, *The Government of Philip Augustus* (1986).

Jean Dunbabin, *France in the Making, 843-1180* (2000).

Horst Fuhrmann, *Germany in the High Middle Ages, 1050-1200* (1986).

THE CHURCH IN THE HIGH MIDDLE AGES, c. 900 to 1216

In 1205 Hubert Walter, the Archbishop of Canterbury, died. His death meant that the most important office of the Roman Catholic Church in the kingdom of England was vacant. Such a Church post was important because it controlled access to a great deal of wealth in the form of Church property in England, as well as revenues of tithes Christians were obliged to give the Church and other fees and gifts that flowed into the Church. Also, with this wealth and property a person serving as Archbishop of Canterbury could be very influential in the political life of England since the kingdom's feudal system of government depended on distributing property as fiefs in exchange for loyalty and service. At the same time, the Archbishop position was important in directing the spiritual affairs of the entire kingdom. Lesser Church posts, implementation of Church policy, issues of morality, and other key religious matters in England were controlled or heavily influenced by the Archbishop of Canterbury.

For all of these reasons, controlling the appointment of the next Archbishop was vitally important to two men in particular in 1205. One was John, King of England. Endlessly restless, given to fits of rage, John was a man that wanted things to go his way. One of the pursuits John cared about was hunting. He had a dozen hunting lodges and traveled with several hundred hunting dogs and their attendants. John was particularly fond of falconry, using trained birds of prey to hunt smaller animals. If one of his falcons failed to return as trained, anyone who found the stray falcon had better return it. John's punishment for anyone attempting to steal a stray falcon points out his capability for cruelty in dealing with someone who dared oppose him: the bird was allowed to eat six ounces of flesh from the guilty man's chest. This imperious nature carried over into his rule of England. John got into a war with the king of France and was notorious for trying, against customary limits of royal power, to rule his kingdom with little or no input from or interference by the barons (the greater English nobles) or anybody else for that matter. Eventually, in 1215, his high-handed approach sparked a revolt of the barons at Runnymeade. Control of the post of Archbishop of Canterbury was something John could use to his advantage in ruling more completely and effectively.

The other man who was interested in the succession at Canterbury was Pope Innocent III, the head of the Roman Catholic Church. Innocent III had his own ideas about who should hold ultimate power in Christian lands such as England. According to him, as the vicar or representative of Christ on earth, the Pope held the highest authority, especially in matters that directly concerned the Church, as did an important Church office like the Archbishopric of Canterbury. Building on earlier developments, Innocent had moved the papacy (the office of the Pope) to its highest level of power and influence.

It is not surprising that these two men came into conflict over the appointment of the next Archbishop of Canterbury. King John very much wanted John de Grey in the post. Grey, although holding a Church post as the bishop of Norwich, was basically a politically involved court favorite *who could be counted on to follow King John's lead. John quickly interfered with the Church officials responsible for selecting the next archbishop, getting them to delay election until he had time to secure Grey's nomination. Some of the electors met in secret, however, and chose another man and sent him along to Rome to be confirmed by the Pope. When John learned of this, he rushed to Canterbury and in his enraged state intimidated the Church officials into rejecting the first election and naming John de Grey instead. Grey set off for Rome as well, and Innocent was faced with two men both claiming to be the rightful successor as archbishop. Innocent eventually dealt with the problem by rejecting both claimants and naming his own replacement, the very capable English scholar and church leader Stephen Langton.*

What followed was a long, heated struggle between John and Innocent over control of the post. John rejected Langton as unacceptable. The Pope confirmed Langton anyway in 1207. In 1208 Innocent placed England under an interdict, which stopped the performance of key Church duties, and he released all of the king's subjects from their oaths of allegiance to the king. John responded by seizing all the Church property in the kingdom, helping himself to revenues as long as he held the property. In 1209 Innocent excommunicated John, which according to Church teaching condemned John to damnation. Eventually, Innocent convinced King Philip Augustus of France to put together an army in preparation for invading England. By this time, 1213, John's position with his barons was such that he needed to avoid trouble with France and to resolve the dispute with the pope, so he caved in to the pope's wishes. John accepted Langton as Archbishop, gave back all of the seized Church property, promised to repay the money he had appropriated, and gave England to the Pope, receiving his kingdom back as a feudal fief from Innocent and becoming the Pope's vassal in the process.

Chronology

910	Monastery at Cluny founded
1049	Pope Leo IX convenes Easter Synod
1059	Lateran Synod reforms papal selection
1073	Hildebrand becomes Pope Gregory VII
1075	Lay Investiture conflict begins
1095	Pope Urban II calls the First Crusade
1098	St. Robert founds monastery at Citeaux
1122	Concordat of Worms ends Lay Investiture conflict
1173	Peter Waldo begins his ministry
1198	Lothario becomes Pope Innocent III
1201	Fourth Crusade begins
1209	*Regula primitiva* approved for the Franciscan order
1209	Crusade against the Cathari in France begins
1215	Fourth Lateran Council meets in Rome
1216	St. Dominic founds Dominican order
1291	Acre, the last Crusader state on the continent, falls to the Muslims

One of the central features of medieval life and the Western Civilization that came together in the medieval era, which most commonly bound provincial Europeans to a common identity, was the overarching presence, importance, and vitality of Christianity, especially in the form of the Roman Catholic Church. In the tenth through the early thirteenth centuries Western Christianity, the Roman Catholic Church that structured it, and the papacy that headed it, experienced a powerful surge of reform energy in the monasteries, in the ranks of the Church hierarchy, and among the common people. Western Christendom saw additional peoples converted, new abbeys and new monastic orders founded, Church governance refined, papal authority asserted against royal authority, crusades waged against heretics within Europe and infidels outside the continent, and various other expressions of a powerful piety. The Church and its Pope reached the high point of authority, influence, and power.

THE ELEVENTH-CENTURY CONDITION AND POSITION OF THE CHURCH

In the disruptive period of the ninth and tenth centuries, which included the disintegration of Charlemagne's empire into rival feudal principalities and the invasions and raids by Vikings, Muslims, and Magyars, Christianity and the Church suffered along with other facets of early Medieval society. Some of the Church's woes, such as the ruin and devastation of many monasteries, were directly related to the violence and disruption of the external invasions and raids in this period. Other problems, such as worldliness, corruption, and lay control of the clergy, stemmed, in part, from the political disintegration of the era and the lack of any effective power other than local warlords. Still other challenges, like the issue of papal authority and control of doctrine, were old problems that extended back to the early days of development of the Church organization.

Though much of Western Europe had been converted to Christianity for several centuries, that conversion at first had been from the top down and in many senses only nominal, leaving many decidedly non-Christian beliefs and behaviors in place that continually demanded the attention of concerned Christians. Many peoples in areas adjacent to the territory that had been incorporated into Charlemagne's empire, such as Slavs in Eastern Europe and the Norse of Scandinavia, remained pagan and offered the challenge of missionary work until conversions were effected in the tenth and eleventh centuries. However, as the challenge of paganism faded, the Church faced numerous internal problems from the perspective of morally scrupulous Christians and those interested in effective, spiritually-driven Church leadership.

Both the regular clergy (those who followed a rule or *regula*) of monastic orders and the secular clergy (those who interacted with the day-to-day world) of the hierarchical Church organization had problems. From the perspective of Christian piety, some of the most serious clerical problems involved moral degeneracy. As it was being defined in Medieval Catholicism, the clergy was a specially ordained group of spiritually empowered Christian leaders. The regular clergy of monasteries were to set examples of Christian devotion and focus on prayer. The secular clergy of priests and bishops had spiritual power to administer sacraments like baptism and the Eucharist that gave the laity access to the saving grace of God. These intercessory clergy ideally followed standards of morality higher than that expected of ordinary lay per-sons (believers who were not professional clergy) because of their key spiritual role and especially because of the example they necessarily presented to ordinary Christians. When the clergy rampantly engaged in immoral behavior, it threatened the legitimacy of the Christian message, as well as of the Church hierarchy.

In the ninth, tenth, and eleventh centuries examples abound of clergy who were anything but moral in the Christian definition. The Church had since the fourth century required candidates for ordination into the clergy to be celibate, that is to refrain from sexual relations with women. But in the tenth and eleventh centuries many priests in Europe were married or had concubines. Whether married or not, incelibate clerics who fathered children often tried to pass on their Church office or offices as an inheritance. Ratherius (ca. 887-974), a conscientious cleric who served as Bishop of Verona from 931-939, had trouble with his clergy in the Verona bishopric, some of whom were married and others who were licentious. When Ratherius tried to reform them, they defied him. This common practice of clerical incelibacy, called Nicolaism from a reference in the second chapter of the book of Revelation in the New Testament to those who professed to be Christians while living immorally, undermined the integrity of not only the local priests but popes as well.

Another major issue confronting the clergy was lay influence and control in the appointment of Church officials. Bishoprics, abbots, and other Church positions brought control of wealth, property, and the subject people living on Church estates, which were valuable benefits that lay rulers needed or craved in an age when taxation authority was limited or nonexistent. At the same time, the survival and success of these Church holdings often depended on local nobles' protection. These two primary factors often meant that lay rulers exerted tremendous influence if not direct control over the selection of candidates for Church positions. In many areas lay rulers not only appointed Church officials but also invested these officials with their spiritual authority by giving them the symbols of that authority, such as the ring and staff of the bishop. This *lay investiture* certainly conflicted with Church (and especially papal) claims to a monopoly on spiritual power and authority. When appointed by lay rulers, Church officials often served as arms of government, loyal to and under the direction of the rulers, and were often there only for the material benefits of the position. In many such cases, appointees did not concern themselves with the spiritual matters that went with the position, and the religious needs dependent on these officials went unmet. Lack of concern was accompanied by ignorance; many of the clergy knew little about theology or other aspects of the religion they represented. Ratherius, the devoted cleric noted above, was scorned for being willing to study his books all day.

Related to the problem of lay control of the clergy was the serious problem of the sale of Church offices, called *simony* after Simon Magus who supposedly tried to buy power from St. Peter. Because higher Church offices controlled wealth and income, they were desirable posts. Those who controlled office appointments, therefore, could, in effect, auction off the positions to the highest bidder, who could then hope to recoup the price of the office from proceeds derived from the wealth of the position while enjoying the remaining income. Simony, therefore, also contributed to the worldliness and lack of spiritual focus of Church officials since those who bought the offices had things other than devotion to religious duty on their minds.

Many of the problems among the clergy stemmed from the lack of effective control by the top of the Church administrative hierarchy, the papacy. Since local or regional political powers superseded the links of clerical authority, popes or other high Church officials could do little to enforce standards of clerical qualifications and behavior. Additionally, popes often were uninterested in trying to enforce such standards since by the eleventh century the papacy itself was very much under lay control and sported pontiffs as guilty of worldliness and serious moral lapses as any of the other clergy. By this time, popes were generally chosen through political maneuverings involving the populace of Rome, Roman aristocrats, and other European rulers, such as the German kings. A good example of political influence in papal selection and of extreme moral corruption in the papacy was Octavian who became Pope John XII in 955. John XII's father, Alberic, held great political power in Rome and had dominated the four previous popes before securing the papacy for his son. Only 18 years old upon assuming the papacy, John XII was known for his love of horses and women. According to one account, he hunted like "a wild man; he adored his collection of women" and was "hateful of the Church, beloved of violent youth." He reportedly consecrated a ten-year-old boy as a bishop, ordained a deacon in his stables, and while gambling with dice called on the pagan gods for help. Also known for his brutality, John XII had a cardinal-deacon castrated as punishment for some offense and, after regaining the papacy after being temporarily deposed by the German king, Otto the Great, he took revenge on some of the clergy who had opposed him, cutting off the hand of one cleric and the nose, tongue, and two fingers of another.

By the eleventh century, German kings were increasingly concerned with the papacy. Since 962 the German king claimed the title of Holy Roman Emperor, the idea of which traced back to Charlemagne and involved casting the kings as not only political heirs of the Roman Empire in the West but also as holy rulers with the religious mission of ruling in the interests of Christianity and with Christian authority. These kings also had designs on Italian territory. Therefore, they had a particular interest in the papacy since control of that office could help them both enhance the notion of the emperor as a religious power and secure control over Italy. On the other hand, since early in papal history, the popes had been concerned with not only religious authority but also political power. This situation points out a fundamental historical theme of the medieval period: the perception of two governmental structures in society, one controlling secular matters and the other controlling spiritual affairs, and the effort to figure out the proper relationship between the two governing hierarchies. Involvement in the papacy by the German throne and conflict between the two would be the springboard for raising the Church and the papacy to the high point of their power and influence.

Even had the papacy been in the hands of serious Christians concerned about spiritual matters, other problems would have competed for their attention. One such problem stemmed from the nature of medieval political economy. In feudal society control of land was a chief basis of power because it provided the financial and other resources needed to exercise both military and political power. The territory in Italy controlled directly by the Pope, known as the Papal States, was, therefore, a constant concern that often consumed a great deal of papal attention. Moreover, threats and opportunities posed by

external powers, such as the Lombards, the Eastern Roman emperors, the Franks, and the German kings, meant that the popes were frequently involved in international alliances and conflicts to protect their position or the office itself.

Another problem popes faced was the challenge to the idea of papal lordship over Christianity posed by the church in the east. East of a line running roughly along the Vistula River, the Carpathian Mountains, and the eastern border of Croatia, the Christian church was under the influence of leadership centered in Constantinople, capital of the Byzantine Empire, rather than Rome. Political concerns, such as Rome's need for protection that Byzantine emperors increasingly could not provide and theological differences such as the monophysite and iconoclastic conflicts dating back to the collapse of the Roman empire in the West, had led to a growing rift between Western Latin Christianity and Eastern Greek Christianity. While Roman popes continued to claim authority over all the Church, the patriarch of Constantinople and the Byzantine emperor actually exerted more control over Eastern Christianity. The Western and Eastern churches became increasingly estranged, and in an eleventh-century dispute Pope Leo IX's legate Cardinal Humbert excommunicated the Constantinople patriarch, Michael Cerularius, in 1054, who returned the favor, a mutual condemnation that would remain in place until 1965. The formal schism between Western Roman Catholic and Eastern Orthodox Christianity dates to this incident.

Yet another challenge confronting the papacy, and Christianity itself in some cases, was the threat of unorthodox (literally "not correct") teachings such as Catharism that occasionally arose in Europe and gained significant followings. By their very existence these *heresies* or "false teachings" and the *heretics* who believed in them presented a challenge to the key concept of a catholic (universal) church and the idea of a single plan of salvation monopolized by that church. Heresies, likewise, challenged the papacy, which claimed to be the penultimate Christian authority. If a group believed in or practiced something contrary to what the Pope's Church taught, they were directly rejecting the Pope's authority.

A final major challenge faced by Roman popes was the competing faith of Islam and, more importantly, the political threat posed by rulers of Islamic states. After the rise of Islam in the seventh century, Muslim rulers had established control over the old Near East, South Central Asia, North Africa, and the Iberian Peninsula of Europe. Frankish power under Charles Martel in the West and Byzantine power under Leo III in the East had blocked further extension of Muslim power toward Europe in the eighth century, though Muslim raids across the Mediterranean posed threats in the ninth and tenth centuries. However, in 1055 the Seljuk Turks, a powerful, nomadic people from the steppe land of Asia, seized control of the Muslim empire centered at Baghdad. The Seljuk Turks, who were members of the Sunni sect of Islam, launched a major attack against the Byzantine empire and routed the Byzantine army at Manzikert in 1071. They seized virtually all of Anatolia (Asia Minor or modern day Turkey) from the Byzantines, leaving that ancient empire with only its eastern European lands and a mere toehold of territory on the Asian continent. With the Byzantine bulwark against Islamic power that had protected Latin Christendom for centuries in danger of collapsing all together, popes had good reason to worry about the future of Christian Europe.

THE BREATH OF SPRING: A REFORM WIND RISES

Even in the depths of decay and corruption in the Church during the post-Carolingian collapse, serious Christians kept alive a more ideal vision of a disciplined Church and a truly Christian society. Although, of course, this vision could never be fully realized and major exceptions and contradictions would always exist, in the High Middle Ages the Church, led by an active papacy, went far toward that vision, creating a society in which Christian beliefs and practices permeated most aspects of life and an organized Church hierarchy with its papal leadership swayed even the obstinate kings of developing national monarchies. Monasteries dotted the landscape, the clergy composed the highest class of the social order, Christian cathedrals were the grandest architectural creations, the calendar was marked by Christian festivals and holy days, Church sacraments paced the life cycle of people great and small from baptism at birth to last rites at death, and disputes in kingdoms throughout Europe were appealed to the pope's courts. The achievements of the Church in the High Middle Ages were built on a reform movement that began in the tenth century among the regular clergy of the monasteries and spread to the papacy by the mid-eleventh century.

One of the first sparks of this reform movement was the establishment of the monastery at Cluny. In 910 reform-minded Christians were able to convince Duke William of Aquitaine to endow and establish a monastery at Cluny near Macon in Burgundy, France. William's charter establishing the abbey of Cluny was designed to prevent the abuses that kept other monasteries away from a spiritual focus. To eliminate lay influence, the land was given to the abbey free and clear without feudal service obligations. The monks had complete authority to elect their own abbot and any lay person that interfered in the selection of the abbot was to be excommunicated.   The monastery was placed under the direct authority of the Pope.   Interestingly, this move occurred at a time when popes had little influence.   This meant that Cluny was, for all intents and purposes, independent.   By attempting to circumvent lay influence by subordinating its members to the Roman Pope, Cluny helped bolster the idea of papal supremacy.

The Cluny charter also emphasized spiritual reform and sought to purify monastic life.   The Benedictine Rule, with some reform-minded revision, was strictly observed.   One modification of the older Benedictine Rule was that the definition of useful labor was broadened to include copying manuscripts.   Another change saw greater emphasis placed on communal prayer and liturgical observance.   Both of these adjustments were designed to reduce idleness and keep the monks occupied.   The Cluniac order also worked vigorously for clerical celibacy and against simony.

In its organizational structure, independence from lay control and devotion to spiritual regeneration, Cluny served as a tremendous inspiration in medieval Europe.   Hundreds of *daughter houses*, that is monasteries under the control of Cluny and following its rule and practices, were founded across Europe though mainly in France and Spain.   Many existing monasteries placed themselves under Cluny's control.   These daughter houses were headed by priors, all of whom were under the authority of the single abbot at Cluny, who regularly traveled to inspect the houses and enforce requirements.   This massive Cluniac expansion provided an active voice for Church reform that eventually influenced the reform of the papacy, as well as provided a virtual army of regular clergy that

reform-minded popes could call upon directly for action.   Most important, perhaps, the Cluniac reform movement helped spark reform of the papacy

By the end of the eleventh century, as wealth poured into Cluny from inspired Christians, its reforming zeal began to relax.   More worldly interests preoccupied the abbots and monks.   For instance, the great basilica of St. Peter and St. Paul built at Cluny mainly between 1088 and 1130, which was the largest church in the world until St. Peter's was constructed in Rome, served as the scene for Cluny's grand ceremonial and liturgical emphasis but also consumed a lot of administrative effort.

The eventual distraction of Cluny from reform certainly points out that even in times of spiritual reform the temptations that wealth and complacence brought were strong.   Many did not share the reformers' zeal. The Christian reform motivation, however, was very powerful in the High Middle Ages, and Cluny was not the only center of monastic reform.   Other houses assumed leadership in monastic reform as Cluny's reformism declined.   In 1098 St. Robert, the abbot of Molesme, founded a monastery at Citeaux, called Cistercium in Latin, in the Bordeaux region of Southern France.   The *Charta Caritatus,* or Charter of Love, that became the basic rule of the Cistercian order centered at this house was issued by St. Stephen Harding around 1120. Citeaux and the 525 new monasteries it founded in the 1100s were usually located in more remote, unimproved areas to emphasize seclusion from worldly influence, a tendency that led Cistercians to become very effective at land reclamation. The White Monks of the Cistercian order, so-called because they wore white mantles instead of the black typically worn by Benedictines, were more ascetic than many.   They ate a vegetarian diet, strictly observed manual labor requirements, and opposed artistic adornment of their places of worship, including the use of stained glass, jeweled crosses, and elaborate architecture. Though Citeaux too would see a decline in its reform impetus, its impact was significant.

In addition to Cluny and the Cistercians, other monastic movements illustrate the reform impulse. In the age of Cluny's great reforms in Western Europe, the abbey at Gorze in Lotharingia exercised tremendous reforming influence in central Europe, emphasizing a simple lifestyle and contributing to literary culture while serving the interests of the German empire and still accepting lay influence. The Carthusian order established in 1084 required its monks to live in cells, spend their time in prayer, meditation, and manual labor, and wear clothing made of hair. The Augustinians, another new order followed a rule significantly different from Benedict's, basing their practice on a letter written by St. Augustine that simply said monks should obey a leader, dress similarly, share their property, and regularly pray collectively. Augustinians focused on preaching, baptizing, hearing confessions, and assisting the poor. In the late tenth century monastic reform in England was pushed through by St. Dunstan, supported by King Edgar.

Perhaps the most important impact of the monastic-centered reform movement exemplified by Cluny was that it inspired the reform of the papacy from a weak post having only grandiose claims to superiority and power to a thriving seat of spiritual influence able to summon armies in defense of Christianity and bring kings into submission. In the High Middle Ages a rejuvenated and reform-minded papacy transformed the Church and its leadership into a powerful shaper of medieval civilization, from its theology to political developments to international confrontations. Hildebrand, who became Pope Gregory VII in 1073, came out of the Cluniac reform tradition to challenge lay control of the Church and other problems and set the stage for the greatness of the Church and the papacy in the High Middle Ages.

The reform of the papacy under Gregory VII was set up interestingly enough by the interference in the papal selection process by German kings. German kings had important reasons for being concerned with the selection of popes and represented important examples of lay influence over the Church. German kings had political motives behind their interest in Church appointments, but they also had religious motives, just as they did in expanding German control and Christianity eastward. In 1046 German emperor Henry III found three rival claimants to the papacy and intervened to place his own candidate on the throne of St. Peter. After two of Henry's appointees died shortly after assuming the papacy, perhaps due to poisoning, Henry III selected his cousin, the German bishop and reformist Bruno of Toul in Lorraine, as Pope. Bruno arrived in Rome dressed as a pilgrim and said he would only accept the papacy if the Roman clergy and populace accepted him. They did, and Bruno became Pope Leo IX in 1049.

Two months into office, Leo IX tackled problems among the clergy, such as incelibacy, at the Easter Synod of 1049. He gathered around himself a group of reformers, including Hildebrand, the future Pope Gregory VII, whom he charged with reforming the finances of the Church. Leo IX did much in the way of establishing the papacy as a center of reform, including travelling endlessly throughout Europe, preaching and holding reform councils to publicize papal decrees. At Reims, where Leo had traveled to dedicate the new basilica of St. Remigius, to press his effort against simony, he

Pope Gregory VII greatly strengthened the Western church. He was among the most powerful and influential popes in the history of the Roman Church.

called on all the bishops and abbots to stand and declare they had received their posts without simony. With all he attempted, the most significant and long-lasting reform Leo IX oversaw was the establishment of the college of cardinals as a body of Church leaders from throughout Europe who would serve as advisors and administrators. After a brief period of uncertainty in the papal succession after Leo IX's demise in 1054, Pope Nicholas II (1058-1061) oversaw the promulgation through the Lateran Synod of 1059 of a decree proclaiming that no priest should receive a church from a layman and that, henceforth, the popes would be selected by the college of cardinals. This helped set up the pos-

sibility of a line of reformist popes and dealt a blow to lay involvement in the papal selection. Nicholas also worked out an alliance with the Norman princes of southern Italy that would provide in the future an important source of support for the papacy against the German emperors.

The election of Hildebrand as Pope Gregory VII in 1073 confirmed the success of the reform movement in the papacy. Hildebrand had been a Cluniac reformer and had served Gregory VI and other popes interested in the extension of reform and papal authority in the direction of ending Nicolaism, simony, and the related problem of lay investiture. In 1075 Gregory issued his *Dictatus Papae*, or Papal Dictate, which asserted papal authority over bishops and emperors and the primacy and Catholicism of the Roman Church in matters of doctrine. Gregory appointed papal legates with full authority to pursue his policies in various countries. In doing these things, Gregory pushed the papacy in the direction of becoming a centralized authority over the Church and, in many senses, over Christendom. In what became the most controversial of his moves, Gregory also decreed in 1075 that, thereafter, no bishop or abbot should receive investiture from a lay ruler. If lay rulers could confer spiritual power, then the power and the authority of the Church was seriously weakened. At the same time, the moves to halt lay investiture challenged the German king's (at that time Henry IV) ability to govern his kingdom since he depended heavily on the support of bishops whom he appointed to provide military forces with which to oppose unruly princes. Gregory's policy and Henry's response led to the struggle between Pope and king known as the Lay Investiture Conflict.

When Henry IV (1056-1106) defied the Pope's directive on lay investiture in a case involving the bishopric of Milan, Gregory threatened to excommunicate the emperor, which meant to cut him off from the Church and thereby deny him the sacraments necessary for salvation. Henry called a meeting of German bishops that declared Gregory unworthy of the papacy. Henry wrote to Gregory telling him to "come down and relinquish the apostolic chair" that he had usurped in order "to be damned throughout all eternity." Gregory learned of this move in February 1076 and excommunicated Henry, as well as declared him deposed as king. This completely undermined Henry's somewhat tenuous authority by giving the rebellious German princes an excuse to openly defy Henry. Steps were taken to have the Pope come to Augsburg in Germany to confer with a diet of bishops and nobles as to Henry's fate as king.

As Gregory journeyed over the Alps in December 1076, Henry made a crafty move designed to have his excommunication lifted and thereby restore his authority as king. With his wife and young son, Henry traveled the narrow path of the Mont Cenis Pass in the cold and snow of winter to meet Gregory at the castle of Canossa in January 1077. According to one chronicler in what may be an apocryphal story, Gregory ordered that Henry be kept waiting, and Henry stood outside the closed castle gate, barefoot in the snow, dressed in the rough clothing of a penitent sinner, for three days and two nights. Finally Gregory admitted Henry who kissed his toe and begged forgiveness, and as was required of a priest confronted with a penitent sinner, Gregory forgave the humbled king, lifting the excommunication.

While this was obviously a personally humiliating experience for Henry, it was a political victory because it took away the justification for the German princes to rebel, and Henry was able to reassert his authority. Once reestablished in power, Henry again defied Gregory's lay investi-

ture policy, and the Pope once again excommunicated the king. This time the king remained in power and sent military forces to Rome where Henry declared Gregory deposed and appointed an antipope, or competing pope, in opposition to Gregory. The antipope crowned Henry Holy Roman Emperor in 1084. Thanks to the alliance forged by Pope Nicholas II with the Normans in southern Italy, Gregory was rescued by the efforts of Robert Guiscard, the Norman ruler of southern Italy, but died shortly afterward in 1085.

Although it seemed at Gregory's death that the Pope had failed, Henry IV suffered several setbacks, including the quick return of reformist popes with Urban II (1088-1099) in 1088. Urban II, famous for calling the First Crusade in 1095, continued to press the reform agenda of Gregory VII, including the lay investiture ban. During Urban II's papacy, the lay investiture struggle was taken to England and France as well. When Henry IV died in 1106, the lay investiture conflict remained unresolved. After the issue was settled in England and France during the pontificate of Pope Pascal II (1099-1118), the German king Henry V (1106-1125) worked out an arrangement with Pope Calixtus II (1119-1124) in 1122 known as the Concordat of Worms. This compromise settlement, similar to the English resolution, recognized the Church's right to elect bishops and confer the spiritual power of the office, symbolized by the ring and staff. The king, however, conferred the feudal lands and secular power that went with the office and so became feudal overlord of the bishop. Since the king could refuse to accept homage from any bishop candidate seeking to become his vassal, the king maintained a power to reject bishop candidates.

The impact of this lay investiture conflict was significant in many ways for medieval and later Western Civilization. An important set of writings by such authors as the unknown "Anonymous of York," Manegold of Lautenbach, Ivo of Chartres, and Hugh of Fleury, arguing one side or the other of the controversy, basically revived the study of political theory in the West. Perhaps more importantly for medieval history, the Church actually saw its power enhanced by this compromise. Even though kings retained a veto power over candidates for office they opposed, this marked a loss of the complete power they previously held. It became harder for the lay rulers to force obviously inappropriate candidates on the Church, and the quality of Church leaders improved as a result. Additionally, the outcome of this struggle was one of several developments enhancing the prestige and influence of the papacy. Finally, this controversy had far-reaching effects on European political development because of its decisive impact on Germany. In Germany, the princes used the opportunity for rebellion offered by the lay investiture conflict to gain the upper hand against kings' efforts to centralize power. After their selection of the weak Lothair of Supplinburg (1125-1137) to succeed heir-less king Henry V, the German princes wound up feudalizing Germany to the point that kings held title but little, if any, real power. The Holy Roman Empire evolved into a loose conglomeration of independent states and principalities that was the most politically decentralized of all areas in Europe.

The lay investiture struggle, while not a complete victory for the papacy and church reform, was a key effort in the papacy's effort to become and have the Church follow as a potent agent for action in the overall political and spiritual life of Europe. In addition to the struggle against lay control of key Church offices, the reformists were active in many endeavors. For example,

one of the more important initiatives of Pope Urban II (1088-1099) was the reorganization of papal government. The papal chancery, or letter writing office, its treasury, and the college of cardinals and other officials composed the papal *curia*, the church's bureaucracy and legal court. Over time this papal government would be highly involved in not only directing the business of the Church as overseen by the popes but also in providing the ultimate resolution of legal matters appealed to the pope's courts. The papal *curia* would become a model for monarchs interested in centralization of power, as well as the ultimate court of appeal in Christian Europe and, therefore, a symbol of papal and Church influence.

In related centralizing developments, popes made increasing use of legates and the Church refined and compiled its canons. Papal legates, officials directly responsible to the Pope, were sent out to the various dioceses to enforce papal policy. Legal scholars in this period busily collected, commented on, and explained Biblical passages, council statements, and decrees and writings of popes and other Church leaders. Ultimately one of these efforts, Gratian's *Decretum*, was adopted as the official law of the Church. The power of a revived Church and papacy, then, would be turned in various directions, including the generation and stimulation of the Crusades and the crusading impulse that in many senses are the quintessence of the High Middle Ages.

THE CRUSADES

One of the most famous and dramatic examples of the vitality and power of Christianity's revival in the High Middle Ages was the series of external holy wars that began in the eleventh century, eventually called *crusades* from the sign of the cross or *Crucesignati* that participants used. For many people, the Crusades refer specifically to the wars launched against the Muslim powers that held the Holy Land of Biblical times in order to place that Near Eastern territory in Christian hands, and usually the term is restricted to the crusades of the late eleventh, twelfth, and thirteenth centuries. Early modern historians' attempts to number and, thus, label the Crusades have contributed to this somewhat narrow view of crusading.

While most of the focus in this chapter is on the major, traditionally numbered Crusades, such a specific designation of the crusades obscures how widespread, varied in scope, and nearly constant the organizing and prosecuting of crusades was in the most intensive period, from 1095 to about 1291, and ignores similar activity that began earlier and extended well after the intensive period. These other crusades need to be mentioned. Many historians in recent years recognize a broader definition of the crusades to include military efforts against Muslim powers that controlled most of Spain, southern Italy, and the southern Mediterranean, including Sicily, in addition to the Holy Land. More attention has also been paid to the continuation of crusading in the fourteenth, fifteenth, and sixteenth centuries, with at least one study noting the fall to Napoleon in 1798 of Malta, a state governed until that time by the crusader order of the Knights Hospitallers of St. John, as the end of the Crusades.

Using a broader definition of the Crusades as being external military efforts fought by Europeans against Muslim-controlled areas, the High Middle Ages still gave rise to the crusading movement, gave ideological and inspirational impetus to later external crusades, and is a particularly important expression of the power of the revived Christianity of that era. In this context, the earliest crusades were waged in Spain as French nobles, primarily Normans and Burgundians and influenced by Cluniac reformers, mounted or assisted in attacks against Muslim territories on the Iberian Peninsula. As early as 1018, Roger de Tony from Normandy waged a war against the Muslims in Spain, and many subsequent attacks and wars followed. Over time, Christian kingdoms developed and expanded control over the peninsula, fighting primarily for territorial reasons, often fighting each other, and willing to ally with or fight against neighboring Muslim princes as the need arose. By the mid-1100s Spain was half-Christian and half-Muslim, with Castile, Aragon, and Portugal having become the most important Christian kingdoms. By 1252, the entire peninsula was in the hands of Christian rulers except the province of Grenada, which would survive as Muslim until the fifteenth century. Although religious crusading was not necessarily the prime motive in many cases for the Spanish princes and kings, the crusading impulse was still an important factor in this *reconquista*, or reconquest of

Church of the Holy Sepulcher in Jerusalem

Spain from the Muslims, especially for the French warriors who provided a lot of the manpower. Additionally, the papacy was able to extend its influence very effectively over Spanish Christianity, replacing the old Visigothic Christian practices with Roman Catholic modes and securing the right of papal legates to hold reforming councils. Elsewhere in the Mediterranean, Western Europeans also established Christian control over southern Italy, the Balearic Islands, Sicily, Corsica, and Sardinia.

The Crusades to recover Christian control of the Holy Land, particularly the Holy Sepulchre in Jerusalem, also began in the eleventh century at the behest of Pope Urban II. Urban II, of

Leaders of the First Crusade included (left to right) Godfrey, Raymond, Bohemund, and Tancred. The forces of these men made up the true military might of the Crusade.

Godfrey of Bouillon marches victoriously through Jerusalem, where mutilated corpses litter the streets.

noble birth and originally named Odo of Chatillon-sur Marne, had served as an archdeacon, a monk, a prior-superior at Cluny, a cardinal, a bishop, and as a papal legate for Gregory VII before being named pope in March 1088. This reform pope, a tall, handsome, bearded man, was attending a church council at Clermont in Auvergne on November 27, 1095, when he preached to the council, calling upon the European nobility to stop fighting each other and go fight a holy war to help fellow Christians of the Byzantine Empire against the Muslims and to recover the Holy Land. The Pope offered spiritual rewards in the form of remission of sins to those who would go. Urban preached his call for a crusade elsewhere in France, and other preachers took up the call throughout Europe.

The response to this call to arms was nothing short of dramatic. Heavily armed knights,

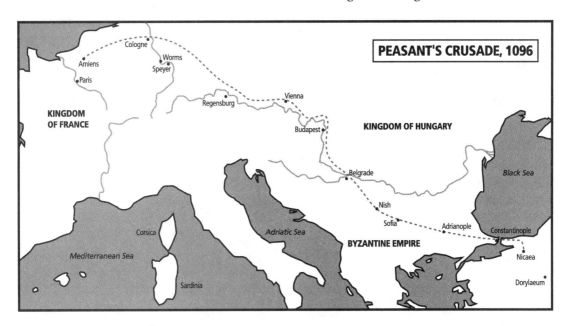

the fighting splendor of Europe, answered the call from across Europe and organized bands under the leadership of notable nobles such as Robert, Duke of Normandy, and Hugh, Count of Vermandois, brothers of the English and French kings, respectively. Raymond de St. Gilles, a count of Toulouse who had fought in wars against the Spanish Muslims, led a contingent from southern France. Godfrey of Bouillon led forces from Lorraine, German territories, and Belgium. Others, like Bohemond and his followers, came from elsewhere in Europe. Urban II appointed Adhemar, the bishop of Le Puy, as leader of the enterprise.

Peasant's Crusade

While the nobles were organizing and preparing their expedition, a remarkable and tragic band of peasants and poor knights formed and set off for the Holy Land in the spring of 1096, gathering additional followers as they went. Inspired by other preachers, such as the popular Peter the Hermit and Walter the Penniless who had taken the call for a crusade to people of all ranks, this hapless, unprepared, and largely unsoldierly bunch had fervor for the cause but little else, not even an understanding of where the Holy Land was. One band of Germans followed a goose they believed to be inspired by God. Referred to as the Peasant's Crusade, this motley crew was primarily led by Peter the Hermit and Walter Sansavoir, a poor knight from France. Peter the Hermit's donkey, which Peter's long and lean face supposedly resembled, had its hairs completely plucked out by followers seeking souvenirs. Having no supplies, these crusaders depended on contributions and, frequently, plunder to survive. They attacked Jewish quarters in the French and German towns along the way, stealing from and killing thousands of Jews. Some who plundered in Hungary were crushed by the Hungarians, and the king of that country annihilated one group at the border, though other groups passed through Hungary without incident. Eventually, a large

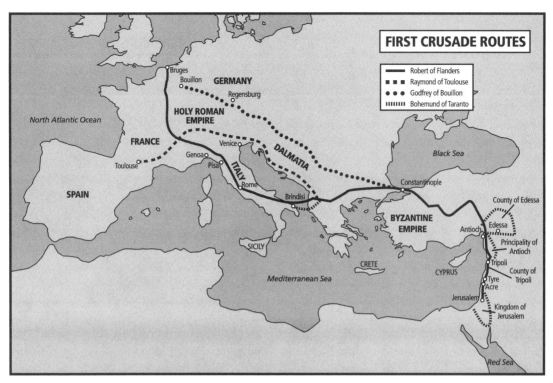

FIRST CRUSADE ROUTES

— Robert of Flanders
▪▪▪ Raymond of Toulouse
●●● Godfrey of Bouillon
ⅡⅡⅡⅡ Bohemund of Taranto

group made it to Constantinople where the Byzantine emperor, Alexis I, who had to be disappointed with the aid that Europe had sent him, got the unruly band out of his city as quickly as possible by transporting them to Muslim-held Anatolia. Being largely untrained and having only limited weaponry, if any, the members of the Peasant's Crusade were easy targets for the Seljuk Turks, who slaughtered many of them at Nicaea. Only a few scattered remnants found haven with some Byzantine forces, with whom they could only wait for the forces led by the barons.

First Crusade

The noble forces, comprised of genuine warriors, arrived in Constantinople in 1097 and moved on into Anatolia. Though not an army sent to serve for pay under Alexis as that emperor had

wanted, this group of crusaders was a formidable fighting force of probably 2000-3000 knights and 8000-12,000 infantrymen. They took Nicaea and, with a good deal of luck, defeated the Seljuk Turks at Dorylaeum, victories that enabled the Byzantines to regain control of western Anatolia. Moving on southeast across Anatolia, this First Crusade conquered Antioch in 1098, which became the center of a western-style feudal state under Bohemond of Tarranto, son of Robert Guiscard, from southern Italy. Baldwin, brother of Godfrey of Bouillon, carved out a principality around Edessa.

After breaking a Turkish siege of Antioch, the bulk of the crusaders headed south along the Mediterranean coast, receiving supplies and troops from an Italian fleet along the way, and reached Jerusalem in June 1099, placing the city under siege. The siege was eventually successful, and the crusaders entered Jerusalem on July

13, 1099. The consequences of this victory were horrific: the crusaders engaged in a terrible massacre of the city's residents. According to Fulcher of Chartres, 10,000 men, women, and children who had fled to Solomon's Temple were beheaded inside where the blood accumulated ankle-deep. While Fulcher's account may certainly exaggerate, the capture of Jerusalem was frightfully bloody.

After securing Jerusalem, the crusaders established a feudal kingdom there as well, the territory of which included much of Palestine and extended north along the Mediterranean coast to just north of Tyre. Godfrey of Bouillon was elected king and took the title of Defender of the Holy Sepulchre. The County of Tripoli, given to Raymond of Toulouse, was formed in the area on the coast between the northern boundary of the Jerusalem kingdom and the southern border of the Antioch principality. A continuous stream of crusaders and pilgrims provided reinforcement for these Latin states in the east, and two military orders established in the area, the Knights of the Temple and the Knights of the Hospital of St. John of Jerusalem, provided a significant military force on an on-going basis.

The First Crusade, then, was largely successful. It had defeated the Muslim forces, established Latin Christian control over the Holy Land and additional territory, and had even assisted the Byzantines against their enemies in the process. This success, however, was due only in part to the crusaders' zeal and skill. Good luck and timing were also important factors. The crusade had happened at a politically advantageous time, with the Muslim empire centered at Baghdad suffering from political fragmentation, particularly in Anatolia where princes were asserting independence from Baghdad and from each other. At the battle of Dorylaeum, the cru-

saders had been moving in two separated columns, out of contact with one another, one under Bohemond and the other under Godfrey. Bohemond's group had been surrounded by the Turks when Godfrey's forces managed to arrive just in time and save the day after a search party finally stumbled upon them and delivered its message of distress. Another critical factor had been the service of the navies of Italian cities, which provided transportation of supplies and reinforcements and kept the Muslim navies from being able to hamper the crusaders. In subsequent years, the role of the Italian naval presence would only become more important in bringing supplies, transporting crusaders, and influencing the direction of events.

What accounts for this response to Urban II's call for a crusade? And why did he call for one in the first place? Why did subsequent Crusades continue to inspire dramatic participation? The causes of the Crusades include several factors. First, increased preaching and Biblical learning, along with significantly increased pilgrimages to the Holy Land in the eleventh century, had heightened European familiarity with the places of the Holy Land and so would be more concerned when Christian access to them seemed threatened. Then, the Seljuk Turks, Muslims from further east, had come on the scene, seizing control of the Holy Land, restricting access to it, and also driving back the Byzantine Empire's control of Asia Minor, or Anatolia. The Seljuk Turks, therefore, posed a threat not only to Christian access to the Holy Land but also a political danger to the Byzantine Empire, which had stood for centuries as a Christian bulwark against Muslim incursions into Europe. Byzantine emperors had called for help from Europe in the form of mercenaries who would help the Byzantines regain their Anatolian territory from the Muslim Turks. At the same time,

Europe was replete with nobles whose main vocation was warfare. When a legitimate reason for war did not present itself, many of these noble warriors had no problem going out and fighting anyway. One primary reason for such unprovoked fighting was economic; second sons and others of little or no inheritance could enhance their position by taking territory or plunder from others. This constant internecine warfare created many problems, including the religious dilemma posed by Christians who were supposed to love one another, even enemies, fighting other Christians, especially at a time of religious revival.

Urban II's call for the First Crusade tapped many of these sources. First, he hoped that a war against non-Christians outside of Europe would provide an outlet for the energy of the warring class. The Church had been attempting to curb the violence of the warrior nobility through the Peace of God and the Truce of God, policies that limited the times and amount of fighting. A crusade would be another way to try to bend the values of a warrior society in a Christian direction. Second, Urban felt a holy war would answer the call for help from the Byzantine emperors, bolstering them as a block against Islam and possibly helping heal the growing rift between the Roman Church and the Byzantine Eastern Church. He also hoped to secure Christian access to the Holy Land and strike a blow to Islam, which was viewed as a false religion in mortal opposition to Christianity, by taking over that territory. Finally, at a time when the papacy was greatly concerned about its own power and influence, particularly in relation to the rulers of Europe, successful leadership of a major endeavor involving the ruling nobility of Europe could enhance papal prestige and power.

Those who answered the call to take the cross and go on a crusade were also motivated by many factors. Certainly, the sense of adventure and the prospect of securing fiefs, or plunder, appealed to many in the noble class. This was especially true for those who had no prospect of future inheritance. Still, it should be remembered that going on a crusade to a far away land was an expensive and dangerous proposition. Many crusaders spent a great deal of wealth, many going into debt, to be able to go. They left the known to go into the unknown with the usual expectation that they might not return. To understand this, it is necessary to see the power of the religious motive. Most crusaders were convinced that they were doing God's will and that they would receive the reward of heaven in the afterlife for their service. Over time, as the crusades were deflected from their original purpose, this motivation would wane, and it became increasingly difficult to recruit fresh crusaders. For nearly two centuries, however, going on a crusade remained a chief way for sincere medieval Christians to demonstrate their faith.

Second Crusade

As it turned out, the First Crusade was the high point of the Crusades from the perspective of the many Europeans who supported them. Eight major subsequent crusades, many lesser crusades, and a nearly constant stream of crusaders going to the Latin East were all mainly concerned with trying to bolster the crusader states established in the First Crusade or with trying to win back these territories after Muslim forces had retaken them. The Second Crusade (1145-1149) was called under Pope Eugenius III and preached by Bernard of Clairvaux when the crusader state of Edessa was conquered by the Muslims in 1144. Emperor Conrad III of the Holy Roman Empire and King Louis VII of France led this ven-

Muslim General Saladin granted Christians access to Jerusalem.

ture but failed completely, being defeated in their effort to take Damascus.

Third Crusade

After the Kurdish Muslim General Saladin defeated the crusader kingdom at Hattin in 1187 and retook Jerusalem, a Third Crusade (1187-1192) was launched under the impressive leadership of Holy Roman Emperor Frederick Barbarossa, King Richard I, the Lionhearted, of England, and King Philip II Augustus of France. Frederick was moving overland through Anatolia where he had some military success when he drowned in the Calycadnus River while bathing. Richard and Philip, arguing constantly, traveled by sea. After successfully besieging the coastal city of Acre, Philip went home. Richard was only able to negotiate an agreement with Saladin to restore a few coastal towns to Latin control and to allow Christian pilgrims to go to Jerusalem. Though not a complete failure, the Third Crusade did not accomplish much and certainly failed to restore the kingdom of Jerusalem.

Fourth Crusade

One of the most corrupted crusades and one that never made it to the Holy Land, the Fourth Crusade (1201-1204), was sidetracked by the Venetian suppliers and transporters of the crusaders into helping Venice take the Dalmatian coastal city of Zara. Then the Venetians got involved in a dispute over the succession of the Byzantine emperorship and used the crusaders to install the Venetian-supported candidate. When the residents of Constantinople rebelled against this

Richard the Lionheart led the Third Crusade but never reached Jerusalem.

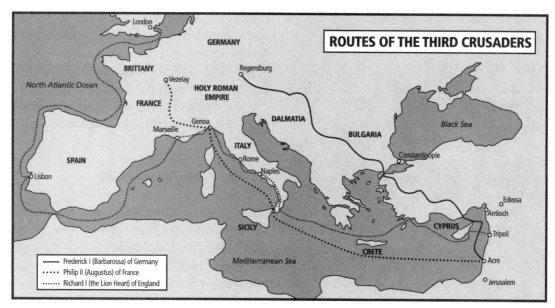

imposed regime, the crusaders ended up looting Constantinople, desecrating Eastern Orthodox Christian churches, and breaking up the empire, setting up several Latin states in part of its territory. The Byzantine Empire that had for centuries protected Christian Europe from Eastern Muslim powers was dealt a blow from which it would never recover, ironically by crusaders who were part of a movement originally called to assist their fellow Christians, the Byzantines.

Children's Crusade

In 1212, two twelve-year-old boys, Stephen in France and Nicholas in Germany, began calling for a crusade of children. They said that angels would serve as guides and that God would open up the sea for them to pass to the Holy Land as He had for the Israelites to escape the Egyptians in the Old Testament. This Children's Crusade saw thousands of boys and girls flock together in a march to the sea. Clergymen, vagabonds, and prostitutes also joined the throng, as did, so credulous accounts claimed, swarms of birds and

butterflies. Some of the German children somehow made it to the Holy Land where they disappeared. When the sea did not part for the French children at Marseilles, they accepted the offer of two shipowners to transport them free-of-charge to the Holy Land. Instead of taking the children to the Holy Land, however, William of Posqueres and Hugh the Iron took them to North Africa and sold them into slavery.

Subsequent Crusades

The story of the other major crusades in the High Middle Ages, the Fifth Crusade (1217-1221), the Sixth Crusade (1228-1229), the Seventh Crusade (1248-1254), and the Eighth Crusade (1270), though not as sordid as that of the Fourth nor as tragic as the Children's Crusade, were failures as well. The Sixth Crusade, led by Holy Roman Emperor Frederick II, brought some results with Jerusalem being regained, but this was done by treaty and Muslim forces retook Jerusalem a little over a decade later. In 1291, the coastal city of Acre fell to the Muslims and the last remaining Latin holding on the mainland was gone.

Outcomes and Failures

One overriding outcome of the Crusades was the ultimate failure to assert Western control over the territory of the Holy Land. This fundamental objective of the crusade preached by Urban II was only achieved temporarily, and in the long run all territorial gains in the Holy Land were lost. Moreover, in trying to accomplish this objective, Europe had expended tremendous resources in people, wealth, supplies, and leadership. So even if one accepts the validity of this objective, the Crusades were expensive failures. If another objective of the Crusades was to support the Byzantines, the Crusades failed on this point as well, the Fourth Crusade in particular contributing to the ultimate demise of that ancient remnant of the Roman Empire. If an objective of individual nobles was to secure territory that they had little hope of acquiring if they remained in Europe, then for most adventurers the Crusades were failures on this point as well since all the territory gained in the Holy Land was eventually lost again to Muslim powers. The only objective for which the Crusades saw resounding success was the effort to siphon off from Europe some of the frenetic warring energy of the nobility and direct it against someone else. Although the crusaders quarreled among themselves, they proved quite capable of fighting and killing Muslims and others. They also did very well at dying, an end that permanently removed some of the warring influence from Europe. A poignant reminder of the nature of the Crusades is that the Crusades' biggest success was in bringing about death.

There are several reasons for the failure of the Crusades. The Crusades as military operations left much to be desired. They lacked cohesive command structure, with various noble leaders bickering among themselves over strategy, power, and rewards. The operations were conducted far from home and presented logistical problems that the crusaders were unable to overcome. Though strategy was increasingly a consideration, there was no overall strategy in place, in part, because there was no overall leadership structure in place. The military forces were insufficient for the task at hand, especially the task of holding the territory once taken. Another factor in the failure of the Crusades was the fact that Europe gained no decisive or critical material or political advantage by taking and holding the Holy Land. The religious purpose of the Crusades was not, therefore, bolstered sufficiently by other purposes. A final reason to consider is the resiliency and fighting capability of the Muslim armies and the quality of their leadership, which contributed much to the demise of the crusaders.

Even though the Crusades were not successful in achieving their primary objectives, their impact on Western Europe was still important. The efforts of medieval kings to strengthen themselves at the expense of the other nobles were aided by the fact that many nobles expended much time, energy, and wealth on Crusades that otherwise might have been used in resisting royal authority or in destabilizing quarrels with other nobles. Kings also used the crusades to extend their power in other ways. For example, Philip Augustus of France used the sense of duty inspired by the Crusades to extend royal taxation power by taxing those who would not go on a crusade, knowing that such individuals would have little support from the larger community in opposing such a penalty. Related to this development, the absence of nobles gone on crusades gave greater opportunity to serfs and other peasants to escape their bonds. Crusaders' financial needs provided opportunity for dependents to bargain for better terms and conditions or buy their freedom. These developments also likely contributed to the movement of population from the countryside to towns.

Another impact of the Crusades was felt in the world of commerce. For one thing, the greater contact between Western Europe and the East increased European awareness of and demand for products of the East like spices and silk cloth. The result was enhanced trade between the East and Europe. Related to this, the Crusades, with the potential profit they offered from supplies and transportation services, gave additional cause for Italian cities like Venice, Genoa, and Pisa to make concerted efforts to completely drive Muslim naval power from the Mediterranean. The result was both increased power and control of trade for the Italian cities. This result was aided by the reduction of Constantinople's commercial power. The crusaders themselves with their need for supplies and transport to the East greatly contributed to the growing wealth of these cities, and the enhanced power and trade helped generate ongoing sources of wealth. While both the increasing trade and enhanced power and wealth of the Italian cities were developing before the Crusades and may have continued without the Crusades, these adventures certainly contributed to and hastened these developments.

One of the longest-lasting impacts of the Crusades was the damage that they caused in the relations between Western European Christian society and other groups. The zeal of the crusaders was turned early on against Jews living throughout Europe, and the root of modern anti-Semitism is found in the crusade-stimulated medieval attitude toward the Jews as internal infidels. The crusaders' mistreatment of Eastern Orthodox Christians, most famously in the Fourth Crusade, helped make the divide between Latin and Greek Christianity a permanent one and contributed to a legacy of mistrust that still lingers. Finally, the Crusades did immeasurable damage to Christian-Muslim relations. The Crusades were conducted against people solely because of religious belief under the sanction and encouragement of the Christian Church and its leadership. Muslims were cast as evil, wicked, and abominable because they were Muslims. Killing them was cast as a noble, holy act. It is understandable that Muslims would continue to feel a strong sense of mistrust and hatred toward Christians and be willing to reciprocate with their own holy wars, especially given the brutal and merciless way in which the Crusaders prosecuted their holy wars. The twenty-first century continues to reap the harvest of hatred and death sown by the Crusades.

Religiously, the Crusades had several impacts. While the papacy stood to gain power and influence from its role in directing great movements in a proclaimed holy cause, the failure of the Crusades and the corruption of purpose of many of them, especially the Fourth Crusade, caused disillusionment and undermined the prestige of the papacy. If these were holy wars fought for God and they failed, many Christians were forced to question either the power of God or the legitimacy of the Church that called for the failed endeavors, and it was easier to decide that the Church was the fallible party. The too liberal use of spiritual rewards and use of the rewards for increasingly political and ignoble purposes also promoted this disillusionment. Still, the Crusades both demonstrated and were an exercise of the prestige and influence that Roman Catholic Christianity held in medieval Europe and so must be seen as an example of the Church's ability in the High Middle

Ages to motivate tremendous effort from its adherents.

INTERNAL CRUSADES

The term crusade was also used to describe the offensives launched against theological foes of Latin Christianity found within Christian Europe: the heretics. The word heresy comes from a Greek word meaning "choice," and so heretics were Christians, or those who held Christian-like beliefs, who chose to believe false teachings, teachings that ran counter to the orthodox, or "straight-thinking," beliefs approved by the Church that were necessary for salvation. Choosing to believe falsehoods, heretics endangered their own immortal soul and the souls of others they might infect with their false teachings. Since religion and its truths were seen as essential to the functioning of medieval society, heretics were like traitors, as well as doctrinal polluters.

Catharism

One of the most famous groups of heretics of the High Middle Ages and one that was the target of a so-called crusade was the Cathari, meaning "the pure." These heretics were also called the Albigensians because the French town of Albi in Languedoc was the center of their religion. Catharism was composed of elements of Christianity but also seems strongly connected to the Eastern religion Manicheanism taught by Mani of the third century, though a direct link between the two has not been proved. Catharism was a dualistic religion that taught that God, the God of goodness and light, created the spiritual world and that Satan, the evil prince of darkness, created the material world. Things of the material world, such as the physical body, meat, and the materialistic Catholic Church, therefore, were

evil. The soul of a human was a good spirit trapped in an evil body. This led the Cathari to see extreme asceticism, the self-denial of physical and material gratification and comforts, as the ideal expression of religion. This view, effectively put into practice by the *perfecti* class of Cathari, stood in stark contrast to the luxurious, worldly living being enjoyed by many of the upper clergy in the Catholic Church, a fact that helped the Cathari win many converts in areas where clerical immorality and worldliness were most prolific. The Cathari also believed that since the body was evil, Christ, whom they saw not as God but an agent of God, could not have been an actual physical man but had only taken the appearance of a man. Likewise, since sexual reproduction created more people and, therefore, more evil material bodies with souls trapped in them, sex was to be avoided.

While Catharism involved more than this brief description, it is easy to see the challenge this belief system posed to Catholic theology, since it cast the Church as an evil part of the material world and even denied the very divinity of Christ. Catharism seems to have emerged in northern Italy and southern France in the tenth century. In the eleventh century it spread elsewhere in Europe, but southern France became its strongest center, where count Raymond VI of Toulouse and other nobles in the region around Albi tolerated and even protected the heresy and its believers. So many people in the region adopted the religion that apparently at one Catholic service the bishop of Albi and his fellow clerics were the only ones in attendance at the cathedral.

The Church at first attempted to deal with the heretics by preaching and conversion. Indeed it was the rampant heresy of southern France that led the Spanish priest, Dominic de Guzman, to begin preaching among the Cathari about 1205 and eventually to found the Dominican order of preaching friars. Innocent III, who became Pope in 1198, tried the preaching and conversion approach for a time. In 1204, however, after being met by indifference from the noble rulers of the area, he listened to advisors who argued that only force would end the heresy. Innocent appealed to King Philip Augustus of France in that year to lead troops to southern France to deal with the Cathari. Preoccupied with other matters, Philip did not oblige the Pope, but finally after a papal legate was murdered in the heretical region in 1208, Philip agreed to give permission to French nobles to engage in a crusade. Accepting what he could get, Innocent called for a crusade against the Cathari heretics, offering spiritual rewards just as for Holy Land crusaders. An army formed in northern France and headed south in the early summer of 1209.

Under the leadership of papal legate Arnold Amalric, the crusaders reached Beziers, a town peopled with many heretics. As the crusaders took the town, the legate was reminded that many Catholics lived there. Amalric responded that the crusaders should "kill all, for God will know his own." The crusaders complied, slaying all the townspeople, some 7000 hiding in a church to which they had fled for safety. After considerable action in which many additional heretics or suspected heretics were killed and the nobles who had supported them deprived of their territories, Catharism was virtually wiped out. As an indirect result, eventually the king of France wound up in personal possession of much of southern France.

Waldensians

Other heresies and non-Christian religions suffered persecution that was certainly tied to the crusading impulse though not targeted by official calls for military action as was the case with Catharism. One such heretical group was the Poor Men of Lyons, also called the Waldensians, who were followers of the preacher Peter Waldo of Lyons. Waldo was a successful merchant who, inspired by the idea that clerics should live in poverty and focus on spiritual matters, in 1173 gave up his wealth and turned to wandering around the countryside preaching in the vernacular language and relying on alms begged from the people for his support in emulation of the life of Christ. Others were inspired to follow suit. Eventually in 1178, the Archbishop of Lyons, concerned about complaints of errors in interpretation, attempted to silence these self-appointed preachers for preaching without a license, a measure the Pope confirmed the following year. Waldo and his followers defied the Pope's decision, and they were condemned as heretics in 1181. Expelled from the archdiocese of Lyons, the Waldensians travelled to nearby regions, establishing a strong presence in southern France and northern Italy. Though the Church was able to return some to orthodox beliefs, others came to deny the necessity of the Church and its sacraments for salvation. Some Waldensian communities in mountain valleys of Savoy and Piedmont were able to maintain their beliefs against repressive measures. Waldensian groups survive today.

Jews

Jews were another group that suffered from the climate that the crusades helped create. The official Church position on the Christian relationship toward Jews remained one of toleration in that Jews were not to be forcibly converted since they provided independent testimony of the prophesies and teaching of the Christian Old

Testament, and many Church leaders condemned and worked to prevent anti-Semitic violence. Other Church attitudes and actions, however, contributed to anti-Jewish sentiment. Innocent III complained to Philip Augustus of France about a Jewish synagogue in Sens that was built taller than the Christian church. The Fourth Lateran Council of 1215 decreed that, in order to help prevent sexual relations between Christians and Jews or Muslims, the Jews and Muslims were to wear distinctive clothing, which most often was enforced by the degrading policy of requiring them to wear a cloth badge, such as a yellow star for Jews, sewn on their outer garments. In addition to these Church actions, the period of the Crusades saw the spread of rumors claiming that Jews kidnapped Christian children and ritually murdered them in mockery of Christ's crucifixion or that Jews stole the host, the consecrated bread used in the Eucharist as the body of Christ, and desecrated it. Such stories were popularly believed despite their ludicrous nature and contributed to a general increase in anti-Jewish sentiment and action in the period of the crusades.

In reality, then, the security of Jews depended on local willingness to tolerate them and nobles' willingness to protect them. As noted earlier, in the First and Peasant's Crusades, European Jews often suffered the wrath of zealous crusaders or those inspired by the call to fight the enemies of Christ, having their property plundered and even their lives taken. Often economic motives for these attacks on Jews were mixed with misplaced religious zeal. In York, England, in 1189 as preparations for a crusade were underway, some knights who owed money to Jewish moneylenders plundered a Jewish home, which set off an anti-Jewish riot, which, inflamed by a hermit preacher, resulted in the death of the entire Jewish community there.

Afterwards, a group of knights seized the records of debts owed to the Jews and burned them.

THE ZENITH OF PAPAL POWER AND CHURCH REFORM

The Crusades, with all their misdirection, hypocrisies, and failures, still represented an often sincerely intended expression of Christian faith that was characteristic of the High Middle Ages. This faith was the basis of the movement that had reformed the Church, revived the papacy, and inspired many Europeans to place their eternal hopes fully in the hands of the Roman Church. The high point of this reform and its impact in many senses was reached in the late twelfth and early thirteenth centuries. Three developments were important facets of this apogee of papal power and Church reform: the pontificate of Innocent III (1198-1216), the rise of the mendicant orders, and the flowering of popular piety.

Though many popes claimed great religious and secular power, few were able to wield such power effectively. Innocent III, despite many failures and limited successes, was able to use the office of Pope more effectively in both religious and secular matters than perhaps any other Pope and represents the high point of the revitalized papacy of the High Middle Ages. Upon the death of 92-year-old Celestine III in 1198, the College of Cardinals selected as successor 37-year-old Lothario, the son of the Count of Segni. Lothario, who was Cardinal-deacon of St. Sergius and St. Bacchus and had received his clerical education in Bologna and Paris, took the papal name Innocent III. He began his pontificate at a time when the papacy had been engaged in a long struggle with the Hohenstauffen emperors of Germany over Italian territory and politics. Pope

Innocent III regained control of the papal bureaucracy and extended papal control of territory in Italy, doubling the size of the papal states by his death in 1216. He also claimed, and worked to use, the authority to approve or reject German candidates for the emperorship.

Although imperial and Italian politics continued to be an issue for Innocent, these problems occupied less of his attention than matters more closely related to his authority and power, as he claimed, as vicar of Christ. Innocent called for the Fourth Crusade (1201-1204) that went terribly astray as the crusaders under Venetian influence pillaged Constantinople and seized control of the Christian Byzantine Empire instead of the Muslim-held Holy Land. Although Innocent deplored the misdirection of the crusade and the brutality and skullduggery of the crusaders and Venetians, it seemed at the time that the developments had led to the reestablishment of Roman Catholic control over the Eastern Christian Church, an important goal since the breach of 1054. In the end, the Latin Christians' actions made the Eastern Christians so irreconcilable that the breach was more permanent than ever, but to the Europe of Innocent's day, it seemed that the papacy had extended control over the Eastern Church.

Innocent was also able to effectively control, to a certain extent, the ambitious and powerful monarchs of Western Europe, such as King John of England and King Philip II Augustus of France, at least in ways that impacted the popes' religious leadership. As the chapter's introductory story recounted, Innocent, after a struggle, compelled John to accept the papal candidate for the Archbishopric of Canterbury and John wound up submitting to the point of not only accepting the papal candidate but also of giving England to the Pope to receive it back as a fief. Philip Augustus of France became a target for

King John did little to endear himself to others. He was a disagreeable man whose cruelty and arrogance eventually led to his political defeat.

Innocent's ire due to Philip's marital activities. The widowered French king took Ingeborg, a princess from Denmark, as his second wife in exchange for a cash dowry payment and the hope that the Danish fleet could help him against England. After deciding that he could not stand Ingeborg, Philip convinced two French clerics to annul the marriage on the grounds that he and Ingeborg were too closely related. Pope Celestine III overturned the annulment after Ingeborg's family appealed the decision. Even though the Pope had declared Philip to be still married to Ingeborg, Philip married Agnes from Bavaria in 1196. When Innocent became Pope in 1198, he sent a legate to France with the power to place France under an interdict if Philip did not repent. When Philip refused to comply with the papal position, the interdict was put in place in January 1200. Concern about the damage the interdict would do to his position in France, as well as the death of Agnes in July, led Philip to agree to the papal voiding of his annulment and the interdict was lifted in September. Still Philip continued to argue the case. Innocent doggedly pursued the matter until Philip finally formally took Ingeborg back as his wife and queen of France in 1213. While political considerations had been important in Philip's submission, this episode still reveals the influence popes could have in matters clearly within the religious sphere.

Perhaps the most far-reaching development of Innocent III's pontificate was the general church council Innocent presided over in Rome in 1215. This Fourth Lateran Council, which was attended by over 400 bishops, 800 abbots and priors, and delegates of all the important European kings and other princes, enacted reform legislation, restated fundamental Catholic theological positions in a dogmatic decree, and dealt with other important issues of the day. For example, the council defined the doctrine of transubstantiation, that in the Eucharist the substance of the bread and wine were transformed into the body and blood of Christ by the consecrating action of the priest. Catholics were required to confess their sins to a priest at least annually, enhancing the need for clergy. A code of moral behavior for the clergy was laid out that emphasized celibacy and sobriety and prohibited gambling, hunting, engaging in trade, and wearing ornate clothing. In these actions and in the attendance of such a body of clerical and political representatives, the council reaffirmed the centrality of the Church in medieval Europe and illustrated the influence a powerful Pope could have.

The importance that people placed on the Church as their means of salvation increased the

powers of popes such as Innocent. The interdict, which if placed on a kingdom by a Pope, cut that kingdom off from receiving most of the sacraments. This put pressure on the king because that kingdom's people were impacted in a very serious way. If the people had not viewed the Church's sacraments as vital, the interdict would have been no weapon at all. This belief in the necessary intermediating role that the Church played in Christian life was but one example of a vital piety felt and expressed by common Europeans across Christendom.

The cult of relics, the veneration of the saints, and pilgrimages were other popular and powerful expressions of Christian sentiment. The cult of relics involved the idea that remnants of a religious figure, such as Jesus or his mother, Mary, or a saint, held significant power that could be tapped by whomever possessed or touched that relic. People sought relics to help achieve healing or as a solution to some problem. Relics were (and still are in the Roman Catholic Church) necessary to found a new church. People went on pilgrimages to churches or monasteries or other sites where relics resided to access the particular power those relics might hold. This, of course, led to abuses. Pig's bones were sold as being saints' bones. Drops of the Virgin Mary's milk and slivers of the True Cross were sold at country fairs. Baldwin II, Emperor of Constantinople, sold for a tidy sum to the French King Saint Louis what was supposed to be the crown of thorns worn by Jesus on the cross. The cult of relics has proved long-lived. Later, in the European Enlightenment, the skeptical Voltaire counted in existence six foreskins of the Lord, which attracted women as pilgrims who could not bear children.

One of the reasons that the trade in relics was so brisk was that Europeans had come to believe strongly in the power of saints, those Christians who had shown particular devotion to the faith or miraculous power during their lives and whose bodies or affects composed a significant amount of the relics in use. Through the veneration of these sanctified Christians, ordinary medieval Christians hoped to gain favor or intercession in their own behalf or that of relatives already departed. Relics of the saints were useful in accessing the power that these saints were supposed to possess. The saints were a more human and closer-at-hand power to consult than Almighty God and offered a tangible means of religious expression.

Related to both the cult of relics and the veneration of saints was the common practice of pilgrimage. To express religious devotion or to seek the power of some saint or relic, thousands of Christians went on religiously inspired journeys to some sacred spot where a miracle had occurred or where relics of a particular saint were housed. Pilgrimages to places such as the Holy Land, Rome, or Compostela in Spain, where according to legend the apostle James was buried, were common as were less grand journeys to lesser holy sites. While pilgrimages were criticized as the occasion of many irreligious activities as Chaucer's *Canterbury Tales* suggest, the practice still illustrates the intense devotion to religious belief that many medieval Christians felt and acted upon.

Connected to the powerful religious sentiment of the common people of Europe and contributing to the larger reform movement within the Church was the rise of the *mendicant*, or "begging," orders of friars. Although several mendicant orders were formed, such as the Carmelites or White Friars and the Friar Hermits of the Order of St. Augustine, the two most prominent and influential orders were the Franciscans and Dominicans. These mendicant orders stressed poverty for members (therefore they depended on contributions "begged" from supporters) and service in the world among the people, particularly in the growing urban areas, usually as preachers and teachers.

The Franciscan order grew out of the life and actions of St. Francis of Assisi (1181-1226). Born in Assisi in central Italy, Francis was the son of a rich cloth merchant named Pietro Bernardone and worked with his father in the family business, enjoying a lavish lifestyle until about the age of twenty-one. After being captured in a war between Assisi and another Italian city, Francis had a conversion experience, went on a pilgrimage to Rome, and decided to give up his wealth and adopt a life of poverty and ministry in imitation of Jesus. Early in this changed life, Francis sold some of his father's cloth to finance the rebuilding of a chapel. His angry father took Francis before the church court where the bishop ordered Francis to give back all his property. Francis complied by taking off all his clothes on the spot and giving them to his father, saying that the only father he would now recognize was God.

Francis attracted people through his simplicity, joy, and sympathy. A growing group of followers sought to follow the example of Christ and his disciples in the Gospels. They gave up worldly possessions, traveled from place to place wearing tunics of coarse gray-brown cloth, and lived in crude shelters, depending for their support on what menial work they might find and gifts from the people. These *Joculatores Dei* (God's Minstrels), as Francis called them, would enter a town singing and then would preach to whomever would listen, urging repentance from sin and proclaiming the salvation that Christ promised. They were received differently by different people: sometimes with suspicion, sometimes with hostility, sometimes with welcome.

Monks lived in poverty and spent their time preaching, performing manual labor, and serving the poor.

But in all cases they posed a contrasting example to the worldly higher Church officials and the reclusive monks of the monasteries, and their simple message and humble approach resonated with ordinary Christians. Francis and his followers took their message and example into various parts of Europe, especially France and Germany. Francis even traveled to Egypt where he was politely granted an audience with the Muslim sultan, whose forces were arrayed against a crusader army. Women followers were organized in convents, the first group at the church of St. Damians by Clare of Assisi who insisted on following Francis' model of absolute poverty. Eventually Franciscan popularity drew so many followers and so much financial support that the emphasis on poverty that Francis held so dear was threatened.

As the movement grew, pressure mounted to organize and become more formalized, with rules and headquarters. In 1209 Pope Innocent III approved a simple rule, called the *regula primitiva*, for this order of friars. In 1223 Pope Honorius III approved an amended rule, the *regula prima*, that became the constitution of the Order of the Little Brothers of St. Francis. Francis was unhappy with moves away from his original inspiration of absolute poverty and simplicity, and he removed himself from direct leadership of the order in 1220, though he remained its spiritual leader until his death in 1226. The Catholic Church officially proclaimed him a saint just two years later. Even while Francis was alive, the Franciscan order had become important as a preaching, evangelizing force in Europe, a good illustration of the vitality of

Christianity among the ordinary people. This role continued to be important, even after the order became more formalized and institutionalized after Francis' death. The order also became an important element in scholarly activity in late medieval Europe, with Franciscans contributing to the study of theology, philosophy, and the sciences in the developing universities and counting among their number such figures as St. Bonaventura, Duns Scot, and William of Ockham.

The "Preaching Friars," commonly called the Dominicans after their founder, St. Dominic (1170-1221), was another mendicant order arising in the High Middle Ages that proved to be especially influential. Born Domingo de Guzman in the village of Calaruega in Castille, one of the chief kingdoms of Spain, St. Dominic was an able administrator and an intellectual, being well educated in theology. He joined the clergy, serving at the Cathedral of Osma. In 1206 he went with the bishop of Osma to preach to the Cathari (Albigensian) heretics in Languedoc in southern France at the urging of Innocent III. In this effort Dominic became convinced that to convert the heretics it was necessary to have preachers who were well educated in theology and who could counter the heretics' arguments but who also had given up all worldly possessions since the Cathari believed that worldly and material things were inherently evil and viewed the Catholic Church as being worldly. Continuing his work among the Cathari, Dominic received approval from Pope Innocent III in 1216 and formal recognition from Honorius III in papal bulls of 1216 and 1217 to found an order with an established rule.

Using the general and easily adaptable Benedictine rule, the *Ordo Praedictatorum* (The Order of Preaching Friars) was primarily concerned with preaching to convert heretics and nonbelievers and to strengthen Christian zeal. They also accepted the idea of poverty, depending on contributions for their support. Due to the requirement for effective preaching and the reliance on donations, the Dominicans did not concern themselves with physical labor but instead devoted themselves to extensive study so that they would be able to counter heresies and win souls. Dominic developed a multi-leveled education program that included study in the arts, philosophy, sciences, and theology, with the highest schools of theology being often connected with universities. Among Dominican figures of intellectual achievement in the Middle Ages are Albertus Magnus, Robert Kilwardby, and the greatest of all medieval scholars, Thomas Aquinas.

The Dominican order, whose members wore distinctive white woolen robes with black travelling capes characteristically worn by Spanish priests, incorporated other important features. It developed a representative governing structure that involved the members of the order not only in selecting leaders, as was common among monastic houses, but also in making policy through representatives working in councils. As the Franciscans did, the Dominicans also incorporated women in their movement. Dominic established the first Dominican convent of nuns in 1206 at Prouille in France from a group of converted Cathari women; other convents soon followed in Bologna and Rome in Italy and Madrid in Spain. The Dominicans became associated with not only scholarly study, anti-heretical preaching, and external missionary work but also with the disciplining effort of the papal Inquisition established in 1233 (not to be confused with the later Spanish Inquisition) that sought to deal with individual heretics and enforce orthodox Catholic teachings. These activities led to the Dominicans being punningly referred to as the *Domini canes*, the "watchdogs of the Lord."

Together the Franciscans and Dominicans represent excellent examples of how the reform impulse and basic Christian piety transformed Christianity and European society in the High Middle Ages. From a state of moral degradation, institutional weakness, and political dependence in the early medieval period, the Church, its papal leadership structure, and Christian society at large had moved to a place where the clergy were effectively disciplined to abide by moral codes, the Church had a predominant voice in selecting its bishops and popes, and the papacy was a strong and vital shaper of policy capable of influencing even the most stubborn kings. As part of this general movement, faith in the teachings of the Church was so strong that new and powerful monastic houses were founded, thousands of people went on crusades, pious Christians devotedly venerated the saints or otherwise demonstrated their sincere beliefs, and vital new orders of friars arose devoted to spreading and strengthening the teachings of the faith. The power and vitality of the Church is such a central feature of the civilization of the High Middle Ages that when the Church suffered problems of corruption and decline over the fourteenth and fifteenth centuries leading to the Protestant Reformation, the resulting decline of power and prestige helped define the end of the medieval age and the beginning of a new, modern era of European civilization.

Suggestions for Further Reading

Morris Bishop, *The Middle Ages* (1970).

Christopher Brooke, *The Monastic World, 1000-1300* (1974).

Rosalind and Christopher Brooke, *Popular Religion in the Middle Ages: Western Europe 1000-1300* (1984).

Nicolas Cheetham, *A History of the Popes* (1982).

Erick Christiansen, *The Northern Crusades: The Baltic and the Catholic Frontier 1100-1525* (1980).

R.I. Moore, *The Origins of European Dissent* (1977).

Colin Morris, *The Papal Monarchy: The Western Church 1050-1250* (1989).

Jonathan Riley-Smith, *What Were the Crusades?* (1977); *The Crusades: A Short History* (1987).

Jeffrey Burton Russel, *A History of Medieval Christianity: Prophecy and Order* (1968).

R.W. Southern, *Western Society and the Church in the Middle Ages* (1970).

Brian Tierney, *Western Europe in the Middle Ages: 300-1475*, 6th edition (1999).

Walter Wakefield, *Heresy, Crusade, and Inquisition in Southern France 1100-1250* (1979).

Chapter 10

Civilization of the Late Middle Ages 1100 – 1300

Westminster Abbey

In 1231, a six-year-old boy named Thomas would stun his teachers at the abbey of Monte Cassino by asking the question, "What is God?" Thomas was born to a noble family in a castle near Naples. Throughout the remainder of his life he continued to ask "what" or "why" when presented with a proposition.

At fifteen, Thomas of Aquino, or Thomas Aquinas, began attending classes at the University of Naples. Under the tutelage of a scholar known as Peter the Irishman, he was introduced to the works of Aristotle.

While still in his teens, Thomas decided to devote his life to God and became a Dominican friar. His family was shocked and disheartened by his decision. On a journey to Bologna, he was kidnapped by his brothers and held in a castle for nearly two years. In an effort to lure him away from the strict discipline of the Dominican Order, his brothers tried to employ carnal lust. A beautiful woman was sent to his chamber to tempt Thomas, but he drove her from his room with a burning log. Unable to corrupt him, his family released him from confinement, and he returned to his life of study and prayer.

Recognizing his brilliance, the Dominicans sent Thomas to the University of Paris, where he studied under the watchful eye of Albertus Magnus. In 1248, master and student moved to Cologne to help the new university in that city. Both men were fascinated by Aristotle's essays and, like so many scholars of their day, chose to ignore warnings issued by Church bureaucrats about the corrupting influence of Greek philosophy.

By 1255, the Dominicans dominated the faculty of Arts at the University of Paris, and they made the works of Aristotle required reading for their students. The following year, Thomas Aquinas was granted the degree of master in theology. As a master, he played an active role in the theological debates that took place at the university. For two years, twice a week, Thomas acted as a challenger in the public debates at the University of Paris. In these debates, he steadfastly maintained that the rational intellect, as a gift from God, could help humanity gain knowledge of God.

In 1265, Thomas was placed in charge of educating young Dominican friars in Rome. There, he began work on the **Summa Theologica**, a comprehensive attempt to explain all that was known about the relationship between God and humanity. In writing the **Summa Theologica**, he returned to answer the question he had raised as a boy at Monte Cassino—"What is God?" By utilizing the logic of Aristotle, Thomas demonstrated that faith and reason were not only compatible, they were complementary.

Thomas died while on a journey to a general council at Lyons. At the time of his death, his great work had not been completed. He is reported to have said: "All I have written seems to me like so much straw compared with what I have seen and what has been revealed to me."

Chronology

926   Work began on St. Vitus Cathedral in Prague. It was completed more than a thousand years later.

981   The great Islamic scholar Abu Ibn Sina (Avicenna) was born in Bukhara in Central Asia. He attempted to reconcile Greek philosophy with the teachings of the Koran.

1113   Peter Abelard moved to Paris and became a teacher of philosophy.

1144   The consecration of the choir at St. Denis would mark the birth of the Gothic style of architecture in France.

1150   Peter Lombard's *Four Books of Sentences* was published. It became the standard theological textbook in the late Middle Ages.

1157   King Henry II of England granted trading privileges in London to the merchants of Cologne.

1159   Lubeck was founded. It became a major trade center in northern Europe.

1163   Work began on the Cathedral of Notre Dame in Paris.

1167   King Henry II ordered the return of English scholars from Paris. Oxford soon emerged as a center of higher learning.

1172   Islamic scholar Abul Ibn Rushd (Averroes) began to translate and condense Aristotle's *de Anima* while serving as a judge in Seville, Spain.

1200   King Philip II of France granted a charter to the masters and students of Paris.

1204   Venetians assisted Fourth Crusade in the conquest of Constantinople.

1241   Lubeck and Hamburg signed a mutual assistance pact that will lead to the creation of the Hanseatic League.

1257   Bonaventure was chosen as Minister General of the Franciscan Order.

1265   Thomas Aquinas was given the responsibility of educating Dominican friars in Rome.

1275   Niccolo Polo presented his son Marco to Kublai Khan.

1278   The Italian painter Cimabue was commissioned to decorate the basilica at Assisi. He was assisted by Duccio and Giotto.

1302   Dante Alighieri was banished from Florence.

1305-06 Giotto painted "the Lamentation" on the wall of the Arena Chapelin Padua.

By the twelfth century, the ingredients of medieval European civilization were all in place. The papal bureaucracy gave spiritual and artistic direction to people throughout western and central Europe. In many regions, kings asserted their supremacy over local warlords. A revival of trade led to a growing prosperity, and prosperity led to greater optimism. Greater stability encouraged innovations in lifestyle, architecture, philosophy, business, and literature. Europeans showed increasing confidence in their ability to control their own destiny and to express themselves in a variety of ways.

TOWNS

The greatest paradox of the Middle Ages is that throughout the entire period, Europe was primarily rural and agricultural. Yet, the beauty of medieval civilization expressed itself most fully in the new and revitalized urban centers during the twelfth and thirteenth centuries.

As noted in Chapter 7, urban growth was closely tied to the revival of trade, which occurred throughout Europe in the eleventh century. Medieval towns usually originated in one of three ways. Some began as centers of lay or church administration. A bishop, abbot, monarch, or great lord would often require the specialized skills of craftsmen to supply his needs. Monarchs

Medieval city wall of Donauworth, Germany

and their vassals needed weapons and armor. Members of the clergy needed ornaments and altar clothes. All people of an elevated station in life desired to set themselves apart from the common people by the clothing they wore. Courts, monasteries, and cathedrals frequently became centers of production.

A second manner of development rested upon the need for security. During the Dark Ages, farmers were plagued by marauding raiders. In response to this danger, they would often flee to a fortification for protection. Some of these local fortifications attracted merchants who viewed local farmers as potential customers. Peasants could exchange a portion of their surplus crop for tools, cloth, or wine. These "farmers' markets" also afforded peasants an opportunity to sell their handicrafts and surplus livestock.

The third explanation for the revitalization of urban centers was put forth by historian Henri Pirenne. Pirenne noted that merchants involved in the new, long-distance trade often united into "companies" or "colonies" for mutual protection as they traveled. Because overland travel was often difficult during periods of inclement weather, merchants tended to congregate at strategically located fortifications along major trade routes. As the trade settlement grew outside of the castle walls, merchants frequently took the initiative in constructing a second, outer wall to protect their homes.

Whether craftsmen, farmers, or merchants were responsible for the rise of an urban center, all medieval towns were centers of production and trade. As such, they brought together the varied classes of medieval society to exchange both goods and ideas. The growth of towns would also lead to the creation of a new and dynamic social class known as the "bourgeoisie" or "middle class." Unlike the peasants and the nobility, they did not derive their wealth from the land. They relied upon skill and intelligence rather than strength and courage. While the incomes of most people in the Middle Ages were fixed by tradition, the wealth of the bourgeoisie was self-generated and unlimited.

The size and appearance of medieval cities varied greatly. The largest urban communities were in northern Italy. Venice, Florence, and Genoa flourished due to their trade connections with the Byzantine Empire and the Levant (the coast of modern Israel and Lebanon). As many as 100,000 people may have lived in Venice by 1200. Centers of production, like London, Bruges, Ghent, and Cologne, could count 20,000 to 40,000 inhabitants. Most medieval towns, however, contained about 5,000 people or less.

Life within metropolitan areas was crude by modern standards. Town dwellers were plagued by fire, disease, unruly livestock, and foul water. Cattle, hogs, rats, and chickens roamed the dirt streets. Human waste was often thrown out in alleyways or dumped into nearby streams. Unsanitary conditions and close quarters made medieval cities fertile breeding grounds for disease. In northern Europe, the popular use of wood and straw as building materials made fire a common hazard.

In spite of the unsavory aspects of urban communities, the lure of wealth, freedom, and entertainment attracted a growing number of Europeans to the cities. In order to succeed, the new middle class needed freedom to run their own affairs. Merchants needed freedom to move about the land in order to trade. Artisans needed the freedom to produce for the market. Money-

lenders wanted freedom from church laws against usury. All town dwellers wanted freedom from servile obligations.

The liberties of an urban population were generally defined in the form of a charter granted to them by its local lord. In exchange for the freedoms granted by the charter, the town's people usually agreed to provide the lord with a fixed cash payment. The local lord might also retain certain monopolies, such as the milling of grain. As a result, the middle class demonstrated to the lord that it would be in the best interest of the lord to encourage the growth of the town.

Virtually all charters granted townsmen or "burghers" personal freedom. The standard custom in most of Europe was that if you lived within a town for a year and a day, you would be considered a free person. This rule did not apply to the serfs of the local lord, but it did apply to the escaped serfs of the lord's rivals.

Charters also defined the revenues the lord could derive from the burghers. In addition to an annual revenue, the lord could collect tolls and levy fines. Maximum fines and tolls were stated in the charter.

By the twelfth century, most towns had gained the right of limited self-government. Usually, the burghers could elect local officials, make rules for their inhabitants, and establish courts to try petty offenses. Lords generally reserved judgment on capital crimes and the approval of new taxes. However, the nobles usually preferred to allow the townsmen to administer their own affairs.

Economic activity within a medieval town was controlled by guilds. Both merchant and craft guilds were organized to promote the interest of their members. A town's merchant guild was primarily interested in preserving a monopoly on the local market. The guild assured uniform prices, placed restrictions on outside merchants trying to trade within the town, and attempted to prevent any one of its members from dominating the market place.

Craft guilds were designed to regulate the methods and quality of production. The guild determined working conditions, such as limiting working hours. Master craftsmen who supervised the work of journeymen and apprentices dominated the craft guilds. The production of a "master piece" was essential for admission into the ranks of the masters. In addition to these functions, craft guilds provided social services to their members.

THE HANSEATIC LEAGUE

The growth of commerce and urban centers in northern Europe led to the creation of a trade association known as the Hanseatic League. By the early twelfth century, England exported large amounts of wool to the Low Countries. Flemish merchants established trading houses in London to facilitate this trade. By the middle of the century, merchants from various German cities were also active in the wool trade. The burghers of Bremen and Cologne used the rivers into the interior of the Holy Roman Empire to access a wide variety of goods that could be sent to England in exchange for wool. In 1157, King Henry II of England granted special trading privileges to the merchants of Cologne to promote trade with the Germanies.

By the mid-twelfth century, the business community in northern Germany was so well developed that the Germans were successfully competing with the Scandinavians in the trade along the coasts of the North and Baltic Seas. In 1159, the ruler of Saxony established Lubeck on the Baltic Sea to give his subjects a competitive edge in their rivalry with the Swedish ship captains

from the island of Gotland. Within two years, Henry the Lion of Saxony arranged a cooperative trade agreement between the two merchant groups. The treaty gave the traders of Lubeck access to the commercial city of Visby on Gotland Island and allowed them to join the Swedes in the Russian fur trade based at Novgorod. By the end of the twelfth century, German merchants were exchanging large quantities of salt and cloth, obtained in western Europe, for furs and forest products originating in northeastern Europe.

The expansion of German trade along the Baltic coast coincided with the migration of Germanic peoples into the region. During the thirteenth century, the Danes and the Teutonic Knights embarked upon crusades against the Slavic-speaking people who inhabited the southern coast of the Baltic Sea. In order to secure their conquests, the German knights encouraged German peasants to immigrate to the region. The interaction of German and Slavic peasants led to improvements in agricultural yields and provided greater incomes for landlords. Many German and Danish lords also sought to enhance their incomes by establishing commercial centers along the Baltic coast. German merchants soon settled permanently in these towns, creating a commercial chain stretching from London to Russia. By the mid-thirteenth century, the Baltic merchants were granted trading privileges in Flanders and London.

In 1241, Lubeck and Hamburg agreed to jointly maintain and police a road that connected the two cities. This vital route also connected the North Sea to the Baltic Sea. Similar agreements were soon negotiated with other cities along the German and Pomeranian coasts. The commercial centers participating in these mutual assistance pacts became known as the Hanseatic League.

The Hanseatic League was never a political entity, but rather it represented a cluster of merchant groups engaged in cooperation for the sake of promoting their international trading privileges. There were actually towns that never sent a delegation to the meetings of the league but were considered members. The merchants of the Hanseatic League not only dominated the trade in furs with Russia, they helped to move grain from northern Europe to the rest of the continent. The sale of fish and metallic ores from Scandinavia also proved profitable. The power of the league actually increased during the fourteenth century when much of Europe was wracked by famine and disease.

GOTHIC ARCHITECTURE

The growing wealth of the middle class combined with the spirituality of medieval culture expressed itself architecturally in the building of great cathedrals throughout Western Europe. Though merchants and artisans pulled the European economy forward, it was the Church that ultimately gave direction to life in the Middle Ages. The Church, with its growing bureaucracy, could raise money from all levels of society. The upper ranks of the clergy also possessed the ability to organize large projects.

From the middle of the eight century until the mid-twelfth century, the churches and abbeys of Western Europe were characterized by a modification of classical Roman architecture known as "Romanesque." By the late Roman Empire, the Christian churches of the western Mediterranean were primarily rectangular in shape with flat roofs. Known as "basilicas," the interiors of these structures were dominated by rows of columns that supported their roofs.

The west front entrance to Westminster Abbey exemplifies several characteristics of English Gothic architecture. The pointed roof and supporting buttresses support a circular, stained-glass window. Statuary adorns the columns and doorway. The archways are severely pointed.

The interior of St. Vitus Cathedral in Prague provides a fine example of the use of ribbed vaults and pointed arches to support the roof. The cathedral was begun in 926 and completed in 1929.

A semi-dome was usually placed over the altar.

Most of the early Romanesque churches continued to resemble the basic structure of the Roman basilicas. However, Romanesque architects replaced the flat roofs with round, stone vaults. The weight of the vaulted roofs required massive walls to support them. Windows were small and usually narrow, giving Romanesque churches a dark and fortress-like appearance. Romanesque structures were also characterized by an extensive use of exterior, ornamental sculptures depicting Christ, his apostles, or various symbols relating to Christianity.

By the mid-twelfth century, medieval builders wanted to add light and elevation to churches to inspire those who worshipped in them. The use of ribbed vaults and pointed arches gave rise to Gothic architecture. In addition to the ribbed vaults, flying buttresses were utilized to eliminate the need for massive walls to support the roof. A flying buttress was a heavy pier of stone used to fortify the walls on the exterior of the building. This new method of construction allowed the builder to incorporate large, stained glass windows into the walls of the church. The interior of Gothic cathedrals were filled with color and light as stained glass windows gradually replaced frescoes as the principal means of decorating the interiors of the great churches of Europe.

The new Gothic style first appeared in the Ile-de-France and quickly spread throughout Western Europe. As always, regional variations

Salisbury Cathedral is considered to be one of the best examples of early English Gothic architecture. Steeply pitched roofs and windows with sharply pointed arches are typical of buildings designed during the late twelfth and thirteenth centuries.

Medieval frescoes on the walls of the parish church in Donauworth, Germany.

would be evident. Italian builders refused to abandon the use of massive walls. The Gothic churches of Spain revealed the ornamental influence of the Moors (Moslem invaders from North Africa). Gothic architecture continued to dominate Western Europe for four centuries, and it would experience a brief revival during the early nineteenth century.

THE TRANSFORMATION OF ART

The growing popularity of Gothic architecture presented medieval artists with both a challenge and an opportunity. Prior to the twelfth century, the most common form of painting was manuscript illumination. The emphasis on light in the interiors of the new Gothic cathedrals meant that their windows were vast in size. The technique of painting stained glass was perfected during the Romanesque period, but the importance of stained glass in decorating Gothic structures cannot be over emphasized.

The stained glass windows were designed in the great cathedral workshops of Europe. The window itself was not a single pane. Each window was composed of large numbers of small pieces of painted glass held together by lead casings. The artist was literally painting with colored glass as he assembled the window. This process encouraged an abstract style. Figures were often monumental but rarely life like.

As the production of stained glass windows was reaching its height in northern Europe during the first half of the thirteenth century, a second artistic revolution began to take hold in Italy. The Franco-Venetian conquest of Constantinople in 1204 led to a renewed interest in Byzantine art. Throughout the thirteenth century,

The west front doorway of Westminster Abbey illustrated the skill of medieval craftsmen in sculpting religious statuary.

Italian painters were increasingly influenced by what they referred to as the "Greek manner." At the same time, Italian architects were increasingly influenced by the Gothic style. Italian sculptors were often employed to decorate the exteriors of the new Gothic structures, and they felt the influence of French and German artists. By the late thirteenth century, a group of Italian painters began to synthesize the two styles.

Cenni di Pepo or Cimabue (1240/1250-1302) was among the first to deviate from the neo-Byzantine tradition. In most respects, this Florentine master conformed to the techniques used in Byzantine paintings, but he experimented with both form and style to satisfy the demands of the huge alter panels that he painted. Sometime around 1278, Cimabue was commissioned to work on the basilica at Assisi in honor of St. Francis. He was assisted in his efforts by Duccio di Buoninsegna (1255-1319) and Giotto di Bondone (1267-1337). Continuing along the path blazed by Cimabue, Duccio and Giotto freed Western art from the rigid and frozen style of the neo-Byzantine school.

Duccio's best known work is the main alter of the cathedral in Siena. Known locally as the *Maesta*, Duccio's alter panels reveal a true blending of Gothic and Byzantine techniques with a new attention given to the humanity of the characters being portrayed. The center panel depicts the "Madonna Enthroned" with the Christ child. The painting has a three-dimensional quality absent in earlier medieval paintings. Both Mary and Jesus are depicted in a natural style with pleasant facial expressions.

Most art historians believe that Giotto served an apprenticeship under the supervision of Cimabue, but the student revealed far more talent than his master. Like Cimabue, Giotto ex-

The Church of San Giacomo is representative of the Romanesque architectural style so popular during the early Middle Ages.

celled when painting on a monumental scale. His most famous murals were painted in the Scrovegni Chapel in Padua during the first decade of the fourteenth century. Like St. Francis of Assisi, Giotto loved the natural world. The realism of his art foreshadowed the works of painters during the Italian Renaissance.

UNIVERSITIES

Christianity permeated the soul of Western Europe in the Middle Ages and the Church re-

garded itself as the embodiment of Christ on earth. In the Book of Genesis, the earth is described as, "a formless wasteland, and darkness covered the abyss, while a mighty wind swept over the waters." Through the act of creation, God brought order out of chaos. In a sense, the Medieval Church attempted to do the same thing.

The invasions, wars and general chaos of the early Middle Ages impeded the intellectual growth of Europeans. Throughout the Dark Ages, monasteries and other institutions of the Church preserved and protected Latin manuscripts from the period of the Roman Empire and continued the traditions of a classical education. Clerics also served in the bureaucracies of medieval rulers because few Europeans outside of the Church were literate.

Schools associated with monasteries were generally designed to train young men in the study of the Bible and in the writings of the early founders of the Christian Church, however, by the twelfth century, schools associated with cathedrals were often surrounded by vibrant urban communities. The growing wealth and stability of Europe fostered an interest in a broader education. An expansion of trade introduced new ideas. In Bologna, wealthy merchants created schools to train their children. Merchants in other Italian cities involved in the Mediterranean trade soon imitated the merchants of Bologna. The earliest universities would emerge from the cathedral schools in northwestern Europe and the more secular schools of Italy.

In a sense, the early universities were associated with the guild system. In the north, master teachers formed educational guilds. In Italy, students controlled the educational guilds.

Due to the Italian focus on trade and municipal government, it is hardly surprising that the scholars of Italy would demonstrate a pro-

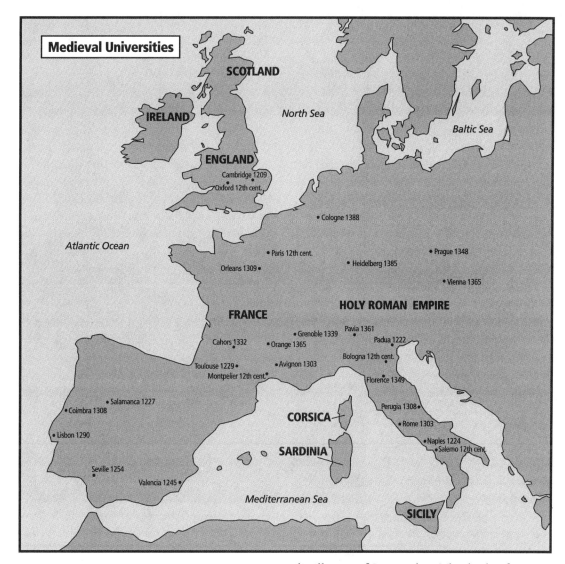

Medieval Universities

SCOTLAND

IRELAND

North Sea

Baltic Sea

ENGLAND

Cambridge 1209
Oxford 12th cent.

Cologne 1388

Atlantic Ocean

Paris 12th cent.

Prague 1348

Orleans 1309

Heidelberg 1385

Vienna 1365

HOLY ROMAN EMPIRE

FRANCE

Grenoble 1339
Pavia 1361
Padua 1222

Cahors 1332
Orange 1365

Bologna 12th cent.

Toulouse 1229
Avignon 1303

Montpelier 12th cent.

Florence 1349

Salamanca 1227
Coimbra 1308

Perugia 1308
CORSICA
Rome 1303

Lisbon 1290

SARDINIA
Naples 1224
Salerno 12th cent.

Seville 1254

Valencia 1245

Mediterranean Sea

SICILY

found interest in the study of law. The rise of the University of Bologna is associated with the revitalization of the study of Roman law.

Irnerius (1055-1130) is generally given credit for sparking a revival of interest in law. Of obscure origins, Irnerius first gained notoriety as a professor of rhetoric. His renown as a legal scholar is based upon his study of the *Corpus Juris Civilis.* During the sixth century, the Emperor Justinian ordered a compilation and distillation of Roman law. This body of Roman law and the legal principles that emerged from it were utilized in the courts of the Byzantine Empire throughout the Middle Ages. However, the customary law of the Germanic barbarians largely replaced the traditions of Roman law in Western Europe. Irnerius offered his students the first comprehensive commentaries on the *Corpus Juris Civilus* of Justinian, as well as contemporary law codes.

One of the most notable features of the Notre Dame de Paris is the flying buttresses. The cathedral was started in 1163 and the flying buttresses were added between 1230 and 1250 to give support to the structure.

To protect themselves from high prices being charged by landlords and store owners, Bologna's students organized two guilds, each headed by a rector. The master teachers (professors) had to agree to the rules set by the guilds and enforced by the rectors. Fines were levied against masters who began their lectures late or who exceeded their time limit. In addition to civil and church law, the young scholars at Bologna could also choose to study rhetoric or medicine.

Greek and Arabs scholars had a great influence on educational developments in southern Italy. Both were intensely interested in finding herbal remedies for diseases. Salerno emerged as the focal point for medical studies in Europe. During the twelfth century, King Roger II of Sicily ordered that those wishing to practice medicine within his kingdom must first be permitted to do so by the masters of Salerno.

The University of Paris was famed for the study of theology and philosophy. By the twelfth century, it had emerged as the greatest center of intellectual life north of the Alps. The strength of the French monarchy offered a stability that helped foster academic pursuits. The prosperity

Oxford University in England grew out of a local school in the town during the twelfth century. The university received its formal charter from King Henry III in 1248.

of the town also aided in attracting teachers to the cathedral school of Notre Dame. However, the transformation of the cathedral school into a university was largely due to the quality of its teachers.

In the early twelfth century, Peter Abelard (1079-1142) was generally regarded as the greatest teacher of his day. By all accounts, he was brilliant, egotistical, controversial, and eloquent. As a student, young Abelard had the audacity to challenge his teacher to a public debate. He first gained fame for a series of lectures on the Book of Ezekiel. Following his triumph, he settled in Paris to teach theology. Having little money, Peter boarded in the home of Fulbert, the canon of Notre Dame. He soon fell in love with Fulbert's niece, Heloise, and impregnated her. The couple secretly married, but they tried to hide the union to preserve Abelard's chances for promotion to a high rank within the Church.

Feeling that his family had been dishonored, Fulbert hired thugs to castrate Abelard. Following the attack, Abelard entered the monastery at St. Denis, and Heloise became a nun. The castration ended their physical passion, but the two would continue to correspond for the remainder of their lives.

Abelard's reputation was based primarily on his willingness to apply the test of critical reasoning to Scripture and the writings of the fathers of the early Christian Church. He would begin with a proposition. He would then cite quotations written by Christian authorities affirming the proposition. Next, he would cite quotations from the same authors denying the validity of the same proposition. He allowed his students to reach their own conclusions after viewing matters from both sides.

Abelard was no enemy of Christianity. He hoped to use logic to defend the teachings of the Church, but he was frequently misunderstood. His work was condemned on two occasions, and St. Bernard of Clairvaux emerged as a bitter rival within the Church. In spite of his controversial teachings, he never failed to delight his students. When forbidden to lecture on French soil, he spoke from the limb of a tree.

Abelard's notoriety attracted other talented teachers to Paris. By the end of the twelfth century, the chancellor of the school had the authority to license instructors and permit masters to lecture in and around the Cathedral of Notre Dame. Due to limited space near the cathedral, teachers began to set up schools on the left bank of the Seine River. Some time during the latter part of the century, the master teachers organized themselves and began to establish standards for admission into their guild. King Philip II of France officially granted a charter to the masters and students of Paris in 1200.

During the course of the thirteenth century, the masters of arts organized themselves under the leadership of a rector while the professors of theology, canon law and medicine organized themselves under the leadership of deans. After a prolonged struggle, the rector was recognized as the leader of the entire university.

In 1167, King Henry II of England ordered the English scholars at Paris to return home. Oxford soon emerged as the center of higher education in England. By 1209, as many as three thousand students were living in the town.

Students paid low fees for their classes. Their greatest expense came from renting books. Most masters taught by reading from the text of a book, then making extensive comments to explain the passages. Students took notes as best they could in the hopes of later passing oral examinations. Strict rules were established at many universities to prevent physical attacks upon the instructors when they administered their examinations.

Medieval universities always sought to exempt their students from the jurisdiction of local courts. Riots often occurred when local authorities attempted to arrest students for criminal conduct. If a conflict between the students and townspeople continued for an extended period, university officials would usually ask the king to intervene.

SCHOLASTICISM

During the remainder of the twelfth and thirteenth centuries, the scholars of Paris and its sister institutions built upon the philosophical foundation laid by Abelard. Peter Lombard (1100-1160) rigorously applied Abelard's method of logic to his analysis of fundamental theological questions. Lombard's *Book of Sen-*

tences became the theological text at universities throughout Western Europe by 1200.

The reintroduction of the works of Aristotle into Europe during the mid-twelfth century helped to fuel the intellectual rebirth of the period. Ironically, Arab Moslems would introduce the Christian scholars of the West to the writings of the Greek philosopher.

As the Arabs conquered the southern and eastern portions of the Byzantine Empire during the eighth and ninth centuries, they absorbed schools of Greek philosophy. For centuries, Islamic scholars attempted to reconcile Greek philosophy with the teachings of the Koran. The greatest of these Islamic philosophers were Ibn Sina (Avicenna) and Ibn Rushd (Averroes).

Abu Ali Al-Hussain Ibn Abdallah Ibn Sina (981-1037) was born near Bukhara in central Asia. As a young man, he studied both the Koran and the natural sciences. During his lifetime, he was better known for his abilities as a physician than for his philosophical writings. In his *Canons of Medicine,* he reviewed all medical knowledge available at the time. This encyclopedic work remained the standard text for students of medicine in the Islamic world for six hundred years. Ibn Sina accurately described the function of heart valves in the pumping of blood through the circulatory system. He also recognized the importance of psychology in human health. *Canons of Medicine* was translated into Latin in the twelfth century and became the text book for most medical schools in Europe during the late Middle Ages.

In the *Book of Healing,* Ibn Sina attempted to compile an encyclopedia of philosophical and scientific knowledge. He divided knowledge into two realms—the theoretical and the practical. In the area of theoretical knowledge, he tried to reconcile ideas drawn from the writings of

Aristotle and Neoplatonic philosophers with the theology of the Koran.

Like the Neoplatonic writers who influenced early Christian theologians, Ibn Sina taught that all being emanated from a single, creative source. He believed that creative source was God. Using Aristotelian logic, Ibn Sina concluded that since God is a creator by nature and since God is eternal, the process of creation must be eternal.

Abul-Waleed Muhammad Ibn Rushd (1128-1198) was both a physician and a jurist. Born in Cordova, Spain, Ibn Rushd was descended from a family of scholars. At 44, he was appointed a judge in Seville. Inspite of his legal duties, he found time to translate and condense Aristotle's *de Anima.* After two years, he returned to Cordova where he continued to translate and comment on Aristotle's metaphysical works.

Ibn Rushd was clearly Aristotelian in his outlook. He believed that the universe was eternal (without beginning or end), yet, he opposed the concept that an individual soul was immortal. Rather, he believed in the existence of a universal intellect that functioned in individual people. Though the individual perished, the universal intellect continued. Ibn Rushd's philosophical writings seemed to contradict the Koran, and he was vigorously attacked by other Islamic teachers.

To defend himself against his critics, Ibn Rushd advocated the "double truth" theory. Truth is understood clearly in philosophy, but it is expressed allegorically in theology. The teachings of the Koran were true but expressed in such a way that ordinary people could understand them.

In addition to Islamic writers, Jewish scholar Moses ben Maimon or Maimonides (1135-1204) had a major impact on the Christian scholars of late Middle Ages. Maimonides fled his native Spain for North Africa when the puritanical Almoravides conquered the Iberian Peninsula. While serving as a physician to the Sultan of Egypt in Cairo, Maimonides wrote ethical works based on the study of the Torah and the Talmud. His *Mishneh Torah* became a standard guide for Jewish practice.

Maimonides is generally considered to be a religious rationalist. He condemned those who advocated a literal interpretation of the Torah. Rather, he felt that when statements in the Torah clearly contradicted reason, they should be interpreted figuratively.

Maimonides used reason and logic to prove the existence of God using Aristotelian logic. He viewed God as both first cause and as necessary Being. In spite of Maimonides' successful attempts to reconcile Greek philosophy with Jewish theology, he was condemned by three leading rabbis in France. Having been forcefully denounced by local Jewish leaders, the French Inquisition burned copies of his books circulating in Paris.

The works of Moslem and Jewish scholars began to reach European Christians by way of Sicily and Spain, regions where Christians, Jews, and Moslems lived in close proximity to one another. During the twelfth century, the archbishop of Toledo patronized scholars who translated the scientific works of Aristotle from Arabic into Latin. European intellectuals quickly developed an insatiable appetite for the writings of Aristotle regarding all fields of study.

The early founders of the Christian Church were primarily influenced by the mysticism of Neoplatonic philosophers. The materialism of Aristotle was difficult to reconcile with the spiritualism inherent in Christianity or Islam. Some Church leaders felt that the writings of Aristotle would lead people into heresy. In spite of attempts by religious leaders to ban some of

Aristotle's scientific essays, the scholars of Paris continued to read them.

Using the dialectical method developed by Abelard and perfected by Lombard, Thomas Aquinas (1225-1274) reconciled Aristotelian knowledge with the divinely revealed truths of Christianity. He maintained that humans could discover many truths about the natural world through experience and reason. However, supernatural truths are revealed to humanity through the grace of God. On topics where Aristotle seemed to contradict the teachings of Christianity, Aquinas employed Aristotelian logic to refute the scientific conclusions of the Greek master. Aquinas maintained that Aristotle never proved that the universe was eternal because such a proposition was impossible to prove. Regarding other areas of conflict, Aquinas argued that Ibn Rushd had misinterpreted Aristotle or had added his own thoughts.

Thomas Aquinas is generally recognized as the greatest philosopher of his day and his *Summa Theologica* the greatest example of medieval scholasticism. Centuries after his death, the Roman Catholic Church would accept the teachings of Aquinas as its official theology. Yet, in his lifetime, he was attacked for emphasizing reason over faith.

Not all Christian theologians of the thirteenth century were influenced by Aristotle. St. Bonaventure's writings continued to show the influence of St. Augustine of Hippo on Christian thought.

Giovanni Fidanza (1221-1274) was born in Bagnorea in northern Italy. It is believed he became known as Bonaventure because his mother petitioned St. Francis of Assisi to pray for her son during a childhood illness. When the boy recovered, she shouted, "O buona ventura!" which, translated into English means, "Oh good fortune!"

Bonaventure entered the Franciscan Order as a young adult and was sent to study under the famed Franciscan teacher Alexander Hales in Paris. While a student, he met and befriended Thomas Aquinas. In 1257, Bonaventure was chosen Minister General of the Franciscan Order, and he worked hard to end the conflict between Spiritual and Conventual Franciscans. The Spirituals demanded that members of the order maintain a strict rule of poverty. The Conventuals supported Pope Innocent IV's decision to allow the papacy to hold property for the use of the Franciscan friars. Though a Conventual, Bonaventure was respected by the Spirituals for his attempt to curb materialism within the order and for his piety and toleration. Bonaventure gained fame for composing the standard biography of St. Francis of Assisi. Pope Gregory X elevated him to the rank of Cardinal and Bishop of Albano.

Bonaventure believed that reason should be used exclusively to support faith. He denied Aristotle's claim to the eternity of the universe. He also argued that the beauty and goodness of humanity was directly related to the fact that we were created by God. As emanations of God, human beings embody a footprint of the divine nature of our Creator.

VERNACULAR LITERATURE AND DANTE

The Christian Church gave Western Europe a spiritual unity during the Middle Ages and the language of the Church was Latin. Virtually all of the theological and scholarly works of the period were written in Latin. In spite of the universality of Latin, some medieval poets preferred the use of their native languages when producing verse.

During the Dark Ages, the epics and sagas of Germanic peoples were recorded in the vernacular, but few of these early manuscripts survived those turbulent centuries. The heroic deeds of the warrior *Beowulf* were written in an early form of English. The poem provides modern readers with the best example of this type of literature.

By 1100, troubadours were writing, and sometimes singing, love poetry in southern France. Eleanor of Aquitaine (1122-1202) made this form of vernacular poetry fashionable throughout France when she married King Louis VII. During the thirteenth century the love songs of the troubadours would spread to Germany and Italy.

The lyrical poetry of the troubadours was primarily written for the benefit of medieval ladies. Men preferred the *chansons de geste*—narrative poems glorifying political conflict and battle. The greatest of the chansons was the *Song of Roland*. It describes a political rivalry within the court of Charlemagne and later a great battle against the Moslem forces in Spain.

By the late twelfth century, medieval writers and poets were entertaining their audiences with fables, legends, and histories drawn from a great variety of sources. English, French, and German authors wrote of the adventures of the legendary King Arthur and his virtuous knights. Geoffrey de Villehardouin would record his memories of the Fourth Crusade. The legend of the great Christian warrior El Cid was memorialized in Spain.

Dante Alighieri (1265-1321) would emerge as the greatest medieval Italian poet. Dante was born in the thriving city of Florence to a middle-class family. Inspired by the beauty of a young woman named Beatrice, Dante began writing love poetry but lost interest in it when Beatrice died. At the age of thirty, Dante became involved in Florentine politics and was an active member of the "White" faction. In 1302, while Dante was on a diplomatic mission, the rival "Black" faction, with the support of Pope Boniface VIII, gained control of Florence. Dante was banished from the republic. He spent the next twenty years in exile. Dante found employment at the courts of various Italian princes, but he hoped for a unification of Italy under the leadership of Emperor Henry VII. He never returned to Florence and was very bitter about his exile.

Dante's fame rests primarily on his composition of the *Divine Comedy*. Set in 1300, the author is taken on a mythical journey through Hell, Purgatory, and Heaven. The Latin poet Virgil escorts Dante through Hell and Purgatory.

Hell was described as a vast pit where the spirits of the damned are tortured according to the nature and gravity of their sins. Some of these spirits are identified by name. Dante placed Pope Boniface VIII in the eighth ring of Hell even though the Pope was still very much alive in 1300. The bottom of the pit was reserved for Judas Iscariot and Brutus, the leader of the conspiracy to assassinate Julius Caesar.

Purgatory was depicted as a mountain reaching into the sky. Like the pit of Hell, Purgatory consisted of levels or rings. The more petty the sins, the higher the elevation of the sinner. Unlike Hell, the suffering souls of Purgatory retained the hope of release from their torment.

Since Virgil was not a Christian, Dante left him as he entered Heaven. Beatrice, the object of Dante's youthful affection, guided the poet through Paradise. In his assent through Heaven, he saw the apostles of Jesus. Eventually, he was allowed to enter the Empyrean of God, where St. Bernard of Clairvaux acted as his escort and led him to Mary, the Mother of Jesus. His journey culminated with a vision of the Holy Trinity.

Because the *Divine Comedy* was written in Tuscan, rather than Latin, it was accessible to a wider audience. The popularity of the poem helped make Tuscan the literary language of the Italian Peninsula. The **Divine Comedy** is also noteworthy as a great synthesis of medieval ideas. Dante presents his reader with an eternal world organized by God. He drew heavily from the philosophy of Thomas Aquinas and the scholars of Paris.

Dante's work indicates that he sympathized with those who wanted to reform the Christian Church of his day. Pope Boniface VIII was placed in Hell for corrupting the Church with his political activities. Controversial figures like Joachim of Floris (1132-1202) were placed in Heaven along side the early founders of the Church. Joachim preached that there were three great epochs of human history. The first was inaugurated by Moses, and it was characterized by the teachings of the Old Testament. Jesus Christ inaugurated the second, and it is spiritually dominated by the teachings of the New Testament. The third epoch would arrive in the future, and the Holy Spirit would direct it. During this final stage of human history, all would live simply and peacefully in a state of Christian anarchy. In the latter part of the thirteenth century, a group known as the Spiritual Franciscans began to preach that St. Francis had inaugurated the coming of the third epoch. The vocal members of the Spiritual Franciscans were persecuted by the Church.

THE ADVENTURES OF MARCO POLO

During the early years of the first millennium A. D. merchants from the Roman world eagerly traded for the spices and herbs of the East Indies and for the raw silk of China. The silk trade survived the fall of Rome and continued to flourish through the early Middle Ages. Greek merchants from the Byzantine Empire gained access to the products of the Far East by establishing trade centers along the coast of the Black Sea and along the coast of Abyssinia (Ethiopia). Wars between the Byzantine Empire and Persia occasionally disrupted the trade but never stopped it. The conquest of North Africa by Arab Moslems put an end to trade between Europe and Ethiopia, but travel along the Silk Roads through Central Asia to China continued throughout the Middle Ages.

The Italian city-state of Venice actively traded with the Greeks of Constantinople (Istanbul) and the Byzantine Empire. The Venetians traded slaves, military equipment, arms, and raw cloth in exchange for the products of the Far East. These same Venetian merchants would transport and assist the warriors of the Fourth Crusade in their conquests of Zara (Zadar) and Constantinople. Once they had conquered the Byzantine capital, the crusading knights established the Latin Empire of Constantinople consisting of Greece, Thrace, and Macedonia. To reward their Venetian allies, the merchants of Venice were granted special trading privileges.

In 1258 Michael Palaeologus (1224-1282) rallied Greek forces in an attempt to drive out the Latin conquerors to recreate the Byzantine Empire. He obtained the aid of Genoese merchants who helped to neutralize the powerful Venetian navy. In 1261, the Byzantine army reconquered Constantinople, and the Genoese were granted commercial concessions within the new empire at the expense of the Venetians.

Just prior to the Greek reconquest of Constantinople, Venetian merchants Maffeo and Niccolo Polo landed in the Crimean Peninsula along the coast of the Black Sea. Traveling eastward into the vast Mongul Empire, the Vene-

The Doge's Palace, Venice, Italy. By the late Middle Ages, Venice had grown wealthy due to her extensive trade connections with Greeks and Arabs in the eastern Mediterranean. Venice was near the height of its power when the Polos began their journey to China.

tian pilgrims stopped to trade at Surai on the Volga River. They later continued their journey until they arrived at the capital of the Great Khan in 1266. The Polo brothers were greatly impressed by both Kublai Khan (1215-1294) and his splendid city, Khanbalig (Beijing).

The Great Khan was extraordinarily curious about Europe, and he questioned the Polos at length about their religion and culture. The year after their arrival in China, Kublai Khan sent the Venetians back to Italy with a letter to the Pope requesting that he dispatch one hundred scholars to China so that his subjects might become better acquainted with European science and Christianity. The Venetian travelers did not return to their homeland until 1269.

After resting two years in Italy, Niccolo and Maffeo Polo began their return journey to China accompanied by Niccolo's teenage son, Marco, (1254-1324) and two Dominican friars, as well as gifts from Pope Gregory X. The hazards of the journey proved too great for the Dominicans, and they turned back. The Venetians continued their long, overland trek through Armenia, Persia, Afghanistan, and the Gobi Desert. In 1275, Niccolo presented his son, Marco, to the Great Khan at his palace. Marco Polo spent the next seventeen years of his life in the service of Kublai Khan. As a bureaucrat in the imperial service, he visited cities and towns throughout China, Siberia, Burma, and India. He was introduced to the use of paper currency, coal, asbestos fabric, and the imperial mail system. He was greatly impressed by the ability of the Chinese to manufacture large quantities of iron and salt.

The Polos were well rewarded for their services to the Khan, and in 1292 they left China to escort a Mongolian princess to Persia where she was scheduled to marry a prince. Upon delivery of the bride, the Polos made their way to the Black Sea and sailed westward to Constantinople and then on to Venice.

Trade wars between Italian city-states were all too common. In 1298, Marco Polo was captured during a naval battle between Venice and Genoa. While spending a year in captivity, he dictated a recollection of his Eastern adventures to Rustichello of Pisa. Certainly, Rustichello embellished Marco's tales. Published as *The Description of the World*, the book would become extremely popular.

In his own day, many questioned the veracity of Marco Polo's account of his travels. Yet his book provided Europeans with the best description of Central and East Asia for the next two centuries. It fascinated generations of readers and stimulated interest in the wealth of the Far East. Both Prince Henry the Navigator of Portugal and Christopher Columbus are reported to have read Rustichello's lively rendition of Polo's journeys.

CONCLUSION

Historian Joseph R. Strayer expressed the belief that medieval society began to stagnate during the course of the thirteenth century. The accomplishments of Europeans in that century lacked the originality and boldness of the twelfth century. He attributes this in part to an emphasis on legalism and rationalism.

In a sense, his analysis of the period is ironic. The lack of a reliable legal structure plagued the people of Western Europe for six centuries following the end of the Roman Empire. The popularity of rationalism among thirteenth-century scholars resulted from the birth of universities in the proceeding century. While Strayer recognizes that the developments of the thirteenth century are a logical outgrowth of trends that first appeared in the twelfth, he fails to see that many innovations appeared in both centuries.

Urban centers continued to show great vigor, and innovation was hardly lacking. In 1241, a mutual assistance pact was signed between the German cities of Lubeck and Hamburg. Smaller cities were later invited to join this association, which came to be known as the Hanseatic League. By 1300, this federation of towns along the Baltic Sea extended from the southern border of Denmark to Novgorod in Russia. The

Roger Bacon argued that logic must be supported with experimentation for a theory to be judged correct.

league also maintained "hanses" or factories in London and Bruges to facilitate its business interests in the North Sea region.

The Hanseatic League successfully dominated the trade in North European products like furs, fish, wax, naval stores, and salt for two centuries. At the height of its power in the fourteenth century, more than seventy towns were associated with the league.

Certainly not all scholastic philosophers employed logic exclusively to speculate about theological matters. Franciscan friar Roger Bacon (1214-1292) abandoned the teaching of philosophy to learn mathematics and to conduct scientific experiments. Unlike many philosophers of his time, he refused to rely exclusively on the writings of acknowledged authorities. He preferred to use empirical evidence as the source for knowledge. Although Bacon was often criticized and censured, Pope Clement IV (1265-1268) recognized his ability and defended him. Like Thomas Aquinas, Bacon believed that wisdom and faith were in harmony.

Few European peasants ever heard of the theological debates conducted by the scholars of Paris. Fewer still would have been able to read the *Divine Comedy* or the *Summa Theologica*. Most of those who could and did appreciate the great writers and teachers of the period lived in the cities and towns. The growing ranks of the new middle class prized literacy and served as a ready audience for new ideas.

Suggestions for Further Reading

Peter Abelard, *The Letters of Abelard and Heloise.* Betty Radice (trans.) (1974).

Thomas Aquinas, *Summa theologiae,* 60 volumes. Thomas Gilby, et al. (trans.) (1964-1973).

John W. Baldwin, *The Scholastic Culture of the Middle Ages, 1000-1300* (1971).

Christopher Brooke, *The Twelfth Century Renaissance* (1969).

Christopher Brooke and Roger Highfield, *Oxford and Cambridge* (1988).

Gabriel Campayre, *Abelard and the Origin and Early History of Universities* (1902).

Alan B. Cobban, *The Medieval Universities: Their Development and Organization* (1975).

Richard C. Dales, *The Intellectual Life in Western Europe in the Middle Ages* (1980).

Elizabeth Hamilton, *Heloise* (1967).

Henry Hersch Hart, *Marco Polo, Venetian Adventurer* (1967).

Charles Homer Haskins, *The Rise of Universities* (1957).

David Knowles, *The Evolution of Medieval Thought* (1962).

David Nicholas, *The Growth of the Medieval City: From Late Antiquity to the Early Fourteenth Century* (1997).

Henri Pirenne, *Medieval Cities: Their Origins and the Revival of Trade* (1956).

Joseph R. Strayer, *Western Europe in the Middle Ages: A Short History,* 3rd edition (1991).

FROM FEAR TO HOPE,
THE 1300'S

Cross from the Ossuary at Sedlec Czech Republic
All the decorations are from skeletons from the Black Death.

ANOTHER SIDE OF THE PICTURE

The history of the fourteenth century is written about men. Men in politics, men in war, men in the Church, and even men in the fields fill the pages of books. We have so few references to women that these few ladies tend to stand out as unique. The image of Joan of Arc leading soldiers in an almost holy crusade is one of those moments. Joan, in the early fifteenth century, belongs to the times as she was fighting in the Hundred Years' War that began in the early fourteenth century. As a woman soldier, Joan was not unique, and many women preceded her valiant efforts.

If we look closely, Joan had many predecessors. Isobel, Countess of Buchan, fought for Scottish independence even against her own husband's wishes. Jeanne de Danpierre fought with her husband for the French cause many years before Joan was born. Records about women in this period are sketchy and are mostly about noblewomen, but a few records stand out giving us clues and showing that women did play significant roles.

Phillipa of Hainault was a noblewoman who involved herself in much of the society and culture of the day. She was born in 1311 (possibly as late as 1314; birth records were not well kept, perhaps because so many children died in early infancy). Philippa was the youngest daughter of William, Count of Hainault, Holland and Zealand. An important man in his region, he became associated with Isabella, the wife of Edward II and Queen of England. Abroad to supposedly help her husband's international causes, Isabella was really looking for allies against Edward. In the complex political intrigues of the day, she introduced the idea that her son, the Crown Prince, marry Phillipa in exchange for her father's loyalty to Isabella's cause.

The Crown Prince met Phillipa briefly and agreed, as he was quite impressed with her. The marriage was quickly organized and performed at Valenciennes, Phillipa's home. Edward, however, was represented by a proxy and not even present at the ceremony. Soon the young bride left for England where, on January 24, 1328, another grand rite was held at York. By this time, Edward was king as his mother's plot had been successful and her husband had been forced to resign. After the wedding ceremony, Phillipa should have been crowned Queen, but Isabella refused to give up her own title.

As Edward's attachment and loyalty to his wife grew and his maturity demanded he be the actual king instead of his mother's puppet, Phillipa grew in power and popularity. In 1330, Edward had his mother sent off to a nunnery and her lover Mortimer executed. The new Queen's coronation was splendid, and the couple began a long and productive reign over their English subjects.

Phillipa was, as some historians have called her, a superwoman involving herself in a whole variety of adventures and interests. She introduced England to the weaving of her Flemish homeland as well as techniques for coal mining, which became important to the English economy. She founded Queens College at Oxford, and although no female would attend the university for many many years, her interest in education was important to English society. She enjoyed and supported the writings of

Geoffrey Chaucer and gave grants to the work of the French chronicler Michel Froissart who was living in England during her reign.

In 1346, Edward was away fighting in France, defending his claim to French lands and its crown. Meanwhile an uprising in Scotland threatened English control there and demanded immediate attention. Phillipa called on her English subjects to follow her, and she led them northward to victory. Her campaign was so successful that her troops captured the Scottish king, David Bruce.

The marriage to Edward was on the whole a happy one. Phillipa gave birth to twelve children, nine of whom survived to adulthood—a near record in those days of disease (the plague would hit England several times during her lifetime) and poor medical knowledge. The children, especially the sons, worked together, another near miracle in an age where claims to the throne could destroy even the closest relationships.

In standards we would find hard to endure, Phillipa did suffer through many of her husband's "indiscretions." Edward, as did most noblemen felt was their privilege, had a roving eye and the power to take whatever, or whomever, he wanted. Even in the scandalous time of the accusation that he raped the Countess of Salisbury, the Queen stood firm in her loyalty. Edward's affair with the notorious Alice Perrers (whom he married after Phillipa's death) was the talk of England, yet Phillipa continued to display her royal dignity.

On the August 14, 1369, Phillipa died at Windsor Castle, just a ways outside London. Only two of her sons, her favorite Edward, the Black Prince, and Thomas, were with her as the others were off fighting again for England. She blessed her children and praised the people of England. The writer Froissart wrote this tribute to the Great Lady:

> *In all her life, she did neither*
> *In thought or deed*
> *Anything whereby to lose her soul*
> *As far as anyone could know.*

Phillipa has few modern day admirers because her story is lost in the times of plague, war and political tensions. Her life, however, proves that on the other side of these cherished historical subjects, real people had to struggle and survive and make their days count in the lives of others.

Chronology

1300	Jubilee Year Proclaimed by the Pope
1305-1377	The Papacy resides in Avignon, France: The Babylonian Captivity
1320	First Western written mention of gunpowder
1324	Marco Polo returns to Italy from China
1337-1453	The First Hundred Years War between France and England
1340	Italians construct first paper mill; 7 water wheels drive the "machinery"
1347-1351	The Bubonic Plague
1350	Edward III introduces the foot, yard and acre as measurements
1356	Hanseatic League formed by Northern European merchants
1358	Jacquerie Revolt in France
1369-1405	Tamerlane, a descendant of Genghis Khan, attacks Russia, Persia, Turkey and India, defeats the Ottoman emperor
1378-1414	Popes in France and Rome: The Great Schism
1388	*Canterbury Tales* by Chaucer
1398	Wat Tyler's Rebellion in England
1431	Joan of Arc burned for witchcraft

THE BAD YEARS

In Western Civilization, the number 12 has a fairly good reputation. There were 12 disciples of Jesus; 12 months in a year; 12 inches in a foot; even 12 days of Christmas. In ancient times, there were 12 cities in the leagues of Ionia and Etruria and 12 tribes of Israel; the Romans composed 12 Tables for their laws. Touching on Western Civilization, there are 12 Proofs of Mohammed as a True Prophet. Even today, success can be measured by 12-Step programs. All of this connotes pleasantry, if not happiness, in the balance of 12. In many myths, 12 is the number of completeness.

The number 13, however, is frequently associated with bad times. That the number 13 is unlucky is probably one of the most consistent superstitions of Western Civilization. In the Bible, Revelations Chapter 13 predicts horrible events; the chapter begins ominously:

> And I stood upon the sand of the sea, and saw the beast rise up out of the sea Having 10 heads an 10 horns, and upon his horns 10 crowns, and upon his head, the name of blasphemy.

The chapter only gets worse in provoking terrors of the end of the world. Eighty-five percent of the references to 13 in the Bible are connected to something bad and usually horrible. Those looking for connections to the evil even count that the letters in the name Judas Iscariot add up to 13.

Many Christians believe Jesus was crucified on Friday 13, making for many fears as that day periodically arrives. There were, of course, 13 people at the Last Supper (Jesus and his 12 disciples—one of whom betrayed him, making only 12 good people). Across the United States, Europe, and Australia many people refuse to seat 13 guests at their tables, and many hotels and buildings skip 13 when numbering their floors.

In the course of Western Civilization, the century following 1300 was perhaps the most unpredictable and devastating to the population. Each year seemed to bring the world closer to its end. In order to find any hope, the people had to turn to new ideas and new social formulations to survive and make sense of their world.

WEATHER

The economic progress of the 1200s brought an increase in the population and the living standard of Europeans. The textile "explosion" brought new and finer material to clothing and "linens," which proved to be successful in trade all over the Mediterranean. As the new century arrived, there was much hope that growth and prosperity would continue. Success, however, depended on continued good luck as the population was quickly outstripping food and water supplies.

Soon after 1300, tell-tale signs of disaster began appearing. Bitter weather patterns loomed over much of the early part of the century. Some historians refer to the period as "The Little Ice Age." Unexpected drops in the temperature and torrential rains damaged crops of grains and flax, the sources of food and fabric, i.e., prosperity. Wheat, oat, hay, pork and beans were the substance of the European diet, as well as the basis for feeding their stock. With transportation of such crops limited to local circulation, any area hit by bad weather was doomed to poverty and starvation. From 1315 to 1317, almost all of Europe was, at the least, malnourished if not at death's door.

The weakened population suffered another blow when an epidemic of typhoid hit town and country during 1316; cities like Ypres in Belgium, the heart of the flourishing textile industry, lost perhaps 10 percent of their population. Animals, also underfed from the poor harvests, fell prey to disease in 1318, and another poor harvest in 1321 brought more suffering and death. By 1322, poor peasants survived on whatever food they could find, whether it was rancid, bug-ridden, or wormy. Unrest and discontent filled the hearts and minds of the few with any energy; families disintegrated and feudal loyalties were strained. With things going wrong everywhere, surely there was some message that God was sending to His People. By the middle of the century, the bubonic plague made it clear that God's wrath was upon the land.

POPES AND KINGS

During the 1200s, the majority of the popes in Rome held a firm hand on Western Christendom. As keeper of the keys to the kingdom of Heaven, they wielded both religious and secular power. In 1295, a new pope was installed, a strangely unsocial but spiritual man who was surely a sign of God's connection to His world. Before his elevation, Celestine V had lived in the wilds of the Abruzzi forests, hiding out in caves and looking for spiritual guidance. The cardinals elected him to show their dedication to holy ways. Five months after his election, however, the former hermit feared for his soul if he remained the chief priest and in an unprecedented move, resigned from the Holy See.

Benedetto Gaetano, one of the leading advisors to the papacy, was primed to take over in the crisis. His reputation as a great jurist of canon law and as a highly skilled diplomat seemed to make him a perfect candidate, and soon he became Boniface VIII. Some even believed that Gaetano had talked the politically incompetent

Celestine to resign in the face of decreasing support for his ascetic ways.

It was definitely a time for a strong leader for many secular controversies were stirring the stability of Europe. Probably the most famous was the long conflict brewing between England and Scotland. The Scots repeatedly declared their independence from the English crown but were dominated by English politics. They appealed to the pope to arbitrate and demanded their freedom from the English, but occupation and control continued. In 1298, William Wallace ("Braveheart") led his troops against the English and, probably betrayed by another jealous Scot, was defeated, sent to England, and executed by drawing and quartering. Boniface warned the English king, Edward I, that Scotland was part of the pope's jurisdiction, but the king continued to rule over the Scots.

Edward seemed unimpressed by papal power. Geographically far from Rome, the king seized every opportunity to increase his own power. In 1294, he had demanded that churches and monasteries pay large sums to gain his protection. Based on an old papal ruling that lords could collect taxes to support holy crusades, Edward demanded that the religious orders pay for his "crusades" against the French.

The Pope had a double problem in dealing with the English. Not only were they defying his edicts, they were constantly tempting the French into war. Such an unstable condition gave increasing powers to the local monarchs at the expense of the Church. In France, Philip the Fair had a similarly disrespectful attitude toward papal positions. He had seized a number of areas previously considered part of the Holy See's possessions. In these wars, Philip had demanded the churches pay large amounts of taxes. France was the most powerful kingdom in all of Europe, and in some ways it was essen-tial that Boniface find some sort of ally. Since working with the kings was impossible, he sought ways to build the power of the papacy above the secular rulers.

The power of the papacy had long been expressed in Papal Bulls, strong statements that carried the punishment of excommunication if disobeyed. (The name has no reference to the animal bull but from the word "bullum," a large lead disk attached to the most important papal documents and then stamped with the holy seal.) Boniface turned to this tool to calm the situation. *Clericis Laicos*, posted in February 1296, declared that secular authorities could not exact any funds or property from the Church unless the Pope gave a special dispensation. Princes who disobeyed the ruling would be excommunicated, meaning that Hell was the final destination of all who broke the rule. While Edward simply ignored the Bull, Philip dealt with it by declaring that no gold, silver, precious stones, weapons or food could be exported from his kingdom, even by the Church. Harassed and pressured by their secular rulers, priests, monks and even cardinals began to petition Boniface to help them. His Holiness responded that he did not mean to forbid voluntary contributions that could aid in the defense of a kingdom. He even added to the compromise by making Philip's grandfather, Louis IX, a saint. The pressure subsided, and for a brief two years the French and English declared a truce.

The year 1300 was a Jubilee year, and Boniface made the most of it. He declared that those who came to Rome to celebrate would be specially blessed. In June, for the Feast of Saints Peter and Paul, 200,000 pilgrims filled the city and rejoiced. Boniface dreamed of reuniting Europe under a papal hegemony. Every country in Europe, and even some from Asia, had answered the call. But, except for the son of the King of

Naples, no king or prince could be found in the crowd. Boniface's plan would quickly fall apart.

Misreading the situation and believing that he had a great deal of support, Boniface issued a new Bull to clarify the papal position. In *Ausculta Fili,* Boniface declared that the Vicar of Christ had been placed by God over kings and all temporal rulers. "He is the keeper of the keys, the judge of the living and the dead, and sits on the throne of justice, with power to extirpate all iniquity."

The Bull brought forth all the enemies of the Pope who quickly decided to support the King of France and his struggle against the Church. In fact, some of these churchmen so opposed the power of Boniface they created a false Bull pretending that the Pope had really announced that he had all power in heaven and earth. This "bull" circulated through France and aroused a patriotic cry against the Roman usurper.

The papacy gathered its supporters and called a council to meet in Rome in October 1302. The king declared that all goods belonging to any ecclesiastic who attended the council would be confiscated. The battle continued, although the council finally met with only a few representatives. Two bulls were then promulgated. The first excommunicated anyone who interfered with persons trying to attend the council; the second, the more famous, reasserted papal claims. In *Unam Sanctam*, the basic foundation for the Church position was set down using the famous fathers of the past, especially Thomas Acquinas and St. Bernard. First, there was only one Church and no salvation beyond its organization. Second, only the Roman Pope could dispense the Church's justice. Third, the world was divided into the realms of the spiritual and the temporal. The second was ruled by princes who understood the leadership of the

first. Clear and logical, the Bull surely placed the King of France and his allies in error.

Philip quickly had his scholars prepare an answer to the Bull that showed the Pope had overstepped his rightful place. In quick succession, he called his supporters to declare that the Roman bishop was a heretic, made peace with England, and called on that kingdom to join him in his opposition to the treasonous Pope, and supported all the claims of temporal leaders who would join his cause. Boniface was declared a "simonist, robber, and a heretic," and many in Europe looked to Philip to save their souls in this time of crisis.

Boniface retreated to his family estate in Agnagi, declaring that if Philip did not stop his accusations he would be excommunicated. Philip responded by appointing a French prosecutor to charge Boniface with all sorts of ethical, moral and legal crimes. Philip sent troops to capture him. On September 7, 1303, the soldiers arrived and demanded their prey, the Pope. They seized him, but papal troops barred their escape. Finally the French retreated, leaving the aged holy man behind. Humiliated and bruised, Boniface returned to Rome, but on October 11, he died from the shock of the confrontation.

Boniface's successor tried to balance the interests of Church and state and even increased the number of French cardinals. His brief tenure led, in 1305, to the election of a Frenchman who took the name Clement V. With a little pressure from the king, the attractiveness of the beautiful French city, and the prospect of an alliance with the most powerful temporal leaders of Europe, Clement took the papacy out of the divisive Rome. He moved to Avignon in Southern France, just across from the German side of the Rhone River. There popes resided until 1378, living in luxury but under the supervision of the French kings.

Tradition connected the papacy with Rome and the time in Avignon, referred to as the Second Babylonian Captivity in reference to the Jewish captivity by the Babylonians many years before, brought an end to the domination of the Church in Western Europe. Although it would remain the only official Christian Church until the early 1500s, Church policies and leadership came under the critical eye of the secular world.

As the kings and princes of Europe turned their attention from Rome to Avignon, they quickly began to distrust the new set up. They considered (rightly so) the Avignon popes were the puppets of the French kings.

The Avignon papacy tried to establish its supremacy over Christian Europe by beautifying the city. It did so, however, by cutting resources to the parishes, taxing bishoprics, and reducing funds throughout Christendom. It made the selling of church offices (simony) a means of increasing revenue, and the sale of indulgences, documents sold to assure the pardon of sins, became a common practice. Encouraging all priests to raise funds, the popes declared that the practice and "sanctity" of poverty was heretical. The spiritual center of Western Christendom seemed to have more in common with business ventures than with its spiritual traditions of its past.

In the years that popes resided at Avignon, the general populace began to see that spiritualism had been translated into materialism. Few reform efforts were implemented, and the papacy's reputation as the spiritual leader began to suffer. As the crises of the fourteenth century increased, the Church failed to serve its people. Wars devastated land and people and revolved only around greedy land disagreements rather than the spiritual causes of the Holy Crusades. Disease and famine left many dead, and when the plague arrived, many priests were so frightened they refused to perform their duty and administer the sacraments, much less the last rites, which meant that the souls of the dead would be sent to Hell. Once the Church had used the devil and his agents to keep the religious faith of its followers; now it seemed to be turning away from its people and leaving them to be victims of the Evil one. Separated from the traditional means for hope and salvation, the people began to rediscover old pagan rituals and mysticism; the decline of papal power also gave more respect to national leaders and local religious leaders. The luxurious lives of the churchmen did not put emphasis on the road to heaven but rather put the worldly needs and desires at center stage.

ENDLESS WARFARE

Ever since human beings began to record their history, there seems to have been a succession of violence. Whether it was over food, territory, or even women, men lined up to hurt and kill each other. The 1300s were an almost continuous succession of battle, including the vaguely accurate title of the "Hundred Years of War" between the English and the French.

In 1066, William of Normandy had arrived on the Dover shore, and as his troops moved inland, they defeated the armies of Harold the Saxon. The Norman vassal of the King of France believed that he was the rightful heir to the throne of England. The former king of England, Edward the Confessor, had looked to William as his heir until his deathbed revision naming Harold the Saxon as King. After William arrived from Normandy and killed Harold, the English crown passed to his line. From that time on, through intermarriage and conquest, England and France were joined, although not united.

By 1300, France was the undeniable leader of the European political scene. With a population of 21 million, it dwarfed its chief competitor with only a fifth of that number. The concept of "nation" was beginning to take hold. There was a firm belief that peoples from similar ancestors were somehow linked under a social and political organization. Kings had begun to assume a special, almost magical role, an almost semi-divine role that paralleled the positions of cardinals and bishops. As far as Philip was concerned, he was on an equal level with the Pope. When, in 1303, the papacy was transferred to Avignon, the reigning French king made certain that the next six popes paid attention to the needs of the French kingdom.

In England, King Edward was similarly claiming that he had a religious role, and he meant to challenge anyone who lessened the claims of his nation. Maneuvering and bluffing, both kings began a series of threats that would bring their people into some of the worst battles Western Civilization had yet to see.

Philip first turned his vengeance on powerful allies of the Church, the most famous was the Templars. Their power was based on the wealth they had accumulated during the Crusades and their reputation for doing good among the populace; the Templars held a supreme respect from both church and secular circles. Philip began his campaign by forcing the members, particularly the old men, to swear that the Order was a treasonous group threatening the monarchy. If they did not give in easily, they were tortured, sometimes to the point of death, and after confessing, were put to death. In the final days of the Order's strength, the Grand Master was burned at the stake and in his last moments asked God to bring his judgement upon Philip and his Pope. The Templar's Curse seemed very real when Clement died within the month, and seven months later, Philip, hale, hearty and enjoying life, fell dead. Then, his three sons died after reigning only a few years. These sudden tragedies left the throne of France vacant, and a war among its claimants became one of the central events of European history for about 125 years.

In 1328, three contenders sought to become the French king. There was the grandson of Philip, who perhaps had the best claim but was the 16-year-old King of England, Edward III. Edward's mother was Philip's daughter, but she was notorious for her political intrigues, including killing her husband so that her son could rule. The French people feared the return of this evil queen and hoped she would stay in England. The other two claimants were Philip of Valois, son of the brother of Philip the Fair, and Philip Evreaux, son of Philip's half brother. A settlement was made that Philip of Valois would be the new king, and temporarily there was peace.

The Valois line began with splendor but it was soon obvious that the young king had no training for his new vocation and was dominated by his wife, Jeanne de Bourgogne, a woman similar to Edward's mother in style and evil conspiracy. Philip on the other hand was similar to his great grandfather, the now revered St. Louis, and he disregarded the significance of the politics of the day. Philip preferred to pray for guidance and left practical matters to others. In 1337, goaded by his wife and greedy politicians, Philip unwisely confiscated the province of Guienne, considered by the English their territory. The fragile peace that had come with Philip's accession was now destroyed, and Edward declared himself the legitimate king of France as well as England. The complicated alliances from heredity and marriage now divided Europe as each side pressed their connections to gain friends and allies.

Medieval Society

Since the end of the Roman empire, European areas fell into local rule with lords and nobles forming armies to both protect and exploit their peasants and serfs. Three major classes divided the society. The nobility counted on hereditary right to maintain an aura of power and control. The clergy depended on their connection to God to gain respect and authority. Last, the Third Estate was a conglomerate of everyone else. Rich businessmen, lawyers, doctors and other professionals were classed with craftsmen, peasants, landless serfs, beggars and anyone else left at the bottom of the population. This last group made up most of society and was denied most civil and political rights. Of course, the biggest right they were denied was to be part of the warrior class to which the nobility claimed exclusive membership. They were, therefore, dependent on the "protective" services of the nobility. For the peasants and serfs, at least most of them, there was grudging acceptance of the situation. The more wealthy of the Third Estate would slowly make demands to separate from them and eventually would form a middle class.

The concept of chivalry permeated the nobility. Fighting was manhood for the upper class, and every able-bodied noble was trained to defend his and his lord's honor. In the previous centuries, protecting the local people and serving their lords through holy crusades made up much of the obligations of knights, as well as princes and kings. With the journeys to the Holy Land limited, these soldiers turned to other ways of proving they were fit and brave. Tournaments and local squabbles became the order of the day. They were far from glorious, and perhaps the lack of honor and high goals turned the events into vicious personal battles.

Violence was not simply a matter of swords and brute strength. Most soldiers donned about 55 pounds of armor and had to balance themselves on horseback. Even on foot, the weight of the metal made the man awkward during battle, increasing his chances of being wounded or simply falling down. Since the suit of metal covered vital parts, wounds were often to the face, neck or underarms, which were not so easily protected. These wounds were easily infected or led to massive blood loss, causing painful death if the injured was "lucky," or a long, slow and very painful existence if the life of the person were "spared," meaning living with debilitating and crippling injuries.

New weapons added horror to the scene. The longbow, about six feet in length, was invented during the reign of Edward I. It made fighting less personal since it allowed a skilled archer to shoot an arrow at an enemy over 300 yards away, as well as permitting him to "load" quickly and send off many shots in a quick period of time. In 1325, the *pot de fer* was a small handheld cannon that fired an iron ball at the enemy. This device was almost as dangerous to the holder as to its target since it frequently blew up in the face of the person discharging the bullet. Still technology beyond sword fighting and spear throwing began to change the face of war. The nobles rose to the challenge and believed that the only course of action was to kill and win. Their horses had made them the best soldiers, but guns and longbows would eventually change the strategy of fighting. War took on a more impersonal tone as soldiers could kill each other without face to face combat.

Europe at War

At first Edward III demonstrated England's military superiority with a naval victory at the Battle of Sluys. The English did not command the seas with a superior navy but won by using their expertise with the longbow. The French soldiers had little chance against the rain of arrows that flew at them while they hurried to find a way to counterattack. Victory was, however, short lived because Edward did not have a land force to follow his triumph.

In the areas disputed between the two kings, the populace often played one side against the other. In France, however, people tended to lean towards a French king who would be there to protect them rather than a far away overlord who might just collect taxes and confiscate their property. Edward was not seen as a noble rescuer from an evil French king but more often a young greedy royal who wanted to increase his wealth for his own personal motives. By claiming he was the rightful heir to the French throne, he could, however, negotiate with any French noblemen opposed to Philip's rule. The alliances would be tangled and fragile, so the war took on horrendous tones.

In a local battle that has now become infamous, the French and English fought for the dukedom of Brittany. Each side backed a candidate for the French throne, and the French choice was Charles de Blois, the nephew of Philip IV. On the one hand, Charles was an extremely pious man. He prayed everyday and confessed every evening. He put pebbles in his shoes and wore rough clothing to scratch his skin. He slept on straw and tied his body with cords to cut into his flesh so that he constantly knew the sad state of being a sinful human. When it came to warfare, however, Charles had a totally different character. Arriving at Nantes that he claimed as his territory, he impressed the citizens with his seriousness by having his catapults hurl into the city the heads of thirty men he had previously captured.

In Flanders, long under the influence of the English because of their commercial ties for wine and wool, different conditions produced other gruesome scenes. The nobility in Flanders were pro-French while the merchants were supporters of the English. In 1302, the French attacked the town of Courtrai, but the Flemish workers came together to stop the line of invaders. As confusion riddled the French troops, the defenders, armed only with wooden pikes, baited them to cross the canals into the city. The French fell into the pits, and their enemy killed them like ancient warriors had speared animals they trapped in deep holes. According to many accounts, seven hundred gold spurs were taken from the dead and triumphantly hung on the city gates. Twenty-five years later, the Flemish would fall in huge numbers as the French gained a victory at Cassel. Although the French knighthood was to some degree vindicated, the success of the Flemish workers still proved that the average citizen was a useful soldier in times of crisis. The little crack in the nobility's control of the military would eventually grow into the earthquake where citizen armies would terrorize society. (See the French Revolution)

The wars between the French and English not only massacred populations and destroyed large sections of land but damaged the European economy, which had begun to grow beyond its old feudal roots. Both Philip and Edward had to borrow heavily to finance their armies, and when they lost, loans could not be repaid. This was especially true of commercial houses in Italy where the beginnings of commercial banking were starting to challenge the old system of barter. In Florence by the early 1340s, three major banking houses failed thus shutting down the growing economy. Goods sat in warehouses, and salaries went unpaid; people feared that they would starve because they were less dependent

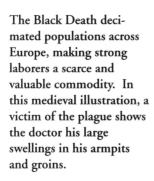

The Black Death deci-
mated populations across
Europe, making strong
laborers a scarce and
valuable commodity. In
this medieval illustration, a
victim of the plague shows
the doctor his large
swellings in his armpits
and groins.

on their land-based economy. Perhaps God was unhappy with their faith in materialism; perhaps wars against fellow Christians <u>were</u> great sins; perhaps they ought to return to simple lives as their ancestors had struggled on earth for preparation of the joys of heaven. Perhaps....

THE ARRIVAL OF SATAN'S KINGDOM

If war and economic upheavals were not enough to convince many that God's wrath had come down upon Europe, the year 1347 brought certainty of the fact for it was in that year death spread across the continent as eerily as Moses' plague had killed the Egyptians thousands of years before. When it was over, one third to one half of Europe was dead and had died horrible and painful deaths at that.

Although it was not clear to the Europeans, the plague resulted from their quest for luxuries and a higher standard of living. Trade, which had slowly grown during and after the Crusades, brought much more than material goods through the Mediterranean routes. In 1347 in the southern Ukraine—the closest port for bringing goods from China—a mysterious illness began killing the local citizens. At this point the plague had moved slowly, as it had been first seen in China in the 1330s. Panic ensued, and the natives blamed the Italian traders who were in the city

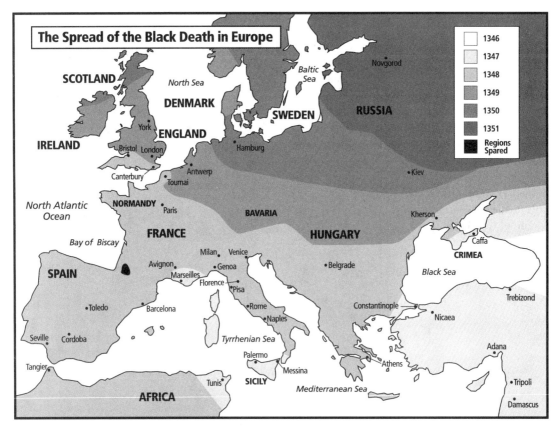

The Spread of the Black Death in Europe

at the time. Dead bodies were thrown at the Europeans hoping to get them to take the disease away. The plan was successful in that the plague arrived in Sicily in October 1347. The dying crew was confined to the ship, but no one noticed the exodus of the black rats onto the shore. The rodents, carrying fleas, quickly contaminated the island, boarded other ships heading for the mainland, and brought about one of the most deadly epidemics western civilization has seen. (The United Nations AIDS Program has predicted that the AIDS epidemic will outnumber the deaths due to the plague in 2004; until then the Bubonic Plague has been the deadliest epidemic.)

    With today's medical knowledge it is hard to understand why the plague was so devastat-ing as many simple sanitary improvements would probably have lessened its effect. Symptoms were, however, so revolting that logical thought may well have been impossible even if scientific knowledge were clearer. The doomed party was bitten by the flea, but fleas were everywhere in society and every class had to deal with the pests—archbishops, merchants, soldiers, peasants, etc. They were so common no one really noticed them; they were simply something to endure. After a bite from a diseased flea, the victim quickly noticed swellings on his body, usually the armpit, groin, or neck. These extremely painful *buboes* could be as large as an apple and gave the disease its name, bubonic plague. As the swelling increased, blood vessels in the patient expanded and burst, leaving black marks on the body. (These did not give the title The Black Death to the epidemic; rather, that came later from a mistranslation of the phrase *altra mors* meaning "dreadful death" but somehow read "black death" around the fifteenth century.)

The dying person gained little consideration from those surrounding him. First of all, the terror caused by the spread of the disease kept family and friends, and even priests, from caring for the sick. Next, everything about the disease was simply disgusting. The body smelled as if it were rotting; breathe, blood, urine, and the oozing sores all created such a stench that it was difficult to approach the person. The wrath of God was not kind, but then the Judeo-Christian God had promised to send his punishment not only to sinners but to their descendants. It seemed as if all the evil of Western Civilization was now being paid for by the residents of the fourteenth century.

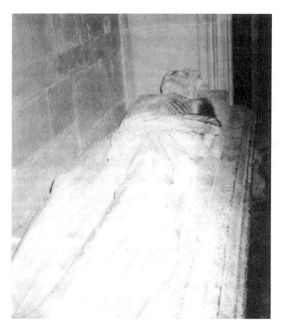

This is a burial image of a person who died from the black plague. (Winchester Cathedral, England)

Explanations

Medical knowledge during the 1300s was mostly superstitious. The most famous medical theorist read during this age was the ancient Roman Galen, who had claimed that disease was spread by poisonous vapors that corrupted the air. People were urged to leave marshy areas and come to the cities. There they could hide inside their homes, cover their windows, and try to keep the air cool as heat helped disease spread. The washing of hands and feet was encouraged, but people should be careful washing the rest of their bodies. The dampened skin might attract the vapors and disease might creep into the person. Many people wore flowers on their filthy clothing to ward away the evil air. The childhood rhyme "Ring Around the Rosy" is really a commentary on the period of the Black Death:

Ring around the Rosy (the pink swellings)...
Pocket full of Posy: (flowers might drive away the disease)
Ashes, ashes; (burning of the infected bodies)
we all fall down! (we shall all die).

This was not a very pleasant picture or interpretation, but surely a realistic view of the despondency of the age.

The plague was uncontrollable. In some places, whole towns were emptied. In some families children died while old people survived. Rich, poor, the plague made no distinction. Some fled the towns and cities for the countryside, bringing the rats and fleas with them, and thus the plague. Some tried lancing the boils and lived; others died of the infections from treatments. There seemed little hope as body after body was placed in the street, and prayers for survival and recovery went unanswered.

There were, in fact, two types of the disease. The fleas and rats carried the first form, and then there was a second that was spread by the sneezing and coughing of the infected person. No one in the fourteenth century knew about germs, viruses, bacteria or other microscopic organisms that caused disease. They knew there must be a cause, and although it scurried right in front of them, they could not see it. At one point, many thought cats carried the disease, and they were killed in large numbers, resulting in another increase in the rat population.

The rats and fleas were simply a sign of the times. Medieval life style wallowed in unhealthy filth. Clothes were seldom changed, and baths were probably infrequent since only public bathing houses, few and far between, existed. Many Christians believed that the only personal cleansing they needed to do was to be baptized by the Church. In homes little housecleaning was done, and the streets of medieval towns were filled with garbage and were sewers for all sorts of waste. Bathrooms were not part of the structure of a house. The custom of building overhangs across the narrow streets might protect the residents from rain and too much sun but suffocated them with stale air and damp conditions that helped breed disease.

The plague was deadly and unrelenting. A person might be active and healthy one day, dead the next. Priests and doctors adopted strange costumes, covering their bodies and faces when they chanced the infection by visiting the sick. Within a year, the plague had spread across continental Europe, and in cities it is estimated that 30 to 60 percent of the population died. In 1349 it spread to Scandinavia, Iceland, and Greenland.

Devoted Christians, the population began turning to God with extraordinary prayers. One group, which grew rapidly, revived the ancient custom of flagellation. By marching through towns and beating themselves, they called on God to forgive the sins of all and remove the plague. Frenzied audiences joined in expressing a notion of collective guilt. Everyone needed to appeal to the saints, to the Virgin Mary, to Jesus. St. Roche and St. Sebastian were particularly called upon to relieve the terrors of the plague. The calls, however, went unheeded, and the suffering continued.

A movement known as The Flagellants had a particular affect. Their masochistic practice of beating themselves to unconsciousness became a public entertainment in a grim time. Each member carried a scourge, a wooden stick that had three or four leather strips at the end. The leather strips were equipped with metal spikes so that when they struck the skin, bleeding and much pain occurred. The group would form a circle, strip to the waist (even women), and begin their self-inflicted martyrdom. Many flocked to their appearances to encourage them to whip themselves even harder. Soon these so-called pious representatives were attacking the organized Church and condemning it for not solving the problem. As the insults grew, as well as the horror shows, the Church began to object to the dissidents.

One of the worst side affects of the Flagellant movement was their appointment of the "true cause" of the plague. Since whipping themselves had had little influence on the course of the disease, there must, they claimed, be a source other than Christian sin. That source was obvious to anyone who looked around Christian Europe: Christians could easily blame the Jewish population for its suffering.

The Jews of Europe lived primarily on the outskirts of towns and cities. They had special "quarters," since they were not permitted to own prime land or be an integral part of Christian society. They had, however, served many purposes, especially when it came to Christians finding ways of circumventing Christian law. The rules of the Church had put a great burden on a growing money economy. Christians were forbidden to charge interest on loans; it was simply the duty of a Christian to help others in need, not to make profit from their troubles. Jews, however, did not have to live by such a rule, and some had managed to accumulate enough wealth in the form of money to become large lenders through the "privilege" of earning interest. No one really likes to be in debt, especially to a group that was socially unacceptable. The Church was one of the first to condemn Jewish traders. During the Crusades, soldiers for the holy venture were forgiven any debts to Jewish lenders by a decree from the Church. This was just part of the long tradition of blaming the Jews for the troubles of Christian society.

Many Jewish rituals made them suspicious to Christian society. For one, the Jews were careful in their food preparation as well as in the processes for cooking, lessening sicknesses due to poisons from rotten food. Cleanliness was a practice of their religious devotions whereas Christians needed only to "bathe in their faith." Because of their outcast position in society, Jews often kept to themselves and, worst of all, seemed to be less affected by the sweep of the plague. All this made them an easy scapegoat for explaining why Christians were dying and Jews were not.

Christians noted that Jews would not take water from town wells. The explanation was simple: according to their laws, they had to get "fresh" water from springs. To the Christians, however, the reason was obvious: the Jews had poisoned the wells. In September 1348, eleven Jewish men in a small southern German town were accused of poisoning the town well and after hours of questioning, accompanied by torture, the men confessed. News of their execution spread through Europe, and other communities began to see the cause of the plague—it was not their sin, but the evilness of those who had crucified Christ!

In Zurich, Jews were forbidden to become citizens, one of the least severe "punishments" of the times. In Basel and Brussels, they were herded into wooden buildings and burned alive. In Strasburg, historians estimate that sixteen thousand Jews were killed in 1349 alone. In Frankfort, the Flagellants entered the Jewish quarter and caused such hysteria that the entire population was destroyed. In Mainz and Cologne, they had the same "success." Jews across Europe huddled in their small ghettos waiting for the worst to happen.

Finally in 1349, after the challenge to Church and Papal authority, Pope Clement IV issued a Bull declaring the Flagellant movement heretical and that members would be excommunicated. A few of the leaders were hanged, priests who had encouraged the movement were unfrocked, and all the members were excommunicated. On the secular side, Philip VI of France forbade public self-flagellation and declared that the punishment for such behavior would be death. Several leading Flagellants were beheaded. Anti-semitism was, however, not eradicated. What saved the few Jews remaining, however, was not the outcry against their torture and death, but, in 1350, the sudden and again unexplainable disappearance of the plague.

A TURNING POINT?

Terrible events are the excitement of historical writers since they can speculate on their causes and results. In 1347, the approximate population of Western Europe was 75 million people; in 1352, it was about 50 million. Twenty five million people died within 5 years, a tremendous toll. Entire families were wiped out; whole towns disappeared. Many historians believe that what happened as a result of the Bubonic Plague was the setting up of the foundations for our modern world. A heavy price was paid to bring about our present social, economic and political systems. By the end of the century, only half the number of people that lived in Europe in 1345 populated its territory. Sporadic outbreaks of the plague continued until 1399, when it disappeared until a brief appearance in the seventeenth century.

The first result of the plague was, of course, the drastic reduction of population. Where competition for status, as well as jobs, had been strong before the plague, now workers and even leaders were desperately needed. The plague had not damaged crops, livestock or land plots, so much more material wealth was available to those who had survived. Wages and benefits increased, providing improved life styles. Workers could leave the land their ancestors had tilled with little success and seek better opportunities. Those with traditional power reacted by supporting laws such as the English Stature of Laborers (1351), which stipulated that wages were to remain the same as in pre-plague days, but these could not be enforced because the need for workers was great while the supply was small.

In some areas, such as Florence, Italy, recovery from the economic ruin caused by loans to Edward in the beginnings of the Hundred Years War was assured as the citizens, organized into guilds, began producing high quality products that were demanded across Europe. The need for funds found a few Christian families wealthy and powerful enough to rule the city with the primary interest of business and suc-

cess determining policy. Roots of the Medici family's control of the city were born out of the plague! Thus, the beginning of the artistic and technological Renaissance came, to at least some degree, from the bite of a tiny flea.

Probably the most significant immediate result of the plague was the negative reaction to the long-term control of society by the Church. For many years, Christianity in Western Europe meant membership in the organization based in Rome. During the plague, the Pope was not in Rome but in Avignon. It was hard not to notice that the city was not protected from the plague. In fact, it suffered as much, if not more, than many other cities.

Also, the Church had preached that living in this world was a time of suffering, a time of preparation for one's journey to Heaven. If life on earth was to be short and miserable, surely God would not mind a few excesses. Even the members of the clergy, especially those at Avignon, indulged in fancy clothes and partying. Years of fear and repression produced a time of celebrating the fact that they had survived the pestilence. Assertiveness replaced compliance; orgies replaced guilt; and European society took on a "this worldly" attitude instead of just seeking the route to Heaven. Many thought it was time to make society a place for the living, not simply a place to prepare for the afterlife.

DIVIDING UP THE WORLD

*The French and the English:
Claims to the Land*

In the complicated realm of allegiances and alliances, European traditions set the stage for a return to war. In some ways, the history of the era can be told through the life of Edward III, King of England from 1327 to 1377. Born in 1312,

French knights charge the enemy during the Battle of Crecy.

he was controlled by his mother, the daughter of the French king; she was a vicious woman who fell in love with an equally unscrupulous man, Roger Mortimer. Together these two plotted against Edward's father and taking advantage of his unpopularity, caused a revolt that put young Edward on the throne at the age of 15. Then they had the old king murdered and took control of the kingdom. Their plan failed when Edward, at 18, showed his own strength and had his mother imprisoned and Mortimer executed. His 50-year rule would bring England into the status of world power.

The early parts of the Hundred Years Wars revolved around Edward's claim, through his mother, to the French crown. The naval battle at Sluys (1340) gave England control of the Channel; and the battles of Crecy ((1346) and Calais (1347) gave the English dominion over much French territory. The catch here was that with these "victories" Edward became the feudal vassal of the King of France and had to pledge his loyalty to him. This meant that even though he was King of England, he was supposed to journey across the Channel, kneel before the Valois dynasty, and promise to protect the French realm from its enemies (some of whom were Edward's allies). Such humiliation was a real problem for Edward, not only ego-wise but in the collection of feudal dues (meaning some of his treasury

would have to go to his enemy, the King of France).

By the early 1350s, with the plague subsiding, both sides began pressing their claims against each other, and war was not far off. The French at first declared that Edward must, as tradition demanded, come and make his feudal promises. When he did not come, they moved their troops on to his land and denied him the collection of his feudal rents. Edward retaliated by declaring that he was the rightful king of France, and in 1355, English soldiers began arriving in France to support his claims.

Led by Edward's oldest son, the Black Prince (because he wore black armor), infantry equipped with their longbows swiftly defeated the French cavalry. In the 1356 Battle of Poitiers, the French King, John (Jean) the Good, was captured with his younger son and sent off to England as a great prize. A huge amount of money and land was demanded for his ransom. At first, only a small amount of money was raised, and the English were so frustrated they allowed John to return to France to help raise the money!

Meanwhile, Charles Valois, called the Dauphin (crown prince), tried to combine and organize the French forces. He called a meeting in Paris of the representatives of French society to consider how they would come to his aid and drive out the English. Barely 18 and not ready to rule, Charles had made a strategic mistake. The delegates quickly disintegrated into a squabbling horde that accused Charles' ministers of losing the war. Robert LeCoq, Bishop of Laon, showed that even the Church had little support for Charles and demanded that he release his primary French opponent for the crown, Charles the Bad, King of Navarre (the Dauphin's brother-in-law).

In a series of disastrous events, the weakness of the French situation came to a head. In 1359, the English surrounded Paris and forced the French into the Treaty of Bretigny. The huge ransom for King John was to be paid in three installments, and more land had to be ceded to the English. It looked like the English would dominate French politics.

Within France itself, society was divided about who should rule the country. With varying support, competing groups caused near chaos. In Paris itself, Etienne Marcel, a wealthy merchant, led the Third Estate, demanding they have a voice in the government that had traditionally been run by the nobles and the clergy. Actually Marcel represented only a small part of his "class," as it was composed of a widely separated group. At one end were the wealthy merchants, doctors, lawyers, and other successful non-nobles who did their best to copy the lives of the hereditary nobility. On the other end were the craftsmen, peasants, and landless workers who struggled for survival. Marcel manipulated the lower class and encouraged them to join him against the traditional leaders, the nobility, and the clergy. He even gave those eager to join with him a symbol for their future liberty, red and blue hoods to signify their inclusion in his projects. He was successful enough to drive the fearful Dauphin from the city.

By 1358 another group began to enter the political scene, the peasants of the countryside.

Beginning around Beauvais, north of Paris, a group of peasants who were totally frustrated by high taxes and noble privilege broke into a castle and killed the knight and his family. Excited by their success, they moved on to another castle and burned the knight at a stake after raping and killing his wife and daughters. The nickname for French peasants was Jacques, and to assure their anonymity, each member of the group called himself Jacques Bonhomme (John Good Man). The movement has since been called the rise of the Jacquerie. Acts of violence spread rapidly across France. Charles of Navarre took these rebels on as his personal challenge, capturing their leader and beheading him. Soon nobles across France rallied and took revenge by massacring thousands of the insurgents, probably many of them innocent.

Marcel, meanwhile, had problems keeping his coalition together and became desperate for allies. He appealed to Charles of Navarre and the English to help him against the Dauphin Charles. As these forces arrived in Paris, the populace turned against Marcel, and on July 31, 1358, he was beaten and murdered, his naked body thrown into the streets to prove that his movement was as dead as he was.

If this were not enough to tear France to near anarchy, a third group began to have its own effect on the scene. As armies came and went on official missions led by royal officers, there were periods of "non-fighting." They could hardly be called peace because throughout the land, marauders or Free Companies attacked whomever and wherever they pleased, taking what they wanted, not only in goods but livestock and women. They left the French countryside as vulnerable as in the days of the Barbarian raiders. It took over thirty years for the French to stabilize the situation.

Both England and France suffered from the years of war. Although a brief peace was made in 1360, war resumed by 1369. A new French commander began to make inroads into English success, including a brief invasion into the English territories. Now it was England's turn to be distracted by troubles at home.

New Ways of Government: The Case of England

The English have long prided themselves with their organized "representative" government and many of the hallmarks of Western Civilization have English precedents. The Magna Carta of 1215 formed the precedent of no taxation without representation; the courts of Henry II and III instituted the notion of a jury of peers for trials. During the passage of these ideas into procedures, the real benefactors were the upper classes, and they were not in any way "democratic" or inclusive when they were first presented.

In 1295, Edward I had reached out to broaden his base of support against the nobles who had forced previous rulers to give up some of their power. Needing money for campaigns and court expenses, he called Parliament but invited two knights from every shire to attend. In an attempt to strengthen royal power, Edward solidified a tradition that would lead eventually to establishment of the House of Commons.

Edward III was similarly a practical man who, especially after the unpopularity and demise of his father, wanted the support of his people. His wars against France demanded that he look favorably on petitions and demands of his subjects. Throughout his reign, Parliament grew stronger and met to consider the needs of the "nation." This did not mean the monarchy felt any desire to represent the common people, but a sort of notion about sharing power began to develop.

The exclusion of the majority of English "citizens" from the government and their exploitation was clearly demonstrated in 1381 with a massive protest that demanded that the rulers consider the needs of the majority. In the early fourteenth century, the Court of Common Pleas, the civil court of England, decided that it did not have time for the legal problems of peasants. This basically denied the lower class access to the protection of the law. It also indicated that there was so much business for the courts that little could get done. For the peasants, local lords equaled justice, and the idea of the King's law was compromised.

During the Bubonic Plague, perhaps as many as half of the English people died. It was particularly devastating to the poor who were the workers of the once-growing English economy. Now the nobles demanded that the peasants work even harder to keep their lowly positions on the manors. If they even tried to understand the law, they were limited because it was written in an almost foreign language, "law French" handed down from the days when William of Normandy became the conqueror of the island.

"Wat Tyler's Rebellion"

The Peasants' Rebellion centered around a specific event against a specific person, but the event and the person symbolized the plight of all the peasants. In 1381, a tax collector arrived at the hovel of a peasant named Wat Tyler. He demanded that Tyler's daughter, aged 15, was of taxable age and grabbed her, stripped her naked, and assaulted her. Tyler, who was working near by, heard the screams of his wife and daughter and came running. Hammer in hand, he

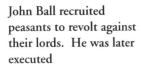
John Ball recruited peasants to revolt against their lords. He was later executed

smashed the tax collector's head to pieces. His neighbors cheered him and agreed to follow him to London to protest their treatment.

As they traveled across England, they were joined by two other groups led by John Ball and Jack Straw, itinerant priests who had called upon the peasants to invade London. By now there were 100,000 followers. They broke into the city, tore open the gates of prisons, and beheaded every judge and lawyer they could find. The leaders demanded that this was a cause for justice not looting and forbid their followers to take any goods as they moved through the area. Now they surrounded the building where Richard II, England's 18-year-old king, huddled among his advisors. As a few nobles tried to escape, they were caught and killed. Richard pleaded with the mob; he asked what they wanted and they cried out, "We will be free forever, our heirs and our lands." Richard, realizing he had little to oppose them, agreed and blessed them.

With the promises of the king, many of the peasants left to go home and take care of

their fields and families. A few days later, Wat Tyler stood at the front of the remaining peasant "army." On horseback, Wat slowly rode toward his king and the Mayor of London. Trusting that all was well, the two men met and exchanged greetings. Suddenly the Mayor of London, who later claimed he thought Tyler had insulted the king, knocked the rebel leader to the ground and slit his throat. Richard charged into the enemy claiming that only he was their rightful lord, and his momentary bravery saved the day. The crowd dispersed. Tyler's head was placed on a pike outside the city; Ball and Straw were soon captured and beheaded.

Richard had promised to forget the violence of the rebels, but when the leaders were dead, he arranged trials for the rebels. Altogether, 1500 peasants were hanged all over England. The trials were presided over by the king's judge who told the jurors that any votes against the crown were treason, and they would be hanged if they did not convict the criminals. Freedom and justice for the lower class would have to wait until another century.

DEFINING CRACKS IN THE SYSTEM

The Rise of Secular Literature

From the beginning of the century, hints of social change slipped between the major political events. Literature in the vernacular encouraged a return to literacy, and legends about the power of the individual began to creep into the expectations of Europeans.

As the fourteenth century developed, more and more writers picked up the theme of the nobility of the individual against the traditional institutions of society. Dante's (see the previous chapter) commentary became very popular, and a new generation of writers began to question the foundations of medieval society.

Born in 1270, Marsillius of Padua was a physician and theologian. In the controversies that arose between popes and secular leaders, the Holy Roman Emperor, Louis IV of Bavaria, was excommunicated and denounced by the Pope. Louis called upon Marsillius to search for sources to justify his rule. The result was the *Defensor Pacis* (Defender of the Peace), a long discourse published in 1324. The basic points were (1) all power is derived from the people; (2) the ruler is the people's delegate; (3) there is no law but popular will; (4) the Church should be under the ruler; (5) it should only deal with worship and it should be governed by councils, not by just one man. Louis was probably as upset by these clearly revolutionary statements as the Church, and the ideas were not, at first, widely circulated. They were, however, another new precedent, and the interest in the role of "the people" began to grow.

In Italy, the poet Francesco Petrarca (known as Petrarch) was similar to Dante. Born in 1304,

Petrarch studied and preserved many of the forgotten works of the ancient Romans and Greeks.

he also fell in love, as a young boy, with "Laura" who inspired him to give up his access to a rich, materialistic life to write poetry. Here he praises the individual whose thoughts and feelings were in conflict with the ideals of medieval asceticism. He rediscovered the writings of Plato and other Greek intellectuals and admired their work. In some ways this set the stage for the next century's "renaissance" of the classics of the ancient world. Petrarch stressed the individual's expressions of love, a sort of spiritual notion. He also condemned the materialism of the Church and pleaded with the popes to return to Rome and a

The Canterbury Tales written by Geoffrey Chaucer is famous for its poetic tales of life during a pilgrimage.

The *Canterbury Tales* again focus on individuals and their trials and tribulations through life. Many tell sad stories of their grief and pain, their humiliation at the hands of others. The tales rapidly became popular, and besides his official positions and military service, Chaucer became well known through the kingdom. He was popular enough that in 1374, the king granted him a gallon of wine every day for the rest of his life. This was improved in 1398 to a ton of wine a year. In 1399, the new King Henry IV granted him all sorts of royal honors for his service to the crown and the people of England. As with the uncertainty of the date of his birth, questions remain about the exact time of his death, but it is usually considered to be in October 1400.

New Ways of Getting to Heaven

With the papacy in Avignon, controlled by the French king, and the Church itself struggling to clarify its doctrinal positions, critics of its message, as well as its organization, began to appear. Muddled within the political and social issues of the day, religious dogma was slowly changing. The universities of Europe were torn by religious feuds. The faculties were primarily made up of clerics with different emphases. French and Italian universities tended to be seats of Church law due to their connection with the papacy. Other Christian intellectuals were less dedicated to orthodox opinions.

John Wyclif

Perhaps related to the political stress between England and France, voices against traditional interpretations of the Church began to be heard and listened to in England. Most noteworthy was that of John Wyclif, professor at Oxford.

simpler style of life than they were practicing in Avignon.

For present day English and American audiences, the most famous of the fourteenth-century "English writers was Geoffrey Chaucer, the poet and chronicler whose *Canterbury Tales* have become a classic. Chaucer was born sometime around 1340 to 1345 to a family that was connected closely with nobles who recommended them for government service. Over his life time he was chosen as a local official and served as a diplomat well into his senior years. In 1359 to 1360 he served with John of Gaunt (one of Edward's III sons) in France and was captured. He was ransomed for a small amount (16 pounds). Not scarred by the episode, he served again in France in 1369 and 1370. These adventures plus his rich imagination made for a fertile source of many stories.

He received support and interest from such powerful men as John of Gaunt, Edward's III son and Richard's II uncle.

Born in 1330, Wyclif studied at Oxford and in 1374 became the Rector of Lutterworth. Here he began writing down his thoughts on Church policy. In his pamphlet, *On Civil Lordship,* he strongly opposed the great accumulation of wealth that the Church had made a major part of its activities. He wrote that the Church should not own property or be involved in any matters other than spiritual issues. He even suggested that a Pope who was involved in worldly power was nothing more than an agent of the devil, and even called such a person the Anti-Christ. In other doctrinal ideas, he declared that priests had no special powers, including the supposed power to turn the bread and wine used in the Holy Eucharist into the Body and Blood of Christ (the Roman Catholic doctrine of transubstantiation). The Scriptures, he claimed, were the only law for the Church and that any conflicting Church policy or doctrine, even Papal Bulls, were irrelevant. Wyclif said that each Christian needed only a personal relationship with God to understand His role on Earth. Because he was so convinced of the need for every person to learn about God's ways, he translated the Latin Bible into English and encouraged its circulation.

Wyclif attracted a large following beyond the circles of the university. His belief in educating the ordinary Christian led him beyond writing, and he sent preachers out to the parishes to speak to their congregations in the vernacular rather than in Latin. Soon his followers became so numerous that they were grouped under the name "Lollards." The name came from a Latin term meaning to sing softly and is loosely meant as "mumblers." Sometimes connected with Way Tyler's rebellion, the Lollards were concerned about the treatment of the lower class but beyond that they were inspired by Wyclif's theological challenges to the traditional Church. In 1382, Wyclif's association with the revolt cost him support in the nobility, and his books were banned. He died at home on December 31, 1384.

The Lollard movement continued and, in 1395, the followers presented their twelve "Conclusions" to Parliament. Much of this was a criticism of the role of the Church and the clergy in English society. They demanded some relief from taxation by the Church and questioned the doctrines of transubstantiation (changing the bread and wine) as well as the "feigned" divinity of Church leaders. In 1398, opposition to the group was so strong that Wyclif's body was dug up, burned at the stake, and his ashes cast into a nearby river. As more religious and political struggles continued, the Lollards played their role as a persecuted group. Many were hanged or burned for their beliefs, but the ideology continued to threaten the orthodox positions.

The Great Schism

The Church went through further challenges and humiliations. In 1377, Gregory XI went to Rome to see if some compromises could be worked out. He realized that he did not have the support of the Italian cardinals so he decided to return to Avignon. He died before he could leave, and the College of Cardinals took this as a divine sign (or at least a political opportunity) and, in 1378, elected Urban VI to lead them as the Holy Father. Soon after, the French cardinals declared Urban's election null and void and elected their candidate, Clement VII, to take charge in Avignon. Now Western Christendom was ruled by two popes, both who excommunicated the other. Europe became split between advocates for each side. Both popes demanded church taxes be sent to them; both declared that any obedience to his opponent would cost the person his soul and heaven. It was a very confusing situation.

This Great Schism caused the rise of the Conciliar Movement, which supported the notion that the Church should be ruled by a group of advisors not just one man. Most of the dogma of the fourteenth century declared, like "Unam Sanctam," that only one person could head the Church but in fact there were now two popes and great arguments about who the "real" pope could be. In 1409, the Council of Pisa met to consider the crisis. They decided that a council could combine the best sense of the Church. The 500 members called upon Gregory VII of Rome and Benedict XIII of Avignon to help bring the schism to an end but neither pope would come and both declared the meeting invalid. The council, however, moved to solve the problem, deposing both popes and declaring a new election. Alexander V was chosen, and the result was that there were now three popes in Western Christendom as well as the Patriarch who ruled the Eastern Church based in Constantinople. (The split of the Roman Empire into Eastern and Western parts was not only political, it was spiritual; Roman Popes claimed supremacy across Christendom, but the Patriarch of Constantinople in the East claimed he was Christendom's spiritual leader. See material in previous chapters.)

In 1414 the Council of Constance met and finally resolved the situation. They deposed the Pisan Pope in 1415; the Roman Pope resigned; and the Avignoese Pope was deposed in the summer of 1417. Now, with no official Pope sitting anywhere, the council met in November 1417 and elected Martin V to return to the Vatican. The turmoil all this confusion had caused greatly lessened the power and the prestige of the papacy.

John Hus

Attacks on Church policy and traditions even began to be heard in the middle of the continent. John Hus (1371 – 1415) had read some of the writings of John Wyclif. The books of the English theologian had arrived in Bohemia (part of modern day Czechoslovakia) as its princess, Anne, married Richard II. Here religious doctrine was bound to the political situation. German and Slavic conflict over control of central Europe gave the Bohemians a strong nationalistic feeling. Many of the Holy Roman Emperors were appointed by a council of electors that was usually controlled by the papacy; their secular power was to rule the area where Germans and the Bohemians resented this "outside" authority. When Hus proclaimed that the Church should only be a spiritual body and that Christ, not the Pope, was the head of the Church, he began a crusade that called Bohemians to formulate their own church doctrines. He preached against the selling of church offices, indulgences, and the abuses of the clergy and the papacy.

At first King Wenceslas IV supported and protected Hus from Church prosecutors. Hus grew bolder and condemned the Church's call for an indulgence to fund a crusade against the King of Naples. Here the Church was asking its people to give money for a war against a fellow Christian. Collection of the indulgence in Bohemia was small, and the Church began to move against Hus. Although the politics of the time would have supported him, Hus refused to cooperate. He preached sermons on the perfection of humans and told his parishioners that only "he who dies, wins." For Hus, there was little to value in this world's existence.

Soon Hus cut himself off from the political forces that were trying to protect him. Summoned to the Counsel of Constance, he was promised safe passage by the Holy Roman Emperor, who at this point was Sigismund the King of Bohemia. Once there, however, he was tried for heresy, convicted, and on July 6, 1415, burned at the stake. Later, Martin Luther and Johannes Eck would argue about Hus' fate. Luther concluded that both popes and councils, being human, could make mistakes.

The Hussites did not disappear when their leader died, and he was pronounced a martyr by his supporters. In fact, they began to become more vocal on the political and religious scenes. Two groups formed around his doctrines. One was the Ultraquists (or Calixtines), a conservative group of nobles and wealthy townsmen that denounced only practices specifically forbidden by the Bible. The other was the Taborites, composed mainly of peasants, who accepted only those practices found in the Bible. The second was closer to Hus' views.

Both suffered as Rome sent, between 1420 and 1434, five "crusades" against them. Jan Zizka led the Hussites against Rome, and in 1420 the "Four Articles of Prague" stating their position was published. War against Rome produced greater friction between the two Hussite groups, and in 1434 the Ultraquists defeated the Taborites. The conservatives then entered into negotiations with the Church and made several compromises. The Taborites continued to resist and became the Bohemian Brethren. Some of this party laid the basis for the present Moravian Church while others would join the Lutherans in their objections to the Roman Church.

Besides the religious significance of the Hussite defiance of the Church was their introduction of an infant technology into their defense. Since the beginning of the 1300s western Europe was toying with gunpowder and its use in military situations. Upon his coronation, Edward III had received a manuscript showing a *pot de fer*, an explosive device that shot a missile into the air. In varying attempts, the device was used to drive a projectile towards the enemy. By 1338, the French were using the techniques to fling iron arrows toward the English, and all noted that with some reliability, this could be the weapon of the future. When the Hussites went to war against the Church, they used handguns and cannon to weaken their enemy and then ran their cavalry into the opposing army. The technique was successful, and a new form of warfare was born. And so in their search for religious and political freedom, reformers changed the way men could efficiently kill each other!

On the other hand, proponents for different religious emphases were not so involved in violence. Both Wyclif and Hus claimed the only authority for Christianity was the Bible. They emphasized the spiritual side of the Church's message. Roman Catholicism was not without its champions for spreading their faith through visions and mysticism. Building on the traditions of, for one, St. Francis of the thirteenth century, Catherine of Sienna (1347-1380) became one of the most notable heroines of the fourteenth century. Born 23rd of 25 children, Catherine was the daughter of a successful dyer and the granddaughter of a poet. At age 6 she began having visions of Christ, and although her family pushed her to have a "normal" life, she gave herself to spiritual missions. When the family sought to set up an engagement to marry, she cut off her hair and stayed prayerfully in her room. Finally they consented, and she became a lay worker for the Dominican order. As Catherine's mission became her life, she called upon the popes to return to Rome from Avignon and give up their extravagant life styles. She wrote beautiful stories and poems focusing on an individual's search for peace with God. These remain Italian classics. Today, Sienna is an attraction to those who wish to perform a modern pilgrimage.

In the fourteenth and early fifteenth centuries, the Church continued to dominate politics and attempt to rule in the secular world. In central Europe, its biggest challenge was the constant pressure from Turkish, meaning Moslem, attacks and inroads. Here the expansion of the "infidels" threatened the survival of Christianity. Local lords, such as Vlad (great grandfather to the famous Vlad Dracul) in Wachovia, traded their religious loyalties for political protection. If the Christian support were stronger, the areas faced Rome, if the Moslems offered more safety, then the choice was to bargain with them.

In the West, Church influence was closely related to the fortunes of the English and French as they continued their wars against each other. The agonies of the rising infant form of nationalism were intimately related to the structure of the Church. Rulers, as well as individuals, began to choose what they thought supported their secular positions, justifying their power. The stage was set for a reformation of the Church.

BACK TO THE WAR

English Dynastic Problems

In 1377, Richard II began his reign at the age of 10, following his grandfather Edward III. The old king, as well as Richard's father, the Black Prince, had been popular heroes, and Richard had a great deal to live up to. His early reign was dominated by John of Gaunt, his uncle. Richard did prove his strength during the Peasants' Rebellion, but soon political battles with the nobility would prove to weaken his powers as king.

Medieval superstition could probably have predicted the outcome of Richard's reign. He married well, first to the daughter of the Holy Roman Emperor and then to Isabella, daughter of the King of France. He had, however, no children from either marriage, and so no heir to the throne.

Richard's choice of advisors was also a sign that all was not well. During the late 1380s, five members of his "loyal opposition" appointed themselves Lords Appellant and found five of Richard's closest advisors guilty of treason. They were executed. In 1397, not realizing the political situation, Richard forced Parliament to find the Lords also guilty of treason. Three were executed, and two were banished. Among those exiled abroad was Henry Bolingbroke, John of Gaunt's son, and Richard's cousin. Soon after this, John of Gaunt died, and Richard foolishly confiscated his land breaking any alliance he had with the powerful Bolingbroke.

With troubles multiplying and an uprising in Ireland, Richard left for the Green Isle to settle things there. Taking advantage of the king's unpopularity and that he was "out of town," Bolingbroke returned and convinced Parliament that he should be king. They elected him and deposed Richard. Henry, with excellent military skills, sent his soldiers off, and they soon captured Richard. It was 1399 and Richard was sent off to prison, where, a year later, he was mysteriously murdered.

Henry's usurpation of throne caused him many problems both politically and personally. Richard's supporters revolted and kept the new king engrossed in suppressing rebels. In a misconceived action against the Church, Henry had the Archbishop executed, antagonizing many across his divided land. In his personal life, he married Joan of Navarre who had many strange habits and, actually, was convicted of witchcraft in 1419.

When he developed (probably) leprosy, and then epilepsy, the popular opinion was that God was punishing him for his misdeeds and sins.

The last two years of Henry V's reign were controlled by his son, Henry VI. Born in 1387, this Henry seemed to have been a natural born soldier. At 14 he fought the Welsh in behalf of his father, and at 16 he was again triumphant at the battle of Shrewsbury. Soon, he put down revolts by the Lollards and an assassination plot by nobles still loyal to Richard II.

Henry's foreign battles slowly distracted his opposition away from other claimants to the throne although he was never secure. He made demands against the French king and in the Treaty of Troyes in 1420, he was "awarded" Catherine, the king's daughter. He then demanded his feudal rights to the duchies of Normandy and Anjou. When Charles ignored him, England went to war with France. At the famous battle of Agincourt, Henry's 5000 exhausted soldiers were pitted against five times as many French soldiers. The conflict between the various French generals, however, gave Henry the day. Shakespeare immortalized Henry with his supposed St. Crispin's day speech, encouraging his troops to follow him to glory. Charles, King of France, was so impressed that he passed over his own son and named Henry as his heir. If Henry had lived only a little longer, he would have worn the crowns of both England and France. A life of warring and partying caught up to Henry, and in 1422 he died, never seeing the son his wife in England had just born him.

With a baby on the throne of England who had a strong claim to the crown of France, English and French politics became more and more intertwined. The struggle for power is never nice,

and the claims to rule rise above civility. The War of the Roses soon ensued, and cousin versus cousin played the English scene in intrigue as well as murder. Now the stage was set for wars between the great grandsons and supporters of Edward III. The War of the Roses would muddle English politics until the victory of the Tudors at Bosworth Field in 1485.

Meanwhile in France

If the English political scene were filled with treachery, the French political scene was filled with insanity. Charles VI was born in 1368 and was crowned at the age of 12. A pleasure loving young man, he left most of the governing to his uncles. In 1382, however, the tax burden on the population caused a series of revolts and Charles, with the help of his brother, Louis of Orleans, took over and began their own style of ruling. They brought back a number of their father's advisors who were of humble origin and could be influenced by the brothers. In 1385, he married Isabeau of Bavaria. She was 14, and he was 16. They filled the court with fun and partying. All this seems pretty much the rule for royal courts.

In 1392, however, Charles suffered an unknown illness. He had high fevers, and his hair and nails fell out. After that, he was subject to strange moods and behaviors. A few years later, he rode with some knights when suddenly he picked up a sword and killed four of them. At a masquerade ball that he and the queen gave, he and some others wore light, flowing costumes. Charles and his revelers caught fire, and only by chance was he saved while the others burned to death. By 1398, the general opinion was that the king was possessed, and even the Church tried to exorcise him. He began to tell people he was made of glass and they must not touch him. He had special clothes made with metal rods to protect him from breaking. In 1405 he decided that he should not even change his clothes and after months of his wandering in filth, his advisors paid some men to paint their faces black, hide in the King's closet, and jump out at him in the middle of the night. This shock treatment did cause a brief return to the king's attention to cleanliness.

During the time Charles was moving back and forth between sanity and insanity, the queen, Isabeau, found it increasingly difficult to behave well. After producing a number of children with the mad king, she began a close relationship with his brother. The queen was never known for her propriety, and she and Louis traveled together and partied as much as she had with the young king. Louis was deeply involved in war with John the Fearless, Duke of Burgundy. When John had Louis killed, the unfaithful Isabeau became John's close friend.

To make matters even worse, the succession to the throne was in doubt. In 1419, the supposed crown prince was discredited by his own mother who claimed he was illegitimate. The prince's reputation was further defeated when, after meeting John the Fearless, the Duke was hacked to death. As turmoil filled the royal palace, the demented king was left to strangers who simply tried to keep him out of trouble. If he wished to be dirty, they agreed; if he had a few sane moments, they humored him back into fantasy. In 1422, the poor disheveled king died, only a few months after his son-in-law and supposed heir, Henry V.

Most of Charles' sons died young and his successor, Charles VII, feared bridges (where he had seen John the Fearless murdered), and had all sorts of food psychoses. Many historians believe that Charles VI had porphyria, which created his mental problems. They point to many relatives who had similar, if less dramatic, symptoms. And as Charles' daughter Catherine married Henry V of England and their oldest son went mad, perhaps this is a connection to the "Madness" of King George III, ruler of the British Isles during the American Revolution.

THE LAST OF THE WAR

The last years of the Hundred Years War are frequently glossed over by historians, suggesting it as not terribly important to European politics. In the Treaty of Troyes, the French princess was given to the English king, and then the French king made Henry his heir instead of his own son. French patriotism began to stir, and a new ending to the war was written. Although the tale of the next few years was written in mysticism and miracles, what probably turned the tide was the introduction of technology.

The romantic symbol of the new patriotism was a saintly young woman, Joan of Arc. The daughter of a small landed peasant, Joan was born in Domremy in the province of Champagne. She began hearing voices as a teenager and soon defined them as Saints sent from God to give her holy messages. Whereas the voices of Catherine of Sienna had led the Italian woman to serve the poor, Joan's voices asked her to save France. Dressing in men's clothing, she traveled to find the Dauphin and aid his cause. Domremy was devoted to the crown prince, even though the Burgundians and their allies, the English, controlled the area.

At first the prince's advisors refused to let her see him, but after several tests, including recognizing the Dauphin even though he was disguised, the idea that Joan held a holy mission began to be considered. At this point, the French had suffered so many defeats that almost any hope would have sounded encouraging to the

Joan of Arc is cheered by townspeople after successfully leading French troops to victory against the English in the north of France.

The crowning of the new king did not unite the French forces, which continued to court English support when it pleased them. In May 1430, Joan was captured and turned over to Bishop Pierre Cauchon for L10,000. Cauchon was an agent of the English, and they greedily accepted the young woman who had defeated their troops and called for the English king to abandon his claims to France.

At first Joan was simply imprisoned; the conditions were dirty, dark, and quite foreboding. She was forced to sign a statement that she would never again wear men's clothing. She tried not to hear the voices and to weather the inquisition but she heard the saints tell her that she did not have long to live, and returned to wear-

desperate French. Joan also validated her claim by asking the men to go to a church and look behind the altar for an ancient sword. When they found it, they were sure Joan had a special calling.

Now Joan, dressed in men's clothing that was strictly forbidden in medieval days, led the Dauphin's troops to Orleans, which had long been controlled by the English. They were victorious in capturing it. It was May 1429 and within the next month, the French had another victory at Patay. On the July 17, Charles VII was crowned at Reims, and Joan felt triumphant.

Joan of Arc was found guilty of sorcery and heresy and burned at the stake. Later, Joan was canonized as a saint.

ing her soldier costume. In 1431, she was tried as a heretic and in late May, only two years after her victory at Orleans, she was condemned. Joan, calling on her saints to lead her to heaven, was burned alive on Rouen's old market square. Her martyrdom was an inspiration to her followers, but she remained unrecognized as a saint until the Church determined that a great mistake had been done; Joan became a saint of the Church in 1920.

Things were rapidly changing on the war front. The alliances between England and various French nobles were falling apart. After the Peace of Arras in 1435, the Burgundians, long tied to the English, abandoned their allies and began to cooperate with the French forces. In 1436, Charles VII retook Paris, and the slow but steady consolidation of France began to have an effect on the war's progress.

In 1450, the French finally found an answer to the English longbow. For many years they had been working on improving the *pot de fer*, the gun, and now had established an improved gun powder that made the weapon more reliable. In the "tradition" of the Hussites, and even the Flemish peasants, the Battle of Formigny saw French gunners decimate the English troops and the French cavalry ride over their mangled bodies. Soon after, the French took back Normandy. The end was in sight.

1453—A REAL TURNING POINT

The events of history are not neat and organized. Historians, however, create orderly time lines. Thus a chronology often confuses the student and places artificial boundaries on the connections of the past. In many ways, the "calamitous" fourteenth century did not end until 1453 when the basis for a new age and new opportunities began to appear.

Two major events framed the year of 1453. On the Western shores of Europe, the guns and cannon of Formigny and Normandy were moved to Castillon where the French destroyed the last English land army. When the fighting was over, the armies just faded away. No formal truce or conditions of peace were signed. Perhaps the long years of war had convinced the rulers, negotiators, and even the people that fighting would surely begin again. But, for awhile the French and English turned to their own matters.

In England, Henry VI became so insane that a Protector, Richard of York, was assigned by Parliament to run the country. Soon the houses of York and Lancaster plotted against each other and the War of the Roses tore England apart. Peace would not be restored until the Battle of Bosworth Field, at the end of the fifteenth century, was won by a new player, Henry Tudor.

For the French, victory allowed them time to concentrate on their own internal confusions. Charles VII died in 1461, and his son Louis XI claimed the crown. The Dauphin had spent much of his earlier years in revolt against his father and had even been exiled for attempts to gain the throne before his father's death. Finally as king, Louis dismissed many of his father's advisors and began to coordinate his power by enticing other nobles to his court. Shifting coalitions gave Louis some general control over the country, and he worked hard to make the crown supreme in France.

In central Europe, the Papacy and the Holy Roman Emperors would continue the struggle for a balance of power. Here was the new battleground for Christianity as the Turks, who now controlled the Muslim empire, increasingly crept towards the prize of Constantinople.

The Eastern capital of Christendom was, by this time, totally surrounded by Moslem lands. On May 29, 1453, Sultan Mohammed

II used "giant bombards" to crash the five walls protecting the city. Once the walls were breached, the city passed into his control, and Christianity became a persecuted religion. The Hagia Sophia, probably Christianity's most spectacular church, was converted to a mosque, and all of Christendom mourned its loss. (Soon, in Rome, the Pope would call for the rebuilding of St. Peter's to take the place of the Hagia Sophia and glorify Christianity.)

Many defeats for the progress of Western Civilization were represented in 1453, but many new opportunities were on the horizon. The mid-fifteenth century would see the birth of people who would change the world and bring Western Civilization into the leading power of world politics and culture, as well as social, political, and religious reform.

In Genoa, Christoforo Columbo was born in 1451. Not too far away, in a little town just outside Vinci, Leonardo arrived; although illegitimate, he would be "adopted" by his father's family and find his way to Florence and great fame. 1456 saw the birth of Henry Tudor who would one day reign over England as Henry VII and produce a line of kings and queens who would change the course of English history. In the same year, Johannes Gutenberg first used moveable type and began a revolution of dispensing information not unlike the explosion which has occurred through the use of the computer. Vasco da Gama, who discovered a route around Africa to India and the Spice Islands, was born in 1467; Copernicus in 1473; and Michelangelo in 1475. Lastly (although this is far from a complete list), 1483 saw the birth of a young German monk and scholar whose soul, tortured by medieval concepts of a judging God and the horrors of Hell, gave Europe new avenues to Heaven. Building on the ideas of Wyclif, Hus and others, Martin Luther declared that each man's soul was his joy and obligation and that faith, not works or even membership in the Roman Church, was the "truth which sets us free."

The traditional institutions of the old world view were giving way, and the importance of each individual, whether they could hold a gun or discover an idea to protect themselves, was becoming part of a new way of looking at this world. The heroes of this new age would be those who took risks and affected the communities around them. The modern world was being born.

Suggestions for Further Reading

Peter F. Ainsworth, *Jean Froissart and the Fabric of History: truth, myth, and fiction in the Chroniques* (1990).

Giovanni Boccaccio: *The Decameron*

Edward P. Chaney, *The Dawn of a New Era, 1250-1453* (1962).

Geoffrey Chaucer: *The Canterbury Tales*

G.G. Coulton, *The Black Death* (1929).

Kenneth A. Fowler, *The Age of Plantagenet and Valois: The Struggle for Supremacy, 1328-1498* (1967).

David Herlihy, *The Black Death and the Transformation of the West* (1997).

Johan Huizinga, *The Waning of the Middle Ages* (1968).

Richard Kieckhefer, *European Witch Trials: Their Foundations in Popular and Learned Culture, 1300-1500* (1976).

Francesco Petrarch, *Letter to Posterity, Canzoniere*

Christine Pizan, *The Book of the City Ladies*

Edward Porroy, *The Hundred Years War* (1965).

Shahar, Shulamith, *The Fourth Estate: A History of Women in the Middle Ages* (1986).

Barbara Tuchman, *A Distant Mirror: The Calamitous 14th Century* (1978).

Chapter 12

THE RENAISSANCE
1350 TO 1650

QUEEN ELIZABETH I

Artemisia Gentileschi, a young eighteen-year-old aspiring painter, sat beside her father, Orazio, in a courtroom in Rome. The time was January 1612. On trial was Agostino Tassi, Artemisia's former teacher and an artist friend of her father. Eight months earlier, in May 1611, Agostino had raped Artemisia. Orazio, seeking justice for his daughter, sued Tassi. The trial, which lasted seven months, was like the rape itself, an ordeal Artemisia hoped never to have to endure again. It seemed as if the Italian legal system favored the rapist rather than his victim. During the seven-month trial the judge had Artemisia tortured with thumbscrews in an effort to pain-fully force her to recant her story about the rape. Fortunately, the heroic young girl endured the pain and testified that Tassi, while teaching her how to paint, tried to seduce her. He became angry when she rejected his sexual advances and forced himself on her. Artemisia fought back, physically resisting the assault. Finding a knife lying nearby, she picked it up, wounding her attacker. Unfortunately, the knife inflicted little permanent damage on Tassi. Infuriated, he began to beat his student, and his strength and brutality were too much for a seventeen-year-old girl to fight off. Tassi completed the rape and then promised to marry his victim. Artemisia then testified that she later consented to have sexual relations with her rapist because she feared he would rape her again and because she hoped sex would make him keep his promise to marry her, which would restore the honor the assault had taken away.

Of course, Tassi never married Artemisia and at the trial denied that he had raped the young woman. His background, however, suggested otherwise. Previously, he had faced trial for murdering his wife but was acquitted for lack of evidence. He had also served a prison sentence for incest after siring several children by his brother's wife. Tassi believed he could beat the rape charge just as he had beaten the earlier murder rap by hiring people to commit perjury during the trial. His strategy backfired when Pietro Stiattesi, a witness Tassi hired to attack Artemisia's character, decided to tell the truth. Stiattesi testified that Artemisia was telling the truth and that Tassi had paid him to lie. Consequently, Tassi was convicted. Artemisia believed for a few minutes that justice had finally prevailed. Her euphoria was short lived, however, when the judge sentenced the rapist to serve only eight months in prison. The judge explained that women were not equal to men, and thus rape was not a serious enough crime to warrant a more severe punishment.

Artemisia, devastated by the rape, the ordeal of the trial, and the lax sentence, felt that she could no longer live in Rome. She married Stiattisi, the man who had testified on her behalf, and moved to Florence where Artemisia became one of the best artists the Italian Renaissance produced. Art historians believe that her victimization by a rapist and an unjust legal system is reflected in her paintings. Strong female figures dominate much of her work. Perhaps, as a rape victim, Artemisia was attempting through her artwork to right the wrongs done to women by the Renaissance legal system and create a more just society.

Chronology

Around 1350	Renaissance Begins
1375	Francesco Petrarch Dies
Around 1385	Jan Van Eyck Born
1397	Manuel Chrysoloras Comes to Florence
1400s	Gunpowder Invented
1422-1461	Charles VII Rules France
1434-1464	Cosimo de' Medici Rules Florence
1452	Leonardo da Vinci Born
1434-1494	Sforza Family Rules Milan
1450	Treaty of Lodi
1453	Mehmed II Captures Constantinople
1455-1471	War of the Roses
1455	Printing Press Invented
1469	Laura Cereta Born
1480	Spanish Inquisition Begins
1484	Charles VIII Invades Italy
1492	Columbus Sails to America
1494	Pietro Medici Forced into Exile
1500-1527	High Renaissance Period
1500	Baldassare Castiglione Writes *The Courtier*
1508	France Invades Italy, forms Cambrian League
1516	Sir Thomas More Writes *Utopia* Erasmus' Greek New Testament Published Concordat of Bologna
1519	Charles V named Holy Roman Emperor
1522	Habsburg-Valois Wars Begin
1527	Charles V Sacks Rome Niccolo Machiavelli Dies
1547	Miguel de Cervantes Born
1594	Shakespeare forms the King's Men
1616	Artemisia Gentileschi joins Florence Academy Of Art
Around 1650	Renaissance Ends

THE ITALIAN RENAISSANCE

A medieval visitor who could transcend time and visit Florence, Italy from the fourteenth to seventeenth centuries might have difficulty believing he or she was in a society and culture much different from the Florence of Dante's time. People still lived in an Aristotelian and Ptolemaic universe and continued to accept the medieval Christian worldview. Both the universe and society were still perceived as hierarchical. The Gothic style of art was still present, especially in northern Europe. In education, scholasticism flourished even though it was under attack by a new liberal arts curriculum, which used literature as its base. Among common people, the pietistic movements that swept Europe during the 1300s continued unabated.

Despite the similarities to medieval Florence, the visitor would have sensed something new in the air. A new tone, a new atmosphere, new attitudes about life, and an important shift in thought had occurred. These changes were the result of secularism, individualism, and humanism. European people had rediscovered classical antiquity and began to appreciate the legacy of Greek and Roman scholars in a new way. While medieval authors, scholars, and poets such as St. Thomas Aquinas and Dante had read, admired, and used ancient writers like Cicero, Aristotle, Plato, and Virgil, their writings emphasized service for God and the Christian faith. Renaissance scholars broke with this tradition, viewing instead the classical world as a culture with its own integrity that was worthy of study for its own sake. In addition to ancient writings, Renaissance people also rediscovered classical art and architecture. The study of antiquity created within the Renaissance person an admiration for the wisdom and achievements of the ancient Greeks, Romans, Egyptians, and Hebrews. This regard for the ancient world was so great that Renaissance scholars began to imitate the elegant literary style, art, architecture, moral realism, politics, and government found within the ancient world. Life within the Greek polis and Roman commonwealth provided standards of civic and personal life that Renaissance scholars found worth imitating.

European nations underwent vast changes that affected virtually all aspects of life on the continent from the fourteenth to the seventeenth century. This interest in and flowering of intellectual and cultural life is called the Renaissance. Italy was the first European kingdom to experience the Renaissance in the late 1300s. After about a century, the Renaissance moved from the Italian Peninsula across the Alps into northern Europe, changing society as it went.

Several factors produced the Renaissance. First, it was the result of urbanization. By the late fourteenth century Italian cities were flourishing economically. Their populations had swelled, their wealth had increased, and their physical size had expanded. Second, was an emphasis on literacy. The trade and commercial relations that developed in the 1300s made literacy necessary for an individual to gain material wealth and prosperity. Merchants had to fluently speak several languages and understand how to use mathematics to be successful. The need for language and math skills gave rise to the need for formal education, which heightened the intellectual development of middle and upper class people. Third, creation of a middle class was necessary for the Renaissance to occur. Prior to the thirteenth century, the wealth of Italy was in the hands of the upper class and the Roman Catholic Church. In the thirteenth and fourteenth centuries the urban middle class was created when trade with Asia and the Middle East increased. The wealth the middle class earned from this trade enabled them to lead a life of comparative luxury and leisure. They now had time and money to enjoy art, literature, and culture. Without the urban middle class sponsorship of artists and writers there likely would not have been a Renaissance. Fourth, feudalism began to wane. The invention of gunpowder in the 1400s enabled kings to defeat feudal knights with standing armies comprised of common men. This caused nobles to lose their monopoly over military defense, which eventually caused them to lose social status. Furthermore, as trade and commerce among the middle class increased, the nobility often had to turn to bankers and merchants for financing, creating huge debts that caused nobles to lose their economic status at the apex of European societies.

Before the Renaissance could occur in any part of Europe, an economic foundation had to be laid. From 1000 to 1300 numerous commercial and financial changes occurred, including an increase in the political power of self-governing cities, an increase in Europe's population, and the opening of new trade routes to Asia and the Middle East that spawned commercial growth. Without such developments, artistic, literary, political, educational, and religious changes associated with the Renaissance could not have occurred.

Venice, Italy, bordered by the sea and crisscrossed by canals, was forced to build upward instead of outward. It was one of the richest cities in Europe. Renaissance merchants gained both wealth and political power.

Northern Italian cities led the way. During the eleventh century a revival of trade and commerce had begun. Venice, Genoa, Milan, and other cities profited handsomely from trade with the Middle East and northern Europe, growing rich as a result. Geography was important in Italian cities monopolizing trade between Europe and Asia. Their location along the Mediterranean coast of southern Europe perfectly situated them to act as middlemen in the trade between East and West. Wealth garnered from this intercontinental trade provided resources that permitted the Renaissance to happen.

Florence was the first Italian city to experience artistic and literary activities that signaled the beginning of the Renaissance. Although Florence was an inland city, not as well suited to profit from foreign trade as were other Italian cities, it nevertheless possessed great wealth derived from control of papal finances. Florentine merchant and banking families served as tax collectors for the Roman Catholic Church, a position they used to provide banking services in North African and European cities, including London, Paris, Barcelona, Marseilles, Morocco, Tunis, and Algiers. These banking families, like

the Medici, profited from their activities and used the money to develop commerce and industry in their native Florence, creating a city that was the most prosperous in Europe for a time. The wool industry was the most important industrial development in Florence. Florence traders acquired fine wool from northern European countries, especially England, Scotland, and Spain, and turned it into high quality cloth. Florence's textile industry employed thousands of workers. Traders then carried this cloth throughout the known world (Europe, Africa, and Asia) where it brought tremendous profits that were plowed back into Florentine industry.

Important also to the Renaissance was the political independence of northern Italian city-states. Milan, Florence, Genoa, Pisa, Siena, and other cities were comprised of independent merchants and craftsmen who did not owe feudal allegiance to Italian nobles. To maintain their independence, northern Italian merchants formed Communes, organizations devoted to keeping merchants and cities free from control of feudal nobles. Communes often had to construct walls around cities, enact ordinances to regulate and control commerce, and maintain law and order to prevent nobles from taking control of Italian city-states. Communes financed these activities by imposing taxes on the city's inhabitants. Most of the cities in northern Italy gained their freedom in the twelfth century when nobles who previously controlled them recognized the economic opportunities independent cities presented them. Nobles also could profit from the riches of cities. They could, for example, form business partnerships with urban merchants engaged in foreign trade, investing heavily in commercial enterprises in return for a share of the profits. Over time these business ventures between noblemen and merchants produced a new social class, an urban aristocracy. Marriages between wealthy merchant families and hereditary noble classes were not uncommon and strengthened the ability of northern Italian cities to maintain their independence.

The urban aristocracy tightly controlled Italian cities. Most residents were not given citizenship, which required that a person own a substantial amount of property, have high social status, and have resided in the city for a lengthy period. Most urban dwellers did not meet these requirements and consequently had no voice in their government. In general, *signori*, an urban king, or *oligarchies*, a small number of urban aristocrats, from 1300 to 1500, ruled Italian city-states. Cosimo de' Medici, for example, ruled Florence from 1434 to 1464 and Lorenzo de' Medici ruled the city from 1469 to 1482 as *signori*. Likewise the Sforza family controlled Milan from 1434 to 1494. Most *signori*, like the Medici and Sforza, were despots who followed no law but their own. They made and enforced ordinances that enabled them and the merchant aristocracy to maintain power, wealth, and influence. *Oligarchies* generally had constitutions, but they were structured to ensure that political power remained in the hands of the urban nobility. Wealthy merchants and other members of the urban aristocracy made the laws, controlled the courts that enforced and administered these laws, and interpreted the constitutions to suit their needs. Venice, for example, had a population that exceeded ninety thousand during the first quarter of the fifteenth century, but less than three hundred of its residents controlled the government. Practically every other Italian city-state not controlled by a *signori* existed under similar conditions. Only a few wealthy men held all the political influence. All challenges to the *signori* or *oligarchies* were crushed. Whenever residents protested their exclusion from power and the heavy tax burden that they bore, the ruling classes in Italian city-states ruthlessly used the military and police power to regain control and "put the lower classes in their place."

ITALIAN STATECRAFT, WAR, AND FOREIGN POLICY

Five Italian city-states—Venice, Florence, Milan, Naples, and the Papal States (Rome and territory governed by the Pope)—controlled Italy during the Renaissance. Of these five "city kingdoms," Venice was perhaps the most important. It was an international power during the fifteenth century. The oligarchy of merchants and bankers that controlled the city dominated its trade around the world and even established colonies outside Italy. While the other four cities were not as powerful as Venice, they exerted much influence over their neighbors. Milan and its ruling Sforza family controlled smaller towns and cities in northern Italy. The Papal States, along with Florence, controlled central Italy, while Naples was dominant in the south. These major city-states influenced politics in and controlled smaller cities in their vicinity while jock-

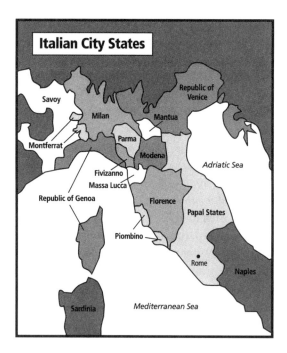

Italian City States

Savoy
Milan
Montferrat
Parma
Mantua
Modena
Fivizanno
Massa Lucca
Republic of Genoa
Florence
Piombino
Rome
Naples
Sardinia
Republic of Venice
Adriatic Sea
Papal States
Mediterranean Sea

eying for influence and fighting for territory among themselves. They made treaties, engaged in spying, arranged marriages between families in other cities, and used any available advantage to enhance their wealth, increase trade, and obtain territory.

Italian cities also took action to prevent one state from becoming dominant. If the military power of one state increased until it was stronger than the other kingdoms, various cities combined against their stronger neighbor. This "balance of power" system, established in 1450 by the Treaty of Lodi, was a prelude to that which countries in northern and western Europe later devised to maintain peace. When Francesco Sforza, the Venetian leader, usurped the position of Duke of Milan in 1450, for example, war broke out between Venice and Milan. Florence and Naples combined their armies with those of Milan to oppose Venice and the Papal States. Cosimo de' Medici, the Florentine prince, aided Milan because he feared that Venice might

become too powerful. Previously, he had made an alliance with Venice but switched sides to prevent Venice from dominating the Italian Peninsula. Naples, likewise, joined the war for similar reasons.

Wars fought by Italian city-states during the Renaissance caused what might be termed "modern diplomacy" to arise. The Italian cities were the first states to build permanent embassies in foreign capitols and staff them with full time ambassadors. This development occurred largely because Italian city-states constantly needed to keep watch on economic and political happenings abroad to protect their own military and economic interests.

The tremendous wealth of Italian city-states attracted attention from foreign powers, which led to numerous invasions of the peninsula. Venice, Florence, Milan, the Papal States, and Naples were unable to stop these invasions because of their inability to unite against a common foe and because they sometimes sought outside help against each other. When Florence and Naples signed a treaty to jointly take territory from Milan in 1493, for example, Milan invited France to defend the duchy. Charles VIII, the French monarch from 1483 until 1498, thus invaded Italy in 1484. French armies were so powerful that they easily defeated the Italian kingdoms, seizing Florence, Rome, and Naples, exiling the Medici from Florence and reestablishing a republic. The French invasion marked the beginning of a period of wars and controversy in Italy that lasted several generations.

France, in an attempt to further its political, economic, and territorial ambitions in Italy, invaded the peninsula a second time in 1508. Louis XII entered into an agreement with the Papal States and Maximilian, the Hapsburg Emperor, to form the Cambrian League. The purpose of this alliance was to take colonial territory from Venice. When France betrayed Rome and the Papal States, Pope Leo X formed a new alliance with Spain and Germany to drive France from Italy. In return, Charles V of the House of Hapsburg was named Holy Roman Emperor in 1519. His success, however, was short lived. French armies again invaded Italy in 1522, beginning a series of conflicts known as the Hapsburg-Valois Wars. Almost continual warfare on the Italian Peninsula took a costly toll on people, livestock, the government, and the economy. Rome, the imperial city, was captured and sacked by Charles V in 1527. For the most part, Italy was controlled by foreign powers until it achieved unification in the nineteenth century. Had Italian kingdoms been able to look beyond parochial interests in the fifteenth and sixteenth centuries and unite as a nation, the history of the western world likely would have been altered. Certainly, Italy could have repelled the foreign invasions and, perhaps, with its wealth and industry assumed a position of dominance in Europe.

One good thing did, however, come out of the wars in Italy. Invading armies exported cultural and intellectual developments achieved by the Italian Renaissance to northern and western Europe. Had these conflicts not occurred, the Renaissance might not have spread outside Italy.

THE ARTISTIC RENAISSANCE IN ITALY

Art is perhaps the feature most associated with the Renaissance. The reappearance of classical styles and an emphasis on harmony and balance were important features of Renaissance art. Many forms of art flourished during the fifteenth and sixteenth centuries, including painting, sculpture, and architecture. From 1500 to 1527, a period historians call the High Renaissance,

Italy's most famous artists—Leonardo da Vinci, Raphael, and Michelangelo—labored in Rome, producing masterpieces like the statue of David, the Mona Lisa painting, the ceiling of the Sistine Chapel, and other equally impressive works. Rome, Florence, Venice, and other Italian cities were centers for artistic achievement.

A distinctive and vitally important feature of Renaissance art was the discovery of perspective and the change it produced in humankind's mental vision of the world. This change is evident in paintings by the masters Botticelli, Masaccio, Ghirlandaio, da Vinci, and other Renaissance artists. The qualities that perspective gives to art—illusion of depth, the capturing of a moment in an event, the sense of movement, careful attention to detail, and an accurate representation of nature—are evident in Renaissance work.

Artists in Renaissance Italy generally did not produce art for art's sake. Rather, they produced art for profit, working on commission for a wealthy merchant or ruler. Production of art for the masses meant the artist had little status as a professional. An individual's reputation as an artist was directly related to the amount of money he or she earned from powerful patrons like the Medici family, who spent vast sums on artistic commissions. Important artists like Leonardo da Vinci and Michelangelo became wealthy on commissions from these art patrons. Da Vinci earned in excess of 2,000 ducats a year at a time when common laborers lived on less than 250 ducats annually. Michelangelo earned 3,000 ducats for painting the ceiling of the Sistine Chapel. This enabled him to turn down a commission for work on St. Peter's Basilica because he was wealthy enough to live comfortably for the rest of his life.

Not only did artists become wealthy, they also achieved high social status within Renaissance society. The Holy Roman Emperor Charles V picked up a paintbrush the artist Titian had dropped, a reflection of the status of artists. Contemporaries sometimes perceived Renaissance artists as geniuses. This marked a break with the Middle Ages. Then, it was generally thought that God expressed himself by giving artists the ability to create. Thus, according to medieval philosophy, God created all artwork by using individual artists. Renaissance people, in contrast, believed that the artist created art. Unlike medieval thought, which did not recognize individual originality, the Renaissance celebrated it. Renaissance people thought that art was not only the creation of the artists but reflected his or her own individuality, personality, and style.

Not only did art enrich the artists but it enhanced the lifestyles of wealthy individuals in Italian city-states. During the Middle Ages homes and castles of princes and wealthy merchants were generally sparsely furnished. As wealth increased in the Renaissance, elaborate and artistic decorations found their way into houses and castles. Rooms were filled with paintings, portraits, statues, elaborately carved furniture, woven tapestries, and other artifacts. Churches and private chapels, likewise, were decorated.

Italian Renaissance society viewed art as power. Individuals in the Italian city-states commissioned artists to complete works to display their wealth and power or to celebrate their family name. Kings, oligarchs, wealthy merchants, and guilds hired artists and commissioned works to make the lower and middle classes aware of their influence and prestige. Such individuals and groups spent enormous sums on paintings, ornate buildings, portraits, and decorative burial chambers to display their wealth. Lorenzo de' Medici, for example, claimed that the Medici had

Lorenzo de' Medici was a patron of the arts.

spent over 650,000 gold florins commissioning works of art and architecture from 1435 to 1470.

Themes Renaissance artists depicted were different than those medieval artists conveyed. Instead of dealing with spiritual themes, as artists in the Middle Ages tended to do, Renaissance art was more secular. Individuals who were the subject of portraits, for example, were often painted in a romantic setting. Giotto, a Florentine painter who lived from 1276 until 1337, was one of the first artists to express realism in portraits. His use of facial expressions and various body poses represented a break from the stiff poses and artificial looks that characterized medieval portraits. Likewise, the Florentine painter Masaccio, often called the father of modern painting by art historians, pioneered the use of light and shade to make his work more accurately reflect the real world.

Sculpture also reflected realism. Donatello, an artist working in Florence during the first half of the fifteenth century, created statues depicting differences in human nature. His work drew from ancient artists in Greece and Rome. He moved away from the medieval display of the naked human body in a spiritual context, creating nude human forms in which individual self-awareness was evident. Other artists, including the famous Michelangelo, also glorified the human body. *David*, Michelangelo's depiction of the Hebrew king in his triumph over the Philistine giant Goliath, shows a male that is youthful, strong, self-confident, and certain of victory over his larger opponent. Female figures were treated in a similar manner. Rather than being depicted as stiff and formal, they were shown as full figured, voluptuous, sensual, and sexual. Artistic treatment of the human body is a reflection of the secularism of the Renaissance. Religion was beginning to lose its grip on the artist as well as the literary scholar.

INTELLECTUAL ACHIEVEMENTS

Renaissance men and women living in fourteenth and fifteenth century Italian towns and cities were conscious that they inhabited a new world vastly different than that of the Middle Ages. The first man to publicize the dawning of a new age was the poet Francesco Petrarch. His poetry and writings indicate that he believed a new age of light had replaced several centuries of darkness that began with the downfall of the Roman Empire. For Petrarch, the first four hundred years of the millennium after the birth of Christ marked the apex of western civilization. When Germanic tribes invaded Western Europe beginning in the fourth century, a "Dark Age" was inaugurated. These Dark or Middle Ages lasted a thousand years, from 400 A.D. to 1400 A.D. During this dark millennium knowledge was stagnant, scholarship almost nonexistent,

and people lived a brutal, barbaric lifestyle largely devoid of art, literature, and the finer things in life that had characterized Greco-Roman civilization. Petrarch, however, believed Greco-Roman civilization was reborn in Italy during the fourteenth century. This rebirth, or Renaissance, as the French called it, witnessed a remarkable record of human intellectual accomplishment. Three intellectual changes marked the Renaissance: secularism, individualism, and humanism. Each of these developments represented a change from medieval European attitudes and is the foundation upon which Western society is built today.

Secularism

Secularism is a fascination with the temporal rather than the spiritual world. Medieval thinkers were more concerned with God and religion than with secular life. Their writings usually focused on heaven and eternal salvation rather than on human life on earth. St. Augustine, for example, maintained that there were two kingdoms, the spiritual one of God and the earthly one of humans. God's kingdom, according to St. Augustine, should be sought while the human kingdom should be shunned. Renaissance scholars, however, tended to be less concerned with the world of God and more concerned with the human condition in the earthly world. Renaissance thinkers did not reject spiritual matters but focused more on the temporal world. Unlike medieval monks and scholars who often abhorred material possessions, Renaissance people often pursued material wealth.

These changing attitudes about materialism had their roots in the economic changes Italy experienced in the thirteenth and fourteenth centuries. As merchants became richer, their attitudes toward wealth changed. The richer they became, the more material comforts and pleasures they could afford. Money gave bankers and merchants in Florence, Rome, Genoa, Venice, Milan, and other Renaissance cities the wherewithal to commission art and the leisure time to enjoy it. Consequently, they began to view life from a different perspective. Instead of seeing the purpose of life as a difficult struggle to obtain heaven, Renaissance men and women viewed existence as an opportunity to enjoy life. What the revival of classical thought in the Renaissance enabled the upper crust of society to do was redirect their attention from preparation for paradise to a concern for living here and now. Renaissance people were unwilling to accept the self-denying, world-rejecting monastic view of life that had dominated medieval culture, and they were dissatisfied with a worldview where human beings were merely pawns in a larger game plan of God. Instead, Renaissance people cultivated family life, endorsed the wise use of wealth, and actively involved themselves in worldly affairs. The temporal world was seen not as a Babylon, or as merely a rest stop on the long pilgrimage to heaven, but as a place where people, using critically and intelligently the wisdom of the ancient past, could realize their potential.

Writings left behind by Renaissance men of letters reflect the temporal world that dominated thought. Lorenzo Valla, an Italian humanist, in *On the False Donation of Constantine* (See Chapter 6) challenges the Catholic Church's claim to have authority over human life. He concluded that an eight-century deed known as the Donation of Constantine, giving the Roman Church and its Pope vast lands in Western Europe, was fake. The Emperor Constantine had not, in fact, given the Church jurisdiction over this land. Valla's evidence that the Donation of Constantine was a forgery questioned Church

claims that it had control of earthly life. How could an institution that purported to be concerned with spiritual matters use a forged document to gain control of a large land area? Valla also discovered serious errors in St. Jerome's translation of the Greek Testament into the Italian language. Valla's work called into question the Church's credibility. He showed that reason and scholarship could be used to challenge previously accepted facts of the medieval world. In another work, *On Pleasure*, he challenged the medieval view that the spiritual world was the highest good, maintaining that earthly pleasures, including food, drink, wealth, art, and sex, were equally as good.

Other writers also concentrated on the sensual. Giovanni Boccaccio in *Decameron* created characters, including husbands, fathers, priests, businessmen, and others, who enjoyed life and pursued temporal and material objects rather than spirituality. Unlike medieval literature, which viewed sensual pursuits with contempt, Boccacio and other Renaissance authors made sensuality and materialism respectable goals to be sought. They supported their views by drawing upon the works of ancient Greek and Roman authors.

Secularism also pervaded the Roman Catholic Church. For the most part, high ranking Church officials—popes, cardinals, and bishops—were scions of wealthy Italian merchants and banking families. They were reared in households who pursued material wealth, patronized art, and sought sensual pleasures. As Church officers, they continued to do these things and seldom did much to discourage the new secular spirit that pervaded upper levels of Italian society. The Church itself spent enormous sums commissioning artists and architects to create works and design buildings that enhanced the power and beauty of Rome. The Papal Chan-

Decameron, by Boccaccio, was the first major prose piece of the Renaissance written in the vernacular tongue.

cellery, constructed from 1483 to 1511, is considered an architectural masterpiece of the Renaissance. St. Peters Basilica was demolished in 1506 and replaced with a new structure; Michelangelo was hired to create the building's dome, which is perhaps his greatest work. Thus, the Church partook of and encouraged secularism rather than condemning and attacking it. The Church's attitude did not mean that it had forsaken spiritual matters altogether. Rather, Church officials tried to strike a balance between the spiritual and temporal worlds, recognizing that both were important to human existence. Most people living in Renaissance society remained Christian, continuing to follow basic teachings of Christ and the apostles. Even learned men who questioned medieval religious doctrine remained loyal to the Church and

Christianity. They were neither atheist nor agnostic but simply viewed religion from a more worldly perspective. Religious themes were still present in Renaissance art, literature, essays, and architecture but so were temporal and material themes, which had been largely absent from medieval works.

Individualism

A second intellectual development that characterized the Renaissance was individualism. While medieval Europe produced renowned personalities like St. Augustine, their achievements were not celebrated as personal accomplishments but as spiritual accomplishments. St. Augustine, as the Bishop of Hippo, wrote his greatest work, *City of God*, to glorify God. Christian beliefs discouraged medieval men from seeking personal glory. This mode of thought and behavior changed with the Renaissance. Individual personality and achievements became important. Artists, architects, and men of letters openly competed with each other and boasted whenever they bested an opponent. Renaissance men sought fame, glory, and attention. Each one tried to accomplish as much as possible while alive so that society would notice. Individual genius was celebrated by Renaissance Europe, and individuals were urged to reach their full potential as human beings. Renaissance men did not follow the "herd mentality." They were not afraid to be different from their neighbors. Consequently, the Renaissance produced individuals who relished their own individuality and who were not afraid to celebrate it. Michelangelo, Gentile Bellini, Leonardo da Vinci, Raphael, Valla, Boccaccio, Benvenuto Cellini, Leon Battista Alberti, Niccole Machiavelli, and other Renaissance figures are remembered for remarkable individual achievements. They and others developed a large body of art and literary work as a result of individualism. Had these men been part of medieval society, the modern world might not have remembered them because most likely they could not have accomplished what they did in a medieval society. They distanced themselves from other people and provided a sense of historical distance from medieval Europe.

Humanism

A third characteristic of the Renaissance was humanism. The Florentine writer Giovanni Pico della Mirandola was its leading advocate. His work, *Oration on the Dignity of Man*, rejected the medieval notion that the distinctive thing about humankind was its place on the Great Chain of Being; instead, he stressed that the individual had an intrinsic worth and that the highest form of religion was to respect human dignity. People can best worship God, Pico held, by respecting themselves and fellow human beings while cultivating individuality to the highest possible level. Intellectual development and the pursuit of knowledge should be goals sought by each individual. Although Pico and other humanists held Christian beliefs and values, their fundamental outlook on life was somewhat different. Whereas medieval Christianity emphasized the sinfulness of humans, the lack of control people had over their destiny, and the unlimited ability of God to forgive, humanists stressed the grandeur of man and viewed God as being relatively uninvolved in the world after creation. While God ultimately judged each human life and decided whether the individual suffered heaven or hell, the deity did not intervene directly in life. Human beings were directly responsible for their life because they had freedom to choose. An important component of humanism was skepticism. Renaissance humanists did not accept Christian, pagan, and classical authors and documents at face value. Rather, they questioned their authority, conscious that time and historical context separated the two ages and knowledgeable that ancient texts often disagreed with and contradicted each other.

The origins of humanism, like most aspects of the Renaissance, lie in antiquity. Italian cities rediscovered ancient texts produced by Greek, Roman, and Egyptian authors. Pope Nicholas V, for example, collected over nine thousand ancient manuscripts, which were eventually housed in the Vatican library that Pope Sixtus IV had constructed. The term "humanism" is derived from ideas of *humanitas* found in ancient texts written by Cicero. In the Ciceronian sense, *humanitas* refers to the educational and literary knowledge needed by civilized beings. Leonardo Bruni, a Florentine historian and lecturer who lived from 1370 to 1444, was the first scholar to use the term humanism to describe the study of ancient texts to understand human nature. These ancient texts focused on individuals, their accomplishments, and their intellectual abilities. Their study led Renaissance scholars to reject the medieval idea that people were merely helpless sinners with no control over life. Instead, humanists emphasized the innate dignity, intellectual abilities, creative talent, free will, and ability to determine the course of life present in all people.

In fact, one can argue that the catalyst for the Italian Renaissance was the rediscovery of ancient texts. Although classical texts were present in monastic libraries, the urban middle classes did not read them during the Middle Ages. At the beginning of the Renaissance, however, the messages ancient texts contained about individualism and secularism were particularly relevant to the new commercial society arising in Italian cities. Furthermore, Renaissance scholars realized that the meaning of ancient texts was often lost or altered by poor translators and thus studied ancient forms of Latin and Greek so that they could read classical texts in their original form. Knowledge of ancient Greek was greatly enhanced when the Byzantine scholar, Manuel Chrysoloras, came to Florence in 1397. This need by Renaissance scholars to find texts closest to the original as possible led to the development of modern philology, textual criticism, and literary and historical scholarship. The study of ancient texts caused Renaissance scholars to admire classical Latin. Because many of the ancient texts they were fascinated with were written in classical Latin, Renaissance intellectuals viewed it as superior to the language used by Latin writers of the Middle Ages. Consequently, men of letters during the Renaissance imitated ancient authors, writing highly stylized manuscripts in classical Latin. They even went so far as to try to recreate Plato's Academy from the fourth century A. D., using the Socratic method of questioning and dialogue to uncover knowledge.

Humanism gave rise to the concept of the Universal or Renaissance person. This was an individual who was well-rounded enough to do many things. The idea of the Universal person first surfaced in *The Courtier* written by Baldassare Castiglione around 1500. According to Castiglione, the Universal person should speak several languages fluently and be knowledgeable about art, literature, and philosophy. If wealthy, the Universal person should patronize artists and authors while always conducting himself in private and public with the grace and dignity that only knowledge could provide. A good example of a Renaissance man was Leonardo da Vinci. During his lifetime (1452-1519) he was a painter, engineer, anatomist,

botanist, optician, and inventor. He theorized about the Law of Gravity two full centuries before Sir Isaac Newton, designed an airplane that influenced other designers, including the Wright brothers, drew the first complete anatomical charts of the human body, studied the principle of optics, and theorized about energy conservation. In addition, his paintings the *Last Supper* and *the Mona Lisa* are among the greatest art works in history.

LITERATURE, WRITING, AND PAINTING

Literature was an important component of the Italian Renaissance. Florence was the dominant city in literary prose, producing great writers, while Ferrara dominated poetry. Francesco Petrarch (1313-1375), the first individual to recognize that a new age had dawned, greatly influenced Renaissance literature. A student of classical literature, he perfected the sonnet as a literary form. His writing style was copied by other Renaissance literary figures. Likewise, Giovanni Boccaccio (1313-1375) helped shape Italian prose and *Decameron*, a collection of stories, influenced novelists into the fifteenth and sixteenth centuries.

Italian Renaissance poetry was centered in Ferrara, a duchy ruled by the Este family located north of Florence and the Papal States. One of the most important Ferraran poets was Matteo Maria Boiardo. He wrote scores of poems during his life from 1434 to 1494. His most famous, *Orlando Innamorato*, was modeled after the medieval *Song of Roland*. He tried to recapture the vitality of the ancient knights long after their time had passed. Ludovico Ariosto (1474-1533) wrote Italy's greatest epic, *Orlando Furisos*, while Torquato Tasso (1544-1595) focused on the First Crusade to the Holy Land in *Jerusalem*

The invention of the printing press eliminated the laborious process of copying books by hand and thus accelerated the spread of literature.

Delivered. Other poets too numerous to mention were also part of the Renaissance.

The Renaissance produced writing in genera other than prose and poetry. Niccolo Machiavelli wrote about politics, government, and statecraft. His most famous work, *The Prince*, rejects metaphysics, theology, and idealism in favor of political realism. Machiavelli distinguished between what ought to be and what is, between the ideal form of government and the pragmatic conditions under which government actually operates. *The Prince* told would-be rulers how to gain and maintain power in the real world. Contrary to the popular view, Machiavelli was not some ogre or Anti-Christ who created a new immorality. He was a diplomat who served the Republic of Florence, the government that came into existence when Pietro Medici, son of Lorenzo, was forced into exile in 1494. For the next eighteen years, Machiavelli lived under and loved the Florentine Republic.

At the age of twenty-nine he joined the government headed by Piero Soderini, who was elected *Gofalonier* (President for Life) in 1502. Machiavelli saw service in the diplomatic corps, where he distinguished himself, until war destroyed the republic in 1512 and again brought the Medici to power. Florence had insisted on allying itself with France against the Papal States and Spain. When France withdrew its protection from Florence in 1512, the city was at the mercy of a hostile pope and his Spanish allies. Machiavelli formed a citizens' army (city militia) to defend Florence but saw it crushed by a stronger Spanish force. Machiavelli was captured and tortured by the Medici before being allowed to retire to the countryside where he wrote numerous books, including *The Prince, A History of Florence, Discourses, The Art of War,* and *Mandragola.* Although he hoped to return to governmental service, the opportunity never presented itself. Machiavelli died in 1527, awaiting a call from a new government that had come to power in Italy. Charles V defeated Papal armies in 1527 and sacked Rome, allowing republican forces in Florence to oust the Medici and restore democratic government for a short period. Machiavelli hurried back to Florence, eager to regain a diplomatic post. Unfortunately, leaders of the new government, like most people, had read and misunderstood *The Prince*, which caused them to fear and distrust Machiavelli. The hopeful Machiavelli became ill and died before learning that the Florentine governing council had voted against employing him as a diplomat. Yet, even after death, Machiavelli survives through the pages of *The Prince*. He was the first politician to truly understand the art of power politics that has shaped the modern world.

THE PRINTING PRESS

The invention of the printed word made literature available to the upper and middle classes. A form of printing that developed in China reached Italy as a result of trade along the Silk Road. The Chinese began to reproduce printed characters carved into blocks of wood that were inked and then pressed onto paper. Using wooden blocks to print characters and words as the Chinese did was expensive and time consuming. Europeans found a more efficient way to print. Johannes Gutenberg of Mainz, Germany is credited with inventing moveable metal type in 1455. There is evidence, however, that Johann Frist and Peter Schoffer also had a hand in creating moveable type and thus modern printing. These men created a system whereby individual letters could be put together to form words and sentences on paper. Since each letter was interchangeable with all other letters, words and sentences could be arranged in any format to print any text in existence.

Paper also was important to Renaissance printing. Medieval European scribes had written on animal hides. Because sheepskin, calfskin, and other animal hide parchments were expensive, few copies of ancient or medieval texts were produced. Arab traders had brought paper, which was relatively inexpensive when compared to animal skins, to Europe during the twelfth century. The Chinese had invented a process to manufacture paper, and Arab traders began to sell the product in European markets. Europeans quickly learned how to make their own paper, which printers could easily acquire.

The invention of the printing press had a tremendous effect on Europe. For the first time, large numbers of people had access to literature. The availability of books increased because their production cost decreased, which enabled middle and upper class merchants to collect their own private libraries. Simultaneously, the printing press facilitated communications among scholars and the general dissemination of knowledge. In 1456 Gutenberg printed his first Bible; within a half-century scores of presses had been established. By 1500 there were over 70 printing presses in Italy, 50 in Germany, 40 in France, and lesser numbers in England, Switzerland, and the Netherlands. The largest and most important press was located in Venice. It was operated by Aldus Manutius and named the Aldine Press. Classic works of ancient Greek and Latin literature, as well as the best works of Renaissance authors, were published. It employed approximately six hundred workers and produced about 15 percent of all books printed in Europe.

Printing affected many aspects of European life. It enabled governments and businesses to effectively use propaganda. Governments could easily disseminate their viewpoints to the masses, while merchants and shopkeepers could engage in a subtle use of propaganda called advertising. Propaganda gave rise to political parties that competed with each other on ideological grounds. Localism and provincialism were eventually replaced by nationalism. People who lived in diverse geographical locations could be united by the printed word and form a common or national identity.

Printing also had an effect on the lives of ordinary people throughout Europe. Because life was tedious, most people sought relief from boredom through reading. Although many books dealt with religion in the early years of printing, printers eventually produced books on practically every imaginable subject.

RENAISSANCE SOCIETY

Although the Renaissance was one of the most important events in Western Civilization, it did not mark the beginning of the modern age. Renaissance society and Renaissance people were, in many respects, closer to medieval men and women than modern people. Yet, the Renaissance concern with secular and religious life laid the intellectual foundations for the modern world. Despite this emphasis on humankind rather than God, most people living during the Renaissance retained their Christian faith. With the exception of a few scholars, most Renaissance people did not question the authority of the Church or the basic tenets of Christianity. Even Italian humanists were not atheist, agnostics, or skeptics. The scores of religious art works and written manuscripts produced by Renaissance scholars that contain religious themes provide evidence that religion remained important during the Renaissance.

A small mercantile elite dominated Renaissance society. It was generally not democratic, and most lower classes of people did not fully participate in it. Renaissance culture and society were created by a small number of highly educated, intellectual writers and artists for an elite population. These elites did not understand, or much care, about the common man and woman. In fact, the Renaissance created and perpetuated a gap between highly educated members of society and the undereducated that persists even today.

Education was a central concern of Renaissance humanists. Numerous essays, letters, and books were written on the subject. The most influential was Castiglione's *The Courtier*. Castiglione maintained that men (not women) should undergo both academic and physical development. The ideal man should have a broad understanding of all academic disciplines, be able to dance, be able to understand music and art, and be proficient at fighting. Education should be structured to teach these things to all young men, especially those from rich merchant or banking families.

Peter Paul Vergerio, another Renaissance scholar, devised a program of education similar to Castiglione's and linked it to the interests of the state. In a letter written to Ubertinus, the ruler of Carraia, Vergerio maintained that the state had an interest in using education to create modern citizens. His program outlined in this letter advised that students study history because it teaches virtue from past examples, ethics so that virtue itself can be learned, and public speaking or rhetoric to develop eloquent oratorical skills. Vergerio also maintained that teachers should be individuals with high moral standards who would provide good examples for students to imitate and who would "repress the first sign of evil." He called his education program "liberal arts" because it was designed to allow the individual to obtain wisdom and practice virtue.

Women

Education, scholarship, and artistic endeavors, like most public activities during the Renaissance, were considered male activities. With a few exceptions, women were not allowed to attend universities and could not practice law or medicine, go into banking, or become teachers. Legally, women were considered to be the property of their fathers until marriage when they became the property of their husbands. (This ideal is still reflected in modern marriage ceremonies when the father traditionally gives the bride away.) Females who attempted to enter male-dominated professions faced much ridicule, suspicion, and opposition. Educational opportunities for women were so limited that less than two hundred women in all Europe owned books, an indication that literacy rates were low.

The status of women during the Renaissance actually declined when compared to the Middle Ages. Access to property and political power for upper class women was less than during medieval Europe, and the ability of women to shape society was almost non-existent during the Renaissance. Ordinary women still performed the same economic functions in Renaissance Europe as their mothers and grandmothers in previous epochs. Farm wives and daughters helped husbands and fathers complete agricultural tasks while urban women performed domestic duties and other feminine tasks. Countless women across Europe functioned as midwives, cooks, seamstresses, maids, laundresses, and house servants. A few women worked in industry. The Italian textile industry, for example, employed women as weavers and silk winders. Shipyards in other European countries often used women to make canvas sails. Widows who possessed the required skills sometimes ran their deceased husband's businesses and were occasionally admitted to membership in guilds.

Occasionally, Renaissance women overcame barriers placed in their way by achieving an education. A few remarkable women from upper class families managed to obtain educations equal to their male counterparts. Such women were taught how to read, write, and do mathematical calculations. They then could learn the ancient languages, which enabled them to read classical literary texts. Such educational advances enabled a few women to produce scholarly works of their own. After the printing press was invented, at least twenty-five Italian women wrote books that were published. Other Renaissance women exchanged letters with male and female colleagues on academic topics, engaged in heated debate with scholars, and produced great works of art.

Isotta Nogarola was one of the most remarkable women the Renaissance produced. She was born in Verona, Italy, in 1418 to a noble family that took pride in educational achievement. Nogarola's aunt, Angela, had been highly educated and when her father died, urged Nogarola's mother to provide her daughter with a classical education, which was atypical for women at that time. Martino Rizzoni, a prominent educator, was hired to tutor Nogarola and her sister, Ginevra. The sisters learned quickly and soon became well known among Italian humanists. Ginevra married in 1438 and, as was customary, completely abandoned her academic pursuits. Isotta moved to Venice, a more cosmopolitan city, where she lived until 1441 when she returned to Verona. Determined never to wed, she spent the majority of her life pursuing academic matters. About 1450 she began to correspond with Ludovico Foscarini, a humanist politician. Their letters provided material that Nogarola drew on to produce several books, including her two most famous, *Dialogue on Adam and Eve* and *Oration on the Life of St. Jerome*.

Another remarkable woman that overcame sexist prejudice was Laura Cereta. Her life from 1469 to 1499 illustrates both the successes and failures of Renaissance women. Like Nogarola, Cereta was a scholar who had difficulty overcoming social prejudices against talented women. Until she was nine years old, she lived in a convent where her education began. She left the convent with her father, a Brescian nobleman and Lombardy government official. He taught Cereta to speak several languages and instructed her in mathematics, philosophy, history, theology, government, and classical literature. Education provided Cereta with self-esteem and a desire to become a scholar like Petrarch, her hero. Marriage to a merchant at the age of fifteen interrupted her studies. Like most Renaissance and some modern women, Cereta was forced to choose between marriage and a career. She could take a husband, bear children, participate fully in social life, and assume domestic duties or live life similar to a hermit, withdrawn from the larger world. After choosing marriage, Cereta fully expected to abandon scholarly pursuits until the unexpected death of her spouse from Bubonic Plague eighteen month after the wedding, which opened new opportunities. The young widow found an outlet for her grief in the pursuit of knowledge. Prior to her death in 1499, Cereta wrote numerous letters to contemporary scholars defending her ideas about a liberal education for women.

Although women labored in studios throughout Italy, credit for the artwork they produced usually went to their husbands and fathers who owned the studios. An exception was Sofonisba Anguissola. Born into an aristocratic Cremonan family about 1532, she, along with her five sisters, were taught music and painting

in accordance with ideas on female education her parents gleaned from Castiglione's *The Courtier*. Sofonisba showed artistic talent as a result of this training and was allowed to study formally with Bernardino Campi, a local painter. Her family encouraged Sofonisba's painting. In 1557, her father persuaded the great Michelangelo to send Sofonisba several drawings that she could paint and return for him to evaluate. Sofenisba's work so impressed Michelangelo that he invited her to serve a two-year apprenticeship under him in Rome. During the apprenticeship she painted a portrait of the Duke of Alba that pleased him so much that he secured her a position at the court of King Philip II of Spain, a job she held for twenty years. The Spanish royal family valued her work so highly that King Philip gave her away when she married a Sicilian nobleman, Fabrizio de Moncada, in 1569. The royal couple, Philip and Queen Isabella, patronized her work. Sofonisba's most famous work is *Portrait of a Couple*, a painting that depicts a husband holding his wife with a tender touch while the couple stare at the viewer, a trait found in most of her work.

Sofonisba inspired other female artists throughout Europe. One of them was Artemisia Gentileschi. Her father, Orazio, himself an artist, taught Artemisia how to paint after her mother died. Orazio also arranged for Artemisia to study under the master painter Caravaggio where she developed a style in which light and dark contrasts were used to convey emotions. Artemisia, at the age of seventeen, completed her first critically acclaimed work, *Susanna and the Elders*, a painting depicting a vulnerable young girl in a world filled with dangerous men. Even after marriage, Artemisia continued working as a painter, one of only a few women to do so. Her signature masterpiece, *Judith Slaying Holofernes*, was painted after she left Rome for

Florence where several members of the Medici family, the scientist Galileo, and descendants of Michelangelo patronized her. In the masterpiece, Judith is depicted as a strong, heroic woman who beheads Holofernes, the Assyrian oppressor of the Hebrews. The painting reveals not only Artemisia's technical talents but her use of bold colors conveys a strong sense of emotion to the viewer. Other works that Artemisia painted also depicted strong female figures, including *Madonna and Child, Self-portrait as the Allegory of Painting*, and portraits of Cleopatra, Lucretia, Minerva, and Mary Magdalene. In 1616 she was the first female artist granted membership in the Florence Academy of Art, the most prestigious artistic society of the seventeenth century.

Despite some success in the literary and artistic world, careers for most Renaissance women were non-existent. Medieval women were relatively equal to men in regards to love and sex, but Renaissance humanists created a double standard for men and women. Castiglione and others proclaimed that woman's proper place was in the home. They maintained that men and men alone participated in public life and separated sex from love. For women, sex was permitted only in the marriage bed, while men, even married ones, pursued sex outside matrimony. Women were required to remain virginal until marriage and then were generally relegated to social roles as wives and mothers. Any talent or career aspirations a wife might harbor were put aside to promote those of her husband and male children. Laura Cereta, Sofonisba Anguissola, Artemisia Gentilischi, Isotta Nogarola, and other Renaissance women who overcame social barriers to achieve scholarly and artistic prominence were the exceptions. Most women had little hope of developing their talents and abilities to their utmost potential.

Females living during the Renaissance were often victimized by rape. Legal evidence from Italian city-states indicates that rape was treated in a casual manner. It was not even classified as a felony. Noblemen committed many rapes. Punishment for a nobleman convicted of raping a noblewoman ranged from a small fine to about six months in prison. Punishment for a nobleman who raped a woman not born to the noble class was non-existent. These light sentences were handed down during a time when shoplifting was punished by bodily mutilation, when heresy was punished by burning at the stake, and when forgery resulted in beheading. The only time rapists were severely punished occurred when a child under the age of twelve was raped or when a common man raped a high-ranking noble woman. Assaults by working class men on noble women were punished more severely because such assaults often had social and political consequences, especially if they resulted in pregnancy. In general, Renaissance society believed that rape did little harm to its victims.

Renaissance women who tried to overcome gender barriers usually faced ridicule and scorn from both lay people and scholars. Females could choose marriage and full participation as women in society or scholarship and social isolation. Marriage prevented most women from fulfilling their scholarly ambitions. With marriage came children and domestic responsibilities that prevented study. Also, males felt threatened by educated females. Most Renaissance men believed that learning was contrary to a woman's basic nature. Education, they believed, would make a woman cease to be a woman. Intelligent women, such as Laura Cereta, who were accomplished scholars faced severe attacks from male counterparts because they threatened to break the male dominance in the intellectual world. Most girls during the Renaissance from upper and middle class families received at most a minimum education in painting, music, and dance. The purpose of this education was to enable them to attract husbands. Girls were educated in various social graces so that after marriage they could grace the husband's household and attract scholars and artists to the manor. Women were not educated to participate in politics or business.

Minorities and Slavery

Women were not the only minorities that suffered from discrimination in Renaissance Europe. Ethnic minorities faced not only discrimination and prejudice but persecution as well. Italy and other Renaissance nations contained a small number of ethnic and religious minorities during the Middle Ages and into the Renaissance. Even though the overwhelming majority of Europe's population was Roman Catholic, a minority of the population in eastern areas of the continent were Eastern Orthodox Christians. In worship services they used either the Greek or Slovonic rites rather than those of the Roman Church. Christians in western nations, however, viewed practitioners of Orthodoxy with suspicion, as Renaissance people did not tolerate religious diversity

Another religious minority in Renaissance Europe were Muslims. Islam reached Europe by two routes—from the Middle East and North Africa. The Moors, Islamic people from northern Africa, invaded Spain and France and controlled parts of both nations from the Middle Ages into the Renaissance. In 1492 Spanish armies controlled by Isabella of Castile, the warrior queen, captured the last Moorish stronghold at Granada. Following a brief period of religious toleration, Isabella demanded that the thousands of Muslims living in Spain convert to Roman

Catholicism. Those who refused were expelled from the Iberian Peninsula. Faced with eviction, thousands became Christian, but thousands more gave up their property and material possessions, fleeing Spain for Africa, Asia, or other European countries. Many lost their lives after leaving Spain due to religious intolerance elsewhere.

Although Islam was virtually destroyed on the Iberian Peninsula, it existed in Eastern Europe as a result of warfare with the Middle East. The Ottoman ruler, Sultan Mehmed II (1451-1481), captured Constantinople, the Turkish city that straddled the boundary between Europe and Asia in 1453. After taking Turkey, Mehmed launched a military campaign in Southern and Eastern Europe. His armies took Athens in 1456 and eventually conquered all of Greece. Later, he captured territories in the Balkans, including Serbia, Bosnia, Herzegovina, and Albania. Mehmed allowed the populations he had conquered to convert to Islam. As a result, Islam became firmly established in Eastern Europe.

Renaissance Europe also had a small population of Jews who managed to survive despite various waves of persecutions. No minority religious or ethnic group was treated as poorly in Europe as were Jews. They often underwent forced expulsions from European countries or were forced to convert to Christianity to escape execution. Occasionally, Jewish populations in Italy and other Renaissance countries were protected by princes or ruling families. However, in most countries Jews were prohibited from owning land, which meant that agriculture was closed to them. Consequently, European Jews became an urban people, working as butchers, peddlers, bankers, pawnbrokers, notaries, writers, servants, and various other occupations not legally closed.

Hatred and prejudice against Jews was so bad that Jewish communities during the fourteenth century were often blamed for any disaster that befell a community. One such example was the Bubonic Plague. Christians throughout Europe accused Jewish neighbors of poisoning wells or placing evil spells on victims of the Black Death. Of course, such accusations were untrue. Bubonic Plague was actually spread by germs that lived in fleas carried by rats that infested Renaissance houses. Many communities afflicted by the plague believed that God was punishing them for allowing unchristian Jews to live within the city. The only way they believed they could rid themselves of the plague was to expel or exterminate their Jewish population. As a result, Jews in hundreds of localities experienced waves of terror that cost them their homes, wealth, and often their lives.

Africans were another minority that lived in parts of Europe during the Renaissance. They came from numerous tribes and religious groups on their native continent. Most were used as domestic slaves in wealthy homes at the height of the Renaissance. African slavery is traceable to the Roman Empire. Africans, along with white slaves, had come into Europe after being captured in war. After the Roman Empire fell, slave traders continued to sell people to rich families. When the Bubonic Plague reduced Europe's population in the fourteenth century, the resulting reduction in the labor force caused the demand for slaves to increase. Thousands of slaves from Africa were brought to Europe. These individuals were captured and sold into slavery by Portuguese and Spanish traders in markets at Barcelona, Marseilles, Seville, Genoa, Pisa, Naples, and other localities. So many Africans were imported into Europe during the Renaissance that they comprised between 3 and 10 percent of the urban population

Europeans often viewed Africans as evil. Prior to the age of discovery, the European world-view was limited. Most Europeans had no contact with Africa. What they knew of it was based on Biblical stories. Europeans generally saw Africa as a far away place inhabited by dark people who were either pagan or heretical Muslims. Contact with an "advanced" European civilization, most believed, would improve the African race. Europeans also suffered from racial prejudice and bias against Africans caused by the scant Biblical knowledge about the continent they valued so highly. European religious scholars maintained that Christ, who was good, was of light skin pigmentation. Black, which represented Satan, was evil. Therefore, theologians speculated that black skinned Africans were created by the devil in his image and were evil while whites, created by a light skinned God in his image, were good. Lucifer, or Satan, was usually depicted as a black man in Renaissance art. Unfortunately, Renaissance scholars ignored historical and archaeological evidence that indicated Christ was most likely dark skinned.

Europeans also regarded Africans as objects of curiosity. Black servants, because of their skin pigmentation, were valued because they were different. Some noble households even kept black servants as "court jesters." In 1491, Isabella, the Duchess of Mantura, gave orders to purchase an African girl with as dark a skin as possible to use for entertainment. Isabella wanted to train the girl to be the "best buffoon in the world." Most Africans, however, were not used for entertainment. They usually performed numerous tasks from farm laborers to prostitutes.

Other minorities, including whites, also served as slaves in Renaissance Europe. Tartars and Turks, for example, were occasionally sold at slave auctions in Ancona, Genoa, Pisa, Venice, and other cities. Like their African counterparts, these slaves performed multiple tasks from serving on ships, working as domestics and in factories to herdsmen, grape pickers, and craftsmen. It appears that race, in contrast to American slavery in later centuries, played little role in Renaissance slavery. Individuals were enslaved not because they were black but because their people sold them into slavery or because they were captured in war. Modern scholarship indicates that race did not become an important factor in slavery until the seventeenth century. Renaissance people kept slaves because, like women and art, they were indications of wealth.

THE NORTHERN RENAISSANCE

Italy was not the only European country to experience the Renaissance. Nations in the northern portion of the continent also underwent a revival of art, learning, and culture, but it occurred somewhat later than in Italy. During the last half of the fifteenth century Italian ideas and culture began to move into European territories across the Alps. At that time, students from Belgium, Holland, France, Germany, England, and Spain ventured to Italy to partake of the new "classical learning." When they returned home, they brought Italian ideas about government, nature, society, people, religion, and the economy with them. Northern Europeans, however, interpreted Italian views on ancient Greece and Rome, individualism, humanism, art, literature, music, religion, and education in light of their own cultural traditions. In general, the northern Renaissance was more Christian and less secular than in Italy. This is not to say that Italian Renaissance scholars and artists were not Christian, for they certainly were; however, Italians focused more attention on worldly themes than did scholars north of the Alps who often emphasized Biblical thought.

The Renaissance was slower to move into Northern Europe because the region did not contain many large cities and lacked the large number of middle class merchants who supported art and literature in Italy. Also, the cultural traditions and languages of people in the North did not have as direct a connection to the Greece and Rome of antiquity as did those in Italy. The court and the knight, rather than the city and merchant, dominated northern European culture until near the close of the fifteenth century.

Humanism as reflected in northern European nations is more aptly labeled "Christian Humanism." Its practitioners were interested chiefly in development of an ethical lifestyle that could best be achieved by fusing together the best parts of Greek, Roman, and Christian cultures. Once Christian and classical values were combined, northern humanists believed an ethical individual and an ethical society would result.

An important component of northern European humanism was its emphasis on logic and reason. Northern scholars adopted Socrates' view that each individual possessed knowledge within that could be extracted through logical reasoning. To arrive at the correct answer, a person had to question preconceived notions. Reason, rather than dogma, was the key to developing an ethical person and society. Humans could, through use of reason, institute reform within society and its institutions. Christian humanists rejected the medieval view that human beings were by nature evil. Instead, they stressed that even though people often committed sins, human nature was basically good. In other words, Christian humanists believed that if given a choice, more often than not, human beings would opt to do good. The key to improving human existence was education, which taught the individual to exercise reason to solve all dilemmas. Only by being educated to use their rational faculties could humans become pious individuals who fashioned just and ethical societies and lived Christian lives in them.

One of the most important Christian humanists was Sir Thomas More, an English lawyer and diplomat. Born in 1478, he lived his teenage and young adult years in London Charterhouse, a Catholic monastery operated by the Carthusian order. He left the monastery, married, and was sent by Henry VIII as ambassador to Flanders. His signature work, which he wrote while in Flanders, was *Utopia*. This work, penned in 1516, represents the first time that a European had written about a socialistic society. In *Utopia,* More creates an island community located somewhere in the Western Hemisphere inhabited by scholars. In this utopian society the government provides each child with a free education. After reaching adulthood, individuals continue learning by dividing their day between work and study, working six hours and studying six hours. Also, in *Utopia* there was absolute equality in society, as property was held in common. All profits from business activities were divided among the population. Greed was not a problem on this island paradise. Precious metals, like gold and silver, were valued so little that they were often used to make chamber toilets. Rather than fighting over money, Utopians used gold and silver to prevent wars. They simply paid enemies not to attack. Utopia's inhabitants lived a carefree, ideal life that was not beset by the problems England faced during More's lifetime. The utopian legal system placed mercy above justice, punishment, and retribution. All people lived in nice houses that contained glass windows (Glass was a symbol of prosperity in sixteenth-century England.), fireproof roofs, and gardens. Water flowed fresh and clean while goods in stores and markets were free. Each individual took only what he or she needed to

live. All people dressed alike except for priests. However, women were somewhat subordinate to men but did receive military training. Wars of conquest were prohibited. Religion was flexible and not bound by dogma. Utopia was a perfect society because its people lived by reason, making their government, social institutions, and economy perfect.

More's career was cut short by his execution in 1535. After his death, his ideas survived. *Utopia* rivals the plays of Shakespeare as the most read sixteenth-century English work. His view that greed and the acquisition of material objects promoted civil disorder and crime were revolutionary in the sixteenth-century world. He clearly rejected earlier Christian notions that crime existed because individuals were sinful. Because legal systems in England and elsewhere protected private property and encouraged the acquisition of material things, society was responsible for war, crime, violence, poverty, and a host of other social ills that plagued humankind. Improvement in the human condition was achievable only by reforming social institutions that were corrupt.

A close friend of Sir Thomas More was the Dutch scholar, Desiderius Erasmus. The illegitimate son of a priest and a physician's daughter, he was born in Rotterdam around 1466. (His exact date of birth is unknown.) When both parents died in his youth, poverty forced Erasmus to enter a monastery. Although he hated the monastic lifestyle, he received an excellent education at the famous Brethren of the Common Life School at Deventer, developing while there an excellent knowledge of the Latin language and profound appreciation for classical literature. The school also instilled into Erasmus its pious *devotio moderna,* a new type of lay spirituality that emphasized free thought and open religious discussion that greatly influenced northern hu-

Eramus was one of the most celebrated humanists in Europe.

manism. Later, Erasmus was ordained as a priest and became a monk at the Steyn, an Augustinian monastery. His stay at the Steyn from 1486 until 1493 was brief. His dislike of other monks, poor health, and love of the classics caused Pope Leo X to grant him a dispensation, allowing Erasmus to permanently leave the monastery. In 1494, he became secretary to the bishop of Cambrai in France, which allowed him to enroll at the College de Montaigue at the University of Paris. He spent several years there but claimed to hate its "stale eggs and stale theology." In particular, Erasmus disliked the scholastic theology and systematic philosophy that dominated theological studies at the university. He was drawn to a new discipline, classical philology, and would place the field in the service of religion. In 1499, Erasmus found employment as a tutor in England where he met humanists John

Colet and Sir Thomas More. He became fast friends with both men. Colet especially influenced Erasmus; his ideas enabled the young Dutchman to apply humanistic principles to Biblical scholarship.

Erasmus was a prolific writer. His first known publication was *Adages*, a collection of eight hundred wise sayings from ancient Latin texts. This work became popular because it made the wit and wisdom of classical texts and authors available to the masses of people who could not read Latin. *Adages* popularized such modern sayings as "to leave no stone unturned," and "where there is smoke, there is fire." After *Adages* established him as an author, Erasmus published *Handbook of the Christian Soldier* in 1503, which stressed the importance of Christian faith in everyday life. In 1504 and 1505 he published an edition of Cicero's and St. Jerome's letters along with Valla's *Annotations on the New Testament*. Erasmus's most important works were *Praise of Folly* (1509) and *The Greek New Testament* (1516). *Praise of Folly* was a work that criticized abuses in both the Catholic Church and European society. Erasmus hoped that his criticism would promote a purer, simpler form of Christianity. Thus, he condemned "the cheats of pardons and indulgences" the Catholic Church dispensed so readily as well as worship of the Virgin Mary before Christ. Even the Pope was not spared criticism. Erasmus wrote: "Now as to the popes of Rome, who pretend themselves Christ's vicar, if they would but imitate his exemplary life...." *Praise of Folly* was popular reading even though the Catholic Church banned it. After moving to Basel, Switzerland to be closer to his publisher, Johann Froben, as his nine-volume edition of the writings of St. Jerome was being printed, Erasmus published his second most important work, *Novum Instrumentum*, a translation of the Greek New

Testament. This work marked progress in higher textual criticism. Erasmus used his knowledge of classical languages to produce an improved version of the Bible translated from the best Greek manuscripts available. He believed, as he explained in the introduction, "that the sacred scriptures should be read by the unlearned translated into their vulgar tongue..." and that "Christ wished his mysteries to be published as openly as possible." The Catholic Church was displeased with Erasmus's improved Bible. Church officials preferred that the official Latin Vulgate be read. Consequently, in the mid-sixteenth century the Greek New Testament, along with all of Erasmus's works, was placed on the Church's *Index of Forbidden Books*.

The phrase, *philosophi Christi,* best describes the fundamental theme found in Erasmus's work. He believed in a simple, ethical piety that imitated Christ. His views contradicted the dogmatic, ceremonial, and factious religious worship present within the Catholic Church. Erasmus criticized anybody or any institution that let doctrine interfere with Christian humility. He taught that Christianity was found within the individual rather than in an institution called church. Christianity is Christ; it is not a building, a priest, a Bible, or a ceremony. To Erasmus, what Christ did and said was more important than anything theologians wrote or anything the Pope decreed. Erasmus, like most humanists, believed the classics from ancient Greece and Rome would prepare the individual's mind to receive God's truth. Furthermore, he believed the classics were worth studying for their own intrinsic value. All people who read from them were bound to improve their outlook on life and likely to become ethical people.

Even though Erasmus is remembered as a critic of the Catholic Church, he was not an early reformer. In fact, he criticized Martin Luther

for breaking with the Catholic faith. When accused of being a "heretic Lutheran," Erasmus said that he did not write *Julius Excluded from Heaven,* a satire published in 1517 that describes a swaggering warrior-pope who is denied admission to heaven. Later, a copy of the work was found in Erasmus's handwriting! In the 1520s Erasmus and Luther engaged in a heated debate over free will and predestination. Erasmus published *The Freedom of the Will* in 1524, which argued that Luther's conception of predestination was incorrect. Because he had disagreed with Luther, Erasmus, fearing for his life, fled Basel in 1529 after the Protestant Reformation came to that city. He settled in Freiburg where he lived for six years before returning to Basel where he died in 1535.

Erasmus was a pacifist who hoped reason would eventually prevent wars. He rejected the idea of St. Augustine that a "just war" was possible. In *Complaint of Peace* (1517) Erasmus argued that "war incessantly sows war, vengeance seethingly draws vengeance, kindness generously engenders kindness." Erasmus was particularly opposed to the Crusades and holy wars of the Middle Ages. He strongly opposed the Catholic Church's involvement in such wars. He thought the Church and all Christians should preach peace and set an example of nonviolence for others to imitate rather than engaging in military alliances, wars, and violence.

Erasmus was one of the first humanists in northern Europe to support classical study for women. Although Erasmus sometimes ridiculed women and believed they were inferior to men, he did not think that they were incapable of learning. He advocated that daughters of the rich, at least, should be educated in the classics. His views were shaped, in part, by having been impressed with the work of Margaret Roper (1504-1544), the daughter of Sir Thomas More, in translating his work on the Lord's Supper into English. This prompted him to write an essay entitled "Dialogue Between an Abbot and a Learned Lady" in which Erasmus has an educated housewife tell an unlearned abbot that "if man can't play their parts, they should get off the stage and let women assume their roles." Erasmus also maintained that study for women was a weapon against an idle mind and would produce a virtuous woman.

Although Erasmus and Sir Thomas More brought recognition for humanistic thought to England and the Netherlands, every country in northern Europe produced a brand of humanism unique to it. In the Germanic kingdoms humanism celebrated nationalism. This nationalistic slant is particularly evident in the work of Conrad Celtis (1459-1508), one of the most important German humanists. Born into a peasant family at Wurzburg, Celtis attended a number of colleges and universities before Holy Roman Emperor Frederick III named him Germany's first poet laureate in 1487. While a student, Celtis became disturbed by Italy's claim to have a superior culture to the "barbarians" in Germany, Poland, Russia, France, and England. This disgust with Italian claims of superiority caused Celtis to urge fellow Germans to challenge Italy culturally much as they had earlier challenged Roman legions militarily. Other than lyric poetry, for which he is well known, Celtis translated *Germania*, the writings of the Roman historian Tacitus, introduced the writings of Hrosvit of Gandersheim, a tenth century author who wrote poetry, history, and drama, and wrote his own history of Germany entitled *Germany Illustrated*. All the translations from antiquity, as well as Celtis' own personal writings, were produced because he wanted to show the world, as well as his countrymen, that German culture was equal to that of Italy or any other nation.

The most celebrated humanist Germany produced was Johann Reuchlin. Born in Pforzheim in 1455, his early education was at the Brethern of the Common Life School. Later, he attended universities at Basel, Freiburg, Orleans, Paris, and Tubingen. He traveled widely and during visits to Italy met the famed humanist Pico whom he came to admire. Trained as a lawyer, Reuchlin served as an aide to the Duke of Wurttemberg and represented the Swambian League from 1502 to 1512. He left the legal profession a few years before his death in 1522 and taught Greek and Hebrew at the universities of Ingolstadt and Tubingen. Reuchlin is most noted for his study of Hebrew. He maintained that it was impossible to understand the Old Testament without reading it in Hebrew, its original language. In 1506, he published a Hebrew grammar book, *The Rudiments of Hebrew*, to guide other scholars interested in the Old Testament and other ancient Hebrew manuscripts. This book represents the first Hebrew grammar book written by a Christian author. Later, in 1517 he wrote *On the Cabalistic Art*, which showed the relationship between ancient Greek, Hebrew, and Christian beliefs.

Reuchlin's work with Hebrew texts provoked much debate within Germany. Johann Pfefferkorn, a scholastic scholar who had converted from Judaism to Christianity, like many religious converts, wanted to advance his new faith at the expense of the old one. Consequently, he attacked Reuchlin and scholars inspired by Reuchlin to study ancient Hebrew texts from a humanistic perspective. In *A Mirror for Jews* Pfefferkorn stated that the government should ban, confiscate, and burn all Hebrew books. Several Catholic monastic orders, including the Dominicans of Cologne, supported Pfefferkorn's ideas, fearing that humanistic Hebrew scholarship threatened traditional scholastic Christian ideas. In 1519 Emperor Maximilian I implemented Pfefferkorn's ideas, ordering all Hebrew books to be burned. This began a controversy known as the Reuchlin Affair. Reuchlin responded that rather than destroying Hebrew books, Christians would become closer to God if they studied these books intensely. Pfefferkorn published a pamphlet directly attacking Reuchlin, stating that he was ignorant. Reuchlin, forced to defend his scholarly reputation, wrote the *Letters of Famous Men*, a collection of statements by noted humanist scholars supporting his idea that the study of Hebrew would enhance Christianity. The Reuchlin Affair continued until 1520 when Pope Leo X issued an edict ordering Reuchlin to stop expressing his views. Even though friends urged him to join Luther in condemning the Catholic Church, Reuchlin refused and obeyed Pope Leo X's order. He died two years later still in the Catholic fold.

Lesser-known German scholars included Ulrich von Hutten (1488-1523), the Humanist Knight, who defended Reuchlin against Pfefferkorn. His most famous work, written with Crotus Rubianus, was the *Letters of Obscure Men*, a work deliberately written using poor Latin grammar to poke fun at those who attacked Reuchlin. Unfortunately, Huten and Rubianus tainted *Letters of Obscure Men* with anti-Semitism, which lessened its value. When the Pope banned *Letters of Obscure Men*, its sales increased, bringing more attention to it authors.

Caritas (1466-1532) and Willibald (1470-1530) Prickheimer, a brother and sister duo, were also part of the German Humanistic Renaissance. Friends of Celtis, the Prickheimers produced numerous works. The most important was Caritas' *Memoirs*, which documented the early history of the Reformation in Nuremberg, the Prikheimers' hometown, and Willibald's translation of major classical Greek and Latin authors,

including Xenophon, Plutarch, Ptolemy, Thucydides, Galen, Aristophanes, Aristotle, and Gregory of Nazianzus.

Jacob Wimpfeling (1450-1528) was the most important Rhenish humanist Germany produced. His most famous work, published in 1500, was *Germania*, a history of the German states. Wimpfeling devoted most of his energy to education, proposing to create a humanist school in Strasbourg. Unfortunately, Strasbourg's leaders rejected his idea.

Humanism also made its way into France and Spain during the European Renaissance. Unlike German humanists, who largely rejected Italian influence, French humanists openly embraced Italian scholarship. One of the most important French humanists was Francois Rabelais. (He lived from about 1490 to 1553; his exact date of birth is unknown.) Like the Italian humanistic work that he used as a model, Rabelais' work was distinctly secular. His most important works, produced between 1532 and 1552, were the literary comedies *Gargantua and Pantagruel*. Modern scholars place them among the world's greatest comic literature. These works are written so that they can be read on several levels: as the funny adventures of the giant Gargantua and his son, Pantagruel, as a romantic comedy starring Gargantua and Pantagruel, as a critique of French society, as a demand for humanistic education, and as a spoof of Christianity. Gargantua and Pantagruel travel throughout the world, meeting numerous people with whom they have comedic chats that provide readers with important information on government, politics, religion, economics, philosophy, and education.

Another important French humanist was Guillaume Bude (1467-1540). As head of the royal national library at Fontainebleau, he was perhaps the chief French authority on classical works. His formal training was as a lawyer, but he rarely practiced. Instead, he studied ancient texts. Because Greek and Latin scholarship was almost non-existent in France, Bude had to teach himself. The work that solidified his place as France's and one of Europe's leading classical authorities was *Commentaries on the Greek Language*, published in 1529.

Lefevre d' Etaples (1450-1536), a contemporary and rival of Bude, also developed a reputation within France and Europe as a humanist scholar. In 1492 he visited Italy where he met and was greatly influenced by Pico. After returning to France, he developed the Aristotelian Renaissance, an educational method that used knowledge of ancient history to study classical texts. Toward the end of his life, Lefevre grew interested in Christian mysticism. His most important publication was *Commentary on the Epistle of St. Paul*. In this work, Lefevre focused on Paul's idea that heaven is attainable only by the grace of God and that the life an individual lived on earth had little to do with salvation.

Cardinal Jimenez de Cisneros (1436-1517) was largely responsible for the flowering of Spanish humanism. Born into poverty, he studied law and theology at the University of Salamanca prior to working for the Catholic Church in Rome. Eventually he returned to Spain as a Franciscan friar and Church officer. When Spanish forces subdued the Moors in 1492, Queen Isabella appointed him as her private chaplain. Cisneros used his influence to promote humanism throughout Spain. His most significant achievement was founding the University of Alcala in 1509. Creation of this university was part of a reform of the Catholic Church throughout Spain that Cisneros oversaw. The Church reforms were intended to force Catholic priests and other Church officials to live morally upstanding lives. Cisneros believed that priests

needed a university devoted to Biblical scholarship. Consequently, the University of Alcala was made into one of Europe's centers for the study of ancient Greek, Hebrew, and Latin texts. Alcalan scholars published the first multilanguage Bible. Greek, Latin, and Hebrew texts were written in parallel columns, much as modern Gospel Parallels will provide texts from different English Biblical translations side by side. Cisneros believed that the study of classical Biblical texts would produce priests who were more moral, who understood more about the Bible, and who, thus, would set a better example for their parishioners.

Another important Spanish humanist was Juan Luis Vives (1492-1540). However, Vives did not spend most of his career in Spain. After completing the early part of his formal schooling in Valencia, his place of birth, he left Spain at the age of seventeen to attend the University of Paris. After graduation, he became a professor at the University of Louvain. While there, he produced one of his most famous early works, *The Fable of Man*, in 1518. Shortly thereafter, the English monarch, Henry VIII, hired Vives as Princess Mary's private tutor. In England, Vives also taught at Oxford. His English sojourn resulted in over fifty books detailing his humanistic ideas. In particular, Vives believed that education should produce a moral citizen, which he held could most easily be achieved by studying ancient classical and Christian texts. Vives, like Erasmus, stressed that women should receive formal education (different than that men received) to create a woman full of wisdom, morality, and goodness. His most famous work on female education is *On the Education of a Christian Woman*, written for Princess Mary in 1523. Vives' success in England did not endure for his entire life. After criticizing Henry VIII for divorcing Catherine of Argon, Vives fled England to avoid execution, settling in Bruges (a town in the Low Countries) where he lived out his life.

Northern Renaissance Art

Art, like literary works, produced as part of the Renaissance in northern Europe also generally contained distinctive literary themes. The center of Renaissance art in northern Europe was the Low Countries ruled by the Duke of Burgundy. Within the Low Countries, Flanders produced some of the greatest artists.

Jan Van Eyck was one of the greatest artists from Flanders. Born about 1385, he is most famous for a type of three-dimensional oil painting. He achieved this effect by using a base of tempera on canvas over which were applied multiple coats of oil-based paints. Van Eyck's use of oil and tempera allowed him to paint with meticulous detail and realism that came to characterize all Flemish art. The Virgin Mary was one of his favorite subjects. Van Eych's technique allowed viewers to approach the Holy Virgin from the familiar perspective of family relations. His most famous painting is *The Virgin Mary and Child*. Viewers of this painting are drawn to the subject's robe and crown jewels. The realism with which Van Eyck depicts them adds an aura to the painting that transfixes the viewer to such an extent that it feels almost as if the subject and viewer are in the same room. Van Eyck was also famous for using a technique in which contemporary subjects were placed in a Biblical setting. Wealthy patrons hired Van Eyck to paint them in the company of the Virgin Mary, Baby Jesus, or other Biblical characters until his death in 1440.

Hieronymus Jerome Bosch (1450-1516), a Flemish contemporary of Van Eyck, also used religious themes in his paintings. Bosch, however, approached art differently than Van Eyck. Rather than producing work with realism, Bosch used fantasy, folk legends, and color to depict his religious message. His *Death and the Miser*, for example, depicts a miser in the throes of death agonizing over his ill-gotten gold that is controlled by rats and toads while an angel offers him the crucifix. In other words, he can choose earthly wealth and eternal damnation or heavenly bliss.

Many art historians regard Peter Paul Rubens as the greatest Flemish school painter of the Baroque period. He studied art in Italy before opening a large studio in Antwerp, Belgium. The Antwerp school attracted students from most European countries. Rubens used his students and instructors to paint sections of massive paintings he designed and became famous for. His work was in great demand at courts across Europe. He was commissioned to paint portraits of royal figures, such as King Philip IV of Spain. Like most Renaissance painters, his work depicted Biblical scenes. One such painting was *Descent from the Cross*.

Germany, like the Low Countries, also produced remarkable artists during the Northern Renaissance. German art stems from the tradition of quality its craftspeople developed. Renaissance artists extended the techniques and styles of German craftspeople to the fine arts. Simultaneously, the German nobility increased its patronage of the arts, which enabled artists to earn a living.

Albrecht Duer of Nuremberg is the best-known German Renaissance artist. His work reflects his craft background. As a youth, Duer served an apprenticeship under his father who was a goldsmith. His work as a goldsmith later enabled Duer to master numerous styles and techniques. In 1486 he found employment with a painter and woodcut designer, Michael Wolgemut. Duer worked for Wolgemut for four years, traveling throughout Germany and the Holy Roman Empire, but realized that if he wanted to become a master artist he must study Italian works. In 1494 and again in 1505 he journeyed to Italy. After each trip he earned important commissions from Holy Roman Emperor Maximilian I. After Maximilian's death in 1519, Duer visited the Netherlands where he studied the Flemish art of Van Eyck and others. Duer also befriended Martin Luther, believing the Protestant reformer had brought Christianity back to its first-century roots. Duer's art work made him wealthy. He lived in a large home near the Nuremberg Castle. Over the course of his life, he produced about 75 paintings, over 100 engravings, over 1,000 drawings, 250 woodcuts, and books on geometry, fortification, and the human body. One of his most famous paintings is the *Self Portrait*, which shows the artist looking like Christ but wearing a fur coat to show his prosperity. The *Self Portrait* was actually one of a series the artist produced. Duer most likely suffered from psychological illness. Throughout life he was prone to bouts of depression that sometimes lasted for weeks.

Two German contemporaries of Duer also became important Renaissance artists. Lucas Cranach (1472-1553) and Hans Holbein (1497-1543) did not master all the techniques and styles that Duer used but, nevertheless, both earned handsome commissions from wealthy patrons. Cranach, like Duer, came from a craft background. As a youngster, the Franconian learned engraving from his father. From 1500 to 1503 he served as court painter for Duke Frederick the Wise in Vienna. He often incorporated Biblical themes in his artwork. His paintings of early leaders of the Protestant Reformation in Saxony, including Martin Luther and Philip Melanchthon, are important to historians studying Reformation art.

Holbein, from Augsburg, was one of the few German artists who did not have a craft background. His father, Hans Holbein the Elder, was a well-known artist in his own right. He sent his son to Italy to study with Italian masters. Following his Italian sojourn, Holbein the Younger traveled throughout Europe creating commissioned art. In Basel, Switzerland he earned excellent fees providing illustrations for books published by Johann Froben, Erasmus's publisher. In addition to book illustrations, he also received commissions for portraits of Swiss nobles. Holbein also spent time in England where he painted portraits of famous people, including Thomas Cromwell, Sir Thomas More, Erasmus, and Anne of Cleves, a German princess who became one of Henry VIII's many wives.

Another famed German artist was the sculptor Tilman Riemenschneider (1460-1531). Although Riemenschneider is not in the category of Michelangelo or Donatello, he was a good artist. He is most remembered for the wooden alters he produced. Born in Heiligenstadt in the Erchsfeld, Thuringia, he moved to Wurzburg where he was admitted to the guild of painters, sculptors, and glaziers. Toward the end of his life, Riemenschneider was tried and tortured because he publicly sympathized with German peasants during the Peasant Revolts from 1524 to 1526. Like Duer, Riemenschneider was most likely afflicted with some sort of psychological disorder as he often experienced long bouts of depression.

The Iberian Peninsula produced El Greco. This famed artist used a style called Mannerism, popularized by Michelangelo. Mannerism was a reaction against the simplicity and symmetry of High Renaissance art. It allowed the artist to incorporate strange, abnormal things into his work. This style allowed artists to reflect individual perceptions and feelings, to paint in a "mannered" or "affected" way.

Literature

Literature, especially that written in the vernacular languages such as English, French, Spanish, and German, flourished in northern and western Europe during the Renaissance. English writers were the most important literary figures during the Renaissance.

Of all English writers, literary scholars regard William Shakespeare (1564-1616) as the most talented. The Bard of Avon, as Shakespeare is sometimes called, came from a wealthy family in Stratford-upon-Avon. His father was a glove maker and government official while his mother's family owned a substantial amount of land. He began writing in his early twenties and continued until his death. By 1592 he had moved to London where he was an actor and playwright. In 1594 he, along with other London actors and playwrights, formed a theatrical company, the King's Men, with whom he remained until he retired to his birthplace in 1611. During the course of his writing career, Shakespeare produced in excess of thirty-five plays, as well as numerous poems. He was an excellent playwright in two different genera—tragedy and comedy. He produced unrivaled masterpieces in both. Tragedies he wrote included *Hamlet, King Lear*, and *Macbeth*. His most beloved comedies included *Much Ado About Nothing*, and *A Midsummer Night's Dream*. Shakespeare's plays convey a sense of history, politics, and world affairs, as well as English and foreign culture. Sev-

Some of Shakespeare's most famous works include: *Hamlet, King Lear, Romeo and Juliet,* and *Macbeth.*

eral of his plays, including *Julius Caesar* and *Antony and Cleopatra,* deal with ancient historical events while others, such as *Richard III* and *Henry VIII,* offer critiques on events closer to Shakespeare's own historical time period. The Bard of Avon did not hesitate to set plays such as *Othello, The Merchant of Venice,* and *Two Gentlemen of Verona* in other countries, including Italy.

Shakespeare was an excellent psychologist. He completely understood many aspects of human behavior, which is evident in his plays. Characters he created bring to life every conceivable mood human beings are capable of experiencing—searing grief, airy romance, rousing nationalism, deadly hatred, betrayal, and humor. His work shows a familiarity with a wide variety of subjects—astronomy, politics, statecraft, alchemy, warfare, seamanship, intrigue, love, hate, life, and death.

Shakespeare was part of what English historians term the Elizabethan Renaissance, sparked by the reign of Elizabeth I (1558-1603). This period produced other remarkable literary figures like Christopher Marlow (1564-1593), Edmund Spenser (1552-1599), Sir Philip Sidney (1554-1586), and his sister, Mary Sidney (1561-1621). Marlow came from a working class background but earned degrees from Cambridge as a result of having received a scholarship to the prestigious university. He wrote seven plays and several volumes of poetry. His most important plays were *Edward II, Dr. Faustus, The Jew of Malta,* and *Tamburlain.* Marlow probably would have produced many more plays had he lived longer. Unfortunately, he died in a barroom brawl at the age of twenty-nine. Spencer was the most important English poet of the Renaissance. His greatest work, *Faerie Queene,* glorifies Elizabeth I. Like most poets and literary figures, Spencer believed Elizabeth I was the greatest monarch

Europe had produced. The Sidneys were friends of Spencer, as well as being important literary figures in their own right. Philip produced several volumes of poetry. His major work was a prose romance entitled *Arcadia* and a scholarly work, *Defense of Poetry.* Mary is noted for writing religious poems, translating Petrarch into English, producing beautiful elegies, and dramatic dialogues. Her most important work was a metrical version of *Psalms.*

Miguel de Cervantes (1547-1616) was Spain's greatest Renaissance literary figure. Cervantes spent most of his life impoverished. Born at Alcala de Henares, he wandered from place to place, holding a variety of low paying jobs. Forced to leave Spain after fighting a duel, he fled to Rome where he worked for a Catholic cardinal until 1570 when he enlisted in the Spanish army to fight against the Ottoman Turks. A

Miguel de Cervantes became a popular Renaissance author when he wrote *Don Quixote.*

few years later he fought in North Africa, where a ship he was on was captured by Moorish pirates who sold Cervantes into slavery in 1575. The Spanish government freed him in 1580 by paying the pirates a ransom. He returned to Spain where he chronicled his mishaps and wartime exploits in *Pictures of Algiers*. Cervantes then married, worked for the Spanish government, and was jailed for financial mismanagement. Despite the hardships, Cervantes wrote his masterpiece, *Don Quixote de la Mancha*, a scathing social satire. In the novel, Cervantes ridicules the Spanish nobility with a knight who was ready to tilt at windmills and who was a born loser. The novel also gives the reader a glimpse of Spanish and European society, especially its intolerances, injustice, and disregard for human beings.

France produced numerous novelists and poets during its Renaissance, including Francois Villon, called the thief, Louise Labe, the ropemaker's wife, Clemont Marot, and Queen Marquerita of Navarre. None of these writers were as important as Christine de Pisan (1363-1434). The daughter of an astrology professor employed by the French monarchy, Thomas de Pisan, Christine was the first woman to write professionally and the first published feminist. As a result of her father's presence at the French court, Pisan attained a superior education, which included instruction in Greek, Latin, French, and Italian literature, despite objections from her mother that learning would hinder Pisan's marital chances. Despite her mother's fears, Pisan married Etienne de Castel, a nobleman from Picardy who served as secretary to Charles V until the monarch died in 1380. Thereafter, her fortunes suffered. Thomas de Pisan lost his position with the new king, Charles VI, and died in 1385. In the fall of 1390 Pisan's husband also died from illness while traveling with Charles

VI to Beauvais. Pisan, at the age of twenty-five, was left with three children, a niece, and mother to support. In addition, she was the defendant in several lawsuits over her late husband's debts. Even though few opportunities for women to support themselves outside marriage existed, Pisan was determined to emulate Petrarch, her idol, and earn a living with the pen. She supported her family by writing poetry, copying books, and working as a notary. About 1393, she began to have success with poetry and literature. Her most important book was *The Book of the City of Ladies* in 1405. This work put forth the revolutionary idea that women were equal to men. She refuted all arguments that supported female inferiority, including those from the Bible. Previously, Pisan had touched off a debate that lasted throughout the Renaissance called the *Querelle de Femmes* (quarrel over women). This debate began when Pisan wrote *The Letter to the God of Love*, criticizing Jean de Meun's work, *Romance of the Rose*, for its misogyny. A heated exchange occurred between Pisan and Meun that attracted attention from other scholars. Pisan published a sequel to *The Book of the City of Ladies* entitled *The Treasure of the City of Ladies*, a handbook on etiquette for all women, including queens, servants, housewives, barmaids, and prostitutes. In this work Pisan urged all women to support each other because they could never be secure in marriage or work. Other works Pisan wrote included *The Body of Policy*, an advice handbook for kings, *The Book of Feates of Arms and Chivalry*, a work Henry VII liked so well he had it translated into English, *Book of Peace*, a text about the need for education, and *Hymn to Joan of Arc*, who Pisan viewed as an heroic woman and example of feminism.

Although German literature developed later than that in other northern European countries, Germany produced important literary figures during the Renaissance. Sebastian Brant (1457-1521) and Hans Sachs (1494-1576) were the most significant figures writing in vernacular German. Brant, a poet and lawyer, was known for poetic satire. His most famous work was *The Ship of Fools* published in 1494. Sachs, like Brant, was a master satirist, who was a prolific author, writing over 4000 songs, 1,700 folk tales, numerous poems, and about 200 plays.

MONARCHS

The literature, art, and other achievements of the Northern Renaissance could not have occurred without the support of strong monarchs. Like the merchant class in Italian city-states, monarchs north of the Alps patronized art, literature, and their creators while simultaneously creating strong nation states. These monarchs, who included Louis XI of France, Henry VII of England, Ferdinand and Isabella of Spain, and others are often called the "new monarchs" because they ruled with a strong hand and pursued nationalistic goals. Even though they had not read Machiavelli's works, they utilized principles he identified to maintain power. The new monarchs believed they were sovereign and tolerated no dissent. All opposition was immediately suppressed. The nobility, which during the Middle Ages had exerted sovereignty over territory within nations, were forcefully subdued. The new monarchs demanded absolute loyalty. Loyalty was achieved by reliance upon civil officials to collect taxes in towns independent of the local nobility. Middle class townspeople, especially merchants and artisans, were willing to pay taxes to a central government in return for protection from armies and knights employed by feudal landowners. This tax revenue was then used to crush local nobles and force their allegiance to the monarch. The ultimate result of

this was the creation of the modern nation-state, which was perhaps the greatest political achievement of the Renaissance.

France

The modern nation-state developed differently in France, England, and Spain. France had been seriously weakened by the Hundred Years' War. The monarchy was weak, the population had declined, business was in disarray, and farm production was low when Charles VII ascended to the throne in 1422. Under his rule, which lasted until 1461, France became one of the strongest nations in Europe. He made peace between the Burgundians and Armagnacs who had fought a civil war in France for more than thirty years and drove English armies from all French provinces except Calais by 1453. In addition, he imposed taxes on various items, including salt and land, to provide the royal treasury with a steady and reliable source of income. Much of the revenue Charles VII received was used to strengthen the French army. He created the first permanent army for the monarchy, organizing it into calvary and archery units. These changes eventually gave France the most formidable army in Europe. Charles VII also curtailed the power of the Roman Catholic Church. In 1438 he proclaimed in the Pragmatic Sanction of Bourges that a general council was superior to the Pope, giving the French monarch authority to appoint Church officials and collect Church revenue. In effect, Charles had taken control of the French Church from the Roman Pope and greatly strengthened the monarchy.

When Charles VII died in 1461, his son, Louis XI, became the French monarch. Nicknamed the Spider King because of his ruthless nature, Louis further strengthened the monarchy. He promoted industry and commerce, using tax revenue generated to enlarge the army. Under Louis XI commercial treaties with England, Portugal, Spain, and the Hanseatic League, allowing foreign craftsmen and products into France and French products into foreign markets, were negotiated. The Spider King also used his strong military to subdue rebellious nobles, take control over independent towns, and annex territory, including Burgundy, Anjou, Bar, Maine, and Provence.

French expansion continued after the Spider King died in 1483. The marriage of Louis XI (1498-1515) to Anne of Brittany added the Duchy of Brittany to France. In 1516 Francis I and Pope Leo X signed the Concordat of Bologna, which repaired the relationship between the papacy and the French monarchy. This agreement overturned the Pragmatic Sanction of Bourges and gave the Pope authority to take the first year's income from French Church officials. In return, the Church gave the French monarchy the right to choose bishops, abbots, and other top Church officials. Since French kings could appoint Church officials, they controlled Church policies and practices. The monarchy had created a national Church.

England

England also experienced nationalism and had strong monarchs during the Renaissance. Several strong monarchs increased the power of the national government. Edward IV (1461-1483) began the process of healing England from the ravages of the War of the Roses. From 1455 to 1471 two noble factions, the Yorks and Lancasters, fought a civil war. This War of the Roses, so called because the Lancaster symbol was a red rose and the York symbol was a white rose, devastated England, hurting commerce, industry, agriculture, and people. Edward IV, a member of the York faction, defeated the Lancasters in 1471 and rebuilt the English monarchy that had lost much of its authority during the war. He, along with his successors, brother Richard III (1483-1485) and Henry VII (1485-1509), the first Tutor king, destroyed the power of the nobility and established law and order throughout England. Methods used by all three rulers were brutal, lethal, ruthless, efficient, and conducted largely in secrecy.

One device these English kings employed to strengthen the monarchy was to bypass Parliament. Before Edward IV became king, the monarch was dependent on Parliament for revenue, a condition made necessary by the high cost of the Hundred Years' War. Since the nobility dominated Parliament, they controlled the monarch by holding the purse strings. It was impossible for the English kings to fight wars without Parliamentary approval and financing. Rather than seek the approval of the nobles who controlled Parliament, Edward IV, Richard III, and Henry VII used diplomacy to conduct foreign policy rather than war. The use of diplomacy meant that the English monarchy was no longer dependent upon Parliament for financing, which curtailed the influence of the nobility within the government.

Another device English monarchs used to increase their power was the Royal Council. This institution consisted of about fifteen middle class men with backgrounds in law or business. Generally, aristocrats were excluded from the Royal Council, which conducted its business at the pleasure of the monarch and dealt with all matters the king requested. Its scope included legislative, executive, and judicial authority. The Royal Council used terror and secrecy to dispose of threats to its authority. The Star Chamber Court was the most notorious device the Royal Council employed, which derived its name from stars painted on the courtroom's ceiling. People tried within this infamous institution were not permitted access to evidence prosecutors had compiled against them. Court sessions were held in absolute secrecy, judges ordered victims tortured to attain bogus confessions, and jury trials were forbidden. Although such practices violated English common law, Henry VII and other English monarchs effectively used the Court of the Star Chamber to control the nobility.

English monarchs also broke the power of the nobility by formulating and pursuing governmental policies that benefited the upper middle class. Influential people engaged in commercial farming or business pursuits disliked violence, chaos, and crime. Consequently, the English national government enacted laws promoting peace and order to secure support from the upper middle class. In return, the upper middle class generally did not object to institutions such as the Star Chamber Court, especially if it was used to punish criminals and prevent future crime.

English kings bypassed nobles in regards to law enforcement. Because England did not have a permanent army or a permanent governmental bureaucracy, Henry VII, Richard III, and Edward IV empowered local judicial officials to act on behalf of the central government. These Justices of the Peace, usually large landowners elected by local voters, enforced laws, punished criminals, collected taxes, controlled wages, set prices, inspected scales, and regulated personal moral behavior in the name of the king. During the Middle Ages, English noblemen had carried out these functions.

Henry VII was the most ruthless English Renaissance monarch. Serious, secretive, economically conservative, and utterly brutal, he made Great Britain one of the leading nations in Europe. He accomplished this by encouraging industrial development, especially in the wool and textile industries, and strengthening the navy and merchant marine so that Albion's products could be sold worldwide. Henry also turned back an Irish invasion and made peace with Scotland by marrying his daughter Margaret to the Scottish king. When Henry VII died in 1509, the England he left was a wealthy, peaceful, prosperous nation on the verge of becoming a world power.

Spain

Spain did not experience the same kind of nationalism during the Renaissance that England and France experienced. Until the eighteenth century Spain existed as a loose confederation of states with each one having its own legislature, courts, system of taxation, and separate monetary system. Two monarchs, Ferdinand and Isabella, did, however, strengthen royal authority in Spain at the expense of Spanish nobles. This was accomplished by investing with royal authority an old medieval institution, the *hermandades*, or brotherhoods. Ferdinand and Isabella gave the *hermandades* power to apprehend, try, and punish criminals. Leaders of the brotherhoods took orders from royal officials and often acted on behalf of the monarchy.

Like their counterparts in England, the Spanish monarchs curtailed the power of the Spanish nobles by using a Royal Council. They prohibited aristocrats from serving on this governmental agency, which greatly reduced the influence of Spain's largest landholders. Ferdinand and Isabella gave themselves the right to appoint council members. They appointed only middle class artisans and businessmen to the Royal Council. Most council members had training in Roman law and owed allegiance to the monarchy. Ferdinand and Isabella invested the Royal Council with tremendous power, making it the central feature of Spanish government during their reign from 1474 to 1516. This institution had complete authority to make, enforce, and interpret Spanish laws.

Ferdinand and Isabella used the Catholic Church to exert control in Spain. Like Charles VII in France, the Spanish monarchs got authority to appoint Church officials. An agreement was negotiated with the Spanish-born Pope, Alexander VI, under which Ferdinand and Isabella was given the authority to appoint bishops throughout Spain and its holdings in Latin America. This authority enabled the Spanish monarchs, whom the Pope gave the title "Catholic Kings of Spain," de facto authority to create and control a national Church. Revenue the monarchy received from the Church enabled the monarchs to create a strong army, which was used to drive the Moors from Granada in 1492 and complete the *reconquista*, a struggle to recapture Spanish lands that Muslim Arabs had held for eight centuries.

Ferdinand and Isabella, like other European Renaissance monarchs, utilized terror to exert control over their subjects. The device they used most frequently was the *Inquisition*. In 1478, Pope Sixtus IV issued a decree allowing governments to establish tribunals to root out religious heretics in Catholic countries. On September 28, 1480, Ferdinand and Isabella ordered tribunals established in Spain. The Spanish Inquisition, as these tribunals were called, was used primarily to curry favor with the Spanish population, which was suspicious of the large minority of Muslim and Jewish converts to Catholicism residing on the Iberian Peninsula. Ferdinand and Isabella realized that most Spanish Catholics hated the Arab and Jewish Christians who had been forced to convert during the fifteenth century. If the royal government protected the

Although Isabella allowed the Inquisition to come to Castile, she demanded that Pope Sixtus relinquish control over the inquisitors and the confiscated wealth to the government.

conversos, it likely would lose support from the population, but if they were not protected, rioting was likely to occur in towns when Spanish Catholics attacked the conversos. Ferdinand and Isabella decided to win popular approval and prevent rioting by establishing the Inquisition.

Compounding the problem was that the conversos, who numbered about 250,000 in the Spanish population of more than 7,000,000, held prominent positions in business and government, which enabled them to exert influence disproportionate to their population. Conversos, for example, held about 30 percent of the positions on the Royal Council, controlled the Spanish treasury, served as archbishops, bishops, and abbots in the Spanish Church, intermarried with the nobility, held prominent positions in medicine and law, created successful businesses, and served as tax collectors. The fact that conversos held prominent positions within Spain produced jealousy and racism within the Catholic population. Traditional Spanish Catholics insisted that the conversos had abandoned Christianity and reverted to their Jewish or Muslim roots. Catholics invoked racism to use against conversos, maintaining that ethnically an individual was what his or her ancestors were before conversion. Thus, a person whose ancestors were Jewish or Muslim remained a Jew or Muslim even after conversion to Christianity. This racial theory, which violated Biblical doctrine, evolved to hold that all conversos were evil and controlled by Satan. Spanish Catholics maintained that the immoral and malicious conversos were by their ethnic nature criminals and thus could not be converted to Christianity. Furthermore, Spanish anti-Semitism alleged that Jews were plotting to control all governmental and religious offices in Spain unless they were stopped. This, anti-Semites believed, posed a threat to Spanish national unity. The Inquisition was thus created and used to rid Spain of these perceived threats and the heretical conversos. The Inquisition, although primarily a Catholic device to uphold Catholic faith, was not controlled by the Church in Spain. Rather, Ferdinand and Isabella controlled and used it to politically unify Spain. The tribunals commonly employed torture to force confessions from Jewish and Muslim converts to Catholicism, as well as from Protestants. After the Inquisition had been created, Ferdinand and Isabella expelled by royal edict all Jews from Spain in 1492. The royal couple demanded that Spain develop as a nation unified by Catholic orthodoxy, free from Muslim and Jewish influences.

Nationalism that developed in the Renaissance produced a wave of overseas exploration that eventually led to the establishment of colonies. Northern European countries led the way across the ocean.

EXPLORATION AND EXPANSION

Toward the end of the Renaissance, the strong monarchies and nationalism they generated caused northern and western European nations to begin a period of overseas exploration and expansion. This "Age of Expansion," as the period from 1415 until 1650 is often called, resulted in the migration of Europeans to other continents and European political, economic, and social control of North and South America, coastal regions of Africa, India, China, Japan, and many Pacific islands.

Before significant oceanic exploration could occur, improvements in navigation and technology had to take place. Before the Renaissance brought its technological revolution to Europe, navigational methods were primitive. Viking sailors, the best medieval Europe produced, calculated their position on the ocean by viewing the sun with the naked eye. They could only guess at the speed their ships traveled and the distance covered. However, all this had changed by the middle part of the fifteenth century.

By that time European sailors were using various mechanical devices to help with navigation on the open ocean. The most important navigational device was the compass. Invented by the Chinese, the compass was a simple tool that consisted of a magnetic needle fastened to a piece of wood marked with directions. Since the magnetized needle always pointed toward the earth's magnetic North Pole, navigators could always determine the direction their ship was traveling. In addition to being able to mechanically determine direction of travel, ship captains could also fix their precise location on the ocean's surface by using the astrolabe, quadrant, and sextant. All three instruments enabled navigators to measure the altitude and position of stars in relation to the earth's surface and thus precisely locate a ship on the ocean. Used in conjunction with the compass, ship captains could correctly and accurately record direction, distance, location, speed, and use maps to plot courses through waters of the known world.

Not only were improvements in navigation made, but Europeans also benefited from better ships. The medieval European ship was a relative small vessel with one sail, high sides, and wide bodies, with a steering rudder on its side. The sail was useful only if the wind blew from behind the ship because it could not be rotated. For locomotion these ships often relied upon slaves to man oars. Over time, modifications in ship design occurred. Important changes included more, larger, and adjustable sails. By using a sailing tactic called "tacking" and a new

type of rigging developed by Arabs called the lanteen sail, ships could position various sails to travel into the wind. No longer did ships have to travel in the direction the wind blew, now they could move against it. European ships in the fifteenth and sixteenth centuries also became longer, sleeker, faster, and more stable and improved rudder designs made them more maneuverable. Such improvements were first manifest in Portuguese caravels and carracks during the 1400s and in Portuguese, Spanish, French, Dutch, and English galleons in the 1600s.

Another important technological innovation that made possible European exploration was the use of gunpowder. Although its origins are not clear, most likely the Arabs invented gunpowder around 1,000 A.D. The Chinese, who had traded with Arabic peoples, were using gunpowder when Marco Polo visited Carthay (the European name for China). Europeans were quick to find a military use for this invention. During the early years of the fourteenth century gunpowder was used to shoot objects from cannons

The triangular sails of the caravel were augmented by square sails to help catch the wind from many directions.

and eventually small arms were invented. Without gunpowder, cannon, and personal firearms, it is doubtful that Europeans could have prevailed in war against Native Americans because of the small number of European soldiers that could be sustained in the New World.

The modern age of exploration began with Portugal during the fifteenth century. Portugal's exploration began largely as a result of Prince Henry the Navigator's quest to make contact with the nation of Prester John. According to legend, Prester John was a Catholic priest who governed a Christian state somewhere in Africa or Asia. Prince Henry, being a devout Catholic and thus anti-Muslim, wanted to contact Prester John in hopes of forming a Christian alliance that would encircle Muslim nations. To achieve this objective, Prince Henry undertook a major exploration along Africa's western coast. Although Prince Henry personally did not sail on any of these voyages, his financial assets were critical to their success. Portuguese explorers, who may or may not have believed in the existence of Prester John, realized there were vast profits to be made in Africa. Portuguese ships left Cape St. Vincent, the westernmost point on the European continent, under the authority of Prince Henry. Their captains, who were paid handsomely by Prince Henry, pushed farther south and west. In 1445, Dinis Dias sailed around Cape Verde and passed beyond the Sahara Desert. On a voyage in 1455, Alivse da Cadamosto sailed up the mouth of the Senegal and Gambia Rivers and discovered the Cape Verde Islands. At the same time, the Portuguese had found and colonized the Madeira and the Azores Islands in the Atlantic Ocean west of Portugal. After Prince Henry died in 1460, his exploration program was continued under various Portuguese monarchs. However, Portugal was no longer concerned with contacting Prester John. The goal was to find the southern tip of Africa, sail around it, and reach India, China, and Japan. If Portugal could discover a water route to Asia, it could control the spice trade, which had been dominated by Italian and Arab traders for centuries.

In 1488 Portugal achieved its goal of sailing around Africa. Bartolomeu Dias rounded the Cape of Good Hope at the southern tip of Africa and saw the Indian Ocean for the first time. Dias had to turn back before reaching Asia because his sailors were afraid to go farther. Ten years later, Portugal finally found its ocean route to Asia. Vasco da Gama set sail in 1497 intending to go beyond the Cape of Good Hope. The

Vasco da Gama

King Ferdinand and Queen Isabella are pictured here with Christopher Columbus.

next year da Gama reached India. Later expeditions reached China. Portugal had achieved its goal of dominating the spice trade. After reaching India, Portugal began to build a commercial empire in Africa and Asia. This was accomplished by establishing numerous trading posts at places such as Sao Tome and the Cape Verde Islands, Ceylon, and Malabar, India. Portuguese control was completed in 1509 when a Muslim fleet was destroyed in a naval battle at Diu in the Indian Ocean. This victory ensured that Portugal would be the dominant power in Asia. By 1550 Portugal had a world monopoly on the spice trade. Its empire stretched from the Persian Gulf to the Pacific.

Portugal, after discovering an oceanic route to Asia, mostly lost interest in further explorations westward across the Atlantic. However, a storm blew the ships of Pedro Alvares Cabral off course in 1500, and he reached the coast of Brazil, which eventually became a Portuguese colony. With the exception of Brazil, Portugal established few colonies in the Western Hemisphere. Exploration and colonization of North

and South America was largely left to other European countries, including Spain, England, France, and the Netherlands.

Jealous of Portugal's success and fearful of its power, Spain wanted to challenge Portugal's mastery of the seas. Like Portugal, Spain sought an ocean route to the riches of Asia. An Italian sea captain, Christopher Columbus, persuaded Ferdinand and Isabella in 1492 that a third trade route to Asia could be discovered by sailing westward across the Atlantic. Spain's fear of Portugal's increasing power, coupled with Columbus' promises of gold, glory, and colonies, caused Ferdinand and Isabella to take a chance on this Italian sailor. Spain provided Columbus with three small ships: the *Nina, Pinta,* and *Santa Maria.* Columbus set sail for China in August 1492. After stopping for repairs and supplies in the Canary Islands, it took Columbus just over

The harbor at Genoa from where Columbus began his journey.

Columbus returned to the court of Ferdinand and Isabella with gifts and natives from the New World. The explorer's tales of vast gold deposits persuaded the king and queen to finance further expeditions.

a month to cross the Atlantic. He landed on a small, flat island in the Bahamas, probably Samana Cay. Columbus erroneously believed he had landed on an island near the Asian mainland and thus called the native people he encountered *Indios* (Spanish for Indian). Columbus then explored parts of Cuba and an island he called Hispaniola (today Haiti and the Dominican Republic). After capturing several Native Americans as proof that he had reached Asia, Columbus returned triumphantly to Spain. There, he was knighted and given the title Admiral of the Ocean. Isabella and Ferdinand believed Spain had found a short route to the wealth of Asia. Columbus made several more voyages to the Americas between 1493 and 1504.

He explored numerous islands in the Caribbean and on his third voyage reached Venezuela in South America. On his fourth voyage in 1504, he visited the southern tip of North America, briefly exploring Honduras, Nicaragua, Costa Rica, and Panama.

Eventually, some Europeans realized that Columbus had not reached Asia but a new continent. One was the adventurer Amerigo Vespucci. An Italian like Columbus, Vespucci was part of a Portuguese expedition that explored the coast of South America in 1499. In 1500, he published a series of vivid and largely fictional descriptions of the lands he visited. Vespucci was the first European to describe the lands Columbus reached as *mundus novus*, or New

World. In 1507, a geographer, Martin Waldseemuller, published a map depicting lands west of Europe as a separate continent, which he labeled America in honor of Vespucci.

Largely as a result of Columbus' exploration, Spain replaced Portugal as Europe's most dominant nation. In 1573, the Spanish explorer Vasco Nunez de Balboa crossed the Isthmus of Panama, seeing the Pacific Ocean for the first time. In 1520, a Portuguese navigator sailing for Spain accomplished what Columbus failed to do—find an ocean route to Asia. Ferdinand Magellan sailed around a passage at the tip of South America into the Pacific Ocean that was named the Straits of Magellan in his honor. Magellan eventually reached the Philippine Islands where he died after a fight with the native people. Finally, one of his ships reached Spain by sailing around the tip of Africa, marking the first time a European ship had circumnavigated the Earth. Other Spanish explorers, including Ponce de Leon in 1513, Cortez in 1519, and Pizarro in

Ferdinand Magellan

1531 continued Spanish explorations throughout the Western Hemisphere. As a result of Columbus' explorations, in the Treaty of Tordesilles Spain claimed all of the Americas with exception of Brazil, which was awarded to Portugal. In 1580 Spain gained control of Portugal and for a time controlled all of the New World where they forced into submission Native American people and largely destroyed their cultures through warfare and disease.

Five years after Columbus' voyage, England sent Giovanni Caboto (John Cabot), a Venetian sea captain, on an exploratory expedition to North America. Cabot, in 1497 and 1498, explored along the Atlantic coast from the Chesapeake Bay to Newfoundland. Like Columbus, Cabot sought an oceanic route to Asia westward across the Atlantic or, as he referred to it, a Northwest Passage. Cabot's voyage in 1497 represents the first recorded Trans-Atlantic voyage by an English ship although some evidence indicates that English fishermen might have accidentally landed in Nova Scotia and Newfoundland in the 1480s. Regardless, English historians give Cabot credit for discovering North America. The English based their territorial claims in the New World upon Cabot's voyages. Perhaps Cabot would have undertaken further explorations had he not died on his second voyage to America in 1498. John's son, Sebastian, continued England's explorations. In 1508 and 1509 he sailed across the Atlantic attempting to find a Northwest Passage to China, but success eluded him. He did, however, explore in the Hudson Bay region of North America, which England claimed.

After Sebastian Cabot failed to find the Northwest Passage, England lost interest in the New World for about seventy-five years. When Elizabeth I took the throne, English interest in overseas exploration revived. The driving force behind exploration under Elizabeth I was Sir

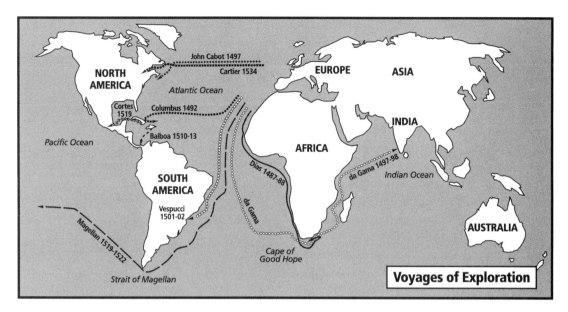

Voyages of Exploration

Humphrey Gilbert. Originally, Gilbert wanted to do what the Cabots had not done, find the Northwest Passage. Earlier, Gilbert published a book on the subject, speculating about where such a passage might be located. He also promised readers, who might be potential investors in an expedition to find a northern route to Asia, that wealth awaited those smart enough to find a new trade route. In 1576, Gilbert convinced Elizabeth I that it was in England's national interest to find the Northwest Passage

In 1576, at the behest of Gilbert, the Queen sent Martin Frobisher to find the Northwest Passage. Frobisher sailed into Labrador where he captured an Eskimo, taking him and the kayak he was paddling from the Atlantic. Frobisher returned to England with the Eskimo and a small sample of gold ore. After assayers determined that the ore contained gold, Elizabeth in 1577 organized a joint stock company to construct a fort and mining operations in Labrador. This company financed two expeditions by Frobisher in 1577 and 1578. During these trips to Labrador Frobisher captured three more Eskimos and

brought back two thousand tons of gold ore. The Eskimos, like the first one in 1576, died soon after arriving in England, and the gold ore was not real after all. Frobisher had brought back "fools gold" (iron pyrite). This mistake ruined his reputation.

Gilbert, distrusting Frobisher, had refused to invest in the 1577 and 1578 expeditions. When Frobisher returned with fools gold, Gilbert took advantage of the explorer's misfortune. He persuaded Elizabeth to grant him a charter to explore, settle, and govern all territory in North America not occupied by Christian people. The English charter completely disregarded all claims Native Americans had upon land in the New World. Gilbert, for some time, had tried to convince the Queen that England should be more interested in land than gold.

Gilbert set sail in 1583. He reached Nova Scotia where the voyage was aborted due to bad weather. On the return voyage to England Gilbert's ship sank during a storm. His death prompted his stepbrother, Sir Walter Raleigh,

Sir Walter Raleigh

nearby tribes of Native Americans. After one year, the colony was abandoned, and the Englishmen returned home. In 1587, Raleigh tried again to settle Roanoke Island. Like the earlier one, this second attempt to plant an English colony in North America was doomed for failure. John White headed the Roanoke Island settlement, which included women and children. Within a year, the Roanoke settlement vanished. Its disappearance is one of the biggest mysteries in history.

England's next attempt at colonization in North America was successful. In 1606 the English government granted a charter to investors for the Virginia Company. Initially, investors in

to attempt to colonize the New World for England. Raleigh received permission from Elizabeth I to explore and establish a colony in North America. The result was the ill-fated adventure at Roanoke Island. In 1584, Raleigh dispatched an exploring party, which surveyed Roanoke Island off the coast of present-day North Carolina. The next year Raleigh dispatched six hundred men to the colony. These men, many of whom were soldiers, raided Spanish ships in the Caribbean before leaving about 108 of their number on Roanoke Island. This attempt at settlement failed due to poor relations with

the Virginia Company dreamed of finding gold and silver but soon realized these minerals were not available along the Atlantic seaboard. They then attempted to make money by trading with Native Americans and establishing an agricultural colony in North America. In December 1606, the Virginia Company sent Captain Christopher Newport and 144 men on three ships, the "Susan Constant," "Godspeed," and "Discovery," to establish a colony near Roanoke Island. Thirty-nine of the men died on the Atlantic crossing, but, in May 1607, the survivors landed at a site they named Jamestown in honor of King James I. This settlement, in territory Raleigh had earlier named Virginia after Elizabeth I, the so-called Virgin Queen, became the first permanent English colony in North America.

The English and Spanish had rivals for control of North America. France and the Netherlands explored and colonized areas in the New World. French claims in North America were based on explorations by Giovanni da Verrazzano in 1524 and Jacques Cartier in 1534. Verrazzano, an Italian mariner, sailed westward across the Atlantic under the authority of Frances I. He explored along the East Coast from South Carolina to New England, claiming all this territory for France. Cartier, following in Verrazzano's wake, led three expeditions between 1534 and 1542 through the St. Lawrence River Valley, reaching sites where the modern cities of Montreal and Quebec are located. Because the French were interested in trading with Native Americans, Cartier established the first French colony in 1541, but the effort failed due to political upheaval in France. It was not until 1608 that the French successfully established a settlement in Canada. Samuel de Champlain built a fort at Quebec on the St. Lawrence River and sent out explorers who claimed the Ohio and Mississippi River Valleys and all territory surrounding the Great Lakes for France.

Dutch claims to North American territory were based on the explorations of Henry Hudson, an English sea captain. In 1609, Hudson, in the employ of the Netherlands, was sent to search for the Northwest Passage. He explored Delaware Bay, New York, the Hudson River, and Hudson Bay. Like the French, Hudson was interested in establishing a fur-trading network with Native Americans. To achieve this objective, the Dutch established forts on Manhattan Island, which they called New Amsterdam and at Albany (Fort Orange) in 1624. For a time New Amsterdam and Fort Orange prospered. The Iroquois people supplied furs in return for Dutch trade goods until England forcefully seized the colony in 1664.

CONCLUSION

The Renaissance in Europe was an exciting time. The continent emerged from the Dark Ages, and a revival of learning took place. The revival of interest in classical texts stimulated one of the greatest periods of human creativity in all recorded history. Italy, because it was the most urbanized part of Europe, first experienced the Renaissance, but northern European countries eventually became as thirsty for knowledge as were the Italians. The Renaissance forever changed western civilization. Humanism, secularism, and individualism became the dominant modes of thought throughout Europe, and scholars imbued with these ideas produced hundreds of works that laid the foundation for the modern world.

Remarkable men and women did remarkable things. Artists produced numerous works influenced by the ancient civilizations. Artists became celebrated figures in Renaissance countries. Wealthy patrons viewed art as power and commissioned artists to produce works to impress others with their status and wealth. Literature and other forms of scholarly writing were also important. Aiding the literary works produced in the Renaissance was the printing press. For the first time in history, it was possible to reproduce the printed word many times over. Nationalism was also an important component of the Renaissance. Strong monarchs in various countries, taking advantage of nationalistic feelings, unified their countries and sent out voyages of exploration to other parts of the world, beginning a process that, over time, saw European influence permeate the entire world. Statecraft became an important component of government, especially in Italy where so many independent city-states existed.

Despite these achievements, the Renaissance was marked by inequality for women, stigmatized by slavery and traumatized by war. However, a few women overcame social barriers and participated in the Renaissance, producing scholarly writings and artwork. Despite the achievements of a few, most women did not fully participate in Renaissance society. They were, at best, second-class citizens who were subject to many inequalities and an unjust legal system.

Even though inequality and injustice were part of society, scholars often date the beginning of the modern world to the Renaissance. This amazing period of artistic, scholarly, political, and literary achievement influenced many events to come. The Protestant Reformation was one such event. The Renaissance emphasis on humanism, individualism, and secularism would, in the sixteenth century, give rise to the Reformation, perhaps the greatest religious upheaval Europe would witness.

Suggestions for Further Reading

Hans Baron, *The Crisis of the Early Italian Renaissance: Civic Humanism and Republican Liberty in the Age of Classicism and Tyranny* (1966).

James Beck, *Italian Painting of the Renaissance* (1981).

Marvin B. Becker, *Civility and Society in Western Europe, 1300-1600* (1988).

Thomas G. Bergin, *Boccacio* (1981).

J. M. Clark, *The Great German Mystics: Eckhart, Tauler and Suso* (1961).

Alistair C. Crombie, *Medieval and Early Modern Science* (1961).

Amos Funkerstein, *Theology and the Scientific Imagination from the Middle Ages to the Seventeenth Century* (1986).

Richard A. Goldthwaite, *The Building of Renaissance Florence: An Economic and Social History* (1980).

J. R. Hale, *Machiavelli and Renaissance Italy* (1966).

J. R. Hale, *Renaissance Europe: The Individual and Society, 1480-1520* (1978).

George Holmes, *Florence, Rome and the Origins of the Renaissance* (1986).

George Holmes, *The Oxford History of Italy* (1997).

George Holmes, ed., *Art and Politics in Renaissance Italy* (1993).

J. Huizinga, *Erasmus of Rotterdam* (1952).

Christiane Klapisch-Zuber *Women, Family and Ritual in Renaissance Italy* (1985).

Christiane Klapisch-Zuber, *A History of Women* (1994).

Paul O. Kristeller, *Renaissance Thought and Its Sources* (1979).

Lauro Martines, *The Social World of the Florentine Humanists* (1963).

M. M. Phillips, *Erasmus and the Northern Renaissance* (1956).

Chapter

13

THE REFORMATION

Martin Luther, the second son of a German copper miner who had become a mine owner, was alone and frightened while crossing a field during a severe thunderstorm. Without warning, a loud clap of thunder and a bolt of lightening knocked Luther, a man in his early twenties, to the ground. The experienced terrified him. He began to see his short life passing in front of his eyes. Thinking that he was dying, Luther cried out to St. Anne, the mother of the Virgin Mary and the patron of travelers in distress, that he would enter a monastery if God allowed him to live. Miraculously, or so he thought, the storm abated. Luther arose, thanked God and St. Anne, and continued on his way. The thunderstorm experience changed Luther's life and the history of Western Christianity. Because Luther had promised St. Anne that he would enter a monastery and devote his life to God if he were spared, the young German faced a dilemma. His father, Hans, an omnipotent figure who dominated the Luther household, was determined that his second son would become a lawyer, a profession that would enable Luther to earn a handsome living and offer many opportunities for the family's upward social mobility. Hans had spent considerable money and endured personal deprivation to see that his son received a good education. Eventually, Luther earned a Masters' degree with distinction in 1505. At his parents' behest, Luther enrolled in law school but never studied law. Without consulting Hans, Luther entered the Order of the Hermits of St. Augustine on July 17, 1505, keeping his vow to St. Anne. Hans was furious. He ranted and raged, thinking that the money and personal sacrifice he had expended to make his son a lawyer had been wasted. Little did he know that Luther would begin a revolution twelve years later that would completely change western civilization.

Luther's decision to enter a monastery was actually an attempt to resolve a long-standing spiritual conflict within his mind. The young German was obsessed with his own sinfulness and tormented by guilt. He joined a monastery hoping that life as a hermit would enable him to be forgiven of his earthly sins and absolve him of guilt. Luther was a conscientious friar, pursuing every possible way of penitence, including lengthy fasts, prayers, self-denial, frequent confessions, and self-flagellation. None of these acts relieved the sense of guilt he felt at being a sinner until another extraordinary experience in a castle tower (restrooms were located in castle towers) at Wittenberg, where he served as a university lecturer on theology, alleviated his guilt. While in the tower, Luther received what he believed to be a visionary insight from God that brought peace to his troubled mind. Prior to the tower experience, he could not understand how a sinner could receive anything from God other than being cast in hell's fiery pits. In the tower vision, however, Luther understood that God was merciful and just. This insight enabled him to develop the principle of "justification by faith" upon which the Protestant Reformation was based. Luther now understood that God forgave sinners and made them righteous through the gift of grace, which was achieved by faith. Luther then began to question activities within the Catholic Church, such as the sale of indulgences, that violated this "truth" God had revealed in the Wittenberg castle tower. In 1517 Luther nailed his Ninety-five Theses to the church door in Wittenberg, beginning the Protestant Reformation that shattered the unity of Western Christendom. Had the young German become a lawyer, as his father wanted, the Protestant Reformation might not have occurred, and Luther most likely would not have had an influence upon the world a half millennium after his life ended.

Chronology

1483	Martin Luther born.
1484	Ulrich Zwingli born.
1509	John Calvin born.
1517	Ninety-Five Theses composed.
1519	Leipzig Debate with John Eck.
1520	Luther branded as a heretic by a Papal Bull.
1521	Luther's ideas published in three pamphlets.
1521	Diet of Worms.
1521-1555	Habsburg-Valois Wars
1524-25	The Peasant's War
1525	Luther marries a former nun.
1527	Henry VIII requests an annulment of his marriage to Catherine of Argon.
1529	Term Protestant first used after Diet of Speyer.
1529	Zwingli meets with Luther at Marburg
1533	Calvin converts to Protestantism.
1534	Calvin flees from France and goes to Geneva.
1534	Acts of Supremacy passed by English Parliament.
1535	Melchiorites gain control of Munster
1535	Order of Ursuline Nuns founded
1536	Calvin publishes *The Institutes of the Christian Religion*.
1541	Calvin establishes a theocracy in Geneva.
1545	Council of Trent convened.
1549	Book of Common Prayer Written.
1553-1558	Bloody Mary reigns in England.
1558	Elizabeth I becomes English Queen.
1560	John Knox creates Calvinist church in Scotland.
1563	Thirty-Nine Articles composed.
1564	Book of Common Order Published.
1572	St. Bartholomew's Day Massacre.
1585	War of the Three Henrys begins.
1588	Spanish Armada defeated.
1598	Edict of Nantes
1618	Thirty Years War begins.

BACKGROUND TO THE REFORMATION

For sixteenth-century Europeans, the most momentous event in their lives was not overseas exploration, nationalism, or the Renaissance but the Protestant Reformation, an event that shattered the unity of Western Europe under the Roman Catholic Church. Two sides within Christianity—the protestors, or Protestants, and Catholics—arose, and each believed that its views and doctrines were righteous while those of the other were heretical. This confrontation between Catholics and Protestants throughout Europe lasted for more than a century, produced countless wars, and killed thousands of people, leading one wit to comment, "more people have been killed in the name of God than for any other reason."

The Protestant Reformation occurred among such a wide complex of change that scholars often regard the sixteenth century as the transition from medieval Europe to the modern age. By 1500, the Renaissance, after a century and a half in Italy, blossomed on both sides of the Alps. In intellectual circles classical antiquity furnished the inspiration for arts and learning, and the courtier had replaced the monk as the "ideal" person. Commercial expansion and overseas exploration had broadened the horizons of Western Europe while secularism and humanism had created a strong interest in temporal things. The emphasis of the medieval manorial and guild economy on community welfare was being replaced by individualistic capitalism that emphasized profit making. Middle class people were challenging nobles and high-ranking church officials for power, privileges, and prestige. Peasants and artisans were becoming impatient with medieval obligations and restrictions. The increasing power of national monarchies, which upheld the principle of state sovereignty, reduced the power of the Catholic Church, its Pope, and the Holy Roman Empire, institutions that during the Middle Ages had largely controlled the Christian Commonwealth (*Corpus Christianum*). Amid all this change, the Protestant Reformation fragmented the ecclesiastical unity of Western Europe.

Despite the secular tendencies the Renaissance stimulated, the sixteenth century was still a religious age, and the Reformation was primarily a religious movement that involved most people in European societies. From one perspective, the Reformation was a religious revival whose main concern was salvation. Individuals took religion seriously, and it was a way of life. Sixteenth-century Europeans looked to both the church and state to foster religious life. Religious issues were closely tied to economic, political, and social issues. Demands for social justice usually were couched in religious language taken from the Bible. It is difficult to understand why people vexed by social, economic, and political changes they did not understand would also support religious reform.

The need for reform in the Church was a theme found within Christianity almost from the time of its inception. Early Christian monasticism, the Benedictine Rule, the Cluniac, Cistercian, and Franciscan movements were all motivated by a desire to bring Christian life into conformity with the highest Christian ideals. The medieval conflict between church and state began as an attempt to free the church from political control, which had subordinated Christian values to political expediency. Medieval reform, however, was not permanent. After a few years the Church, like the ancient Israelites, strayed from the "will of God" and needed to be taken back to its original commitment. In the century and a half before Luther began his reformation, most serious efforts within the Church had failed. The Englishman, John Wyclif, for example, had been declared a heretic. Jan Hus and Girolamo Savonarola had been burned at the stake. Desiderius Erasmus had been ordered to keep quite, and the Roman Church banned his books. Church councils, which had been called from time to time, accomplished little. Popes, bishops, abbots, and priests often behaved immorally. Monks were perceived as being fat and lazy. Not all Church officials fit these perceptions but enough did to give the Church a bad reputation. The behavior of Church officials, coupled with the corruption, was enough to undermine respect lay people had for the institution. When various individuals began criticizing the Catholic Church, common people, aware of problems within the Church, began to take allegations of the detractors seriously.

PROBLEMS IN THE CHURCH AND ORIGINS OF THE REFORMATION

Dissatisfaction within the Roman Catholic Church was apparent by the first decade of the sixteenth century. The authority of the Pope had been declining for over two centuries. Three events—conflict with German Emperor Frederick II in the thirteenth century, the Babylonian Captivity from 1309 to 1376 when Philip the Fair forced the Pope to live in Avignon, France so that he could control the Church, and the Great Schism from 1378 to 1418 when three individuals claimed to be the true Pope—weakened the Church. Even though the Council of Constance had ended the Great Schism by 1418, it encouraged the Concilian Movement, an attempt to give papal authority to Church councils and make the papacy a constitutional monarchy. The Concilian Movement failed largely because Wyclif and Hus convinced secular rulers to oppose it. Their action, which probably delayed the Reformation for a century, was an indication that Western Christendom faced serious trouble.

Further weakening the authority of the Church was secularization produced by the Renaissance. Popes, like many people in Europe, became increasingly concerned with worldly things. They behaved like kings, employing diplomacy and war to gain territory, surrounding themselves with an elaborate court, and patronizing artists and writers. From the perspective of many observers, the papal concern with temporal matters seemed more important than the Pope's religious duties. Various popes, including Alexander VI and Julius II, used their spiritual authority to raise money for non-religious activities, such as building palaces, funding private armies, etc. Although funds available to the Church increased as a result of these prac-

tices, corruption within the Church became widespread. Wealthy individuals and families could purchase high ecclesiastical offices. Usually nobles who bought Church offices did so not to further religion but because such offices could be used to attain wealth and power.

Abuses were also apparent at lower levels within the Catholic Church where the religious life of most Europeans took place. Priests at parishes in local villages, like most of the European population, were peasants who lived in abject poverty. To raise funds for themselves and the Church, parish priests sometimes granted forgiveness for sins in return for money. Some lay people viewed such practices as an attempt to sell divine grace. Parish priests also vulgarized religion, sometimes combining religious and pagan symbols into daily life.

By the beginning of the sixteenth century, critics of the Catholic Church attacked it on three fronts: immorality within the Church, the lack of knowledge of parish priests, and clerical pluralism. These things made it seem that the Church was not fulfilling its religious mandate and meeting the spiritual needs of parishioners. These attacks occurred largely because over the centuries the Church had become more institutionalized, more formal, and its doctrines were supported by a detailed system of canon law, theology, pomp, and ritual. Increasingly, Church officials promoted as important the sacraments and the role of priests in performing them. Moreover, the doctrine that good works, fasting, self-denial, and charity must accompany faith was becoming more dominant within the Church.

Immorality was a big problem. It particularly manifested itself in the requirement that priests and Church officials remain celibate. This practice, which dates to the fourth century, was often violated. Parish priests, as well as higher-

Public burnings ensured that the crowds would witness the execution and hear the agonizing screams of the dying.

ranking Church officials, including Pope Alexander VI, commonly had sexual relations with females in their congregations. Sometimes these priests even lived with concubines, sired children, and raised families. Immorality was not confined solely to sexual transgressions. Clergy often appeared in public wearing fancy clothes, gambled, and drank alcoholic beverages to excess. Such conduct, which contradicted Church doctrine and teaching, caused lay people to view Church officials as hypocrites.

Clerical ignorance was another problem. Even though Church law required priests to be educated, bishops rarely enforced this regulation because it was difficult to find educated people who wanted to become priests. Consequently, priests were often poorly educated. Many could barely read and write. They understood the Bible little better than the parishioners they ministered to. Church record books were usually not well maintained. Records of deaths, births, and marriages were sometimes inaccurately recorded, if they were recorded at all. Financial records were usually in disarray. Because of these problems, which could be solved by having an educated clergy, Christian humanists and other Renaissance intellectuals who valued learning criticized the poorly educated priests, mocking them as they recited Latin words in Mass that neither priest nor parishioner could understand.

Clerical pluralism also provided ammunition critics used to attack the Church. Many Church officials held several *benefices* or Church offices simultaneously. This meant that absenteeism was a problem. It was impossible for one official to regularly visit different offices they held in various countries and carry out the spiritual duty each office required. However, these officials collected revenue from all offices held. Priests were usually hired by absentee office holders to perform the spiritual duties each office entailed. These priests were paid a small fraction of the revenue the office holder collected. Thomas Wolsey, an advisor to England's Henry VIII, for example, held the position as Archbishop of York for a decade and a half before he visited the diocese he controlled. Antoine du Prat, the French diplomat under Louis XII, served as Archbishop of Sens without ever visiting a church in his diocese. The only time he was ever in a church in the diocese he controlled was for his own funeral. It was common for Italian church officials to hold high offices in foreign countries that they seldom, if ever, visited. Yet, these absentee foreign officials collected revenue from benefices in England, France, Spain, Germany, and other countries. Clerical pluralism and absenteeism created resentment within congregations and others at the local level, leading to harsh condemnation of the Catholic Church. Critics complained about the way money changed hands every time a new bishop was appointed.

A fundamental problem with the Roman Catholic Church by the sixteenth century was that it simply did not provide for the spiritual needs of local parishioners in an acceptable manner. Most laypersons wanted a more personal relationship with God than the elaborate pomp and ritual present in the Church enabled them to have. They found little comfort in formalized institutional rituals because such practices had little meaning unless the believer could find within them the presence of God. Part of the difficulty was due to the fact that the Catholic Mass was conducted in Latin, which most people did not understand.

Some individuals who wanted a closer personal relationship with God turned toward mysticism because its practitioners stressed religious freedom and individualized worship. Mystics rejected Scholastic theology that dominated the Catholic Church, denounced its authority, and turned to the ancient scriptures and writings of early figures within the Christian Church for guidance. St. Augustine's writings particularly influenced Mysticism. Mystic religious groups had arisen in European cities by the sixteenth century. Such groups were particularly numerous in Germany. By allowing individuals to engage in private devotions, they met the spiritual needs of Christians in ways the Catholic Church could not. One of the largest Mystic organizations in Germany was the Brotherhood of the Eleven Thousand Virgins. Its members met regularly to sing hymns and read psalms. By 1450 over one hundred Mystic societies existed in Hamburg, a city that contained only about eleven thousand people. Other cities in Germany, Italy, and other countries contained similar groups.

Officials within the Roman Catholic Church tried to suppress Mysticism and ordered Mystic societies to disband. These efforts at suppression met with little success. Itinerant preachers traveled throughout Europe spreading Mystic doctrines and beliefs. At every place they preached Mystic evangelists exhorted listeners to communicate directly with God. Mystic ministers told the large crowds they drew to rid themselves of corrupt priests, free themselves from the institutionalized doctrine and ritual of the Catholic Church, and seek a deeply personal relationship with God.

One of the most famous and popular Mystic preachers was Girolamo Savonarola, a Dominican friar who wanted to outlaw materialism and secularism present throughout the

Catholic Church. Everywhere this Italian friar preached hundreds, and perhaps thousands, of lay Christians flocked to receive his message. In 1496, for example, he preached in Florence, Italy and presided over a tremendous bonfire fueled by the burning of secular items that included "heathen literature," art, cosmetics, gambling devices, and other worldly items. The tremendous following Savonarola attracted, along with his condemnation of secularism within the Church, drew the attention of Catholic officials. Eventually the Pope issued a warrant for his arrest and had Savonarola executed for heresy.

Another Mystic group was the Brethren of the Common Life. This group was active in Holland. The lay people that organized it tried to imitate Christ in their daily lives. They lived simple lives and performed daily acts of charity, such as feeding the hungry, providing shelter for the homeless, and aid to the sick. The Brethren did these things because they believed Christ taught all Christians to do them. In addition, members of this Mystic society also taught in local schools. Through their teaching, the Brethren of the Common Life urged students, many of whom were training to be Catholic priests, to develop an inner, personal relationship with God and to provide opportunities for future parishioners to develop the same kind of relationship with their God. Thomas Kempis, a member of the Brethren of the Common Life, even wrote *The Imitation of Christ* that was widely read in Holland. In this book he exhorted Christians to view Christ as their role model and lead a simple, unadorned life similar to that the Savior had led. By the mid-fifteenth century the Brethren of the Common Life had spread beyond Holland into Germany. There they would influence many people, including Martin Luther.

LUTHER AND THE BIRTH OF PROTESTANTISM

The problems in the Catholic Church prior to and during the first two decades of the sixteenth century caused Martin Luther (1483-1546), a German Augustinian monk, to officially break with the Church and launch the Protestant Reformation. Even though he did not intend to break away from the Church, Luther was appalled at conditions within the institution. He believed the institution had strayed from practices, beliefs, and teachings of Christ, the Apostles, and first-century Christians.

Luther was particularly troubled by the Catholic practice of selling indulgences. An indulgence allowed sinners to be forgiven of their sins and repair the relationship with God the sin had broken. According to Catholic teaching, individuals who sin become estranged from God. Reconciliation can only occur if the sinner confesses the sin before a priest and is given penance to perform. Penance usually amounted to requiring sinners to reject the wrong and then reciting certain prayers or performing some kind of community service or good deed as atonement for the evil. However, the Pope insisted that because the Church was the embodiment of Christ upon earth it had the authority to grant sinners forgiveness for any sin they might have committed. The doctrine of indulgences was originally developed in the twelfth century so that the Pope and bishops could reward crusader knights for fighting to free the Holy Land from Muslim infidels. Individuals who received an indulgence from the Church, it was believed, would not face punishment for their sins while alive on earth or after entering purgatory. These individuals, at the moment of death, would be granted immediate entry into heaven. Luther was especially upset that people who bought in-

Martin Luther, German scholar, was one of the fathers of the Protestant movement.

cal pluralism), had received a special papal dispensation to simultaneously hold all three offices. He had borrowed money from the Fuggers, a wealthy Jewish banking family in Augsburg, to pay Leo X for the dispensation allowing him to hold all three offices. As part of the agreement, Leo X had authorized Albert to sell indulgences to raise money to repay the Fuggers and fund construction of St. Peter's Basilica. Albert hired John Tetzel, a Dominican friar, to sell the indulgences near Wittenberg where Luther was teaching in 1517. Tetzel was one of the first people to engage in modern advertising. To sell indulgences, he constructed a chart with different prices for different sins and composed a "cute" but disturbing slogan "As soon as coin in coffer rings, from purgatory the soul springs." Individuals could purchase indulgences not only for themselves but also for dead relatives.

Frederick of Saxony, one of the seven electors within the Holy Roman Empire, and the ruler of the German principality where Wittenberg was located, forbade Tetzel to sell indulgences in the Duchy of Saxony. Tetzel simply moved across the border to Jutenborg, Thuringia where he continued to preach and sell indulgences. Many Saxony residents, including some of Luther's students at the University of Wittenberg, crossed the border and purchased forgiveness for their sins. Luther, a Biblical scholar, had found no scriptural authority allowing the Church to grant indulgences. Furthermore, he believed that Tetzel was cheating German citizens out of their hard-earned money. He found it objectionable that the Catholic Church was making worthless promises to people that their sins would be forgiven when the Church did not have the authority to grant forgiveness. Luther's studies told him only Christ could forgive sin. Since the Church had no official doc-

dulgences believed they could commit any sin afterwards without having to confess the sin and do penance.

The event that disturbed Luther most was Pope Leo X's selling of indulgences to raise funds to construct St. Peter's Basilica. In 1517 Albert of Magdeburg, the Archbishop of Mainz, Halberstadt and Magdeburg (an example of cleri-

trine on the sale of indulgences, Luther believed the matter was open for academic discussion.

Luther wrote a letter to Archbishop Albert stating his objections to the sale of indulgences. This letter contained a document written in Latin called the "Ninety-five Theses on the Power of Indulgences." After Luther's death, Philip Melanchthon, one of his disciples, claimed that on All Hallow's Eve in 1517 Luther posted the Ninety-five Theses on the door of Wittenberg Castle Church. Whether Luther nailed this document to the church door is controversial. Some historians have concluded that the event never occurred. Nevertheless, Luther's argument in the Ninety-five Theses was that the sale of indulgences trivialized the penance sacrament, contradicted Biblical teaching, and caused Christians to forgo charitable penance. By the end of 1517 the Ninety-five Theses had been translated into German and were being read and discussed throughout the German principalities.

Luther's Ninety-five Theses was not intended to signal a break with Catholicism. The document stated what Luther believed to be the Biblical position on indulgences. Luther maintained that there was no Biblical basis for indulgences and rejected the notion that salvation could be purchased through an indulgence or achieved by performing good deeds. Instead, Luther maintained that salvation came only by the grace of God. There was nothing that an individual could do in the earthly life to obtain salvation. God granted salvation to individuals for reasons known only to the deity. Luther also maintained that the Pope could only remit temporal punishment imposed by the Church, that every Christian was saved so long as they accepted grace even if they did not purchase an indulgence and criticized papal wealth.

As word of Luther's attack on indulgences spread across Germany, the money Tetzel collected from their sale declined. This caused the Dominican Order to launch an attack on Luther, whom they perceived to be a presumptuous Augustinian. The Dominican attack was based in part on a longstanding rivalry with the Augustinian order. Augustinian beliefs were more liberal (more likely to question church practices) than those held by the Dominicans, who were defenders of Church orthodoxy and who would later play a prominent role in the Catholic Inquisition. In fact, Luther and other Augustinians often mockingly split the Dominican name into its two Latin parts *Domini canes*, which means dogs of the Lord. Initially, church officials, including Pope Leo X, took little interest in the controversy, regarding it as simply a dispute between friars. Eventually the controversy became so widespread that the Church could not ignore it. In 1519 Luther, in a public debate with John Eck, a prominent scholar, at Leipzig that attracted a large audience, challenged the authority of both the Pope and the Council of Constance, maintaining that both had been wrong when John Hus was convicted of heresy and burned at the stake.

In 1520 Luther wrote three brief essays outlining his views. The first, entitled *An Address to the Christian Nobility of the German Nation*, was an appeal to German nationalism. In this essay Luther urged his countrymen to reject the authority of a foreign pope. All Christians, said Luther, constitute the body of Christ (the Church) and have a responsibility to heal a defective institution and rid it of abuses such as indulgences. The second essay, *The Babylonian Captivity*, criticized the seven sacraments from which the Catholic Church derived much of its power. Luther argued that the Bible authorized only three sacraments—penance, baptism, and the Lords Supper (the Eucharist). The third letter, *Liberties of the Christian Man*, outlined

Luther's position on salvation, faith, good works, and grace.

Pope Leo X responded by condemning Luther's theology, ordering that his books be burned, and excommunicating him unless he publicly recanted within two months. Luther responded by burning Leo X's letter and calling the pontiff an Antichrist. Charles V, the Holy Roman Emperor, ordered Luther to defend his views before a diet (assembly) at Worms, a city on the Rhine, in 1521. When directed to disavow what he had previously said and written, Luther refused, stating that he could not go against his conscience or Biblical scripture. His refusal to recant prompted Charles to brand Luther an outlaw and issue an order for his arrest. Even though it was illegal to do so, Duke Frederick III of Saxony offered Luther protection against German and Church authorities, officials he viewed as foreign usurpers. Frederick had Luther taken to Wartburg Castle where the monk lived for a year. Ironically, Frederick never broke with the Catholic Church. His actions, however, enabled the Protestant Reformation to continue. Without his protection Charles V would probably have had Luther burned at the stake.

Luther's break with the Catholic Church was complete. From 1520 to 1530 he developed a theology different from Catholic orthodoxy. The theological principles Luther devised became the basic tenants all Protestant sects who were part of the Reformation followed. Lutheran theology was firmly rooted in Biblical scholarship.

Luther devised five primary doctrines that became the foundation for all Protestant theology. First was the principle of salvation. Traditional Catholic doctrine held that salvation resulted from faith and good works. Luther rejected the notion that good deeds played any role in salvation. Instead, he taught that the Bible clearly indicated salvation results solely from faith. There is nothing, Luther said, that humankind does to achieve salvation. Individuals are saved because God arbitrarily decides, for reasons known only to the deity, to grant certain people grace. Taking the sacraments, giving to charity, or doing good in everyday life would not save someone unless God granted that person grace. God, not people, Luther believed, initiated salvation.

Second, Luther rejected the Catholic notion that religious authority resides in two places— the Bible and traditional Church teachings. Rather, Luther stated that religious authority resides only in the Bible, which he believed was the word of God revealed to humans. Each person was free to interpret the Bible as his or her conscience dictated. For Luther, it was important that each individual read and study the Bible and then reflect on its teachings amid the presence of other Christians in a communal or church setting.

Third, Luther maintained that the church was the body of Christ and that all Christians, not just clergymen, were part of the institution. Catholics had previously taught that only priests were part of the Church, and, therefore, only priests were allowed to partake of wine during the Eucharist. Luther allowed the congregation to drink the wine, which lessened the authority of priests. Furthermore, Luther abolished much of the Catholic pomp in religious services, which simplified the liturgy and further decreased the power of priests.

Fourth, Luther developed the concept known as the *priesthood of the believer*. This is the idea that individuals can understand God's will as revealed in the Bible through prayer without the aid of priests. Nor, do people need a priest or church to attain salvation. God will grant grace outside church without the presence of a priest endowed with special powers. In other words, each believer can serve as his or her own priest and together all Christians share responsibilities Catholics reserved for priests. This idea was completely alien to Catholics whose theology made a clear distinction between clergy and laity. Since the doctrine of the priesthood of the believer meant that it must be possible for every person to read the Bible, Luther translated the Latin Bible into German, finishing the task in 1534.

Fifth was the doctrine of *consubstantiation*, which differed from the Catholic idea of *transubstantiation*. Catholics believed that during the Eucharist words uttered by the priest consecrated the wafer and wine, miraculously transforming them into the actual body and blood of Christ. Luther rejected this idea. His doctrine of consubstantiation held that after consecration the bread and wine changed spiritually so that the presence of Christ was found, but the wafer and wine were not really transformed into the body and blood.

Luther's basic principles were first codified in the Augsburg Confession of 1530. After his German Bible was published in 1534, Luther's new Christianity was doctrinally complete. Although Luther lived until 1546, he did little after 1534 to further spread his beliefs. Yet, the revolution he launched over the sale of indulgences would spread throughout Europe and around the world, producing wars and social change in its wake.

RELIGIOUS VIOLENCE AND THE PEASANT REBELLION

Luther's condemnation of the Catholic Church and its religious authority encouraged oppressed people across Germany to revolt. The first violence related to Luther's new theology occurred in the summer of 1522 between German princes and knights. Imperial knights, who usually owned only one castle and owed their allegiance to the Holy Roman Emperor, felt oppressed by the growing power of independent towns and the local princes who controlled vast territories in Germany. Since German princes usually held ecclesiastical offices, the imperial knights, who believed they represented the emperor, used Lutheranism to justify launching an attack on the Archbishop of Trier. This war, which lasted about a year before the knights were defeated, caused Luther's opponents to criticize Protestantism for inciting violence and undermining law, order, peace, and stability.

Lutheranism also was used to justify the peasant revolts that swept across sixteenth-century Germany. German peasants were particularly attracted to Luther's doctrines because he came from a peasant background. Peasants generally looked upon Luther as a hero because he had defied the authority of the Catholic Church, which was viewed by peasants as perhaps their greatest economic oppressor. German peasants took Luther literally when he proclaimed in *On Christian Liberty* in 1520 that Christianity makes humans "the most free lord of all and subject to none." Uneducated peasants who followed Luther's teachings understood the words to mean that Christ would liberate them from their earthly oppressors—the Church and government.

The peasant revolt began in Swabia in 1524 and within a few months spread throughout southern and central Germany. Citing Luther's beliefs, peasant representatives gathered at Memmingen in 1525 to compose a list of twelve grievances. The articles of grievance condemned ecclesiastical and temporal lords for practices that made peasant life difficult. Among the grievances, peasants wanted common land that nobles had seized returned to villages, freedom for serfs, an end to religious taxes or tithes, prohibitions on hunting and fishing lifted, excessive rents and fees for religious services lowered, unlawful punishments abolished, an end to death duties (the practice of peasant families being forced to give the church and nobles their best horses or cows when a death occurred in a peasant family), and the right to choose their own pastors. They also insisted that their revolt be judged by Biblical scripture rather than temporal law.

At first, Luther personally sympathized with the peasants' cause because he admired their unceasing toil and as a peasant child himself had experienced the drudgery of everyday life peasants endured. In 1525 Luther published *An Admonition to Peace*, which criticized German nobles and blamed them for causing the revolt: "We have no one…to thank for this…rebellion, except…lords and princes, especially…blind bishops, mad priests, and monks…. You do nothing but flay and rob your subjects…until the poor common folk can bear it no longer." However, when Luther realized that peasants were rebelling against all authority using his theology, he turned against the peasant rebellion, ignored the oppressive life they endured, and wrote *Against the Rapacious and Murdering Peasants*, a pamphlet that authorized German nobles to destroy rebellious peasants unmercifully until peace was restored. A few months later the Peasant Rebellion was crushed; its participants believed Luther had turned his back on a just cause, ignoring Biblical teachings that supported revolt. However, Luther did not see it this way. When he used the word "freedom," Luther meant freedom to obey the word of God without interference from the Roman Church. Freedom did not mean opposition to legally instituted governments. In fact, as Luther refined his theology, he increasingly demanded that

Christians support the state, that the church be subordinate to government, and condemned rebellion. Luther wrote "that nothing can be more poisonous, hurtful, or devilish than a rebel." Luther's critics maintained that he opposed the Peasant Revolt and supported the state because he realized that he and his faith needed the protection of German princes to oppose Roman Catholicism. Had Luther supported the Peasant Revolt, Germany's secular rulers likely would have denied him protection from Catholic authorities, condemning him and his movement to an early death. Regardless of why Luther opposed the Peasant Rebellion, historians estimate that German princes killed over seventy-five thousand peasants before crushing the revolt in 1525.

THE SPREAD OF PROTESTANTISM

Despite violence, such as the Peasant Rebellion that was associated with Lutheranism, the new faith spread across Germany and throughout Europe. Important to its spread was the printing press, which enabled publishers to rapidly reproduce Luther's writings and disseminate his ideas everywhere. Equally important was Luther's ability to turn a phrase. He was a gifted writer and speaker who expressed himself extremely well. Some scholars have maintained that only Shakespeare equals his use of language. Nevertheless, language was the sword that Luther, the peasant's son, used to seriously wound the Catholic Church.

Many people were attracted to Luther's ideas. Peasants, Renaissance humanists, nobles, merchants, and princes found desirable Luther's call for a simple religion based on personal faith and scripture and the abolition of elaborate ceremonies. Humanists across Renaissance Europe had advocated many of the same reforms. Ulrich von Hutten (1488-1523), for example, was a celebrated German humanist who joined Luther in advancing the Reformation. The conservatism within Lutheranism made it possible for anyone who accepted the idea of justification by faith and the authority of scripture to join the church. Converts could, with some modification, keep much from the Catholic faith they had grown up with, including the liturgy, music, and church organization.

One of the most important things that attracted rulers and nobles to Lutheranism was materialism. Since Lutheran theology did not permit the church to hold vast amounts of land or acquire substantial wealth, any prince who accepted the Protestant faith could confiscate the land and wealth controlled by Catholic monasteries, churches, and high officials in their kingdom. Although this strategy was risky because Emperor Charles V was a staunch supporter of the Catholic faith and could take away the title of prince from any German nobleman, if successful it could enrich the prince. Eventually, enough German princes risked alienating the Emperor by becoming Protestant that they developed enough strength to resist Charles. Protestant rulers convened at the Diet of Speyer in 1529 and produced a document protesting the Emperor's order that no new religious idea would be allowed in Germany. In fact, this is the origin of the word "Protestant." After Speyer, all non-Catholic Christians would be called Protestants. In 1530 the Lutheran princes further upset Charles V by voting to support the Confession of Augsburg, a document containing the basic principles of the Lutheran faith. Faced with this opposition, Charles threatened to use military force to crush Protestant princes. They responded by forming a military alliance against the Holy Roman Emperor at Schmalkalden, Saxony in 1531.

War did not occur between German Protestant princes and Charles V until 1546. From 1531 until 1546 German Protestants consolidated their power, enticed other princes to join their ranks, and negotiated with the Pope about returning to the Catholic fold. When the Roman Church was not willing to accept Protestant demands that Lutheran theology be made part of the Catholic faith, it became clear that war could not be averted. In 1546 German princes and Charles V fought a brief conflict. Charles easily defeated the weaker German princes, but his victory did not destroy Protestantism. Luther's theology had advanced too far by the time Charles acted. About half of the German population had become Protestant by 1546. There were so many Protestants in Germany, particularly in the northern and eastern principalities, that it was impossible for the Holy Roman Emperor to destroy Lutheranism. There were also pockets of Protestantism in southern cities like Nuremberg, which was the German center of Renaissance Humanism.

Catholic princes in Germany also made it difficult for Charles to destroy Protestantism. They feared the power the Holy Roman Emperor had amassed and were reluctant to help him assert control across Germany, refusing to provide German troops. Thus, Charles had to use Spanish troops to fight Protestant princes, which caused the German populace to resent this foreign intrusion. Historians believe that the use of Spanish troops caused even more Germans to become Protestant.

From 1546 to 1555 sporadic fighting occurred in Germany. Although Charles V was a staunch defender of the Catholic faith, his actions were partly responsible for the spread of Lutheranism. The Holy Roman Emperor did not understand or try to solve political, religious, social, and economic problems Germany faced in the sixteenth century. Rather than devoting attention to Germany, he was more concerned about Flemish, Spanish, and Italian territories he controlled. He also faced a threat from Turkish Muslims who besieged Vienna, ruled by Charles' brother, Ferdinand, in 1529 and went to war with the Valois kings of France five times between 1521 and 1555. Consequently, Catholic rulers of France supported German Protestant princes when they challenged Charles V's power. France wanted to keep Germany divided to weaken Charles. This struggle between Catholic France and Charles V, called the Habsburg-Valois Wars, fought over Habsburg lands due to the marriage of Maximilian and Mary of Burgundy, ironically promoted the spread of Protestantism.

As Protestant numbers increased, they became more formidable, and in 1555 a diet at Augsburg was held. This meeting produced a settlement between Catholics and Protestants in Germany. According to the agreement, known as the Peace of Augsburg, each German prince could determine what religion his kingdom would follow without interference from the Roman Pope or the Holy Roman Emperor. The Peace of Augsburg signaled that the unity of Western Christendom had ended and that Lutheranism would be safely entrenched in Germany. Other reformers, imitating Luther's example, also broke with the Catholic Church and carried Protestantism throughout Europe.

REFORMERS AND RADICALS

One of the most important reformers was the Swiss humanist Ulrich Zwingli (1484-1531). He introduced the Reformation into Switzerland. On January 1, 1519, less than two years after Luther composed his Ninety-five theses, Zwingli, a Catholic priest and disciple of Erasmus, in-

formed his congregation that he would no longer preach sermons taken from official Catholic sources. Using the New Testament Erasmus had translated, he stated that he would cover the entire book from Matthew to Revelation. Like Luther, Zwingli believed a personal study of scripture was necessary to lead a Christian life. From 1519 to 1522 he developed a theology similar to Luther's. Zwingli's doctrine rejected priests serving as intermediaries between God and humankind, allowed ministers to marry, and disavowed the notion of purgatory.

Despite similarities, Zwingli's theology was vastly different from Luther's. Unlike Luther, Zwingli believed individuals were basically good and only needed discipline imposed by the church to lead Christian lives. To accomplish this, he created a magisterial tribunal comprised of ministers and lay people to enforce religious law. Whereas Luther made a distinction between religious and secular authority, Zwingli saw the two as being one and the same. Zwinglian tribunals were thus given authority to enforce all laws, secular and religious, excommunicate wayward Christians, rule on moral questions, require church attendance, and spy on parishioners using a network of informers. In short, Zwingli created a Protestant faith more dependent on the individual and less reliant on grace than Luther could accept. When Luther and Zwingli met in 1529 to work out differences in their theology, a disagreement over the importance of the sacraments prevented them from reaching an accord. Zwingli saw the sacraments as symbols of grace God previously bestowed on the individual whereas Luther believed God was actually present in the ceremony to bestow grace when the sacraments were administered. Under Zwingli's system, baptism and communion, for example, were not necessary; Luther saw them as central to the Christian faith.

The most important reformer other than Luther was John Calvin (1509-1564). Born in Noyon, France, Calvin studied law at the University of Paris before beginning a crusade to make the world Protestant. As a young man, Calvin underwent an experience that changed his life. He called this event his "sudden conversion" but refused to elaborate about it. Whatever the experience was, after its occurrence in 1533, Calvin converted to Protestantism, becoming its foremost sixteenth-century spokesperson. The theology he developed had a greater impact on subsequent generations than any other reformer, including Luther. Calvinistic doctrine greatly influenced the government, economy, society, attitudes, and character of Europeans and their settlers in various American colonies.

After his sudden conversion French authorities charged Calvin with heresy. Thereafter, he hid from authorities for more than a year until he moved to Basel, Switzerland. While living at Basel, Calvin wrote *Institutes of the Christian Religion* (1536) that discussed his religious doctrine. This essay contained the five principles central to Calvin's theology. First is the idea that humankind is totally depraved. Calvin theorized that humans, by nature, are evil and will almost always do wrong. Second is the concept of unmerited grace. Calvin maintained that all people who became sinners when Eve consumed the forbidden fruit in the Garden of Eden were damned to hell. However, for reasons known only to God, some sinners were given salvation. Yet, this grace was not earned. People who were saved could do nothing to earn or merit heaven. God arbitrarily chose the saints and condemned all others to spend eternity in hell. In other words, according to Calvin, God, not human beings, was sovereign. It did not matter how morally upright a life people lived on earth. They still could go to hell. Third is the notion of limited

atonement. Calvin stressed that although God granted salvation to undeserving human sinners, the number of people who receive atonement for their sins was limited. God chose only a few people to enjoy heavenly bliss in the afterlife. Calvinists referred to the chosen ones as the Saints or the elect. The vast majority of people were condemned to eternal hell. Fourth was the idea of predestination. Calvin concluded that God had decided who was damned and who was saved before people were born. This decision, which was made before a child was even in his or her mother's womb, was completely independent of the earthly life an individual might lead. Fifth is the idea of irresistible grace. Calvin declared that God's will would be done regardless of what any human might do. Individuals granted grace had no choice but to accept salvation just as those sentenced to hell could not change their fate. God's grace was irresistible, and the deity's power was absolute. People were, Calvin said, "as meaningless to God as grains of sand upon the seashore."

Shortly after defining his basic theology in the *Institutes of the Christian Religion*, Calvin moved to Geneva, where he remained until his death. In 1541 he accepted an invitation from Geneva's citizens to establish the Protestant faith in the Swiss city after it deposed its prince who was also a Catholic bishop. Calvin established a theocracy to govern both Geneva and his church. A group of deacons and church elders controlled the theocracy. A body of lay elders, called the consistory, made decisions about both church and state in Geneva, enforced laws, excommunicated wayward Christians, and punished sinners. Strict discipline and a high degree of organization characterized Geneva and other communities controlled by Calvinists.

The Reformation produced individuals and religious sects even more radical than Luther,

Zwingli, and Calvin, who primarily represented moderate to conservative Protestantism. Left wing Protestant sects that embraced the Reformation were called Anabaptists. Controversy between mainstream and liberal Protestants erupted over the sacrament of baptism. Calvin, Luther, and most mainline reformers, wanting to preserve church authority, held that the individual became part of the body of Christ (the church) at the moment of baptism. This meant that infants who were baptized became Christians at the moment of immersion. Anabaptists, however, rejected infant baptism. They believed that only mature adults should undergo baptism. Radicals insisted that only mature adults, capable of exercising free will, could consciously accept grace and become Christian. Thus, Anabaptists insisted that all adults who had undergone infant baptism be re-baptized. (The term Anabaptist means to baptize again.) They maintained that there was no scriptural basis for infant baptism because immature children could not understand the concept of grace.

Generally, Anabaptist sects, each one unique, are characterized by several commonalities. All accepted the idea of religious diversity. They did not reorganize the church in an institutional form, did not allow priests, believed that personal communication between God and the individual was paramount, and valued religious tolerance. Anabaptists sought to recreate the Christian community they believed had existed during the first century after Christ's execution, a voluntary group of believers who had attained salvation. Anabaptist sects rarely numbered more than one hundred individuals. Many sects wanted to completely isolate themselves from the world, live a Christian life as they saw it, and set an example for worldly sinners to follow. Anabaptist sects were also generally eschatological, that is, they believed in the im-

minent coming of Christ. Some even went so far as to create "communistic" societies in which members held everything in common, including material possessions and husbands and wives. Mystical Anabaptist sects lived isolated, hermit-like lives completely apart from the world. They often experienced some sort of psychological trance, which they believed indicated direct contact with God. Each Anabaptist church and sect was completely independent of all other groups, chose its own ministers and officials, made its own laws, and devised its own theology. Some Anabaptist sects were the first Christian churches to accept women ministers while others allowed only males to preach. Most Anabaptists refused to hold civil offices and some were pacifists, refusing to serve in national militaries or fight for any reason.

Anabaptists also held that only a few "true believers" really achieved salvation and that church and state should be separated. Anabaptists believed that no government should promote any religious view. Nor did Anabaptists think individuals should proselytize, meaning Anabaptist sects did not force their religious views on others. Instead, Anabaptists allowed people to make up their own minds about religion.

Radical views meant that Anabaptists were destined to remain in the religious minority. Mostly, such sects attracted the poor, the dispossessed, the uneducated, and the downtrodden from Europe's urban areas. Also, because Anabaptist ideas threatened the church/state relationship during an age that made no distinction between the two institutions, these minority sects often faced persecution, religious hatred, and violence. Political and religious leaders in Protestant countries, including Luther, Calvin, and Zwingli, believed that separation of church and state would inevitably led to the creation of a completely secular society, which they opposed. Since Anabaptist ideas threatened existing governments, churches, and societies, members of radical sects often experienced brutality sanctioned by mainstream religious leaders. Some European towns drove Anabaptists out of the community while others maimed, tortured, and killed members of these radical groups. Many Anabaptists were burned at the stake for heresy, while others were brutally beaten to death, drowned, hanged, or drawn and quartered.

The assault on Anabaptist sects began in the mid-1520s in Germany and quickly spread throughout Europe. An imperial diet in 1529 condemned to death all Anabaptists. Consequently, most of their leaders were violently executed. One of the best examples of violence against an Anabaptist sect was suppression of the Melchiorites at Munster, Germany. The Melchiorites attracted a large number of industrial workers and craftspeople. In 1534 this Anabaptist sect gained political control of Munster and established a Christian community according to Melchiorite ideas. They instituted a legal code that, among other things, established the death penalty for wives who did not obey their husbands and forced women to marry or face banishment from the community. Women who refused to marry or leave the city were executed. Melchiorites rule also introduced into Munster polygamy, burned all books except the Bible, and preached an eschatological religion.

Religious and secular leaders perceived what the Melchiorites had done at Munster as threatening society. Catholic and Protestant rulers united, sent an army to attack Munster and rid the city of Melchiorite ideas. This assault was successful. Many Melchiorites were killed; a few escaped to Poland, England, and the Netherlands.

THE ENGLISH REFORMATION

Across the English Channel the Reformation took a different turn, having economic and political causes in addition to religious ones. The official split with the Catholic Church occurred when King Henry VIII, wanting a male heir in 1527, requested that Pope Clement VII grant an annulment to his marriage to Catherine of Argon. Previously, Pope Julius II had given Henry a special dispensation, which allowed him to wed Catherine who had been married to Henry's brother, Arthur. In asking for the annulment Henry stated that if Princess Mary, the child produced by his union with Catherine, inherited the English throne, anarchy would result. He also maintained a legal marriage to Catherine had never existed because of her prior marriage. Clement VII was a weak pontiff whose focus at the time was on Luther's Reformation in Germany and on the Habsburg-Valois War in Italy. Clement refused Henry's request for an annulment because he did not want to provide more ammunition to Protestant reformers who criticized the Church by saying that popes replaced God's law as revealed in scripture with their own rules. Henry's divorce petition claimed that Julius II erred because his special dispensation violated God's rule that a man could not marry his brother's widow. Had Clement recognized Henry's argument and granted the annulment, Lutherans would have used this to convince more people to join the Reformation. Compounding the situation was the sack of Rome in 1527 by Charles V, Catherine's nephew. Since Charles was in complete control of Rome, Pope Clement delayed action on Henry's request; he was afraid to annul the marriage of Charles V's aunt while the Holy Roman Emperor controlled Rome.

After Clement refused to grant the annulment, Henry joined the Reformation. He removed the English church from papal control and made himself head of the institution. In 1533, at Henry's request, Parliament passed the Act in Restraint of Appeals, which legalized the English Reformation by forbidding church officials to submit legal appeals to the Roman Pope. Instead, English churchmen were required to submit all religious disputes to the English monarch. Thus, Henry VIII became the highest religious authority in England. Later, Parliamentary laws more firmly codified the Reformation in Britain. The Act for the Submission of Clergy in 1534 required priests and all other church officials to obey the king's rules and forbade Christians from publishing theological principles without consent of the monarch. The Supremacy Act, also passed in 1534, made the English monarch the official head of the Anglican Church. Henry's opposition was unexpected because he had previously written an essay attacking Luther and the Reformation, for which the Pope had named him "Defender of the Faith" in England. While these acts made the break with Rome official, they caused controversy within England. A few Parliamentary representatives and other officials opposed passage of England's Reformation laws. Sir Thomas More, for example, resigned his chancellorship because he could not support leaving the Catholic fold and making the English monarch head of the Anglican Church. John Fisher, the Bishop of Rochester, also objected to the English Reformation, accusing the English clergy of cowardice when most did not protest when Henry removed the church from Rome's control. More, Fisher, and others who opposed the English Reformation were beheaded.

From 1535 to 1539 the English Reformation continued. Henry and Thomas Cromwell, his most influential advisor, abolished the monastery as an institution and confiscated its wealth. Monks, nuns, and abbots were driven from their homes. All monastic lands were taken; much of it was later sold to the upper and middle classes because the government needed money to finance various wars. The redistribution of lands also strengthened the rich and made them dependent upon the English king.

Because the English Reformation occurred more for secular than religious reasons, initially the Anglican Church kept many Catholic beliefs, doctrine, and practices, such as transubstantiation, celibacy for priests, and confession.

Edward VI wanted the country to be Protestant.

Anne Boleyn, mistress of Henry VIII, demanded that he annul his marriage to Catherine, causing an international controversy.

After Henry VIII's death, however, the English church became more Protestant. During the seven-year reign of Edward VI (1547-1553), Henry's son, Catholic practices and theology were replaced with Protestant ideas. Archbishop Thomas Cranmer ordered a simplification of the Anglican liturgy. The *Book of Common Prayer* was written in 1549. Protestant ministers began to roam the English countryside, spreading Calvinistic, Lutheran, and other religious doctrines.

After Edward's death, his half-sister, Mary Tudor, the daughter of Catherine of Argon, tried to undo the English Reformation. During her brief reign from 1553 to 1558 England faced religious instability. She rescinded most laws Henry VIII and Edward VI had enacted to further the Reformation. In their place, Mary passed legislation that completely returned England to the Catholic fold. Mary's religious changes, along with her marriage to the Spanish prince Phillip, son of Holy Roman Emperor Charles V, were not received well by her English subjects. When Mary began a campaign to persecute Protestants, many fled England, settling in countries where the Reformation was more firmly established. Under Queen Mary's rule, hundreds of Protestants, especially ministers and other leaders, were executed, earning her the name "Bloody Mary."

Mary's death brought her sister, Elizabeth I, to the throne. Under Elizabeth's reign from 1558 to 1603, religious stability slowly came to England. Because Elizabeth was raised Protestant, she rescinded Mary's laws that had returned England to Catholicism. However, Elizabeth was not overly zealous initiating religious reforms. When she became queen, she faced pressure from Catholics who wanted England to remain part of the Roman Church and a group of Protestants called Puritans who wanted the Anglican Church to become Calvinistic. Puritans were especially vocal and political. They wanted Elizabeth to rid the English church of all vestiges of Catholicism. Elizabeth, who was perhaps the best monarch in English history, steered a middle course between Catholic and Protestant extremists. She gave England more religious freedom and toleration than it had ever had. Even though all English people were legally required to be Anglican, Elizabeth generally allowed her subjects to practice whatever religion they wanted so long as they did not try to force their beliefs on others. Nor was the Queen a strict doctrinalist. She demanded that peace and order be maintained throughout her realm and in religious services but did not precisely define how English services were to be conducted. Laws enacted by Parliament during her reign, called the Elizabethan

Settlement, were not unreasonable. They required that every English man and woman attend Anglican services; those that refused faced fines rather than execution or imprisonment. English bishops in 1563 drew up and approved the *Thirty-nine Articles* that briefly outlined Anglican beliefs. All Anglican services were required to be conducted in a uniform manner. The English language was used in services, Anglican priests were allowed to marry, and monasteries were prohibited from reopening. Still, these reforms were modest when considered in light of what Catholic and Protestant extremists wanted.

The Reformation in Scotland and Ireland was more radical than in England. John Knox, a staunch Calvinist, was the most important Reformation figure in Scotland. In 1560 he persuaded the Scottish legislature to pass legislation creating a Calvinistic Church. The Catholic Mass was forbidden. Any Scottish citizen who attended mass could be executed. Everyone was required to attend the Presbyterian Church, which was controlled by ministers called presbyters instead of bishops, which Knox founded. Calvinistic theology was introduced into Scotland. Knox, who previously had studied with Calvin in Geneva, attempted to create a theocracy in Scotland. The Presbyterian Church utilized a simple worship service dominated by hell fire and brimstone preachers. The *Book of Common Order* that Knox published in 1564 was adopted as the official liturgical tool in the Presbyterian Church.

Both James V and his daughter, Mary, Queen of Scots, opposed the Scottish Reformation. The Scottish monarchs were staunch Catholics who allied themselves with other Catholic monarchs in Europe. Because the Scottish monarchy was weak, James and Mary were powerless to stop the spread of Calvinism throughout their realm. Numerous Scottish nobles, who dominated Parliament, supported the Reformation. They saw religious change as a means whereby they could wrest more power from an already weak monarchy.

Ireland did not undergo a complete Reformation as Scotland did. In 1536 the English government ordered the Irish Parliament to pass legislation instituting the Reformation. These laws abolished the Catholic Church, made the English monarch head of the Irish church, outlawed monasteries, and created an Irish church similar to the English Church. The ruling class, which was primarily comprised of English nobles, quickly converted to Protestantism. However, the largest majority of the Irish population remained Catholic because they did not accept the political legitimacy of their English rulers and Parliament. Maintaining their Catholic faith was a way for the masses to defy their oppressive English rulers. The Catholic Church had to function as an underground institution. Its property was confiscated and sold. Profits went to England. Monasteries were destroyed. Despite these hardships, Catholicism survived in Ireland. Catholic priests and bishops became national leaders in the Irish resistance to English rule.

THE CATHOLIC REFORMATION
(Counter Reformation)

After Luther began the Reformation in 1517 it quickly spread across Europe. By 1547 all England and Scandinavia had become Protestant. Most of Germany and Scotland, as well as parts of France and Switzerland, were following the doctrines of Luther, Calvin, Zwingli, Knox, or some other reformer. The spread of Protestantism meant that the Catholic Church had lost its control over millions of Christians and had witnessed the confiscation of thousands of acres of real estate property and had lost millions of dollars in annual income. Faced with these problems, Catholics began to put the Church's affairs in order. Reforms within the Church were instituted as a result of the Protestant Reformation. Catholics refer to these reforms at the Catholic Revival while Protestants call it the Counter Reformation. Whatever its name, lasting changes in the Catholic Church resulted, and after 1540, with the exception of the Netherlands, no substantial number of people in a European geographic area would become Protestant.

Certainly, reform within the Catholic Church was needed. Protestantism had spread across Europe, taking several countries out of the Catholic fold. Even in countries that remained loyal to the faith, the Church had lost much of its influence. There also was no unified Catholic doctrine on justification, salvation, or the sacraments. This situation began to change in 1534 when Paul III was elected Pontiff. When his reign ended in 1549, the Catholic Revival was firmly established. Pope Paul III began to root out abuses within the Church. He tolerated little corruption from lay priests, high ranking bishops, or abbots and created the Roman Inquisition, which used violence to stifle dissent.

Paul's primary strategy to reform the Church was convening an ecumenical council that met at Trent, Italy in 1545. The Council of Trent, as it was known, met off and on for eighteen years until the work was finished in 1563. Delegates to the Council of Trent were instructed to reform the Catholic Church and induce reconciliation with wayward Protestants. Lutherans, Calvinists, and other Protestants were initially asked to participate. Those who attended insisted that the Bible was the sole authority of God, which made reconciliation difficult to achieve.

Throughout the Council's existence, national politics intruded on its religious mission. Representatives from Western European countries demanded that Rome share power while delegates from Italian states wanted the Church's power centralized under the Pope. Charles V refused to allow discussion on any topic he believed would upset Lutherans in his realm. If Lutherans were upset too much, Charles was likely to lose more land to Protestant German princes. Likewise, French representatives opposed reconciliation with Protestants because they wanted to keep Germany weak. So long as Lutheranism divided the German states, the less authority Charles V had. A religiously divided Germany meant that France, unified under Catholicism, would be stronger.

Despite the intrusion of national politics and the stubbornness of Protestants regarding the importance of Scripture, achievements of the Council of Trent were remarkable. Numerous decrees were issued at the meeting. The most important one rejected Protestant positions on Scripture, sacraments, and free will. The Bible was not, according to this decree, the sole authority on religious matters. Tradition, as well as rulings by the Pope and church officials, was also important. Moreover, the Council of Trent decided that all seven sacraments are valid representations of God's grace. Priests were the only people authorized to administer the sacraments. Delegates also reaffirmed the Catholic position that humans possess free will and that good works in conjunction with faith are necessary for salvation. The elaborate rites and ceremonies that had become part of Catholic worship remained part of the faith.

Numerous decisions of less importance were also handed down from Trent. Many abuses within the Church were corrected. Ecclesiastical discipline was strengthened; bishops were now required to live within the diocese they governed. The sale of indulgences was abolished, priests who lived with women were ordered to embrace celibacy, bishops were required to visit every church within their diocese at least once every two years, and every diocese was ordered to create a seminary to educate priests. St. Jerome's Latin translation of the Bible was made a holy book, and priests were required to preside over marriage ceremonies. The Council also established the Inquisition and the *Index of Forbidden Books* to root out dissent and inform Catholics about books the Church considered heretical.

Although the Council of Trent did not affect reconciliation with Protestants, it did create a renewed spirituality within the Church. Criticism of the Catholic Church abated after most abuses were abolished. Decisions made at Trent remained important to Catholics for centuries afterward.

The Catholic Reformation involved more than simply the Council of Trent. New Religious orders also came into existence. They developed primarily for two reasons—to improve morality within the Church and provide education for clergy and lay people. The two foremost orders were the Society of Jesus (Jesuits) and the Ursuline Nuns. Ignatius Loyola (1491-1556) founded the Jesuit Order in 1540. He believed the Protestant Reformation had occurred because of low spiritual moral within lay people. The antidote for the Reformation, he believed, was found in ministering to the spiritual needs of individual Catholics. Loyola molded the Jesuits into a highly centralized group whose members were willing to go to the far corners of the world in service to the Church. Individuals who wanted to become Jesuits had to undergo a novitiate (probationary period) of two years rather than the standard one-year period required of other religious orders. The Je-

suits became known for the schools they established. Jesuit monks educated children from both common and noble families. Over time, Jesuits exerted tremendous political influence, especially on the nobles and kings who had been educated in the order's schools.

The Ursuline Order of Nuns, founded by Angela Merici (1474-1540), focused on educating women. Originally established in 1535 to battle Protestant heresy by educating girls according to Catholic doctrine, the order eventually spread outside Italy, becoming known worldwide for its mission. The Ursuline goal was to make society more moral by teaching women who would become wives and mothers about Christian love. It was then hoped these Christian women could influence husbands and sons to exercise greater morality both inside and outside the home.

New religious orders were not the only institutions established as part of the Catholic Reformation. In 1542 Pope Paul III created the Inquisition to fight the spread of Protestantism within Catholic countries. The Roman Inquisition consisted of six cardinals who were given authority to act as a court to try individuals accused of heresy. This institution was given the power to issue warrants, arrest, try, imprison, and execute heretics. Trials run by the Inquisition were not fair to the accused. Judges accepted hearsay evidence. Accused heretics were not always informed of what they were charged with and torture was often applied to extract confessions. In countries controlled by Catholic monarchs Protestant heretics were effectively destroyed; in non-Catholic countries the Inquisition was not effective.

RELIGIOUS WARS

Wars plagued Europe for almost a century. From the 1560s to the 1650s countries fought over many issues, but religion was a common denominator in all the conflicts. Religion caused Catholics and Protestants to oppose each other. Both faiths saw the other as heretics and were convinced that God wanted all heretics destroyed. Catholics and Protestants developed a hatred for each other that bordered on fanaticism. This hatred caused members of both Christian sects to treat each other cruelly. Catholics executed Protestants by burning them at the stake; Protestants executed Catholics by drawing and quartering (ripping the body apart by hitching horses to all four limbs). Even corpses were not spared. Dead bodies were often mutilated as a warning to other heretics.

One of the most fervent anti-Protestant rulers was Philip II of Spain (1556-1598), the most powerful monarch in the world at the time. He ruled Spain, most of Italy, the Netherlands, most of South America, and parts of North America. Despite his vast possessions and wealth, Philip was not satisfied. He intensely disliked the Protestant Reformation and also hated Muslims who controlled parts of Africa and the Middle East. Philip believed that Islam and Protestantism were enemies of the Catholic Church; consequently, he wanted to destroy both. Philip waged a successful campaign in the Mediterranean against the Muslims. A naval victory at the Battle of Lepanto against Muslim forces curtailed Islamic power in the Mediterranean and made Philip a hero in the Catholic world. However, his successes against Islam did not translate into victory against Protestant forces.

One of the most serious setbacks for Philip was in the Netherlands, which he had inherited when his father Charles V abdicated in 1556, dividing his territories between Ferdinand (Charles's brother) and Philip. Problems arose because the Dutch considered Philip to be Spanish whereas Charles was one of their own, having been born in Ghent and raised in the Netherlands. Unlike Charles, who was Flemish in language and lifestyle, Philip spoke Spanish and the Dutch perceived him as a foreign ruler. In 1559 Philip named Margaret, his half sister, as ruler of the Netherlands and ordered her to destroy Protestantism in the kingdom. She quickly established the Inquisition to root out Protestantism. The problem in the Netherlands was not Lutheranism but Calvinism. Calvin's teachings had attracted a following among the Dutch middle and working classes. By the 1560s, Calvinist enclaves existed in most Dutch towns and the religion was well financed by bankers and merchants throughout the seventeen provinces that comprised the Netherlands. Margaret's immediate problem was raising capital to finance efforts to destroy Protestantism. Despite protests from the Dutch legislature that taxes were already too high, Margaret raised them. Her actions caused Dutch merchants, businessmen, and bankers who opposed the tax increase to unite with Calvinist leaders being persecuted by the Queen.

In 1566 working class Calvinists, faced with high food costs coupled with high taxes, revolted. Incited by Calvinist preachers, fanatical mobs attacked Catholic churches and their parishioners. The Catholic cathedral of Notre Dame at Antwerp, along with thirty other churches, was destroyed. Alters were smashed, windows broken, tombs opened, books were burned, and priests were killed. From Antwerp the violence spread across the Netherlands and throughout the Low Countries.

Philip II dispatched a Spanish army commanded by the Duke of Alva to crush the Dutch rebellion. In addition to using the Inquisition against Protestants, Alva established an institution called the Council of Blood. To finance the Spanish campaign, he increased taxes even more. On March 3, 1568, Alva's troops executed over fifteen hundred Protestant heretics. Protestants were publicly hanged, and rebel bands were ruthlessly slaughtered by Spanish forces as the troops sought to suppress treason and heresy. Often innocent people were killed. Two Dutch noblemen, for example, were executed because they demanded that Philip alter his repressive policy. The executions and tax increases, which produced economic hardship, caused Dutch Protestants to completely turn against their Spanish oppressors. Over the next ten years a civil war was fought between Protestants and Catholics in the Netherlands. Generally, Protestant forces won the war. In 1572 a group of Dutch sailors, whom the Spanish called "sea beggars," captured Brill, a North Sea fishing village. Their success prompted revolts in other Dutch towns. Spanish troops were dispatched to recapture Brill and other towns that had fallen to rebel forces but were defeated in 1574 when the dikes were opened, flooding Spanish troops who were only twenty-five miles from Amsterdam. In 1576 Protestants in all seventeen Dutch provinces united under the leadership of William of Orange.

Philip II sent his nephew, Alexander Farnese, the Duke of Parma, to crush the revolt. Farnese captured numerous towns in the southern provinces, including Ghent, Bruges, Maastricht, Tournai, and Antwerp. The fall of Antwerp was the last significant Spanish victory in the Netherlands. Farnese's success also meant that the Netherlands would be divided religiously. In the ten southern provinces Farnese conquered, Calvinism was stamped out. Protestants residing within them were either forced to become Catholic or migrate to a Protestant province. These ten provinces, called the Spanish Netherlands, remained under control of the Habsburg dynasty, eventually becoming the country of Belgium.

The seven northern provinces William of Orange controlled remained Protestant. In 1581, led by Holland, they signed the Treaty of Utrecht, declared their independence from Spain, and created the country of Holland.

Philip and Farnese refused to accept the political division of the Netherlands. They tried to subdue the northern provinces after 1581. Protestant Holland repeatedly asked Elizabeth I, the English monarch, for military assistance. England faced a serious dilemma. If Elizabeth helped the Dutch she would anger Philip II and likely produce war with Spain. But, if Spain conquered all the Netherlands provinces Philip would likely attack England to restore the Catholic religion in Albion. Compounding the problem, the Dutch revolt had harmed the English wool industry. The Netherlands was the largest market for English wool cloth. When it collapsed, Elizabeth's government lost tax revenue. The execution of William of Orange in July 1584 and the Spanish victory at Antwerp frightened Elizabeth. She believed that if Spain crushed the Dutch resistance Farnese would turn his army against England. Thus, Elizabeth I sent money and soldiers to help Dutch Protestants confront the Catholic armies of Spain in 1585.

Farnese insisted that before Spain could defeat the Dutch it must also defeat England and halt Elizabeth's support of the Protestant Netherlands. Philip agreed with Farnese because he had spent a fortune fighting the Dutch but had little to show for it. Upsetting Philip even more was the execution of Mary, Queen of Scots, Elizabeth I's cousin and heir to the English throne, on February 18, 1587. Mary, a staunch Catholic, had hatched a plot to assassinate Elizabeth and take the English throne for herself. Philip II, wanting to restore England to the Catholic fold, had provided Mary financial support. Had Mary's plot worked, English support of the

The powerful Spanish Armada set sail to attack England. Bad weather and superior English naval tactics, however, forced the crippled fleet to withdraw in defeat.

Dutch rebellion would have ended and Spain could have completed its Dutch conquest. After the plot failed, Elizabeth had Mary beheaded. Pope Sixtus V (1585-1590), after learning of Mary's death, was so upset that he offered Philip one million Italian gold ducats if Spain invaded England. Philip, after consultation with his military advisors, decided to assemble a large fleet to attack England.

On May 9, 1588, the Spanish Armada left Lisbon. This fleet, which consisted of about 130 ships, was one of the largest ever dispatched against an enemy. Unfortunately for Spain, England could assemble a larger fleet. About 150 English ships fought the Spanish Armada in the English Channel. The English ships, which were generally smaller, faster, more maneuverable, and had greater firepower than their Spanish counterparts, carried the day. Particularly damaging to Spain was England's use of fire ships that ignited and burned Spanish vessels. England de-

stroyed about a third of the Spanish fleet. On the return voyage to Spain several more ships sank in a storm off the Irish coast. Less than seventy Spanish ships survived to return home.

The defeat of the Spanish Armada did not immediately end the Netherlands war. Fighting continued between Protestants backed by England and Spain until 1609 when Philip III (1598-1621) signed a treaty in which Spain recognized the independence of the seven northern Dutch provinces. The English victory over the Spanish Armada meant that Philip II had failed to restore Catholicism to most parts of Europe. It also marked the ascension of England as the world's foremost naval power. Spain never again seriously threatened England.

France, like England, experienced war as a result of religious differences. Luther's writings had reached France by 1518 but attracted few converts. When Calvin's *Institutes of the Christian Religion* was published in 1536, large num-

The Spanish galleon was a mainstay of the powerful Spanish Armada.

bers of French Catholics adopted the Protestant faith. These converts were called Huguenots. Calvinism appealed to them in part because Calvin was French and wrote in the French language. Most French Huguenots lived in cities such as Paris, Lyons, Meaux, and Grenoble. Despite widespread persecution, which included burning at the stake, the numbers of French Calvinists grew, reaching about 9 percent of the population by 1560.

Civil war, rooted in religion, engulfed France in 1559 and lasted for thirty-six years. The weak French monarchs, all sons of Henry II, the last strong king France produced for a generation, were unable to maintain order. Francis II, who became king in 1159 after Henry II's death, died after ruling for only seventeen months. His successor, Charles II, who ruled from 1560 to 1574, was controlled by his Mother, Catherine de' Medici. Henry III, who succeeded to the throne in 1574 and ruled to 1589 experienced psychological problems due to guilt he experienced because he was homosexual in a society that did not tolerate gay people. It was not until Henry

The English ship was narrower, with gun ports along her side, which made her clearly superior to the Spanish galleon.

IV (ruled 1589-1610) became king that peace and stability came to France.

French nobles took advantage of royal weakness. Various nobles adopted Calvinism in an attempt to intimidate Lutheran princes in Germany and use religion to declare their independence from the king. In southern France Huguenot leaders, for a time, created a semi-autonomous state. Estimates indicate that perhaps half of all French nobles adopted Calvinism at some time. Clashes between Protestant and Catholic nobles were inevitable given the weakness of the monarchy. Among the nobility the real issue was power while among the working classes it was religion. Calvinists and Catholics viewed each other as heathens. Violence erupted throughout France. Not only did Catholic and Protestant armies led by various nobles clash, but violence often occurred at daily events, such as weddings, funerals, baptisms, and worship services. Catholics attacked Protestants and Protestants attacked Catholics. Huguenot ministers often exhorted their flocks to raid Catholic churches and destroy statues and art objects that Protestants viewed as idols. Likewise, Catholic priests urged parishioners to kill the Huguenot heretics.

The most notorious act of violence in France occurred on August 24, 1572. Called the Saint Bartholomew's Day Massacre, the event occurred when Huguenot nobles gathered for a wedding uniting Margaret of Valois, sister to the Catho-

Queen Elizabeth went to St. Paul's Cathedral for a service to celebrate the defeat of the Armada dressed in elaborate garb.

lic King Charles IX, to Henry of Navarre, the foremost Protestant leader. The marriage was intended to bring reconciliation to the warring Catholic and Protestant factions in France. Catherine de' Medici, who several times in the French civil war switched sides, felt that her Huguenot allies were becoming too strong and apparently ordered attacks on Protestant leaders gathered for the wedding. On the eve of the wedding Henry of Guise had Admiral Gaspard de Coligny, a Protestant leader who had replaced Catherine de Medici as primary advisor to King Charles, attacked. This event touched off rioting and violence in Paris that killed most of the Calvinist leadership. Only Henry of Navarre escaped. Within a short time, religious violence spread from Paris to the countryside. All French Provinces were engulfed in war. From the Saint Bartholomew's Day Massacre until early October Catholics slaughtered over ten thousand Huguenots throughout France.

This bloodshed produced the War of the Three Henry's. The conflict was a civil war between factions led by Henry of Guise, a Catholic nobleman, Protestant nobleman Henry of Navarre, and King Henry III who succeeded Charles IX in 1574. For fifteen years France experienced civil conflict. Even though Henry III was Catholic, he fought against Henry of Guise because the Catholic Guise faction had formed an alliance of Catholic nobles called the Holy League whose goals were to eradicate the Huguenots as well as overthrow the monarchy.

Several events brought the War of the Three Henry's to an end. One was the defeat of the Spanish Armada. When England defeated the

Armada, Henry of Guise lost his principal backer, Philip II of Spain. Henry III then had Henry of Guise assassinated. A few months later Henry III was also assassinated. The deaths of two of the three Henry's meant Henry of Navarre, the lone survivor, could take the French throne. He ruled as King Henry IV from 1589 to 1610. Even though he was Protestant, Henry IV realized that the majority of the French people were Catholic; therefore, he converted to Roman Catholicism in 1593 so that most French citizens would accept him as king. However, he issued the Edict of Nantes in 1598, which allowed Huguenots to legally hold worship services and exist as a religious minority throughout France.

THE THIRTY YEARS WAR

The Holy Roman Empire in Germany and central Europe were not immune from religious war. Conflict between Protestants and Catholics rocked the region, killing millions from 1618 until 1648. Known as the Thirty Years War, this conflict was the bloodiest of all wars that resulted from the Reformation. Central Europe was ravaged by this conflict, and every principal monarch in Europe eventually became involved.

Problems leading to the Thirty Years' War date to the Augsburg settlement in which each German prince acquired the right to determine whether his lands would be Catholic or Protestant. Catholics became alarmed when Protestants violated the Augsburg peace by expanding into German Catholic bishoprics. Catholics were particularly concerned about the aggressive spread of Calvinism. Since the Augsburg agreement was between Lutherans and Catholics, Calvinists ignored it, converting German princes at an alarming rate. Lutherans, like Catholics, also feared the spread of Calvinism into Germany. They believed that the Augsburg peace

was in danger of collapse if the advances of both Calvinists and Catholics were not halted. Compounding the problem was that Jesuit missionaries had convinced several Lutheran princes to become Catholic. Lutheran principalities responded by forming the Lutheran League in 1608; Catholics in turn created the Catholic League in 1609. The primary goal of both alliances was to stop the other from enlarging its territory.

The war began after Ferdinand of Styria, a staunch Catholic, was elected king of Bohemia in 1617. He angered Bohemian Protestants in 1618 when he abolished laws enacted by the previous ruler, Emperor Rudolf II, that in 1609 had allowed Protestants to worship freely within Bohemia. Bohemians rebelled. Since the Bohemian king was elected, the electors declared that Ferdinand had been deposed. In his place they chose Fredrick II of Palatinate, the leader of Bohemian Calvinists. Violence erupted with the occurrence of the Defenestration of Prague. Protestants, upset with Ferdinand, threw two government officers from the window of a Prague castle on May 23, 1618. Both men miraculously survived after falling approximately seventy feet to the ground. Catholics maintained that angels caught the men, gently lowering them to the earth while Protestants claimed that a deep pile of horse manure softened the fall. Regardless of what happened, the Defenestration of Prague marked the onset of the Thirty Years' War.

The conflict escalated over time. From 1618 to 1625 it was primarily fought in Bohemia. This conflict was essentially a religious civil war between Ferdinand and his Catholic allies trying to reclaim the throne from Fredrick and his Calvinists allies. In 1620 Catholics won a major victory when they defeated Fredrick's army at the Battle of White Mountain. Ferdinand, who had also been named Holy Roman Emperor, took back the Bohemian crown. He unleashed persecution on Bohemian Protestants, forcing most to become Catholic and executing those who refused. By 1630 Protestantism no longer openly existed in Bohemia.

In 1625 the war escalated. King Christian IV of Denmark (ruled 1588-1648) intervened on the Protestant side. Largely ineffective as a military commander, Christian was unable to stop advances by Ferdinand's forces. Albert von Wallenstein, the commander of Catholic forces, won numerous victories over Protestant armies. By 1627 his army had began to attack Protestant strongholds in the northern regions of the Holy Roman Empire. Catholic forces took control of Silesia, Pomerania, Jutland, and Schlesuwig. Protestants had lost so much territory in Germany by 1629 that Ferdinand issued the Restitution Edict, which ordered all property taken from Catholics since 1552 returned. The Restoration Edict alarmed Lutheran princes throughout Germany. They feared that Ferdinand and the House of Habsburg he represented would eventually subdue all of Germany. Consequently, they united against Ferdinand, forcing the Holy Roman Emperor to fire Wallenstein at an electoral diet in 1630.

Protestant fortunes began to improve in 1630 when Swedish king Gustavus Adolphus (ruled 1594-1632) brought an army to support oppressed Lutherans. The French king, Louis XIII, wanting to weaken the Habsburgs in central Europe, provided financial support for Sweden. In 1631 Adolphus decisively defeated a Habsburg army at Breitenfeld. After Adolphus was killed in a victory over Catholic forces at Lutzen in 1632 and after a Swedish army was defeated at the Battle of Nordlingen in 1634, France entered the war. Even though France was a Catholic nation, its forces supported Protestants because the French monarch wanted to sty-

mie the advance of Habsburg power. The French intervention marked the beginning of the international phase of the Thirty Years' War. Over the next fourteen years French and Swedish armies ravaged Germany. More than a third of Germany's population was killed, agriculture was virtually destroyed, and economic devastation occurred when several German princes debased their currency. The war caused an economic depression that engulfed the entire European continent, causing deflation and falling commodity prices for the first time in over a century.

The Thirty Years' War lasted so long because no ruler had the ability and resources to win a complete victory. Fortunately, the primary conflict ended in October 1648 when the Peace of Westphalia was signed. Peace was achieved when two agreements, the Treaties of Munster and Osnabruck, were signed. France and the Habsburgs agreed that German princes would be sovereign and independent. Each prince could rule his territory as he saw fit, make any law he wanted, and determine what religion his subjects would follow. The Holy Roman Empire was effectively destroyed. Germany was now controlled by over three hundred princes, which meant that centralized authority represented by the Holy Roman Empire had ended. The position of France and Sweden in the European power structure improved. France received two new territories, the provinces of Alsace and Lorraine. Sweden received territory in Pomerania, Bremen, and Verden. In addition, the independence of Protestant Holland was recognized, and France got the right to intervene in German affairs. The issue between Catholics and Protestants was settled when the Westphalia Peace expanded the Augsburg agreement of 1555 to include Calvinists as well as Lutherans and Catholics. All three religions could legally exist in central Europe. This did not mean that religious toleration was accepted. German citizens usually followed the religion of their prince. In practice, principalities in northern Germany were Protestant while those in southern Germany remained Catholic.

WOMEN AND WITCHCRAFT

The Reformation introduced new ideas regarding women, marriage, and sexuality. Whereas Catholics saw marriage as a holy sacrament that could not be dissolved once the union was completed, Protestants viewed marriage as a legal contract between two individuals. Each partner under this contractual arrangement was legally required to fulfill various marital responsibilities. Wives were expected to maintain and manage the home, engage in charitable work, help husbands with farm or business work as the need arose, bear, rear, and tend children, and provide sex for husbands on demand. Women were generally discouraged from working outside the home because outside employment would interfere with homemaking duties. A husband's responsibilities, in contrast, included providing food, shelter, and clothing for his wife and children. Men generally worked on the farm or ran the business from which he earned the family's livelihood.

Although Protestant thought, as evidenced in literature about marriage, stressed that husbands, as head of the household, should rule their families fairly and justly, many husbands behaved like tyrants. Protestant writers justified the verbal and physical abuse women suffered as punishment for sins committed by the Biblical Eve. Men, they said, were also punished because God required them to work on a daily basis, earning their family's living "by the sweat of his brow."

Like Catholics, Protestants stressed sexual fidelity within marriage. Because marriage was perceived as a contract, Protestants permitted divorce for various reasons, including adultery. Protestants also allowed ministers to marry, which lessened the problem created by priests taking female lovers. Women who had been priests's concubines could legally become their lovers' wives.

Although civil governments in both Catholic and Protestant nations licensed prostitution houses, the world's most ancient profession was frowned upon. Legally licensed prostitution establishments catered only to single males. Some Protestant countries paid government employees to live in the houses to ensure that married men did not partake of their sensual pleasures. Even though prostitution was legal throughout Europe, it reflected a double standard in sexual morality for men and women. Single males were free to satisfy their sexual cravings while women, with the exception of prostitutes, were expected to refrain from sexual intercourse outside marriage.

Even though Protestant women were expected to remain virginal until marriage, Luther, Calvin, Zwingli, and other Reformation leaders believed that celibacy was not necessary to lead a religious life. Luther maintained that God delighted in sexual activity so long as it occurred as part of marriage. Words Luther wrote a friend in a letter provide evidence of his views regarding sex: "Dear lad, be not ashamed that you desire a girl, nor you my maid, the boy. Just let it lead you into matrimony and not into promiscuity, and it is no more cause for shame than eating or drinking." Nuns in former Catholic countries were encouraged to marry after their convents were abolished. Marriage, Protestant reformers believed, provided women with economic, emotional, and cultural benefits while alleviating repression of sexual desires. Still, the emphasis was upon sex within marriage. Women who expressed their sensuality too openly or who behaved differently from the norm might be accused of practicing witchcraft.

The century of the Reformation witnessed the persecution of numerous women for practicing witchcraft. A belief in witchcraft was widespread throughout Europe. Educated and non-educated people alike believed that witches were real. Most people believed the earth was the battlefield between God and the Devil. Illness, injury, bankruptcy, deaths, or any misfortune were often blamed on witchcraft. Witches were generally thought to be older women who consorted with Satan and as a result possessed mysterious powers. Occasionally, younger women and children might be accused of witchcraft. Tradition held that witches rode broomsticks to *sabbats* (meetings with the Devil and other witches). At these sabbats witches supposedly engaged in wild sexual orgies with Satan and male witches called warlocks. These sexual escapades, which people believed included lesbian sex with other witches, supposedly lasted all night. Between bouts of sex, witches were believed to dine on the flesh of human babies.

Europeans generally believed that witches were married or widowed women who desired more sex than they were having. Women older than fifty were especially prone to accusations of witchcraft largely because they possessed some of the characteristics Europeans attributed to witches—aged, wrinkled skin, limbs crippled with arthritis or other diseases, deafness, poor eyesight, malnutrition, thinning hair, and various psychological disorders. Moreover, these women might practice midwifery and folk medicine, healing sick people with roots, herbs, and other folk cures. Moreover, most women accused of witchcraft did not follow the mild, meek roles assigned women in European society. Instead, they behaved aggressively, spoke their mind, and refused to be subservient to men.

The Protestant Reformation contributed to the witch hysteria that swept across the European continent from 1560 to 1660. Protestants, especially Calvinists, feared Satan's power and the religious wars wrecked havoc across Europe, creating much insecurity. Because reformers believed witches worshipped Satan, witchcraft was considered heresy. As a result, governments and religious reformers denounced witchcraft. Anyone suspected of witchcraft was subject to horrible prosecution. Thousands of women accused of witchcraft were executed across the European continent. Authorities in several southern German principalities burned over three thousand witches. Switzerland killed even more. Although the exact number of women tried for witchcraft will likely never be known, one estimate is that over nine million throughout the world stood accused over several centuries. Between 1450 and 1700 at least nine thousand people were tried for witchcraft on the European continent. Over half were found guilty and condemned to death. England, for example, executed about one thousand witches from 1560 to 1740.

Scholars differ about the cause of the European witch hysteria after the Reformation occurred. Most likely the fear of witches and the executions resulted from a variety of factors. First, most people believed in witchcraft. They tended to blame witches for life's misfortunes and feared the power of witches. Anything that could not be readily explained was usually blamed on witchcraft. Second, Protestant ministers preached strong sermons warning congregations about the Devil's power. These sermons created fear in the minds of ordinary people. Some began to look for signs of witchcraft in neighbors. Third, Christianity stressed a repression of sexual desire. All the sexual activities attributed to witches, some scholars believe, represented the repressed urges of sexually frustrated Christians. Fourth, witchcraft provided an easy means for tight knit, local communities that stressed social and cultural conformity to rid themselves of nonconformists. Anyone who did not behave like others in the community was likely to be accused of witchcraft. Fifth, the Christian belief that women were more susceptible to the Devil's intrigues likely played a role in the witch hysteria. European Christians believed that women inherited a tradition from Eve of being deceived by Satan. In light of this belief it is no wonder that women were accused of practicing witchcraft far more often than men. Whatever the reason for the witch persecutions, they took a tremendous toll on European women. Thousands were executed as witches at various times in European history.

CONCLUSION

When Luther nailed his Ninety-five Theses to the church door in Wittenberg, Western Christianity was forever changed. All of Western Europe would never again practice the same faith. Religious unity under the Catholic Church was forever broken. Other reformers, following Luther's example, disavowed Catholic doctrines and formed numerous Protestant denominations. John Calvin was the most strident of these reformers, creating a theocracy in Geneva. Calvinist ministers fanned out across Europe preaching the gospel as they saw it. Anabaptists, the most radical of Protestant groups, gained a foothold in parts of Europe. Henry VIII created a state controlled church in England as part of the Reformation.

Suggestions for Further Reading

Roland H. Bainton, *Here I Stand: A Life of Martin Luther* (1955).

William Bangert, *A History of the Society of Jesus* (1772).

William J. Bouwsma, *John Calvin: A Sixteenth Century Portrait* (1988)

John Calvin, *On God and Political Duty.* John T. McNeil, ed. (1950).

Owen Chadwick, *The Reformation* (1964).

Patrick Collinson, *The Religion of Protestants* (1982).

Jean Delumeau, *Catholicism Between Luther and Voltaire: A New View of the Counter-Reformation* (1977).

H. J. Hillerbrand, *The Reformation in its Own Words* (1964)

Anthony Kenny, *Thomas More* (1983).

James M. Kittelson, *Luther the Reformer: The Story of the Man and His Career* (1986).

Bernd Moeller, *Imperial Cities and the Reformation* (1972).

E. A. Payne, *The Free Church Tradition in the Life of England* (1952).

Bob Scribner and Benecke, Gerhard (eds.), *The German Peasant War of 1525: New Viewpoints* (1979).

W. A. Shaw, *A History of the English Church 1640-1660.*

Max Weber, *The Protestant Ethic and the Spirit of Capitalism* (1958).

Index